Fundamentals of
Business Mathematics

Fundamentals o

Business Mathematics

Walter E. Williams
University of South Florida

James H. Reed
University of South Florida

wcb

Wm. C. Brown Company Publishers

Dubuque, Iowa

Book Team

Ed Bowers, Jr., Publisher
Ed Bowers, Jr., Editor
David Corona, Designer
Mary Jo Wentz, Design Layout Assistant
Ruth Richard, Manager, Production-Editorial Department
Patricia L. A. Hendricks, Production Editor

Wm. C. Brown Company Publishers

Wm. C. Brown, President
Larry W. Brown, Executive Vice President
Ann Bradley, Director of Marketing Strategy
Jim Buell, Director of Information Management
John Carlisle, Assistant Vice President, Production Division
Robert Chesterman, Comptroller
David Corona, Design Director
Lawrence E. Cremer, Vice President, Product Development
Richard C. Crews, Publisher
John Graham, National Marketing Manager
Ray Deveaux, National College Sales Manager
Linda Judge, Director of Personnel/Public Relations
Roger Meyer, Assistant Plant Superintendent
Paul Miller, Vice President/Director, University Services
Roy Mills, Assistant Vice President/Plant Superintendent
Ed O'Neill, Vice President, Manufacturing
Dennis Powers, Director of Information Services

To Our Parents

Contents

4 Selected Topics 387

Preface

This textbook provides the student with basic skills in business mathematics. It is written for the first year community college or university student and is intended as an introductory course for the potential business major. However, the topics in the book are pertinent to consumers as well as employers, thus the book is appropriate as a core course in basic mathematics.

There is no prerequisite for using this text other than standard high school math courses. In fact, the opening chapters of the text are a review of basic arithmetic and provide the student with an opportunity to solidify and sharpen his arithmetic foundation before applying these skills to business applications.

The philosophy of the text is learning by doing, and the pedagogy follows the successful formula of explanation—example—exercise. Reinforcement of new material is immediate and includes examples and exercise sets geared to business situations. A unique feature of the text is the wealth of "word" problems. These augment the topic of each section and provide valuable training for actual business operations.

Another feature of the book is its flexibility. With an understanding of the material in Part I, virtually any choice of topics from the remaining chapters is possible. This enables the book to be used successfully in courses ranging from one term to a full year.

The text is divided into four parts.

Part I—Basics.   This subdivision presents the foundation material of the book. In addition to a review of basic arithmetic, an understanding of equations and graphs is acquired, and the fundamental formula of business mathematics, $P = BR$, is studied in detail.

Part II—Retailing/Accounting.   In addition to the fundamentals of buying and selling, the chapters in this subdivision introduce the student to the basic terminology and record keeping found in contemporary business operations.

Part III—Finance.   This part covers the principles of basic finance from the point of view of both the consumer and the businessperson. The emphasis is on an understanding of the basic formulas rather than rote or memorization.

Part IV—Selected Topics.   In addition to the changes brought about by advances in technology, businesses must adjust to rapidly changing social conditions. Insurance has become a business necessity, and the entire nation must cope with the inevitable conversion to the metric system. Computers now dominate business operations and along with statistics are an integral part of the decision process. The chapters of this subdivision examine the basic principles of these topics in their modern-day perspective.

A textbook is the work of many people other than the authors, and we take this opportunity to pay tribute to their contributions. Many excellent suggestions and improvements are due to the reviewers of the manuscript; they are: Rhosan Stryker, Delta College; George Philbrick, Prince

George's Community College; Helen Scoon, Madison Area Technical College; Nell Edmundson, Miami-Dade Junior College North; Howard Propes, San Antonio College; Darrell DeGeeter, Waubonsee College; and Thomas Barrett, Moraine Valley Community College. A special thanks is also due to David Strong, Prince George's Community College for providing further insight into the business mathematics course.

Mr. Wm. C. Brown deserves our gratitude for assembling the finest and most cooperative publishing team one could ask for. Especially we must mention Larry Cremer, Ed Bowers, John Carlisle, Ruth Richard, Dave Corona, Louise Klein, Linda Judge, John Graham, Patricia Hendricks, and Jean Heins.

We are grateful to June Bobbitt for her expertise and tireless effort in typing the manuscript. Also, our thanks to Beverly McMillan, Janet Earles, and Diane Gossett for their cheerful assistance on several occasions.

Finally, we wish to thank Liz, Debbie, Vicky, June, Steve, J.M., Jennifer and Jimbo for their understanding during those many nights that we spent with the manuscript instead of with them.

W. E. Williams
J. H. Reed

This text, *Fundamentals of Business Mathematics,* is accompanied by the following learning aids:

Instructor's Resource Manual
Student Workbook

1 Basics

Review of Arithmetic

Chapter Objectives for Chapter 1

I. Learn the meaning of the following terms:

A. *Whole numbers,* 4
B. *Addend* and *sum,* 5
C. *Minuend, subtrahend,* and *difference,* 11
D. *Multiplicand, factor, partial product,* and *product,* 14
E. *Dividend, divisor, quotient,* and *remainder,* 17

II. Understand the principles of:

A. Positional notation, 4
B. Carrying and borrowing, 5, 11
C. Casting out nines, 7, 15
D. Grouping symbols, 18

III. Compute:

A. Sums of whole numbers, 5
B. Differences of whole numbers, 11
C. Products of whole numbers, 14
D. Quotients of whole numbers, 17

Introduction

The foundation of business mathematics is the ten digits of the decimal system, 0, 1, 2, 3, 4, 5, 6, 7, 8, 9. All numbers are written with these ten digits—a remarkable feat considering the set of numbers is infinite. This is possible because of the Hindu-Arabic* positional notation that emphasizes the position of the digits. For example, 467 and 764 have the same three digits; the position of each digit with respect to the other digits distinguishes them as different numbers. The same distinction is used in written language. The words "teach" and "cheat" contain the same letters; it is the arrangement of the letters that creates two different words.

In the decimal system, each position represents a product of tens, as shown in Figure 1–1.

Figure 1–1

By the notation depicted in Figure 1–1, 467 means 4 hundreds (400) plus 6 tens (60) plus 7 ones (7) or 400 + 60 + 7, and 5,029 means 5 thousands (5,000) plus 0 hundreds (0) plus 2 tens (20) plus 9 ones (9) or 5,000 + 20 + 9.

The numbers 0, 1, 2, 3, 4, 5, 6, 7, 8, 9, 10, 11, . . . are called the **whole numbers.** In the sections to follow, we review the arithmetic of the whole numbers.

Addition

Not only is the Hindu-Arabic positional notation an efficient method for writing numbers, it also lends itself to an algorithm† for the shortcut method of counting that we call addition. We add two or more numbers by adding the digits in each positional column separately, beginning with the "ones" column. If the sum of the digits in a column results in a two-digit number, the first digit of that number is "carried" to the next column

---

* This notation is named after the Hindus who invented it and the Arabs who refined it and exported it to the Western world.
† An algorithm is a step-by-step process for performing a calculation.

and added with the digits in that column. The addition algorithm is illustrated in Example 1.

Example 1

Find: a.   427   b.   14
          + 62   53
                    +96

Solution:

a.   427 addend   b.   14 addend
   + 62 addend   53 addend
   489 sum   + 96 addend
                    163 sum

In (a) of Example 1, the sum of the digits in the ones column is $2 + 7 = 9$, in the tens column $6 + 2 = 8$, and in the hundreds column $0 + 4 = 4$, hence $427 + 62 = 489$. In (b), the sum of the digits in the ones column is $6 + 3 + 4 = 13$. Because 13 is a two-digit number, the 1 is "carried" to the tens column and added with the other digits in that column, or $9 + 5 + 1 + 1 = 16$. Thus $14 + 53 + 96 = 163$.

The electronic calculator has eliminated much of the need for manual addition, but instances arise where columns of numbers must be added by hand, and the sum checked. In such instances, addition is often simplified by grouping combinations of digits whose sum is 10. For instance, in the problem

$$
\begin{array}{r}
8 \\
6 \\
2 \\
+4 \\
\hline
\end{array}
$$

the sum is found more quickly by combining $8 + 2 = 10$, $6 + 4 = 10$, then $10 + 10 = 20$.

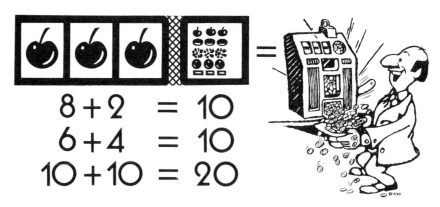

$$8 + 2 = 10$$
$$6 + 4 = 10$$
$$10 + 10 = 20$$

Example 2

Find: 86
         68
         42
         35
        +14

Solution:

$\overset{2}{86}$ $6 + 4 = 10, \ 8 + 2 = 10, \ 10 + 10 + 5 = 25;$

68   Write 5, carry 2

42

35 / $2 + 8 = 10, \ 6 + 4 = 10, \ 10 + 10 + 3 + 1 = 24;$

+ 14   Write 24

245

For particularly long columns of numbers, it may be simpler to split the problem into two or more problems, then add the subtotals.

Example 3

Find: 407
         939
         701
         463
         442
         565
        +848

Solution:

  407
  939
  701
+463   2,510 Subtotal
 ─────
  442
  565
+848   1,855 Subtotal
 ─────
        4,365 Total

Checking Addition

Numerous methods exist for checking addition; reversing the order of the addition is one method. That is, add beginning from the top of the column instead of the bottom (or vice versa). A second method is to readd using the grouping technique illustrated in Example 3.

With either method, if reading results in the same sum, odds are that the solution is correct.

A third method of checking addition is called "casting out nines." The method is illustrated best by an example.*

Example 4

Find and check your result: $467 + 231 + 189 + 493$

Solution:

$$
\begin{array}{rcll}
467 & \rightarrow & 4+6+7 = 17 & \rightarrow \quad 1+7 = 8 \\
231 & \rightarrow & 2+3+1 = \ 6 & \rightarrow \qquad\qquad 6 \\
189 & \rightarrow & 1+8 \ \ = \ 9 & \\
+\ 493 & \rightarrow & 4+3 \ \ = \ 7 & \rightarrow \qquad\quad +\ 7 \\
\hline
1380 & & & \qquad\quad 21 \rightarrow 2+1 = 3
\end{array}
$$

$$1 + 3 + 8 + 0 = 12 \longrightarrow 1 + 2 = 3 \longleftarrow \text{Checks}$$

Horizontal and Vertical Addition

The previous examples illustrated addition of numbers in vertical columns; numbers may be added horizontally if one continues to observe the positional place of the digits. A number of business situations occur where both horizontal and vertical addition are required. Consider the following sales information:

	Mon.	Tues.	Wed.	Thurs.	Fri.	Total
Brand A	10	9	14	11	14	58
Brand B	17	22	19	15	23	96
Brand C	8	6	9	5	10	38
Total	35	37	42	31	47	192

By adding horizontally and vertically, it is possible to determine both the sales of a particular brand and the total sales on a given day. The addition is checked by adding the totals to obtain the grand total of 192.

HOURLY PRODUCTIVITY REPORT

(Do Not Show Cents)

	MON	TUES	WED	THURS	FRI	SAT	SUN	TOTAL
7 A.M.	108.00	117.00	112.00	110.00	107.00	116.00	129.00	799.00
8 A.M.	123.00	132.00	129.00	126.00	119.00	121.00	133.00	883.00
9 A.M.	134.00	139.00	140.00	129.00	131.00	137.00	142.00	952.00
10 A.M.	147.00	149.00	152.00	147.00	147.00	148.00	159.00	1,049.00
11 A.M. OR 11:30 A.M.	159.00	164.00	162.00	159.00	161.00	173.00	183.00	1,161.00
SUBTOTAL	671.00	701.00	695.00	671.00	665.00	695.00	746.00	4,844.00

* The method of casting out nines fails to detect errors that are multiples of nine.

In problems 1–20, find the indicated sums.

1. 531
   +223

2. 274
   +715

3. 8,422
   + 431

4. 2,431
   + 562

5. 1,002,143
   + 471,242

6. 7,472,143
   + 213,415

7. 427
   +842

8. 971
   +217

9. 529
   +311

10. 723
    +137

11. 446
    +475

12. 278
    +643

13. 546
    +774

14. 727
    +473

15. 7,435,758
    + 947,762

16. 4,539,743
    + 842,051

17. 746
    529
    +872

18. 514
    655
    +927

19. 70,123,547
    290,182
    5,421,714
    + 8,921,546

20. 213,415,819
    4,572,113
    8,549,637
    + 40,219,517

In problems 21–26, find the indicated sum and check by casting out nines.

21. 1,473
    891
    + 273

22. 2,476
    472
    + 231

23. 2,721
    3,273
    +4,529

24. 3,472
    7,231
    +4,273

25. 7,423
    8,291
    4,726
    +1,429

26. 2,721
    7,214
    2,143
    +9,256

In problems 27–32, find the indicated sum and check by the method of grouping.

27.   43
   187
    21
   231
+143

30.   384
   192
   726
   427
+532

28.   123
    49
    63
   721
+ 82

31.   4,271
   872
9,536
4,279
+ 873

29.   127
   723
   496
   873
+421

32.   3,273
4,521
3,426
   572
+ 831

33. Professor Porter has the following amounts withheld from his monthly check: $243 for Federal income tax, $35 for hospitalization insurance, $63 for retirement, and $123 for a credit union loan payment. Find the total amount withheld from his monthly check.

34. The Corner Grocery paid invoices to wholesalers in the following amounts: bakery items, $74; dairy products, $219; produce, $198; meat products, $1,723. What was the total expenditure for the invoices?

35. The monthly payroll of the ABC Machine Shop is summarized as follows: machinists, $7,829; draftsmen, $3,587; maintenance men, $1,720; executives, $5,280; consultants, $1,240. Find the total monthly payroll.

36. During the first week in September, an inspector at a manufacturing plant rejected 793 items on Monday, 1,021 items Tuesday, 821 items Wednesday, 1,129 items Thursday, and 998 items Friday. How many items did this inspector reject during the week?

37. A three-story warehouse is offered for lease. The warehouse has 5,427 square feet of storage space on the first floor, 5,272 square feet on the second floor, and 2,742 square feet on the third floor. Find the total storage space in the warehouse.

38. An apartment building contains four types of apartments: efficiency, one-bedroom, two-bedroom, and three-bedroom. The rental income per month from the efficiencies is $2,842; from the one-bedroom apartments, $7,423; from the two-bedroom apartments, $5,243; and

from the three-bedroom apartments, $1,422. How much rental income does the building produce?

39. Dr. Denton made deposits in his savings account in the following amounts: January, $1,729; February, $2,341; March, $1,927; April, $2,542; and May, $2,143. Find the total of his deposits for the five months.

40. The Atlas Manufacturing Company is divided into five departments. During the month of January, the operating expenses for each department were as follows: department A, $672; department B, $7,422; department C, $927; department D, $4,898; department E, $2,747. What was the company's total operating expense for the month?

41. A telephone company warehouse contains five coils of steel cable. The lengths of the coils are 7,421 feet, 11,422 feet, 4,281 feet, 2,973 feet, and 13,271 feet. How much cable is stored in the warehouse?

42. A real estate salesman received commissions on the sale of five pieces of property during the month of August. The commissions were $128, $293, $179, $423, and $42. Find the salesman's total commission for the month.

43. A public utilities commission survey showed that a community paid the following amounts for energy in one month: electricity, $13,472,321; natural gas, $2,729,431; fuel oil, $1,272,431; gasoline, $147,242,155; bottled gas, $12,421; other, $2,022. What was the total expenditure for energy for the month?

44. Use horizontal and vertical addition to fill in the missing entries in the following chart showing the daily sales of each department at Waldo's Grocery during the first week in April.

	Monday	Tuesday	Wednesday	Thursday	Friday	Saturday	Total
Bakery	$420	$360	$540	$490	$585	$310	____
Meats	760	840	910	429	719	554	____
Produce	510	485	547	493	604	641	____
Dairy Products	314	219	337	408	373	381	____
Grocery Items	2,342	2,719	1,921	2,567	2,681	2,501	____
Total	____	____	____	____	____	____	____

45. The following chart shows the departmental operating expenses at Orion, Inc., during the first six months of 1976. Use horizontal and vertical addition to fill in the missing entries in the chart.

	January	February	March	April	May	June	Total
Office	$2,132	$1,814	$1,701	$2,147	$2,211	$1,982	____
Showroom	714	841	902	893	721	746	____
Sales	3,142	3,015	3,257	3,419	3,221	3,657	____
Storage	517	631	597	551	492	481	____
Total	____	____	____	____	____	____	____

Subtraction

The operations of addition and subtraction are closely related. For example, if 8 is the sum of 5 plus 3 ($8 = 5 + 3$), then 8 subtract 5 equals 3 ($8 - 5 = 3$). That is, to subtract 5 from 8, we seek that number that when added to 5 equals 8. When subtracting, we observe the same positional rules used in addition.

Example 1

Find: a. $49 - 28$ b. $44 - 18$

Solution:

a.
$$
\begin{array}{ll}
49 & \text{Minuend} \\
-28 & \text{Subtrahend} \\
\hline
21 & \text{Difference}
\end{array}
$$

b.
$$
\begin{array}{ll}
\overset{3}{\cancel{4}}4 & \text{Minuend} \\
-18 & \text{Subtrahend} \\
\hline
26 & \text{Difference}
\end{array}
$$

In the ones column of problem (b) there is no positive number that added to 8 equals 4. This difficulty is overcome by the device of borrowing. The procedure is a rearrangement of the positional notation of the minuend to permit subtraction. The number 44 means 4 tens + 4 ones in the positional notation; to facilitate subtraction we write 44 as 3 tens + 14 ones. That is,

$$
\begin{array}{ll}
44 = & 3 \text{ tens} + 14 \text{ ones} \\
-18 = & 1 \text{ ten } + \ 8 \text{ ones} \\
\hline
& 2 \text{ tens} + \ 6 \text{ ones} = 26
\end{array}
$$

Borrowing may be necessary in any positional column when subtracting one number from another.

Checking Subtraction

The relationship between subtraction and addition provides a means for checking the answer to a subtraction problem. The answer (difference) is added to the subtrahend; if the result is the minuend, the subtraction was correctly performed.

Example 2

Find and check your answer: $834 - 263$

Solution:

$$
\begin{array}{r}
7 \\
\cancel{8}34 \\
-263 \\
\hline
571
\end{array}
\qquad
\begin{array}{r}
\text{Check:} \\
263 \\
+571 \\
\hline
834
\end{array}
$$

Exercises for Section 1.3

In problems 1–15, perform the indicated subtraction and check your result.

1. $\begin{array}{r} 27 \\ -15 \\ \hline \end{array}$ 9. $\begin{array}{r} 5{,}601 \\ -\ \ \ 42 \\ \hline \end{array}$

2. $\begin{array}{r} 53 \\ -42 \\ \hline \end{array}$ 10. $\begin{array}{r} 3{,}705 \\ -\ \ \ 76 \\ \hline \end{array}$

3. $\begin{array}{r} 153 \\ -\ 21 \\ \hline \end{array}$ 11. $\begin{array}{r} 3{,}251 \\ -\ \ 172 \\ \hline \end{array}$

4. $\begin{array}{r} 785 \\ -\ 43 \\ \hline \end{array}$ 12. $\begin{array}{r} 4{,}536 \\ -\ \ 347 \\ \hline \end{array}$

5. $\begin{array}{r} 5{,}496 \\ -\ \ 273 \\ \hline \end{array}$ 13. $\begin{array}{r} 14{,}732 \\ -\ 2{,}159 \\ \hline \end{array}$

6. $\begin{array}{r} 7{,}487 \\ -\ \ 276 \\ \hline \end{array}$ 14. $\begin{array}{r} 34{,}867 \\ -\ \ \ 778 \\ \hline \end{array}$

7. $\begin{array}{r} 741 \\ -\ 27 \\ \hline \end{array}$ 15. $\begin{array}{r} 54{,}837 \\ -27{,}549 \\ \hline \end{array}$

8. $\begin{array}{r} 543 \\ -\ 39 \\ \hline \end{array}$

16. Sam Smooth purchased some real estate. The total price of the property was $42,725. He paid $22,750 cash and mortgaged the balance. What was the amount of the mortgage?

17. Mary Mackey wishes to buy a new house. The cost of the house is $67,750, and she agrees to a down payment of $32,350. Find the amount she will owe on the house.

18. The owner's equity in a business is the total assets minus the total liabilities. Belcher's Bakery has total assets of $42,793 and total liabilities of $19,275. Find the owner's equity.

19. A recent balance sheet for a small restaurant listed total assets of $27,492 and total liabilities of $13,745. What is the owner's equity? (See exercise 18.)

20. A department store offers to sell a dining room set at a sale price of $763. If the regular price of the set was $819, how much would one save by buying the set on sale?

21. The Furniture Mart purchases some used furniture for $2,314. The furniture was then sold for $2,703. How much profit was realized?

22. Professor Porter's total salary is $372 per week. Of this amount, $93 is deducted for taxes and other items. What amount does he receive each week (take-home pay)?

23. During the month of January, a small business had total sales of $7,492 of which $4,593 were for cash. Find the credit sales for the month.

24. It cost $17,217 to stock the shelves of the Corner Drug Store. The sales value of the stock is $27,129. If the stock is sold at sales value, what is the profit?

25. A contractor built four houses at a total cost of $287,543. He sold them at a total cost of $342,722. How much profit did he realize?

Section 1.4 Multiplication

Multiplication began as a shortcut for repeated addition. For example, $3 \times 5 = 5 + 5 + 5 = 15$, and $4 \times 7 = 7 + 7 + 7 + 7 = 28$. The multiplication table is a listing of these products, and our first training in multiplication is to memorize a portion of this table. However, we soon are

RABBIT LIFE

The average life-span of a cottontail rabbit is nine years. Most live and die in an area less than a mile from their birthplace. Almost everything preys on the hapless bunnies. They are fair game for cats, dogs, foxes, hawks and owls, many snakes, weasels, lynx. Floods, heavy rains, extreme cold and deep snow can decimate rabbit populations. Their enormous fecundity is their sole defense. Females normally bear four litters, averaging five animals apiece, annually. And cottontails born in early spring will breed by the summer of the next year. Each female produces 20 animals, half of which are capable of reproducing themselves 20 times over within a year. Without predation and decimation the world would soon be filled with cottontails.

taught an efficient algorithm for multiplying two numbers. The process involves multiplying each digit in the multiplicand by each digit in the multiplier to obtain a partial product. The product is the sum of the partial products as shown in the next example.

Example 1

Find: 24×7

Solution:

```
 24  Multiplicand or Factor
× 7  Multiplier or Factor
───
 28  Partial Product (7 × 4 = 28)
140  Partial Product (7 × 2 tens = 14 tens = 140)
───
168  Product (sum of the partial products)
```

With practice we learn to condense the above solution by employing the carrying device.

```
  2
 24
× 7
───
168
```

The reasoning is: $7 \times 4 = 28$; write 8, carry 2. $7 \times 2 = 14, 14 + 2 = 16$; write 16.

Example 2

Find: 36×18

Solution:

```
 36  Multiplicand
× 18  Multiplier
───
 48  Partial Product (8 × 6 = 48)
240  Partial Product (8 × 3 tens = 24 tens = 240)
 60  Partial Product (1 ten × 6 = 6 tens = 60)
300  Partial Product (1 ten × 3 tens = 10 × 30 = 300)
───
648  Product
```

The same problem solved using carrying is:

```
 36  Multiplicand
× 18  Multiplier
───
288  Partial Product (8 × 6 = 48; write 8, carry 4.
              8 × 3 = 24, 24 + 4 = 28; write 28)
360  Partial Product (10 × 36 = 360)
───
648
```

Checking Multiplication   There are a number of acceptable methods for checking the solution to the product of two numbers. Two such methods will be illustrated.

A.   Transposition of multiplicand and multiplier

Solution: Check:

$$
\begin{array}{r}
53 \\
\times\ 28 \\
\hline
424 \\
106 \\
\hline
1484
\end{array}
\qquad
\begin{array}{r}
28 \\
\times\ 53 \\
\hline
84 \\
140 \\
\hline
1484
\end{array}
$$

B.   Casting out nines

Solution: Check:

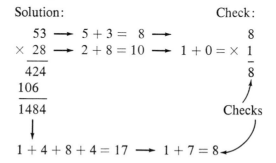

$$
\begin{array}{r}
53 \\
\times\ 28 \\
\hline
424 \\
106 \\
\hline
1484
\end{array}
$$

53 → 5 + 3 = 8 →   8
× 28 → 2 + 8 = 10 → 1 + 0 = × 1
                                 8

Checks

1 + 4 + 8 + 4 = 17 → 1 + 7 = 8

Multiplication Shortcuts   Several mathematical shortcuts exist when either the multiplicand or multiplier contains zeros. The simplest case is when the multiplier is a product of tens; that is, the multiplier is 10, 100, 1,000, etc. The product is found by appending to the multiplicand the number of zeros in the multiplier. For example,

$$
\begin{array}{r}
21 \times\ \ \ \ \ 10 =\ \ \ \ \ 210 \\
433 \times\ \ \ 100 = 43{,}300 \\
91 \times 1{,}000 = 91{,}000
\end{array}
$$

Other multipliers ending in zero are handled as follows.

Example 3

Find: a.   74 × 80   b.   5,300 × 76

Solution:

a.   Long Method   Shortcut   b.   Long Method   Shortcut

$$
\begin{array}{cc}
\begin{array}{r}
74 \\
\times\ 80 \\
\hline
00 \\
5{,}920 \\
\hline
5{,}920
\end{array}
&
\begin{array}{r}
74 \\
\times\ \ 80 \\
\hline
592 \\
\\
5{,}920
\end{array}
\end{array}
\qquad
\begin{array}{cc}
\begin{array}{r}
5{,}300 \\
\times\ \ \ \ 76 \\
\hline
31{,}800 \\
371{,}000 \\
\hline
402{,}800
\end{array}
&
\begin{array}{r}
5{,}300 \\
\times\ 76 \\
\hline
318 \\
3{,}710 \\
\hline
4{,}028 \\
402{,}800
\end{array}
\end{array}
$$

In problems 1–14, perform the indicated multiplication and check by casting out nines.

1. $\begin{array}{r} 12 \\ \times \quad 3 \\ \hline \end{array}$

2. $\begin{array}{r} 21 \\ \times \quad 4 \\ \hline \end{array}$

3. $\begin{array}{r} 376 \\ \times \quad 4 \\ \hline \end{array}$

4. $\begin{array}{r} 547 \\ \times \quad 3 \\ \hline \end{array}$

5. $\begin{array}{r} 579 \\ \times \quad 67 \\ \hline \end{array}$

6. $\begin{array}{r} 766 \\ \times \quad 78 \\ \hline \end{array}$

7. $\begin{array}{r} 905 \\ \times \quad 319 \\ \hline \end{array}$

8. $\begin{array}{r} 872 \\ \times \quad 407 \\ \hline \end{array}$

9. $\begin{array}{r} 51{,}273 \\ \times \quad 17 \\ \hline \end{array}$

10. $\begin{array}{r} 63{,}192 \\ \times \quad 53 \\ \hline \end{array}$

11. $\begin{array}{r} 7{,}893 \\ \times \quad 2{,}471 \\ \hline \end{array}$

12. $\begin{array}{r} 9{,}356 \\ \times \quad 3{,}271 \\ \hline \end{array}$

13. $\begin{array}{r} 7{,}283 \\ \times \quad 2{,}406 \\ \hline \end{array}$

14. $\begin{array}{r} 8{,}173 \\ \times \quad 4{,}057 \\ \hline \end{array}$

15. A shipping clerk dispatched 127 packages averaging 43 pounds each. Find the total weight of the packages.

16. A small office building contains 14 offices, each renting for $323 per month. What is the total rental income from the building per month?

17. A university charges tuition at the rate of $15 per credit. If a student decides to take 17 credits of course work, how much tuition will he pay?

18. A lathe operator in a machine shop produces 37 units per day. Each unit sells for $14. Find the daily income from the operation of the lathe.

19. A discount store purchases 123 television sets at a wholesale cost of $322 per set. How much did the store pay for the sets?

20. Professor Porter's take-home pay per month for the nine months of September through May is $927 per month. In addition he teaches summer school and receives $572 take-home pay per month for the three months of June through August. Find his total take-home pay for the year.

21. A trucking company hauls citrus at the rate of $13 per mile per truckload. A citrus grower estimates his crops to be 572 truckloads, and he wishes to ship 327 truckloads to packing plant A and the remainder of his crop to packing plant B. If the distance to packing plant A is 123 miles and the distance to packing plant B is 67 miles, what will be the total shipping charge?

22. The M & M Motel has a total of 137 rooms, 93 of which are double occupancy and the remainder single occupancy. If the doubles rent for $17 per day and the singles rent for $13 per day, what is the total rental income per day at full occupancy?

Division

Just as subtraction "reverses" the operation of addition, division reverses the operation of multiplication. That is, if $3 \times 12 = 36$, then $36 \div 12 = 3$. Similar to the other operations, there is an algorithm for division. In the division problem $504 \div 6$, the algorithm is illustrated in the following steps:

```
  8  (8×6 = 48)          8          84 (4×6 = 24)          84—Quotient
┌6) 504 ────┐        6) 504    6) 504                    6) 504
│   48      │          −48↓      48                         48
│           │          ───       ──                         ──
│           │           24       24                         24
│ Dividend ─┘                     24                        −24
│                                                           ───
└ Divisor                                                     0—Remainder
     Step 1            Step 2      Step 3                    Step 4
```

Steps in the division algorithm are repeated until all of the digits in the dividend are used and the subtraction step yields a number less than the divisor; then the solution is the quotient along with this number (the remainder). In the above illustration, the solution is 84 with remainder 0. When the remainder is zero as in the illustration, the divisor is said to divide the dividend evenly.

Checking Division The relationship between multiplication and division furnishes a method for checking division problems. The procedure is to multiply the divisor by the quotient and add the remainder; the result should equal the dividend. That is,

$$(\text{Divisor} \times \text{Quotient}) + \text{Remainder} = \text{Dividend}$$

Example 1

Find and check your result: $7,329 \div 24$

Solution:

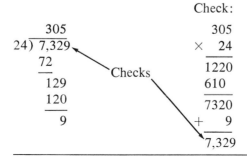

Check:

```
        305                      305
 24) 7,329                     ×  24
     72                        ─────
     ──          Checks         1220
     129                         610
     120                       ─────
     ───                       7320
       9                     +    9
                             ─────
                             7,329
```

Parentheses

For clarity, parentheses ( ) or brackets [ ] are used to group numbers when more than one operation is involved. In the absence of such grouping symbols, it is a mathematical convention that multiplication is performed first, then division, then addition, then subtraction. Thus

$$8 + 12 \div 4 \times 3 - 2$$

means

$$8 + 1 - 2 = 7$$

However,

$$(8 + 12) \div [(4 \times 3) - 2]$$

means

$$20 \div 10 = 2$$

If a grouping symbol is preceded by a number, multiplication is implied. Thus

$$4(12 - 7)$$

means

$$4 \times 5$$

Exercises for Sections 1.5 and 1.6

In problems 1–20, perform the indicated division and check your result by multiplication.

1. $96 \div 8$
2. $84 \div 7$
3. $235 \div 5$
4. $376 \div 8$
5. $581 \div 7$
6. $522 \div 9$
7. $168 \div 12$
8. $840 \div 24$
9. $756 \div 54$
10. $986 \div 34$
11. $3{,}551 \div 53$
12. $3{,}230 \div 34$
13. $23{,}968 \div 428$
14. $16{,}864 \div 248$
15. $310{,}648 \div 412$
16. $380{,}304 \div 684$
17. $636{,}519 \div 741$
18. $544{,}993 \div 827$
19. $2{,}774{,}912 \div 4{,}256$
20. $1{,}540{,}203 \div 7{,}231$

In problems 21–30, find the quotient and remainder.

21. $245 \div 9$
22. $375 \div 6$
23. $219 \div 4$
24. $612 \div 7$

25. $3,068 \div 75$

26. $5,569 \div 64$

27. $2,799 \div 43$

28. $4,188 \div 57$

29. $7,897 \div 83$

30. $3,967 \div 48$

In problems 31–40, perform the indicated operations and simplify.

31. $6 + 4 \div 2$

32. $4 \times 3 - 2$

33. $2(4 - 1) + 3$

34. $5 - 1(3 - 2)$

35. $7 + 4(6 - 2)$

36. $8 + 2 \times 3 \div 6$

37. $5 - 3 \times 1 + 4 \div 2$

38. $[7 + (3 \times 2 - 5)] \div 4$

39. $16 \div [(4 - 2) \times 2]$

40. $3[4 \div 2 - 1] - 2$

41. The A.B.C. Clothing Outlet purchases 225 men's suits from the manufacturer for $7,875. Find the cost of each suit.

42. A businessman decides to construct an office building containing 26 offices. He plans to rent each office at the same monthly rate, and he wants a total rental income (at full occupancy) per month of $8,450. How much rent per month should he charge for each office?

43. Professor Porter's take-home pay for the year was $13,524. Assuming he received equal pay each month, what was his take-home pay per month?

44. The Mighty-Mite Manufacturing Company receives a purchase order for 996 units of its best quality electric shaver motors. The company computes the cost of the order to be $7,968. Find the price per unit that the buyer is paying for the motors.

45. A business executive has carpeting installed in her conference room for a total cost of $1,190. If 85 square yards of carpeting were required, what did she pay per square yard?

46. W. L. Mercer purchased 56 shares of a certain stock for $1,512, excluding the broker's commission. Find the cost of one share of the stock.

47. A manufacturing plant produced 4,297 golf carts in one month. The production cost for the carts was $77,346. How much did it cost to produce one cart?

48. Reliable Furniture and Appliance Company sold 223 color television sets during a recent sale for a profit of $6,021. What profit was made on each set?

49. Jack Edwards sells water softeners on a commission basis. In one month he sold 37 softeners and received a total commission of $925 for the month. Find Jack's commission for each sale.

50. A machine shop receives an order for 1,562 units of a part to be used in the construction of jet engines. The tooling costs required to fill the order amount to $46,860. Find the tooling cost per unit.

51. Fiberglass Industries, Inc., manufactures canoes and all of its products have the same selling price. The total sales for the month of April amounted to $19,596 for 92 units. What was the selling price per unit?

52. The owner of a small twelve-unit apartment building received a total rental income of $26,114 in 1976. Due to increasing overhead expenses, the owner needs to receive $29,282 in 1977 in order to make a satisfactory profit. How much should the rent of each unit per month be increased? (Assume full occupancy.)

53. A company filled a purchase order for 1,472 of its best quality electronic calculators at a total cost of $401,856. The company then filled a second purchase order for 927 of the calculators at the same price per unit. Find the cost of the second purchase order.

Review of Fractions

Chapter Objectives for Chapter 2

I. Learn the meaning of the following terms:

A. *Numerator* and *denominator* of a fraction, 24
B. *Proper, improper,* and *complex fractions,* 24
C. *Common divisor,* 28
D. *Least common denominator,* 36
E. *Mixed number,* 36
F. *Decimal point,* 40

II. Understand:

A. The four interpretations of a fraction, 24
B. The procedure for multiplying fractions, 24
C. The concept of equal fractions, 26
D. Reducing fractions to lowest terms, 27
E. The technique of cancelling, 28
F. The procedure for dividing fractions, 31
G. The procedure for adding fractions, 34
H. The process for converting mixed numbers to fractions, 36
I. The procedure for subtracting fractions, 37
J. The process for rounding a number, 46

III. Compute:

A. Products of fractions, 24
B. Quotients of fractions, 32
C. Sums of fractions, 34
D. Differences of fractions, 37
E. Sums, differences, products, and quotients of decimal fractions, 41, 42

A fraction consists of two numbers separated by a horizontal or slanting bar; for example, the fraction one-sixth may be written $\frac{1}{6}$ or ⅙. In either event the number to the top or left of the bar is called the **numerator,** while the number below or right of the bar is called the **denominator.**

There are at least four different interpretations for a number like $\frac{1}{6}$.

Interpretation 1.   A Part of a Whole.

If *one* pie is cut into *six* equal slices, then a slice is $\frac{1}{6}$ of the whole pie.

Interpretation 2.   A Part of a Group.

$\frac{1}{6}$ of 36 bottles is 6 bottles, or 1 six-pack out of 6 six-packs.

Interpretation 3.   Division of Two Numbers.

The number $\frac{1}{6}$ can mean $1 \div 6$. In this sense, the bar is just another symbol for the division sign $\div$.

Interpretation 4.   Ratio of Two Numbers.

If during a baseball game a batter gets one hit in six times at bat, then we can say he hit safely $\frac{1}{6}$ of the time. Here the fraction implies a comparison between the numbers 1 and 6.

Before discussing the arithmetic of fractions let us consider the different kinds of fractions.

A **proper fraction** is a fraction with numerator less than the denominator. $\frac{1}{6}$, $\frac{3}{8}$, and $\frac{5}{7}$ are examples of proper fractions.

An **improper fraction** is a fraction with numerator greater than or equal to the denominator. $\frac{9}{7}$, $\frac{8}{3}$, and $\frac{7}{7}$ are examples of improper fractions.

A **complex fraction** is a fraction consisting of a fractional numerator, a fractional denominator, or both. $\frac{\frac{6}{7}}{14}$, $\frac{1\frac{5}{2}}{3}$, and $\frac{\frac{1}{2}}{\frac{3}{4}}$ are examples of complex fractions.

It should be emphasized that fractions are numbers, and like other numbers they can be added, subtracted, multiplied, and divided. However, because a fraction consists of a pair of numbers, the algorithms for these operations differ from those for whole numbers. Multiplication is considered first because it is the simplest.

The product of two fractions is a fraction found by multiplying the numerators and multiplying the denominators of the given fractions. This is true whether the fractions are proper, improper, or complex. Thus,

$$\frac{2}{3} \times \frac{5}{7} = \frac{2 \times 5}{3 \times 7} = \frac{10}{21},$$

$$\frac{11}{4} \times \frac{3}{8} = \frac{11 \times 3}{4 \times 8} = \frac{33}{32}$$

Example 1

Find: a. $\dfrac{2}{7} \times \dfrac{5}{3}$ b. $\dfrac{\frac{5}{24}}{\frac{4}{5}} \times \dfrac{\frac{2}{3}}{\frac{7}{18}}$

Solution:

a. $\dfrac{2}{7} \times \dfrac{5}{3} = \dfrac{2 \times 5}{7 \times 3} = \dfrac{10}{21}$

b. $\dfrac{\frac{5}{24}}{\frac{4}{5}} \times \dfrac{\frac{2}{3}}{\frac{7}{18}} = \dfrac{\frac{5}{24} \times \frac{2}{3}}{\frac{4}{5} \times \frac{7}{18}} = \dfrac{\frac{5 \times 2}{24 \times 3}}{\frac{4 \times 7}{5 \times 18}} = \dfrac{\frac{10}{72}}{\frac{28}{90}}$

Exercises for Section 2.2

In problems 1–10, find the product of the given fractions.

1. $\dfrac{1}{2} \times \dfrac{1}{3}$

2. $\dfrac{1}{4} \times \dfrac{1}{3}$

3. $\dfrac{3}{5} \times \dfrac{2}{3}$

4. $\dfrac{4}{5} \times \dfrac{3}{4}$

5. $\dfrac{9}{7} \times \dfrac{6}{7}$

6. $\dfrac{8}{9} \times \dfrac{4}{5}$

7. $\dfrac{12}{17} \times \dfrac{9}{11}$

8. $\dfrac{13}{15} \times \dfrac{12}{11}$

9. $\dfrac{\frac{1}{2}}{\frac{3}{4}} \times \dfrac{\frac{2}{3}}{\frac{3}{2}}$

10. $\dfrac{\frac{5}{9}}{\frac{2}{7}} \times \dfrac{\frac{3}{4}}{\frac{7}{8}}$

11. A manufacturing plant normally employs 28 men. During a recent recession, 6 men received temporary layoffs. What fraction of the work force was laid off? What fraction continued to work?

12. An office building has a total floor space of 12,400 square feet. Of this space, 11,200 square feet is used for offices and the remaining space consists of hallways, storage rooms, etc. Find the fraction of the total floor space that is used for offices. What fraction of the total floor space is used for other purposes?

13. New refrigerators have been installed in each apartment of a thirty-six-unit complex that is being remodeled. Thirty-one of the old refrigerators were sold to used appliance dealers and five were so badly damaged they were sold as junk. Find the fraction of the refrigerators that was junked. What fraction was sold to dealers?

14. Waldo's Supermarket received a shipment of thirty-two cases of corn-meal, four of which were later discovered to be infested with insects. What fraction of the shipment was damaged?

15. Professor Porter's calculus class had an enrollment of 42 students at the beginning of the term. Thirty-six students completed the course and the rest dropped. Find the fraction of the students that completed the course.

16. Universal Products, Inc., purchased 46 acres of land on which to construct a new plant. Ten acres will be used for parking and 4 acres will be used for buildings. What fraction of the land will remain unused?

17. A produce dealer purchased ¾ of a truckload of watermelons and sold ⅞ of it. He donated the rest of the watermelons to a church picnic. What fraction of a truckload did he sell?

18. A contractor ordered ½ ton of sand to be used for a construction project and used only ¾ of it. How much sand did he use?

19. A farmer purchased ¼ ton of seed and planted ⅚ of it. How much seed did he plant?

20. A warehouse is rented by an appliance dealer, who uses ¾ of the storage capacity of the warehouse to store a shipment of washing machines. When all but ⅓ of the machines are sold, how much of the storage capacity of the warehouse will the dealer need to store the remaining machines?

Section 2.3 Equality of Fractions

Equality of fractions can be determined by cross multiplication. **Cross multiplication** consists of multiplying the numerator of the first fraction by the denominator of the second fraction, and multiplying the numerator of the second fraction by the denominator of the first fraction. **Two fractions are said to be equal if their cross products are equal.**

Example 1

Show that $\frac{4}{7} = \frac{12}{21}$.

Solution:

The cross products are

$$4 \times 21 = 84$$
$$12 \times 7 = 84$$

The cross products are equal, hence $\frac{4}{7} = \frac{12}{21}$.

It is possible to construct a fraction equal to a given fraction by multiplying the numerator and denominator of the given fraction by the same nonzero number. For instance,

$$\frac{2}{5} \times \frac{3}{3} = \frac{2 \times 3}{5 \times 3} = \frac{6}{15}.$$

The two fractions are equal because their cross products are equal; that is, $2 \times 15 = 6 \times 5$. Multiplying $\frac{2}{5}$ by $\frac{2}{2}, \frac{3}{3}, \frac{4}{4}, \frac{5}{5}, \ldots$, we see there are an infinite number of fractions equal to a given fraction; that is,

$$\frac{2}{5} = \frac{4}{10} = \frac{6}{15} = \frac{8}{20} = \frac{10}{25} = \cdots$$

Example 2

Find four fractions equal to $\frac{3}{2}$.

Solution:

$$\frac{3}{2} \times \frac{2}{2} = \frac{3 \times 2}{2 \times 2} = \frac{6}{4} \qquad \frac{3}{2} \times \frac{4}{4} = \frac{3 \times 4}{2 \times 4} = \frac{12}{8}$$

$$\frac{3}{2} \times \frac{3}{3} = \frac{3 \times 3}{2 \times 3} = \frac{9}{6} \qquad \frac{3}{2} \times \frac{5}{5} = \frac{3 \times 5}{2 \times 5} = \frac{15}{10}$$

Example 3

Find a fraction with denominator 48 that is equal to the fraction $\frac{5}{6}$.

Solution:

In symbols the problem is $\frac{5}{6} = \frac{?}{48}$. Since $48 \div 6 = 8$, we multiply $\frac{5}{6} \times \frac{8}{8} = \frac{40}{48}$. Thus, $\frac{5}{6} = \frac{40}{48}$.

Reducing Fractions

Utilizing the fact that a fraction with the same numerator and denominator is equal to the number one, the procedure for constructing equal fractions can be reversed. For example,

$$\frac{16}{40} = \frac{2 \times 8}{5 \times 8}$$
$$= \frac{2}{5} \times \frac{8}{8}$$
$$= \frac{2}{5} \times 1$$
$$= \frac{2}{5}$$

This process is called **reducing fractions.** When a fraction is reduced to the point that the resulting fraction cannot be further reduced, then the fraction is said to be reduced to **lowest terms.** For example, $\frac{48}{72} = \frac{4}{6}$, but the reduction is not to lowest terms because $\frac{4}{6}$ can be reduced as follows:

$$\frac{4}{6} = \frac{2 \times 2}{3 \times 2} = \frac{2}{3} \times \frac{2}{2}$$
$$= \frac{2}{3} \times 1 = \frac{2}{3}$$

Thus, $\frac{48}{72}$ reduced to lowest terms is $\frac{2}{3}$.

The reduction procedure can be simplified: **to reduce a fraction, divide** (without remainder) **the numerator and denominator of the fraction by the same nonzero whole number.**

Example 4

Reduce: a. $\frac{27}{36}$ b. $\frac{40}{28}$

Solution:

a. $27 \div 9 = 3$

    $36 \div 9 = 4$ hence $\frac{27}{36} = \frac{3}{4}$

b. $40 \div 4 = 10$

    $28 \div 4 = \ 7$ hence $\frac{40}{28} = \frac{10}{7}$

Divisors used to reduce fractions are called **common divisors** or **common factors.** The largest common divisor of a fraction will reduce the fraction to lowest terms. The divisors in Example 4 are largest common divisors, thus each of the fractions has been reduced to lowest terms. Clearly, a fraction reduced to lowest terms is simpler to use than the fraction in higher terms. It is considerably easier to find $\frac{3}{4} \times \frac{2}{3}$ than $\frac{3}{4} \times \frac{48}{72}$.

$$\frac{32}{96} = \frac{16}{48} = \frac{8}{24} = \frac{4}{12} = \frac{2}{6} = \frac{1}{3}$$

Multiplication by Cancelling By modifying the technique for reducing fractions, the product of fractions can be simplified. To illustrate:*

$$\frac{20}{9} \times \frac{27}{8} = \frac{20 \times 27}{9 \times \ 8}$$

$$= \frac{20 \times 27}{8 \times \ 9}$$

$$= \frac{20}{8} \times \frac{27}{9} = \frac{5 \cdot 4}{2 \cdot 4} \times \frac{3 \cdot 9}{1 \cdot 9}$$

$$= \frac{5}{2} \times \frac{3}{1}$$

$$= \frac{15}{2}$$

* Step 2 uses the **commutative property of multiplication.** This property states that the product of two numbers is not affected by a rearrangement of the numbers. That is, $9 \times 8 = 8 \times 9$.

However, this procedure is usually shortened further by a shortcut called **cancellation.**

$$\frac{\overset{5}{\cancel{20}}}{\underset{1}{\cancel{9}}} \times \frac{\overset{3}{\cancel{27}}}{\underset{2}{\cancel{8}}} = \frac{5}{1} \times \frac{3}{2} = \frac{15}{2}$$

Example 5

Using cancellation wherever possible, find:

a. $\dfrac{25}{6} \times \dfrac{3}{10}$ b. $\dfrac{63}{12} \times \dfrac{60}{21}$

Solution:

a. $\dfrac{25}{6} \times \dfrac{3}{10} = \dfrac{\overset{5}{\cancel{25}}}{\underset{2}{\cancel{6}}} \times \dfrac{\overset{1}{\cancel{3}}}{\underset{2}{\cancel{10}}}$

$\qquad\qquad = \dfrac{5}{2} \times \dfrac{1}{2}$

$\qquad\qquad = \dfrac{5}{4}$

b. $\dfrac{63}{12} \times \dfrac{60}{21} = \dfrac{\overset{3}{\cancel{63}}}{\underset{1}{\cancel{12}}} \times \dfrac{\overset{5}{\cancel{60}}}{\underset{1}{\cancel{21}}}$

$\qquad\qquad = \dfrac{3}{1} \times \dfrac{5}{1}$

$\qquad\qquad = \dfrac{15}{1} = 15$

Exercises for Section 2.3

In problems 1–15, find three fractions that are equal to the given fraction.

1. $\frac{3}{4}$
2. $\frac{5}{8}$
3. $\frac{3}{2}$
4. $\frac{7}{15}$
5. $\frac{15}{16}$
6. $\frac{11}{3}$
7. $\frac{5}{17}$
8. $\frac{7}{20}$

9. $\frac{9}{4}$
10. $\frac{21}{43}$
11. $\frac{18}{31}$
12. $\frac{16}{14}$
13. $\frac{38}{82}$
14. $\frac{42}{84}$
15. $\frac{105}{120}$

In problems 16–21, find a fraction with denominator 60 equal to the given fraction.

16. $\frac{1}{6}$

17. $\frac{5}{12}$

18. $\frac{14}{5}$

19. $\frac{7}{15}$

20. $\frac{19}{30}$

21. $\frac{3}{4}$

In problems 22–27, find a fraction with denominator 90 equal to the given fraction.

22. $\frac{3}{5}$

23. $\frac{14}{15}$

24. $\frac{17}{9}$

25. $\frac{12}{3}$

26. $\frac{27}{45}$

27. $\frac{13}{30}$

In problems 28–35, use cross multiplication to decide whether or not the given pair of fractions are equal.

28. $\frac{3}{4}$ and $\frac{15}{20}$

29. $\frac{5}{7}$ and $\frac{25}{35}$

30. $\frac{5}{4}$ and $\frac{30}{23}$

31. $\frac{7}{8}$ and $\frac{14}{15}$

32. $\frac{27}{28}$ and $\frac{81}{94}$

33. $\frac{21}{17}$ and $\frac{84}{68}$

34. $\frac{13}{41}$ and $\frac{65}{205}$

35. $\frac{32}{33}$ and $\frac{192}{198}$

In problems 36–45, reduce the given fraction to lowest terms.

36. $\frac{7}{14}$

37. $\frac{15}{30}$

38. $\frac{21}{28}$

39. $\frac{27}{36}$

40. $\frac{12}{8}$

41. $\frac{28}{21}$

42. $\frac{95}{100}$

43. $\frac{118}{124}$

44. $\frac{81}{90}$

45. $\frac{54}{36}$

In problems 46–57, use cancellation when possible and compute the given products of fractions.

46. $\frac{3}{5} \times \frac{15}{12}$

47. $\frac{7}{8} \times \frac{12}{21}$

48. $\frac{5}{6} \times \frac{9}{15}$

49. $\frac{12}{5} \times \frac{15}{8}$

50. $\frac{7}{9} \times \frac{81}{14}$

51. $\frac{64}{5} \times \frac{105}{8}$

52. $\frac{39}{26} \times \frac{13}{26}$

53. $\frac{21}{72} \times \frac{12}{7}$

54. $\frac{27}{35} \times \frac{70}{81}$

55. $\frac{46}{54} \times \frac{48}{92}$

56. $\frac{33}{28} \times \frac{7}{11}$

57. $\frac{44}{15} \times \frac{30}{132}$

Express the answers to problems 58–67 as fractions reduced to lowest terms.

58. The Daisy Dairy Farm purchased 35 dairy cows and resold 20 of them. What fraction of the cows were resold? What fraction of the cows did the dairy keep?

59. Sunshine Hardware received a shipment of 64 chain saws and sold 24 of them in one week. Find the fraction of the shipment that was sold during the week.

60. Professor Potter gave an examination to her class of 44 students, and 33 of them passed. What fraction of her students passed the exam?

61. A restaurant's total receipts for one day totaled $810. Of this amount, $90 was for the sale of liquor. Find the fraction of the total receipts that was due to liquor sales.

62. A warehouse contains 28,000 square feet of floor space. Of the total floor space, 2,000 square feet is used for offices and the rest is used for storage. What fraction of the total floor space is used for offices? What fraction is used for storage?

63. A contractor maintains a fleet of 275 trucks, of which 240, on the average, are in service at any given time. Find the fraction of the total fleet that is not in service (on the average) at any given time.

64. Kirby's Electronics, Inc., specializes in used television sets. Recently, Mr. Kirby bought a color set for $312 and sold it for $364. What fraction of the selling price was his profit?

65. W. L. Mercer bought 575 shares of stock in a land development company. A year later she sold 252 shares of the stock. Find the fraction of stock that was sold.

66. Arlin Lackey inherited $266,000 and used $210,000 to pay off his creditors. What fraction of his original inheritance did he have left after paying off his debts?

67. Sally Smith and Dr. Denton entered into a joint business venture from which they realized a profit of $48,000. Because Sally initially put more money into the venture than Dr. Denton, they agreed that Sally would receive $32,000 and Dr. Denton would receive $16,000. Find the fraction of the total profit that Sally received.

Division of Fractions

Multiplying the numerator and denominator of a fraction by the same nonzero whole number results in a fraction equal to the given fraction. This is true even when the fraction is complex and the multiplier is itself a fraction. Thus

$$\frac{\frac{5}{7}}{\frac{3}{2}} = \frac{\frac{5}{7} \times \frac{2}{3}}{\frac{3}{2} \times \frac{2}{3}} = \frac{\frac{10}{21}}{\frac{6}{6}} = \frac{\frac{10}{21}}{1} = \frac{10}{21}$$

Note that the multiplier is the **reciprocal*** of the denominator $\frac{3}{2}$. This step is the key to an algorithm for dividing fractions:

To divide a number by a nonzero fraction, multiply the dividend by the reciprocal of the fraction.

Example 1

Solve: a. $\dfrac{3}{17} \div \dfrac{1}{4}$ b. $12 \div \dfrac{1}{3}$ c. $\dfrac{3}{8} \div \dfrac{8}{5}$

Solution:

a. $\dfrac{3}{17} \div \dfrac{1}{4} = \dfrac{3}{17} \times \dfrac{4}{1} = \dfrac{12}{17}$

b. $12 \div \dfrac{1}{3} = \dfrac{12}{1} \div \dfrac{1}{3} = \dfrac{12}{1} \times \dfrac{3}{1} = \dfrac{36}{1} = 36$

c. $\dfrac{3}{8} \div \dfrac{8}{5} = \dfrac{3}{8} \times \dfrac{5}{8} = \dfrac{15}{64}$

The division algorithm for fractions presents a method for simplifying complex fractions. For example, by Interpretation 3 (See Section 2.1),

$\dfrac{\frac{4}{6}}{\frac{19}{7}} = \frac{4}{6} \div \frac{19}{7}$. But by the division algorithm for fractions, $\frac{4}{6} \div \frac{19}{7} =$

$\frac{4}{6} \times \frac{7}{19} = \frac{28}{114}$. Hence, $\dfrac{\frac{4}{6}}{\frac{19}{7}} = \frac{28}{114}$.

Example 2

Simplify: a. $\dfrac{\dfrac{5}{9}}{\dfrac{11}{12}}$ b. $\dfrac{24}{\dfrac{5}{3}}$ c. $\dfrac{\dfrac{17}{4}}{15}$

Solution:

a. $\dfrac{\dfrac{5}{9}}{\dfrac{11}{12}} = \dfrac{5}{9} \div \dfrac{11}{12} = \dfrac{5}{\overset{}{9}} \times \dfrac{\overset{4}{12}}{11} = \dfrac{20}{33}$

b. $\dfrac{24}{\dfrac{5}{3}} = 24 \div \dfrac{5}{3} = \dfrac{24}{1} \times \dfrac{3}{5} = \dfrac{72}{5}$

c. $\dfrac{\dfrac{17}{4}}{15} = \dfrac{17}{4} \div \dfrac{15}{1} = \dfrac{17}{4} \times \dfrac{1}{15} = \dfrac{17}{60}$

---

* Two numbers are said to be reciprocals if their product is equal to 1.

In problems 1–10, write the reciprocal of the given fraction reduced to lowest terms.

1. $\frac{4}{14}$

6. $\frac{6}{38}$

2. $\frac{27}{18}$

7. $\frac{91}{65}$

3. $\frac{63}{28}$

8. $\frac{77}{42}$

4. $\frac{90}{55}$

9. $\frac{152}{133}$

5. $\frac{8}{18}$

10. $\frac{170}{51}$

In problems 11–24, perform the indicated division and express the result in lowest terms.

11. $\frac{5}{7} \div \frac{3}{8}$

18. $\frac{5}{17} \div \frac{5}{28}$

12. $\frac{3}{11} \div \frac{5}{6}$

19. $5 \div \frac{6}{54}$

13. $\frac{2}{3} \div \frac{9}{13}$

20. $\frac{73}{13} \div 9$

14. $\frac{3}{4} \div \frac{5}{13}$

21. $\frac{61}{11} \div 1\frac{3}{5}$

15. $\frac{7}{13} \div \frac{19}{32}$

22. $\frac{125}{124} \div \frac{3}{4}$

16. $\frac{5}{32} \div \frac{1}{16}$

23. $\frac{121}{110} \div 1\frac{1}{5}$

17. $\frac{7}{13} \div \frac{7}{26}$

24. $\frac{143}{69} \div 1\frac{1}{23}$

In problems 25–35, simplify the given complex fraction and express the result in lowest terms.

25. $(\frac{3}{4})/(\frac{7}{8})$

31. $(\frac{19}{25})/(\frac{7}{25})$

26. $(\frac{15}{17})/(\frac{3}{4})$

32. $(\frac{14}{137})/(\frac{7}{137})$

27. $5/(\frac{7}{8})$

33. $(\frac{36}{219})/(\frac{6}{219})$

28. $7/(\frac{16}{11})$

34. $(\frac{43}{71})/(\frac{83}{55})$

29. $(\frac{11}{15})/111$

35. $(\frac{57}{61})/(\frac{63}{31})$

30. $(\frac{37}{29})/142$

36. Apco Land Co. purchased $\frac{1}{5}$ of an acre of land and divided it equally into four lots. How large was each lot?

37. Farmer Jones bought $\frac{3}{4}$ of a truckload of seed. If it requires $\frac{1}{8}$ of a truckload to plant one acre, how many acres can he plant?

38. A contractor estimates that $\frac{7}{8}$ of his fleet of trucks is in service at any given time. He also estimates that he needs $\frac{1}{16}$ of his fleet of trucks for each job he undertakes. How many jobs can the contractor undertake at any given time?

39. An office building is under construction in which $\frac{3}{5}$ of the total floor space is to be used for offices. If each office uses $\frac{1}{20}$ of the total floor space of the building, how many offices will the building contain?

40. A tract of land is to be planted in apple trees. If the tract is $5/6$ of an acre and if each tree occupies $1/90$ of an acre, how many trees will be planted on the tract?

41. Fancy Foods, Inc., purchased $7/10$ of a truckload of potatoes. If one bushel is $1/1{,}500$ of a truckload, how many bushels of potatoes were purchased?

42. A cable manufacturing company leases $3/4$ of the total floor space of a warehouse to store its cable. The company estimates that each 100 rolls of cable will occupy $1/80$ of the total floor space of the warehouse. How many hundreds of rolls of cable can the company store in the warehouse?

43. Luigi's Restaurant is being remodeled. Mr. Luigi plans to use $5/6$ of the total floor space for the dining area and the remainder of the space for the kitchen. He estimates that each table in the dining area will require $1/24$ of the total floor space of the restaurant. How many tables will the dining room contain?

44. A produce dealer received a shipment of 224 crates of grapes, which are to be repacked in boxes for retail sale. If each box holds $2/5$ of a crate, how many boxes of grapes can be packed?

45. Louisa's Dress Shop received a shipment of ladies' coats. Some of the coats were damaged and thus returned, but $4/5$ of the shipment was accepted. Louisa estimates that she will sell $1/10$ of the number of coats in the original shipment per day. How many days will it take for the unreturned coats to be sold?

Section 2.5 Addition of Fractions

To add fractions we must consider two cases: (a) fractions with the same (common) denominator and (b) fractions with unlike denominators.

The sum of two fractions with a common denominator is a fraction with the same denominator and whose numerator is the sum of the numerators of the given fractions.

Example 1

Find: a. $\frac{8}{5} + \frac{11}{5}$ b. $\frac{8}{27} + \frac{19}{27}$

Solution:

a. $\frac{8}{5} + \frac{11}{5} = \frac{8 + 11}{5} = \frac{19}{5}$

b. $\frac{8}{27} + \frac{19}{27} = \frac{8 + 19}{27} = \frac{27}{27} = 1$

Addition of fractions with unlike denominators is accomplished by converting the given fractions to fractions with a common denominator, then using the above algorithm. A common denominator will always be the product of the denominators of the given fractions. For example,

$$\frac{2}{3} + \frac{4}{5} = (\frac{2}{3} \times \frac{5}{5}) + (\frac{4}{5} \times \frac{3}{3}) = \frac{10}{15} + \frac{12}{15} = \frac{10 + 12}{15} = \frac{22}{15}.$$

Note that we have multiplied the numerator and the denominator of $\frac{2}{3}$ by the denominator of $\frac{4}{5}$, and similarly we have multiplied the numerator and denominator of $\frac{4}{5}$ by the denominator of $\frac{2}{3}$. The resulting fractions have the common denominator 15, which is the product of the denominators of the given fractions.

Example 2

Find: a. $\frac{2}{9} + \frac{1}{4}$ b. $4 + \frac{3}{4}$

Solution:

a. $\frac{2}{9} + \frac{1}{4} = (\frac{2}{9} \times \frac{4}{4}) + (\frac{1}{4} \times \frac{9}{9}) = \frac{8}{36} + \frac{9}{36} = \frac{17}{36}$

b. $4 + \frac{3}{4} = \frac{4}{1} + \frac{3}{4} = (\frac{4}{1} \times \frac{4}{4}) + (\frac{3}{4} \times \frac{1}{1}) = \frac{16}{4} + \frac{3}{4} = \frac{19}{4}$

There is a shortcut that simplifies the above work. The sum of two fractions with unlike denominators is a fraction determined as follows:

1. The numerator is the sum of the cross products of the given fractions.
2. The denominator is the product of the denominators of the given fractions.

We rework the previous example to illustrate this method.

a. $\frac{2}{9} + \frac{1}{4} = \frac{(2 \times 4) + (1 \times 9)}{9 \times 4} = \frac{8 + 9}{36} = \frac{17}{36}$

b. $4 + \frac{3}{4} = \frac{4}{1} \times \frac{3}{4} = \frac{(4 \times 4) + (3 \times 1)}{1 \times 4} = \frac{16 + 3}{4} = \frac{19}{4}$

We can always find a common denominator for fractions with unlike denominators, but this may not be the smallest such denominator. For example, $216 = 12 \times 18$ is a common denominator for the two fractions $\frac{1}{12}$ and $\frac{1}{18}$, but other common denominators are:

$$108 \text{ found by multiplying } \frac{1}{12} \times \frac{9}{9} \text{ and } \frac{1}{18} \times \frac{6}{6}$$

$$72 \text{ found by multiplying } \frac{1}{12} \times \frac{6}{6} \text{ and } \frac{1}{18} \times \frac{4}{4}$$

$$36 \text{ found by multiplying } \frac{1}{12} \times \frac{3}{3} \text{ and } \frac{1}{18} \times \frac{2}{2}$$

The smallest of all possible common denominators is called the **least common denominator.** The least common denominator is the smallest nonzero whole number divisible by the denominators of the given fractions. The number 36 is the least common denominator in the preceding example.

Example 3

Find: a. $\frac{1}{4} + \frac{1}{6}$ b. $\frac{1}{3} + \frac{1}{15}$ by finding the least common denominators.

Solution:

a.   The smallest whole number divisible by both 4 and 6 is 12, hence,

$$\frac{1}{4} + \frac{1}{6} = (\frac{1}{4} \times \frac{3}{3}) + (\frac{1}{6} \times \frac{2}{2}) = \frac{3}{12} + \frac{2}{12} = \frac{5}{12}$$

b.   The smallest whole number divisible by both 3 and 15 is 15 itself, hence we need change only the first fraction,

$$\frac{1}{3} + \frac{1}{15} = (\frac{1}{3} \times \frac{5}{5}) + \frac{1}{15} = \frac{5}{15} + \frac{1}{15} = \frac{6}{15} = \frac{2}{5}$$

The addition algorithm for fractions makes it possible to discuss mixed numbers. A **mixed number** is the sum of an integer and a fraction, written as one number. For example, $6 + \frac{3}{4}$ is written $6\frac{3}{4}$.

But

$$6 + \frac{3}{4} = \frac{6}{1} + \frac{3}{4} = (\frac{6}{1} \times \frac{4}{4}) + \frac{3}{4} = \frac{24}{4} + \frac{3}{4} = \frac{27}{4},$$

hence we have $6\frac{3}{4} = \frac{27}{4}$. Note that the number $27 = (6 \times 4) + 3$, where these last three numbers are found in the mixed number $6\frac{3}{4}$. This suggests a shortcut for converting mixed numbers to improper fractions. Observe that

$$2\frac{3}{5} = \frac{13}{5} \text{ where } 13 = (5 \times 2) + 3$$

$$8\frac{1}{2} = \frac{17}{2} \text{ where } 17 = (2 \times 8) + 1$$

Example 4

Convert to improper fractions: a. $1\frac{2}{3}$ b. $4\frac{7}{8}$

Solution:

a. $(3 \times 1) + 2 = 5$, hence $1\frac{2}{3} = \frac{5}{3}$

     Check: $1 + \frac{2}{3} = \frac{3}{3} + \frac{2}{3} = \frac{5}{3}$

b. $(8 \times 4) + 7 = 39$, hence $4\frac{7}{8} = \frac{39}{8}$

Check: $4 + \frac{7}{8} = (\frac{4}{1} \times \frac{8}{8}) + \frac{7}{8} = \frac{32}{8} + \frac{7}{8} = \frac{39}{8}$

The reverse process of converting an improper fraction to a mixed number can be accomplished by using Interpretation 3 (Section 2.1) for a fraction. Consider the improper fractions in the previous example; dividing numerator by denominator we have $\frac{5}{3} = 5 \div 3 = 1$ with remainder 2, thus $\frac{5}{3} = 1 + \frac{2}{3} = 1\frac{2}{3}$; $\frac{39}{8} = 39 \div 8 = 4$ with remainder 7, thus $\frac{39}{8} = 4 + \frac{7}{8} = 4\frac{7}{8}$.

Example 5

Convert to mixed numbers: a. $\frac{9}{4}$ b. $\frac{26}{3}$

Solution:

a. $9 \div 4 = 2$ with remainder 1, hence $\frac{9}{4} = 2\frac{1}{4}$

b. $26 \div 3 = 8$ with remainder 2, hence $\frac{26}{3} = 8\frac{2}{3}$

Section 2.6 Subtraction of Fractions

The algorithm for subtracting fractions is identical to the addition algorithm except for the replacement of + by −.

Example 1

Find: a. $\frac{13}{20} - \frac{9}{20}$ b. $\frac{12}{5} - \frac{1}{4}$

Solution:

a. $\frac{13}{20} - \frac{9}{20} = \frac{13 - 9}{20} = \frac{4}{20} = \frac{1}{5}$

b. $\frac{12}{5} - \frac{1}{4} = (\frac{12}{5} \times \frac{4}{4}) - (\frac{1}{4} \times \frac{5}{5}) = \frac{48}{20} - \frac{5}{20} = \frac{48 - 5}{20} = \frac{43}{20}$

Exercises for Sections 2.5 and 2.6

In problems 1–10, find the least common denominator of the given pair of fractions. Then add the fractions and express the sum in lowest terms.

1. $\frac{1}{4}$, $\frac{3}{8}$
2. $\frac{2}{5}$, $\frac{1}{6}$
3. $\frac{1}{3}$, $\frac{3}{4}$
4. $\frac{1}{5}$, $\frac{2}{3}$

5. $\frac{4}{5}, \frac{6}{7}$ 8. $\frac{3}{16}, \frac{23}{64}$

6. $\frac{11}{12}, \frac{1}{9}$ 9. $\frac{21}{23}, \frac{8}{69}$

7. $\frac{5}{17}, \frac{7}{34}$ 10. $\frac{7}{15}, \frac{19}{20}$

In problems 11–20, express the given mixed number as an improper fraction.

11. $3\frac{3}{5}$ 16. $4\frac{1}{5}$

12. $5\frac{1}{4}$ 17. $7\frac{3}{11}$

13. $3\frac{5}{8}$ 18. $8\frac{1}{7}$

14. $6\frac{2}{9}$ 19. $13\frac{21}{22}$

15. $3\frac{1}{13}$ 20. $11\frac{14}{17}$

In problems 21–30, express the given improper fraction as a mixed number.

21. $\frac{14}{3}$ 26. $\frac{21}{4}$

22. $\frac{11}{4}$ 27. $\frac{24}{13}$

23. $\frac{15}{6}$ 28. $\frac{62}{7}$

24. $\frac{17}{8}$ 29. $\frac{51}{15}$

25. $\frac{14}{8}$ 30. $\frac{80}{9}$

In problems 31–40, perform the indicated operation. Express your answer as either a mixed number or as a proper fraction reduced to lowest terms.

31. $\frac{1}{7} + \frac{3}{10}$ 36. $\frac{7}{6} - \frac{8}{14}$

32. $\frac{5}{6} - \frac{3}{8}$ 37. $\frac{21}{19} + \frac{7}{3}$

33. $\frac{7}{6} - \frac{7}{8}$ 38. $\frac{39}{21} - \frac{8}{42}$

34. $\frac{2}{13} + \frac{14}{9}$ 39. $\frac{33}{38} - \frac{9}{19}$

35. $\frac{13}{6} - \frac{13}{14}$ 40. $\frac{23}{11} - \frac{5}{7}$

In problems 41–60, convert the mixed numbers to improper fractions and perform the indicated operation. Express your answer as either a mixed number or as a proper fraction reduced to lowest terms.

41. $2\frac{3}{4} + 5\frac{3}{8}$ 47. $7\frac{3}{7} + 4\frac{5}{21}$

42. $3\frac{5}{6} + 1\frac{2}{3}$ 48. $17\frac{2}{5} - 4\frac{1}{3}$

43. $4\frac{3}{5} - 4\frac{1}{10}$ 49. $15\frac{2}{3} - 8\frac{5}{6}$

44. $3\frac{2}{6} - 1\frac{1}{4}$ 50. $13\frac{3}{4} - 5\frac{1}{6}$

45. $9\frac{7}{8} + 3\frac{5}{6}$ 51. $7\frac{3}{8} + 5\frac{2}{6}$

46. $11\frac{3}{6} + 9\frac{2}{3}$ 52. $8\frac{7}{11} - 7\frac{5}{22}$

53. $6\frac{2}{3} \cdot 4\frac{5}{8}$ 57. $3\frac{5}{7} \cdot 6\frac{2}{3}$

54. $7\frac{2}{5} \cdot 11\frac{5}{9}$ 58. $7\frac{1}{4} \cdot 9\frac{1}{6}$

55. $11\frac{1}{3} \div 12\frac{3}{4}$ 59. $5\frac{7}{8} \div 3\frac{1}{4}$

56. $4\frac{1}{5} \div 13\frac{2}{3}$ 60. $11\frac{7}{9} \div 13\frac{3}{11}$

61. Mary Mackey spent $\frac{1}{6}$ of her monthly paycheck for rent and $\frac{1}{5}$ for food. What fraction of her paycheck did she spend for food and lodging?

62. A land developer deeded $\frac{1}{9}$ of a tract of land to the county for roads and $\frac{2}{7}$ of the tract to a creditor for payment of debts. Find the fraction of the tract that he had left.

63. Comtek, Inc., had $\frac{1}{6}$ of its capital invested in merchandise, $\frac{2}{7}$ in equipment, $\frac{3}{8}$ in real estate, and the balance in cash. What fraction of the company's capital was invested in equipment and real estate? What fraction of the company's capital was cash?

64. Robison's Music Store received a shipment of record albums and sold $\frac{1}{5}$ of the shipment in one week. During the next week $\frac{4}{9}$ of the shipment was sold, and $\frac{4}{15}$ of the shipment was sold in the third week. What fraction of the albums was sold during the three-week period?

65. Sybil's Flower and Gift Shop received a shipment of merchandise that was $\frac{1}{7}$ flowers, $\frac{2}{5}$ glassware, $\frac{3}{7}$ leather goods, and $\frac{1}{35}$ miscellaneous items. What fraction of the shipment was glassware and leather goods? What fraction was flowers and miscellaneous items?

66. Eastern Storage, Inc., leases $\frac{2}{5}$ of the floor space of its Charlottesville warehouse to company A, $\frac{4}{15}$ of the floor space to company B, and $\frac{2}{9}$ of the floor space to company C. How much of the floor space is leased to company A and company B? How much is leased to all three companies?

67. The inventory of a sporting goods store is found to be $\frac{5}{9}$ sporting equipment, $\frac{2}{7}$ clothing, $\frac{2}{21}$ books, and the remainder miscellaneous merchandise. What fraction of the inventory is equipment and clothing? What fraction is miscellaneous merchandise?

68. A company finds that $\frac{3}{7}$ of its total production cost for the year was for employees' wages, $\frac{4}{9}$ was for equipment and supplies, $\frac{2}{21}$ was for plant maintenance, and the remainder was for miscellaneous expenses. Find the fraction of the total production cost due to equipment, supplies, and wages. Find the fraction due to miscellaneous expenses.

69. A man left $\frac{2}{5}$ of his estate to his widow, $\frac{1}{10}$ each to his two sons, $\frac{2}{7}$ to his daughter, and the remainder to charity. How much of his estate did he leave to his family? How much did he leave to charity?

70. Weber Enterprises, Inc., presented a petition to the zoning commis-

sion to subdivide a $14\frac{2}{3}$ acre tract into twenty parcels of equal size. If the petition is approved, how many acres will each parcel contain?

71. Smith's Poultry Farm bought 735 pounds of poultry feed for $22\frac{1}{3}$ cents a pound. How much did the feed cost?

72. Delta Rock & Gravel Co. purchased $3\frac{1}{2}$ truckloads of decorative gravel and sold $\frac{2}{5}$ of it the day it was delivered. The next day $\frac{3}{8}$ of the original shipment was sold. Find the number of truckloads sold during the two days.

73. One lathe in the M & M Machine Shop can produce $9\frac{3}{5}$ units of a certain item per hour. How many lathes will be required to produce $67\frac{1}{5}$ units per hour?

74. A citrus grower produced $112\frac{3}{4}$ tons of fruit from one grove and $97\frac{2}{3}$ tons of fruit from another. How much fruit was produced from the two groves? If $\frac{7}{8}$ of the fruit was sold to a packing house and the remainder was sold at roadside stands, how many tons of fruit were sold at roadside stands?

75. The J & J Lumber Co. receives an order for 326 feet of two-by-fours and $48\frac{1}{2}$ square feet of plywood. If the two-by-fours cost $12\frac{1}{4}$¢ per foot and the plywood costs $27\frac{1}{3}$¢ per square foot, find the cost of the order.

76. B. J. Rockwell's net income after taxes is $17,500. He estimates that $\frac{2}{9}$ of the money is spent for food, $\frac{3}{16}$ for rent, $\frac{1}{5}$ for savings, and $\frac{3}{20}$ for clothing. How much of the $17,500 is still unaccounted for?

Section **2.7** **Decimal Fractions**

Decimal fractions are an extension of the Hindu-Arabic positional notation, as shown in Figure 2–1.

Figure 2–1

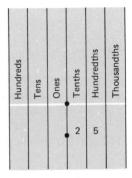

The dot or **decimal point** separates columns that are products of 10 from columns that are products of $\frac{1}{10}$. Using this notation 0.25 means 2 tenths $\left(\frac{2}{10}\right)$ + 5 hundredths $\left(\frac{5}{100}\right)$ or $\frac{2}{10} + \frac{5}{100} = \frac{25}{100}$.

There is an immediate relationship between decimal fractions and fractions:

$$0.1 = \frac{1}{10}$$

$$0.01 = \frac{1}{100}$$

$$0.001 = \frac{1}{1,000}$$

$$0.0001 = \frac{1}{10,000}$$

etc.

Operations with decimal fractions use the same algorithms as for whole numbers. In addition and subtraction of decimal fractions, positional notation is observed by aligning the numbers according to positional columns. The decimal point is a natural alignment guide.

Example 1

Find and check your answer: a.   1,204.685 + 322.96

b.   129.77 − 32.604

Solution:

		Check (Reversing Addends):
a.	1,204.685 Addend	322.96
	+ 322.96 Addend	+1,204.685
	1,527.645 Sum	1,527.645

		Check:
b.	129.770 Minuend	32.604
	− 32.604 Subtrahend	+ 97.166
	97.166 Difference	129.770

Multiplication of decimal fractions requires a different technique. **If the multiplier is a product of tens, the solution is found by moving the decimal point in the multiplicand to the right one place for each zero in the multiplier.** For example,

1.865 × 10 = 18.65 (1 zero; move decimal point 1 place)

1.865 × 100 = 186.5 (2 zeros; move decimal point 2 places)

1.865 × 1000 = 1865. (3 zeros; move decimal point 3 places)

If the multiplier is a decimal fraction, the numbers are written and multiplied as if they were whole numbers, then the decimal point is inserted in the answer. **The product will contain digits to the right of the decimal point equal to the sum of the digits to the right of the decimal point of the factors.**

Example 2

Find: 2.63×5.7

Solution:

$$
\begin{array}{r}
2.63 \text{ Multiplicand or Factor} \\
\times\ \ 5.7 \text{ Multiplier or Factor} \\
\hline
1841 \\
1315 \\
\hline
14.991 \text{ Product}
\end{array}
$$

There are $2 + 1 = 3$ digits to the right of the decimal points in the factors, thus the decimal point is located in the product so that there are 3 digits to its right.

Example 3

Find: 0.03×0.6

Solution:

$$
\begin{array}{ll}
0.03 & \text{2 digits to right of decimal point} \\
\times\ \ 0.6 & +\text{1 digit to right of decimal point} \\
\hline
0.018 & \text{3 digits to right of decimal point}
\end{array}
$$

Note that a zero was inserted in the product to obtain the answer. Since

$$
0.03 \times 0.6 = \frac{3}{100} \times \frac{6}{10} = \frac{18}{1000}
$$

this procedure is justified.

There are three cases to consider in the division of decimal fractions:

a.   the divisor is a product of 10

b.   the divisor is a nonzero whole number

c.   the divisor is a decimal fraction.

Case (a):   If the divisor is a product of tens, the solution is found by moving the decimal point in the dividend to the *left* for each zero in the divisor. For example:

$26.47 \div 10 = 2.647$ (1 zero; move decimal point 1 place)

$26.47 \div 100 = 0.2647$ (2 zeros; move decimal point 2 places)

$26.47 \div 1000 = 0.02647$ (3 zeros; move decimal point 3 places)

Case (b): If the divisor is a nonzero whole number, the decimal point in the quotient is located directly above its position in the dividend. Thus, to divide 704.96 by 32,

$$\begin{array}{r} 22.03 \\ 32 \overline{)\ 704.96} \\ 64 \\ \hline 64 \\ 64 \\ \hline 96 \\ 96 \\ \hline 0 \end{array}$$

Case (c): If the divisor is a decimal fraction, convert it to a whole number by multiplying both dividend and divisor by a product of tens, then divide as in Case (b).

Example 4

Find and check your answer: $40.096 \div 1.79$

Solution:

Multiplying both numbers by 100, $40.096 \div 1.79 = 4{,}009.6 \div 179$, hence,

$$\begin{array}{r} 22.4 \\ 179 \overline{)\ 4{,}009.6} \\ 358 \\ \hline 429 \\ 358 \\ \hline 716 \\ 716 \\ \hline \end{array}$$

Check:
$$\begin{array}{r} 1.79 \\ \times\ 22.4 \\ \hline 716 \\ 358 \\ 358 \\ \hline 40.096 \end{array}$$

Exercises for Section 2.7

In problems 1–32, perform the indicated operation.

1. $\begin{array}{r} 27.4 \\ +32.3 \\ \hline \end{array}$

2. $\begin{array}{r} 42.7 \\ +53.2 \\ \hline \end{array}$

3. $\begin{array}{r} 213.6 \\ +\ \ 34.7 \\ \hline \end{array}$

4. $\begin{array}{r} 21.9 \\ +34.4 \\ \hline \end{array}$

5. $\begin{array}{r} 21.23 \\ +34.71 \\ \hline \end{array}$

6. $\begin{array}{r} 43.71 \\ +23.28 \\ \hline \end{array}$

7. $\begin{array}{r} 189.349 \\ 272.58 \\ +357.152 \\ \hline \end{array}$

8. $\begin{array}{r} 498.31 \\ 217.576 \\ +929.915 \\ \hline \end{array}$

9. 542.075 −391.477	21. 41.07 × 3.15
10. 872.054 −425.947	22. 57.62 × 2.73
11. 974.3 − 27.95	23. 80.02 ×40.07
12. 547.86 − 29.476	24. 70.09 ×61.07
13. 473.1 − 52.854	25. 4.7856 ×3.726
14. 429.8 − 47.726	26. 7.6543 ×2.097
15. 492.83 − 47.2	27. 72.68 ÷ 2.33
16. 72.95 − 1.4	28. 45.56 ÷ 6.88
17. 85.746 −19.0172	29. 89.22 ÷ 4.56
18. 49.239 − 7.9459	30. 96.35 ÷ 6.71
19. 4.015 ×2.14	31. 543.56 ÷ 6.43
20. 7.107 ×4.67	32. 745.38 ÷ 9.58

NO.	CHECKS DRAWN IN FAVOR OF	DATE	BAL. BR'T. FR'D.	✓	$ 1,382	47
223	TO Jones' Hardware FOR tools	1/6	AMOUNT OF CHECK OR DEPOSIT		27	05
			BALANCE		$ 1,355	42
224	TO The Corner Market FOR snacks for party	1/7	AMOUNT OF CHECK OR DEPOSIT		4	18
			BALANCE		$ 1,351	24
225	TO Master Charge FOR Jan. payment	1/9	AMOUNT OF CHECK OR DEPOSIT		107	00
			BALANCE		$ 1,244	24
226	TO Interstate Electric Co. FOR Jan. payment	1/9	AMOUNT OF CHECK OR DEPOSIT		21	00
			BALANCE		$ 1,223	24
227	TO City Savings and Loan FOR house payment	1/9	AMOUNT OF CHECK OR DEPOSIT		324	45
			BALANCE		898	79
228	TO The Mart FOR	1/12	AMOUNT OF CHECK OR DEPOSIT		2	19
			BALANCE		896	60
229	TO Foxy Lady Boutique FOR party dress	1/15	AMOUNT OF CHECK OR DEPOSIT		41	16
			BALANCE		855	44

33. During the month of June, Denise Denton wrote seven checks in the following amounts: $27.05, $4.18, $107.00, $21.00, $324.45, $2.19, and $41.16. What is the total amount of the checks?

34. A sporting goods store reported monthly sales for the six months of January through June as follows: January, $6,482.35; February, $8,749.87; March, $11,493.73; April, $13,473.71; May, $14,973.71; and June, $12,372.42. Find the total sales for the six-month period.

35. A citrus grower operates five groves. During the past year the income from the crops of each of the groves was as follows: grove A $11,293.14; grove B $22,492.36; grove C $9,403.26; grove D $7,413.19; and grove E $4,297.93. How much income did the grower receive from the five groves?

36. Belcher's Bakery leases space in a warehouse to store supplies. The monthly charge for storage depends upon the amount of goods stored. The storage fees for the past six months were $219.72, $413.39, $327.72, $523.78, $319.47, and $209.42. Find the amount paid for storage during the six months.

37. Dr. Denton purchased new equipment for her office with $1,000 down and twelve payments of $972.31 each for a total cost of $12,667.72. If the cash price of the equipment was $10,727.35, what is the difference in the cash price and the amount she paid?

38. W. L. Mercer purchased 183.43 acres of land at $525 per acre for a total cost of $96,300.75. She then sold 172.85 acres for a total price of $115,722.81. How many acres of land did she have left? How much cash profit did she realize from the transaction?

39. A small manufacturing business has total sales of $76,728.72 for one year. The operating expenses for the same year are as follows: rent $8,723.42, labor $21,742.41, machinery $12,242.79, supplies $13,742.57, and incidentals $5,429.73. Compute the profit for the year.

40. An apartment complex has 178 units, each unit providing rental income of $233.50 per month. Assuming all units are rented, what is the total rental income of the complex per month?

41. A citrus grower has 2,743.47 acres of groves. He estimates the gross income from the year's crop to be $176 per acre. How much income will he realize from his citrus?

42. A storage warehouse agrees to store 7,263 barrels of salt at the rate of 7¢ per barrel per month. Find the total storage fee for the salt in dollars per month.

43. The owner of a restaurant decides to have 572 square yards of carpeting installed. The carpet he selects is $6.23 per square yard and

it will cost $1.19 per square yard for padding and 79¢ per square yard for installation. How much will the carpeting cost?

44. The inventory of men's suits in a department store was as follows: 27 suits (grade A) at $120.50 per suit; 32 suits (grade B) at $97.25 per suit; 63 suits (grade C) at $72.50 per suit. What was the total value of the suits?

45. A discount store purchases 273 refrigerators at a cost of $153 per unit. The regular retail price per unit is $225.50. The store offers the refrigerators on sale at $199.95 each. Assuming all refrigerators are sold at the sale price, what is the total profit? How much more profit would the store have made if all the refrigerators were sold at the regular price?

46. A firm manufactures steel cable that it sells for 52.5¢ a foot. A construction company purchases some of the cable for a total price of $301.35. How many feet of the cable were purchased?

47. An estate of $137,281.20 was to be equally divided among five heirs. A sixth heir was then found who also was entitled to an equal share of the estate. How much less did each of the original five heirs receive?

48. A produce dealer paid a farmer $1,137.93 for 2,742 crates of lettuce and $2,016.84 for 1,372 boxes of tomatoes. The farmer's profit on the lettuce was $425.01 and on the tomatoes was $987.84. How much did it cost the farmer to grow a crate of lettuce? How much to grow a box of tomatoes?

Section 2.8 Rounding

A calculation is no more accurate than the accuracy of its components. For example, in the sum

$$
\begin{array}{r}
12.863 \\
24.02 \\
+47.259 \\
\hline
84.142
\end{array}
$$

the answer cannot be considered accurate beyond the hundredths place, the accuracy of 24.02. It is true that 24.02 = 24.020, but there is no assurance that zero is the correct digit for that space; that information is missing.

In problems such as the above, the answer is frequently "rounded" to the accuracy of the least accurate component. The procedure for rounding a number is described by the following three steps:

Step 1. Examine the first digit to the right of the decimal place to which the number is to be rounded.

Step 2. If the digit from Step 1 is 4 or smaller, change it and all digits to its right to zero.

Step 3.   If the digit from Step 1 is 5 or greater, add one to the preceding digit and change all digits to its right to zero.

Example 1

Round to hundredths: a.   35.1426   b.   35.1476

Solution:

a.   35.14②6 rounds to 35.14

b.   35.14⑦6 rounds to 35.15

Example 2

Round 1.72546 to the: (a) thousandths place, (b) hundredths place, (c) tenths place, and (d) ones place.

Solution:

a.   1.725④6 rounds to 1.725

b.   1.72⑤46 rounds to 1.73

c.   1.7②46 rounds to 1.7

d.   1.7246 rounds to 2

Example 3

Round 8,671.56 to: (a) hundreds (b) thousands

Solution:

a.   8,700

b.   9,000

In problems 1 through 10, round the given numbers to (a) ones, (b) tenths, and (c) hundredths.

1.	23.413	6.	7,429.867
2.	46.341	7.	217,499.981
3.	217.483	8.	456,799.974
4.	548.372	9.	23,452.899
5.	4,219.785	10.	97,876.979

In problems 11 through 20, round the given numbers to (a) thousands, (b) hundreds, and (c) hundredths.

11.	4,872.576	16.	17,596.991
12.	3,729.049	17.	927,399.954
13.	6,974.997	18.	743,899.639
14.	9,294.372	19.	149,891.691
15.	19,942.193	20.	199,996.797

Money answers resulting from computations in mathematics of finance are rounded off to values that can be paid in standard coinage. In problems 21–28, round the money values accordingly.

21.   Dr. Denton's electric bill was computed from the meter reading in March to be $37.3252. For what amount was she actually billed?

22.   Professor Porter's salary for teaching summer school was to be 28.2 percent of his nine-month salary. On this basis he computed the amount he would be paid for the summer and arrived at the figure $3,721.54731. How much was he actually paid?

23.   Sam Smooth, the salesperson, receives 23.7 percent of his total monthly sales as commission. In September, his computed commission was $533.45831. What commission was he paid?

24.   A retail firm computed that the selling price for its product should be $37.7152 per unit. What will be the actual price per unit?

25. A businesswoman is given a travel allowance based on the number of miles travelled and the number of days spent enroute. For a recent trip, her travel allowance was $37.2992. How much did she receive?

26. A city council decided to spend 12.3 percent of the city's receipts from parking meters on the development of parks and recreation areas. Computation of meter receipts yielded the figure $56,723.72514. How much money can the city spend on parks?

27. Professor Porter computed his deduction for home office space for his income tax and arrived at the figure $407.6952. What amount will he deduct?

28. A real estate salesperson is allowed a depreciation on an automobile for tax purposes, since it is essential to the occupation. Last year the depreciation was computed at $301.247. What figure did the salesperson use on the tax return?

Equations and Formulas

Chapter Objectives for Chapter 3

I. Learn the meaning of the following terms:

II. Understand the concepts of:

III. Learn to:

Introduction

Many ideas in business are expressed as formulas: interest, bank discounts, annuities, and installment accounting are familiar examples. To use formulas effectively in business decisions, it is necessary to understand the basic properties of equations. This chapter begins with a discussion of these properties.

Section **3.2** **Equations and Variables**

An **equation** expresses the equality of two quantities. The equation

$$(3–1) \qquad 6 = 4 + 2$$

means that 6 and $4 + 2$ are symbols for the same number.

One fundamental property of an equation is that the equality is preserved if the same number is added to both sides of the equation. Thus, if 3 is added to both sides of (3–1) we have

$$(3–2) \qquad 6 + 3 = (4 + 2) + 3.$$

Since each side equals 9, the equality is preserved.

This property is inherently nonrestrictive; that is, *any* number added to both sides of an equation preserves the equality. To emphasize this we write

$$(3–3) \qquad 6 + x = (4 + 2) + x$$

The letter x in equation (3–3) acts as a placeholder for any number. Such a placeholder is called a **variable.**

Variables are an important concept in mathematics. The purpose of a variable is to act as a placeholder for numbers. In equation (3–3), if the variable x were replaced by 10, $\frac{3}{2}$, and 0.75 respectively, then the equations would be

$$(3–4) \qquad 6 + 10 = (4 + 2) + 10$$

$$(3–5) \qquad 6 + \tfrac{3}{2} = (4 + 2) + \tfrac{3}{2}$$

$$(3–6) \qquad 6 + 0.75 = (4 + 2) + 0.75$$

Equation (3–3) is an example of an equation with one variable. The equation

$$(3–7) \qquad x + y = y + x$$

is an example of an equation of two variables, where both letters are placeholders for numbers. For particular values of x and y, say 5 for x and 7 for y, equation (3–7) becomes

$$(3–8) \qquad 5 + 7 = 7 + 5.$$

Similarly, if $x = 9$ and $y = 3$, we have

$$(3–9) \qquad 9 + 3 = 3 + 9$$

Clearly, there is no limit to the number of values we could choose for x and y.*

3.3   Identities and Conditional Equations

Equations 3–3 and 3–7 are examples of identities. An **identity** is an equation for which the left side equals the right side for any substitution of the variable(s). However, most equations are of another type called conditional equations. A **conditional equation** is an equation for which the left side does *not* equal the right side for all substitutions of the variable(s). The equation

(3–10) $x = 7$

is a conditional equation. The variable in this equation is x, but only one replacement for x (namely 7) will cause the left side of the equation to equal the right side. All other substitutions fail to produce an equality. Other examples of conditional equations† are

(3–11) $4 \cdot x = 24,$

(3–12) $3 \cdot x + 8 = 17$

The left side is equal to the right side for only one substitution of x, 6 in equation 3–11 and 3 in equation 3–12.

   Like identities, conditional equations may have more than one variable. The equation

(3–13) $y = x + 1$

is a conditional equation of two variables. Again, not all substitutions for the variables will result in equality. For example, the substitution of 1 for x and 5 for y does not result in equality, but 2 for x and 3 for y does.

**Exercises for
Sections 3.2 and 3.3**

In problems 1–8, replace the variable(s) in the given equation with the specified value(s) and write the resulting numerical equation. For example, the equation $3z - z = 2z$ yields the numerical equation $3 \cdot 2 - 2 = 2 \cdot 2$ when $z = 2$.

1. $4x + 2 = 10; x = 2$

2. $7x + 3x = 30; x = 3$

3. $5x + 2 = 3x + (2x + 2); x = 0$

---

* Equation (3–7) is an important property of addition. It shows that a rearrangement of the addends does not affect the sum. This is called the **Commutative Property of Addition.**

† To avoid possible confusion between the variable x and the cross ($\times$) for multiplication, it is customary to use a dot ($\cdot$) as the symbol for multiplication or to omit the symbol entirely. Thus, $4 \times x = 24$, $4 \cdot x = 24$, and $4x = 24$ all have the same meaning.

4. $6(x + 2) = 6x + 6; x = 4.$

5. $xy + 3 = 3 + yx; x = 3, y = 2.$

6. $x(4 + y) = 2x + 2(x + xy) - xy; x = 2, y = 3.$

7. $x(y + z) = xy + xz; x = 2, y = 3, z = 5.$

8. $(x + y) + z = x + (y + z); x = 3, y = 1, z = 2.$

In problems 9–20, state the number of variables in the given equation and classify the equation as either (1) an identity or (2) a conditional equation.

9. $2x - 3 = 0$

10. $xy = 4$

11. $x(y + 3) = xy + 3x$

12. $(x - 1)(2 + 4) = 6x - 6$

13. $(x + y)7 = 7x + 5y$

14. $x(x + y) = x + xy$

15. $x(y + z) = xy + xz$

16. $(x + y)(z + 1) = xz + yz + x + y$

17. $(x + y)(z + w) = xz + xw + yz + yw$

18. $(x + 2y)/2 = (\frac{1}{2})x + y$

19. $x/(y + z) = x/y + x/z$

20. $(x + y + z)/9 = (x + y)/9 + z/9$

21. Write a conditional equation in one variable that is true for exactly one numerical substitution of the variable.

22. Give an example of a conditional equation in one variable that is true for more than one numerical substitution of the variable.

Section **3.4** **Solving Conditional Equations**

A **solution** to a conditional equation is any numerical substitution for the variable(s) that results in equality between the left side of the equation and the right side. Thus 7 is a solution to equation 3–10, 6 is a solution to equation 3–11, and 3 is a solution to equation 3–12. This section is devoted to techniques for finding solutions to conditional equations.

It is easy to see that the solution to equation 3–10 is 7, but the solutions to equations 3–11 and 3–12 are less obvious. However, if these equations could be restructured to a form similar to that of equation 3–10, then their solutions would also be obvious. This is precisely what is done in solving conditional equations.

One set of tools needed to restructure a conditional equation is the arithmetic of chapter 1, because every conditional equation is composed of numbers and placeholders for numbers. The following properties of equations are also needed. An equality is preserved if (A) the same number is added to both sides of the equation; (B) the same number is subtracted from both sides of the equation; (C) both sides of the equation are multiplied by the same number; and (D) both sides of the equation are divided by the same nonzero number.

Other tools frequently used are the following identities:

$(3–14)$ $x + y = y + x$ Commutative Property of Addition

$(3–15)$ $x \cdot y = y \cdot x$ Commutative Property of Multiplication

$(3–16)$ $\left. \begin{aligned} x \cdot z + y \cdot z &= (x + y) \cdot z \\ x \cdot z - y \cdot z &= (x - y) \cdot z \end{aligned} \right\}$ Distributive Properties

We illustrate the use of these tools with a series of examples.

Example 1

Solve: $4 \cdot x = 20$

Solution:

Dividing both sides of the equation by 4, we obtain

$$\frac{4 \cdot x}{4} = \frac{20}{4} \qquad \text{(Property D)}$$

Since $\dfrac{4 \cdot x}{4} = \dfrac{4}{4} \cdot \dfrac{x}{1} = 1 \cdot x = x$ and $\dfrac{20}{4} = 5$, we have

$x = 5$

Check: $4 \cdot 5 = 20$, hence 5 is the correct solution to $4 \cdot x = 20$.

Example 2

Solve: $3 \cdot x + 8 = 17$

Solution:

We eliminate 8 and 3 from the left side of the equation by subtracting 8 from both sides, then dividing both sides by 3.

$3 \cdot x + 8 - 8 = 17 - 8$ (Property B)

$3 \cdot x + 0 \quad\ = 9$ $(8 - 8 = 0,\ 17 - 8 = 9)$

$3 \cdot x \quad\ \ = 9$ $(3 \cdot x + 0 = 3 \cdot x)$

$\dfrac{3 \cdot x}{3} \quad\ \ = \dfrac{9}{3}$ (Property D)

Since $\dfrac{3 \cdot x}{3} = \dfrac{3}{3} \cdot \dfrac{x}{1} = 1 \cdot x = x$ and $\dfrac{9}{3} = 3$ we have

$x = 3$

Check: $3 \cdot 3 + 8 = 17$, hence 3 is the solution.

Example 3

Solve: $\frac{1}{2}x - 6 = 8$

Solution:

We eliminate 6 and $\frac{1}{2}$ from the left side by adding 6 to both sides, then multiplying both sides by 2.

$\frac{1}{2}x - 6 + 6 = 8 + 6$ (Property A)

$\frac{1}{2}x + 0 \quad = 14$ $(6 - 6 = 0, 8 + 6 = 14)$

$\frac{1}{2}x \quad\quad = 14$ $(\frac{1}{2}x + 0 = \frac{1}{2}x)$

$2 \cdot \frac{1}{2}x \quad = 2 \cdot 14$ (Property C)

Since $2 \cdot \frac{1}{2}x = 2 \cdot \frac{1}{2} \cdot x = 1 \cdot x = x$ and $2 \cdot 14 = 28$

we have

$x = 28$

Check:

$\frac{1}{2} \cdot 28 - 6 = 8$, hence 28 is the solution.

Example 4

Solve: $5x + x = 30$

Solution:

$5x + x = 5 \cdot x + 1 \cdot x$, and by equation (3–16)
$5 \cdot x + 1 \cdot x = (5 + 1) \cdot x = 6 \cdot x$, hence

$6 \cdot x = 30$

$\dfrac{6 \cdot x}{6} = \dfrac{30}{6}$ (Property D)

But $\dfrac{6 \cdot x}{6} = x$ and $\dfrac{30}{6} = 5$, thus

$x = 5$

Check: $5 \cdot 5 + 5 = 30$, hence, 5 is the solution.

Example 5

Solve: $10x + 7 = 3x + 56$

Solution:

First 7 then $3x$ is subtracted from both sides, then both sides are divided by 7.

$$10x + 7 - 7 = 3x + 56 - 7 \qquad \text{(Property B)}$$

$$10x + 0 \quad\;\; = 3x + 49 \qquad (7 - 7 = 0, 56 - 7 = 49)$$

$$10x \qquad\;\; = 3x + 49 \qquad (10x + 0 = 10x)$$

$$10x - 3x \quad = 3x - 3x + 49 \qquad \text{(Property B)}$$

By equation $(3–16)$

$$10x - 3x = (10 - 3) \cdot x \text{ and}$$

$$3x - 3x = (3 - 3) \cdot x, \text{ hence we have}$$

$$7 \cdot x \quad\;\; = 0 \cdot x + 49 \qquad (10 - 3 = 7, 3 - 3 = 0)$$

$$7 \cdot x \quad = 49 \qquad\qquad\quad (0 \cdot x = 0)$$

$$\frac{7 \cdot x}{7} \quad = \frac{49}{7} \qquad\qquad \text{(Property D)}$$

$$x \quad\;\; = 7$$

Replacing x by 7 in the original equation, we have

Check: $10 \cdot 7 + 7 = 3 \cdot 7 + 56$

$$77 = 77$$

Exercises for Section 3.4

In problems 1–30, solve the given conditional equation.

1. $2x = 14$ $x = 7$
2. $6x = 24$ $= 4$
3. $3x + 2 = 11$ $x = 3$
4. $4x - 5 = 6$
5. $3x = \frac{7}{2}$
6. $5x = \frac{11}{3}$
7. $(\frac{1}{2})x = 5$
8. $(\frac{1}{4})x = 3$
9. $(\frac{3}{5})x = 6$
10. $(\frac{2}{7})x = 4$
11. $7x + \frac{2}{3} = 4$
12. $3x - \frac{3}{5} = 2$
13. $3x + 2x = 10$

14. $2x + 7x = 18$
15. $(\frac{2}{5})x = 4 - x$
16. $(\frac{3}{4})x = 7 - 3x$
17. $3x - 14 = 2x + 9$
18. $6x - 5 = 3x + 2$
19. $7x - 6 = 3x + 2$
20. $12x + 3 = 7 - 4x$
21. $9x - 3x = 12 + 2x$
22. $20x + 4x - 2 = 14x + 10$
23. $(\frac{2}{3})x = \frac{4}{9}$
24. $(\frac{3}{5})x = \frac{12}{15}$
25. $(\frac{7}{9})x - \frac{1}{2} = \frac{3}{4}$
26. $(\frac{4}{5})x + \frac{2}{3} = \frac{7}{9}$

27. $(\frac{5}{9})x + (\frac{1}{3})x = \frac{1}{2}$ 29. $(\frac{3}{4})x - 2 = (\frac{4}{5}) - (\frac{1}{5})x$

28. $(\frac{2}{3})x - (\frac{5}{9})x = \frac{3}{4}$ 30. $(\frac{5}{6})x + 3 = \frac{1}{2} + (\frac{1}{3})x$

31. Does the equation $2x = 2(x + 4)$ have a solution? Explain your answer.

3.5 Conditional Equations and Word Problems

The Grayson Wholesale Plumbing Company has outlets in Atlanta and Knoxville. During April the sales of the Atlanta office were three times the sales of the Knoxville office. Together their sales totaled $24,000. What were the sales of each outlet?

"Word" problems such as the above have two parts to the solution: (a) expressing the problem as a conditional equation and (b) solving the conditional equation.

While no algorithm exists for converting a word problem to a conditional equation, there are steps that are often helpful.

1. Read the problem carefully to ascertain the "known" and "unknown" information.
2. Denote one item of the unknown information by a variable, then express the remaining unknown items in terms of this variable.*
3. Write a conditional equation that combines the known and unknown information.
4. Solve the equation for the variable and check your answer.

In the plumbing company problem cited earlier, these steps are as follows:

1a. Unknown Information

    (1)   The April sales of the Atlanta office
    (2)   The April sales of the Knoxville office

  b. Known Information

    (1)   Total Sales = $24,000
    (2)   Total Sales = Atlanta sales + Knoxville sales
    (3)   Atlanta sales = 3 times Knoxville sales

2.   Let x = April sales of the Knoxville office

          $3x$ = April sales of the Atlanta office

3. $x + 3x = \$24,000$

          $4x = \$24,000$ (Equation (3–16))

---

* In many word problems more than one variable may be required, but such problems are beyond the scope of this text.

4. $\dfrac{4x}{4} = \dfrac{\$24{,}000}{4}$ (Property D)

$x = \$6{,}000,$

$3x = 3 \cdot \$6{,}000 = \$18{,}000$

Check: $x + 3x = \$6{,}000 + \$18{,}000 = \$24{,}000$

Thus, for the month of April the Knoxville sales were $6,000 and the Atlanta sales were $18,000.

Example 1

The Toast-Eze Company sells its economy toaster for % of the production cost plus $3. If the selling price of the toaster is $27, what is the production cost per unit?

Solution:

1a.   Unknown Information

    (1)   The production cost per unit

  b.   Known Information

    (1)   Selling price for one unit $= \$27$
    (2)   Selling price per unit $=$ % of production cost plus $3

2.   Let $x =$ the production cost per unit

3. $27 \quad\ = (\%)x + 3$

    $27 - 3 = (\%)x + 3 - 3$ (Property B)

    $24 \quad\ = (\%)x$

    $5 \cdot 24 \ = (5)(\%)x$ (Property C)

Since $5 \cdot (\%) = 6$, we have

    $120 = 6x$

Thus $\dfrac{120}{6} = \dfrac{6x}{6},$ (Property D)

and $20 = x$

Check: Substituting $x = 20$ into the equation, we have

    $27 = (\%)(20) + 3$

    $27 = 24 + 3$

    $27 = 27$

thus, the production cost per unit is $20.

Example 2

Walker's Produce Market received a shipment of tomatoes and avocados. The cost of the tomatoes was $7.50 a box and the avocados cost $12.00 a box. The total cost of the shipment was $360 and there were 36 boxes in the shipment. Find the number of boxes of tomatoes and the number of boxes of avocados received in the shipment.

Solution:

1a. Unknown Information

    (1)   The number of boxes of tomatoes

    (2)   The number of boxes of avocados

  b. Known Information

    (1)   Total number of boxes in the shipment $= 36$

    (2)   Total cost of shipment $= \$360$

    (3)   Cost of tomatoes per box $= \$7.50$

    (4)   Cost of avocados per box $= \$12.00$

    (5)   Total cost of avocados plus total cost of tomatoes $= \$360$

2.   If $x =$ number of boxes of avocados, then $36 - x =$ number of boxes of tomatoes.

3. $12x + (7.5)(36 - x) = 360$

4. $12x + (36 - x)(7.5) = 360$ (Equation (3–15))

      $12x + 36(7.5) - x(7.5) = 360$ (Equation (3–16))

      $12x - (7.5)x + 36(7.5) = 360$

      $(12 - 7.5)x + 270 \; = 360$ (Equation (3–16))

      $(4.5)x + 270 - 270 = 360 - 270$ (Property B)

      $(4.5)x \qquad\qquad = 90$

      $\dfrac{(4.5)x}{4.5} \qquad\qquad = \dfrac{90}{4.5}$ (Property D)

                $x = 20$

           $36 - x = 16$

Check: $12(20) + (7.5)(16) = 360$

Thus, 20 boxes of avocados and 16 boxes of tomatoes were in the shipment.

Express the given problem as a conditional equation in one variable and solve.

1. The C and J Appliance Store sold 125 refrigerators during a recent five-day sale. If the same number of refrigerators were sold each day of the sale, how many were sold each day?

2. One fifth of the sales of the Fit-N-Trim Sporting Goods Store are charges. Find the total sales of the store on a day when charges total $225.

3. A television set is on sale for $83, which is $\frac{5}{6}$ of the regular price. What is the regular price?

4. A supermarket chain purchased two tracts of land on which to build new stores. Tract A cost $3,000 more than tract B, and the two tracts together cost $47,500. How much did each tract cost?

5. Professor Porter's salary is $72 a month less than Professor Smith's. If their combined salary is $1,750 per month, what is the monthly salary of each?

6. An apartment complex contains only one and two-bedroom units, and there are twice as many one-bedroom units as two-bedroom units. If there are a total of 120 units, how many one-bedroom apartments are there?

7. Sam Smooth's commission for February was $15 more than half his commission for March, and his total commission for the two months was $633. Find his commission for each month.

8. The number of administrative employees at a plant is $\frac{1}{11}$ the number of assembly line workers. If the company employs 240 people in administrative and assembly line work, how many are administrators? How many are assembly line workers?

9. Elsie's Restaurant spent 3.2 times as much for television advertising last year as for all other types of advertising. If the total amount spent on advertising for the year was $9,240, how much was spent on television advertising? How much was spent on other types of advertising?

10. Cool Pool, Inc., built 539 swimming pools last year. If they build $4\frac{1}{2}$ times as many rectangular pools as nonrectangular pools, find the number of rectangular pools constructed. How many nonrectangular pools were built?

11. J. W. Masterson, a building contractor, purchased sand and gravel for a construction project. He bought $3\frac{1}{4}$ times as much sand as gravel, and the total amount of sand and gravel purchased was 42 tons. Find

the number of tons of sand and the number of tons of gravel that he bought.

12. An estate is valued at $225,000 and is to be distributed to a son and a daughter so that the daughter receives four times as much as the son. What is the son's share of the estate? What is the daughter's share?

13. A warehouse contains 440,000 square feet of storage space. Company A leases three times as much as company B. How much space does each company lease, if together they lease the entire warehouse?

14. The Brite-Lite Company produces 1,100 reading lamps a day when it operates on two shifts. The first shift produces only ⅚ as many lamps as the second shift. Find the number of lamps that each shift produces per day.

15. The inventory of the Comfort-Step Shoe Store totaled $56,000. If the inventory for ladies' shoes was 2½ times the inventory for men's shoes, what was the inventory for men's shoes?

16. Bud's Hardware Store makes a profit of $3 on each economy model electric hand drill it sells, and it makes a $4 profit on each deluxe drill sold. In one week, the store made $289 profit from the sale of drills. If four more deluxe drills were sold than economy drills, how many drills of each type were sold during the week?

17. Two more than one-fifth of the employees of a company have 20 years or more of service. If 15 employees have 20 or more years of service, find the number of people employed by the company.

18. The Bargain Furniture Store pays $112 a unit for one type of office desk and $45 a unit for the matching file cabinet. A recent shipment of 22 units of the office furniture cost the store $1,660. How many desks and how many file cabinets were in the shipment?

19. A manufacturing company finds that to produce one unit of its product, it costs $140 for labor and $230 for material. The total cost for labor and material during the month of January was $14,060. How many units did the company produce in January?

Section 3.6 Formulas

As noted in equation (3–13), a conditional equation may contain more than one variable. Conditional equations with more than one variable are sometimes called **formulas.** The equations

(3–17) $$y = 3x + 7$$

(3–18) $$P = B \cdot R$$

(3–19) $$I = Prt$$

are formulas. Generally, formulas have one variable on the left side of the equation and the remaining variables on the right side of the equation.

Primarily, formulas are used to evaluate the variable on the left side for given substitutions of the variables on the right side. This is illustrated by the following examples.

Example 1

In formula $(3-17)$ evaluate y if:

a. $x = 4$ b. $x = 7$

Solution:

a.   If $x = 4$, then $y = 3 \cdot 4 + 7$ b.   If $x = 7$, then $y = 3 \cdot 7 + 7$

$\qquad\qquad\qquad y = 19$ $\qquad\qquad\qquad\qquad\qquad\qquad y = 28$

Example 2

In formula $(3-18)$ evaluate P if:

a. $B = 16$ and $R = 12$

b. $B = 480$ and $R = \frac{3}{4}$

Solution:

a. $P = BR$ $\qquad\qquad$ b. $P = BR$

$\quad P = 16 \cdot 12$ $\qquad\qquad\qquad P = 480 \cdot \frac{3}{4}$

$\quad P = 192$ $\qquad\qquad\qquad\qquad P = 360$

Example 3

Evaluate I in formula $(3-19)$ if:

a. $P = 14, r = 6, t = 8$

b. $P = 25, r = 14, t = \frac{3}{4}$

Solution:

a. $I = Prt$ $\qquad\qquad$ b. $I = Prt$

$\quad I = 14 \cdot 6 \cdot 8$ $\qquad\qquad\qquad I = 25 \times 14 \times \frac{3}{4}$

$\quad I = 672$ $\qquad\qquad\qquad\qquad I = 262\frac{1}{2}$

Since formulas are equations, it is possible to restructure formulas using the properties of equations. For example, to solve formula (3–17) for x in terms of y,

$$y = 3x + 7$$

$$3x + 7 = y$$

$$3x = y - 7 \qquad \text{(Property B)}$$

$$x = \frac{y - 7}{3} \qquad \text{(Property D)}$$

Example 4

a. Solve formula (3–18) for R.

b. Find R if $P = 3,460$ and $B = 20$.

Solution:

a. $P = BR$

$BR = P$

$R = \dfrac{P}{B} \qquad \text{(Property D)}$

b. $R = \dfrac{P}{B}$

$R = \dfrac{3,460}{20}$

$R = 173$

Example 5

a. Solve formula (3–19) for t.

b. Find t if $I = 540$, $r = 0.045$, $P = 6,000$.

Solution:

a. $I = Prt$

$Prt = I$

$t = \dfrac{I}{Pr} \qquad \text{(Property D)}$

b. $t = \dfrac{I}{Pr}$

$t = \dfrac{540}{6,000 \times 0.045}$

$t = 2$

Example 6

The H & N Candy Company has determined that the demand for their deluxe box of Valentine candy is

$$x = 18{,}000 - \frac{8{,}000p}{3}$$

where p is the selling price per box to dealers and x is the number of boxes that can be sold. Find the number of boxes that can be sold if

a. $p = \$1.95$ b. $p = \$2.85$ c. $p = \$4.50$

Solution:

a. $x = 18{,}000 - \dfrac{8{,}000p}{3}$

$\quad = 18{,}000 - \dfrac{8{,}000 \times 1.95}{3}$

$\quad = 18{,}000 - \left(8{,}000 \times \dfrac{1.95}{3}\right)$

$\quad = 18{,}000 - 5{,}200$

$\quad = 12{,}800$

b. $x = 18{,}000 - \dfrac{8{,}000p}{3}$

$\quad = 18{,}000 - \dfrac{8{,}000 \times 2.85}{3}$

$\quad = 18{,}000 - \left(8{,}000 \times \dfrac{2.85}{3}\right)$

$\quad = 18{,}000 - 7{,}600$

$\quad = 10{,}400$

c. $x = 18{,}000 - \dfrac{8{,}000p}{3}$

$\quad = 18{,}000 - \dfrac{8{,}000 \times 4.50}{3}$

$\quad = 18{,}000 - \left(8{,}000 \times \dfrac{4.50}{3}\right)$

$\quad = 18{,}000 - 12{,}000$

$\quad = 6{,}000$

Example 7

The formula for gross sales is $G = np$ where G = gross sales, n = number of items sold, and p = price per item. Which of the prices in Example 6 produces the largest gross sales?

Solution:

a. $G = np$

$= 12,800 \times \$1.95$

$= \$24,960$

b. $G = np$

$= 10,400 \times \$2.85$

$= \$29,640$

c. $G = np$

$= 6,000 \times \$4.50$

$= \$27,000$

Thus, a price of \$2.85 produces the largest gross sales.

Exercises for Section 3.6

In problems 1–8, evaluate the variable on the left side of the given formula when the variables on the right side of the formula are given the indicated values.

1. $y = x + 2z$; $x = 3$, $z = 10$

2. $P = 2l + 2w$; $l = 4$, $w = 5$

3. $V = lwh$; $l = 2$, $w = 5$, $h = 2$

4. $A = (bh)/2$; $b = 8$, $h = 3$

5. $I = Prt$; $P = 2,000$, $r = 0.05$, $t = 2$

6. $R = (abc)/4K$; $a = 2$, $b = 1$, $c = 3$, $K = \frac{1}{2}$

7. $K = [(a + b)h]/2$; $a = 3$, $b = 1$, $h = 0.5$

8. $V = (\frac{1}{6})h(b + B + 4M)$; $M = 3$, $B = 9$, $b = 3$, $h = 1$

9. Solve the formula in problem 1 for z. Find z if $y = 4$ and $x = 0$.

10. Solve the formula in problem 2 for l. Find l if $P = 20$ and $w = 5$.

11. Solve the formula in problem 6 for c. Find c if $R = 2$, $K = 4$, $a = 1$, and $b = 4$.

12. Solve the formula in problem 8 for B. Find B if $V = 12$, $h = 3$, $b = 4$, and $M = 2$.

In problems 13–20, solve the given formula for x and find the value of x when y and z are given the indicated values.

13. $z = xyz - 2y$; $y = 2$, $z = 3$

14. $y = (z - 4)/(xz)$; $y = 3$, $z = 8$

15. $y = xz + yz - z$; $y = 1$, $z = 6$

16. $z = (yx + y)/(y + 1)$; $y = 2$, $z = 6$

17. $z = x/y - 5$; $y = 2$, $z = 7$

18. $z = x/(zy) - y$; $y = 4$, $z = 8$

19. $y = 1/(xyz) - 2z$; $y = 2$, $z = 3$

20. $z = (xyz)/(y + z)$; $y = 4$, $z = 5$

21. The formula $G = np$ is used to compute the gross sales G from the sale of n units of a product at a selling price of p dollars per unit. Solve this formula for n. If a product is sold for $8 per unit and the gross sales are $3,200, how many units are sold?

22. Simple interest is computed by the formula $I = Prt$, where $I =$ interest, $P =$ principal, $r =$ rate of interest, and $t =$ time. Find the interest paid on $2,000 invested for two years at rate $r = 0.05$.

23. Solve the formula $I = Prt$ for r in terms of I, P, and t. Find the value of r if a principal of $4,000 earns $800 interest over a period of four years. (See problem 22.)

24. The formula $N = G - C$ is used to compute the net profit N where G is gross profit and C is production cost. Solve this formula for C and find the production cost if the gross profit is $280,520 and the net profit is $42,520.

25. The checking accounts at the West End Bank are subject to a monthly charge of C dollars, where C is given by the formula $C = 1 + (0.01)x$ and x is the number of checks written during the month. Find the charge C for a month where (a) 25 checks are written, (b) 30 checks are written, and (c) 40 checks are written.

26. The amount S of Sam Smooth's weekly paycheck is given by the formula $S = 125 + x/10$, where x is the amount of his sales during the week (in dollars). Find the amount of Sam's paycheck for a week in which he sells (a) $700 worth of merchandise, (b) $950 worth of merchandise, and (c) $1,200 worth of merchandise.

27. A company estimates that its production cost C to produce x units of its product is given by the formula $C = 5x + 1,000$. Find C when (a) 1,000 units are produced, (b) 1,200 units are produced, and (c) 2,000 units are produced.

28. The Sporty Shirt Company finds that the amount S of its weekly gross sales is given by the formula $S = 1,500 + 100x$, where x is the

number of 30-second television commercials per week. Find the weekly gross sales if (a) 8 commercials are run, (b) 15 commercials are run, and (c) 20 commercials are run.

29. The cost S (in dollars) of an order of x pounds of premium grade fertilizer from the Gro-Green Fertilizer Company is given by the formula $S = (0.6)x + 1$. Find the cost of an order of (a) 60 pounds, (b) 100 pounds, and (c) 120 pounds.

30. Magnum Corporation determines the retail price p for its product by using the formula $p = 18 - x/250$, where x is the number of units produced by the company. Determine the price p if the company produces (a) 250 units, (b) 750 units, and (c) 1,000 units.

31. The Drill-Rite Company determines that the demand x for their deluxe electric drill is given by the formula $x = 3,000 - (200/3)p$ where p is the selling price per drill to dealers and x is the number of drills that can be sold. How many drills can be sold if the price p is (a) $12, (b) $15, and (c) $18?

32. Use the formula $G = np$, when $G =$ gross sales, $n =$ number of units sold, and $p =$ price per unit to determine which of the prices in problem 31 yields the maximum gross sales.

33. Budget Beans, Inc., estimates that the demand x for their small size can of baked beans is given by the formula $x = 24,000 - 1,250p$, where p is the selling price (in cents) per can and x is the number of cans that can be sold. Find the number of cans that can be sold if the price p is (a) 8¢, (b) 10¢, and (c) 13¢.

34. Use the formula $G = np$, where $G =$ gross sales, $n =$ number of units sold, and $p =$ price per unit to determine which of the prices in problem 33 yields the maximum gross sales.

4

Percentage, Base, and Percent

Chapter Objectives for Chapter 4

I. Learn the meaning of the following terms:

II. Understand:

III. Learn to convert:

Learn to:

Introduction

Progress is measured by comparison with a predetermined base. For example, we compare this week's production with last week's production, this month's sales with last month's sales, this year's earnings with last year's earnings. Whether increase or decrease, these changes are frequently measured in percent.

MANAGEMENT'S DISCUSSION AND ANALYSIS OF
CONSOLIDATED STATEMENT OF EARNINGS

Category	Change (Millions of Dollars)		Principal Causes
	1975	1974	
Net Shipments Mining Machinery Construction Machinery Industrial Products Total	Up $ 99 (79%) Down $ 12 (10%) Up $ 5 (24%) Up $ 92 (35%)	Up $ 42 (51%) Up $ 25 (27%) Up $ 7 (54%) Up $ 74 (40%)	Increased demand in both years for mining machinery and oil related construction machinery due to energy crisis, but construction machinery overall down in 1975 due to recession in construction industry
Interest, Royalties & Miscellaneous Revenues	Down $ 0.2 (6%)	Up $1.0 (33%)	Variation in interest on short-term investments and notes receivable
Cost of Products Sold	Up $ 61 (32%)	Up $ 59 (44%)	Increased volume
Gross Margins (Net Shipments Less Cost of Products Sold)	Up $ 31 (44%) to 29% margin from 27%	Up $ 15 (28%) but margin dropped to 27% from 29%	Favorable effect, after late 1974, of broader mining machinery escalation clauses and current pricing of construction machinery

Courtesy of the Bucyrus-Erie Company. From the company's Annual Report 1975, page 43.

Salesmen are often paid according to the dollar amount of their sales. A portion of the total amount is paid in commissions, bonuses, and override. The unit of measurement for these payments is percent.

Banks and savings and loan companies pay investors and charge borrowers according to fixed rates. Again, the unit of measurement for these rates is percent.

The Meaning of Percent

As illustrated above, percent is an important business term. In fact, no other word dominates the quantitative language of business as does percent. The word stems from the Latin *per centum* meaning "by the hundred." With time, the phrase was shortened to per cent, and now it appears as the single word percent.

Because our number system is the decimal system and because our monetary system is decimal based, it is natural to subdivide units into "hundredths." In business, these "hundredths" are called percent.

The symbol for percent is %. Thus 5% means "5 hundredths" and 75% means "75 hundredths." From chapter 2, we conclude that

$$5\% = \frac{5}{100} = 0.05$$

and

$$75\% = \frac{75}{100} = 0.75$$

The following examples demonstrate simple methods for converting percents to fractions or decimal numbers and vice versa.

Example 1

Convert the following percents to decimal numbers:

a. 2%   b. 47%   c. 6.5%   d. $12\frac{3}{4}\%$

e. $\frac{1}{2}\%$ f. 130%

Solution:

a. $2\% = \frac{2}{100} = 0.02$

d. $12\frac{3}{4}\% = 12.75\% = \frac{12.75}{100} = 0.1275$

b. $47\% = \frac{47}{100} = 0.47$

e. $\frac{1}{2}\% = 0.5\% = \frac{0.5}{100} = 0.005$

c. $6.5\% = \frac{6.5}{100} = 0.065$

f. $130\% = \frac{130}{100} = 1.30$

Observe from this example that a shortcut method for converting a percent to a decimal number is to move the decimal point two places to the left and drop the % symbol.

Example 2

Convert the following decimal numbers to percents:

a.   0.03   b.   0.1   c.   0.045   d.   0.8525

e.   0.00075   f.   1.25

Solution:

a. $0.03 = \dfrac{3}{100} = 3\%$

b. $0.1 = 0.10 = \dfrac{10}{100} = 10\%$

c. $0.045 = \dfrac{4.5}{100} = 4.5\%$ (or $4\frac{1}{2}\%$)

d. $0.8525 = \dfrac{85.25}{100} = 85.25\%$ (or $85\frac{1}{4}\%$)

e. $0.00075 = \dfrac{.075}{100} = 0.075\%$ $\left(\text{or } \dfrac{75}{1000}\%\right)$

f. $1.25 = \dfrac{125}{100} = 125\%$

Thus, a shortcut method for converting decimal numbers to percents is to move the decimal point two places to the right and affix the % symbol.

Example 3

Convert the following percents to fractions:

a.   20%   b.   45%   c. $\frac{3}{4}\%$ d.   0.5%

e. $\frac{9}{4}\%$ f.   110%

Solution:

a. $20\% = \dfrac{20}{100} = \dfrac{1}{5}$

b. $45\% = \dfrac{45}{100} = \dfrac{9}{20}$

c. $\frac{3}{4}\% = \dfrac{\frac{3}{4}}{100} = \dfrac{3}{400}$

d. $0.5\% = \frac{1}{2}\% = \dfrac{\frac{1}{2}}{100} = \dfrac{1}{200}$

e. $\frac{9}{4}\% = \dfrac{\frac{9}{4}}{100} = \dfrac{9}{400}$

f. $110\% = \dfrac{110}{100} = \dfrac{11}{10}$

The next examples illustrate converting fractions to percents. To convert a fraction to a percent, divide the numerator of the fraction by the denominator for two places to the right of the decimal point; the percent consists of the digits of the quotient plus the fraction whose numerator is the remainder and whose denominator is the divisor.

Example 4

Find the percent equal to $\frac{1}{8}$.

Solution:

$$
\begin{array}{r}
0.12 \\
8)\overline{1.00} \\
\underline{8} \\
20 \\
\underline{16} \\
4
\end{array}
$$

Thus, $\frac{1}{8} = 12\frac{4}{8}\% = 12\frac{1}{2}\%$

Example 5

Find the percent equal to $\frac{3}{20}$.

Solution:

$$
\begin{array}{r}
0.15 \\
20)\overline{3.00} \\
\underline{2\,0} \\
1\,00 \\
\underline{1\,00} \\
0
\end{array}
$$

$\frac{3}{20} = 15\%$

Example 6

Find the percent equal to $\frac{1}{3}$.

Solution:

$$
\begin{array}{r}
0.33 \\
3\overline{)\,1.00} \\
\underline{9} \\
10 \\
\underline{9} \\
1
\end{array}
$$

$\frac{1}{3} = 33\frac{1}{3}\%$

Example 7

Find the percent equal to $\frac{7}{5}$.

Solution:

$$
\begin{array}{r}
1.4 \\
5\overline{)\,7.00} \\
\underline{5} \\
20 \\
\underline{20}
\end{array}
$$

$\frac{7}{5} = 1.40 = \frac{140}{100} = 140\%$

Certain percents occur frequently in business because they are equivalent to simple fractions, which facilitates computations. For example, $33\frac{1}{3}\% = \frac{1}{3}$, $50\% = \frac{1}{2}$, etc. Table 4–1 shows some of the more common percents and their equivalent fractions.

Table 4–1*

$\frac{1}{2}$=50%	$\frac{1}{3}$=33$\frac{1}{3}$%	$\frac{1}{4}$=25%	$\frac{1}{5}$=20%	$\frac{1}{6}$=16$\frac{2}{3}$%	$\frac{1}{8}$=12$\frac{1}{2}$%	$\frac{1}{12}$=8$\frac{1}{3}$%
	$\frac{2}{3}$=66$\frac{2}{3}$%	$\frac{3}{4}$=75%	$\frac{2}{5}$=40%	$\frac{5}{6}$=83$\frac{1}{3}$%	$\frac{3}{8}$=37$\frac{1}{2}$%	$\frac{5}{12}$=41$\frac{2}{3}$%
			$\frac{3}{5}$=60%		$\frac{5}{8}$=62$\frac{1}{2}$%	$\frac{7}{12}$=58$\frac{1}{3}$%
			$\frac{4}{5}$=80%		$\frac{7}{8}$=87$\frac{1}{2}$%	$\frac{11}{12}$=91$\frac{2}{3}$%

* An aliquot part of 100 is any number that divides 100 evenly. Each of the percents in line 1 of the table represents an aliquot part of 100.

Exercises for Section 4.2

In problems 1–18, convert the given percents to decimal numbers.

1. 4%

2. 9%

3. 52%

4. 43%

5. 92.6%	12. $4\frac{3}{4}\%$
6. 87.4%	13. $\frac{1}{4}\%$
7. 7.31%	14. $\frac{3}{4}\%$
8. 5.39%	15. 321%
9. 92.42%	16. 142%
10. 61.37%	17. 172.5%
11. $11\frac{1}{2}\%$	18. 849.3%

In problems 19–36, convert the given decimal numbers to percents.

19. 0.01	28. 0.6421
20. 0.04	29. 0.0052
21. 0.53	30. 0.0047
22. 0.71	31. 4.32
23. 0.7	32. 5.17
24. 0.9	33. 6.241
25. 0.053	34. 8.992
26. 0.019	35. 7.0263
27. 0.5934	36. 8.5752

In problems 37–60, convert the given percents to fractions reduced to lowest terms.

37. 14%	49. $\frac{3}{5}\%$
38. 28%	50. $\frac{7}{12}\%$
39. 35%	51. $\frac{1}{4}\%$
40. 82%	52. $\frac{3}{5}\%$
41. 0.2%	53. 102%
42. 0.4%	54. 240%
43. 0.25%	55. 122%
44. 0.75%	56. 340%
45. 0.44%	57. 98.4%
46. 0.86%	58. 72.6%
47. $\frac{7}{8}\%$	59. 166.6%
48. $\frac{5}{6}\%$	60. 148.2%

Convert each of the fractions given in problems 61–76 to percents.

61.	¼	69.	$^{15}\!/_{16}$
62.	⅕	70.	$^{21}\!/_{25}$
63.	¾	71.	$^{9}\!/_{11}$
64.	⅘	72.	$^{7}\!/_{9}$
65.	$^{7}\!/_{20}$	73.	$^{1}\!/_{15}$
66.	$^{9}\!/_{20}$	74.	$^{8}\!/_{5}$
67.	⅞	75.	$^{9}\!/_{4}$
68.	⅝	76.	$^{12}\!/_{11}$

Section **4.3** **Percentage and Base**

Percent is related to two other quantities, base and percentage. The sentence

$$\text{"\$46.00 is 40\% of \$115.00"}$$

illustrates the relationship of these three quantities. The **base** is a quantity one calculates a percent "of;" in the above sentence, $115.00 is the base. The **percentage** is the product of the percent and the base. Since $0.40 \times \$115.00 = \$46.00$, $46.00 is the percentage in the above sentence. This relationship between percent, base, and percentage is summarized by the formula

(4–1) $P = B \cdot R$

where P = percentage, B = base, and R = percent or "rate."

Because the words percent and percentage are similar, they are frequently used incorrectly. Many times percent is used in conversation by someone who is actually discussing percentage, or vice versa. Formula (4–1) clarifies the distinction between the two words; percentage is a quantity determined by multiplying the base quantity by the percent.

When the base and percent are known, formula (4–1) is used to find the percentage. When the percent and percentage are known, a formula for finding the base is found by dividing both sides of formula (4–1) by R to obtain

(4–2) $B = \dfrac{P}{R}$

When the percentage and base are the given quantities, a formula for finding the percent is found by dividing both sides of formula (4–1) by B to obtain

(4–3) $R = \dfrac{P}{B}$

Many problems that involve percent, percentage, or base can be solved using formulas (4–1), (4–2), and (4–3). Choosing the correct formula for a given problem depends upon correctly identifying the known and unknown quantities. It is helpful to keep in mind that the base is the quantity that we find the percent "of."

American League

TEAM BATTING

	AB	R	H	HR	RBI	Pct
Kansas City	4091	565	1121	55	520	.274
Minnesota	4130	527	1117	57	491	.270
New York	4099	550	1105	94	509	.276
Cleveland	4089	475	1082	67	435	.265
Detroit	4077	469	1072	81	438	.263
Boston	4023	489	1022	89	447	.254
Chicago	4174	444	1060	61	407	.254
Texas	4116	483	1027	57	449	.250
Milwaukee	3879	421	967	69	399	.249
Oakland	4005	537	988	85	485	.247
Baltimore	3949	446	950	88	415	.241
California	4006	415	937	50	384	.234

INDIVIDUAL BATTING
225 or more at bats

		AB	R	H	HR	RBI	Pct
McRae	KC	373	61	132	7	55	.354
G.Brett	KC	487	78	166	6	53	.341
Poquette	KC	250	34	84	2	28	.336
LeFlore	Det	459	78	153	3	37	.333
Carew	Min	452	72	146	6	68	.323
Garr	Chi	400	48	127	4	28	.318
Bostock	Min	337	46	106	3	51	.315
Staub	Det	437	52	135	11	71	.309

Munson	NY	457	67	141	13	77	.309
Carty	Cle	410	54	126	12	65	.307
Lynn	Bos	401	56	122	9	48	.304
Manning	Cle	471	59	142	5	38	.301
Chambliss	NY	482	61	144	15	81	.299
Rivers	NY	490	77	146	8	57	.298
Hargrove	Tex	404	66	120	6	51	.297
Lezcano	Mil	343	35	100	6	38	.292
B.Bell	Cle	452	57	130	5	44	.288
Cooper	Bos	306	44	88	10	51	.288
W.Stein	Chi	239	23	68	3	27	.285
Otis	KC	446	77	126	16	70	.283
North	Oak	439	78	124	2	27	.282
Orta	Chi	484	60	135	12	57	.279
Burleson	Bos	392	54	109	4	27	.278
Braun	Min	314	48	87	3	44	.277
Piniella	NY	235	27	65	3	27	.277
A.Johnson	Det	363	35	100	5	39	.275
R.White	NY	468	80	128	12	51	.274
G.Scott	Mil	447	53	122	12	57	.273
Rudi	Oak	356	41	97	10	72	.272
Money	Mil	386	50	105	11	51	.272
Grich	Bal	387	71	105	11	38	.271
Hisle	Min	443	60	120	11	66	.271
Yount	Mil	452	43	122	2	48	.270
ReJackson	Bal	356	57	96	21	76	.270
Hendrick	Cle	413	57	111	20	60	.269
Campaneris	Oak	411	54	110	0	38	.268

Example 1

What amount is 5% of $3,000?

Solution:

The key is "5% of." $P = ?$, $B = \$3,000$, $R = 5\%$. Using formula (4–1),

$$P = B \cdot R$$

$$= \$3,000 \times 0.05$$

$$= \$150$$

$150 is 5% of $3,000.

Example 2

Twenty-five percent of what number is 30?

Solution:

The key is "25% of." $B = ?$, $P = 30$, $R = 25\%$. Using formula (4–2),

$$B = \frac{P}{R}$$

$$= \frac{30}{.25}$$

$$= 120$$

25% of 120 is 30.

Example 3

This month's inventory of 248 cases is 80% of last month's inventory. What was the inventory of the previous month?

Solution:

The key is "80% of." $B = ?, P = 248, R = 80\%$. Using formula (4–2),

$$B = \frac{P}{R}$$

$$= \frac{248}{.80}$$

$$= 310$$

The inventory of the previous month was 310 cases.

Example 4

If the commission on a sale of $42.00 is $3.78, what percent commission is paid?

Solution:

The key is "sale of." $R = ?, P = \$3.78, B = \$42.00$. Using formula (4–3),

$$R = \frac{P}{B}$$

$$= \frac{3.78}{42}$$

$$= 0.09$$

$$= 9\%$$

Exercises for Section 4.3

In problems 1–12, find the indicated amounts.

1. 4% of 200
2. 8% of 600
3. 12% of 40
4. 16% of 120
5. 42% of 16
6. 36% of 43
7. 5% of the amount is 12
8. 12% of the amount is 14
9. 15% of the amount is 10.215
10. 18% of the amount is 18.432
11. 21% of the amount is 6.5541
12. 47% of the amount is 8.7796

13. What percent of 240 is 12?   *5%*

14. What percent of 120 is 18?   *15*

15. What percent of 96 is 2.88?   *3%*

16. What percent of 112 is 10.08?

17. What percent of 45.6 is 3.192?

18. What percent of 68.4 is 9.576?

19. Mary Mackey purchased a new refrigerator priced at $275. She made a down payment of 15% of the price. Find the amount of the down payment.   *41.25*

20. Pete's Pet Shop spent $1,825 for advertising this year. Last year the store spent 82% of this amount. How much was spent on advertising last year?

21. The Quality-Wise Furniture Store recorded total sales of $21,000 for January, of which $4,200 were charges. What percent of the sales were charges?   *20%*

22. Barb Fox had a total income of $11,362 for the year and paid $1,477.06 in taxes. Find the percent of her income that she paid in taxes.   *13%*

23. Sam Smooth earned $32 commission on the sale of a color television set. If the commission rate is 4%, find the selling price of the set.   *800.00*

24. The annual dividend returns from an investment in preferred stock is $450. If this return is 7% of the investment, how much did the stock cost?   *6428.57*

25. Northwest Motors, Inc., accepted 160 used cars as trade-ins during February. Of these, 25% were wholesaled to a used car dealer and 5% were sold as junk. The remaining cars were reconditioned and sold through the company's used car division. How many cars were reconditioned? How many cars were sold as junk?

26. Cameron Industries employs 580 people, of which 493 are union members. What percent of the company's work force are members of the union?

27. Peabody & Sons, Inc., reduced its monthly office expense by 5% after consulting efficiency experts. If the monthly office expense was $3,200 before the efficiency study, how much per month did the company save?

28. Paxton Products, Inc., reported a profit of $17,500 for the month of January, which was 5.4% of the company's sales. Find the amount of the company's January sales.

29. Professor Porter places $81 each month in a savings account, which is 4.5% of his monthly take-home pay. How much take-home pay does he receive each month?

30. The Eltek Corporation reported profits of $26,730 in April on sales of $356,400. What percent of the company's April sales are its profits?

31. William Martin bought corporate stock for $7,400 and sold it for $7,998. What percent of his original investment was his profit?

32. During a recent sale at Stan's Music store, the profit made on Regal transistor radios was 5% of the sale price. If the profit on each radio was 75¢, find the sale price of the radios.

33. The manager of the men's department decides to close out a certain line of sports coats, so he reduces the price of the coats from $60 to $48. What percent of the original price is the reduced price?

34. Lotus Industries reports that due to rising expenses, the development of one of its new products costs 20% more than originally projected. If it cost $12,000 more than projected to develop the product, find the original estimate of the cost.

    60,000

35. Frances Thomas purchased the Children's Apparel Shop. At the end of the first year she had $21,200 invested in the shop. If the net income from the shop was $9,200 for the year, what percent of the investment did she receive as income? (Round to the nearest percent.)

36. The Fairview Meat Market pays 3% of its monthly net sales to the landlord for rent. In February the market's net sales were $39,472.40. How much rent did the market pay for February? (Round to the nearest cent.)

37. Jan Foster paid $3,671.10 in federal income taxes based on an adjusted gross income of $17,468.20. What percent of her adjusted gross income did she pay in taxes? (Round to the nearest percent.)

38. Bill Curtis has $32.67 deducted from his monthly check for health insurance, which is 7% of his gross pay. What is Bill's monthly gross pay? (Round to the nearest cent.) *466.71*

39. A salesman sold $885 worth of fittings. At a commission rate of 7% of sales, how much commission will he receive?

40. Bob Snyder purchased a new television set for a total price of $734.50. If the sales tax was $23.50, what percent of the total price was sales tax? (Round to the nearest percent.)

    3.2

4.4 Variations of the Percentage Formula

At the beginning of this chapter, we pointed out that percents are often used to describe increases or decreases. In this section, we discuss formulas used to solve problems of this type. The first problems involve changes in the base.

(4-4)
$$R = \frac{\text{increase (or decrease) in base}}{\text{base}}$$

The base in formula 4–4 is the smaller of the two quantities if there has been an increase, the larger of the two quantities if there has been a decrease.

Example 1

The sale price of a men's nylon jacket is $10.90 compared to the regular price of $11.90. By what percent was the price reduced on the jacket?

Solution:

The new base of $10.90 is a decrease from the initial base of $11.90. Using formula (4–4),

$$R = \frac{\text{decrease in base}}{\text{base}}$$

$$= \frac{\$11.90 - \$10.90}{\$11.90}$$

$$= \frac{\$1.00}{\$11.90}$$

$$= .084$$

The price of the jacket was reduced by 8.4%.

Example 2

From December, 1973 through January, 1974 the average retail price of regular gasoline increased from 40.9 cents per gallon to 51.9 cents per gallon. Calculate the percent increase in price for this period of time.

Solution:

The initial base is 40.9 cents; the new base is 51.9 cents, an increase. Using formula (4–4),

$$R = \frac{\text{increase in base}}{\text{base}}$$

$$= \frac{51.9 - 40.9}{40.9}$$

$$= \frac{11}{40.9}$$

$$= .2689$$

$$= 26.89\%$$

The average retail price of gasoline increased 27% (rounded) from December, 1973 through January, 1974.

Example 3

Railway freight revenue in 1961 was 8.395 billion dollars compared to 8.665 billion in 1960. Calculate the percent decrease in freight revenue for the one year period.

Solution:

$$R = \frac{8.665 - 8.395}{8.665} \text{ (decrease in base)}$$

$$= \frac{0.270}{8.665}$$

$$= 0.031$$

$$= 3\% \text{ (rounded)}$$

Freight revenues decreased 3% from 1960 to 1961.

A second variation of the percentage formula occurs in situations where the base is increased or decreased by a known percent. If the base B is increased or decreased by R percent to the quantity B_1, the formula is

(4–5) $$B_1 = (1.00 \pm R) \times B$$

The symbol $\pm$ means "plus or minus." Only one of the signs is used in a given problem. The plus sign is used if the base is increased; the minus sign is used if the base is decreased. We illustrate the use of formula (4–5) by examples.

Example 4

The Addison Appliance Company decided to raise its retail prices on home freezers by 5%. One of the freezers currently sells for $179.88. What is the new retail price of the freezer?

Solution:

$R = 5\% = 0.05$ and $B = \$179.88$. The base is increased, hence

$$B_1 = (1.00 + R) \times B$$

$$= (1.00 + 0.05) \times \$179.88$$

$$= 1.05 \times \$179.88$$

$$= \$188.87$$

The new retail price of the freezer is $188.87.

Example 5

The Dixon Corporation reported that profits for the year 1974 had declined by 7% to $102,500. Calculate the profits of the previous year.

Solution:

$R = 0.07$ and $B_1 = \$102,500$. The base B has decreased, hence

$$B_1 = (1.00 - R) \times B$$

$$\$102,500 = (1.00 - 0.07) \times B$$

$$\$102,500 = 0.93\ B$$

$$\frac{\$102,500}{0.93} = B$$

$$\$110,215 = B$$

Profits in 1973 were \$110,215.

Example 6

During the period from 1964 to 1973, the weekly earnings of employees engaged in transportation and public utilities rose 72.42%. If the weekly earnings in 1964 were \$118.37, find the 1973 weekly earnings.

Solution:

$R = .7242$ and $B = \$118.37$, hence

$$B_1 = (1.00 + R) \times B$$

$$= (1.00 * 0.7242) \times \$118.37$$

$$= 1.7242 \times \$118.37$$

$$= \$204.09$$

The 1973 weekly earnings were \$204.09.

Exercises for Section 4.4

In problems 1–10, compute the percent increase or decrease of the given base B.

1. $B = 50$ to 75

2. $B = 400$ to 380

3. $B = 48$ to 36

4. $B = 92$ to 115

5. $B = 136$ to 145.52

6. $B = 472$ to 401.2

7. $B = 14.2$ to 18.46

8. $B = 52.04$ to 117.09

9. $B = 4,752$ to $4,134.24$

10. $B = 8,628.02$ to $12,942.03$

In problems 11–20, compute the value B_1 obtained by increasing or decreasing the given value B by the given percent.

11. $B = 42$, increased by 50%

12. $B = 108$, decreased by 25%

13. $B = 254$, increased by 13%

14. $B = 147$, decreased by 31%

15. $B = 65.6$, increased by 110%

16. $B = 474.2$, decreased by 80%

17. $B = 86.4$, increased by 17.5%

18. $B = 202.5$, decreased by 18.8%

19. $B = 4{,}612.24$, increased by 14.2%

20. $B = 17{,}462.8$, decreased by 21.7%

21. Smithfield Enterprises normally employs 240 full-time employees. During a recent recession, the company cut its work force to 216 people. Find the percent decrease in the company's work force. 10%

22. Southern Auto Company increased the base price of its automobiles by 4%. What is the new selling price of a car that previously sold for $2,100? 2184.00

23. The cosmetics department lost $324 of its inventory last month due to theft. This month $420 worth of merchandise was stolen. Find the percent increase in stolen goods. (Round to the nearest percent.) 30%

24. The sales at Lambert's Delicatessen increased this month by 3% over last month's sales. If last month's sales were $1,240, what were this month's sales? 1277.20

25. The manager of Mom's Restaurant discovers that supplies that cost $150 a year ago now cost $169.50 because of rising prices. What is the percent increase in the cost of supplies? 13%

26. Chuck's Marine Equipment cut the price on outboard motors by 6% for a special sale. Find the sale price of a motor that regularly sells for $379.50. 356.73

27. Bernard Bonds owns a pet shop. Last year the gross sales were $38,420 as compared to $41,877.80 for this year. What is the percent increase in sales? 9%

28. The manager of the ladies' apparel department increased the price of a certain line of dresses by 7.5%. Find the new price of a dress in this line that originally sold for $24. 25.80

29. The office expenses at J & B Enterprises were reduced from $1,420

last month to $1,290 this month. Find the percent decrease (rounded to the nearest percent).   *9%*

30. The retail value of the stock at Simon's Pharmaceuticals is $22,484. If the wholesale cost of the stock is 28% less than the retail value, what is the wholesale cost?   *16188.48*

31. Ray Richards purchased an air conditioner for his automobile at a sale price of $429.75. If the regular price was $472.50, what percent of the regular price did he save? (Round to the nearest percent.)   *10%*

32. The value of the inventory in the sporting goods section of a large department store increased from $46,400 to $52,200 during the first quarter of the year. Find the percent increase.   *12.5%*

33. The J and J Construction Company estimates a building that cost $115,000 to construct three years ago costs $145,000 to construct today. What is the percent increase in the construction cost? (Round to the nearest percent.)   *26%*

34. A truckload of apples arrived at the Super Sweet Cannery. If 15% of the apples were spoiled, and if there were 1,250 pounds of apples in the shipment, how many pounds of apples were usable?   *1062.5*

35. A university had 8,420 students in attendance last year. This year, the enrollment has increased to 9,240. Find the percent increase in enrollment. (Round to the nearest percent.)   *10%*

36. B and D Hardware sells its lighting fixtures for 32% more than cost. Find the selling price of a fixture with a cost price of $104.50.   *137.94*

37. The operating expenses at the Pick-A-Pare shoe store were $340 a week last year. This year the operating expenses have been reduced to $320 a week. What percent reduction is this? (Round to the nearest percent.)   *6%*

38. Built-Well Furniture sold a living room suite for $540, which was $80 less than the regular price. What percent of the regular price did the customer save? (Round to the nearest percent.)   *13%*

39. The selling price of a motorcycle at Sol's Scooter Shack is 18% more than the wholesale cost. Find the wholesale cost of a motorcycle that sells for $1,450. (Hint: Use the formula $B_1 = (1 + R)B$ with $B_1 = \$1,450$ and $R = 0.18$. Solve for B.)

40. The inventory of 520 sacks of fertilizer at Larry's Lawn and Garden Shop was 15% short of the amount required. Find the required number of sacks. (Hint: Use $B_1 = (1 - R)B$ with $B_1 = 520$ and $R = 0.15$. Solve for B.)

41. The sales at Henry's Harness & Feed Store were $824 this month, which was 4% less than last month's sales. Find the sales for last

month. (Hint: Use $B_1 = (1 - R)B$ with $B_1 = \$824$ and $R = 0.04$. Solve for B.)

42. Mrs. Prentice wishes to sell her house, so she lists the house with a real estate agency. If she wishes to receive $27,500 for the house and the realtor's fee is 8% of the selling price, find the price at which the realtor will advertise the house. (Hint: Let $B_1 = \$27,500$ and $R = 0.08$ in the formula $B_1 = (1 - R)B$ and solve for B. Round your answer to the nearest hundred dollars.)

43. Peerless Products, Inc., installed new equipment that reduced the production cost per unit of its product by 12%. If the new production cost per unit is $120, what was the old cost? (Hint: Use the formula $B_1 = (1 - R)B$ with $B_1 = \$120$ and $R = 0.12$. Solve for B and round your answer to the nearest cent.)

5

Graphs

Chapter Objectives for Chapter 5

I. Learn the meaning of the following terms:

A. *Line graph,* 93
B. *Bar graph,* 100
C. *Pictogram,* 107
D. *Circle graph,* 110

II. Understand:

A. Variations of line graphs, 95
B. Variations of bar graphs, 103
C. Graph distortions, 114

III. Learn to:

A. Construct graphs representing business information, 95-112
B. Recognize distorted graphs that convey misleading information, 115

Introduction

"One picture is worth more than ten thousand words." Attributed to a Chinese philosopher, this familiar adage emphasizes that pictures supply instant information. Since "time is money" (another familiar adage), it is natural that people turn to pictures for instant communication.

In this chapter we concentrate on particular kinds of pictures called graphs. In business, graphs are used to transmit statistical information. A graphical presentation of data is often more meaningful than charts or aggregates of figures, and graphs are particularly useful in spotting trends. We shall study four of the more popular graphs used in business: line graphs, bar graphs, pictograms, and circle graphs.

Line Graphs

The line graph is the most widely used graph. The basis for a line graph is two mutually perpendicular lines called **axes.** See Figure 5–1. The horizontal line is called the **x-axis** and the vertical line is called the **y-axis.** Equally spaced points on each axis are assigned numbers or other identifying information. The intersection point of the two axes is called the **origin** and is the initial point of measurement.

Figure 5–1

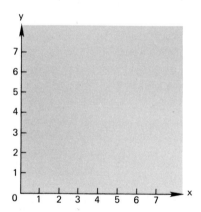

Consider a line through one of the labeled points on the x-axis and perpendicular to that axis. Consider a similar line perpendicular to the y-axis. (See Figure 5–2.) The intersection point of these two lines is called a **point** of the graph. It is the points of a graph that contain the information to be communicated.

For example, suppose a manufacturing plant machines a part used in the assembly of farm tractors. Let us use the numbers on the x-axis of Figure 5–2 to represent the number of parts produced, measured in hundreds. Thus, the number 2 means 200 parts were produced, the number

Figure 5–2

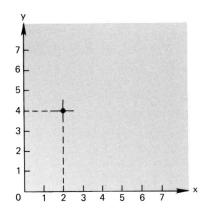

3 means 300 parts were produced, etc. Let us further use the numbers on the y-axis to represent the production cost per part in dollars; that is, the number 1 means the cost is $1.00 per part, the number 2 means the cost is $2.00 per part, etc. Then a point on the graph describes the cost of production. For example, the point in Figure 5–2 indicates that if 200 parts are produced, the cost is $4.00 per part.

Refer to Figure 5–3. Here we show two additional points on the graph. These points indicate if 400 parts are produced, the cost per part is $3.00, and if 500 parts are produced, the cost per part is $2.00. If we use a straightedge to connect the three points as shown in Figure 5–4, the result is a **line graph**.

Figure 5–3

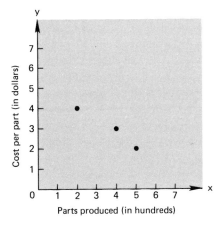

Two important items of information emerge from Figure 5–4. First, the immediate visual impact of the graph is its downward slope, which indicates that the more parts produced, the less the cost per part. The graph clearly demonstrates this. Second, the graph permits us to estimate the production cost for points not shown on the graph. For instance, we can

Figure 5–4

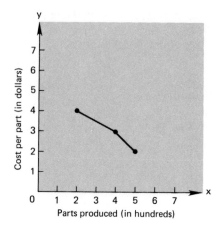

estimate the production cost to be $3.50 per part if 300 parts are produced. This is determined by constructing a line perpendicular to the x-axis at the number 3 and intersecting the line graph. (See Figure 5–5.) At this point of intersection we construct a line perpendicular to the y-axis. The point of intersection with the y-axis will be the estimated cost per part. (See Figure 5–6.)

Figure 5–5

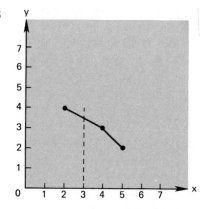

Figure 5–6

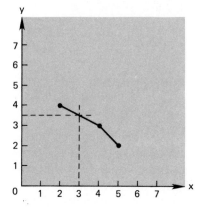

Line graphs may be constructed from data or from formulas. Example 1 shows a line graph made from profit data of the Armstrong Company.

Example 1

In 1972, the profits of the Armstrong Company resulted in earnings per share of $0.40. In succeeding years the earnings were: 1973—$0.36, 1974—$0.32, and 1975—$0.30. Construct a line graph of the company profits for the four years.

Solution:

Since time is customarily shown on the horizontal axis, the years are indicated on the x-axis. The y-axis is marked in cents, and we choose a scale that insures clarity, but results in a graph that is not oversized. We locate the points on the graph, then connect the points with line segments (Figure 5–7).

Figure 5–7

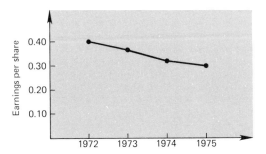

Again, let us comment on the visual impact of the graph. This graph should cause concern to both management and stockholders, for its downward slope indicates a decline in the company's return to investors. The graph demonstrates this decline.

The line graphs have several variations. For example, Figure 5–8 shows the six-month sales record of a company where the area below the line graph has been shaded to emphasize the changes that the graph portrays.

Figure 5–8

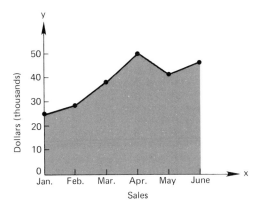

Figure 5–9 is a graph of cotton prices in 1972. Note that the vertical scale of the graph has been shortened as indicated by the break in the y-axis. This permits a smaller, more detailed graph; and it is possible because the price of cotton varied only about eleven cents per pound during the year. Shortening the vertical scale should be practiced with care, since this can lead to misinterpretation. See Section 5.6 on graph distortions.

Figure 5–9

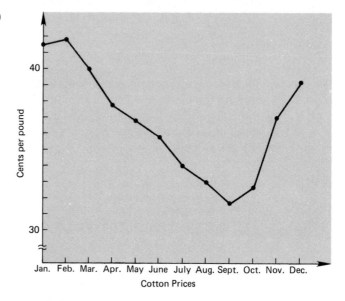

Cotton Prices

Figure 5–10 is another variation of a line graph in which two graphs are drawn on the same set of axes so comparisons may be made. In Figure 5–10, which depicts the production and labor costs of a company, it is clear that production costs are rapidly approaching labor costs.

Figure 5–10

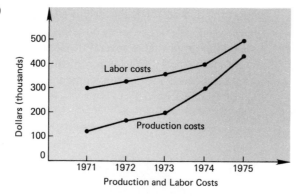

Production and Labor Costs

Exercises for Section 5.2

1. The profit per share of stock in the Sutton Company is shown in the following line graph.

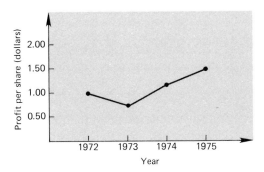

What was the profit per share in 1972? In 1973? In 1974?

2. The following line graph shows the production cost per unit for a certain part used in the manufacturing of jet engines.

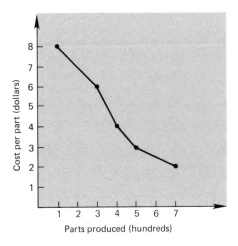

What is the cost per part if 300 parts are produced? If 200 parts are produced? If 600 parts are produced?

3. The Golden State Corporation reported profits of $1.25 per share in 1972, $1.75 in 1973, $2.00 in 1974, and $1.50 in 1975. Construct a line graph of the company's profits for the four years.

4. The annual maintenance costs of the Omega Manufacturing Company for the past five years are as follows: 1971, $50,000; 1972, $70,000; 1973, $85,000; 1974, $90,000; 1975, $95,000. Prepare a line graph to illustrate this data.

5. Superior Products, Inc., manufactures blade housings for lawn mowers. The table on page 98 gives the production cost per unit depending upon the number of units produced per month.

Number of units produced	600	800	1,000	1,200
Production Cost per unit	$8	$7.00	$6.50	$6.25

Construct a line graph for this data. Use the graph to estimate the production cost per unit if 700 units are produced per month.

6. The following table gives the gross sales and production costs of the Braxton Company for the first six months of 1975:

Month	Jan.	Feb.	March	April	May	June
Gross Sales	$27,000	$31,000	$26,000	$27,500	$33,000	$33,500
Production Costs	$18,000	$20,000	$17,000	$17,500	$21,500	$22,000

On the same set of axes, draw a line graph of the gross sales and a line graph of the production costs.

7. Gross profit is gross sales less production costs. Use the data in problem 6 to prepare a line graph of the gross profit of the Braxton Company for the first six months of 1975.

8. Bennett Clothiers reported the following data for the years 1971–1975:

Year	Sales	Cost of Goods Sold	Expenses
1971	$280,000	$180,000	$ 80,000
1972	450,000	280,000	120,000
1973	580,000	390,000	140,000
1974	780,000	510,000	150,000
1975	920,000	620,000	170,000

On the same set of axes, construct (1) a line graph of the sales, (2) a line graph of the cost of goods sold, and (3) a line graph of the expenses.

9. Using the data given in problem 8, prepare a line graph of the net profit of Bennett Clothiers for the years 1971–1975. (Net profit is sales less cost of goods sold and expenses.)

10. The sales record of the Fabric Mart for the years 1971–1975 is given in the following table:

Year	Sales	Cost of Goods Sold	Expenses
1971	$160,000	$ 80,000	$50,000
1972	270,000	140,000	70,000
1973	310,000	150,000	80,000
1974	330,000	160,000	85,000
1975	340,000	180,000	90,000

On the same set of axes, construct (1) a line graph of the sales, (2) a line graph of the cost of goods sold, and (3) a line graph of the expenses.

11. Prepare a line graph of the net profit of the Fabric Mart for the years 1971–1975, using the data given in problem 10. (Net profit is sales less cost of goods sold and expenses.)

12. Abbott Aluminum Products manufactures portable storage buildings. The following table gives the number of units produced at Abbott for each of the first six months of last year and the production cost per unit.

	Number of Units Produced	Production Cost per Unit
January	195	$75
February	205	65
March	210	60
April	220	55
May	210	60
June	180	90

Construct (1) a line graph of the number of units produced and (2) a line graph of the production cost per unit.

13. Prepare a line graph of the total monthly production costs of Abbott Aluminum Products for the first six months of last year, using the data provided in problem 12. (The total monthly production cost is the cost per unit times the number of units produced.)

14. Use the data given in problem 12 to construct a line graph of the production cost per unit, with values on the x-axis representing the number of units produced and values on the y-axis representing the production cost per unit. From the graph, estimate (1) the production cost per unit during a month when 200 units are produced and (2) the production cost per unit during a month when 185 units are produced.

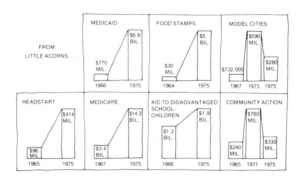

Bar graphs are similar to line graphs in that they are also drawn in reference to a pair of axes, but bar graphs use bars projecting from an axis instead of points. In Figure 5–11 we have drawn a bar graph of the data of Example 1 of Section 5.2. Note the height of the bars corresponds to the points on the line graph. This is the basic relationship between the bar graph and the line graph.

Figure 5–11

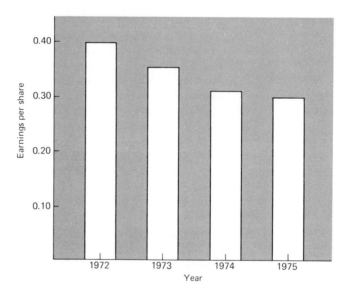

Bar graphs may have horizontal or vertical bars. The use of household appliances shown in Figure 5–12 is an example of a graph with horizontal bars. Note how easy it is to read this graph compared with the graph of paper box sales in Figure 5–13. Both scales are easy to read in Figure 5–12, but it is necessary to turn the graph on its side to read Figure 5–13. The use of shaded and unshaded bars in this graph is also undesirable. The bar graph in Figure 5–12 was constructed more thoughtfully than the bar graph in Figure 5–13.

Figure 5–12

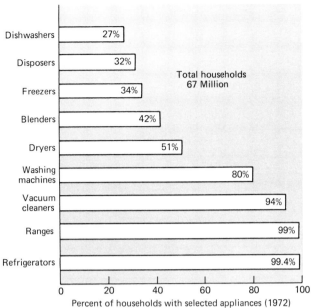

Total households
67 Million

Percent of households with selected appliances (1972)

Source: Merchandising Week, Bureau of Competitive Assessment and Business Policy

Figure 5–13

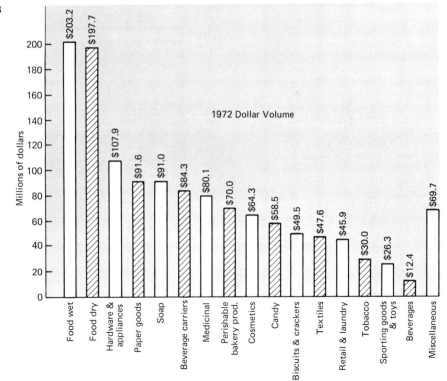

1972 Dollar Volume

Example 1

A building supply company reported the following sales of building materials:

Lumber	$38,000	Sand and gravel	$19,100
Gypsum wallboard	29,700	Plumbing fixtures	16,400
Insulation materials	31,700	Copper tubing	26,800

Draw a bar graph of the company sales.

Solution:

In order to present a readable graph, the materials are shown on the vertical axis and the sales are placed on the horizontal axis. (See Figure 5–14.) Sales are scaled in thousands of dollars.

Figure 5–14

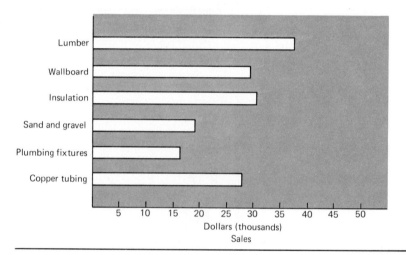

Figure 5–15   Women Workers in the Labor Force*

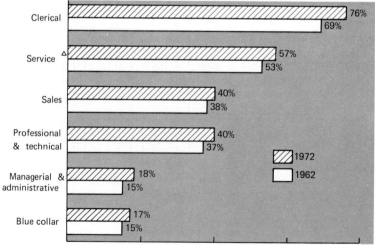

*By percentage of total workers in each occupational group
Δother than private household   Source: Bureau of Labor Statistics

U.S. Department of Agriculture

NEG. ARS6065-73 (8) Agricultural Research Service

Variations of a bar graph include two or more graphs on the same set of axes and shortening of an axis. In Figure 5–15, a graph of women workers in the labor force, the 1962 and 1972 data is shown side by side on the same set of axes. In the graph of educational attainment (Figure 5–16), the college and high school data is shown on the same bar.

Figure 5–16

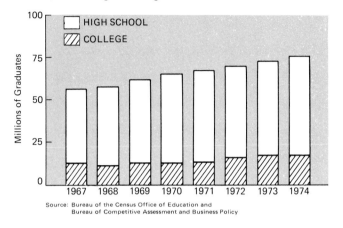

Source: Bureau of the Census Office of Education and
Bureau of Competitive Assessment and Business Policy

Example 2

The Green Company reported the following tons of fertilizer sold:

	1971	1972	1973	1974
Ammonia	31.38	34.60	39.68	36.36
Potash	20.52	21.68	22.63	24.53

Construct a bar graph of the company sales.

Solution:

Since the sales range between 20.52 and 39.68 tons, let us shorten the vertical scale of the graph. The graph is shown in Figure 5–17.

Figure 5–17

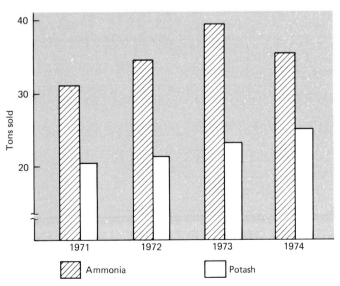

1. The following bar graph shows the cash and credit sales of the Glover Company for the first six months of last year.

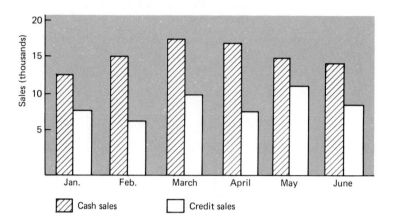

What were the company's credit sales in February? What were the cash sales in March? For which of the six months were the company's total sales the greatest?

2. Culver Enterprises presented the following bar graph to summarize the number of male and female employees on its work force at the beginning of each of the years shown.

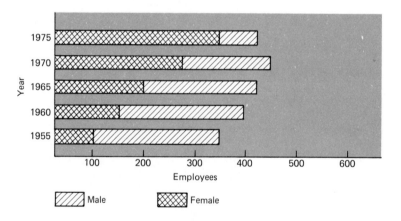

How many female employees were at Culver at the beginning of 1970? What was the total work force at the beginning of 1960? How many male employees were there at the beginning of 1975?

3. Construct a vertical bar graph that shows the number of units produced each month at the Concord Manufacturing Company: January, 4,500; February, 4,800; March, 5,200; April, 5,800; May, 4,200; June, 3,800.

4. Using the data given in the following table, construct a horizontal bar graph of the sales of the five branch stores of the Friendly Wholesale Farm Supply Company.

Branch	Sales
Riverview	$230,000
Eastport	320,000
Gulf	280,000
Brooksville	360,000
Sumter	220,000

5. The Brookline Publishing Company reported the following sales record for its publications during the years 1971–1975:

Year	Books	Periodicals
1971	$520,000	$180,000
1972	580,000	200,000
1973	610,000	170,000
1974	720,000	220,000
1975	840,000	310,000

On the same set of axes, construct side-by-side horizontal bar graphs for the five-year period, one representing book sales and the other representing periodical sales.

6. The employment records of the Bradston Company yield the following data on the number of male and female employees at the company at the beginning of the years 1950, 1955, 1960, 1965, 1970, and 1975:

Year	Male	Female
1950	800	50
1955	850	250
1960	900	400
1965	1,150	700
1970	1,250	950
1975	1,300	1,150

On the same set of axes, construct side-by-side vertical bar graphs, one representing the number of male employees for each of the six years and the other representing the number of female employees.

7. Construct a vertical bar graph for the data given in problem 5, with book sales and periodical sales shown on the same bar for a given year.

8. Construct a horizontal bar graph for the data given in problem 6, with the number of male employees and the number of female employees shown on the same bar for a given year.

9. The following table gives the cash and credit sales of each department at Anderson's Variety Store for the past year.

Department	Cash Sales	Credit Sales
Lawn and Garden	$140,000	$ 60,000
Appliances	210,000	190,000
Hardware	180,000	110,000
Sporting Goods	70,000	30,000
Toys	240,000	150,000
Clothing	190,000	120,000

On the same set of axes, construct side-by-side horizontal bar graphs, one representing the cash sales of each department and the other representing the credit sales.

10. Construct a vertical bar graph for the data given in problem 9, with cash sales and credit sales shown on the same bar for each of the given departments.

11. The sales record of the Kingsford Company for the years 1971–1975 is given in the following table:

Year	Sales	Cost of Goods Sold	Expenses	Net Income
1971	$420,000	$280,000	$ 80,000	$60,000
1972	470,000	340,000	95,000	45,000
1973	510,000	350,000	105,000	55,000
1974	640,000	420,000	150,000	70,000
1975	740,000	510,000	140,000	90,000

On the same set of axes, construct side-by-side vertical bar graphs, one representing the sales for each of the five years and the other representing the cost of goods sold.

12. Using the data given in problem 11, construct a horizontal bar graph showing the expenses and net income on the same bar for each of the five years.

13. Design and construct a bar graph that shows all of the data given in problem 11.

14. Repeat problem 13 for the data given in problem 8 of the previous set of exercises.

15. Repeat problem 13 for the data given in problem 10 of the previous exercise set.

16. Repeat problem 13 for the data given in problem 12 of the previous exercise set.

Section 5.4   Pictograms

A pictogram is a modified form of a bar graph in which pictures are used to represent quantity. Consider, for example, the record of the Century Corporation, a builder of low-cost retirement homes. In 1950 the corporation built 500 houses; in 1960, 900 homes were built; and in 1970 the corporation constructed 1,250 houses. A pictogram of this record might be drawn as follows:

Figure 5–18

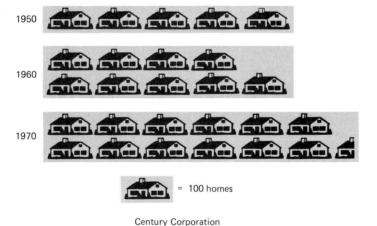

Century Corporation
Homes constructed

An examination of Figure 5–18 shows we have eliminated the horizontal scale by using a picture to depict quantity. In this case, each house represents 100 homes built by the corporation. The number of homes constructed in a given year is the number of pictures in that line, 5 pictures for 1950, 9 for 1960, and 12½ for 1970.

The advantage of a pictogram lies in its simplicity. However, simplicity is gained at the loss of accuracy. For example, it is difficult to determine from the graph that 1,250 homes were constructed in 1970, rather than 1,240 or 1,260.

A variation of the basic pictogram is to place two graphs on the same set of axes.

Example 1

In 1966, the Whitman Company employed 50 men and 20 women. In 1970, 65 men and 40 women were employed, and in 1974 the company employed 70 men and 55 women. Construct a pictogram of the Whitman Company employment record.

Solution:

We must choose an appropriate scale so that the graph may be easily read. In this case, one picture for each 10 persons is suitable. Pictograms are almost always displayed horizontally, thus years are scaled on the vertical axis (See Figure 5–19).

Figure 5–19

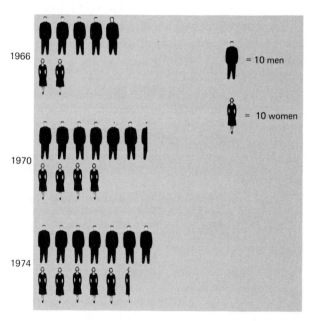

Employment record
The Whitman Company

1. Huffman Industries manufactures farm equipment. The company produced 40,000 tractors in 1950, 45,000 in 1960, and 55,000 in 1970. Let the symbol ⬛ represent 10,000 tractors and prepare a pictogram showing the company's production for the three years.

2. Universal Freightways, a trucking company, transported 30,000 tons of freight in 1971, 40,000 tons in 1972, 55,000 tons in 1973, and 70,000 tons in 1974. Using the symbol ⬛ to represent 10,000 tons of freight, construct a pictogram showing the tons of freight transported for the four years.

3. The Riverview Electric Company uses both coal and fuel oil to generate its electricity. The following table gives the percent of electricity generated from each fuel during four past years:

Year	Percent of Electricity Generated by Coal	Percent of Electricity Generated by Fuel Oil
1972	60%	40%
1973	40%	60%
1974	50%	50%
1975	70%	30%

    Construct a pictogram of the percent of electricity generated from each fuel for the four years, using the symbol 🏭 to represent each 10% of electricity generated by coal and the symbol 🗼 to represent each 10% of electricity generated by fuel oil.

4. Employment records at the Hammond Company reveal that the company employed 20 women and 40 men in 1950, 40 women and 45 men in 1960, and 55 women and 50 men in 1970. Prepare a pictogram for this data, using the symbol 👤 to represent 10 men and the symbol 👤 to represent 10 women.

5. The net income of the Kenyon Company for the years 1971–1975 is as follows: 1971, $60,000; 1972, $70,000; 1973, $90,000; 1974, $80,000; 1975, $110,000. Construct a pictogram that shows the net income for each year, using the symbol 💰 to represent $20,000.

6. Sterling Auto Sales sold 2,500 cars in 1960, 3,750 cars in 1965, 4,000 cars in 1970, and 3,500 cars in 1975. Using the symbol 🚗 to represent 500 cars, construct a pictogram of the company's sales for the four years.

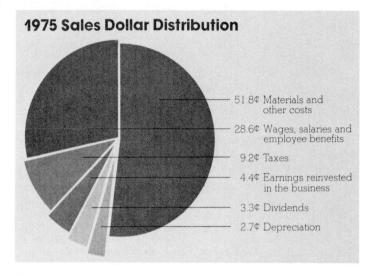

Circle graphs, also known as pie charts, use a circle as a base for the graph. Circle graphs are used to illustrate the distribution of goods or money and to make comparisons of these distributions. Figure 5–20 is an example of a circle graph and depicts the 1974 use of cleaning compounds in the United States. Note that the sum of the percents of the graph is 100%. This is one of the requirements of a circle graph.

Figure 5–20

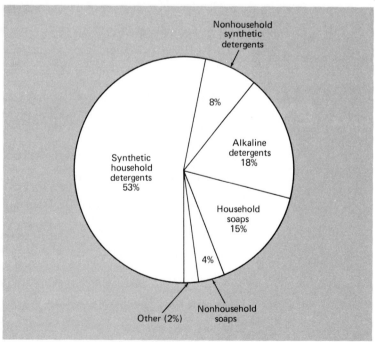

Total shipments 1974: $2,900 million
Source: Bureau of the Census and Bureau of Competitive Assessment and Business Policy

Figure 5–20 is an example of a circle graph in which the distribution is in the form of percents. Another common circle graph is the distribution of a dollar in cents. Figure 5–21 shows the use of each dollar earned by the Logan Manufacturing Company.

Figure 5–21

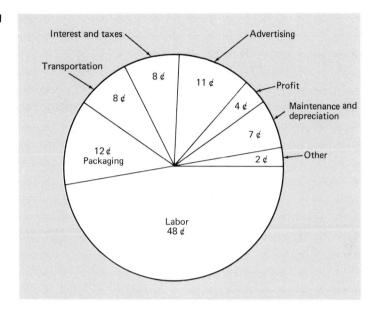

To construct a circle graph, we must convert each item of the data to a corresponding area of the circle. This is not difficult if we recall some fundamentals of angle measurement. A circle is subdivided into 360 equal units called **degrees.** Thus, the entire circle contains 360 degrees (in symbols 360°), one-half of the circle contains 180°, one-sixth contains 60°, one-fourth contains 90°, etc. See Figure 5–22.

Figure 5–22

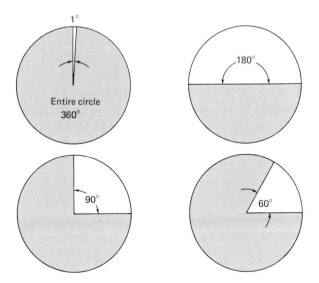

Note there is a direct relationship between the measure of an angle and a region of the circle. Thus to construct a circle graph we need only convert our data to degrees, then draw angles with these measurements on a circle. Data can be converted to degrees by multiplying by 3.6.* Let us illustrate this by example.

Example 1

King Drugs consists of a chain of 14 drug stores. Tobacco sales in the chain for the past quarter were distributed as follows:

Cigarettes	42%
Cigars	32%
Pipe Tobacco	18%
Chewing Tobacco	6%
Snuff	2%

Construct a circle graph of the King tobacco sales.

Solution:

Converting the percents to degrees, we have:

$$
\begin{array}{ll}
42 \times 3.6 = 151 & \text{(rounded)} \\
32 \times 3.6 = 115 & \\
18 \times 3.6 = 65 & \\
6 \times 3.6 = 22 & \\
2 \times 3.6 = 7 & \\
\hline
100\% 360° &
\end{array}
$$

Using a protractor like the one pictured in Figure 5–24, we draw angles on a circle with these degrees of measurements. See Figure 5–23.

---

* If n = number of cents or percent of an item of data
  100 = total cents or percent of all the data
  x = measure of the angle in degrees
  360 = total degrees of a circle

then we have

$$\frac{n}{100} = \frac{x}{360}$$

Cross multiplying and solving for x, we have

$$100\,x = 360\,n$$
$$x = \frac{360\,n}{100}$$
$$x = 3.6\,n$$

Figure 5–23

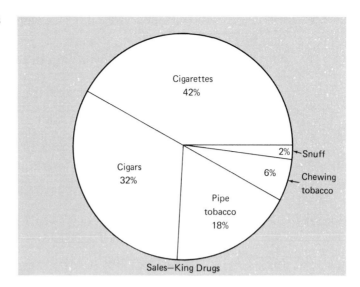

Figure 5–24

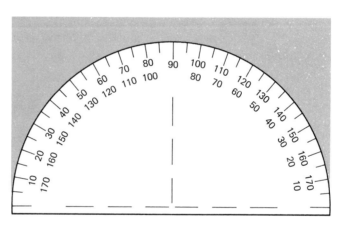

In problems 1–6, convert the given percents to degrees.

1. 10%, 15%   4. 48%, 22%

2. 50%, 20%   5. 37%, 12%

3. 5%, 85%   6. 79%, 57%

7. The Concord Manufacturing Company reported at its annual stockholder's meeting that each dollar of production expense is used as follows: 54¢ for labor, 38¢ for raw materials, and 8¢ for overhead. Draw a circle graph that represents the distribution of each dollar of production expenses.

8. The first quarter sales of Adamson's Men's Store were distributed as follows: suits, 32%; sportcoats, 25%; slacks, 18%; shirts, 16%;

shoes, 6%; miscellaneous, 3%. Construct a circle graph of the first quarter sales.

9. The Eagle Manufacturing Company reported the following use of the company's sales dollar: production, 40¢; operating expenses, 25¢; research, 15¢; taxes, 15¢; miscellaneous, 5¢. Construct a circle graph that represents the use of the sales dollar.

10. The sales last year at Sander's Sporting Goods Store were distributed as follows: sports equipment, 64%; clothing, 28%; books, 6%; miscellaneous, 2%. Prepare a circle graph of the store's sales.

11. John and Pat Weber prepared the following monthly budget for their family: food, $320; housing, $230; clothing, $160; savings, $100; recreation and miscellaneous, $120. Find the percent of each expenditure and construct a circle graph of the budget.

12. The Samford Company reported sales last year of $424,000, distributed as follows: cost of goods sold, $210,000; operating expenses, $154,000; net income, $60,000. Prepare a circle graph of the company's sales. Hint: First find the percent of the sales used for (1) cost of goods sold, (2) operating expenses, and (3) net income.

13. Tinker Industries prepared the following budget for the coming year: salaries, $46,000; rent, $15,000; utilities, $7,500; supplies, $11,000; miscellaneous, $10,500. Construct a circle graph of the company's budget. Hint: First find the percent of the total budget represented by each expense.

14. Production expenses at the Higgins Company last year were $375,000, distributed as follows: materials, $180,000; labor, $145,000; maintenance, $30,000; overhead, $20,000. Prepare a circle graph of the company's production expenses. Hint: First find the percent of the production expenses used for (1) materials, (2) labor, (3) maintenance, and (4) overhead.

Section 5.6 Graph Distortions

Care must be exercised in the construction of a graph, since it is possible to present a graph that is accurate, yet misleading. To see this, let us reexamine the data of Example 1 of Section 5.2 from the viewpoint of

a. the board of directors of the company and

b. a dissident stockholder seeking control of the company.

The board of directors naturally wants to minimize the declining earnings of the company. Therefore, in their annual report to stockholders, they present Figure 5–25 as a graph of the company earnings. By stretching the scale of the x-axis and shortening that of the y-axis, the decline in earnings appears minimal. Compare with Figure 5–7.

Figure 5–25

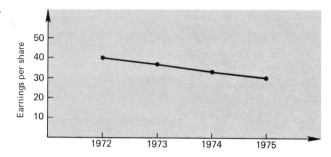

On the other hand, in an open letter to stockholders, Mr. Dissident Stockholder charges the company with mismanagement and calls for an immediate change in the company leadership. He supports his charge with the following graph of the company's earnings record:

Figure 5–26

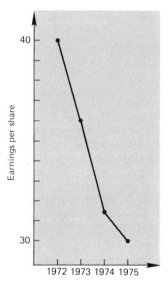

By stretching the scale on the y-axis, shortening the scale of the x-axis, and eliminating most of the vertical portion of the graph, Mr. D.S. has presented an earnings record that appears calamitous. In both cases the graphs were accurately drawn, but created opposite impressions.

The preceding is an example of how graphs can be manipulated to create an impression. Such manipulations may be accidental, but all too often they are deliberate attempts to deceive. In pointing out these distortions our purpose is to help the student avoid unintentional errors in graph construction and to encourage a critical examination of all published graphs.

Bar graphs are susceptible to the same distortions as line graphs. For example, in a report to the home office on reduction of energy consumption, a branch manager submitted the graph shown in Figure 5–27.

Figure 5–27

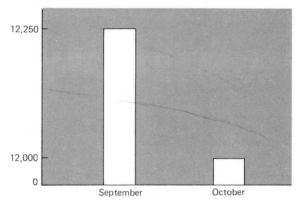

Kilowatt hours consumed
Oregon branch

As we have seen, information can be viewed from many different perspectives; likewise, graphs can be prepared from different perspectives. It is important to avoid deliberate attempts to deceive with graphs by allowing a particular viewpoint or perspective to distort the information.

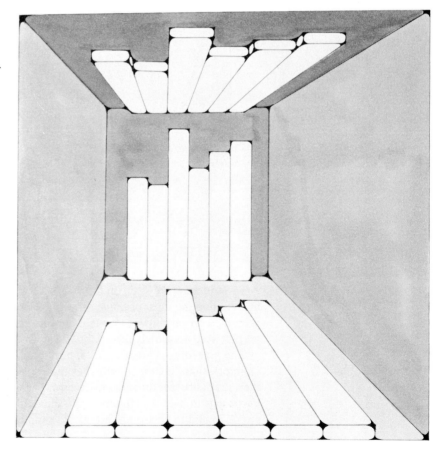

At first glance, the decrease seems impressive; the actual reduction is only about 2%. In this instance, a false impression was created by using a detailed scale, then omitting most of the vertical portion of the graph. The correct relationship is shown in Figure 5–28.

Figure 5–28

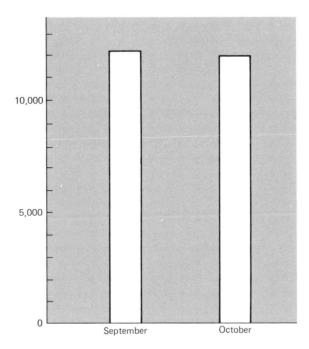

In Figure 5–29, we show a distortion of a pictogram. In this case, a twofold increase in company assets has been depicted by a figure whose radius is twice that of the 1974 figure. Although the radius is only twice as large, the *area* of the 1975 figure is *four times* that of the 1974 figure!

The correct method of graphing the increase is shown in Figure 5–30.

Figure 5–29

1974

1975

Assets

Figure 5–30

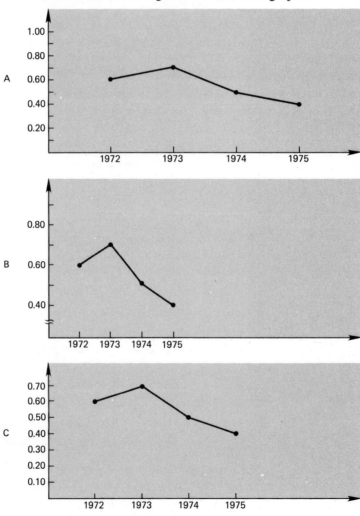

1974

1975

Assets

1. Kelsey Industries reported profits of $0.60 per share in 1972, $0.70 per share in 1973, $0.50 per share in 1974, and $0.40 per share in 1975. Which of the following line graphs most accurately represents this data? What is wrong with the other two graphs?

2. Robertson's Electrical Supply recorded sales of $19,000 in January, $21,500 in February, $17,000 in March, and $15,000 in April. Which of the following bar graphs most accurately represents this information? What is wrong with the other two?

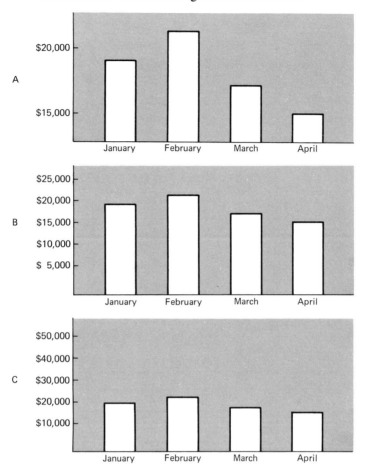

3. Americana Builders constructed 1,000 new homes in 1960 and 4,000 new homes in 1970. If the symbol ⌂ represents 1,000 homes, which of the following pictograms most accurately reflects the construction record at Americana?

4. Employment records at the Bradshaw Company show that in 1960, 15% of the employees were members of minority groups; in 1965, the figure rose to 20%; and in 1970, 30%. Which of the following line graphs most accurately represents this data? What is wrong with the other two graphs?

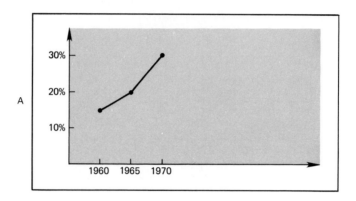

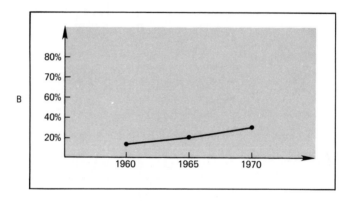

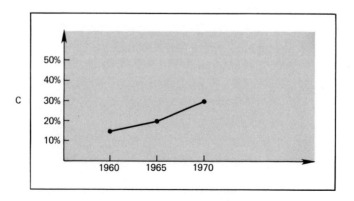

5. The sales record at the Clayton Candy Co. for the first quarter of this year is as follows: January, $12,000; February, $16,000; March, $8,000; and April, $10,000. Which of the following bar graphs most accurately represents this information? What is wrong with the other two graphs?

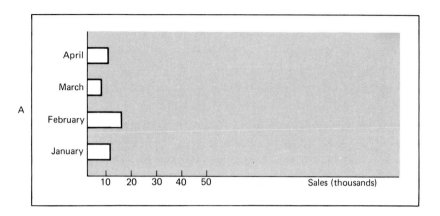

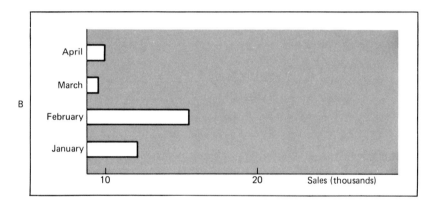

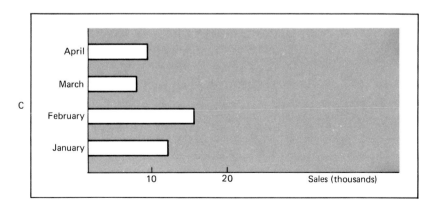

6. Braxton Builders reported net income of $20,000 in 1972 and $40,000 in 1973. Using the symbol [$] to represent $10,000, which of the following pictograms most accurately represents the net income of the company for the two years?

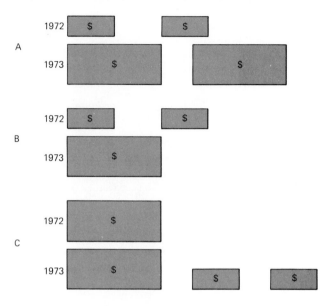

2 Retailing / Accounting

Retailing Decisions

Chapter Objectives for Chapter 6

I. Learn the meaning of the following terms:

A. *List Price,* 126
B. *Cost Price,* 126
C. *Selling Price,* 126
D. *Net Price,* 126
E. *Discount,* 126
F. *Overhead,* 126
G. *Markon,* 126
H. *Net Profit,* 126
I. *Markdown,* 150

II. Understand the concepts of:

A. Trade Discount, 127
B. Complement of the Discount, 128
C. Chain Discounts, 131
D. Quantity Discounts, 134
E. Cash Discounts, 139
F. Ordinary Dating, 143
G. End of the Month Dating, 143
H. Receipt of Goods Dating, 143
I. Extra Dating, 143
J. The Basic Markon Equation, 145
K. Conversion of the Markon Base, 147
L. Operating Loss, 152
M. Gross Loss, 152

III. Learn to use:

A. The basic percentage formula $P=BR$ to calculate discounts, markon, markdown, 128, 145, 150
B. The basic markon equation to calculate selling price, 145
C. The formulas for markon based on selling or cost price to calculate selling price, 146, 147
D. The formulas to convert from one markon base to the other, 148

The retail store is the final step of the marketing process that begins with raw materials and ends with a product for purchase by the public.

Retail stores may be large or small, may be independently owned or part of a nationwide chain, but they have one thing in common—their managers are engaged in buying merchandise for resale to the public. Approximately 13 percent of the country's work force is engaged in some aspect of retailing, and annual sales of retail stores now approach 500 billion dollars. The basic mathematics of retailing is the subject of this chapter.

A number of special terms are required for the discussion of retail mathematics; the definitions of these terms are listed below for future reference.

> The **list price** or **suggested retail price** is the catalog price or the price on a price list or price tag.
>
> The purchase price of an item is the **cost price** to the buyer, the **selling price** to the seller.
>
> The **net price** is the cost price less any discounts.
>
> The **billing price** is net price plus freight, transportation, or other charges.
>
> A **discount** is a percentage reduction from either the cost price or the billing price.
>
> **Overhead** is the expenses of operation; it includes rent, taxes, salaries, utilities, etc.
>
> **Markon** is the difference between the selling price and the cost price. Also known as gross profit or margin, markon includes overhead and net profit.
>
> **Net profit** is markon less overhead.

COMPANY	SALES				PROFITS				MARGINS			RETURN COM. EOY. 12 MOS. ENDING 12-31	P-E 2-27	12 MONTHS EARNINGS PER SHARE
	4TH QTR. 1975 $ MIL.	CHG. FROM 1974 %	12 MO. 1975 $ MIL.	CHG. FROM 1974 %	4TH QTR. 1975 $ MIL.	CHG. FROM 1974 %	12 MO. 1975 $ MIL.	CHG. FROM 1974 %	4TH QTR. 1975 %	4TH QTR. 1974 %				
RETAILING (NONFOOD): Department, discount, mail order, variety, specialty stores														
Allied Stores (11)	418.0	12	1691.8	5	9.4	127	44.6	25	2.3	1.1		12.6	9	5.47
Amfac	306.9	-5	1133.8	-1	9.4	-24	38.5	-40	3.1	3.8		13.0	6	3.25
Arlen Realty & Development (10)	206.9	-6	731.5	-12	0.0	NM	-42.2	NM	NM	NM		-34.4	NM	-2.14
Associated Dry Goods (11)	337.3	7	1335.0	3	8.8	72	36.5	-12	2.6	1.6		9.0	14	2.70
Best Products (6)	142.2**	38	259.1	31	6.5	118	6.4	165	4.6	2.9		17.7	13	2.22
Carter Hawley Hale (11)	292.2	8	1185.8	7	7.6	32	33.7	-11	2.6	2.1		8.9	14	1.74
Cunningham Drug Stores (3)	41.3	9	132.9	11	1.2	36	1.1	184	2.8	2.2		4.4	8	0.93
Dayton-Hudson (11)	415.1	13	1608.3	8	10.7	173	37.4	32	2.6	1.1		10.4	15	2.34
Drug Fair (6)	58.1	11	210.6	11	1.0	74	3.0	107	1.7	1.1		13.7	7	1.88
Eckerd (Jack) (5)	132.7	13	570.3	13	3.4	15	25.3	-11	2.6	2.5		17.0	20	1.34
Eckerd Drugs (9)	67.9	15	222.9	16	3.4	27	7.7	26	5.0	4.5		20.1	13	1.67
Edison Brothers Stores	146.7	23	489.6	16	10.4	65	24.0	43	7.1	5.3		23.4	9	5.94
Empire Gas (6)	28.0	24	80.0	25	1.4	-42	4.6	18	5.1	10.8		14.1	5	2.63
Fed-Mart (4)	94.2**	18	396.2	20	0.3	-36	3.4	-8	0.3	0.7		12.4	6	2.80
Federated Department Stores (11)	882.8	13	3534.8	11	34.0	43	139.3	20	3.8	3.0		14.4	18	3.14
Fingerhut (6)	57.4**	-24	210.4	-24	2.0	NM	-4.7	NM	3.6	NM		-9.5	NM	-0.72
Gamble-Skogmo (11)	390.1	3	1500.2	1	3.9	-31	19.8	-22	1.0	1.5		8.9	6	4.26
Gordon Jewelry (4)	42.4	3	174.5	-1	1.7	5	10.7	-2	3.9	3.8		12.2	7	1.96
Heck's	46.8	17	151.1	11	2.6	2	5.4	5	5.5	6.3		14.4	9	1.75
Interstate United (6)	62.7	0	260.2	4	0.8	8	2.6	-25	1.2	1.1		5.8	7	0.88
Kay	75.6**	7	245.0	-12	2.1	107	2.9	108	2.8	1.4		8.5	7	0.45
Kresge (S.S.) (11)	1656.0	22	6430.4	19	39.7	55	129.1	0	2.4	1.9		12.2	34	1.06
Longs Drug Stores (11)	100.6	19	390.1	21	3.2	24	13.9	21	3.2	3.1		21.9	29	2.64
Lowe's (5)	106.8	20	359.0	0	3.5	16	11.0	-24	3.2	3.4		NA	34	3.14
Macke (3)	46.5**	1	177.5	-3	0.8	91	-1.2	NM	1.8	1.0		-3.2	NM	-0.42
Macy (R.H.) (5)	352.9	14	1340.7	5	9.6	125	32.5	12	2.7	1.4		10.7	11	3.29

Reprinted from *Business Week*, March 22, 1976, page 92.

Trade Discounts

A **trade discount** is a percentage reduction from the list price offered to certain categories of customers by the seller. Often, the manufacturer's list price is approximately the resale price of the retailer. Therefore, if the retailer is to sell at the suggested price, the merchandise must be bought at a discount if the retailer is to cover his overhead and earn a net profit.

An invoice illustrating a trade discount is shown in Figure 6–1. Note the trade discount of 50% reduces the list price of $436.00 by $218.00. Thus the net price is $436.00 − $218.00 = $218.00.

Figure 6–1

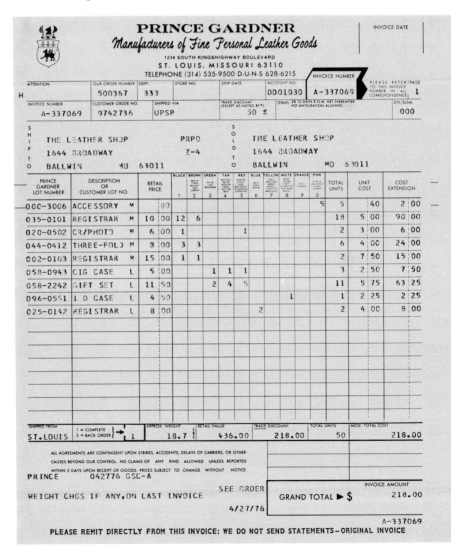

Example 1

The Appleton Company buys refrigerators from a wholesale appliance dealer. The list price of one model is $478 with a trade discount of 40%. Find the trade discount percentage and the net price.

Solution:

The amount of a discount is just an application of the basic percentage formula $P = BR$ where P = trade discount percentage, B = list price, and R = discount percent. In this problem $P = ?$, $B = \$478$, and $R = 40\%$.

$$P = BR$$
$$= \$478 \times 0.40$$
$$= \$191.20$$

$$\begin{array}{rl} \$478.00 & \text{List price} \\ - \ 191.20 & \text{Trade discount percentage} \\ \hline \$286.80 & \text{Net price} \end{array}$$

Example 2

A wholesale hardware company lists a water heater at $246 with a trade discount of 30%. Find the net price.

Solution:

$$\begin{array}{rl} \$246.00 & \text{List price} \\ - \ \ \ 73.80 & \text{Trade discount percentage } (\$246 \times 0.30) \\ \hline \$172.20 & \text{Net price} \end{array}$$

An alternate method exists for calculating the net price in the previous example. A trade discount of 30% means that the net price is 70% $(100\% - 30\%)$ of the list price. Multiplying the list price by 0.70 yields

$$\begin{array}{rl} \$246.00 & \text{List price} \\ \times \ \ \ 0.70 & \\ \hline \$172.20 & \text{Net price} \end{array}$$

Relative to the 30% discount, 70% is called the **complement of the discount.** A discount and its complement are related by the formula

(6–1) $$100\% - D = C$$

where D = discount and C = complement of the discount.

An alternate method for calculating the net price is to multiply the list price by the complement of the discount.

Example 3

A dining room suite with a list price of $1,268 carries a trade discount of 70%. The freight charges are $24.60. Find the net price using the complement of the discount and find the billing price.

Solution:

$$
\begin{array}{rl}
\$1,268.00 & \text{List price} \\
\times \qquad 0.30 & \text{Complement of the discount} \\
\hline
\$\;\; 380.40 & \text{Net price} \\
+ \quad 24.60 & \text{Freight charges} \\
\hline
\$\;\; 405.00 & \text{Billing price}
\end{array}
$$

Frequently, discounts will be in fractional percents such as $16\tfrac{2}{3}\%$, $33\tfrac{1}{3}\%$, etc. In such instances, it may be simpler to multiply the list price by the fractional equivalent of the discount percent. Recall that

$$
16\tfrac{2}{3}\% = \frac{16\tfrac{2}{3}}{100} = \frac{50}{3} \times \frac{1}{100} = \frac{1}{6} \text{ and}
$$

$$
33\tfrac{1}{3}\% = \frac{33\tfrac{1}{3}}{100} = \frac{100}{3} \times \frac{1}{100} = \frac{1}{3}.*
$$

The complement of the discount may be found by subtracting the fractional equivalent of the discount percent from 1; for example,

$$
100\% - 16\tfrac{2}{3}\% = 83\tfrac{1}{3}\% \qquad\qquad 100\% - 33\tfrac{1}{3}\% = 66\tfrac{2}{3}\%
$$
$$
1 \;-\; \tfrac{1}{6} \;=\; \tfrac{5}{6} \qquad\qquad\qquad 1 \;-\; \tfrac{1}{3} \;=\; \tfrac{2}{3}
$$

Example 4

A load of fertilizer with a list price of $880 carries a trade discount of $12\tfrac{1}{2}\%$. Find the net price using the complement of the discount.

Solution:

$$
12\tfrac{1}{2}\% = \frac{12\tfrac{1}{2}}{100} = \frac{25}{2} \times \frac{1}{100} = \frac{1}{8}
$$

$$
100\% - 12\tfrac{1}{2}\% = 87\tfrac{1}{2}\%
$$
$$
1 \;-\; \tfrac{1}{8} \;=\; \tfrac{7}{8}
$$

List Price

$$\$880 \times \tfrac{7}{8} = \$770 \text{ Net Price}$$

Complement of the Discount

---

* See Section 4.2.

1. Century Electronics Company buys its television sets from a wholesale appliance dealer. One model has a list price of $575 with a trade discount of 32%. Find the trade discount percentage and the net price.

2. If a wholesale appliance dealer lists an air conditioning unit at $428 with a trade discount of 38%, find the net price of the unit.

3. Walt's Water Conditioning Service buys water softeners from a wholesaler at a list price of $620 with a trade discount of 28%. Find the trade discount percentage and the net price.

4. What is the net price of a washing machine that lists for $424 with a trade discount of 32%?

5. A set of bedroom furniture with a list price of $1,420 carries a trade discount of 65%. If the freight charges are $62.70, find (a) the net price using the complement of the discount and (b) the billing price.

6. A furniture wholesaler lists a living room suite at $1,840 with a trade discount of 54%. Find the net price using the complement of the discount. If the freight charges are $47.30, what is the billing price?

7. The net price of a self-cleaning oven at a wholesale outlet is $288.60. If the list price is $390, what percent is the trade discount? What is the complement of the trade discount?

8. The list price of a refrigerator is $630 and the net price is $415.80. Find the trade discount percent and the complement of the trade discount.

9. The Quality Appliance Company recently purchased a shipment of vacuum cleaners from a wholesaler. Each unit had a list price of $219 with a trade discount of 33⅓%. Find the trade discount percentage and the net price for each unit.

10. An appliance wholesaler lists a color television set at $525 with a trade discount of 16⅔%. Find the net price using the complement of the discount. If the freight charges are $12.23, what is the billing price?

11. A building supply store purchased a load of lumber for a net price of $807.50. If the lumber was purchased at a trade discount of 15%, what was the list price?

12. Find the list price of a set of office furniture that was purchased at a net price of $680.40 if the trade discount was 58%.

13. Find the list price of a fur coat that was purchased at a net price of $341 if the trade discount was 8⅓%.

6.3 Chain Discounts

Changes in market conditions may affect the price of an already discounted product. Improved technology, reduction in the price of raw materials, or wholesale price adjustments may necessitate a price change to maintain a competitive position. Rather than changing the entire price structure, the seller may add an additional trade discount. For instance the price of an item may be quoted at $100 less 40% less 20%. This means that the list price is discounted 40%, then the result discounted an additional 20% to obtain the net price. Two or more discounts on a single item are called **series discounts** or **chain discounts.**

Example 1

A load of paneling has a list price of $684 less 30% less 15%. What is the net price?

Solution:

$684.00 List price
− 205.20 First discount ($684 × 0.30)

$478.80
− 71.82 Second discount ($478.80 × 0.15)

$406.98 Net price

Example 2

What is the net price of a musical instrument with a list price of $500 less 60% less 30% less 10%?

Solution:

$500.00 List price
− 300.00 First discount ($500 × 0.60)
─────────
$200.00
−   60.00 Second discount ($200 × 0.30)
─────────
$140.00
−   14.00 Third discount ($140 × 0.10)
─────────
$126.00 Net price

The previous example can be used to illustrate that it is *not* correct to add the chain discount percents to obtain a single discount percent. Had this been done in Example 2 the single discount percent would be 60% + 30% + 10% = 100%, and the net price would be

$500.00 List price
− 500.00 Trade discount ($500 × 1.00)
─────────
$ 0.00 Net price

A vendor using this kind of mathematics will have a difficult time making a profit!

There is a single discount percent equal to the chain discounts of the previous example. Referring again to Example 2

the complement of 60% is 40%,
the complement of 30% is 70%,
the complement of 10% is 90%,

and the product of these complements is

$$0.40 \times 0.70 \times 0.90 = 0.252.$$

Multiplying by this product,

$500.00 List price
×   0.252 Product of the complements
─────────
$126.00 Net price

Thus, an alternate method for solving Example 2 is to multiply the list price by the product of the complements of the chain discounts. This means that the product of the complements is the complement of the equivalent single discount. Thus, to find the single discount percent equivalent to a chain discount, the product of the complements is subtracted from 100%. In Example 2,

$$100\% - 25.2\% = 74.8\% \qquad (0.252 = 25.2\%)$$

This is the correct single discount percent because

$$
\begin{array}{ll}
\$500.00 & \text{List price} \\
-\ \ 374.00 & \text{Discount } (\$500 \times 0.748) \\
\hline
\$126.00 & \text{Net price}
\end{array}
$$

Example 3

A stereophonic tape recorder listing at $369.95 has trade discounts of $33\frac{1}{3}/16\frac{2}{3}/10$ (list less $33\frac{1}{3}\%$ less $16\frac{2}{3}\%$ less 10%). Find the net price using a single discount percent equivalent to the chain discounts.

Solution:

The product of the complements is

$$\frac{2}{3} \times \frac{5}{6} \times \frac{9}{10} = \frac{1}{2} = 50\%$$

hence the single discount percent is

$$100\% - 50\% = 50\% = 0.50$$

$$
\begin{array}{ll}
\$369.95 & \text{List price} \\
-\ \ 184.98 & \text{Discount } (\$369.95 \times 0.50) \\
\hline
\$184.97 & \text{Net price}
\end{array}
$$

Exercises for Section 6.3

1. A stereo amplifier has a list price of $460 less 20% less 15%. What is the net price?

2. If a platform rocker has a list price of $240 less 12% less 5%, what is the net price?

3. Find the net price of a camera listed at $340 less 30% less 4%.

4. What is the net price of a washer-dryer combination with a list price of $800 less 30% less 20% less 10%?

5. A pocket calculator has a list price of $180 less 15% less 10% less 8%. What is the net price?

6. A home entertainment center has a list price of $720 less $16\frac{2}{3}\%$ less $8\frac{1}{3}\%$. What is the net price?

7. An executive office desk has a list price of $842 less $33\frac{1}{3}\%$ less $16\frac{2}{3}\%$. Find the net price of the desk.

8. Find the single discount percent equivalent to the following chain discounts:

   a. 40%, 20%   c. 30%, 10%
   b. 35%, 20%   d. 60%, 40%

9. Find the single discount percent equivalent to the following chain discounts:

   a. 50%, 20%, 10%   c. 40%, 20%, 10%
   b. 70%, 40%, 20%   d. 30%, 15%, 5%

10. Find the single discount percent equivalent to the following chain discounts:

    a. 66⅔%, 33⅓%   c. 16⅔%, 8⅓%, 3⅓%
    b. 33⅓%, 16⅔%   d. 66⅔%, 16⅔%, 8⅓%

11. A home heating system listing at $950 has trade discounts of 30/20/10. Find the net price using a single discount percent equivalent to the chain discounts.

12. Some bedroom furniture is listed at $1,200 with trade discounts of 40/20/20. Find the net price using a single discount percent equivalent to the chain discounts.

13. Use a single discount percent to find the net price of some office furniture listed at $1,600 with trade discounts of 60/50/30.

14. Find the net price of a piece of furniture listed at $800 with discounts of 40/10/5.

15. Some display cases for a jewelry store are listed at $1,140 each with trade discounts of 20/10/5. What is the net price of the cases?

16. A living room suite is listed at $1,450 with trade discounts of $33\frac{1}{3}/16\frac{2}{3}$. Find the net price using a single discount percent equivalent to the chain discounts.

17. Find the net price of a home freezer listed at $480 with discounts of $16\frac{2}{3}/8\frac{1}{3}/3\frac{1}{3}$.

Quantity Discounts

A **quantity discount** is a reduction in price because of the amount purchased. Quantity discounts may be based on:

   a. the number of units purchased
   b. the dollar value of the entire order
   c. the size of the package purchased

The following examples illustrate quantity discounts.

Example 1

The list prices of a manufacturer are subject to the following discounts:

Units	Discount from List Price
1–24	40%
25–49	43%
50 or more	46%

If an item has a list price of $25.00, what is the net price on an order of 30 units?

Solution:

Quantity discounts are also an application of the basic percentage formula where P = quantity discount, B = cost price, and R = discount %. Thus,

$$\begin{array}{r} \$750.00 \\ -\ \ 322.50 \\ \hline \$427.50 \end{array} \quad \begin{array}{l} \text{Cost price (\$25} \times \text{30)} \\ \text{Quantity discount (\$750} \times \text{0.43)} \\ \text{Net price} \end{array}$$

The solution could have been found using the complement of the discount.

$$\begin{array}{r} \$750.00 \\ \times\ \ \ \ 0.57 \\ \hline \$427.50 \end{array} \quad \begin{array}{l} \text{Cost price (\$25} \times \text{30)} \\ \text{Complement of the discount (100\%} - \text{43\%)} \\ \text{Net price} \end{array}$$

Example 2

An invoice* of the Jok Sports Company contains the following at the bottom of the page:

Quantity Discounts Allowed	
$100–$500	3%
$500–$900	5%
$900 and over	7%

Find the billing price for an order totaling $750.88 if transportation charges are $9.65.

Solution:

$$\begin{array}{r} \$750.88 \\ -\ \ \ \ 37.54 \\ \hline \$713.34 \\ +\ \ \ \ \ 9.65 \\ \hline \$722.99 \end{array} \quad \begin{array}{l} \text{Cost price} \\ \text{Quantity discount (\$750.88} \times \text{0.05)} \\ \text{Net price} \\ \text{Transportation charges} \\ \text{Billing price} \end{array}$$

---

* An itemized statement showing the merchandise sold to the buyer.

Example 3

A brand of toothpaste with a list price of $8.00 per dozen tubes has a trade discount of 33⅓%. An additional 2% discount is offered for orders by the case (a case contains twelve dozen tubes). What is the net price on an order of two cases?

Solution:

$192.00   List price ($8.00 × 24)

−   64.00   Trade discount ($192.00 × ⅓)

$128.00

−   2.56   Quantity discount ($128.00 × 0.02)

$125.44   Net price

Quantity discounts are offered to induce customers to purchase in larger quantities and are possible because of certain economies realized by the seller. On large orders there may be a reduction in the salesman's expenses or in packaging, accounting, or transportation costs. In fact, this is a requirement by federal regulations. Quantity discounts are subject to the Robinson-Patman Act of 1936, which prohibits lower prices for large orders unless such prices reflect a reduction in the cost of doing business or are needed in order to meet the prices of a competitor. The purpose of the Robinson-Patman Act is to preserve competition and to prevent the creation of monopolies.

1. The list prices of a manufacturer are subject to the following discounts:

Units	Discount from List Price
1–49	30%
50–99	35%
100 or more	40%

   If each unit has a list price of $20, what is the net price of an order of 70 units?

2. The following discounts apply to merchandise purchased at Ralph's Wholesale Plumbing Supply:

Quantity	Discount Allowed
$500–$1,000	5%
$1,000–$1,500	7%
$1,500 and over	10%

   Find the net price for an order totaling $954.75.

3. Merchandise purchased at Universal Hardware Supply is subject to the following discounts:

Quantity	Discount Allowed
$100–$300	2%
$300–$600	5%
$600–$1,000	8%
$1,000 and over	10%

   Find the billing price for an order totalling $578.25 if freight charges are $14.78.

4. A wholesale distributor of appliances offers the following discounts on built-in dishwashers:

Units	Discount from List Price
1–10	20%
11–20	33⅓%
21 or more	60%

   If each dishwasher has a list price of $225, what is the net price of an order for 12 dishwashers?

5. Stone's Building Products offers the following discounts:

Quantity	Discount Allowed
$400– $600	10%
$600–$1,000	12%
$1,000–$1,400	16⅔%
$1,400 and over	18%

   Find the billing price for an order totalling $1,238 if transportation charges are $73.52.

6. The following discounts apply to refrigerators purchased at Atlas Appliance Wholesalers:

Units	Discount from List Price
1– 5	20%
6–15	33⅓%
16–25	40%
26 and over	45%

If each refrigerator has a list price of $423, what is the net price of an order for 40 refrigerators?

7. Trim-Eze Hair Clippers list at $23 each with a trade discount of 26%. An additional 8⅓% discount is offered for orders of a shipping case of 20 clippers. What is the net price of an order of 5 cases?

8. A brand of electric carving knives lists at $32 each with a trade discount of 34%. An additional 4% discount is offered for orders of a shipping case of 12 knives. Find the net price for an order of 6 cases if freight charges are $41.61.

II Terms of Payment

Section 6.5 Credit Terms

The majority of sales by manufacturers or wholesalers to retailers are on credit; that is, the retailer is permitted a period of time following the sale before payment must be made. Credit sales have become widespread because they permit the retailer to carry a larger assortment of merchandise. This means a potential increase in sales, an advantage to both the retailer and the supplier.

INVOICE

Packerland Packing Co. of Texas, Inc.

Phone (806) 669-6811
Shipped From: E. FREDERICK - HWY 60   PAMPA, TEXAS 79065

INVOICE NO.   006206
DATE   10/03/76
TERMS   NET

SOLD TO:
PACKERLAND PACKING CO INC
P.O. BOX 1184
GREEN BAY, WIS.
54305

SHIP TO:
PACKERLAND PACKING CO INC
P.O. BOX 1184
GREEN BAY, WIS.
54305

Remit To: P.O. BOX 1184   GREEN BAY, WI 54305
Phone (414) 468-4000   SHIP VIA: FFE 918 PREPAID

Cust P.O.	Date	Salesman 18	Manifest 040486	B.O.L. No. 007292

Quantity	Selling Unit	Description	Weight	Price	Unit of Measure	Amount
32	CARCASS	GOOD HEIFER	FR 17,848.0	56.75	CWT	10,128.74
5	CARCASS	CH. HFR 2 & 3 5/6	FR 2,844.0	57.25	CWT	1,628.19
1	CARCASS	CH. HFR 2 & 3 4/5	FR 448.0	65.25	CWT	292.32
5	CARCASS	CH. HFR 2 & 3 6/7	FR 3,096.0	57.25	CWT	1,772.46
1	CARCASS	CH. HFR 2 & 3 7/8	FR 748.0	57.25	CWT	428.23
3	CARCASS	BULL	FR 2,260.0	61.00	CWT	1,378.60
3	CARCASS	L. BULL	FR 1,278.0	61.00	CWT	779.58
1	CARCASS	BULL #2	FR 982.0	61.00	CWT	599.02
1	CARCASS	BULL #3	FR 954.0	61.00	CWT	581.94

FILE COPY   30,458.0 $17,589.08

Credit terms are shown on the invoice, usually in an abbreviated notation. The most common credit period is thirty days, and will appear on an invoice as

"net 30 days" or "n/30."

This notation means that the buyer has thirty days after the date on the invoice during which payment may be made. If the bill is not paid, after thirty days it is considered overdue and may be subject to penalty charges. Similarly, the notations

n/60   or   n/90

mean that the credit period is sixty days and ninety days after the date of the invoice, respectively. If credit is not extended by the seller, the invoice will contain the notation "C.O.D.," which stands for **cash on delivery.**

Section

6.6   Cash Discounts

While credit may be a competitive necessity, the delay in payment can be costly to the seller. With prompt payment, the seller could reinvest the money or use it to pay bills of his own. As a result, it is a common practice to offer an inducement to buyers to pay promptly in the form of an additional discount called the cash discount. A **cash discount** is a percentage reduction from the net price for payment within a specified time. Cash discounts usually range from 1 to 3 percent and are indicated on the invoice along with the credit period, as follows:

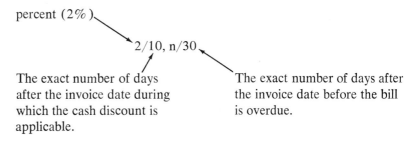

The cash discount

percent (2%)

2/10, n/30

The exact number of days after the invoice date during which the cash discount is applicable.

The exact number of days after the invoice date before the bill is overdue.

Suppose, for example, the above notation is on an invoice dated May 1. Thus:

May 2–11   2% discount applicable
May 12–31 Net price applicable
June 1   Bill is overdue.

Cash discounts are calculated in the same manner as trade discounts and quantity discounts, except that cash discounts are taken after all discounts have been applied. Cash discounts are not applicable to freight charges.

Example 1

The list price on an invoice dated November 1 is $195.50, with terms of 2/10, n/30. How much should be remitted if the bill is paid on (a) November 10 or (b) November 30?

Solution:

a. November 10 falls within the cash discount period of 10 days following November 1, hence

$195.50 List Price
−   3.91 Cash discount ($195.50 × 0.02)
_____
$191.59 Amount to be remitted

b. November 30 is in the period of the 11th through the 30th day after the invoice date, thus the amount to be remitted is the list price of $195.50.

Example 2

The invoice in Figure 6–2 contains the following information: office desk, list $478.95; trade discounts, 70/10; freight charges, $12.68; and terms, 2/30, n/60. If the bill is paid on May 10, how much should be remitted?

Solution:

May 10 is well within the cash discount period, hence both the trade discounts and the cash discount are to be taken.

$478.95 List price
− 349.64 Total trade discounts
_____
$129.31
−   2.59 Cash discount ($129.31 × 0.02)
_____
$126.72
+   12.68 Freight charges
_____
$139.40 Amount to be remitted

More than one cash discount may be offered on a given sale. The notation

$$3/15, 1/30, n/60$$

on an invoice dated June 10 means:

June 11–June 25   3% cash discount applicable
June 26–July 10   1% cash discount applicable
July 11–August 9 Billing price due
August 10   Bill overdue

Figure 6–2

SHIP TO	Britton Office Supply 2824 Dennison Boulevard Detroit, Michigan	STORE NO. **12**	CUSTOMER DEPT.	CUSTOMER ORDER NO. **11378**
		INVOICE DATE **4/20**	TERMS (NO ANTICIPATION ALLOWED) **2/30, n/60**	
SOLD TO	Britton Office Supply 2824 Dennison Boulevard Detroit, Michigan	ROUTING INSTRUCTIONS		
		NO. OF CNTS. **1**	WGT. **236**	OUR REFERENCE NO. **21823** INVOICE NO. **67021**

STORE USE	STYLE OR LOT	DESCRIPTION	PCS	PRICE	EXTENDED AMOUNT
	113-M	Desk, Executive	1	478.95	478.95

SALESMAN	PAGE NO.	TOTAL NUMBER OF UNIT ➡	SHIPMENT COMPLETE PARTIAL	SUB TOTAL MDSE. AMOUNT	478.95
			Less 70% Less 10%		349.64
				FRT. CHARGES	12.68
				GRAND TOTAL	141.99

Example 3

An invoice for floor coverings shows a billing price of $659.82, including freight charges of $42.16. If the invoice is dated July 16 and indicates terms of 5/15, 4/45, n/60, what amount should be remitted if the bill is paid on August 30?

Solution:

Since freight charges are not subject to cash discounts, they must be deducted from the billing price then readded after the cash discount is taken.

$$
\begin{array}{rl}
\$659.82 & \text{Billing price} \\
-\quad 42.16 & \text{Freight charges} \\
\hline
\$617.66 & \\
-\quad 24.71 & \text{Cash discount } (\$617.66 \times 0.04) \\
\hline
\$592.95 & \\
+\quad 42.16 & \text{Freight charges} \\
\hline
\$635.11 & \text{Amount to be remitted}
\end{array}
$$

1. The list price on an invoice dated June 12 is $372.60, with terms of 3/10, n/30. How much should be remitted if the bill is paid on (a) June 19 (b) July 11?

2. If the list price on an invoice is $742.42 and if the terms of the invoice are 4/15, n/60, what amount should be remitted on March 26 if the date of the invoice is March 12?

3. An invoice dated September 5 contains the following information: plumbing supplies—list $1,142; trade discounts 20/5; freight charges $75.40; terms 3/30, n/60. If the bill is paid on October 2, how much should be remitted?

4. Find the net price for an invoice dated January 7 and paid on February 20 if the terms of the invoice are as follows: list price $973.38; trade discounts 30/10; freight charges $62.50; terms 4/45, n/90.

5. An invoice for draperies is dated April 5 and shows a list price of $1,455. If the terms are 5/10, 3/30, n/60, how much should be remitted if the bill is paid on (a) April 15, (b) May 1, (c) June 3?

6. An invoice for lighting fixtures is dated December 8 and contains the following information: list price $743.62; terms 4/15, 3/30, n/60. How much should be remitted if the bill is paid on (a) December 22, (b) January 5, (c) February 5?

7. Find the net price for an invoice dated August 27 and paid on September 21 if the terms of the invoice are as follows: list price $2,279.60; trade discounts 20/5; freight charges $112.40; terms 3/30, 2/60, n/90. How much would be remitted if the bill were paid on October 25?

8. The list price on an invoice for electronic equipment is $1,972.32. The invoice is dated May 17 and contains the following information: trade discounts 30/15; freight charges $37.20; terms 5/10, 4/30, n/60. How much should be remitted if the bill is paid on May 25? If it is paid on June 14?

9. Including freight charges, the billing price of an invoice dated November 11 is $527.93. If the freight charges are $11.24 and if the terms of the bill are 5/15, 4/30, n/60, how much should be remitted if the bill is paid on November 24?

10. An invoice for optical equipment dated March 19 shows a billing price of $1,326.12, including freight charges of $78.46. The invoice contains the following information: trade discounts 25/10; terms 6/10, 4/30, n/45. How much should be remitted if the bill is paid on March 30? If it is paid on April 15?

Section 6.7 Dating

The terms of payment in the previous examples are called **ordinary dating.** Other forms of dating are used in conjunction with cash discounts; three of these are discussed here.

A. End of the Month

An invoice dated October 12 with terms 2/10, E.O.M. means that the cash discount period would begin the first day of the following month and that the bill becomes overdue 20 days after the expiration of the cash discount period.

October 12	Invoice date
November 1–10	Cash discount period
November 11–30	Billing price due
December 1	Bill is overdue

An exception to the above occurs when the invoice date is after the 25th day of a month. Then the cash discount period begins the first day of the second month after the month of the invoice date. Thus, for an invoice dated October 29,

October 29	Invoice date
December 1–10	Cash discount period
December 11–30	Billing price due
December 31	Bill is overdue

E.O.M. dating is a convenience to retailers who make frequent purchases from the same supplier in that it permits a single payment for all purchases made during the month.

B. Receipt of Goods

Receipt of goods dating is used when the transport time is relatively long. In this case, the cash discount period begins upon receipt of the merchandise by the buyer. Suppose, for example, an invoice dated April 16 and marked 3/10, R.O.G. is received by the buyer on May 12. Then

April 16	Invoice date
May 13–22	Cash discount period
May 23–June 11	Billing price due (20 days)
June 12	Bill is overdue

C. Extra Dating

In extra dating, the seller allows an added number of days before the cash discount period ends. Thus, an invoice dated July 7 with terms 2/10, 30X, net 60 means

July 7	Invoice date
July 8–August 16	Cash discount period (10 days + 30 extra days)
August 17–September 5	Billing price due
September 6	Bill is overdue

Extra dating is used most frequently in the sale of seasonal items in advance of the peak market demand. For example, air conditioners may be sold in the winter in anticipation of summer sales. For the supplier, the sales effected by extra dating helps to stabilize production and to eliminate storage costs.

Example 1

An invoice for $196.13 is dated March 12 and the merchandise is delivered on April 2. What is the last day of the cash discount if the invoice terms are (a) 2/10, n/30; (b) 2/10, E.O.M.; (c) 2/10, R.O.G.; and (d) 2/10, 60X.

Solution:

a. Ten days after March 12 is March 22.

b. Ten days after March 31 is April 10.

c. Ten days after April 2 is April 12.

d. Seventy days after March 12 is May 21.

Exercises for Section 6.7

1. An invoice for $472.56 is dated April 22 with terms 4/10, E.O.M. How much should be remitted if the bill is paid on May 9? If it is paid on May 27? When does the bill become overdue?

2. If an invoice dated July 27 has a list price of $946.70 with terms of 5/10 E.O.M., how much should be remitted if the bill is paid on September 8? If it is paid on September 19? When does the bill become overdue?

3. An invoice dated October 17 is marked 4/10, R.O.G. and is received by the buyer on November 21. If the list price on the invoice is $472.50, how much should be remitted if the bill is paid (a) on November 30 or (b) on December 10.

4. Find the amount that should be remitted for a $273.60 invoice dated January 10 and marked 5/10, R.O.G., if the invoice was received February 14 and is paid on February 20.

5. The invoice for a shipment of swimming pool chemicals is marked 3/15, 20X, net 60. The invoice is dated March 6 and the list price is $874.50. How much should be remitted if the bill is paid on April 18?

6. Find the amount to be remitted on August 10 for an invoice dated July 2, with list price $1,322.72 and terms 3/10, 30X, net 60.

7. An invoice for $324.75 is dated May 6 and the merchandise is delivered on May 23. Find the amount to be remitted on June 2 if the terms are (a) 3/10, n/30; (b) 3/10, E.O.M.; (c) 2/10, R.O.G.; (d) 4/10, 20X, net 60.

8. Find the amount to be remitted on December 12 for an invoice for $579.20 dated November 15, if the merchandise is delivered on November 2 and the terms of the invoice are (a) 4/10, 2/60, n/90; (b) 2/10, E.O.M.; (c) 3/10, R.O.G.; (d) 3/10, 30X, net 60.

III Pricing

Section **6.8**

The Basic Markon Equation

To be successful, the retailer must sell merchandise at a price higher than the cost price. This difference, called **markon,** must be sufficient to cover overhead and provide a net profit. Judicious pricing is one of the keys to any successful retail operation. If the price is too high, sales are reduced or lost to a competitor. If the price is too low, the markon may not be sufficient to cover operating expenses and earn a reasonable net profit. For these reasons, pricing is as much an art as it is a science and requires experience coupled with sound judgment.

The selling price of an item is equal to the cost price plus the markon. This fundamental concept can be expressed by the equation

$$(6–2) \qquad\qquad\qquad C + M = S$$

where C = cost, M = markon, and S = selling price. Markon* is usually a percentage of either the cost price or the selling price.

A. Markon Based on Cost Price

Small retail businesses frequently express markon in terms of the cost price. Markon based on cost price is a straight application of the basic percentage formula with P = amount of markon, B = cost price, and R = markon percent.

Example 1

What is the selling price of an article if the cost price is $42.00 and the markon is 30% of the cost price?

Solution:

Using equation (6–2) and the basic percentage formula,

$$
\begin{array}{rl}
\$42.00 & \text{Cost price} \\
+\ \ 12.60 & \text{Markon ($\$42 \times 0.30$)} \\
\hline
\$54.60 & \text{Selling price}
\end{array}
$$

---

* The terms markon and markup are often used interchangeably in this equation, but in modern terminology markup is reserved for an increase in an original selling price.

The above problem can be solved by an alternate method using formula (4–5). In this case, the increase in the base is the increase from the cost price to the selling price. Thus, with $C = B$, $S = B_1$ and $R_c =$ markon percent,

$$(6–3) \qquad\qquad S = (1 + R_c) \cdot C$$

Example 1 is solved using formula (6–3) as follows:

$$S = (1 + R_c) \cdot C$$
$$= (1 + 0.30) \cdot \$42.00$$
$$= 1.30 \times \$42.00$$
$$= \$54.60$$

Example 2

The invoice for a group of furniture pieces indicates a list price of $528.60, a trade discount of 40%, and transportation charges of $9.25. The retailer determines a markon of 60% of the cost price. What should be the selling price of the furniture?

Solution:

	$528.60	List price
−	211.44	Trade discount ($528.60 × 0.40)
	$317.16	
+	9.25	Transportation charges
	$326.41	Cost price
+	195.85	Markon ($326.41 × 0.60)
	$522.26	Selling price

The selling price could have been determined by formula (6–3) once the cost price was determined.

$$S = (1 + R_c) \cdot C$$
$$= (1 + 0.60) \times \$326.41$$
$$= 1.60 \times \$326.41$$
$$= \$522.26$$

B. Markon Based on Selling Price

Most large retail establishments base markon on the selling price. There are several reasons for this: sales data is more available than cost data, trade statistics are expressed using a sales base, and a number of internal operations such as sales commissions, taxes, and advertising are based on sales.

The formula for computing selling price when the markon is based on the selling price is

$$(6\text{–}4) \qquad\qquad S = \frac{C}{1 - R_s}$$

where S = selling price, C = cost price, and R_s = markon percent. (This is equivalent to formula $(4\text{–}5)$ solved for B.)

Example 1

A hardware item that costs $4.60 is to have a markon of $33\frac{1}{3}\%$ of the selling price. Find the selling price.

Solution:

With a markon of $33\frac{1}{3}\%$, calculations are simplified using the fraction* $\frac{1}{3}$. Using equation $(6\text{–}4)$,

$$
\begin{aligned}
S &= \frac{C}{1 - R_s} \\
&= \frac{\$4.60}{1 - \dfrac{1}{3}} \\
&= \frac{\$4.60}{\dfrac{2}{3}} \\
&= \$4.60 \times \frac{3}{2} \\
&= \$6.90
\end{aligned}
$$

Section 6.9 Conversion of the Markon Base

If an item costs $10 and sells for $15, the markon of $5 is 50% of the cost price and $33\frac{1}{3}\%$ of the selling price. The markon based on selling price appears to be smaller, another reason that this base is used to determine markon. Under certain conditions, it is desirable to convert from one markon base to the other. Dividing both sides of formula $(6\text{–}3)$ and $(6\text{–}4)$ by C, we have

$$\frac{S}{C} = 1 + R_c$$

$$\frac{S}{C} = \frac{1}{1 - R_s}$$

Thus, $\qquad\qquad 1 + R_c = \dfrac{1}{1 - R_s}$

* See Example 6 of Section 4.2.

This equation can be solved for either R_c or R_s:

$$(6\text{–}5) \qquad\qquad R_c = \frac{R_s}{1 - R_s}$$

$$(6\text{–}6) \qquad\qquad R_s = \frac{R_c}{1 + R_c}$$

The above formulas are used for conversion of one markon base to the other.

Example 1

The markon on an item is 40% of the selling price. What is the markon percent of the cost price?

Solution:

$$R_c = \frac{R_s}{1 - R_s}$$

$$R_c = \frac{0.40}{1 - 0.40}$$

$$= \frac{0.40}{0.60}$$

$$= \frac{2}{3} = 66\tfrac{2}{3}\%$$

Example 2

The markon on an item is 20% of the cost price. What is the markon percent of the retail price?

Solution:

Using formula (6–6) with $R_c = 20\%$, $R_s = ?$,

$$R_s = \frac{R_c}{1 + R_c}$$

$$= \frac{0.20}{1 + 0.20}$$

$$= \frac{0.20}{1.20}$$

$$= 0.1666 \ldots$$

$$= 16\tfrac{2}{3}\%$$

1. Find the selling price of an article of clothing if the cost price is $47 and the markon is (a) 20% of the cost price and (b) 26% of the cost price.

2. If the cost price of a digital clock radio is $22.50, find the selling price if the markon is (a) 25% of the cost price and (b) 32% of the cost price.

3. The cost price of a certain lighting fixture is $79. What is the selling price if the markon is (a) 40% of the cost price and (b) 45% of the cost price?

4. An invoice for a color television set shows a list price of $724.24, a trade discount of 35% and freight charges of $11.40. The retailer decides on a markon of 40% of the cost price. What should be the selling price for the television set?

5. The list price for a washing machine is $424.50. If the trade discount is 45% and freight charges are $14.70, find the cost price. If the markon is 55% of cost price, what is the selling price of the washer?

6. The invoice for a photographic enlarger shows a list price of $324.50, a trade discount of 55%, and freight charges of $7.56. If the retailer decides on a markon of 60% of the cost price, what should be the selling price for the enlarger?

7. An article of clothing whose cost price is $47.50 is to have a markon of 25% of the selling price. Find the selling price.

8. The cost price for a piece of electronic equipment is $82.32. What should the selling price be if the markon is to be 45% of the selling price?

9. The manager of Atlas Building Supplies decides on a markon of 32% of the selling price for a table saw. If the cost price of the saw is $120.70, what is the selling price?

10. The markon on an item is 25% of the selling price. Find the markon percent of the cost price.

11. If the markon of an item is 25% of the cost price, what is the markon percent of the selling price?

12. A retailer decides on a markon of 42% of the cost price for one model of a microwave oven. What is the markon percent of the selling price?

13. Find the markon percent of the cost price if the markon percent of the selling price is (a) 30% and (b) 35%.

14. What is the markon percent of the selling price if the markon percent of the cost price is (a) 40% and (b) 30%?

15. A trash compactor has a markon of 38% of the selling price. What is the markon percent of the cost price? If the cost price is $142.50, what is the selling price?

16. Find the markon percent of the selling price for a refrigerator that has a markon percent of 48% of the cost price. If the selling price is $382.40, what is the cost price?

6.10 Markdown

The dynamics of retailing require a continuous adjustment in pricing. Economic conditions and competition cause prices to fluctuate both upward and downward. Price adjustments include discounts to employees, markup (an additional markon), and the most significant of all, markdowns.

A **markdown** is a reduction in the selling price of an item, and it is one of the principal means by which the retailer adjusts his inventory to internal and external conditions. Markdowns occur for a number of reasons: special sales and promotions, the need to meet competition, and the need to clear out merchandise that is obsolete, shopworn, unpopular, or part of broken assortments. Markdowns are ordinarily expressed as a percentage of the selling price and are calculated as a straight application of the percentage formula, with P = amount of markdown, B = selling price, and R = markdown percent.

Example 1

The price of a book was marked down from $4.95 to $3.95. What was the markdown percent?

Solution:

The amount of the markdown P was $4.95 − $3.95 = $1.00, B = $4.95, R = ?

$$R = \frac{P}{B}$$

$$= \frac{1.00}{4.95}$$

$$= 0.202$$

$$= 20.2\%$$

Example 2

A department store advertised better women's blouses on sale at 20% off the regular price. If the blouses sold originally at $15.00, what is the new selling price?

Solution:

The new selling price is the original selling price less the markdown.

$15.00 Original selling price
− 3.00 Markdown ($15.00 × 0.20)

$12.00 New selling price

Alternatively, a markdown of 20% means that the new selling price is 100% − 20% = 80% of the original selling price. By using this complement of the discount,

$15.00 Original selling price
× 0.80 Complement of the discount

$12.00 New selling price

Example 3

A large scratch was discovered on a dining room table on display in a furniture store. The selling price of the table included a markon of 50% of the selling price. It was determined to mark down the table 30% of the selling price because of the scratch. If the cost price of the table was $78.00, find (a) the original selling price and (b) the new selling price.

Solution:

a. $S = \dfrac{C}{1 - R_s}$

$= \dfrac{\$78.00}{1 - 0.50}$

$= \dfrac{\$78.00}{0.50}$

$= \$156.00$ Original selling price

b. $156.00 Original selling price
× 0.70 Complement of the markdown
$109.20 New selling price

Section 6.11 Extent of Markdown

The question of how much to mark down an item is as difficult to answer as the question of how much markon should be applied. The general rule is that the markdown must be sufficiently large to induce customers to purchase the merchandise. A dress reduced from $20.00 to $18.50 is not likely to attract attention, but a markdown to $16.00 may result in a quick sale. An old adage in retailing is "the first markdown is the least expensive," meaning that efforts to clear out merchandise should be in one step rather than a series of successive markdowns.

While the markdown should be large enough to sell the merchandise, there are practical restraints to consider when making a markdown. These can be made clear by a reexamination of the price structure. From equation (6–1), the selling price equals the cost price plus markon. As previously mentioned, markon includes overhead plus net profit. Thus

(6–1)
$$S = C + M$$

and

(6–7)
$$M = O + P$$

where O = overhead and P = net profit. Substituting

(6–8)
$$S = C + O + P$$

This structure is illustrated in Figure 6–3.

Figure 6–3

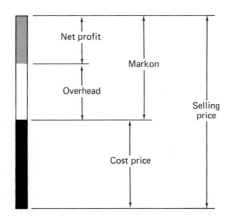

If possible, the markdown on an item should be confined to the net profit region, so that the retailer recovers at least the cost price and operating expenses. In this event, there may be no profit, but neither is there a loss. If the price reduction falls into the overhead region, the retailer is said to suffer an **operating loss.** If the markdown falls into the cost price, then the result is called a **gross loss.** This is illustrated in Figure 6–4.

Expressed differently, if the markdown is less than the markon but exceeds the net profit, there is an operating loss; if the markdown exceeds the markon, there is a gross loss.

Figure 6–4

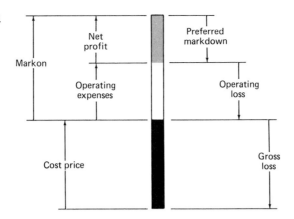

Example 1

The R. J. Taylor Department Store sells an item of toddler's wear at $6.95. Included in this price is a markon of $2.78. Estimated overhead on the item is $2.08. During an end-of-season sale, the item was marked down to $5.00. Determine if a sale results in a profit or a loss.

Solution:

$6.95 Original selling price
$-$ 5.00 New selling price
$1.95 Markdown

From (6–7) $P = M - O$

$2.78 Markon
$-$ 2.08 Overhead
$0.70 Net profit

The markdown ($1.95) is less than the markon ($2.78) but greater than the net profit ($0.70), thus an operating loss is incurred.

Example 2

As part of a sales promotion, a stereo was advertised at $25.00 off of the selling price of $369.95. The cost price is $231.84, and overhead is estimated at 40% of the cost price. Determine whether a sale results in a profit or loss.

Solution:

$369.95 Original selling price
$-$ 231.84 Cost price

$138.11 Markon
$-$ 92.74 Overhead ($231.84 × 0.40)

$ 45.37 Net profit

The markdown of $25.00 is less than the net profit, hence there is no loss. A profit of $45.37 $-$ $25.00 = $20.37 is earned on the sale.

---

1. The price of an air conditioning unit was marked down from $275 to $206.25. Find the markdown percent.

2. A clothing store advertised men's suits on sale at 15% off the regular price. If the suits sold originally for $98.00, find the sale price.

3. A dent in the side of a washing machine dictated a markdown in the price of the machine by 30%. The cost price of the machine was $150, and the markon was 40% of the selling price. Find (a) the original selling price and (b) the new selling price.

4. A living room easy chair was found to have a small tear in the fabric. The cost price of the chair was $54.75, and the markon was 55% of the cost price. It was decided to mark down the selling price of the chair by 25%. Find (a) the original selling price and (b) the new selling price.

5. A man's jacket at Quality Clothiers was originally priced at $78, but during a recent sale was marked down to $65. The estimated overhead on the jacket was $4.75. If the markon was $28, determine whether selling the jacket at $65 will yield a profit or a loss.

6. A power saw at Hall's Hardware is priced at $23.78. The overhead on the saw is $3.25, and the markon is $4.78. If the saw is marked down to $17.95, will a sale result in a profit or a loss?

7. Frank's Furniture Store advertised a record cabinet for $49.95 during a recent sale. The original price of the cabinet was $69.95. The cost price of the cabinet was $39.95, and overhead is estimated to be 20% of cost price. Will the sale of the cabinet at $49.95 result in a profit or a loss?

8. Samson's Stereo Shop marked down a tape recorder from $295.75 to $260.00. If the cost price of the recorder was $195.25 and overhead is 30% of cost, will a sale at $260.00 result in a profit or a loss?

9. A coffee table at Fred's Furnishings was originally priced at $79.95. The cost price of the table was $51.25, and overhead is estimated to be 40% of cost. What is the smallest sale price for the table that will not result in an operating loss?

10. Dempsey's Department Store sells an outdoor barbecue for $49.50. The cost price of the barbecue is $27.24, and the overhead is estimated to be 30% of cost. By how much can Dempsey's reduce the price of the barbecue and still not incur an operating loss?

11. A picnic table at Del's Discount Center is on sale at $30.60. The original price of the table was $36.00. What is the markdown percent? If the markdown is 20% of cost, what is the cost price of the table? If the overhead is estimated to be $2.20, will the sale of the table at $30.60 result in an operating loss?

Payrolls

Chapter Objectives for Chapter 7

I. Learn the meaning of the following terms:

A. *Gross earnings,* 159
B. *Net earnings,* 159
C. *Salary,* 159
D. *Commissions,* 161
E. *Wages,* 169
F. *Piecework,* 170
G. *Overtime,* 176
H. *Exemption,* 186

II. Understand:

A. The concept of payroll deductions, 159, 185
B. The purpose of employer contributions, 201
C. The information required on payroll records, 204

III. Learn to:

A. Compute gross earnings
  1. Salary, 159
  2. Commissions, 161
  3. Wages, 169
B. Compute overtime
  1. Salary, 176
  2. Commissions, 178
  3. Wages, 178
C. Calculate payroll deductions, 185

Payment for services rendered is the most fundamental of employer-employee relationships. The record of these payments is the company payroll. Fifty years ago this may have consisted of little more than a simple entry in a paybook; today payroll clerks record an array of items such as hours worked, regular and overtime rates, federal income and social security taxes, hospitalization insurance, union dues, and pledges to the United Fund. Much of the complexity of the payroll is due to social legislation and labor laws enacted by the federal government, while other items are the result of union contracts or trade competition. Today, keeping payroll records has become a time-consuming task requiring careful preparation using specialized knowledge. Accuracy is essential; not only are mistakes damaging to employee morale, but penalties may be imposed by governmental agencies for incorrect reports.

Gentlemen:—The following is a complete list of all warrants issued by me during the month of June, 1898:

Name.	For what Purpose.	Amt.
C. H. Berg,	salary as mayor	$116 65
H. B. Gniffke,	treasurer	133 35
H. B. Gniffke,	clerk hire	75 00
L. M. Langstaff,	recorder	116 65
F. B. Hoffman,	auditor	100 00
E. O. Duncan,	assessor	125 00
T. H. Duffy,	city attorney	150 00
Edw. Morgan,	city marshal	83 35
Jos Reinfried,	fire chief	100 00
Wm. Fitzpatrick,	committee clerk	75 00
Wm. A. Kaep,	clerk recorder's office	50 00
Edw Herron,	clerk treasurers office	50 00
Edw C Blake,	city engineer	125 00
E S Hyde,	assistant engineer	91 65
P. Cassidy,	chainman	40 00
Jas Boyce,	street commissioner	91 65
Wm Hippmann,	electrician	83 35

Since employees are paid at specified intervals called pay periods, the payroll is a recurring responsibility. Most pay periods are either weekly, biweekly, or monthly.

The basic structure of the payroll is contained in the meanings of the terms gross earnings and net earnings. **Gross earnings** refer to the total earnings of an employee within a pay period. **Net earnings** are gross earnings less deductions, that is, gross earnings less amounts withheld from the employee's pay. It is the responsibility of the payroll department to calculate gross earnings, withhold deductions, and remit net earnings. The actions of the payroll department are summarized in Figure 7–1.

Figure 7–1

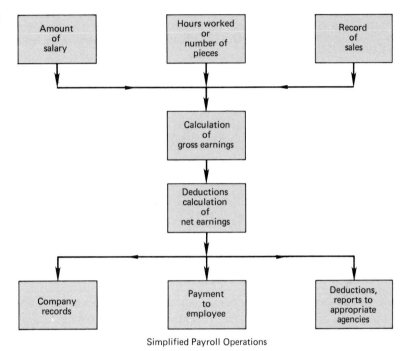

Simplified Payroll Operations

Section 7.2   Gross Earnings

There are three forms of gross earnings: salaries, commissions, and wages.

A. Salaries   The word **salary** is used to describe earnings of executives, supervisors, office personnel, and others who are paid according to a specified period of employment. A salary is independent of both production and working time.

The gross earnings of salaried employees are calculated by dividing the annual earnings by the number of pay periods per year; that is,

(7–1)   Gross Earnings (Salary) $= \dfrac{\text{Annual Earnings}}{\text{Number of pay periods per year}}$

Example 1

The president of the Triton Manufacturing Company earns a salary of $60,000 per year. The salary of his private secretary is $1,200 per month. If the company pay period is biweekly, calculate the gross earnings per pay period of the president and his private secretary.

Solution:

There are 26 pay periods per year when the pay period is biweekly. Thus,

a.   Gross earnings (President) $= \dfrac{\$60,000}{26} = \$2,307.69$ per pay period.

b.   The annual earnings of the secretary are $\$1,200 \times 12 = \$14,400$.

   Gross earnings (Secretary) $= \dfrac{\$14,400}{26} = \$553.85$ per pay period.

Exercises for Section 7.2A

Round all answers to the nearest cent.

1.   Leon Allen earns an annual salary of $8,000 at S.M.C. Industries where the pay period is biweekly. Find his gross earnings per pay period.

2.   Wendy Miller is a computer programmer at the Coughlin Corporation where she earns $850 per month. If the company's pay period is weekly, find her gross earnings per pay period.

3.   The Britton Company pays draftsmen a beginning salary of $11,400 per year. If the pay period at Britton is biweekly, find the gross earnings of a beginning draftsman per pay period.

4.   John Elliot earns $940 per month at Wellington Motors where the pay period is biweekly. Compute his gross earnings per pay period.

5.   The Carter Chemical Company pays its vice president a salary of $56,000 per year. If the pay period is biweekly, compute the vice president's gross earnings per pay period.

6.   Find the gross earnings per pay period of an employee who earns $724 per month at the Atlas Manufacturing Company where the pay period is weekly.

7.   The president of Union Mills, Inc., is paid $82,000 a year. Find her gross earnings per pay period if the pay period is weekly.

8.   Ed Mason receives a monthly salary of $860 as a bookkeeper for the Barrett Construction Company. Compute his gross earnings per pay period if the pay period is biweekly.

9.   Judy Hill is an office manager at Ampek Enterprises. She earns a

salary of $1,470 per month, and the pay period is weekly. Find her gross earnings per pay period.

10. Graham Johnson is the senior vice president of Sutton Foodstores. His annual salary is $78,000, and the pay period is biweekly. Find his gross earnings per pay period.

11. The Bookshire Company is presently operating on a weekly pay period. James Richards, an employee, has gross earnings of $260 per pay period. Next year the company will switch to a monthly pay period. What will his gross earnings be after the switch? (Hint: First compute his annual salary.)

12. The biweekly gross earnings of Patricia Cook at the Lakeside Loan Agency currently amount to $356. When the company converts to a monthly pay period next January, what will Ms. Cook's gross earnings be per month? (Hint: First compute her annual salary.)

13. Find the monthly salary of an employee whose weekly gross earnings amount to $185. (Hint: First compute the annual salary.)

14. Jack Pharr has biweekly gross earnings of $424 at the Preston Clothing Outlet. Compute his monthly salary. (Hint: First compute his annual salary.)

B. Commissions

Commissions are the earnings of sales personnel. Three common commission plans are: (1) straight commission, (2) graduated commissions, and (3) salary and commission.

1. Straight Commission

Salespeople on straight commission earn according to the amount of their net sales (total sales less returns and cancellations). This may be a set amount per item sold, but more often it is a percentage of the dollar amount of their net sales. Thus, calculation of gross earnings is simply an application of the percentage formula $P = BR$. The commission (percentage) equals the net sales (base) times the rate of commission (percent).

(7–2)   Gross Earnings (Commissions) = Net sales × Commission Rate.

Example 1

Herbert Wesley is paid a straight commission of 12 percent on his net sales. During April his net sales totaled $8,600. Find his gross earnings for the month.

Solution:

Using formula (7–2),

Gross earnings = $8,600 × 0.12

$\qquad$ = $1,032

Example 2

Charles Schultz submitted orders for $16,450 worth of machinery during the month of September. During the same month, the company received cancellation of two orders from a customer of Schultz totaling $1,220. At a straight commission rate of 8%, calculate Schultz's gross earnings for the month.

Solution:

The net sales are $16,450 - $1,220 = $15,230. Using Formula (7-2),

Gross earnings $= \$15,230 \times 0.08$

$= \$ \ 1,218.40$

The advantage of the straight commission plan is its simplicity. However, because sales tend to vary from month to month, the income of a sales representative will also fluctuate. In addition, new or inexperienced sales personnel initially may not produce sufficient volume to earn a reasonable income. To offset these disadvantages, a company may augment a straight commission plan with a drawing account. A **drawing account** is essentially an advance on future commissions; it is repaid from future commissions.

Example 3

During her first three months of employment with the Glover Company, sales representative Carol Cook had sales of $2,800, $4,500, and $3,400. Carol receives a straight commission of 12½% of net sales with a draw of $450 per month. Calculate Carol's gross earnings for the three-month period.

Solution:

Using formula (7–2) the commissions for the three months are $350, $562.50, and $425 respectively. Her earnings are calculated as follows:

1	2	3	4	5	6
		Deficit			*Deficit*
	Earned	*Brought*	*Total*	*Gross*	*Brought*
Sales	*Commissions*	*Forward*	*(2–3)*	*Earnings*	*Forward*
$2,800	$350.00	—	$350.00	$450.00	$100.00
$4,500	$562.50	$100.00	$462.50	$462.50	—
$3,400	$425.00	—	$425.00	$450.00	$ 25.00

As a result of her drawing account, Carol would receive $450.00, $462.50, and $450.00 respectively as gross earnings for each of the three months.

2. *Graduated Commissions*

As an additional incentive, commissions may be established on a graduated scale. In other words, the commission rate increases as sales volume increases. Companies offer this kind of commission plan because travel, meals, and other sales expenses absorbed by the company remain relatively constant regardless of the sales volume.

Example 1

The Shelby Corporation pays its sales personnel monthly according to the following graduated scale:

> 6% of the first $5,000 in net sales
> 7¼% of the next $5,000 in net sales
> 8% of all net sales over $10,000

Last month Travis Clark had net sales of $14,750. Calculate his gross earnings.

Solution:

Sales		Commissions
$5,000 × 0.06	=	$300.00
$5,000 × 0.0725	=	$362.50
$4,750 × 0.08	=	$380.00
$14,750		$1,042.50

3. Salary and Commission

Sales personnel under this plan receive a salary plus a percentage of net sales. Since the sales representative receives a guaranteed salary, the commission rate is usually less than a straight commission rate.

Example 1

During a week that Harry Carson sold $1,630 worth of supplies, the company had returns of $208 from one of his customers. Harry receives a salary of $90 a week plus a commission of 3% of his net sales. Calculate his gross earnings for the weekly pay period.

Solution:

Gross Sales	= $ 1,630.00
Returns	= − 208.00
Net Sales	= $ 1,422.00
Commission	= $ 42.66 ($1,422 × 0.03)
Salary	= $ 90.00
Gross Earnings	= $132.66

Retail stores commonly offer a salary and commission plan wherein a commission is paid only when sales exceed a specified quota.

Example 2

Nancy Sherman, Sharon Blake, and Sarah Brennan are salesclerks in the women's wear section of a large department store. Each is paid a weekly salary of $88.00 for a 35-hour workweek plus a commission of 4% of net sales in excess of $800 per week. Calculate their gross earnings during a week when Nancy recorded sales of $960.00, Sharon's sales were $880.00, and Sarah's sales were $840.00.

Solution:

	Nancy Sherman	*Sharon Blake*	*Sarah Brennan*
Salary	$88.00	$88.00	$88.00
Commission	$ 6.40 (160 × 0.04)	$ 3.20 (80 × 0.04)	$ 1.60 (40 × 0.04)
Gross Earnings	$94.40	$91.20	$89.60

Department heads or sales managers often are paid a commission that is a percentage of the net sales of the people they supervise. This type of commission is called an **override.**

Example 3

Joan Littlefield heads the women's wear section of the department store in Example 2. In addition to her weekly salary of $120, she receives a commission of 4% of her personal net sales in excess of $800, plus an override of ½% of the net sales of the three clerks in her section. Using the information in Example 2, calculate her gross earnings if her personal sales for the week were $1,140.

Solution:

Salary	$120.00
Commission	13.60 ($340 × 0.04)
Override	13.40 ($2,680 × 0.005)
Gross Earnings =	$147.00

Exercises for Section 7.2B

1. Joe Prentice is paid a straight commission of 11% on his net sales. During March his net sales totaled $12,350. Find his gross earnings for the month.

2. In September, Marcia Peters sold $14,720 worth of merchandise. At a straight commission rate of 9%, how much are her gross earnings for the month?

3. During the month of January, Bob Reynolds submitted orders for $18,472 worth of fittings. Two of the orders totaling $3,250 were subsequently cancelled. Calculate his gross earnings for the month if he is paid a straight commission of 7%.

4. Yvonne Parker is paid a straight commission of 6% on net sales. In May her sales were $21,420 with returns and cancellations totaling $3,942. What was her commission for the month?

5. Last month, Walter Lewis sold $15,314 worth of furniture with returns and cancelled orders totaling $1,323. If he is paid a straight commission rate of 9% of net sales, find his gross earnings for the month.

6. Jack Randall sells plumbing fixtures on a straight commission of 8% of net sales. Find his gross earnings for a month during which he submitted orders totaling $16,316 and cancellations amounted to $4,115.

7. Marla Davis is paid a straight commission of 4% of her net sales. During the past week she had sales of $370 on Monday, $411 on Tuesday, $437 on Wednesday, $392 on Thursday, and $406 on Friday. Returned merchandise for the week totaled $51. What are her gross earnings for the week?

8. Joan Nichols sold $273 worth of merchandise on Monday, $314 on Tuesday, $342 on Wednesday, $290 on Thursday, and $315 on Friday. If returned merchandise for the week totaled $104, find her gross earnings for the week at a straight commission rate of 5%.

9. Conway Higgins, a stockbroker, received a commission of $69.30 for purchasing some stock for one of his customers. The sale price of the stock was $9,240. If he is paid a straight commission on the sale price, what is his commission rate?

10. Real estate salesperson Howard Burke received a commission of $1,290 on the sale of a home. If his commission rate is 6% of the selling price, how much did the home sell for?

11. Glenn Chapman recently accepted a position as a salesperson with Hoffman Industries where he receives a straight commission of 9% of net sales with a draw of $575 per month. Complete the following record of his monthly gross earnings for his first three months with the company.

Month	1 Net Sales	2 Commis- sion	3 Deficit Forward	4 Total (2–3)	5 Gross Earnings	6 Deficit
Jan.	$5,200	$468	$ 0		$575	$107.00
Feb.	6,850		107			65.50
March	8,450					0

12. Fashion Flair, Inc., a wholesale clothing firm, pays its sales personnel 7% of net sales with a draw of $420 per month. Complete the following record of the monthly gross earnings for sales representative Patricia Wolfe:

Month	1 Net Sales	2 Commis- sion	3 Deficit Forward	4 Total (2–3)	5 Gross Earnings	6 Deficit
Sept.	$5,650		$71.50			$96.00
Oct.	7,225		96.00			10.25
Nov.	7,140					

13. Redmund Industries pays salesperson Martin Wells a straight commission of 6% with a monthly draw of $550. Complete the following record of his monthly gross earnings:

Month	1 Net Sales	2 Commis- sion	3 Deficit Forward	4 Total (2–3)	5 Gross Earnings	6 Deficit
April	$ 8,842		$70.00			
May	11,540					
June	12,760					

14. Shirley Jenkins is paid a straight commission of 12% with a draw of $400 per month. Complete the following record of her monthly gross earnings:

Month	1 Net Sales	2 Commis- sion	3 Deficit Forward	4 Total (2–3)	5 Gross Earnings	6 Deficit
August	$3,525		$44.00			
Sept.	3,850					
Oct.	3,975					

15. Donald Ross is paid a monthly graduated commission of 5% of the first $5,000 in net sales and 6.5% of net sales over $5,000. Last month he had net sales of $9,420. Find his gross earnings for the month.

16. The Shelby Corporation pays its sales personnel a monthly graduated commission of 7% of the first $3,000 in net sales and 9% of net sales over $3,000. Compute the gross earnings of one of the company's salespersons for a month during which net sales were $6,250.

17. Pickwick Products, Inc., pays its sales personnel a monthly graduated commission of 6% of the first $4,000 in net sales, 6.75% of the next $3,000, and 7.5% of net sales in excess of $7,000. In January, salesperson Bill Walker reported net sales of $8,124. What were his gross earnings for the month?

18. Leslie Maynard is paid a weekly graduated commission of 8% of the first $1,000 of net sales, 9.25% of the next $500, and 10.5% of net sales in excess of $1,500. Find her gross earnings for a week during which her net sales total $1,622.

19. During the month of October, salesperson Jerry Roberts submitted orders totaling $25,483. Jerry is paid a monthly graduated commission of 5% of the first $10,000 in net sales, 6.5% of the next $8,000, and 7% of net sales over $18,000. Compute Jerry's gross earnings for the month if $4,120 worth of his orders were subsequently cancelled.

20. Lisa Taylor submitted orders totaling $17,563 in February with cancellations totaling $2,657. Lisa is paid a monthly graduated commission of 5.5% of the first $9,000 in net sales, 6.5% of the next $4,000, and 7.25% of net sales in excess of $13,000. What were Lisa's gross earnings for the month?

21. Linda Roberts is employed as a salesclerk in the ladies' wear department of a large store. She is paid a salary of $85 a week plus a commission of 3.25% of her weekly net sales. Find her gross earnings for a week during which she sold $1,242 worth of merchandise and returns totaled $165.

22. Patton's Home Improvement Center pays salesperson Mark Watson $110 per week plus a commission of 2.75% of net sales. Last week Mark sold $2,720 worth of supplies with returns totaling $323. What were his gross earnings for the week?

23. Dennis Putnam is paid a monthly salary of $450 plus a commission of 5% of net sales in excess of $5,500. During the past month he sold $11,424 worth of goods with cancellations totaling $2,720. How much were his net earnings for the month?

24. Laura Lindsey is employed by Griffin's Gift Shoppe where she is paid a weekly salary of $92.00 plus a commission of 3.25% of net sales in excess of $1,200. Find her gross earnings for a week during which she sells $1,572 worth of merchandise with returns of $117.

25. Tom Weber is the manager of the men's wear section in a department store. He is paid a salary of $110 a week plus a commission of 4% of net sales over $800 and an override of ¾% of the net sales of the clerks working under him. His sales last week totaled $2,300 with returns of $143. The people working under him had sales of $7,240 with returns of $619. What were his gross earnings for the week?

26. Michele Turner manages the Hillside branch of the Tidy-Tot children's clothing chain. She receives a salary of $115 a week plus a commission of 3.5% of net sales over $500 and an override of 0.5% of the net sales of the people working in her store. Find her gross earnings for a week when she sold $3,125 worth of merchandise with returns of $217 and her employees sold $12,420 worth of merchandise with returns of $757.

27. The following payroll record gives the net sales, commission rate, quota, amount of returns, and salary for each of the five salespeople employed at Sam's Style Shoppe. Find the gross earnings of each of the salespeople for the week.

| Sam's Style Shoppe | | | Net | | Commis- | | Week Ending 4/6/76 |
Name	Sales	Returns	Sales	Quota	sion	Salary	Gross Earnings
Mazurek, S.	$2,452	$47		$800	6.5%	$105	
Reese, S.	3,187	63		—	4.0	115	
Taylor, J.	2,740	18		1,200	7.0	110	
Velasco, R.	3,416	27		—	5.5	90	
Williams, P.	3,141	36		1,000	5.75	120	
					Totals		

28. Frieda's Card & Gift Shop employs five salespeople. Complete the following payroll record for the week ending June 7, 1976.

| Frieda's | | | Net | | Commis- | | Week Ending 6/7/76 |
Name	Sales	Returns	Sales	Quota	sion	Salary	Gross Earnings
Darke, L.	$1,720	102		$500	8%	$120	
Hargraves, E.	1,542	182		600	8.5	125	
Lynam, J.	1,912	94		—	4.5	110	
Robinson, M.	2,004	114		—	5.25	105	
Ullrich, J.	1,643	83		700	9	130	
					Totals		

C. Wages

The majority of American workers are paid according to actual time at work. Their earnings are called **wages** and are calculated on a per hour basis. Gross earnings for hourly workers are found by multiplying the hourly rate by the number of hours worked per pay period; that is,

(7–3)   Gross earnings (Wages) =
Rate per hour $\times$ number of hours worked

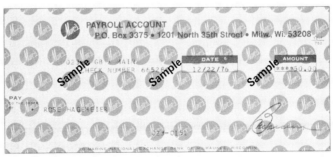

Example 1

A baker earns $4.06 per hour. Calculate her gross earnings for a 40-hour workweek.

Solution:

Using formula (7–3),

$$\text{Gross earnings} = \$4.06 \times 40$$
$$= \$162.40$$

Example 2

An electrician wiring apartments in a new complex works the following hours in a two-week period:

	Sun.	Mon.	Tues.	Wed.	Thur.	Fri.	Sat.
Week 1	0	8	6	4	8	8	4
Week 2	0	8	8	8	8	4	4

At an hourly rate of $7.56, calculate his gross earnings for the biweekly pay period.

Solution:

The electrician worked 38 hours in week 1 and 40 hours in week 2 for a total of 78 hours.

$$\text{Gross earnings} = \$7.56 \times 78$$
$$= \$589.68$$

In addition to the hourly rate, the term wages also refers to compensation based on production. The oldest form of production wages is called **piecework** or **piece-rate.** Workers under this payment plan earn according to the number of units produced.

Example 3

A plastics company pays a worker $0.28 for each load of sheets fed into a baking press. Calculate the gross earnings of the worker on a day that 72 loads are fed into the press.

Solution:

The gross earnings are found by multiplying the number of loads by the rate per load; that is,

$$\text{Gross Earnings} = \$0.28 \times 72$$
$$= \$20.16$$

Piecework of this kind is called **straight piece-rate.** Prior to World War II, piecework was used more than any other wage plan, but since that time its popularity has declined rapidly. Part of this is due to requirements imposed by the Federal Labor Standards Act (discussed later in the section entitled Overtime), but the primary reason is union dissatisfaction. Piecework rewards the fast, efficient worker who can exceed the average production, but it penalizes the slower, below-average worker. Today there is considerable pressure to guarantee a minimum wage to the pieceworker regardless of production. These minimum wages are set near a "standard," a production requirement per unit of work time established by work measurement methods. The following is an example of how a straight piece-rate plan can be coupled with a minimum wage. The worker is paid the higher of the piece-rate or the minimum wage.

Example 4

A lathe operator is paid $0.45 for each part machined with a guaranteed weekly wage of $126.00. His production for the week was

Sun.	Mon.	Tues.	Wed.	Thur.	Fri.	Sat.
0	50	57	56	60	52	0

Calculate his gross earnings for the week.

Solution:

The worker turned out a total of 275 pieces during the week. His piece-rate is:

$$\text{Piece-rate} = \text{No. of Pieces} \times \text{Rate per piece}$$
$$= 275 \times \$0.45$$
$$= \$123.75$$

Since this is less than the guaranteed rate, his weekly gross earnings are $126.00.

A popular wage plan today is called the **standard hour plan.** This is also a production plan, but the units are expressed in terms of time instead of money as does piece-rate. That is, the variable is changed from units produced to time per units produced. Suppose, for instance, the lathe operator in the previous example normally takes 0.143 hours per piece machined. At an hourly wage of $3.15, this amounts to $0.45 per piece ($3.15 × 0.143). Note this is the piece-rate of the previous example, but now the unit of measurement is time and an hourly wage is paid. In an era when hourly wage equivalents are required by the federal government, this simplifies the clerical work of the payroll department.

The standard production for a day or week is the basis for a guaranteed minimum wage in the standard hour plan. Production exceeding standards is paid in the form of an "incentive bonus."

Example 5

A worker in a company manufacturing electrical devices normally can assemble 340 units in a week's time (40 hours). At an hourly rate of $2.50, calculate the gross earnings in a week when 374 units were assembled.

Solution:

A production of 374 units is 34 units above the weekly standard. This is an efficiency of $\frac{374}{340} = 110\%$. Accordingly, the worker receives the regular wage plus a 10% incentive bonus.

$$\begin{aligned} \text{Regular pay} &= \$2.50 \times 40 &= \$100.00 \\ \text{Incentive Bonus} &= \$100.00 \times 0.10 = &\underline{\quad 10.00} \\ & \text{Gross Earnings} &= \$110.00 \end{aligned}$$

Production plans such as piecework or the standard hour plan fall under the general category of **incentive wage plans.** For workers engaged in production, it has long been evident that extra or sustained effort is possible only if some incentive exists. Numerous incentive wage plans have been developed, ranging from piecework to the profit sharing plans of today. Some of the plans are discussed in the exercises. The appropriate wage plan for a given institution will depend upon a number of factors, including size, type of business, unionization of the work force, and competitive practices. Wage plans are continually changing and this evolutionary process will continue as long as the free enterprise system exists.

Exercises for Section 7.2C

1. Max Goddard earns $6.35 per hour as a mechanic. Compute his gross earnings for a week in which he worked 36 hours.

2. Last week Elsie Davis worked 32 hours, and the previous week she worked 28 hours. At a wage rate of $3.56 per hour, find her gross earnings for the two-week period.

3. Fred Geiger, a carpenter, worked the following hours during the past two weeks:

	Sun.	Mon.	Tues.	Wed.	Thurs.	Fri.	Sat.
Week 1	0	8	6	5	7.5	8	0
Week 2	0	6	6.5	4	8	8	0

Find his gross earnings for the two-week period, if he earns $7.15 per hour.

4. John Killian earns $8.23 per hour working for a local air conditioning contractor. Calculate his gross earnings for a two-week period during which he worked the following hours:

	Sun.	Mon.	Tues.	Wed.	Thurs.	Fri.	Sat.
Week 1	0	7	5.5	8	4.5	7	0
Week 2	0	6.5	4	7	8	2	0

5. Nell Phillips assembles electrical components at Mohawk Industries. She is paid on a straight piecework basis of $0.42 per component assembled. Find her gross earnings for a day during which she assembles 54 components.

6. Eugene Maycroft is paid on a straight piecework basis of $0.87 per piece. What are his gross earnings for a day during which his production is 37 pieces?

7. The Chandon Company employs Louise Reeves to operate a machine that produces components for electric motors. Louise is paid $0.37 per unit produced with a guaranteed weekly wage of $132. Find her gross earnings for a week during which her production is as follows:

Sun.	Mon.	Tues.	Wed.	Thurs.	Fri.	Sat.
0	68	69	74	70	65	0

8. Dandy Draperies, Inc., pays Ruby Nesbit, a sewing machine operator, $0.87 per unit produced with a guaranteed weekly wage of $122. Calculate her gross earnings for a week in which her production rate is as follows:

Sun.	Mon.	Tues.	Wed.	Thurs.	Fri.	Sat.
0	30	32	27	31	28	0

9. Wilma Hogue is a packer for Wellington Industries. She is paid $0.08 per item packed for shipping with a guaranteed wage of $105 per week. Last week she packed the following number of items each day:

Sun.	Mon.	Tues.	Wed.	Thurs.	Fri.	Sat.
0	257	265	261	259	255	0

Compute her gross earnings for the week.

10. Theresa Dinsmore is an assembler at the Merritt Company. She receives $0.57 per unit assembled with a guaranteed wage of $138 per week. Find her gross earnings for a week during which she assembled the following number of units per day:

Sun.	Mon.	Tues.	Wed.	Thurs.	Fri.	Sat.
0	52	49	47	53	49	0

11. In problem 7, suppose the Chandon Company decides to convert to the standard hour plan and sets Louise Reeves's standard level of production at 360 units per week (40 hours). Using her piecework rate of $0.37 per unit produced, find her hourly wage.

12. In problem 8, calculate Ruby Nesbit's hourly wage (using her piecework rate of $0.87 per unit produced) if the company converts to the standard hour plan and sets Ruby's weekly (40 hours) production level at 145 units per week.

13. Clyde Shaw is an assembler in a manufacturing company that uses the standard hour plan. Clyde is paid $2.85 per hour, and his standard production level is 210 units per 40-hour workweek. Find his gross earnings for a week during which he produces 215 units.

14. Sally Greer is paid according to the standard hour plan. Her production level is 280 units per week (40 hours) and her hourly wage is $2.90. What are her gross earnings for a week during which she produces 305 units?

15. In problem 9, if Wellington Industries converts to the standard hour plan and sets Wilma's weekly (40-hour) production level at 1,350 units, find her gross earnings for a week during which she produces 1,340 units. (Hint: First find her hourly wage, using her piecework rate of $0.08 per unit.)

16. In problem 10, the Merritt Company converts to the standard hour wage plan and sets Theresa's weekly (40-hour) production level at 250 units. What are her gross earnings for a week during which she produces 275 units? (Hint: First find her hourly wage, using her piecework rate of $0.57 per unit.)

A common variation of the straight piecework wage plan is a method of wage compensation called **differential piecework.** This plan offers additional production incentive by providing two different piece-rates, one for all units up to a specified standard and a second (higher) one for all units if the worker's production exceeds the standard. For example, a worker might be paid $0.25 a unit if production is 100 units or less and $0.27 a unit if production exceeds 100 units. Thus for 100 units the worker receives $25 and for 101 units he/she receives $27.27.

17. Carol Rhodes is employed by Western Textiles, Inc., where she operates a knitting machine to produce infant footwear. She is paid

under a differential piecework plan as follows: she receives $0.19 a unit on a day when her production is 100 units or less and $0.23 a unit for a day during which her production exceeds 100 units. Find her gross earnings for a week during which her daily production is as follows:

Sun.	Mon.	Tues.	Wed.	Thurs.	Fri.	Sat.
0	105	96	97	110	100	0

18. Ken Methi is paid on a differential piecework basis of $0.40 per unit on a day when his production is 70 units or less and $0.43 per unit for a day during which his production exceeds 70 units. Calculate his gross earnings for a week during which his daily production is as follows:

Sun.	Mon.	Tues.	Wed.	Thurs.	Fri.	Sat.
0	71	68	70	72	69	0

The *efficient production bonus* plan is another piecework incentive plan. Under this system, if a worker's production is less than or equal to a set standard, only a guaranteed hourly wage is paid. However, if the worker's production exceeds the standard, the hourly wage is increased by a predetermined percentage. For example, a worker might be paid $2.70 per hour for a day when production is less than or equal to 25 units and 10% more per hour ($2.97 per hour) for a day when production exceeds 25 units.

19. Ruth Goodnik operates a machine that assembles a component part used in the production of vacuum cleaners. She is paid $3.80 an hour for an eight-hour day during which she produces 56 units or less. If her production exceeds 56 units, her hourly wage for the day is increased by 18%. Compute her gross earnings for a day during which she produces (a) 54 units and (b) 59 units.

20. Joe Gentner receives $2.95 an hour for an eight-hour day during which he produces 35 units or less. If he produces more than 35 units, his hourly wage for the day is increased by 15%. Find his gross earnings for a day during which he produces (a) 34 units and (b) 36 units.

Section 7.3 Overtime

For some 47 million workers in the United States covered by the Fair Labor Standards Act, hours on the job must be separated into two categories, regular and overtime. First passed by Congress in 1938, this act (also known as the Federal Wage and Hour Law) establishes minimum wages, overtime pay, and other labor standards for every employee engaged in interstate or foreign commerce or in the production of goods for such commerce. Under the latest amendment to the act, regular hours consist of a workweek of 40 hours. Hours worked in excess of 40 hours during a workweek constitute **overtime** hours. The act specifies the rate of pay for overtime to be 1½ times the rate for regular hours.

No.				PAY PERIOD ENDING		
Name						

			Daily Totals R.T. Hours O.T.	R.T. HOURS	O.T. HOURS
M	08.0				
M	12.0				
M	12.9		RATE		
M	17.1				
TU	08.0		AMOUNT		
TU	17.0				
W	08.0		Total Earnings		
W	12.0		NO. OF EXEMPTIONS		
W	13.0				
W	17.0				
TH	08.3		F.I.C.A.		
TH	12.0				
TH	12.9		FED. W.T.		
TH	17.0				
TH	19.1				
TH	22.3		CITY/ST W.T.		
FR	08.2				
FR	12.0		STATE U.C.		
FR	13.0				
FR	17.0		BONDS		
SA	06.8				
SA	08.8				
			Total Deductions		
			BALANCE DUE		

TOTAL HOURS SHOWN IS CORRECT.   Signature
84151   SIMPLEX TIME RECORDER CO., GARDNER, MASS., PRINTED IN U.S.A.

While the act is aimed primarily at wage earners, its overtime provisions also apply to certain categories of salaried and commissioned employees. For the latter it is standard practice to convert their earnings to an hourly wage equivalent, then compute regular and overtime wages. In the examples to follow we will illustrate overtime payments for each form of compensation.

A. Salaries

If a salary is paid to an employee for a specified number of hours to be worked per week, then the employee is covered by the Fair Labor Standards Act and must be paid the overtime rate for hours in excess of the specified workweek. An hourly rate of pay for salaried workers is determined by dividing the weekly salary (or the monthly salary reduced to a weekly basis) by the specified weekly hours.

Example 1

Vivian Moore is employed as a secretary. Her salary is $98.80 for a specified workweek of 40 hours. Calculate her gross earnings during a week that she worked 46 hours.

Solution:

A salary of $98.80 for a 40-hour workweek amounts to a regular hourly rate of $\frac{\$98.80}{40} = \$2.47$ per hour. The overtime rate is $\$2.47 \times 1\frac{1}{2} = \$3.705$ per hour. Thus,

$$
\begin{array}{lll}
\text{Regular Pay} & = \$2.47 \times 40 = & \$ \ 98.80 \\
\text{Overtime Pay} & = \$3.705 \times \ 6 = & 22.23 \\
\hline
\text{Gross Earnings} & = & \$121.03
\end{array}
$$

Example 2

The Spring Pure Water Company pays one of its office workers a salary of $546 per month. The salary is paid for a workweek of 35 hours, but during a two-week period, the following hours were worked.

	S	M	T	W	T	F	S
Week 1	0	7	7	8	8	8	4
Week 2	0	7	7	7	7	7	4

Calculate the gross earnings of the office worker if the pay period is biweekly.

Solution:

The monthly salary is converted to an hourly rate in two steps:

$$
\begin{array}{ll}
\text{Weekly Salary} & = \$546 \times \frac{12}{52} = \$126 \\
\text{Hourly Rate} & = \$126 \div 35 = \$3.60 \\
\text{Overtime Rate} & = \$3.60 \times 1\frac{1}{2} = \$5.40
\end{array}
$$

$$
\begin{array}{lll}
\text{Week 1} \quad \text{Regular Pay} & = \$3.60 \times 35 = \$126.00 \\
\qquad\qquad \text{Overtime Pay} & = \$5.40 \times 7 = \quad 37.80 \\
\hline
\qquad\qquad \text{Subtotal} & & \$163.80 \\
\\
\text{Week 2} \quad \text{Regular Pay} & = \$3.60 \times 35 = \$126.00 \\
\qquad\qquad \text{Overtime Pay} & = \$5.40 \times \ 4 = \quad 21.60 \\
\hline
\qquad\qquad \text{Subtotal} & & \$147.60 \\
\hline
\qquad\qquad \text{Gross Earnings} & & \$311.40
\end{array}
$$

B. Commissions

"Outside" sales personnel, that is, sales representatives who spend most of their time away from their employer's place of business are exempt from the Fair Labor Standards Act. However, "inside" sales personnel are covered by the act and their commissions must be included in the regular rate when calculating overtime pay. This is true whether the commissions are a percentage of total sales or sales in excess of a quota.

Example 1

A salesclerk for Gilbert's Department Store is paid $90 a week for a 40-hour week and 3% of her sales in excess of $700. Calculate her gross earnings for a week that she worked 44 hours and recorded sales of $780.

Solution:

This is an inside sales position, hence the employee is entitled to four hours overtime pay. To determine the overtime pay we first calculate a regular hourly rate for both the salary and the commission, then multiply by $1\frac{1}{2}$.

For the salary, the regular rate is $\frac{\$90}{40} = \$2.25$ per hour and the overtime rate is $\$2.25 \times 1\frac{1}{2} = \$3.375$ per hour. The total commission for the week is $\$80 \times 0.03 = \$2.40$, thus the "regular commission rate" is $\frac{\$2.40}{40} = \$0.06$ and the "overtime commission rate" is $\$0.06 \times 1\frac{1}{2} = \$0.09$.

Regular Weekly Pay	$= \$2.25 \times 40 = \$90.00$	
Overtime Weekly Pay	$= \$3.375 \times 4 = \$13.50$	
Subtotal		$103.50
Regular Commission	$= \$0.06 \times 40 = \$ 2.40$	
Overtime Commission	$= \$0.09 \times 4 = \$ 0.36$	
Subtotal		$ 2.76
Gross Earnings		$106.26

C. Wages

Overtime for employees paid an hourly wage is $1\frac{1}{2}$ times the hourly rate for hours in excess of a 40-hour workweek.

Example 1

A switchboard operator for a metropolitan telephone company earns $3.66 an hour for a 40-hour workweek. Calculate her gross earnings for a week that she worked 48 hours.

Solution:

The overtime rate is $\$3.66 \times 1\frac{1}{2} = \$5.49$. Thus:

Regular wages	$= \$3.66 \times 40 = \$146.40$
Overtime wages	$= \$5.49 \times 8 = \ \ 43.92$
Gross Earnings	$= \$190.32$

Many payroll employees will compute the overtime wages of the previous example by multiplying the number of overtime hours by 1½ instead of the hourly rate by 1½. The result is the same.* For example,

$$\text{Regular wages} = \$3.66 \times 40 = \$146.40$$
$$\text{Overtime wages} = \$3.66 \times 12 = \$\ \underline{43.92}\ (12 = 8 \times 1\tfrac{1}{2})$$
$$\text{Gross Earnings} \qquad\qquad\ = \$190.32$$

Since employees are paid a higher rate for overtime, it is important that the employer keep accurate records of the hours worked. Most employers accomplish this by means of individual time sheets or by clock time cards. An example of a time card is shown in Figure 7–2. A more sophisticated procedure utilizes an individual plastic card that is inserted into a timing device directly linked to a computer. The computer records and stores the time worked and during the payroll-run calculates the regular and overtime wages.

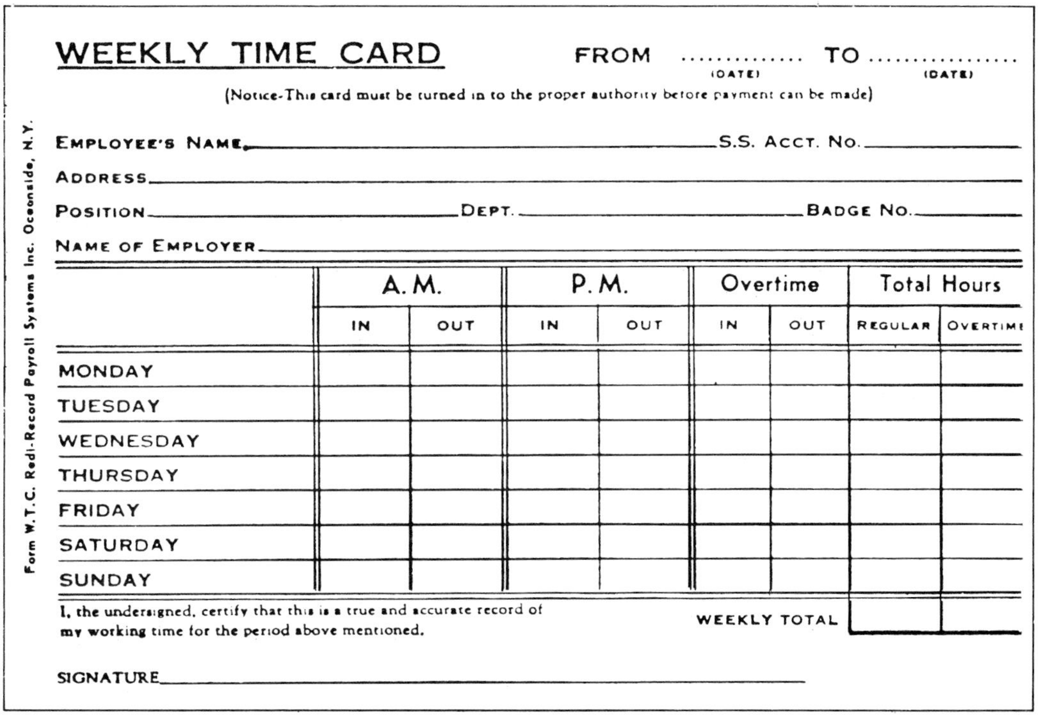

WEEKLY TIME CARD		FROM .... TO					

Figure 7–2

---

* This is an immediate consequence of the associative law of multiplication that states that for any numbers a, b, and c,

$$(a \times b) \times c = a \times (b \times c).$$

In the regular calculation of overtime we multiply (hourly rate $\times$ 1½) $\times$ hours worked. However, by the associative law this is equivalent to hourly rate $\times$ (1½ $\times$ hours worked).

Example 2

WEEKLY TIME CARD								FROM 3/7 TO 3/13	

(Notice-This card must be turned in to the proper authority before payment can be made)

EMPLOYEE'S NAME _George C. Welch_ S.S. ACCT. NO. _321-54-9876_

ADDRESS _110 Oak Street_

POSITION _____ DEPT. _Production_ BADGE NO. _10479_

NAME OF EMPLOYER _____

	A.M.		P.M.		Overtime		Total Hours	
	IN	OUT	IN	OUT	IN	OUT	REGULAR	OVERTIME
MONDAY	8:00	12.01	12:30	4:30			8	
TUESDAY	8:02	12.00	12:30	4:30	6:00	9:30	8	3½
WEDNESDAY	8:01	12.01	12:30	4:32	4:32	6:35	8	3½
THURSDAY	8:00	12:00	12:31	4:31			8	
FRIDAY	8:00	12:05	12:35	4:30			8	
SATURDAY								
SUNDAY								

I, the undersigned, certify that this is a true and accurate record of my working time for the period above mentioned.

WEEKLY TOTAL | 40 | 7

SIGNATURE _George C. Welch_

Mr. Welch earns $3.10 an hour for a 40-hour workweek. Calculate his gross earnings for the week.

Solution:

The overtime rate is $3.10 × 1½ = $4.65 per hour.

$$\text{Regular wages} = \$3.10 \times 40 = \$124.00$$
$$\text{Overtime wages} = \$4.65 \times 7 = \quad 32.55$$
$$\text{Gross earnings} \qquad\qquad = \$156.55$$

While the wage and hour law defines overtime as work in excess of 40 hours per workweek, some wage agreements recognize other forms of overtime. "Time and a half" (one and one-half times the regular rate) may be paid for hours in excess of 8 hours per day, and "double time" (two times the regular rate) is often paid for work on Sundays or holidays.

Example 3

The time card of an employee indicated the following hours worked during the week of Sunday, June 30 through Saturday, July 6.

6/30	7/1	7/2	7/3	7/4	7/5	7/6
8	0	8½	8	4½	8	8

The regular hourly rate for the employee is $3.40 and he receives time and a half for work in excess of 8 hours a day or 40 hours per week plus double time for Sundays or holidays. Find his gross earnings for the week.

Solution:

The hours worked are distributed as regular (R), overtime or time and a half (OT), and double time (DT).

	6/30	7/1	7/2	7/3	7/4	7/5	7/6	Total Hours	Rate	Total Wages
R			8	8		8	3	27	$3.40	$ 91.80
OT			½				5	5½	$5.10	$ 28.05
DT	8				4½			12½	$6.80	$ 85.00
								Gross Earnings		$204.85

Employees on piecework also receive overtime pay for work in excess of a 40-hour workweek. In order to calculate overtime pay, the total wages earned by piecework first must be converted to an hourly rate; the overtime rate is one and one-half times the hourly equivalent.

Example 4

An employee on piecework earned $112.00 during a week that he worked 50 hours. What are his gross earnings for the week?

Solution:

The regular hourly rate is $\dfrac{\$112.00}{50} = \$2.24$ per hour, and the overtime rate is $\$2.24 \times 1\frac{1}{2} = \$3.36$ per hour.

$$\begin{aligned}
\text{Regular wages} &= \$2.24 \times 40 = \$\ 89.60 \\
\text{Overtime wages} &= \$3.36 \times 10 = \$\ 33.60 \\
\hline
\text{Gross earnings} &\qquad\quad\ = \$123.20
\end{aligned}$$

Example 5

Donna Appleton is paid a piece-rate of $0.32 with a guaranteed weekly wage of $88.00. She produced 300 pieces during a week that she worked 44 hours. Calculate Donna's gross earnings for the week.

Solution:

The guaranteed weekly wage amounts to $\dfrac{\$88.00}{40} = \$2.20$ per hour. The total amount earned by piecework is $\$0.32 \times 300 = \$96.00$, which converts to only $\dfrac{\$96.00}{44} = \$2.18$ per hour. Since this is less than the guaranteed wage of $2.20 per hour, she is paid the guaranteed wage. The overtime rate is $\$2.20 \times 1\frac{1}{2} = \$3.30$.

$$\begin{aligned}
\text{Regular wages} &= \$2.20 \times 40 = \$\ 88.00 \\
\text{Overtime wages} &= \$3.30 \times\ 4 = \$\ 13.20 \\
\hline
\text{Gross earnings} &\qquad\quad\ = \$101.20
\end{aligned}$$

1. John James is paid a salary of $104.40 per 40-hour workweek. Calculate his gross earnings for a week during which he works 44 hours.

2. Diane Mathis is a salaried employee at the Decker Company where she earns $96.80 per 40-hour workweek. Find her gross earnings for a week during which she works 46 hours.

3. Frank Larkin is an office manager at the Bissett Paint Company. He is paid a monthly salary of $940 for a workweek of 35 hours. The pay period at the Bissett Company is biweekly, and during the last two-week period Frank worked the following hours:

	Sun.	Mon.	Tues.	Wed.	Thurs.	Fri.	Sat.
Week 1	0	8	6	7	6	8	6
Week 2	0	6	5	8	8	6	4

Compute Frank's gross earnings for this two-week period.

4. The Amazon Marine Equipment Company pays one of its office workers a monthly salary of $760 for a specified workweek of 35 hours. If the pay period at Amazon is biweekly, find the worker's gross earnings for the following two-week period:

	Sun.	Mon.	Tues.	Wed.	Thurs.	Fri.	Sat.
Week 1	0	7	8	6	7	7	5
Week 2	0	6	7	8	8	6	6

5. Robinson's Metal Works pays Joan Schyler an annual salary of $11,640. The workweek at Robinson's is 35 hours and the pay period is biweekly. Find Joan's gross earnings for a pay period during which she worked the following hours:

	Sun.	Mon.	Tues.	Wed.	Thurs.	Fri.	Sat.
Week 1	0	8	8	6	6	7	5
Week 2	0	6	8	7	7	6	6

6. Hallamore Industries pays one of its branch office managers an annual salary of $18,790 for a 35-hour workweek. The pay period at Hallamore is biweekly, and during the last two weeks the manager worked the following hours:

	Sun.	Mon.	Tues.	Wed.	Thurs.	Fri.	Sat.
Week 1	0	8	8	7	5	7	8
Week 2	0	8	7	7	6	8	2

Calculate his gross earnings for this two-week period.

7. Vernon Kyle works in the sporting goods section of a department store. He is paid a salary of $120 for a 40-hour workweek plus a commission of 4% of sales in excess of $1,500. Find his gross earnings for a week during which he works 46 hours and sells $1,720 worth of merchandise.

8. Isabel Keene sells leisure wear at the Fun-N-Frolic Shoppe. She receives a salary of $125 per 40-hour workweek plus a commission of 2.5% of sales in excess of $600. Calculate her gross earnings for a week during which she works 45 hours and records sales of $1,120.

9. The sales personnel at Apple's Appliance Store are paid $115 per 35-hour workweek plus a commission of 3.5% of sales in excess of $2,000. What are the gross earnings of a sales representative for a week during which the representative works 38 hours and sells $2,430 worth of merchandise?

10. Ed Alexander worked 42 hours last week at the Futura Furniture Store. He is paid a salary of $130 per 40-hour workweek plus a commission of 3% of sales in excess of $1,800. If he recorded sales for the week totalling $2,672, what were his gross earnings?

11. If Bruce Jackson is paid $4.75 per hour for a 40-hour workweek, what are his gross earnings for a week during which he works 48 hours?

12. Find Camille Jordan's gross earnings for a week during which she works 43 hours if she receives $5.40 an hour for a specified 35-hour workweek.

13. Doug Johnson earns $3.60 per hour for a 35-hour workweek. Calculate his gross earnings for a week when his time report is as follows:

TIME REPORT							
Week Beginning 7/15						Week Ending 7/21	
Day of Week	Time Worked						Total Hours
	Start	Stop	Start	Stop	Start	Stop	
Sunday							
Monday	7:00	11:30	12:30	3:00			
Tuesday	7:00	11:30	12:30	3:00			
Wednesday	7:00	11:30	12:30	3:00	3:00	7:00	
Thursday	7:00	11:30	12:30	3:00	3:00	4:30	
Friday	7:00	11:30	12:30	3:00			
Saturday	7:00	11:30					
Name: Johnson, Douglas M.						Total	
I hereby certify that the above is correct. Employee Signature: *Douglas M. Johnson*							

14. Diane Gaskins filed the following time report for the week of April 15 through April 21. If she is paid $4.20 per hour for a 40-hour workweek, compute her gross earnings for the week.

TIME REPORT							
Week Beginning 4/15							Week Ending 4/21
Day of Week	Time Worked						Total Hours
	Start	Stop	Start	Stop	Start	Stop	
Sunday							
Monday	8:00	12:02	1:15	5:15	7:00	8:30	
Tuesday	8:02	12:04	1:00	5:00			
Wednesday	8:00	12:00	1:00	5:00	7:00	8:00	
Thursday	8:00	12:00	1:10	5:10	7:00	9:00	
Friday	9:04	12:05	2:00	6:00			
Saturday	9:00	12:00	1:00	3:00			
Name: Gaskins, Diane P.						Total	

I hereby certify that the above is correct.
Employee Signature: *Diane P. Gaskins*

15. The Buckline Company pays its employees time and a half for work in excess of 8 hours a day or 40 hours a week plus double time for Sundays and holidays. Richard Sneyd, an accountant at Buckline, is paid $5.80 per hour. Compute his gross earnings for the week of Sunday, December 30, through Saturday, January 5, during which he worked the following hours:

	12/30	12/31	1/1	1/2	1/3	1/4	1/5
Hours	4	4	6	7½	9	8½	4

16. Julia Mays is employed at the Fulwood Company, where she receives $4.40 per hour with time and a half for work in excess of 8 hours per day or 40 hours per week and double time for Sundays and holidays. Find her gross earnings for the week of Sunday, July 1, through Saturday, July 7, during which she worked the following hours:

	7/1	7/2	7/3	7/4	7/5	7/6	7/7
Hours	3	6	8½	5	9½	4	0

17. Gene Walters is an assembler at Fairline Industries, where he is paid on a piecework basis of $0.42 per part assembled. Last week he worked 48 hours and assembled 358 units. Calculate his gross earnings for the week.

18. An employee at the Brookwood Company is paid a piecework rate of $0.65 per piece. Find the gross earnings for a week during which the person worked 45 hours and produced 210 units.

19. Lillian Brink is paid a piece-rate of $0.26 per piece with a guaranteed weekly wage of $102.00. What are her gross earnings for a week during which she works 46 hours and produces 420 pieces?

20. The Waterford Company pays its employees in the shipping department $0.82 per unit packed for shipment, with a guaranteed weekly wage of $115.00. Compute the gross earnings of an employee for a week during which he works 47 hours and packs 170 units.

21. Maude Richardson is paid a piece-rate of $0.62 per piece with a guaranteed weekly wage of $108.00. Find her gross earnings for a week during which she works 42 hours and produces 192 pieces.

22. John Lopez works for the Winters Company where he is paid a piece-rate of $0.38 per piece with a guaranteed weekly wage of $120.00. Calculate his gross earnings for a week during which he worked 45 hours and produced 337 pieces.

Section 7.4 Net Earnings

Following the computation of gross earnings, the next step in preparation of the payroll is the calculation of net earnings. As previously stated, net earnings are gross earnings less deductions. Deductions are amounts that are withheld from the employee's earnings by the employer. The payroll department subtracts deductions from gross earnings and remits the difference or net earnings to the employee. A record is maintained of all deductions and periodically these sums are sent to the appropriate agency.

Deductions may be voluntary or required by law. We examine the latter category first.

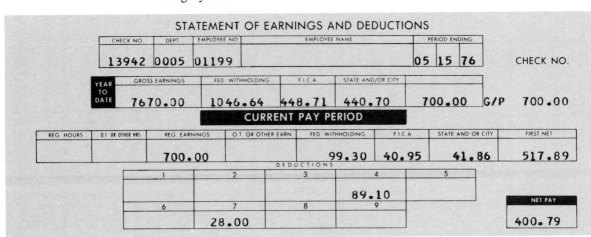

A. Federal Income Tax

The payment of federal income tax in a lump sum would create a financial hardship for most citizens, thus the federal government has authorized employers to withhold a percentage of the employee's gross earnings each payday as advance payment of the employee's personal income tax. The percentage subtracted from gross earnings depends upon three factors: (1) gross earnings, (2) marital status, and (3) number of exemptions. An **exemption** is a tax allowance for a person supported by the employee. At the time of employment each employee is required to complete an Employee's Withholding Allowance Certificate (Form W-4) on which the employee declares the number of exemptions he/she wishes to claim. See Figure 7–3. A person with a spouse and two children may claim four exemptions, one for the employee and one for each of the other family members. If both work, then the couple may split the exemptions as they see fit.

A detailed discussion of exemptions and eligible dependents is beyond the scope of this text, but it should be noted that an employee may claim fewer exemptions than the number to which he/she is entitled. Since the amount of tax withheld is only an approximation, the employee may owe additional taxes on April 15, the deadline for filing income tax returns. By claiming fewer exemptions, a greater amount will be withheld thus reducing the likelihood of owing additional tax upon filing the return. The government will refund any amount in excess of the taxes the employee owes.

To assist the payroll clerk in computing the amount of income tax to be withheld, the Internal Revenue Service has prepared tables. The table most frequently used is the Wage Bracket Table. This table categorizes employees by the three factors previously mentioned, marital status, gross earnings, and number of exemptions. A portion of this table is shown in Figures 7–4 through 7–6.

To illustrate the use of these tables, consider a married employee claiming four exemptions who is paid weekly a salary of $225. To determine the tax to be withheld, we locate the table entitled Married Persons—Weekly Payroll (Figure 7–5), and find the employee's wage bracket in the left column headed "And the Wages Are."* A weekly salary of $225 falls in the wage bracket "at least $220 but less than $230." We then proceed to the right along this line until we reach the column for four exemptions. The amount to be withheld is $22.40.

---

* As used in this table, wages means all forms of compensation, including salaries and commissions.

Form **W-4**
(Rev. Dec. 1971)

Department of the Treasury—Internal Revenue Service
Employee's Withholding Exemption Certificate

Type or print full name	Social security number

Home address (Number and street or rural route)	City or town, State and ZIP code

Marital status—check one (if married but legally separated, or spouse is a nonresident alien, check "Single"): ☐ Single   ☐ Married

If you expect to owe more tax than will be withheld, you may either claim
fewer or zero exemptions or ask for additional withholding on line 8.

1 Personal exemption for yourself. Write "1" if claimed . . . .

2 If married, personal exemption for your wife (or husband) if not separately claimed by her (or him). Write "1" if claimed . . . .

3 Special withholding allowance.¹ (See instruction 2.) Write "1" if claimed . . . .

4 Exemptions for age and blindness (applicable only to you and your wife but not to dependents):

  (a) If you or your wife will be 65 years of age or older at the end of the year, and you claim this exemption, write "1"; if both will be 65 or

    older, and you claim both of these exemptions, write "2" . . . .

  (b) If you or your wife are blind and you claim this exemption, write "1"; if both are blind, and you claim both exemptions, write "2" . . . .

5 Exemptions for dependents. (Do not claim an exemption for a dependent unless you are qualified under instruction 5.) . . . .

6 Additional withholding allowances for itemized deductions. See table on reverse . . . .

7 Add the exemptions and allowances (if any) which you have claimed above and enter total . . . .

8 Additional withholding per pay period under agreement with employer . . . . $

Under the penalties of perjury, I certify that the number of withholding exemptions and allowances claimed on this certificate does not exceed the number to which I am entitled.

(Date) ...., 19...... (Signed)..

Figure 7–3

SINGLE Persons—WEEKLY Payroll Period

And the wages are—		And the number of withholding allowances claimed is—										
At least	But less than	0	1	2	3	4	5	6	7	8	9	10 or more
		The amount of income tax to be withheld shall be—										
$0	$25	$0	$0	$0	$0	$0	$0	$0	$0	$0	$0	$0
25	26	.10	0	0	0	0	0	0	0	0	0	0
26	27	.20	0	0	0	0	0	0	0	0	0	0
27	28	.40	0	0	0	0	0	0	0	0	0	0
28	29	.60	0	0	0	0	0	0	0	0	0	0
29	30	.70	0	0	0	0	0	0	0	0	0	0
30	31	.90	0	0	0	0	0	0	0	0	0	0
31	32	1.00	0	0	0	0	0	0	0	0	0	0
32	33	1.20	0	0	0	0	0	0	0	0	0	0
33	34	1.40	0	0	0	0	0	0	0	0	0	0
34	35	1.50	0	0	0	0	0	0	0	0	0	0
35	36	1.70	0	0	0	0	0	0	0	0	0	0
36	37	1.80	0	0	0	0	0	0	0	0	0	0
37	38	2.00	0	0	0	0	0	0	0	0	0	0
38	39	2.20	0	0	0	0	0	0	0	0	0	0
39	40	2.30	0	0	0	0	0	0	0	0	0	0
40	41	2.50	.20	0	0	0	0	0	0	0	0	0
41	42	2.60	.30	0	0	0	0	0	0	0	0	0
42	43	2.80	.50	0	0	0	0	0	0	0	0	0
43	44	3.00	.70	0	0	0	0	0	0	0	0	0
44	45	3.10	.80	0	0	0	0	0	0	0	0	0
45	46	3.30	1.00	0	0	0	0	0	0	0	0	0
46	47	3.40	1.10	0	0	0	0	0	0	0	0	0
47	48	3.60	1.30	0	0	0	0	0	0	0	0	0
48	49	3.80	1.50	0	0	0	0	0	0	0	0	0
49	50	3.90	1.60	0	0	0	0	0	0	0	0	0
50	51	4.10	1.80	0	0	0	0	0	0	0	0	0
51	52	4.20	1.90	0	0	0	0	0	0	0	0	0
52	53	4.40	2.10	0	0	0	0	0	0	0	0	0
53	54	4.60	2.30	0	0	0	0	0	0	0	0	0
54	55	4.70	2.40	.10	0	0	0	0	0	0	0	0
55	56	4.90	2.60	.30	0	0	0	0	0	0	0	0
56	57	5.00	2.70	.40	0	0	0	0	0	0	0	0
57	58	5.20	2.90	.60	0	0	0	0	0	0	0	0
58	59	5.40	3.10	.70	0	0	0	0	0	0	0	0
59	60	5.50	3.20	.90	0	0	0	0	0	0	0	0
60	62	5.80	3.50	1.10	0	0	0	0	0	0	0	0
62	64	6.10	3.80	1.50	0	0	0	0	0	0	0	0
64	66	6.40	4.10	1.80	0	0	0	0	0	0	0	0
66	68	6.70	4.40	2.10	0	0	0	0	0	0	0	0
68	70	7.10	4.70	2.40	.10	0	0	0	0	0	0	0
70	72	7.50	5.10	2.70	.40	0	0	0	0	0	0	0
72	74	7.90	5.40	3.10	.80	0	0	0	0	0	0	0
74	76	8.30	5.70	3.40	1.10	0	0	0	0	0	0	0
76	78	8.70	6.00	3.70	1.40	0	0	0	0	0	0	0
78	80	9.10	6.30	4.00	1.70	0	0	0	0	0	0	0
80	82	9.50	6.70	4.30	2.00	0	0	0	0	0	0	0
82	84	9.90	7.00	4.70	2.40	0	0	0	0	0	0	0
84	86	10.30	7.40	5.00	2.70	.40	0	0	0	0	0	0
86	88	10.70	7.80	5.30	3.00	.70	0	0	0	0	0	0
88	90	11.10	8.20	5.60	3.30	1.00	0	0	0	0	0	0
90	92	11.50	8.60	5.90	3.60	1.30	0	0	0	0	0	0
92	94	11.90	9.00	6.30	4.00	1.60	0	0	0	0	0	0
94	96	12.30	9.40	6.60	4.30	2.00	0	0	0	0	0	0
96	98	12.70	9.80	6.90	4.60	2.30	0	0	0	0	0	0
98	100	13.10	10.20	7.30	4.90	2.60	.30	0	0	0	0	0
100	105	13.80	10.90	8.00	5.50	3.20	.90	0	0	0	0	0
105	110	14.80	11.90	9.00	6.30	4.00	1.70	0	0	0	0	0
110	115	15.80	12.90	10.00	7.20	4.80	2.50	.20	0	0	0	0
115	120	16.90	13.90	11.00	8.20	5.60	3.30	1.00	0	0	0	0

Figure 7–4

And the wages are—		And the number of withholding allowances claimed is—										
At least	But less than	0	1	2	3	4	5	6	7	8	9	10 or more
		The amount of income tax to be withheld shall be—										
$120	$125	$18.00	$14.90	$12.00	$9.20	$6.40	$4.10	$1.80	$0	$0	$0	$0
125	130	19.20	15.90	13.00	10.20	7.30	4.90	2.60	.20	0	0	0
130	135	20.30	17.00	14.00	11.20	8.30	5.70	3.40	1.00	0	0	0
135	140	21.50	18.20	15.00	12.20	9.30	6.50	4.20	1.80	0	0	0
140	145	22.60	19.30	16.00	13.20	10.30	7.40	5.00	2.60	.30	0	0
145	150	23.80	20.50	17.10	14.20	11.30	8.40	5.80	3.40	1.10	0	0
150	160	25.50	22.20	18.90	15.70	12.80	9.90	7.00	4.60	2.30	0	0
160	170	27.80	24.50	21.20	17.80	14.80	11.90	9.00	6.20	3.90	1.60	0
170	180	30.10	26.80	23.50	20.10	16.80	13.90	11.00	8.10	5.50	3.20	.90
180	190	32.40	29.10	25.80	22.40	19.10	15.90	13.00	10.10	7.20	4.80	2.50
190	200	34.50	31.40	28.10	24.70	21.40	18.10	15.00	12.10	9.20	6.40	4.10
200	210	36.60	33.50	30.40	27.00	23.70	20.40	17.10	14.10	11.20	8.30	5.70
210	220	38.70	35.60	32.60	29.30	26.00	22.70	19.40	16.10	13.20	10.30	7.50
220	230	40.80	37.70	34.70	31.60	28.30	25.00	21.70	18.40	15.20	12.30	9.50
230	240	42.90	39.80	36.80	33.80	30.60	27.30	24.00	20.70	17.40	14.30	11.50
240	250	45.20	41.90	38.90	35.90	32.80	29.60	26.30	23.00	19.70	16.30	13.50
250	260	47.80	44.00	41.00	38.00	34.90	31.90	28.60	25.30	22.00	18.60	15.50
260	270	50.40	46.60	43.10	40.10	37.00	34.00	30.90	27.60	24.30	20.90	17.60
270	280	53.00	49.20	45.50	42.20	39.10	36.10	33.10	29.90	26.60	23.20	19.90
280	290	55.80	51.80	48.10	44.30	41.20	38.20	35.20	32.10	28.90	25.50	22.20
290	300	58.80	54.50	50.70	46.90	43.30	40.30	37.30	34.20	31.20	27.80	24.50
300	310	61.80	57.50	53.30	49.50	45.80	42.40	39.40	36.30	33.30	30.10	26.80
310	320	64.80	60.50	56.20	52.10	48.40	44.60	41.50	38.40	35.40	32.40	29.10
320	330	67.80	63.50	59.20	54.80	51.00	47.20	43.60	40.50	37.50	34.50	31.40
330	340	70.80	66.50	62.20	57.80	53.60	49.80	46.10	42.60	39.60	36.60	33.60
340	350	73.80	69.50	65.20	60.80	56.50	52.40	48.70	44.90	41.70	38.70	35.70
350	360	77.40	72.50	68.20	63.80	59.50	55.20	51.30	47.50	43.80	40.80	37.80
360	370	81.00	75.80	71.20	66.80	62.50	58.20	53.90	50.10	46.40	42.90	39.90
370	380	84.60	79.40	74.20	69.80	65.50	61.20	56.90	52.70	49.00	45.20	42.00
380	390	88.20	83.00	77.80	72.80	68.50	64.20	59.90	55.50	51.60	47.80	44.10
390	400	91.80	86.60	81.40	76.20	71.50	67.20	62.90	58.50	54.20	50.40	46.70
400	410	95.40	90.20	85.00	79.80	74.60	70.20	65.90	61.50	57.20	53.00	49.30
410	420	99.00	93.80	88.60	83.40	78.20	73.20	68.90	64.50	60.20	55.90	51.90
420	430	102.60	97.40	92.20	87.00	81.80	76.60	71.90	67.50	63.20	58.90	54.60
430	440	106.20	101.00	95.80	90.60	85.40	80.20	75.00	70.50	66.20	61.90	57.60
440	450	109.80	104.60	99.40	94.20	89.00	83.80	78.60	73.50	69.20	64.90	60.60
450	460	113.40	108.20	103.00	97.80	92.60	87.40	82.20	77.00	72.20	67.90	63.60
460	470	117.00	111.80	106.60	101.40	96.20	91.00	85.80	80.60	75.40	70.90	66.60
470	480	120.60	115.40	110.20	105.00	99.80	94.60	89.40	84.20	79.00	73.90	69.60
480	490	124.20	119.00	113.80	108.60	103.40	98.20	93.00	87.80	82.60	77.40	72.60
490	500	127.80	122.60	117.40	112.20	107.00	101.80	96.60	91.40	86.20	81.00	75.80
500	510	131.40	126.20	121.00	115.80	110.60	105.40	100.20	95.00	89.80	84.60	79.40
510	520	135.00	129.80	124.60	119.40	114.20	109.00	103.80	98.60	93.40	88.20	83.00
520	530	138.60	133.40	128.20	123.00	117.80	112.60	107.40	102.20	97.00	91.80	86.60
530	540	142.20	137.00	131.80	126.60	121.40	116.20	111.00	105.80	100.60	95.40	90.20
540	550	145.80	140.60	135.40	130.20	125.00	119.80	114.60	109.40	104.20	99.00	93.80
550	560	149.40	144.20	139.00	133.80	128.60	123.40	118.20	113.00	107.80	102.60	97.40
560	570	153.00	147.80	142.60	137.40	132.20	127.00	121.80	116.60	111.40	106.20	101.00
570	580	156.60	151.40	146.20	141.00	135.80	130.60	125.40	120.20	115.00	109.80	104.60
580	590	160.20	155.00	149.80	144.60	139.40	134.20	129.00	123.80	118.60	113.40	108.20
590	600	163.80	158.60	153.40	148.20	143.00	137.80	132.60	127.40	122.20	117.00	111.80
600	610	167.40	162.20	157.00	151.80	146.60	141.40	136.20	131.00	125.80	120.60	115.40
610	620	171.00	165.80	160.60	155.40	150.20	145.00	139.80	134.60	129.40	124.20	119.00
620	630	174.60	169.40	164.20	159.00	153.80	148.60	143.40	138.20	133.00	127.80	122.60
630	640	178.20	173.00	167.80	162.60	157.40	152.20	147.00	141.80	136.60	131.40	126.20
		36 percent of the excess over $640 plus—										
$640 and over		180.00	174.80	169.60	164.40	159.20	154.00	148.80	143.60	138.40	133.20	128.00

Figure 7–4 (*continued*)

And the wages are—		And the number of withholding allowances claimed is—										
At least	But less than	0	1	2	3	4	5	6	7	8	9	10 or more
		The amount of income tax to be withheld shall be—										
$0	$48	$0	$0	$0	$0	$0	$0	$0	$0	$0	$0	$0
48	49	.10	0	0	0	0	0	0	0	0	0	0
49	50	.20	0	0	0	0	0	0	0	0	0	0
50	51	.40	0	0	0	0	0	0	0	0	0	0
51	52	.60	0	0	0	0	0	0	0	0	0	0
52	53	.80	0	0	0	0	0	0	0	0	0	0
53	54	.90	0	0	0	0	0	0	0	0	0	0
54	55	1.10	0	0	0	0	0	0	0	0	0	0
55	56	1.30	0	0	0	0	0	0	0	0	0	0
56	57	1.40	0	0	0	0	0	0	0	0	0	0
57	58	1.60	0	0	0	0	0	0	0	0	0	0
58	59	1.80	0	0	0	0	0	0	0	0	0	0
59	60	1.90	0	0	0	0	0	0	0	0	0	0
60	62	2.20	0	0	0	0	0	0	0	0	0	0
62	64	2.50	.10	0	0	0	0	0	0	0	0	0
64	66	2.90	.40	0	0	0	0	0	0	0	0	0
66	68	3.20	.80	0	0	0	0	0	0	0	0	0
68	70	3.60	1.10	0	0	0	0	0	0	0	0	0
70	72	3.90	1.40	0	0	0	0	0	0	0	0	0
72	74	4.20	1.80	0	0	0	0	0	0	0	0	0
74	76	4.60	2.10	0	0	0	0	0	0	0	0	0
76	78	4.90	2.50	0	0	0	0	0	0	0	0	0
78	80	5.30	2.80	.40	0	0	0	0	0	0	0	0
80	82	5.60	3.10	.70	0	0	0	0	0	0	0	0
82	84	5.90	3.50	1.00	0	0	0	0	0	0	0	0
84	86	6.30	3.80	1.40	0	0	0	0	0	0	0	0
86	88	6.60	4.20	1.70	0	0	0	0	0	0	0	0
88	90	7.00	4.50	2.10	0	0	0	0	0	0	0	0
90	92	7.30	4.80	2.40	0	0	0	0	0	0	0	0
92	94	7.60	5.20	2.70	.30	0	0	0	0	0	0	0
94	96	8.00	5.50	3.10	.60	0	0	0	0	0	0	0
96	98	8.30	5.90	3.40	1.00	0	0	0	0	0	0	0
98	100	8.70	6.20	3.80	1.30	0	0	0	0	0	0	0
100	105	9.40	6.80	4.30	1.90	0	0	0	0	0	0	0
105	110	10.40	7.70	5.20	2.70	.30	0	0	0	0	0	0
110	115	11.40	8.60	6.00	3.60	1.10	0	0	0	0	0	0
115	120	12.40	9.60	6.90	4.40	2.00	0	0	0	0	0	0
120	125	13.40	10.60	7.70	5.30	2.80	.40	0	0	0	0	0
125	130	14.40	11.60	8.70	6.10	3.70	1.20	0	0	0	0	0
130	135	15.40	12.60	9.70	7.00	4.50	2.10	0	0	0	0	0
135	140	16.40	13.60	10.70	7.80	5.40	2.90	.50	0	0	0	0
140	145	17.40	14.60	11.70	8.80	6.20	3.80	1.30	0	0	0	0
145	150	18.40	15.60	12.70	9.80	7.10	4.60	2.20	0	0	0	0
150	160	19.90	17.10	14.20	11.30	8.40	5.90	3.50	1.00	0	0	0
160	170	21.90	19.10	16.20	13.30	10.40	7.60	5.20	2.70	.30	0	0
170	180	23.90	21.10	18.20	15.30	12.40	9.50	6.90	4.40	2.00	0	0
180	190	25.60	23.10	20.20	17.30	14.40	11.50	8.60	6.10	3.70	1.20	0
190	200	27.30	24.80	22.20	19.30	16.40	13.50	10.60	7.80	5.40	2.90	.50
200	210	29.00	26.50	24.10	21.30	18.40	15.50	12.60	9.80	7.10	4.60	2.20
210	220	30.70	28.20	25.80	23.30	20.40	17.50	14.60	11.80	8.90	6.30	3.90
220	230	32.40	29.90	27.50	25.00	22.40	19.50	16.60	13.80	10.90	8.00	5.60
230	240	34.10	31.60	29.20	26.70	24.30	21.50	18.60	15.80	12.90	10.00	7.30
240	250	35.80	33.30	30.90	28.40	26.00	23.50	20.60	17.80	14.90	12.00	9.10
250	260	37.50	35.00	32.60	30.10	27.70	25.20	22.60	19.80	16.90	14.00	11.10
260	270	39.20	36.70	34.30	31.80	29.40	26.90	24.50	21.80	18.90	16.00	13.10
270	280	41.70	38.40	36.00	33.50	31.10	28.60	26.20	23.70	20.90	18.00	15.10
280	290	44.20	40.60	37.70	35.20	32.80	30.30	27.90	25.40	22.90	20.00	17.10
290	300	46.70	43.10	39.50	36.90	34.50	32.00	29.60	27.10	24.70	22.00	19.10
300	310	49.20	45.60	42.00	38.60	36.20	33.70	31.30	28.80	26.40	23.90	21.10
310	320	51.70	48.10	44.50	40.90	37.90	35.40	33.00	30.50	28.10	25.60	23.10

Figure 7–5

And the wages are—		And the number of withholding allowances claimed is—										
At least	But less than	0	1	2	3	4	5	6	7	8	9	10 or more
		The amount of income tax to be withheld shall be—										
$320	$330	$54.20	$50.60	$47.00	$43.40	$39.80	$37.10	$34.70	$32.20	$29.80	$27.30	$24.90
330	340	56.70	53.10	49.50	45.90	42.30	38.80	36.40	33.90	31.50	29.00	26.60
340	350	59.20	55.60	52.00	48.40	44.80	41.20	38.10	35.60	33.20	30.70	28.30
350	360	62.00	58.10	54.50	50.90	47.30	43.70	40.10	37.30	34.90	32.40	30.00
360	370	64.80	60.80	57.00	53.40	49.80	46.20	42.60	39.00	36.60	34.10	31.70
370	380	67.60	63.60	59.50	55.90	52.30	48.70	45.10	41.50	38.30	35.80	33.40
380	390	70.40	66.40	62.30	58.40	54.80	51.20	47.60	44.00	40.40	37.50	35.10
390	400	73.20	69.20	65.10	61.10	57.30	53.70	50.10	46.50	42.90	39.30	36.80
400	410	76.00	72.00	67.90	63.90	59.80	56.20	52.60	49.00	45.40	41.80	38.50
410	420	78.80	74.80	70.70	66.70	62.60	58.70	55.10	51.50	47.90	44.30	40.70
420	430	81.60	77.60	73.50	69.50	65.40	61.40	57.60	54.00	50.40	46.80	43.20
430	440	84.50	80.40	76.30	72.30	68.20	64.20	60.20	56.50	52.90	49.30	45.70
440	450	87.70	83.20	79.10	75.10	71.00	67.00	63.00	59.00	55.40	51.80	48.20
450	460	90.90	86.30	81.90	77.90	73.80	69.80	65.80	61.70	57.90	54.30	50.70
460	470	94.10	89.50	84.90	80.70	76.60	72.60	68.60	64.50	60.50	56.80	53.20
470	480	97.30	92.70	88.10	83.50	79.40	75.40	71.40	67.30	63.30	59.30	55.70
480	490	100.50	95.90	91.30	86.60	82.20	78.20	74.20	70.10	66.10	62.10	58.20
490	500	103.70	99.10	94.50	89.80	85.20	81.00	77.00	72.90	68.90	64.90	60.80
500	510	107.10	102.30	97.70	93.00	88.40	83.80	79.80	75.70	71.70	67.70	63.60
510	520	110.70	105.50	100.90	96.20	91.60	87.00	82.60	78.50	74.50	70.50	66.40
520	530	114.30	109.10	104.10	99.40	94.80	90.20	85.60	81.30	77.30	73.30	69.20
530	540	117.90	112.70	107.50	102.60	98.00	93.40	88.80	84.20	80.10	76.10	72.00
540	550	121.50	116.30	111.10	105.90	101.20	96.60	92.00	87.40	82.90	78.90	74.80
550	560	125.10	119.90	114.70	109.50	104.40	99.80	95.20	90.60	86.00	81.70	77.60
560	570	128.70	123.50	118.30	113.10	107.90	103.00	98.40	93.80	89.20	84.60	80.40
570	580	132.30	127.10	121.90	116.70	111.50	106.30	101.60	97.00	92.40	87.80	83.20
580	590	135.90	130.70	125.50	120.30	115.10	109.90	104.80	100.20	95.60	91.00	86.30
590	600	139.50	134.30	129.10	123.90	118.70	113.50	108.30	103.40	98.80	94.20	89.50
600	610	143.10	137.90	132.70	127.50	122.30	117.10	111.90	106.70	102.00	97.40	92.70
610	620	146.70	141.50	136.30	131.10	125.90	120.70	115.50	110.30	105.20	100.60	95.90
620	630	150.30	145.10	139.90	134.70	129.50	124.30	119.10	113.90	108.80	103.80	99.10
630	640	153.90	148.70	143.50	138.30	133.10	127.90	122.70	117.50	112.40	107.20	102.30
640	650	157.50	152.30	147.10	141.90	136.70	131.50	126.30	121.10	116.00	110.80	105.60
650	660	161.10	155.90	150.70	145.50	140.30	135.10	129.90	124.70	119.60	114.40	109.20
660	670	164.70	159.50	154.30	149.10	143.90	138.70	133.50	128.30	123.20	118.00	112.80
670	680	168.30	163.10	157.90	152.70	147.50	142.30	137.10	131.90	126.80	121.60	116.40
680	690	171.90	166.70	161.50	156.30	151.10	145.90	140.70	135.50	130.40	125.20	120.00
690	700	175.50	170.30	165.10	159.90	154.70	149.50	144.30	139.10	134.00	128.80	123.60
700	710	179.10	173.90	168.70	163.50	158.30	153.10	147.90	142.70	137.60	132.40	127.20
710	720	182.70	177.50	172.30	167.10	161.90	156.70	151.50	146.30	141.20	136.00	130.80
720	730	186.30	181.10	175.90	170.70	165.50	160.30	155.10	149.90	144.80	139.60	134.40
730	740	189.90	184.70	179.50	174.30	169.10	163.90	158.70	153.50	148.40	143.20	138.00
740	750	193.50	188.30	183.10	177.90	172.70	167.50	162.30	157.10	152.00	146.80	141.60
750	760	197.10	191.90	186.70	181.50	176.30	171.10	165.90	160.70	155.60	150.40	145.20
760	770	200.70	195.50	190.30	185.10	179.90	174.70	169.50	164.30	159.20	154.00	148.80
770	780	204.30	199.10	193.90	188.70	183.50	178.30	173.10	167.90	162.80	157.60	152.40
780	790	207.90	202.70	197.50	192.30	187.10	181.90	176.70	171.50	166.40	161.20	156.00
790	800	211.50	206.30	201.10	195.90	190.70	185.50	180.30	175.10	170.00	164.80	159.60
800	810	215.10	209.90	204.70	199.50	194.30	189.10	183.90	178.70	173.60	168.40	163.20
810	820	218.70	213.50	208.30	203.10	197.90	192.70	187.50	182.30	177.20	172.00	166.80
820	830	222.30	217.10	211.90	206.70	201.50	196.30	191.10	185.90	180.80	175.60	170.40
830	840	225.90	220.70	215.50	210.30	205.10	199.90	194.70	189.50	184.40	179.20	174.00
840	850	229.50	224.30	219.10	213.90	208.70	203.50	198.30	193.10	188.00	182.80	177.60
850	860	233.10	227.90	222.70	217.50	212.30	207.10	201.90	196.70	191.60	186.40	181.20
860	870	236.70	231.50	226.30	221.10	215.90	210.70	205.50	200.30	195.20	190.00	184.80
		36 percent of the excess over $870 plus—										
$870 and over		238.50	233.30	228.10	222.90	217.70	212.50	207.30	202.10	197.00	191.80	186.60

Figure 7-5 *(continued)*

MARRIED Persons — BIWEEKLY Payroll Period

And the wages are—		And the number of withholding allowances claimed is—										
At least	But less than	0	1	2	3	4	5	6	7	8	9	10 or more
		The amount of income tax to be withheld shall be—										
$0	$96	$0	$0	$0	$0	$0	$0	$0	$0	$0	$0	$0
96	98	.10	0	0	0	0	0	0	0	0	0	0
98	100	.50	0	0	0	0	0	0	0	0	0	0
100	102	.80	0	0	0	0	0	0	0	0	0	0
102	104	1.20	0	0	0	0	0	0	0	0	0	0
104	106	1.50	0	0	0	0	0	0	0	0	0	0
106	108	1.80	0	0	0	0	0	0	0	0	0	0
108	110	2.20	0	0	0	0	0	0	0	0	0	0
110	112	2.50	0	0	0	0	0	0	0	0	0	0
112	114	2.90	0	0	0	0	0	0	0	0	0	0
114	116	3.20	0	0	0	0	0	0	0	0	0	0
116	118	3.50	0	0	0	0	0	0	0	0	0	0
118	120	3.90	0	0	0	0	0	0	0	0	0	0
120	124	4.40	0	0	0	0	0	0	0	0	0	0
124	128	5.10	.20	0	0	0	0	0	0	0	0	0
128	132	5.80	.90	0	0	0	0	0	0	0	0	0
132	136	6.40	1.50	0	0	0	0	0	0	0	0	0
136	140	7.10	2.20	0	0	0	0	0	0	0	0	0
140	144	7.80	2.90	0	0	0	0	0	0	0	0	0
144	148	8.50	3.60	0	0	0	0	0	0	0	0	0
148	152	9.20	4.30	0	0	0	0	0	0	0	0	0
152	156	9.80	4.90	0	0	0	0	0	0	0	0	0
156	160	10.50	5.60	.70	0	0	0	0	0	0	0	0
160	164	11.20	6.30	1.40	0	0	0	0	0	0	0	0
164	168	11.90	7.00	2.10	0	0	0	0	0	0	0	0
168	172	12.60	7.70	2.70	0	0	0	0	0	0	0	0
172	176	13.20	8.30	3.40	0	0	0	0	0	0	0	0
176	180	13.90	9.00	4.10	0	0	0	0	0	0	0	0
180	184	14.60	9.70	4.80	0	0	0	0	0	0	0	0
184	188	15.30	10.40	5.50	.60	0	0	0	0	0	0	0
188	192	16.00	11.10	6.10	1.20	0	0	0	0	0	0	0
192	196	16.70	11.70	6.80	1.90	0	0	0	0	0	0	0
196	200	17.50	12.40	7.50	2.60	0	0	0	0	0	0	0
200	210	18.90	13.60	8.70	3.80	0	0	0	0	0	0	0
210	220	20.90	15.30	10.40	5.50	.60	0	0	0	0	0	0
220	230	22.90	17.10	12.10	7.20	2.30	0	0	0	0	0	0
230	240	24.90	19.10	13.80	8.90	4.00	0	0	0	0	0	0
240	250	26.90	21.10	15.50	10.60	5.70	.80	0	0	0	0	0
250	260	28.90	23.10	17.30	12.30	7.40	2.50	0	0	0	0	0
260	270	30.90	25.10	19.30	14.00	9.10	4.20	0	0	0	0	0
270	280	32.90	27.10	21.30	15.70	10.80	5.90	1.00	0	0	0	0
280	290	34.90	29.10	23.30	17.60	12.50	7.60	2.70	0	0	0	0
290	300	36.90	31.10	25.30	19.60	14.20	9.30	4.40	0	0	0	0
300	320	39.90	34.10	28.30	22.60	16.80	11.80	6.90	2.00	0	0	0
320	340	43.90	38.10	32.30	26.60	20.80	15.20	10.30	5.40	.50	0	0
340	360	47.80	42.10	36.30	30.60	24.80	19.00	13.70	8.80	3.90	0	0
360	380	51.20	46.10	40.30	34.60	28.80	23.00	17.30	12.20	7.30	2.40	0
380	400	54.60	49.70	44.30	38.60	32.80	27.00	21.30	15.60	10.70	5.80	.90
400	420	58.00	53.10	48.20	42.60	36.80	31.00	25.30	19.50	14.10	9.20	4.30
420	440	61.40	56.50	51.60	46.60	40.80	35.00	29.30	23.50	17.70	12.60	7.70
440	460	64.80	59.90	55.00	50.10	44.80	39.00	33.30	27.50	21.70	16.00	11.10
460	480	68.20	63.30	58.40	53.50	48.60	43.00	37.30	31.50	25.70	20.00	14.50
480,	500	71.60	66.70	61.80	56.90	52.00	47.00	41.30	35.50	29.70	24.00	18.20
500	520	75.00	70.10	65.20	60.30	55.40	50.50	45.30	39.50	33.70	28.00	22.20
520	540	78.50	73.50	68.60	63.70	58.80	53.90	48.90	43.50	37.70	32.00	26.20
540	560	83.50	76.90	72.00	67.10	62.20	57.30	52.30	47.40	41.70	36.00	30.20
560	580	88.50	81.30	75.40	70.50	65.60	60.70	55.70	50.80	45.70	40.00	34.20
580	600	93.50	86.30	79.00	73.90	69.00	64.10	59.10	54.20	49.30	44.00	38.20
600	620	98.50	91.30	84.00	77.30	72.40	67.50	62.50	57.60	52.70	47.80	42.20
620	640	103.50	96.30	89.00	81.80	75.80	70.90	65.90	61.00	56.10	51.20	46.20

Figure 7–6

And the wages are—		And the number of withholding allowances claimed is—										
At least	But less than	0	1	2	3	4	5	6	7	8	9	10 or more
		The amount of income tax to be withheld shall be—										
$640	$660	$108.50	$101.30	$94.00	$86.80	$79.60	$74.30	$69.30	$64.40	$59.50	$54.60	$49.70
660	680	113.50	106.30	99.00	91.80	84.60	77.70	72.70	67.80	62.90	58.00	53.10
680	700	118.50	111.30	104.00	96.80	89.60	82.40	76.10	71.20	66.30	61.40	56.50
700	720	124.00	116.30	109.00	101.80	94.60	87.40	80.20	74.60	69.70	64.80	59.90
720	740	129.60	121.50	114.00	106.80	99.60	92.40	85.20	78.00	73.10	68.20	63.30
740	760	135.20	127.10	119.00	111.80	104.60	97.40	90.20	83.00	76.50	71.60	66.70
760	780	140.80	132.70	124.60	116.80	109.60	102.40	95.20	88.00	80.80	75.00	70.10
780	800	146.40	138.30	130.20	122.20	114.60	107.40	100.20	93.00	85.80	78.60	73.50
800	820	152.00	143.90	135.80	127.80	119.70	112.40	105.20	98.00	90.80	83.60	76.90
820	840	157.60	149.50	141.40	133.40	125.30	117.40	110.20	103.00	95.80	88.60	81.30
840	860	163.20	155.10	147.00	139.00	130.90	122.80	115.20	108.00	100.80	93.60	86.30
860	880	169.00	160.70	152.60	144.60	136.50	128.40	120.30	113.00	105.80	98.60	91.30
880	900	175.40	166.30	158.20	150.20	142.10	134.00	125.90	118.00	110.80	103.60	96.30
900	920	181.80	172.50	163.80	155.80	147.70	139.60	131.50	123.50	115.80	108.60	101.30
920	940	188.20	178.90	169.70	161.40	153.30	145.20	137.10	129.10	121.00	113.60	106.30
940	960	194.60	185.30	176.10	167.00	158.90	150.80	142.70	134.70	126.60	118.60	111.30
960	980	201.00	191.70	182.50	173.30	164.50	156.40	148.30	140.30	132.20	124.10	116.30
980	1,000	207.40	198.10	168.90	179.70	170.50	162.00	153.90	145.90	137.80	129.70	121.60
1,000	1,020	214.20	204.50	195.30	186.10	176.90	167.60	159.50	151.50	143.40	135.30	127.20
1,020	1,040	221.40	211.00	201.70	192.50	183.30	174.00	165.10	157.10	149.00	140.90	132.80
1,040	1,060	228.60	218.20	208.10	198.90	189.70	180.40	171.20	162.70	154.60	146.50	138.40
1,060	1,080	235.80	225.40	215.00	205.30	196.10	186.80	177.60	168.40	160.20	152.10	144.00
1,080	1,100	243.00	232.60	222.20	211.80	202.50	193.20	184.00	174.80	165.80	157.70	149.60
1,100	1,120	250.20	239.80	229.40	219.00	208.90	199.60	190.40	181.20	171.90	163.30	155.20
1,120	1,140	257.40	247.00	236.60	226.20	215.80	206.00	196.80	187.60	178.30	169.10	160.80
1,140	1,160	264.60	254.20	243.80	233.40	223.00	212.70	203.20	194.00	184.70	175.50	166.40
1,160	1,180	271.80	261.40	251.00	240.60	230.20	219.90	209.60	200.40	191.10	181.90	172.70
1,180	1,200	279.00	268.60	258.20	247.80	237.40	227.10	216.70	206.80	197.50	188.30	179.10
1,200	1,220	286.20	275.80	265.40	255.00	244.60	234.30	223.90	213.50	203.90	194.70	185.50
1,220	1,240	293.40	283.00	272.60	262.20	251.80	241.50	231.10	220.70	210.30	201.10	191.90
1,240	1,260	300.60	290.20	279.80	269.40	259.00	248.70	238.30	227.90	217.50	207.50	198.30
1,260	1,280	307.80	297.40	287.00	276.60	266.20	255.90	245.50	235.10	224.70	214.30	204.70
1,280	1,300	315.00	304.60	294.20	283.80	273.40	263.10	252.70	242.30	231.90	221.50	211.10
1,300	1,320	322.20	311.80	301.40	291.00	280.60	270.30	259.90	249.50	239.10	228.70	218.30
1,320	1,340	329.40	319.00	308.60	298.20	287.80	277.50	267.10	256.70	246.30	235.90	225.50
1,340	1,360	336.60	326.20	315.80	305.40	295.00	284.70	274.30	263.90	253.50	243.10	232.70
1,360	1,380	343.80	333.40	323.00	312.60	302.20	291.90	281.50	271.10	260.70	250.30	239.90
1,380	1,400	351.00	340.60	330.20	319.80	309.40	299.10	288.70	278.30	267.90	257.50	247.10
1,400	1,420	358.20	347.80	337.40	327.00	316.60	306.30	295.90	285.50	275.10	264.70	254.30
1,420	1,440	365.40	355.00	344.60	334.20	323.80	313.50	303.10	292.70	282.30	271.90	261.50
1,440	1,460	372.60	362.20	351.80	341.40	331.00	320.70	310.30	299.90	289.50	279.10	268.70
1,460	1,480	379.80	369.40	359.00	348.60	338.20	327.90	317.50	307.10	296.70	286.30	275.90
1,480	1,500	387.00	376.60	366.20	355.80	345.40	335.10	324.70	314.30	303.90	293.50	283.10
1,500	1,520	394.20	383.80	373.40	363.00	352.60	342.30	331.90	321.50	311.10	300.70	290.30
1,520	1,540	401.40	391.00	380.60	370.20	359.80	349.50	339.10	328.70	318.30	307.90	297.50
1,540	1,560	408.60	398.20	387.80	377.40	367.00	356.70	346.30	335.90	325.50	315.10	304.70
1,560	1,580	415.80	405.40	395.00	384.60	374.20	363.90	353.50	343.10	332.70	322.30	311.90
1,580	1,600	423.00	412.60	402.20	391.80	381.40	371.10	360.70	350.30	339.90	329.50	319.10
1,600	1,620	430.20	419.80	409.40	399.00	388.60	378.30	367.90	357.50	347.10	336.70	326.30
1,620	1,640	437.40	427.00	416.60	406.20	395.80	385.50	375.10	364.70	354.30	343.90	333.50
1,640	1,660	444.60	434.20	423.80	413.40	403.00	392.70	382.30	371.90	361.50	351.10	340.70
1,660	1,680	451.80	441.40	431.00	420.60	410.20	399.90	389.50	379.10	368.70	358.30	347.90
1,680	1,700	459.00	448.60	438.20	427.80	417.40	407.10	396.70	386.30	375.90	365.50	355.10
1,700	1,720	466.20	455.80	445.40	435.00	424.60	414.30	403.90	393.50	383.10	372.70	362.30
1,720	1,740	473.40	463.00	452.60	442.20	431.80	421.50	411.10	400.70	390.30	379.90	369.50
		36 percent of the excess over $1,740 plus—										
$1,740 and over		477.00	466.60	456.20	445.80	435.40	425.10	414.70	404.30	393.90	383.50	373.10

Figure 7–6 (*continued*)

Example 1

Derek Tracy is single and claims one exemption (S-1). His job at the Carson Publishing Company pays $4.22 per hour for a 40-hour workweek. Because of a broken press he worked 56 hours during one workweek. How much income tax was withheld for that weekly pay period?

Solution:

The tax to be withheld is found in Figure 7–4, Single Persons—Weekly Payroll Period, but first we must calculate his gross earnings for the week in order to determine the appropriate wage bracket. The regular rate is $4.22 and the overtime rate is $4.22 × 1½ = $6.33 per hour, hence:

$$\text{Regular wages} = \$4.22 \times 40 = \$168.80$$
$$\text{Overtime wages} = \$6.33 \times 16 = \underline{\$101.28}$$
$$\text{Gross earnings} = \$270.08$$

The gross earnings lie in the wage bracket of "at least $270 but less than $280." The tax for one exemption is $49.20.

Example 2

Perry Watson sells chemical products on a straight commission of 30%. During the last biweekly pay period, his sales were $748 for the first week and $1,232 for the second week. Perry's wife works in an office and they have one child. How much tax should be deducted from Perry's gross earnings if he claims two exemptions on his W-4 form?

Solution:

Perry's total sales for the pay period are $1,980.

$$\text{Commissions} = \$1,980 \times 0.30 = \$594.$$

In the table entitled Married Persons—Biweekly Payroll Period (Figure 7–6), Perry's tax bracket is "at least $580 but less than $600." His tax for two exemptions is $79.00.

B. Social Security   The economic depression of the 1930s spawned a number of emergency measures and legislation. Perhaps the most significant of these was the Federal Insurance Contributions Act of 1937. Better known as the Social Security Act, it established a fund to provide monthly benefits to retired or disabled workers and to pay burial and survivor's benefits to the surviving family of a deceased worker. A recent amendment to the act provides health insurance benefits under the Medicare Program.

More a compulsory insurance program than a tax, the act requires employers to withhold a percentage of the employee's gross earnings as contributions to the benefit fund. These contributions are matched by the employer until the total annual contribution reaches a maximum established by the act. Both the contribution percent and the maximum to be withheld have been amended by Congress a number of times in order to liberalize benefits. This has been necessary because of the continued rise in the cost of living and inflation. At this writing, the current contribution is 5.85 percent. The maximum contribution is tied to changes in the cost of living. In 1976, the maximum was 5.85 percent of the first $15,300 of gross earnings, or $895.05. The contributions of the employee are matched by the employer, and periodically these sums are deposited with a bank authorized to accept F.I.C.A. taxes.

Tax tables for F.I.C.A. are furnished by the Internal Revenue Service, or one may compute the tax by multiplying the employee's gross earnings by 5.85 percent. A portion of these tax tables are reproduced in Figure 7–7. Note they are similar to the income tax tables in that the tax is in the line to the right of the appropriate wage bracket.

Social Security Employee Tax Table—Continued

5.85 percent employee tax deductions

Wages		Tax to be withheld	Wages		Tax to be withheld	Wages		Tax to be withheld	Wages		Tax to be withheld
At least	But less than		At least	But less than		At least	But less than		At least	But less than	
$133.25	$133.42	$7.80	$144.36	$144.53	$8.45	$155.48	$155.65	$9.10	$166.59	$166.76	$9.75
133.42	133.59	7.81	144.53	144.71	8.46	155.65	155.82	9.11	166.76	166.93	9.76
133.59	133.77	7.82	144.71	144.88	8.47	155.82	155.99	9.12	166.93	167.10	9.77
133.77	133.94	7.83	144.88	145.05	8.48	155.99	156.16	9.13	167.10	167.27	9.78
133.94	134.11	7.84	145.05	145.22	8.49	156.16	156.33	9.14	167.27	167.44	9.79
134.11	134.28	7.85	145.22	145.39	8.50	156.33	156.50	9.15	167.44	167.61	9.80
134.28	134.45	7.86	145.39	145.56	8.51	156.50	156.67	9.16	167.61	167.78	9.81
134.45	134.62	7.87	145.56	145.73	8.52	156.67	156.84	9.17	167.78	167.95	9.82
134.62	134.79	7.88	145.73	145.90	8.53	156.84	157.01	9.18	167.95	168.12	9.83
134.79	134.96	7.89	145.90	146.07	8.54	157.01	157.18	9.19	168.12	168.30	9.84
134.96	135.13	7.90	146.07	146.24	8.55	157.18	157.36	9.20	168.30	168.47	9.85
135.13	135.30	7.91	146.24	146.42	8.56	157.36	157.53	9.21	168.47	168.64	9.86
135.30	135.48	7.92	146.42	146.59	8.57	157.53	157.70	9.22	168.64	168.81	9.87
135.48	135.65	7.93	146.59	146.76	8.58	157.70	157.87	9.23	168.81	168.98	9.88
135.65	135.82	7.94	146.76	146.93	8.59	157.87	158.04	9.24	168.98	169.15	9.89
135.82	135.99	7.95	146.93	147.10	8.60	158.04	158.21	9.25	169.15	169.32	9.90
135.99	136.16	7.96	147.10	147.27	8.61	158.21	158.38	9.26	169.32	169.49	9.91
136.16	136.33	7.97	147.27	147.44	8.62	158.38	158.55	9.27	169.49	169.66	9.92
136.33	136.50	7.98	147.44	147.61	8.63	158.55	158.72	9.28	169.66	169.83	9.93
136.50	136.67	7.99	147.61	147.78	8.64	158.72	158.89	9.29	169.83	170.00	9.94
136.67	136.84	8.00	147.78	147.95	8.65	158.89	159.06	9.30	170.00	170.18	9.95
136.84	137.01	8.01	147.95	148.12	8.66	159.06	159.24	9.31	170.18	170.35	9.96
137.01	137.18	8.02	148.12	148.30	8.67	159.24	159.41	9.32	170.35	170.52	9.97
137.18	137.36	8.03	148.30	148.47	8.68	159.41	159.58	9.33	170.52	170.69	9.98
137.36	137.53	8.04	148.47	148.64	8.69	159.58	159.75	9.34	170.69	170.86	9.99
137.53	137.70	8.05	148.64	148.81	8.70	159.75	159.92	9.35	170.86	171.03	10.00
137.70	137.87	8.06	148.81	148.98	8.71	159.92	160.09	9.36	171.03	171.20	10.01
137.87	138.04	8.07	148.98	149.15	8.72	160.09	160.26	9.37	171.20	171.37	10.02
138.04	138.21	8.08	149.15	149.32	8.73	160.26	160.43	9.38	171.37	171.54	10.03
138.21	138.38	8.09	149.32	149.49	8.74	160.43	160.60	9.39	171.54	171.71	10.04
138.38	138.55	8.10	149.49	149.66	8.75	160.60	160.77	9.40	171.71	171.89	10.05
138.55	138.72	8.11	149.66	149.83	8.76	160.77	160.95	9.41	171.89	172.06	10.06
138.72	138.89	8.12	149.83	150.00	8.77	160.95	161.12	9.42	172.06	172.23	10.07

Figure 7–7

Example 1

Juan Hernandez earns a salary of $145.25 per week. How much is deducted for F.I.C.A. taxes?

Solution:

By straight computation,

$$\$145.25 \times 0.0585 = \$8.50$$

Using Figure 7–7, $145.25 is in the bracket of "at least $145.22 but less than $145.39." The tax for this bracket is $8.50. At the end of a year Juan will have contributed a total of $8.50 × 52 = $442.00 in F.I.C.A. taxes.

Example 2

In 1975, the comptroller of the Barrett Corporation was paid a salary of $21,000. How much was deducted each monthly pay period for F.I.C.A. taxes?

Solution:

An annual salary of $21,000 amounts to gross earnings of $21,000 ÷ 12 = $1,750 per month. This amount is not covered by the Social Security Tables, but by direct computation his F.I.C.A. tax was:

$$\$1750 \times 0.0585 = \$102.38$$

per month. After eight months the comptroller had contributed $819.04, hence the contribution for the ninth month was $895.05 − $819.04 = $76.01. No further deductions were made for the rest of the year.

Example 3

Wade Taylor is a salesperson whose commission rate is 18% of net sales with a guaranteed draw of $200 per week. Last week his sales were $1,100. How much F.I.C.A. tax should be deducted?

Solution:

The earned commission for the week is $1,100 × 0.18 = $198.00, hence his gross earnings for the week will be the draw of $200.00. The F.I.C.A. tax on this amount is:

$$\$200 \times 0.0585 = \$11.70$$

C. Other Deductions

Deductions for Social Security and federal income tax are the main required payroll deductions. Some states may have compulsory deductions for state income tax or disability insurance. Additionally, there may be voluntary deductions made by the employer as a service to the employee. Group insurance premiums, union dues, United States Savings Bonds, credit union loan payments, or contributions to charitable organizations are examples of such deductions.

Example 1

Harrison Keely is a diemaker earning $6.15 per hour for a 40-hour workweek. In addition to deductions for federal income tax (S-1) and Social Security, union dues of $3.25 per month are also withheld from his pay. Find Keely's net earnings for a 40-hour workweek if the company pay period is weekly.

Solution:

Gross earnings = $6.15 × 40		= $246.00
Income Tax	= $41.90	
F.I.C.A.	= 14.39	
Union Dues ($3.25 × $\frac{12}{52}$)	= 0.75	
Total Deductions		$ 57.04
Net earnings		$188.96

Example 2

Charles Patton is paid weekly and earns $4.40 per hour for a 35-hour workweek. He has joined the payroll savings plan and purchases a bond a month (Cost $18.75). He also participates in the company group insurance plan, which costs him $35.10 a month to insure his family. He is classified M-4. Calculate his net earnings for a week during which he worked 42 hours.

Solution:

The overtime rate is $4.40 × 1½ = $6.60 per hour.

Regular Wages	= $4.40 × 35	= $154.00
Overtime Wages	= $6.60 × 7	= $ 46.20
Gross earnings		= $200.20
Federal Income Tax		= $ 18.40
F.I.C.A.		= $ 11.71
Savings Bond	= ($18.75 × $\frac{12}{52}$)	= $ 4.33
Group Insurance	= ($35.10 × $\frac{12}{52}$)	= $ 8.10
Total Deductions		= $ 42.54
Net earnings		= $157.66

Example 3

Virginia Krisloff sells cosmetics. She receives a salary of $200 per week plus 5% of all sales in excess of $1,500. During the last biweekly pay period, her weekly sales were $1,800 and $1,600. Virginia is married and claims three exemptions for income tax purposes. In addition to Social Security, she contributes $12.20 per month to the company retirement plan. To insure her family under the group insurance plans costs $37.00 per month, and Virginia has agreed to a deduction of $1.00 per month as a pledge to the United Fund. What are her net earnings for the last pay period?

Solution:

The commission for the pay period is $400 \times 0.05 = \$20.00$, hence:

Salary	$= \$200 \times 2$	$= \$400.00$
Commissions		$= \$\ 20.00$
Gross earnings		$= \$420.00$
Income Tax (M-3)		$= \$\ 46.60$
F.I.C.A.	$= \$420 \times 5.85\%$	$= \$\ 24.57$
Retirement	$= \$12.20 \times \frac{12}{26}$	$= \$\ \ 5.63$
Group Insurance	$= \$37.00 \times \frac{12}{26}$	$= \$\ 17.08$
United Fund	$= \$1.00 \times \frac{12}{26}$	$=\ \ \ \ 0.46$
Total deductions		$= \$\ 94.34$
Net earnings		$= \$325.66$

1. Tony Di Salvo is married, has three children, and claims three exemptions. His weekly salary is $314. How much income tax is withheld from his weekly gross earnings?

2. Find the income tax withheld from the biweekly gross earnings of an employee who is married, claims two deductions, and is paid a monthly salary of $920.

3. Joanne McMannis is an office manager at the Carleton Company, where she receives a salary of $18,450 per year. She is married with two children, and she claims all four exemptions. If the pay period at Carleton is biweekly, how much income tax is withheld from her biweekly gross earnings?

4. Ray Baker earns $3.75 an hour for a 40-hour workweek at the Calvert Manufacturing Company. He is single, claims one deduction, and is paid weekly. Find the amount of income tax withheld for a week during which he works 47 hours.

5. Accutex Scientific Equipment, Inc., operates on a biweekly pay period. Richard Thaxton, an employee at Accutex, is married with four children and claims three exemptions. He is paid $4.20 per hour for a 40-hour workweek. How much income tax is withheld from his gross earnings for a pay period during which he works 43 hours the first week and 47 hours the second week?

6. Glenn Darnell sells office furniture on a straight commission of 11% of net sales. He is married with one child and claims three deductions. How much income tax was withheld from his last biweekly gross earnings if he sold $2,340 worth of merchandise the first week and $2,984 the second week?

7. Beverly Morrow is employed by Cory Products Company where she is paid weekly a straight commission of 14% of her net sales. She is single and claims one exemption. Find the amount of income tax withheld from her gross earnings for a week during which she sells $2,142.60 worth of merchandise, with returns of $211.40.

8. Cecil Beamon is paid a biweekly graduated commission of 6% of the first $3,500 in net sales and 7.5% of net sales in excess of $3,500. He is married with two children and claims four deductions. How much income tax is withheld from his gross earnings for a pay period in which he sells $9,842.40 worth of merchandise with cancellations and returns of $622.50?

9. The Doyle Company pays its sales personnel a weekly graduated commission of 7% of the first $1,500 in net sales and 9% of net sales in excess of $1,500. Find the income tax withheld from the gross earnings of a married salesperson claiming two deductions for a week during which sales total $3,240 with returns of $519.20.

10. Judy Roberts receives a salary of $90 per week plus a commission of 3.25% of net sales. Judy is married, but claims only one exemption. How much income tax is withheld from her gross earnings for a week during which she has sales of $2,140.51 with returns of $291.72?

11. Nelson's Novelty and Gift Shop pays its salesclerks $125 a week plus 4.25% of weekly net sales in excess of $500. If the pay period is biweekly, find the income tax withheld from the gross earnings of a married salesclerk claiming three deductions who reports the following sales:

	Total Sales	Returns
Week 1	$1,142.41	$203.72
Week 2	$1,003.39	$114.78

In the following problems use the 1976 F.I.C.A. contribution rate of 5.85% of the first $15,300 in gross earnings when calculating F.I.C.A. deductions.

12. Ted Lee is paid $179.42 per week. How much is deducted from his gross earnings for F.I.C.A. taxes each biweekly pay period? How much will Ted have contributed in F.I.C.A. taxes in a year?

13. George Tibbetts is a department manager for the Drexel Company and is paid an annual salary of $27,500. How much is deducted each biweekly pay period from his gross earnings for F.I.C.A. taxes? For how many pay periods of the year will he contribute to F.I.C.A.?

14. David Bland, a salesperson, receives a commission of 16% of net sales with a guaranteed draw of $210 per week. How much F.I.C.A. tax is deducted from his gross earnings for a week during which his net sales total $1,242.50?

15. Nancy Miller sells cookware on a biweekly commission basis of 14.5% of net sales with a guaranteed biweekly draw of $375. During the last two-week period, she reported the following sales:

	Total Sales	Returns and Cancellations
Week 1	$1,352.63	$72.41
Week 2	$1,411.71	$53.69

How much was deducted for F.I.C.A. taxes this pay period?

16. Morehouse Metal Works employs Charles McDonald as a machinist. He receives $4.15 per hour for a 40-hour workweek. In addition to deductions for federal income tax (his classification is S-2) and Social Security, he also has deducted from his weekly gross earnings (1) union dues of $5.90 per month and (2) a group insurance payment of $32.14 per month. Find his net earnings for a week during which he works 43 hours.

17. John Ritch is paid biweekly at Timsco Industries. He is paid $3.90 per hour for a 40-hour workweek. His group insurance payment is $37.42 per month, his union dues are $10.11 per month, and he has $50.00 per pay period deducted from his earnings and deposited with the company credit union. His classification is M-3. Compute his net earnings for the last two-week period during which he worked 47 hours the first week and 40 hours the second week.

18. Madison's Department Store employs Cheryl Watts as a salesclerk. She is paid biweekly a salary of $160 per week plus a commission of 4.75% of weekly sales in excess of $1,200. She is classified M-2. In addition to F.I.C.A., she contributes $13.75 per month to the company retirement plan. She also has $32.14 per month for insurance, $5.00 per month for the United Fund, and $3.72 per month for union dues deducted from her earnings. Calculate her net earnings for a pay period when she sold $1,432.71 worth of merchandise the first week and $1,563.42 the second week.

19. Terry Gilbreath is paid weekly a salary of $225 per week plus a commission of 7.5% of net sales in excess of $1,400. He is classified M-3, and in addition to F.I.C.A. he contributes $22.72 per month to the company retirement plan. He also has deductions to cover (1) his union dues of $8.43 per month, (2) his group insurance payment of $47.15 per month, (3) his credit union payment of $50 per month, and (4) his United Fund contribution of $10 per month. Find his net earnings for a week during which he sells $1,873.17 worth of merchandise with returns and cancellations totalling $94.12.

20. Ben Darlington earns $14,720.00 per year as a supervisor at the Busbee Corporation. He is classified M-1, and in addition to F.I.C.A. he contributes $19.31 per month to the company retirement plan. He also has deductions for (1) $14.42 per month union dues, (2) $41.17 per month group insurance, and (3) $18.75 per month for savings bonds. If the pay period at Busbee is biweekly, find his net earnings for the first pay period in February.

21. The vice president of Holstrum Enterprises is paid $37,500 per year. He is classified M-3. He has deductions from his weekly earnings to cover (1) $87.21 per month for the company retirement plan, in addition to F.I.C.A., (2) $56.25 per month for savings bonds, (3) $200 per month for savings in the credit union, and (4) $56.82 per month for group insurance. If the pay period at Holstrum is weekly, what are his net earnings for the first week in March? What are his net earnings for the last week in October?

Employer Contributions

Except for income tax, most payroll deductions are payments for employee benefits. Ordinarily, the employee pays only a portion of the total cost of these benefits; the remainder is paid by the employer. Some employer contributions are required by law, while others are voluntary in the form of fringe benefits to the employee. Let us consider some of these benefits and the employer's share of their cost.

A. Social Security

The employer is required to match the F.I.C.A. contributions of the employee.

Example 1

An employee had gross earnings of $136.42 for a weekly pay period. Find the total amount to be deposited for F.I.C.A.

Solution:

Employee F.I.C.A. Deductions = $136.40 × 0.0585 = $ 7.98
Employer F.I.C.A. Contributions   =   7.98

Total F.I.C.A. tax $15.96

B. Federal Unemployment Tax

Employees who lose their job or who are temporarily laid off may receive limited compensation through a provision of the F.I.C.A. A fund called the Federal Unemployment Trust Fund has been established from taxes on industry. From this fund payments are made to unemployed workers either for a limited time period or until reemployment, whichever comes first.

The federal tax is 3.28% of the first $4,200 of the employee's gross earnings and is paid entirely by the employer. However, most states also have unemployment tax laws, and if an employer pays state unemployment taxes, the federal tax rate is reduced to 0.58% of the first $4,200. In other words, if there is a state unemployment tax, the total tax paid by the employer is the state tax plus a federal tax of 0.58%. Each state sets its own tax rate. In many states, the lower the company's unemployment rate, the lower the tax. Thus employers with a history of stable employment may pay a total tax less than the maximum rate of 3.28%.

Example 1

The K & C Company is located in Miami. Florida has a standard unemployment tax of 3% of the first $3,000 of gross earnings of each employee. However, as a result of favorable employment experience, the current tax rate for the K & C Company is 1%. If the company employed 36 people last year and all 36 employees earned in excess of $4,200, calculate the total unemployment taxes paid by the employer.

Solution:

The state of Florida tax rate is $3,000 × 0.01 = $30.00 per person. The federal tax rate is $4,200 × 0.0058 = $24.36 per person. Thus:

Florida tax   = $30.00 × 36 = $1,080.00
Federal tax   = $24.36 × 36 = $ 876.96

Total unemployment tax   = $1,956.96

C. Group Life and Health Insurance

A common employee fringe benefit is group insurance. Under a master policy issued to the company, employees may be insured for life insurance, hospitalization, surgical, and other medical expenses. In addition, most policies extend the health benefits to the employee's family, if he/she wishes to contract for this option. Group insurance is usually available without medical examination and is less expensive than individual insurance for two reasons: first, the policy is sold to a group thus reducing paperwork and administrative expenses and second, it is customary for the employer to pay a portion of the cost.

The employer's share of the insurance premium varies from company to company. Some employers pay the entire premium; others pay a percentage, say 50%. A common arrangement is for the employer to pay the employee's premium while the employee in turn pays the cost of insuring his family. Group insurance will be discussed again in chapter 16.

Example 1

The Bradford Dry Goods Company has a group insurance plan whereby each employee is covered under a Major Medical health plan. In addition, each employee is insured for $5,000 term life insurance except the officers of the company who are insured for $12,000. The premiums are as follows:

Life Insurance   —$0.68 per $1,000 per month.
Major Medical
   Employee Only —$15.42 per month
   Dependents Only—$36.15 per month.

The company has agreed to pay for the cost of the employee benefits; the employee must pay for any dependents. If the company has 42 employees and 4 officers, and if 24 of the 28 married employees elect to insure their families, what is (a) the total monthly premium and (b) the cost to the employer?

Solution:

The life insurance costs $0.68 × 5 = $3.40 per month for $5,000 insurance and $0.68 × 12 = $8.16 for $12,000 of coverage.

Life Insurance Premiums		
Officers ($8.16 × 4)	$ 32.64	
Other employees ($3.40 × 42)	142.80	
Subtotal		$ 175.44
Major Medical Premium		
Employee ($15.42 × 46)	$709.32	
Dependents ($36.15 × 24)	$867.60	
Subtotal		$1,576.92
Total Monthly Premium		$1,752.36
Cost to the Employer ($709.32 + $175.44)		$ 884.76

Records and Reports

The records maintained by a payroll department vary according to the size of the organization. However, all companies are required by the Fair Labor Standards Act to keep accurate records of each employee that include the following information:

Identifying information

Employee's full name, address, Social Security number, birth date, sex, and occupation.

Hours (Wage earners)

Time and day of week when the workweek begins, hours worked each day, total hours worked each workweek.

Earnings

Basis on which earnings are paid, regular hourly rate, total regular earnings, total overtime earnings, all additions to or deductions from the employee's earnings for each pay period.

One method of recording the above information is an employee earnings record. A sample earnings record is shown in Figure 7–8. Often this form will have quarterly totals because quarterly reports are required by federal and state governments. The calendar quarters of a year are January 1–March 31, April 1–June 30, July 1–September 30, and October 1–December 31.

The Employer's Quarterly Tax Return (Form 941) is an example of a quarterly report required by the Federal government. See Figure 7–9.

Figure 7–8

- RECAPITULATION BY QUARTERS -

EMPLOYEE RECORD

QTR.	EARNINGS	FICA	FED WHLDG	STATE WHLDG	INS.	UNION DUES	NET PAID
1st	3272 —	191 44	432 40		136 50	24 —	2487 66
2nd							
3rd							
4th							
TOT.							

NAME James Harvard Lyon EXEMPTIONS M-3
ADDRESS 201 Debra Lane PHONE 622-1212
S. S. ACC'T NO. 987-65-4321 SEX M SINGLE ☐ MARRIED ☒
CLOCK NO. 123 POSITION Welder DATE BORN 8-1-50
HRS. PER DAY_____ PER WEEK_____ DATE EMPLOYED 6/70 TERMINATED_____
REMARKS_____
RATE OF PAY: DATE 7/74 $ 6.20 PER HR : DATE_____ $_____ PER_____

W 152
MADE IN U. S. A.

FIRST QUARTER — 19 75

PAYROLL PERIOD	REGULAR TIME		OVERTIME		TOTAL EARNINGS	NON-TAXABLE SICK PAY ETC.	AM'T TAXABLE	DEDUCTIONS						NET EARNINGS	
	TIME	RATE	HRS.	RATE				F.I.C.A.	FED. WHLDG.	STATE WHLDG.	DISA-BILTY	INS.	UNION DUES	AMOUNT	DATE PAID
JAN 12/30–1/3	40	6.20	8	12.30	345 60			20 22	55 20			10.50	8.00	251 68	1-10
6–10	40		8	9.30	322 40			18 86	50 40			10.50		242 64	1-17
13–17	40		8		322 40			18 86	50 40			10.50		242 64	1-24
20–24	40				248 —			14 51	31 40			10.50		191 59	1-31
27–31	40				248 —			14 51	31 40			10.50		191 59	2-7
FEB 2–7	32				198 40			11 61	22 00			10.50	8.00	146 29	2-14
10–14	32				198 40			11 61	22 00			10.50		154 29	2-21
17–21	40				248 —			14 51	31 40			10.50		191 59	2-28

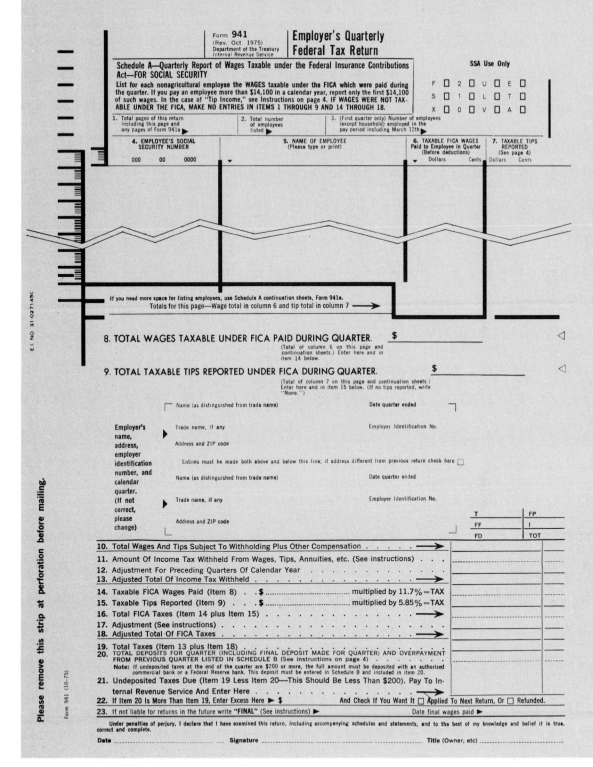

Figure 7-9

Deductions for both F.I.C.A. and federal income tax are reported on this form. The report must be filed on or before the last day of the month following the end of the calendar quarter. At the same time the employer must remit to the U. S. Treasury Department (through a Federal Reserve Bank or any commercial bank authorized to receive federal taxes) the F.I.C.A. tax levied on him as an employer, the F.I.C.A. tax withheld from his employee's wages, and the federal income tax he has deducted from his employees' wages, provided the total remittance is between $200 and $2,000. Special rules apply if the total is less than $200 or more than $2,000.

8

Topics in Accounting

Chapter Objectives for Chapter 8

8.1 Introduction

A requisite of efficient business operation is accurate data. The collection, summarization, and communication of accurate information are essential to sound planning. The kinds of information needed by management and analysts are records of past activities, data concerning current operating efficiency, and projections for future activities. These three items summarize the role of accounting in business. Accounting techniques are the most widely used means of describing and communicating business operations. This chapter examines some of the basic accounting procedures central to all businesses.

8.2 The Income Statement

Periodically, a company must appraise its progress. Managers and owners need to check the financial health of the enterprise and note its economic activity. There are two documents that summarize this information, the income statement and the balance sheet.

The **income statement** is a report on the company income for a period of time, generally a month or a year. The income statement describes the general manner in which the income of the business is earned. The basic format of the statement is the fundamental business equation:

$$(8–1) \qquad R - E = I$$

where $\qquad R =$ revenue (sales and gains)

$\qquad E =$ expenses (costs incurred to generate income)

$\qquad I =$ income (net earnings)

Figure 8–1 is an example of an income statement.*

Income statements are used in an analysis of company operations. To management, the income statement is a report on the success or failure of the firm's activities; to owners, it is a measure of the efficiency of management.

---

* Financial statements such as income statements and balance sheets are not uniform in either content or arrangement. The income statement in Figure 8–1 is an illustration of a single-step statement and has been adopted by many companies because of its simplicity and readability. Other forms of income statements will also be illustrated in this chapter.

Figure 8–1

Meyer Company Income Statement for the Year Ended December 31, 19__		
Revenue		
	Sales	$ 960,000
	Gain from Sale of Land	46,000
	Interest and Other	72,000
		$1,078,000
Expenses		
	Cost of Merchandise Sold	$ 450,000
	Operating Expenses	320,000
	Interest Expenses	96,000
	Federal and State Taxes	120,000
		$ 986,000
Net Income		$ 92,000

Section 8.3 The Balance Sheet

The **balance sheet** presents the financial condition of a firm at a given moment of time. It is developed from past activities of the company and involves the classification and valuation of the firm's resources.

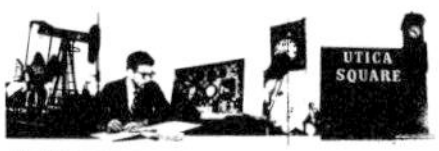

Helmerich & Payne, Inc.
and
Consolidated Subsidiaries

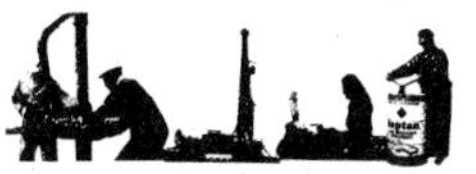

Statement of Income

	Quarter Ended 6-30-76	Quarter Ended 6-30-75*	Nine Months Ended 6-30-76	Nine Months Ended 6-30-75*
SALES AND OTHER OPERATING REVENUE	$18,042,000	$16,191,000	$52,004,000	$47,414,000
DIVIDEND AND INTEREST INCOME	455,000	491,000	1,433,000	1,778,000
Total Revenue	18,497,000	16,682,000	53,437,000	49,192,000
OPERATING COSTS				
Operating Expenses	7,595,000	7,979,000	23,125,000	23,017,000
General and Administrative Expenses	210,000	339,000	998,000	1,060,000
Interest Expense	366,000	405,000	1,200,000	1,308,000
Taxes, other than Federal Income Taxes	850,000	748,000	2,414,000	2,147,000
	9,021,000	9,471,000	27,737,000	27,532,000
INCOME BEFORE OTHER CHARGES AND FEDERAL INCOME TAXES	9,476,000	7,211,000	25,700,000	21,660,000
OTHER CHARGES				
Depreciation and Depletion	1,745,000	1,553,000	5,111,000	4,444,000
Dry Holes and Retirements	896,000	502,000	2,436,000	1,482,000
	2,641,000	2,055,000	7,547,000	5,926,000
INCOME FROM CONTINUING OPERATIONS BEFORE FEDERAL INCOME TAXES	6,835,000	5,156,000	18,153,000	15,734,000
Federal Income Taxes	2,746,000	1,757,000	6,602,000	5,954,000
INCOME FROM CONTINUING OPERATIONS	4,089,000	3,399,000	11,551,000	9,780,000
DISCONTINUED OPERATIONS NET OF FEDERAL INCOME TAXES				
Income from Discontinued Manufacturing Division	—	300,000	45,000	915,000
Gain on sale of Manufacturing Division	—	—	609,000	—
NET INCOME	$ 4,089,000	$ 3,699,000	$12,205,000	$10,695,000
PER SHARE OF COMMON STOCK OUTSTANDING (NOTE):				
From Continuing Operations	$ .98	$ .83	$ 2.76	$ 2.39
From Discontinued Operations	—	.07	.16	.22
Net Income	$ .98	$ .90	$ 2.92	$ 2.61
SHARES OUTSTANDING**	4,186,891	3,618,643	4,186,891	3,618,643
**Excluding Shares Held in Company Treasury	273,855	282,103	273,855	282,103

*Restated

NOTE: During 1976 the 5% convertible subordinated debentures outstanding since 1968 were called; therefore the potential for dilution which existed in prior years no longer exists. This dilutive effect on primary EPS in prior years was shown as fully diluted EPS. Accordingly, primary EPS for 1976 should be compared with fully diluted EPS for 1975 and prior years. Although not considered comparable, primary EPS for the third quarter of 1975 were $.92 for continuing operations and $.08 for discontinued operations.

Balance Sheet

	Balance as of 6-30-76	Balance as of 6-30-75*
Assets		
CURRENT ASSETS		
Cash and Time Deposits	$ 8,587,000	$ 9,279,000
Accounts and Notes Receivable	15,795,000	15,825,000
Other Current Assets	13,071,000	8,626,000
	37,453,000	33,730,000
INVESTMENTS AND ADVANCES	39,774,000	34,733,000
PROPERTY, PLANTS AND EQUIPMENT	112,368,000	102,767,000
Less: Accumulated Depreciation and Depletion	49,178,000	45,263,000
	63,190,000	57,504,000
OTHER ASSETS AND DEFERRED CHARGES	881,000	1,757,000
	$141,298,000	$127,724,000
Liabilities and Capital		
CURRENT LIABILITIES		
Current Portion of Mortgages and Notes Payable**	$ 8,564,000	$ 5,274,000
Accounts Payabie	5,404,000	8,457,000
Accrued Liabilities	3,743,000	6,084,000
	17,711,000	19,815,000
NONCURRENT LIABILITIES		
Mortgages and Notes Payable (Less Current Portion)**	12,148,000	14,013,000
5% Convertible Subordinated Debentures	—	10,209,000
Deferred Income Taxes	6,917,000	4,704,000
Other	2,379,000	1,769,000
	21,444,000	30,695,000
CAPITAL		
Capital Stock	446,000	390,000
Capital Surplus	35,162,000	25,053,000
Reinvested Earnings	67,763,000	53,036,000
	103,371,000	78,479,000
Less: Treasury Stock, at Cost	1,228,000	1,265,000
	102,143,000	77,214,000
	$141,298,000	$127,724,000

*Restated

**As of 6/30/76, $9,170,000 was the debt of subsidiaries, with no recourse to the parent company.

All figures are subject to audit and adjustment at the end of the fiscal year. The Company's Annual Report is available upon request.

Helmrich Payne, Inc., Quarter Report.

The balance sheet is a representation of the basic accounting equation

(8–2)   Assets = Liabilities + Owner's Equity

Defined in a broad sense, the term **assets** refers to the dollar value of everything the company owns, the term **liabilities** means the dollar value of everything the company owes, and the difference between the two is the **owner's equity.*** The term **equities** is used for the sum of liabilities plus owner's equity and represents the claims upon the assets if the business is dissolved.

Traditionally, assets are reported on the left-hand side of the balance sheet and equities on the right-hand side (account form). Alternatively, assets may be at the top of the report and equities at the bottom (report form). In either event, since assets and equities are just two dimensions of the same investment, it follows that the two sides balance—hence the name balance sheet.

The two forms of balance sheets are illustrated in Figures 8–2 and 8–3.

Figure 8–2

THE VARGAS COMPANY				
Balance Sheet				
December 31, 19__				
Assets			**Equities**	
Current Assets		Current Liabilities		
Cash	$ 4,500	Due to Bank		$ 3,000
Accounts Receivable	6,000	Notes Payable		4,500
Merchandise Inventory	4,700	Total Current Liabilities		$ 7,500
Prepayments	1,300			
Total Current Assets	$16,500	Long-Term Liabilities		
		Mortgage		$20,000
Fixed Assets		Total Liabilities		$27,500
Equipment	$ 5,000			
Building	22,000	Owner's Equity		
Land	3,000	M. Vargas, Owner		$19,000
Total Fixed Assets	$30,000			
Total Assets	$46,500	Total Equities		$46,500

* Assets may also be thought of as the location of investment, liabilities the source of the funds.

Figure 8–3

The Brown Corporation
Statement of Financial Condition
At December 31, 19___

Assets

Current Assets	
Cash	$ 16,288,000
Marketable Securities (at Cost)	60,883,000
Receivables	90,061,000
Inventory	109,758,000
	$276,990,000
Fixed Assets	
Investments in Foreign Branches	$ 50,310,000
Property, Plant, and Equipment	130,964,000
	$181,274,000
Total Assets	$458,264,000

Liabilities and Stockholder's Equity

Current Liabilities	
Payables and Accruals	$ 38,285,000
Accrued Taxes	26,270,000
Current Installments on Long-Term Debt	1,229,000
Dividends Payable	2,882,000
Customers Deposits	2,005,000
Customers Service Prepayments	22,917,000
	93,588,000
Long—Term Debt	123,187,000
Total Liabilities	$216,775,000
Stockholder's Equity	
Common Stock, 8,607,000 shares, $5 par value	$154,187,000
Earnings Retained for Use in the Business	87,302,000
Total Stockholder's Equity	$241,489,000
Total Liabilities and Stockholder's Equity	$458,264,000

On a balance sheet, the general headings of assets and liabilities are subdivided according to short-term and long-term categories. Current assets and current liabilities are short-term transactions; fixed assets and long-term liabilities are long-term transactions.*

---

* Fixed assets are items that normally will not be converted to cash within a period of one year. Similarly, long-term liabilities are those the firm does not expect to retire in one year.

Horizontal and Vertical Analysis

As public statements, the income statement and the balance sheet describe the economic activities of a company. Properly analyzed, these two statements disclose the company's earnings capability and its financial strength. In the short run, a company must have sufficient funds for current needs. In the long run, the company must have sufficient earning and borrowing capacity to provide for continued growth and productivity.

The measure of a company's financial health requires an assessment that is both qualitative and quantitative. Qualitative evaluation is subjective and requires good intuition coupled with sound judgment. Quantitative analysis uses the mathematics of percents and ratios. Thus, financial analysis is both an art and a science.

There are two basic forms of quantitative analysis, vertical analysis and horizontal analysis. **Vertical analysis** expresses in percentage form component parts in relation to a whole. The computations in vertical analysis are an application of the basic percentage equation solved for R,

$$R = \frac{P}{B}.$$

On an income statement, the base B typically is the value of net sales. This relates all other entries in the statement to sales, as percentages. An example of vertical analysis is shown in Figure 8–4.

Figure 8–4

The Turner Company
Income Statement
For the Year Ended December 31, 19__

	Amount	Percent
Net Sales		$375,000	100.0
Less:		
Cost of Sales	$335,000		89.3
Depreciation	6,000		1.6
Maintenance and Repairs	4,200		1.1
Taxes (Other than Federal Income)	6,500		1.7
Total Cost and Operating Expenses		$351,700	93.8
Operating Income		23,300	6.3
Interest Expense		2,500	0.7
Federal Income Taxes		9,900	2.6
Net Income		$ 10,900	2.9

The vertical analysis in Figure 8–4 answers the question, "Where did the sales dollar go?" In this instance, 89.3% of each dollar (89.3¢) went for cost of goods, 1.6% for depreciation (1.6¢), etc.

The second type of financial analysis is horizontal analysis. **Horizontal analysis** compares dollar amounts for different periods shown on the same line of a comparative statement.* Figure 8–5 illustrates horizontal analysis. Note that the earlier year is the base for computing percent increase or decrease. This is standard practice.

Horizontal analysis is applicable to income statements as well as balance sheets. The primary advantage of horizontal analysis is in disclosing trends.

Figure 8–5

Troy Manufacturing Co., Inc.

Comparative Balance Sheet

As of December 31, 19_8, 19_9

	19_9	19_8	Increase or (Decrease) Amount	Increase or (Decrease) Percent
Current Assets				
Cash	$ 250,000	$ 249,000	$ 1,000	0.4
Short-term Investments	382,000	400,000	18,000	(4.5)
Accounts Receivable	237,000	175,000	62,000	35.4
Inventories	300,000	330,000	30,000	(9.1)
Unexpired Insurance	40,000	30,000	10,000	33.3
Total Current Assets	$1,209,000	$1,184,000	$25,000	2.1
Fixed Assets				
Land	$ 135,000	$ 130,000	$ 5,000	3.8
Buildings (Net)	370,000	340,000	30,000	8.8
Machinery and Equipment (Net)	180,000	186,000	6,000	(3.2)
Total Fixed Assets	$ 685,000	$ 656,000	$29,000	4.4
Total Assets	$1,894,000	$1,840,000	$54,000	2.9
Liabilities				
Accounts Payable	$ 64,000	$ 70,000	$ 6,000	(8.6)
Bank Loans	100,000	85,000	15,000	17.6
Wages Payable	40,000	30,000	10,000	33.3
Federal Income Tax Payable	215,000	195,000	20,000	10.3
Bonds Payable	300,000	300,000	-0-	-0-
Total Liabilities	$ 719,000	$ 680,000	$39,000	5.7
Owner's Equity				
Common Stock	$ 850,000	$ 832,000	$18,000	2.2
Retained Earnings	325,000	328,000	3,000	.9
Total Owner's Equity	$1,175,000	$1,160,000	$15,000	1.3
Total Liabilities and Owner's Equity	$1,894,000	$1,840,000	$54,000	2.9

* A comparative statement is one that provides financial data for more than one reporting period.

1. Fill in the missing entries in the following income statement, if the sales for the Topkin Company were $870,000 and the operating expenses were $122,000.

The Topkin Company Income Statement for the Year Ended December 31, 1976	
Revenue	
Sales	_____
Rental Income	$ 73,500
Interest	17,400
Total	_____
Expenses	
Cost of Merchandise Sold	$642,500
Operating Expenses	_____
Interest Expenses	7,200
Federal and State Taxes	97,000
Total	_____
Net Income	_____

2. Fill in the missing entries in the following balance sheet for the Clinton Corporation, if the current assets in cash are $10,200, fixed assets in land are $7,300, and the long-term mortgage liability is $42,700.

The Clinton Corporation Balance Sheet December 31, 1976			
Assets		**Equities**	
Current Assets		**Current Liabilities**	
Cash	_____	Due to Bank	$111,200
Accounts Receivable	$12,500	Notes Payable	18,800
Merchandise Inventory	72,300	Total Current	
Prepayments	3,200	Liabilities	_____
Total Current Assets	_____		
		Long-term Liabilities	
Fixed Assets		Mortgage	_____
Equipment	$58,000	Total Liabilities	_____
Buildings	97,000		
Land	_____	**Owner's Equity**	
Total Fixed Assets	_____	R. H. Clinton, Owner	_____
Total Assets	_____	Total Equities	_____

3. Fill in the missing entries in the following balance sheet for the Elkhorn Company, if the current accounts receivable are $218,400, fixed assets in plant and equipment are $430,000, and long-term debts total $257,000.

```
                The Elkhorn Company
                   Balance Sheet
                 December 31, 1976

                      Assets
Current Assets
    Cash                              $ 47,500
    Marketable Securities               82,000
    Accounts Receivable               _____
    Inventories                        249,000
        Total Current Assets          _____

Fixed Assets
    Land                              $ 98,000
    Plant and Equipment               _____
        Total Fixed Assets            _____
        Total Assets                  _____

                     Equities
Current Liabilities
    Payables                          $748,200
    Accrued Taxes                       37,400

Long-term Liabilities
    Long-term Debts                   _____

Owner's Equity
    P. H. Elkhorn, Owner              $ 82,300
        Total Equities                _____
```

4. Fill in the missing entries and complete the vertical analysis of the following income statement, using net sales as the base for computing percents (to the nearest tenth).

```
                The Hamilton Company
                  Income Statement
             Year Ended December 31, 1976

                                        Amount    Percent
Net Sales                              $450,000   _____

Less:
    Cost of Sales       $375,000                  _____
    Depreciation           9,700                  _____
    Maintenance            6,300                  _____
        Total Cost and Operating Expenses  _____ _____

Operating Income                       _____   _____

Interest Expense                          4,500   _____

Federal Taxes                             7,200   _____

Net Income                             _____   _____
```

5. Complete the vertical analysis of the following income statement, using total income as the base for computing percents (to the nearest tenth).

Houser Wholesalers
Income Statement
December 31, 1976

	Amount	Percent
Revenue		
Sales	$730,000	_____
Rentals	60,000	_____
Interest	7,000	_____
Total Income	797,000	_____
Expenses		
Cost of Merchandise	$540,000	67.75
Operating Expenses	92,000	11.54
Interest Expenses	6,000	.75
Taxes	46,000	5.77
Total Expenses	684,000	85.8
Net Income	113	14.

6. Complete the vertical analysis of the following balance sheet, using total assets as the base for computing percents (to the nearest tenth).

William Mullins, Inc.
Balance Sheet
December 31, 1976

Working Capital = current assets minus current liabilities

Assets

Current Assets	Amount	Percent
Cash	$105,000	10.6
Accounts Receivable	140,000	14.1
Inventory	350,000	35.4
Total Current Assets	595,000	60.1
Fixed Assets		
Land	$ 75,000	7.6
Plant and Equipment	320,000	32.3
Total Fixed Assets	395,000	39.9
Total Assets	990,000	100.0

Equities

Current Liabilities		
Payables	$720,000	72.7
Accrued Taxes	42,000	4.2
Long-term Liabilities		
Long-term Debts	$150,000	15.2
Owner's Equity		
W. E. Mullins, Owner	$ 78,000	7.9
Total Equities	990,000	_____

7. Complete the horizontal analysis of the following income statement (compute percents to the nearest tenth).

Oswald Enterprises
Income Statement for Years
Ending December 31, 1975 and 1976

	1976	1975	Increase or Decrease Amount	Percent
Net Sales	$450,000	$370,000	80,000	21.6
Less:				
Cost of Sales	310,000	240,000	70,000	29.2
Depreciation	8,000	6,200	1,800	29
Maintenance	5,200	4,800	400	8.3
Total Cost and Operating Expenses	323,200	251,000	72,200	28.8
Operating Income	126,800	119,000	7,800	6.6
Interest Expense	14,000	12,000	2,000	16.7
Federal Taxes	22,000	18,000	4,000	22.2
Net Income	90,800	89,000	1,800	2.0

8. Complete the horizontal analysis of the following balance sheet (compute percents to the nearest tenth).

J. W. Wall, Inc.
Balance Sheet for Years Ending
December 31, 1975 and 1976

	1976	1975	Increase or Decrease Amount	Percent	Percent of Total Assets 1976	1975
Assets						
Cash	$ 92,000	$ 74,000				
Accounts Receivable	260,000	240,000				
Inventory	374,000	370,000				
Total Current Assets		684,000				
Fixed Assets	420,000	470,000				
Total Assets						
Equities						
Payables	$816,000	$810,000				
Accrued Taxes	57,000	51,000				
Total Current Liabilities		861,000				
Long-term Liabilities	170,000	190,000				
Total Liabilities		1,051,000				
Owner's Equity	103,000	103,000				
Total Equities						

9. Complete the horizontal analysis of the following balance sheet (compute percents to the nearest tenth).

			Increase or Decrease		Percent of Total Assets	
Brooker Enterprises Balance Sheet for Years Ending December 31, 1975 and 1976						
	1976	**1975**	**Amount**	**Percent**	**1976**	**1975**
Assets						
Cash	$ 3,220,000	$ 4,110,000	_____	_____	____	____
Marketable Securities	11,700,000	9,100,000	_____	_____	____	____
Accounts Receivable	8,756,000	8,386,000	_____	_____	____	____
Inventory	16,750,000	14,200,000	_____	_____	____	____
Total Current Assets	_____	_____	_____	_____	____	____
Fixed Assets	110,000	70,000	_____	_____	____	____
Total Assets	_____	_____	_____	_____	____	____
Equities						
Payables	$15,700,000	$14,100,000	_____	_____	____	____
Accrued Taxes	2,700,000	2,200,000	_____	_____	____	____
Dividends Payable	4,100,000	3,476,000	_____	_____	____	____
Deposits	1,842,000	1,040,000	_____	_____	____	____
Total Current Liabilities	_____	_____	_____	_____	____	____
Long-term Debt	6,214,000	5,470,000	_____	_____	____	____
Total Liabilities	_____	_____	_____	_____	____	____
Common Stock	$ 9,740,000	$ 8,840,000	_____	_____	____	____
Retained Earnings	240,000	740,000	_____	_____	____	____
Total Stockholders' Equity	_____	_____	_____	_____	____	____
Total Liabilities and Stockholders' Equity	_____	_____	_____	_____	____	____

Financial Ratios

Recall that a ratio is another name for a fraction. The fraction $\frac{5}{1}$ in ratio form is $5:1$. The fraction $\frac{216}{648}$ can be expressed as $\frac{1}{3}$ or $1:3$ by reduction of fractions, or $33\frac{1}{3}\%$ by division and conversion to percent.

In financial analysis, numerous ratios have been developed to interpret a company's economic activities. A select group of these will be examined; these are:

Ratios Measuring Liquidity

1. Current Ratio
2. Acid-test Ratio

Ratios Measuring Profitability

3. Gross Profit Margin
4. Operating Ratio

Ratios Measuring Long-term Financial Condition

5. Stockholder's Equity Ratio
6. Debt-Equity Ratio

In discussing these basic ratios, the balance sheet and income statement of Space-Tronics, Inc., Figures 8–6 and 8–7, will be used.

Figure 8–6

Space-Tronics, Inc.
Balance Sheet
December 31, 19___

Current Assets		Current Liabilities	
Cash	$ 12,200	Accounts Payable	$ 13,400
Accounts Receivable	21,900	Notes Payable	4,700
Inventory	18,300	Wages Payable	1,400
Prepaid Insurance	1,200	Income Tax Payable	2,400
Total Current Assets	$ 53,600	Total Current Liabilities	$ 21,900
Fixed Assets		Long-Term Liabilities	
Plant and Machinery	$ 97,000	Bonds Payable	$ 12,000
Land	12,400	Stockholder's Equity	
		Capital Stock	$120,000
		Retained Earnings	9,100
Total Assets	$163,000	Total Liabilities and Stockholder's Equity	$163,000

Liquidity is the ability of a company to convert assets into cash quickly without incurring a significant loss. The current ratio (also called the working capital ratio) offers a rough measure of whether a company can meet its liabilities in the near future as they come due. The **current ratio** is the ratio of current assets to current liabilities.

(8–3) $$\text{Current Ratio} = \frac{\text{Current Assets}}{\text{Current Liabilities}}$$

Figure 8–7

Space-Tronics, Inc.

Income Statement

December 31, 19___

Sales	$250,000
Expenses	
Cost of Goods Sold	$150,000
Operating Expenses	75,000
Interest Charges	600
Common Stock Dividend	12,500
Total	$238,100
Net Income	$ 11,900

Example 1

Find the current ratio for Space-Tronics, Inc.

Solution:

$$\text{Current Ratio} = \frac{53,600}{21,900}$$

$$= 2.4$$

The current ratio is 2.4 to 1.

The current ratio assumes that current assets could be used to pay current liabilities. Most creditors want more than just a 1:1 ratio, and traditionally a 2:1 ratio is considered a minimum.

A variation of the current ratio is the acid-test ratio. The inference is that the real measure or the acid-test of liquidity is to eliminate inventories and prepaid expenses from current assets. Prepaid expenses is money already spent, and inventories, it is argued, require both sales and collection before cash can be obtained. Thus, the **acid-test ratio** is the ratio of cash and receivables to current liabilities.

$$(8\text{--}4) \qquad \text{Acid-test Ratio} = \frac{\text{Cash} + \text{Receivables}}{\text{Current Liabilities}}$$

Example 2

Find the acid-test ratio of Space-Tronics, Inc.

Solution:

$$\text{Acid-test Ratio} = \frac{\$12,200 + \$21,900}{\$21,900}$$

$$= 1.6$$

The acid-test ratio is 1.6 to 1.

An acid-test ratio of 1:1 is considered acceptable, but a more practical analysis is to compare the results with the acid-test ratio of other companies in the specific trade or industry.

The difference between net sales and the cost of goods sold is called gross margin. Gross margin should be sufficient to cover all expenses of operation, interest expense, and profit for the owners. The percent found by dividing gross margin by net sales is called the **gross profit margin,** and it shows the average spread between the cost of goods sold and the selling price.

$$(8\text{--}5) \quad \text{Gross Profit Margin} = \frac{\text{Net Sales} - \text{Cost of Goods Sold}}{\text{Net Sales}}$$

Example 3

Find the gross profit margin of Space-Tronics, Inc.

Solution:

$$\text{Gross Profit Margin} = \frac{\$250,000 - \$150,000}{\$250,000}$$

$$= .40$$

$$= 40\%$$

Diminishing earnings over a period of time may be explained by a corresponding decline in gross profit margin.

The **operating ratio** is the ratio of cost of goods sold plus operating expenses to net sales.

$$(8\text{--}6) \quad \text{Operating Ratio} = \frac{\text{Cost of Goods Sold} + \text{Operating Expenses}}{\text{Net Sales}}$$

Expressed as a percent, this ratio reflects the amount of sales dollars used to defray the cost of goods and administrative expenses. The higher the operating ratio, the less income to meet interest payments, dividends, and other financial obligations.

Example 4

Determine the operating ratio of Space-Tronics, Inc.

Solution:

$$\text{Operating Ratio} = \frac{\$150,000 + \$75,000}{\$250,000}$$

$$= 0.90$$

$$= 90\%$$

The ratio of owner's equity to total assets is called the **stockholders equity ratio.**

[handwritten: Tells how own much they own]

(8–7) $\text{Stockholders Equity Ratio} = \dfrac{\text{Owners Equity}}{\text{Total Assets}}$

Expressed as a percent, this ratio indicates the investment in assets that is financed by the owners or stockholders.

Example 5

Find the stockholders equity ratio of Space-Tronics, Inc.

Solution:

$$\text{Stockholders Equity Ratio} = \frac{\$120,000 + \$9,100}{\$163,000}$$

$$= 0.79$$

$$= 79\%$$

A high stockholders equity ratio is regarded as favorable by creditors, since it indicates a large cushion of security.

Another safety indicator is the debt-equity ratio. The **debt-equity ratio** is the ratio of total debt to total ownership equity.

(8–8) $\text{Debt-Equity Ratio} = \dfrac{\text{Current Liabilities} + \text{Long-term Liabilities}}{\text{Owner's Equity}}$

Example 6

Determine the debt-equity ratio of Space-Tronics, Inc.

Solution:

$$\text{Debt-Equity Ratio} = \frac{\$21,900 + \$12,000}{\$120,000 + \$9,100}$$

$$= 0.26$$

$$= 26\%$$

A ratio of 1:1 (100%) is considered acceptable for established manufacturing firms; for small firms a 1:4 (25%) ratio may be the acceptable
minimum.

**Exercises
for Section 8.5**

1. The Bilford Company lists current assets of $47,400 and current
    liabilities of $16,700. Find the current ratio. 2.9 : 1

2. In problem 1, if inventories and prepaid expenses total $24,300 of the
    company's current assets, find the acid-test ratio. 1.4 : 1

3. Find the current ratio and the acid-test ratio for the Sanderson
    Company, which reported current liabilities of $21,400 and current
    assets of $53,800. $29,100 of the current assets were inventories and
    prepaid expenses.

4. The Concord Company reported net sales of $174,000. Find the
    gross profit margin if the cost of the goods sold was $92,000. 47.1 %

5. Tamtek, Inc., reported net sales of $324,000 with operating expenses
    of $120,000. If the cost of the goods sold was $190,000, find the
    gross profit margin and the operating ratio.

6. The net sales of Taylor Enterprises was $520,000 with operating 97.1
    expenses of $260,000. The cost of goods sold was $245,000. Find
    the gross profit margin and the operating ratio.

7. The owner's equity of the Lewis Company is $91,000, and last 70%
    year's total assets were $130,000. Find the stockholder's equity ratio.

8. Lerch Enterprises reported current liabilities of $34,000, long-term
    liabilities of $11,400, and total assets of $210,000. If the owner's
    equity in the company is $152,000, find the stockholder's equity ratio
    and the debt-equity ratio. 72.4 29.9

9. The owner's equity of the Thresher Company is $119,000, and last
    year's total assets were $183,000. The current liabilities are
    $31,500 and long-term liabilities are $9,700. Find the stockholder's
    equity ratio and the debt-equity ratio. 65% 34.6

10. The common stock outstanding in the Scott Corporation totals
    $120,000. Last year the company retained $14,000 in earnings and
    reported total assets of $273,000. The current liabilities were
    $42,300, and the long-term liabilities were $13,200. Find the
    stockholder's equity ratio and the debt-equity ratio. 41% 49%

For problems 11–15, refer to page 226 for the balance sheet and income
statement of the Brewster Company.

```
                    The Brewster Company
                      Balance Sheet
                    December 31, 1976
```

Current Assets		Current Liabilities	
Cash	$18,500	Accounts Payable	$ 15,400
Accounts Receivable	32,000	Notes Payable	5,200
Inventory	28,000	Wages Payable	2,100
Prepaid Insurance	1,750	Income Tax Payable	2,450
Total Current Assets	_80250_	Total Current Liabilities	_25,150_
Fixed Assets		**Long-term Liabilities**	
Plant and Equipment	$82,500	Bonds Payable	$ 18,400
Land	_21700_	**Stockholder's Equity**	
Total Assets	_184450_	Capital Stock	$138,000
		Retained Earnings	_2400_
		Total Liabilities and Stockholder's Equity	$184,450

```
                    The Brewster Company
                     Income Statement
                    December 31, 1976
```

Sales	$321,000
Expenses	
Cost of Goods Sold	$182,000
Operating Expenses	92,400
Interest Charges	_2400_
Common Stock Dividend	8,200
Total Expenses	$285,000
Net Income	_36,000_

11. Fill in the missing entries in the Balance Sheet and the Income Statement for the Brewster Company.

12. Find the current ratio for the Brewster Company. What is the acid-test ratio?   3.2   2.8

13. Compute the gross profit margin and the operating ratio for the Brewster Company.   43%   76.4%

14. Find the stockholder's equity ratio.   76.4%

15. What is the debt-equity ratio for the Brewster Company?   30.4

Section **8.6** **Depreciation**

Depreciation is the loss in utility or earning power of a fixed asset. This loss is measured in dollars and may be due to physical wear, obsolescence, or exhaustion of the asset's service life. Because depreciation is a factor in the cost of operating a business, it is recognized by the Internal Revenue Service as a tax deductible item.

While the federal government acknowledges depreciation as a legitimate business expense, it does not specify any particular method of calculation. The general rule is that any method or formula is acceptable provided it is logical, reasonable, and consistently applied. Consistent application means that once a method is chosen, it must continue to be used; changing from one method to another requires prior approval from the Internal Revenue Service.*

Depreciation is a means of recovering an investment in a property that has a useful life of more than one year, but it should be emphasized that a depreciation formula does not necessarily follow the decline in market value. Depreciation charges are intended to spread the cost of the asset during the period of its usefulness in an equitable manner; thus, the accounting emphasis is on the assignment of cost rather than physical deterioration.

As previously mentioned, the Internal Revenue Service does not advocate any particular depreciation formula, however, it does recognize three as acceptable. They are (1) the straight-line method, (2) the declining balance method, and (3) the sum-of-the-years-digits method. In discussing these methods, we shall use the most familiar item of depreciation, the automobile.†

Consider a company car purchased by the Scott Company for $5,000 (**cost of the asset**). It is estimated that after six years (**the useful life**) the car will be worth $800 in **trade-in value** (also called **salvage value‡**).

A. The Straight-line Method

The simplest and most commonly used, the straight-line method spreads the depreciation uniformly over the useful life. The formula for the straight-line method is:

(8–9)
$$d = \frac{c - s}{n}$$

where

d = depreciation amount per period

c = cost of asset

s = salvage value

n = periods of useful life

---

* It is possible to change from the declining balance or the sum-of-the-years-digits to the straight-line method without permission, but not vice versa.
† Only automobiles used for business purposes may be depreciated.
‡ The salvage value is also the minimum depreciation amount; that is, no asset may be depreciated below a reasonable salvage value. The salvage value is sometimes called scrap value.

For the Scott Company car,

$$d = \frac{\$5,000 - \$800}{6}$$

$$= \$700$$

The depreciation expense is $700 per year. Note this is at a constant rate of $16\frac{2}{3}\%$ per year ($\frac{700}{4,200} = 0.166\ldots$).

A **depreciation schedule** is used to keep track of the depreciation expense for each asset. A depreciation schedule for the above computation is:

Year	Depreciation	Accumulated Depreciation	Book Value*
0	—	—	$5,000
1	$700	$ 700	4,300
2	700	1,400	3,600
3	700	2,100	2,900
4	700	2,800	2,200
5	700	3,500	1,500
6	700	4,200	800

* Book value is the current depreciated value of an asset. This is not necessarily the current market value.

The advantage of the straight-line method is its simplicity; a disadvantage is it penalizes the later years when repairs are heaviest.

B. The Declining Balance Method

The declining balance formula is:

(8–10) $d = b \times r$

where $d =$ depreciation amount per period

$b =$ book value of the preceding period

$r =$ depreciation rate

The depreciation rate may be any percent up to twice the straight-line rate; the normal is $1\frac{1}{4}$ to $1\frac{1}{2}$ times the straight-line rate.

Suppose the Scott Company decided on a rate of 20%. Then a depreciation schedule for the company car would be as shown in Figure 8–9 (the formula calculations are shown in parentheses).

The declining balance method results in high depreciation in the early life of the asset, an advantage for income tax purposes. A disadvantage is that this is opposite to the probable maintenance and repair costs.

Figure 8–9

Year	Depreciation	Accumulated Depreciation	Book Value
0	—	—	$5,000.00
1	$1,000 ($5,000 × 0.20)	$1,000.00	4,000.00
2	800 ($4,000 × 0.20)	1,800.00	3,200.00
3	640 ($3,200 × 0.20)	2,440.00	2,560.00
4	512 ($2,560 × 0.20)	2,952.00	2,048.00
5	409.60 ($2,048 × 0.20)	3,361.60	1,638.40
6	327.68 ($1,638.40 × 0.20)	3,689.28	1,310.72

C. The Sum-of-the-Years-Digits Method

In the previous two formulas, the rate per period remained constant. In the sum-of-the-years-digits method, the rate is different for each period. The formula for this method is:

$$(8–11) \qquad\qquad d = (c - s) \times r$$

where r is a fraction determined as follows: The denominator is the sum of the digits representing the useful life of the asset and the numerator is the number of years of useful life remaining at the beginning of the year for which the computation is made.* To illustrate, the Scott Company car has a useful life of six years, hence the denominator is $1 + 2 + 3 + 4 + 5 + 6 = 21$. The number of years of useful life remaining at the beginning of each year is 6, 5, 4, 3, 2, 1, hence the fractions used are $\frac{6}{21}, \frac{5}{21}, \frac{4}{21}, \frac{3}{21}, \frac{2}{21}, \frac{1}{21}$. The depreciation schedule is as follows (the formula calculations are in parentheses):

Figure 8–10

Year	Depreciation	Accumulated Depreciation	Book Value
0	—	—	$5,000
1	$1,200 ($4,200 × $\frac{6}{21}$)	$1,200	3,800
2	1,000 ($4,200 × $\frac{5}{21}$)	2,200	2,800
3	800 ($4,200 × $\frac{4}{21}$)	3,000	2,000
4	600 ($4,200 × $\frac{3}{21}$)	3,600	1,400
5	400 ($4,200 × $\frac{2}{21}$)	4,000	1,000
6	200 ($4,200 × $\frac{1}{21}$)	4,200	800

* The denominator may also be found using the formula $\frac{n(n+1)}{2}$ where $n =$ number of years. This formula is useful when the useful life of the asset is a large number of years.

The sum-of-the-years-digits method has the same advantages and disadvantages as the declining balance method.

D. Comparison of the Methods

A visual comparison of the three methods can be made by graphing their depreciation schedules on the same graph. See Figures 8–11 and 8–12.

Figure 8–11

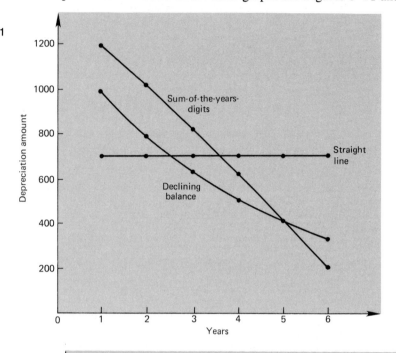

Figure 8–12

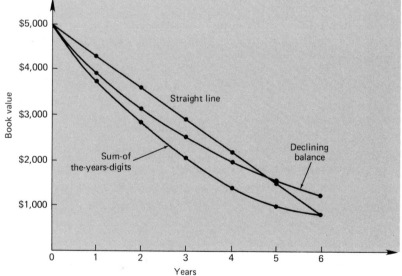

E. Additional First-Year Allowance

For special kinds of rapidly depreciating assets, such as machinery and transportation equipment, the Internal Revenue Service permits an additional first-year depreciation allowance of 20%. This allowance is in addition to the regular depreciation and is subject to the following conditions:

1. The allowance must be taken in the first year.
2. The asset must have a useful life of at least six years.
3. The asset must be tangible personal property for use in business or for production of income.
4. The allowance is limited to $10,000 on separate returns, $20,000 on joint returns.

The first-year allowance reduces the cost of the asset in the calculation of the regular depreciation amount. In the case of the Scott Company car, the first-year allowance is $5,000 \times 0.20 = $1,000$. If the straight-line depreciation method is used, then:

$$d = \frac{\$4,000 - \$800}{6}$$

$$= \$533.33$$

and the depreciation schedule is shown in Figure 8–13.

Figure 8–13

Year	Depreciation	Accumulated Depreciation	Book Value
0	—	—	$5,000.00
1	$1,533.33 ($1,000 + $533.33)	$1,533.33	3,466.67
2	533.33	2,066.66	2,933.34
3	533.33	2,599.99	2,400.01
4	533.33	3,133.32	1,866.68
5	533.33	3,666.65	1,333.35
6	533.35*	4,200.00	800.00

* The additional $0.02 compensates for rounding in the calculation of d.

A comparison of the regular straight-line method and the formula using the additional first-year allowance is shown in Figures 8–14 and 8–15.

Figure 8–14

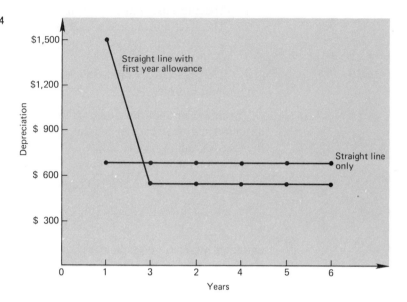

Figure 8–15

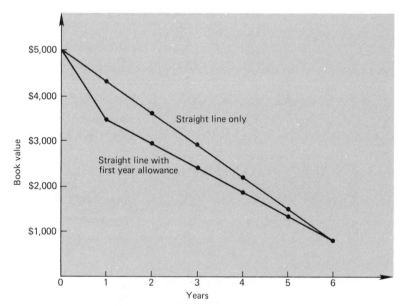

1. The Madison Manufacturing Company purchased a new conveyor for $10,000. The useful life of the conveyor is ten years and its salvage value is $1,000. Find the amount of depreciation per year using the straight-line method.

2. Prepare a depreciation schedule for the conveyor in problem 1 (see Figure 8–8).

3. Halpen Enterprises purchased some tooling equipment for $23,500. The salvage value of the equipment is $4,000 and its useful life is eight years. Find the amount of depreciation per year using the straight-line method.

4. Prepare a depreciation schedule for the tooling equipment in problem 3 (see Figure 8–8).

5. Processing equipment at Central Food Packers with an initial purchase cost of $18,000 has a useful life of six years. The equipment is depreciated at 20% per year using the declining balance method. Prepare a depreciation schedule for the equipment (see Figure 8–9).

6. The Carson Company uses the declining balance method at a rate of 25% to depreciate its equipment. If the purchase price of the equipment is $52,000 and the useful life is eight years, prepare a depreciation schedule for the equipment (see Figure 8–9).

7. Nelson Meat Packers purchased new meat cutting equipment for $36,000. The useful life of the equipment is eight years. Prepare a depreciation schedule for the equipment using a depreciation rate of 15% and the declining balance method.

8. The Prescott Company purchased an automobile for $6,000. The salvage value of the car is $1,000, and its useful life is five years. Prepare a depreciation schedule for the car using the sum-of-the-years-digits method (see Figure 8–10).

9. A new platform loader at Holden Industries cost $16,000 and has a useful life of eight years. If the salvage value of the loader is $2,000, prepare a depreciation schedule for the loader using the sum-of-the-years-digits method (see Figure 8–10).

10. Use the sum-of-the-years-digits method to prepare a depreciation schedule for a $25,000 piece of machinery at Holden Industries, if the machinery has a useful life of six years and salvage value of $5,000.

11. A packing machine costs $10,000, has a salvage value of $4,000 and a useful life of five years. Prepare depreciation schedules for the machine using (a) the straight-line method, (b) the declining balance method with $r = 25\%$, and (c) the sum-of-the-years-digits method. Draw a graph comparing the book value of the machine over its useful life under the three methods of depreciation (see Figure 8–12).

12. Repeat problem 11 for a piece of machinery that costs $8,000, has a useful life of four years, and salvage value $2,000. Use a depreciation rate of 30% in the declining balance method.

13. A crane purchased by the Decker Construction Company cost $15,000 and has a useful life of eight years. Its salvage value is $5,000. Use the first-year depreciation allowance of 20% and the straight-line method and prepare a depreciation schedule for the crane.

14. Use the declining balance method with $r = 15\%$ and prepare a depreciation schedule for the crane in problem 13, using the first-year depreciation allowance of 20%.

15. Use the sum-of-the-years-digits method and the first-year depreciation allowance of 20% and prepare a depreciation schedule for the crane in problem 13.

Section 8.7 Overhead

Overhead, as previously defined, is a general term for operating expenses such as rent, utilities, maintenance, etc. Since overhead contributes to the cost of doing business, it must be kept to a minimum. One mechanism for controlling overhead is to allocate a portion of the total amount to each department or subunit of the company. If this distribution is equitable, management will have a standard to measure the efficiency of each department or subunit. Two methods of distribution widely used are (1) allocation according to floor space and (2) allocation according to net sales.

Example 1

The Banning Corporation distributed its total overhead expense of $24,000 according to the square feet of floor space occupied by each department. Determine the distribution if the floor space of each department is as follows:

Department		Ratio to Total Space
Offices	1,500	$\dfrac{1,500}{30,000} = \dfrac{1}{20}$
Accounting	2,500	$\dfrac{2,500}{30,000} = \dfrac{1}{12}$
Production	14,000	$\dfrac{14,000}{30,000} = \dfrac{7}{15}$
Warehouse	12,000	$\dfrac{12,000}{30,000} = \dfrac{2}{5}$
Total	30,000	

Solution:

The allocation is an application of the basic percentage equation $P = BR$ with $P =$ allocation amount, $B = \$24,000$, and $R =$ ratio of department space to total space.

$$\text{Office Allocation} \quad = \$24{,}000 \times \frac{1}{20} = \$1{,}200$$

$$\text{Accounting Allocation} = \$24{,}000 \times \frac{1}{12} = \$2{,}000$$

$$\text{Production Allocation} = \$24{,}000 \times \frac{7}{15} = \$11{,}200$$

$$\text{Warehouse Allocation} = \$24{,}000 \times \frac{2}{5} = \$9{,}600$$

As a check, the sum of the departmental allocations should equal the total overhead expense (i.e., $\$1{,}200 + \$2{,}000 + \$11{,}200 + \$9{,}600 = \$24{,}000$).

A second method of distributing overhead is by net sales.

Example 2

The Lombard Company had monthly net sales in its departments as follows:

Department		Ratio to Total Sales
Appliances	$ 1,000	$\dfrac{1{,}000}{12{,}000} = \dfrac{1}{12}$
Automotive	2,800	$\dfrac{2{,}800}{12{,}000} = \dfrac{7}{30}$
Ladies' Wear	6,200	$\dfrac{6{,}200}{12{,}000} = \dfrac{31}{60}$
Men's Wear	1,200	$\dfrac{1{,}200}{12{,}000} = \dfrac{1}{10}$
Toys	800	$\dfrac{800}{12{,}000} = \dfrac{1}{15}$
	$12,000	

If the month's overhead of $2,400 is distributed according to net sales, what was the allocation to each department?

Solution:

$P = ?$, $B = \$2{,}400$, $R =$ ratio to total net sales

$$\text{Appliances Allocation} \ = \$2{,}400 \times \frac{1}{12} = \$200$$

$$\text{Automotive Allocation} = \$2{,}400 \times \frac{7}{30} = \$560$$

$$\text{Ladies' Wear} \qquad = \$2{,}400 \times \frac{31}{60} = \$1{,}240$$

$$\text{Men's Wear} \qquad = \$2{,}400 \times \frac{1}{10} = \$240$$

$$\text{Toys} \qquad = \$2{,}400 \times \frac{1}{15} = \$160$$

Check: $\$200 + \$560 + \$1{,}240 + \$240 + \$160 = \$2{,}400.$

1. The Stratford Corporation distributed its overhead expense of $32,000 according to the floor space occupied by each department. Determine the distribution of overhead if the floor space of each department is as follows:

Department	Floor Space	Ratio to Total Floor Space
Offices	1,000	$\dfrac{1,000}{40,000} = \dfrac{1}{40}$
Accounting	3,000	$\dfrac{3,000}{40,000} = \dfrac{3}{40}$
Production	16,000	$\dfrac{16,000}{40,000} = \dfrac{2}{5}$
Warehouse	20,000	$\dfrac{20,000}{40,000} = \dfrac{1}{2}$
Total	40,000	

2. The floor space of the Nelson Company is distributed as follows:

Department	Floor Space	Ratio to Total Floor Space
Offices	1,400	$\dfrac{1,400}{8,000} = \dfrac{7}{40}$
Accounting	1,300	$\dfrac{1,300}{8,000} = \dfrac{13}{80}$
Showroom	2,200	$\dfrac{2,200}{8,000} = \dfrac{11}{40}$
Maintenance	900	$\dfrac{900}{8,000} = \dfrac{9}{80}$
Warehouse	2,200	$\dfrac{2,200}{8,000} = \dfrac{11}{40}$

Determine the distribution of the company's overhead of $47,000 if the overhead is distributed according to the floor space occupied by each department.

3. For the month of June, the departmental net sales at the Parker Company were as follows:

Department		Ratio to Total Sales
Clothing	$ 4,900	$\dfrac{4,900}{16,000} = \dfrac{49}{160}$
Hardware	2,500	$\dfrac{2,500}{16,000} = \dfrac{5}{32}$
Appliances	3,200	$\dfrac{3,200}{16,000} = \dfrac{1}{5}$

Toys	1,300	$\dfrac{1,300}{16,000} = \dfrac{13}{160}$
Home Furnishings	4,100	$\dfrac{4,100}{16,000} = \dfrac{41}{160}$
Total	$16,000	

The total overhead for the month of June was $3,400. If the overhead is distributed according to net sales, find the allocation to each department.

4. The total overhead at Braxton Industries for the month of February was $4,850. The net sales for the month totaled $50,000, distributed among the departments as follows:

Department		Ratio to Total Sales
Garden Supplies	$ 6,250	$\dfrac{6,250}{50,000} = \dfrac{1}{8}$
Glassware	8,450	$\dfrac{8,450}{50,000} = \dfrac{169}{1,000}$
Hardware	12,100	$\dfrac{12,100}{50,000} = \dfrac{121}{500}$
Carpets	16,200	$\dfrac{16,200}{50,000} = \dfrac{81}{250}$
Lighting	7,000	$\dfrac{7,000}{50,000} = \dfrac{7}{50}$
Total	$50,000	

If the month's overhead was distributed according to net sales, what was the allocation to each department?

5. The W. T. Southerd Company reported total overhead of $3,250 for the month of November. The net sales for November were $40,000, distributed as follows:

Department	Net Sales
Office Supplies	$11,200
Furnishings	7,700
Floor Coverings	5,200
Office Machines	15,900
Total	$40,000

Find the overhead allocation to each department, if the distribution is made according to net sales.

6. The floor space of Frederick's, Inc., is distributed as follows:

Department	Floor Space
Offices	1,200
Accounting	1,600
Home Furnishings	3,200
Hardware	2,100
Paints	1,800
Draperies	2,700
Carpets	2,400
Total	15,000

Determine the distribution of the company's overhead of $42,500 if it is distributed according to the floor space occupied by each department.

7. Elco Enterprises reported total overhead of $5,620 for the month of June. The net sales for June were $65,000, distributed as follows: office equipment, $17,500; business forms, $3,500; furnishings, $23,200; art supplies, $4,700; and chemicals, $16,100. The month's overhead was distributed according to net sales. Prepare a table showing the ratio of the net sales of each department to total net sales and the allocation of overhead to each department.

8. The floor space at Prindles, Inc., is distributed as follows: accounting, 1,400; offices, 900; men's clothing, 2,600; women's clothing, 3,600; children's wear, 1,800; and shoes, 1,000. Prepare a table showing the ratio of the floor space of each department to total floor space and the allocation of the company's overhead of $54,200 to each department if the overhead is distributed according to floor space.

3 Finance

9

Simple Interest

Chapter Objectives for Chapter 9

I. Learn the meaning of the following terms:

A. *Interest*, 242
B. *Time Fraction*, 246
C. *Exact Time*, 247
D. *Ordinary Time*, 247
E. *Exact Interest-Ordinary Interest*, 250
F. *Maturity Value*, 258
G. *Present Value*, 260

II. Understand:

A. The formula for simple interest and its variations, 243–244
B. The difference between exact time and ordinary time, 247
C. The difference between ordinary interest and exact interest, 250
D. The formulas for maturity value and present value, 258, 260

III. Apply:

A. The simple interest formula to solve problems involving loans, 243–245, 251–252
B. The 6%-60-day method to compute simple interest, 254
C. The formulas for maturity value and present value for simple interest loans, 258, 260

Introduction

Money paid for the use of money is called **interest.** Much of the American economy depends on keeping in circulation money that people have but temporarily do not need. The charge for use of this money is called interest.

Nearly everyone either pays or receives interest at some point during their lifetime. We receive interest from savings accounts or bonds because we in effect loan our money for others to use. On the other hand, in the mortgage payments for our house, in the monthly payments for our automobile, or in our charge account at the department store we are borrowing money, and our payments include charges for interest.

Businesses and governmental agencies frequently need money to finance special projects, thus loans are obtained from banks, life insurance companies, or by the issuance of bonds. In each case interest is paid to the party supplying the money.

In this chapter we begin a study of the kinds of interest and the methods used to determine interest for a given loan or investment.

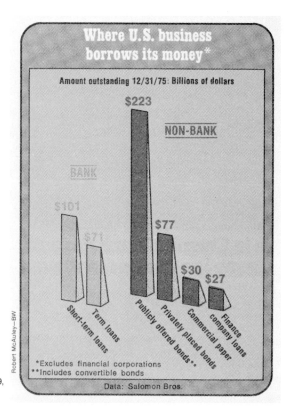

Reprinted from *Business Week*, April 19, 1976, page 69.

Section **9.2** **Simple Interest**

Simple interest is an annual percentage of the amount borrowed or invested. The formula for simple interest is a modification of the basic percentage formula. The equation is:

(9–1) $I = Prt$

where I = interest

   P = principal, the amount of money borrowed or invested

   r = rate

   t = the length of time (in years) the principal is borrowed or invested

Thus simple interest is a function of three variables—principal, rate, and time. The principal is expressed in dollars, the rate in percent, and the time in years.

Example 1

A man borrows $500 for 2 years at a simple interest rate of 8%. (See Figure 9–1.) How much interest does he pay?

Solution:

$I = ?, P = \$500, r = 8\%, t = 2$. Using Formula (9–1),

$$I = Prt$$

$$= \$500 \times \frac{8}{100} \times 2$$

$$= \$80$$

The interest charge is $80. Note that the rate is expressed as a fraction rather than a decimal. This permits the use of the arithmetic of fractions to simplify the computation; that is,

$$\$500 \times \frac{8}{100} \times 2 = \$\overset{5}{\cancel{500}} \times \frac{8}{\cancel{100}} \times 2 = \$80$$

Example 2

What is the interest on a $2,800 loan for 8 months at 7¼% simple interest?

Solution:

$I = ?, P = \$2,800, r = 7\frac{1}{4}\% = \frac{29}{400}, t = \frac{8}{12}$. Using Formula (9–1),

$$I = Prt$$

$$= \$2,800 \times \frac{29}{400} \times \frac{8}{12}$$

$$= \$135.33$$

The charge for interest is $135.33. Note that time is always expressed in years, hence the time fraction $\frac{8}{12}$ is used for 8 months.

In Formula (9–1), the interest I is the unknown. However, it may be necessary to solve for one of the other variables. From

$$I = Prt$$

(9–2) $\qquad P = \dfrac{I}{rt}$ [dividing both sides of (9–1) by rt]

(9–3) $\qquad r = \dfrac{I}{Pt}$ [dividing both sides of (9–1) by Pt]

(9–4) $\qquad t = \dfrac{I}{Pr}$ [dividing both sides of (9–1) by Pr]

Example 3

At a simple interest rate of $6\frac{1}{2}\%$, how much money would one have to invest for one year to earn \$400 in interest?

Solution:

$I = \$400$, $P = ?$, $r = 6\frac{1}{4}\%$, $t = 1$. Using Formula (9–2),

$$\begin{aligned} P &= \frac{I}{rt} \\[2mm] &= \frac{\$400}{\frac{1}{16} \cdot 1} \qquad (6\frac{1}{4}\% = \frac{25}{400} = \frac{1}{16}) \\[2mm] &= \frac{\$400}{\frac{1}{16}} \\[2mm] &= \$400 \times \frac{16}{1} \\[2mm] &= \$6,400 \end{aligned}$$

Example 4

Find the simple interest rate necessary for \$3,000 to earn \$270 interest in 9 months.

Solution:

$I = \$270$, $P = \$3,000$, $r = ?$, $t = \frac{9}{12}$. Using Formula (9–3),

$$\begin{aligned} r &= \frac{I}{Pt} \\[2mm] &= \frac{\$270}{\$3,000 \times \frac{9}{12}} \\[2mm] &= \frac{\$270}{\$2,250} \\[2mm] &= 0.12 \\[2mm] &= 12\% \end{aligned}$$

Example 5

How long must \$1,800 be invested to earn \$72 in interest if the simple interest rate is 6%?

Solution:

$I = \$72$, $P = \$1,800$, $r = 6\%$, $t = ?$ Using Formula (9–4),

$$t = \frac{I}{Pr}$$

$$= \frac{\$72}{\$1,800 \times \dfrac{6}{100}}$$

$$= \frac{72}{108}$$

$$= \frac{2}{3} \text{ years or 8 months}$$

Exercises for Section 9.2

In problems 1–12, solve the formula $I = Prt$ for the appropriate variable and compute the value of the indicated quantity.

1. $I = \$1,500$, $r = 5\%$, $t = 2$; find P.

2. $r = 7\%$, $P = \$4,000$, $I = \$720$; find t.

3. $P = \$8,000$, $I = \$1,280$, $t = 2$; find r.

4. $P = \$6,000$, $r = 7\%$, $t = 5$; find I.

5. $I = \$975$, $r = 6.5\%$, $t = 2$; find P.

6. $r = 9\%$, $P = \$1,250$, $I = \$56.25$; find t.

7. $P = \$1,600$, $I = \$216$, $t = 2$; find r.

8. $P = \$2,000$, $r = 7\frac{1}{4}\%$, $t = 9$ months; find I.

9. $I = \$500$, $r = 6\%$, $t = 2$; find P.

10. $I = \$281.25$, $P = \$2,250$, $t = 2$; find r.

11. $I = \$483$, $P = \$2,800$, $r = 5\frac{3}{4}\%$, find t.

12. $P = \$3,500$, $r = 7\frac{1}{4}\%$, $t = 8$ months; find I.

13. Bob Parker borrowed \$1,200 for four years at a simple interest rate of 6%. How much interest will Bob pay for the loan?

14. Find the interest paid for a loan of \$1,800 for three years at 9% simple interest.

15. What is the interest on a \$1,500 loan for six months at $8\frac{3}{4}\%$ simple interest?

16. Myra Williams borrowed $2,400 for thirty months at a simple interest rate of 6½%. How much interest will she pay for the loan?

17. Sue Cunningham owns a $5,000 bond that pays 5¼% simple interest. How much does she receive quarterly from the bond?

18. During the first quarter of last year, Bill Foster had $3,250 in his savings account. How much interest did he receive at the end of the quarter if the interest rate is 5¾%?

19. At an interest rate of 7%, how much money would have to be invested in order to earn $700 in two years?

20. Mel Phillips wishes to invest $5,000 for one year. Find the interest rate necessary for him to earn $300 in interest from his investment.

21. Brenda Jones invested $6,000 at 8% interest. How long will it take for her investment to earn $1,920?

22. In order to earn $85 in eight months, how much money would have to be invested at 8½% interest?

23. Find the simple interest rate necessary for $2,500 to earn $243.75 in eighteen months.

24. How long will it take $1,300 invested at 7½% to earn $48.75 in interest?

25. Wilma Smith arranged for a loan of $7,500 for four and one-half years at 6¾% interest. How much interest will she pay?

26. Brett Walker needs to borrow $5,000 to pay for remodeling his store. If the rate of interest Brett must pay is 8¼% and if he is not willing to pay more than $1,000 in interest, can he borrow the money for two years? Can he borrow it for three years?

27. Mr. Peters needs to borrow $8,000 for two years. If he cannot pay more than $1,000 in interest, and if the least interest rate at which he can borrow the money is 6¾%, can he obtain the loan?

28. The new owner of a small business wishes to borrow some money for operating capital. At an interest rate of 6¼%, how much can she borrow for three years and not pay more than $1,200 in interest?

29. Mrs. Richardson has arranged to loan $5,000 to a friend for four years. In order to receive at least $1,500 in interest, what is the smallest interest rate that she can charge?

Section **9.3** **Time**

Time is measured in years in the simple interest formula, hence a **time fraction** is used in problems where the term of the loan is specified in months (See Examples 2 and 4 of Section 9.2). In this time fraction, the numerator consists of the term of the loan in months, and the denominator consists of the number of months in a year. That is,

(9–5)
$$t = \frac{\text{term of the loan in months}}{\text{number of months in a year}}$$

If the term of a loan is specified in days, a time fraction again is necessary. In this case,

(9–6)
$$t = \frac{\text{term of the loan in days}}{\text{number of days in a year}}$$

When time is measured in days, Equation (9–6) is complicated by the use of two calendars, an astronomical calendar and a financial calendar.

The astronomical calendar, called **exact time,** is based on the revolution of the earth around the sun. One orbit requires 365¼ days, hence our year consists of 365 days with a leap year of 366 days every fourth year.* The year is divided into months of 28 (29), 30, or 31 days, irregularly spaced.

The financial calendar, called **ordinary time** or **Banker's year,** eliminates the irregularities of the astronomical calendar by defining a year to consist of twelve months of 30 days per month. A year in ordinary time thus consists of 360 days. Ordinary time is a calendar of convenience; it is true that 360 days is nearly an exact year, but more importantly, 360 is a multiple of numbers such as 60 and 90, frequently the term of a loan.

In most interest transactions, if the term of the loan is expressed in days, the numerator of the time fraction will be exact time. Calculation of exact time may be simplified by the use of Appendix A—The Number of Each Day, found in the appendix. The following examples illustrate the use of this table in finding exact time. Unless specified, the years are non-leap years.

The Equibank, Philadelphia

* Leap years account for the ¼ day accumulation each year, with the extra day added to the month of February (February 29). Leap years occur on years divisible by 4; 1972 and 1976 were leap years. Likewise, 1980, 1984, 1988, etc., will be leap years.

Example 1

Using exact time, find the number of days from May 14 to September 20 of the same year.*

Solution:

Using Appendix A and subtracting the first date from the second,

Date	Day
September 20 =	263
May 14 =	−134
	129

There are 129 days from May 14 to September 20.

Example 2

Find the exact number of days from January 4, 1976 to April 30, 1976.

Solution:

The year 1976 is a leap year, thus

Date	Day
April 30, 1976 =	121
January 4, 1976 =	− 4
	117

Example 3

Find the number of days from November 14, 1976 to January 10, 1977, using exact time.

Solution:

Because this period includes two different years, the interval must be separated in 1976 time and 1977 time, then the solutions added to obtain the total time.

Date	Day
December 31, 1976 =	365
November 14, 1976 =	−318
	47
January 10, 1977 =	+ 10
	57

There are 57 days from November 14, 1976 to January 10, 1977.

---

* An interest-bearing document begins to earn interest on the day following its execution and continues to earn interest until the day it is paid. Thus in counting the days between two dates, the last day is counted, but the first is not.

Example 4

A loan is executed on June 10 for a term of six months. Find the due date of the loan using exact time.

Solution:

Since the term of the loan is stated in months, six months from June 10 is December 10. This is true using either exact time or ordinary time.

One exception to the reasoning of the last example occurs when the term of a loan ends on a day that does not exist. For instance, a one-month loan executed on March 31 would be due on April 30, since there is no April 31.

Example 5

A loan is executed on June 10 for 180 days. Find the due date of the loan using exact time.

Solution:

The term of the loan is in days, hence:

$$\begin{array}{rl} \textit{Date} & \textit{Day} \\ \text{June 10} \longrightarrow & 161 \\ & +180 \ \text{days} \\ \hline \text{December 7} \longleftarrow & 341 \end{array}$$

When the term of a loan is in days, the numerator of the time fraction is usually exact time, but depending on the loan, the denominator may be either exact time or ordinary time. That is, there are two possibilities:*

$$(9\text{--}7) \qquad\qquad t = \frac{\text{exact time}}{365}$$

$$(9\text{--}8) \qquad\qquad t = \frac{\text{exact time}}{360}$$

In time fraction (9–7) both numerator and denominator are in exact time, while in time fraction (9–8) the numerator is in exact time and the denominator is in ordinary time. In the next section the use of these time fractions in solving simple interest problems will be discussed.

Exercises for Section 9.3   In problems 1–10, find the number of days from the first date to the second using (a) exact time and (b) ordinary time. Use the table in the appendix when computing exact time.

1. March 6, 1976 to October 12, 1976

2. June 19, 1976 to December 27, 1976

---

* Actually, there are two additional possibilities, $\dfrac{\text{ordinary time}}{365}$ and $\dfrac{\text{ordinary time}}{360}$, but these are infrequently used.

3. April 24, 1976 to August 15, 1976

4. May 12, 1976 to November 2, 1976

5. February 6, 1977 to July 15, 1977

6. January 19, 1977 to September 12, 1977

7. April 18, 1976 to January 24, 1977

8. June 14, 1976 to February 15, 1977

9. November 18, 1975 to September 13, 1976

10. August 6, 1975 to May 3, 1976

In problems 11–20, find the due date of a loan executed on the given date for the given term, using (a) exact time and (b) ordinary time.

11. May 24, 3 months

12. September 15, 8 months

13. August 21, 60 days

14. March 6, 180 days

15. February 10, 1977, 90 days

16. January 14, 1976, 60 days

17. February 18, 1976, 180 days

18. January 7, 1977, 90 days

19. November 18, 1975, 180 days

20. December 16, 1976, 90 days

Section 9.4 Exact Interest—Ordinary Interest

Interest calculations using time fraction (9–7) are called **exact interest.** Exact interest is used by the federal government and by federal reserve banks in their transactions with member banks. Interest calculations using time fraction (9–8) are called **ordinary interest, Banker's interest,** or **Banker's rule.** Ordinary interest is used by most commercial institutions because it generates more interest. This is illustrated by the following example.

Example 1

A loan for $500 is executed on January 10 at a simple interest rate of 6% and is due on February 20. Calculate the interest using (a) exact interest and (b) ordinary interest.

Solution:

Using Appendix A, the exact time from January 10 to February 20 is 41 days. Thus, with $P = \$500$ and $r = 6\%$:

a. $I = Prt$

$= \$500 \times \dfrac{6}{100} \times \dfrac{41}{365}$

$= \$3.37$

b. $I = Prt$

$= \$500 \times \dfrac{6}{100} \times \dfrac{41}{360}$

$= \$3.42$

In this case ordinary interest earned $0.05 more than exact interest.

The following are additional examples of exact and ordinary interest.

Example 2

Find the exact interest on $3,000 at 6¾% from August 12 to December 5.

Solution:

The exact time from August 12 to December 5 is 115 days. Thus $I = ?$, $P = \$3,000$, $r = 6\frac{3}{4}\% = \dfrac{27}{400}$, $t = \dfrac{115}{365}$.

$$I = Prt$$

$$= \$3,000 \times \dfrac{27}{400} \times \dfrac{115}{365}$$

$$= \$63.80$$

Example 3

A loan of $1,200 for 90 days earned ordinary interest in the amount of $24. What was the interest rate?

Solution:

$P = \$1,200$, $I = \$24$, $r = ?$, $t = \dfrac{90}{360} = \dfrac{1}{4}$.

$$r = \dfrac{I}{Pt}$$

$$= \dfrac{24}{\$1,200 \times \dfrac{1}{4}}$$

$$= 0.08$$

$$= 8\%$$

Example 4

How many days would it take to earn $300 ordinary interest on $20,000 invested at 5%?

Solution:

$$I = \$300,\ P = \$20,000,\ r = \frac{5}{100},\ t = \frac{x}{360}.$$

$$t = \frac{I}{Pr}$$

$$\frac{x}{360} = \frac{\$300}{\$20,000 \cdot \dfrac{5}{100}}$$

$$\frac{x}{360} = \frac{\$300}{\$1,000}$$

$$\frac{x}{360} = \frac{3}{10}$$

$$10x = 1,080 \qquad \text{(cross multiplying)}$$

$$x = 108 \text{ days}$$

Exercises for Section 9.4

In problems 1–15, find (a) the exact interest and (b) the ordinary interest for the given loans. (Always assume non-leap years.)

1. $7,500 at 6% for 90 days.

2. $4,500 at 7% for 180 days.

3. $3,200 at 8¼% for 60 days.

4. $2,700 at 9½% for 180 days.

5. $5,600 at 8¾% for 45 days.

6. $8,200 at 7¾% for 65 days.

7. $2,000 at 7½% from May 15 to August 13.

8. $6,200 at 10¼% from July 8 to September 6.

9. $3,500 at 9¾% from February 4 to August 3.

10. $9,200 at 10½% from January 18 to August 6.

11. $7,800 at 6¾% from September 26 to February 3.

12. $5,700 at 8½% from November 12 to July 10.

13. $7,450 at 9½% from October 23 to February 15.

14. $8,230 at 10¾% from August 18 to January 20.

15. $12,720 at 9¼% from December 5 to February 18.

In problems 16–25, find the interest rate for the given loans.

16. $1,000 earns $35 ordinary interest in 180 days.

17. $2,400 earns $32 ordinary interest in 60 days.

18. $4,500 earns $99.86 exact interest in 90 days.

19. $5,700 earns $112.44 exact interest in 120 days.

20. $2,800 earns $140 ordinary interest from March 15 to November 10.

21. $3,800 earns $140.39 ordinary interest from May 6 to September 23.

22. $6,400 earns $153.42 exact interest from November 11 to February 19.

23. $7,200 earns $300.33 exact interest from December 4 to July 2.

24. $5,200 earns $136.50 ordinary interest from October 28 to February 5.

25. $3,100 earns $151.34 ordinary interest from September 18 to March 27.

In problems 26–31, find the number of days necessary to earn the given amount of interest on the given loan.

26. $350 ordinary interest on $10,000 at 7%.

27. $37.50 ordinary interest on $2,500 at 9%.

28. $136.50 ordinary interest on $4,200 at 9¾%.

29. $452.38 exact interest on $8,600 at 8%.

30. $128.71 exact interest on $7,200 at 7¼%.

31. $330.82 exact interest on $9,200 at 8¾%.

In problems 32–39, an investment of P dollars yields the given amount of interest. Find P (round to the nearest dollar).

32. $80 ordinary interest in 180 days at 8%.

33. $60 ordinary interest in 60 days at 9%.

34. $94.93 exact interest in 90 days at 11%.

35. $57.53 exact interest in 120 days at 7%.

36. $41.25 ordinary interest at 7½% from May 6 to August 4.

37. $142.92 ordinary interest at 8¾% from September 5 to January 23.

38. $573.25 exact interest at 9¼% from July 22 to April 8.

39. $483.29 exact interest at 10½% from August 10 to June 6.

The 6%-60-Day Method

In an era of sophisticated electronic calculators, it is comforting that some interest calculations can be done just as quickly by hand, using a technique for computing ordinary simple interest known as the 6%-60-day method.

When the interest rate is 6% and the term of the loan is 60 days, then for any principal P:

$$I = Prt$$

$$= P \cdot \frac{6}{100} \cdot \frac{1}{6} \qquad (\frac{60}{360} = \frac{1}{6})$$

$$= P \cdot \frac{1}{100}$$

$$= \frac{P}{100}$$

But, division by 100 simply means moving the decimal point two places to the left, thus ordinary interest at 6% for 60 days is found by moving the decimal point of the principal two positions to the left.

Example 1

Find the ordinary interest on (a) $650, (b) $7,200, and (c) $1,450.80 at 6% for 60 days.

Solution:

a. Principal = $650.00

    Interest = $6.50

b. Principal = $7,200.00

    Interest = $72.00

c. Principal = $1,450.80

    Interest = $14.5080

           = $14.51

A. Variations in Time

Variations of the 6%-60-day method utilize the fact that if two variables in the formula are fixed, then the third variable multiplied by a constant changes the interest by the same constant multiple. For example, the interest on a 60-day note is twice that of a 30-day note, all other things being equal. Likewise, the interest on a 12% note is twice that of a 6% note, and a $10,000 note earns twice the interest of a $5,000 note, again all other things being equal in the formula. This principle is utilized in the following examples.

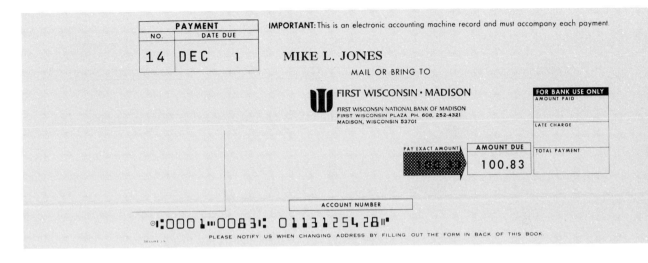

Example 1

Find the ordinary interest earned on $1,800 invested at 6% for 90 days.

Solution:

$$\text{Principal} = \$1,800.00$$

$$\text{Interest } 6\%\text{-}60 \text{ days} = \$18.00$$

$$6\%\text{-}30 \text{ days} = \$\ 9.00 \quad (30\text{-day interest} = \tfrac{1}{2} \times 60\text{-day interest})$$

$$6\%\text{-}90 \text{ days} = \$27.00 \quad (\text{adding interest})$$

Example 2

Find the ordinary interest on $2,400 at 6% for 186 days.

Solution:

$$\text{Principal} = \$2,400.00$$

$$\text{Interest } 6\%\text{-}\ 60 \text{ days} = \$24.00$$

$$6\%\text{-}\ \ 6 \text{ days} = \$\ 2.40 \quad (6\text{-day interest} = \tfrac{1}{10} \times 60\text{-day interest})$$

$$6\%\text{-}180 \text{ days} = \$72.00 \quad (180\text{-day interest} = 3 \times 60\text{-day interest})$$

$$6\%\text{-}186 \text{ days} = \$74.40 \quad (\text{adding last two lines})$$

B. Variations in Rate

Example 1

What is the ordinary interest on $400 at 12% for 60 days?

Solution:

$$\text{Principal} = \$400.00$$

Interest   6%-60 days = $4.00

12%-60 days = $8.00   (12% interest = $2 \times 6\%$ interest)

Example 2

Find the ordinary interest on $1,500 invested at 8% for 60 days.

Solution:

$$\text{Principal} = \$1,500.00$$

Interest 6%-60 days = $15.00

2%-60 days = $ 5.00   (2% interest = $\frac{1}{3} \times 6\%$ interest)

8%-60 days = $20.00   (adding last two lines)

C. Variations in Time and Rate

Example 1

How much will the ordinary interest be on $1,000 invested at 9% for 120 days?

Solution:

$$\text{Principal} = \$1,000.00$$

Interest 6%- 60 days = $10.00

6%-120 days = $20.00   (120-day interest = 2×60-day interest)

3%-120 days = $10.00   (3% interest = $\frac{1}{2} \times 6\%$ interest)

9%-120 days = $30.00   (adding last two lines)

Example 2

Find the ordinary interest on $600 invested at 18% for 30 days.

Solution:

$$\text{Principal} = \$600.00$$

Interest   6%-60 days = $6.00

6%-30 days = $3.00   (30-day interest = $\frac{1}{2} \times 60$-day interest)

18%-30 days = $9.00   (18% interest = $3 \times 6\%$ interest)

The advantage of the 6%-60-day method is that the formula reduces to multiplying the principal by $\frac{1}{100}$ or 1%. There are other combinations of rate and time that result in the same fraction. For example, if $r = 8\%$ and $t = 45$ days:

$$I = Prt$$

$$= P \times \frac{8}{100} \times \frac{45}{360}$$

$$= P \times \frac{1}{100}$$

Other common variations of rate and time whose product is $\frac{1}{100}$ are summarized in Table 9–1:

Table 9–1

r	t	rt
4 %	90 days	$\frac{1}{100}$
$4\frac{1}{2}\%$	80 days	$\frac{1}{100}$
6 %	60 days	$\frac{1}{100}$
8 %	45 days	$\frac{1}{100}$
10 %	36 days	$\frac{1}{100}$
12 %	30 days	$\frac{1}{100}$

Problems with any of these combinations may be solved by moving the decimal point of the principal two places to the left.

Exercises for Section 9.5

In problems 1–30, use the 6%-60-day method, with appropriate variations, to compute the ordinary interest for the given loan.

1. $8,750 at 6% for 60 days
2. $12,400 at 6% for 60 days
3. $2,400 at 6% for 90 days
4. $5,620 at 6% for 180 days
5. $4,240 at 6% for 30 days
6. $3,200 at 6% for 120 days
7. $6,800 at 6% for 126 days
8. $7,200 at 6% for 36 days
9. $24,000 at 6% for 252 days

10. $16,400 at 6% for 192 days

11. $860 at 12% for 60 days

12. $1,640 at 12% for 60 days

13. $1,280 at 9% for 60 days

14. $1,860 at 9% for 60 days

15. $4,260 at 8% for 60 days

16. $3,600 at 8% for 60 days

17. $24,000 at 7% for 60 days

18. $42,000 at 5% for 60 days

19. $5,600 at 11% for 60 days

20. $3,000 at 10% for 60 days

21. $4,000 at 9% for 30 days

22. $8,400 at 8% for 90 days

23. $7,600 at 12% for 240 days

24. $1,620 at 7% for 120 days

25. $3,300 at 11% for 180 days

26. $5,400 at 10% for 150 days

27. $6,200 at 9% for 126 days

28. $4,800 at 11% for 192 days

29. $6,600 at 5% for 234 days

30. $1,320 at 7% for 114 days

Section **9.6** **Maturity Value—Present Value**

When a loan is repaid, the borrower pays the principal plus interest. This sum is called the **amount** or **maturity value.** In symbols:

(9–9) $$A = P + I$$

where

$$A = \text{amount or maturity value}$$

$$P = \text{principal}$$

$$I = \text{interest}$$

In Example 1 of Section 9.2, the maturity value is,

$$A = P + I$$
$$= \$500 + \$80$$
$$= \$580$$

Thus the borrower paid $580 at the end of two years. In Example 2 of Section 9.2,

$$A = P + I$$
$$= \$2,800 + \$135.33$$
$$= \$2,935.33$$

The maturity value can be expressed by a different formula. We have:

$$A = P + I$$

and $\qquad I = Prt$

hence $\qquad A = P + Prt$ (Substitution)

(9–10) $\qquad A = P(1 + rt)$ (Distributive Property)

If the principal, rate, and time are given, the maturity value may be found directly from Formula (9–10).

Example 1

Find the maturity value of $1,280 invested at a simple interest rate of 7% for three years.

Solution:

$A = ?, P = \$1,280, r = 7\%, t = 3$. Using Formula (9–10),

$$A = P\,(1 + rt)$$
$$= \$1,280 \left(1 + \frac{7}{100} \times 3\right)$$
$$= \$1,280 \left(\frac{100}{100} + \frac{21}{100}\right)$$
$$= \$1,280 \left(\frac{121}{100}\right)$$
$$= \$1,548.80$$

The result can be checked using Formula (9–1) and (9–9).

$$I = Prt$$

$$= \$1{,}280 \times \frac{7}{100} \times 3$$

$$= \$268.80$$

$$A = P + I$$

$$= \$1{,}280 + \$268.80$$

$$= \$1{,}548.80$$

Example 2

What investment at 12% simple interest would have a maturity value of $500 in eighteen months?

Solution:

$A = \$500$, $P = ?$, $r = 12\%$, $t = 1\frac{1}{2}$. Formula (9–10) is used, but since P is the unknown, first (9–10) is solved for P.

$$A = P\,(1 + rt)$$

$$P(1 + rt) = A$$

(9–11) $\qquad P = \dfrac{A}{1 + rt}$ $\qquad$ [dividing both sides by $1 + rt$]

$$= \frac{\$500}{1 + \left(\dfrac{12}{100} \times \dfrac{3}{2}\right)}$$

$$= \frac{\$500}{\dfrac{100}{100} + \dfrac{18}{100}}$$

$$= \frac{\$500}{\dfrac{118}{100}}$$

$$= \$423.73$$

Formula (9–11) in Example 2 is an important variation of Formula (9–10). When Formula (9–11) is used, P is referred to as **present value.**

Formulas (9–10) and (9–11) solve opposite kinds of problems. Formula (9–10) answers the question, "What amount A results from the investment of principal P at rate r for time t?" On the other hand, Formula (9–11) answers the question, "What principal P invested at rate r for time t will result in amount A?"

The following are additional examples of finding present value.

Example 3

Find the present value of $2,000 at 6% for eight months.

Solution:

$$A = \$2,000, P = ?, r = 6\%, t = \frac{8}{12}$$

$$P = \frac{A}{1 + rt}$$

$$= \frac{\$2,000}{1 + \left(\frac{6}{100} \times \frac{8}{12}\right)}$$

$$= \frac{\$2,000}{1 + \frac{1}{25}}$$

$$= \frac{\$2,000}{\frac{26}{25}}$$

$$= \$1,923.08$$

Example 4

In one year John Sparks plans to modernize his shop by buying new equipment. He estimates it will require $6,000 for the new machines. In order to have the money to purchase the equipment, he wishes to make an investment that will yield $6,000 one year from now. At 8½% simple interest, how much must he invest now in order to have a total of $6,000 in one year?

Solution:

$$A = \$6,000, P = ?, r = 8\frac{1}{2}\%, t = 1$$

$$P = \frac{A}{1 + rt}$$

$$= \frac{\$6,000}{1 + \left(\frac{17}{200} \times 1\right)}$$

$$= \frac{\$6,000}{\frac{217}{200}}$$

$$= \$5,529.95$$

Exercises for Section 9.6

In problems 1–8, use the formula $A = P(1 + rt)$ to compute the maturity value A for the given value of P, r, and t.

1. $P = \$2,000$, $r = 5\%$, $t = 3$ years

2. $P = \$4,000$, $r = 8\%$, $t = 2$ years

3. $P = \$1,800$, $r = 7\frac{1}{2}\%$, $t = 4$ years

4. $P = \$2,400$, $r = 6\frac{1}{4}\%$, $t = 5$ years

5. $P = \$1,850$, $r = 7\frac{3}{4}\%$, $t = 6$ months

6. $P = \$3,250$, $r = 8\frac{1}{4}\%$, $t = 9$ months

7. $P = \$2,750$, $r = 9\frac{1}{4}\%$, $t = 8$ months

8. $P = \$2,250$, $r = 8\frac{3}{4}\%$, $t = 4$ months

In problems 9–16, use the formula $P = A/(1 + rt)$ to find the present value P for the given values of A, r, and t.

9. $A = \$2,280$, $r = 7\%$, $t = 2$ years

10. $A = \$1,270$, $r = 9\%$, $t = 3$ years

11. $A = \$4,275$, $r = 8\frac{1}{2}\%$, $t = 5$ years

12. $A = \$2,555$, $r = 9\frac{1}{4}\%$, $t = 3$ years

13. $A = \$2,922.50$, $r = 8\frac{3}{4}\%$, $t = 6$ months

14. $A = \$2,376.56$, $r = 7\frac{1}{2}\%$, $t = 9$ months

15. $A = \$2,000$, $r = 6\frac{3}{4}\%$, $t = 3$ months

16. $A = \$3,000$, $r = 9\frac{3}{4}\%$, $t = 4$ months

17. John Richards borrowed $1,500 from Leslie Small at 7% interest for three years. How much will John repay Leslie at the end of three years?

18. Dick Welch loaned his neighbor $2,000 for two years at 8¼% interest. What amount of money will the neighbor repay Dick at the end of two years?

19. Find the maturity value for a loan of $4,500 for four years at 7½% interest.

20. If $2,800 is borrowed for five years at 8½% interest, what is the maturity value of the loan?

21. Joan Parker is planning to spend $2,000 two years from now for a European tour. How much should she invest now at 8¾% interest in order to have the money for her trip?

22. In order to have $10,000 ten years from now for his son's education, how much should Bob Schmidt invest now at 8¼% interest?

23. What investment at $10\frac{1}{4}\%$ simple interest will have a maturity value of $4,000 in six years?

24. How much money should Arthur Samuels invest at $9\frac{1}{4}\%$ in order to have $6,000 four years from now?

25. Find the present value of $1,500 at $6\frac{1}{4}\%$ interest for nine months.

26. What is the present value of $2,400 at $8\frac{1}{2}\%$ interest for three months?

27. Bob Simmons borrowed $1,800 for eighteen months at $7\frac{3}{4}\%$ interest to pay for new equipment for his auto repair shop. What amount will he repay for the loan?

28. Paul Baker estimates that he will need $4,500 three years from now to replace some aging equipment in his grocery store. How much should he invest now at $9\frac{1}{4}\%$ interest in order to have the money?

29. Max Phillips plans to remodel his store two years from now. He estimates it will cost $3,000, and he has $2,500 to invest. Find the least interest rate at which he can invest his money so as to meet his remodeling expenses. (Hint: Solve the formula $A = P(1 + rt)$ for r.)

30. At an interest rate of $7\frac{1}{2}\%$, how long will it take for an investment of $4,200 to have a maturity value of $6,090? (Hint: Solve the formula $A = P(1 + rt)$ for t.)

31. June Porter has an opportunity to invest $2,400 at $8\frac{3}{4}\%$ interest. How long will it take for the maturity value of the investment to reach $3,240? (Hint: Solve $A = P(1 + rt)$ for t.)

32. At what rate of interest will $2,800 have a maturity value of $4,095 in five years? (Hint: Solve $A = P(1 + rt)$ for r.)

10

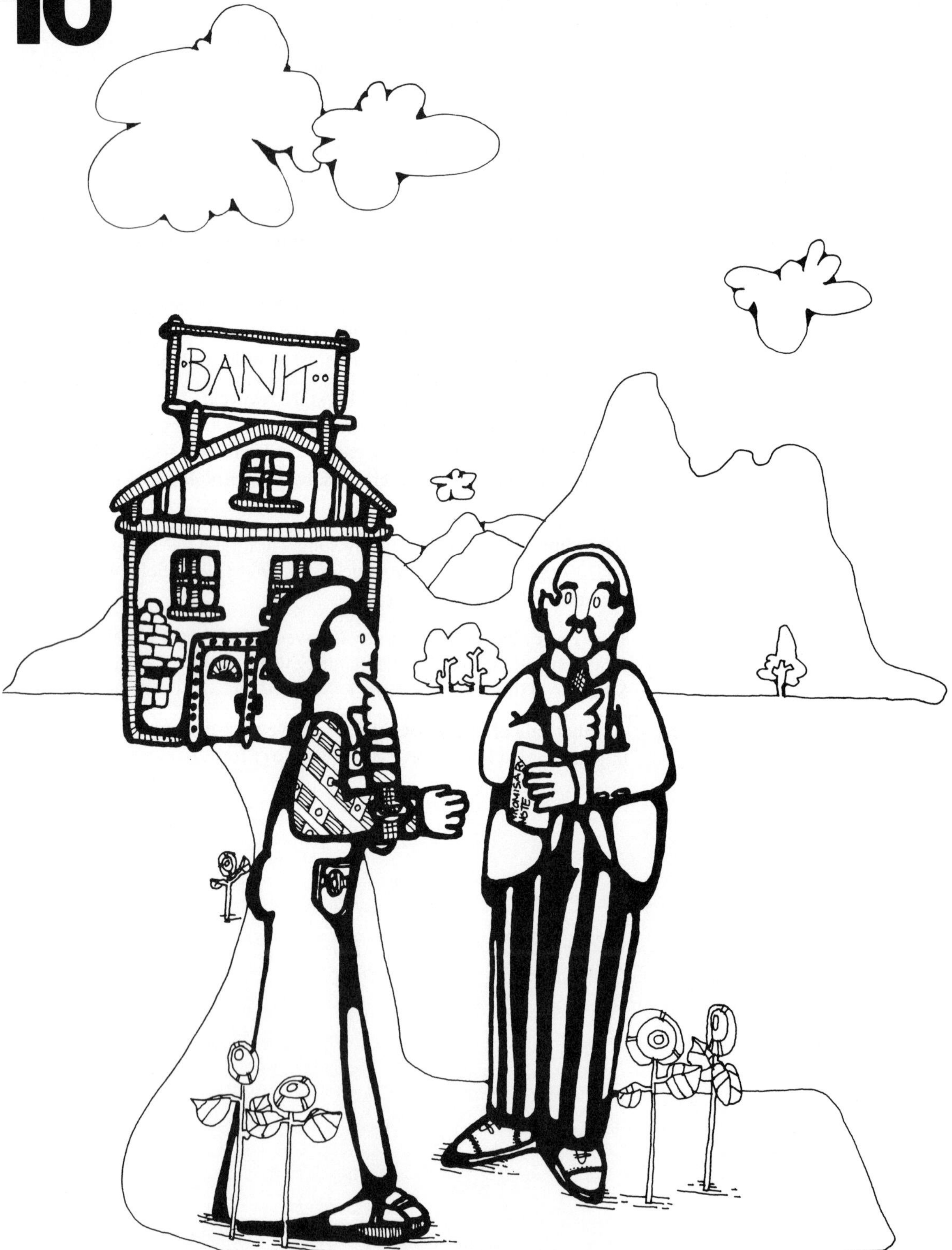

Simple Discount

Chapter Objectives for Chapter 10

I. Learn the meaning of the following terms:

II. Understand:

III. Learn to:

Introduction

Another kind of interest is called **simple discount.** Simple discount is often described as "interest in advance." The following is an illustration of simple discount. John Webster asks the bank for a loan of $1,000 for one year. The bank draws up a promissory note for $1,000 due in one year, but presents Webster with $940, indicating the $60 difference as a 6% interest charge payable in advance ($1,000 × 0.06 = $60). Webster signs the note, receives $940, and in one year will owe the bank $1,000.

There are two differences in the above transaction from a simple interest loan. First, the interest was calculated on the maturity value instead of the principal; second, the interest is paid at the beginning of the loan instead of the due date of the loan. These differences are worth repeating to avoid confusing simple interest with simple discount. **Simple interest is a percentage of the principal; simple discount is a percentage of the maturity value.** Second, **simple interest is paid upon expiration of the loan; simple discount is paid upon execution of the loan.**

Section **10.2** **The Simple Discount Formula**

Simple discount is another application of the basic percentage equation. The formula is:

(10–1)
$$D = Adt$$

where

D = amount of discount

A = maturity value

d = discount percent

t = term of the loan in years

In the John Webster loan, the calculations were: $D = ?$, $A = \$1,000$, $d = 6\%$, $t = 1$.

$$D = Adt$$

$$= \$1,000 \times \frac{6}{100} \times 1$$

$$= \$60$$

The amount paid to the borrower in a simple discount loan is called the **proceeds** of the loan rather than the principal. The proceeds of a simple discount transaction are equal to the maturity value minus the discount. That is:

(10–2) $P = A - D$

where

$$P = \text{proceeds}$$

$$A = \text{maturity value}$$

$$D = \text{amount of discount}$$

In the Webster transaction,

$$P = A - D$$

$$= \$1,000 - \$60$$

$$= \$940$$

The proceeds may also be thought of as the **present value** of the loan at simple discount.

Example 1

The Farmers State Bank offered to discount a note of $900 at 7% for six months. Find (a) the discount and (b) the proceeds of the loan.

Solution:

a. $D = ?, A = \$900, d = 7\%, t = \dfrac{1}{2}$ b. $P = ?, A = \$900, D = \$31.50$

$\quad D = Adt$ $\quad P = A - D$

$\quad\quad = \$900 \times \dfrac{7}{100} \times \dfrac{1}{2}$ $\quad\quad = \$900 - \$31.50$

$\quad\quad = \$31.50$ $\quad\quad = \$868.50$

Example 2

For a $680 note discounted at 6¼% for two months, find (a) the discount and (b) the present value.

Solution:

a. $D = ?, A = \$680, d = 6\frac{1}{4}\%, t = \dfrac{1}{6}$ b. $P = ?, A = \$680, D = \$7.08$

$\quad D = Adt$ $\quad P = A - D$

$\quad\quad = \$680 \times \dfrac{1}{16} \times \dfrac{1}{6}$ $\quad\quad = \$680 - \$7.08$

$\quad\quad = \$7.08$ $\quad\quad = \$672.92$

It should be noted that for a given transaction, 6% simple discount is not equivalent to 6% simple interest. To see this, let us return to the John Webster loan and calculate the simple interest rate. We have $I = \$60$, $P = \$940$, $r = ?$, $t = 1$, hence:

$$r = \frac{I}{Pt}$$

$$= \frac{\$60}{\$940 \times 1}$$

$$= 0.0638$$

$$= 6.38\%$$

Thus a 6% simple discount rate on this loan is equivalent to a simple interest rate of 6.38%. In other words, for a given simple discount percent, it takes a higher simple interest percent to produce the same amount of interest.

Because simple discount earns more interest than the same simple interest percent, simple discount has long been popular with banks for short-term loans. Therefore, it is not surprising that ordinary interest is used when the term of a simple discount loan is in days, since this is the time fraction used by most commercial lending institutions.

Example 3

Find the discount on a $1,200 note at 8% for forty-five days.

Solution:

$$D = ?, A = \$1,200, d = 8\%, t = \frac{45}{360} = \frac{1}{8}$$

$$D = Adt$$

$$= \$1,200 \times \frac{8}{100} \times \frac{1}{8}$$

$$= \$12.00$$

Example 4

A loan of $575 is executed on November 28 and is due on January 15. What is (a) the discount and (b) the proceeds if the loan is discounted at 12%?

Solution:

Using Appendix A, there are 48 days from November 28 to January 15. Thus with $A = \$575$, $d = 12\%$, and $t = \frac{48}{360}$:

a. $D = Adt$

$$= \$575 \times \frac{12}{100} \times \frac{48}{360}$$

$$= \$9.20$$

b. $P = A - D$

$$= \$575 - \$9.20$$

$$= \$565.80$$

Exercises
for Section 10.2

In problems 1–15, find the discount and the present value of the given note.

1. $1,000 discounted at 7% for 3 years

2. $3,000 discounted at 9% for 2 years

3. $720 discounted at 7½% for 1 year

4. $1,420 discounted at 8¼% for 9 months

5. $2,250 discounted at 6¾% for 6 months

6. $450 discounted at 5½% for 3 months

7. $875 discounted at 8¾% for 10 months

8. $1,150 discounted at 9½% for 8 months

9. $1,275 discounted at 7½% for 18 months

10. $1,800 discounted at 9¼% for 6 months

11. $900 discounted at 7% for 30 days

12. $1,400 discounted at 8¾% for 60 days

13. $350 discounted at 7¾% for 50 days

14. $760 discounted at 8½% for 200 days

15. $1,350 discounted at 9¼% for 170 days

16. Find the simple interest rate for the note in problem 1.

17. Find the simple interest rate for the note in problem 4.

18. Find the simple interest rate for the note in problem 11.

19. Find the simple interest rate for the note in problem 14.

20. A $1,200 loan is executed on April 10 and is due July 15. If the loan is discounted at 7%, find the discount and the proceeds.

21. John Blocker negotiates a loan at the bank for $1,500 for two years, discounted at 7½%. Find the discount and the proceeds of the loan.

22. The Midwest Bank offers to lend Janice Baxter $1,200 discounted at 8¾% for forty days. Find the discount and the proceeds for the loan. What is the simple interest rate?

23. To obtain additional operating capital for his new business, Bob Perkins borrows $2,000 from his bank, discounted at 8¼% for 245 days. Find the discount and the proceeds for the loan. What is the simple interest rate?

Section 10.3 Other Discount Formulas

As in the case with simple interest, formula (10–1) can be solved for any of the other variables.

(10–3) $A = \dfrac{D}{dt}$ [dividing both sides of (10–1) by dt]

(10–4) $d = \dfrac{D}{At}$ [dividing both sides of (10–1) by At]

(10–5) $t = \dfrac{D}{Ad}$ [dividing both sides of (10–1) by Ad]

Example 1

If a bank discounts a note at 10% for four months, what is the maturity value if the discount is $40?

Solution:

$D = \$40, A = ?, d = 10\%, t = \frac{1}{3}$

$$A = \frac{D}{dt}$$

$$= \frac{\$40}{\dfrac{1}{10} \times \dfrac{1}{3}}$$

$$= \frac{\$40}{\dfrac{1}{30}}$$

$$= \$1,200$$

Example 2

Gilbert Evans signed a promissory note agreeing to pay the Citizens Bank $400 in nine months. If the bank charged $25.50 for the loan, what is the simple discount rate?

Solution:

$D = \$25.50,\ A = \$400,\ d = ?,\ t = \frac{3}{4}$

$$d = \frac{D}{At}$$

$$= \frac{\$25.50}{\$400 \times \dfrac{3}{4}}$$

$$= \frac{\$25.50}{\$300}$$

$$= 0.085$$

$$= 8\frac{1}{2}\%$$

Example 3

J. D. Godwin received $192.50 from Clyde McKeever and agreed to repay him $200. If the note Godwin signed was discounted at a simple discount rate of 9%, what was the term of the loan?

Solution:

$D = \$200 - \$192.50 = \$7.50,\ A = \$200,\ d = 9\%,\ t = ?$

$$t = \frac{D}{Ad}$$

$$= \frac{\$7.50}{\$200 \times \dfrac{9}{100}}$$

$$= \frac{\$7.50}{\$18} = \frac{7\frac{1}{2}}{18} = \frac{15}{36} = \frac{5}{12}$$

$$= 5 \text{ months}$$

As in the case with simple interest, the student should learn to solve formula (10–1) for the appropriate variable rather than attempt to memorize formulas (10–3), (10–4), and (10–5).

An alternate formula for the proceeds can be derived.

$$P = A - D$$

and $\qquad D = Adt$

hence $\qquad P = A - Adt \qquad$ (Substitution)

or

(10–6) $\qquad P = A\,(1 - dt) \qquad$ (Distributive Property)

Example 4

Find the proceeds of a $670 loan discounted at 12% for five months.

Solution:

$P = ?, A = \$670, d = 12\%, t = \frac{5}{12}$

$$P = A\,(1 - dt)$$

$$= \$670\,(1 - \frac{12}{100} \cdot \frac{5}{12})$$

$$= \$670\,(1 - \frac{5}{100})$$

$$= \$670\,(\frac{95}{100})$$

$$= \$636.50$$

Example 5

The proceeds of a loan are $1,580. What is the maturity value of the loan if the discount rate is 6% and the term of the loan is seventy-five days?

Solution:

$P = \$1,580, A = ?, d = 6\%, t = \frac{75}{360}$

$$P = A\,(1 - dt)$$

$$A = \frac{P}{1 - dt} \qquad \text{(dividing both sides by } 1 - dt)$$

$$= \frac{\$1,580}{1 - (\frac{6}{100} \cdot \frac{75}{360})}$$

$$= \frac{\$1,580}{1 - \frac{75}{6,000}}$$

$$= \$1,600$$

In problems 1–12, solve the formula $D = Adt$ for the appropriate variable and compute the value of the indicated quantity.

1. $A = \$800, d = 7\%, D = \$112$; find t.

2. $d = 6\%, t = 3$ years, $D = \$216$; find A.

3. $A = \$450, t = 2$ years, $D = \$76.50$; find d.

4. $A = \$750$, $d = 9\frac{1}{2}\%$, $t = 4$ years; find D.

5. $A = \$600$, $t = 6$ months, $D = \$24$; find d.

6. $A = \$1,300$, $d = 11\%$, $D = \$107.25$; find t.

7. $d = 10\frac{1}{2}\%$, $t = 4$ months, $D = \$59.50$; find A.

8. $A = \$2,400$, $t = 7$ months, $D = \$157.50$; find d.

9. $A = \$1,440$, $d = 12\frac{1}{2}\%$, $t = 40$ days; find D.

10. $A = \$1,300$, $t = 72$ days, $D = \$22.75$; find d.

11. $d = 11\frac{3}{4}\%$, $t = 180$ days, $D = \$82.25$; find A.

12. $A = \$900$, $t = 64$ days, $D = \$15.60$; find d.

13. Bill Harris borrowed $700 for six months discounted at 11%. Find the proceeds from the loan.

14. What is the discount on a loan of $1,200 discounted at 12%, if the loan is executed on May 24 and is due on November 2?

15. Clementine Williams executed a loan on October 12 for $1,100, discounted at 8½%. If the loan is due February 16, what are the proceeds?

16. Karen Peters can borrow money from her bank discounted at 8% for two years. If she needs proceeds of $840, how much should she borrow?

17. John Butcher needs to borrow $2,000 to cover operating expenses for his new store. How much should he borrow, if the loan is to be discounted at 12% for six months?

18. The First City Bank will approve a loan of $2,000 for two years. If the proceeds are $1,700, what is the discount rate?

19. If the proceeds on a $1,200 loan for six months are $1,149, what is the discount rate?

20. Jennifer Smith needs $1,400 to remodel her store. What is the least amount that she can borrow if the loan is discounted at 7¼% for 120 days?

21. John Baxter signed a promissory note agreeing to pay the bank $950 in forty-five days. If the bank charged $7.42 for the loan, what is the discount rate?

22. Paula Forsythe received $228.75 from P. J. Thomas and agreed to repay him $250. If the note Paula signed was discounted at 8½%, what was the term of the loan?

10.4 Discounting Interest-bearing Notes

An individual who borrows money is usually required to sign a written agreement that states the conditions of the loan—the term, the rate of interest or discount, and the principal or maturity value of the loan. An example of such an agreement is the promissory note shown in Figure 10–1. Promissory notes can be written at simple interest, simple discount, or no interest at all. In any event, a note is a promise to pay the maturity value of the loan on the date specified.

Figure 10–1
Sample Promissory Note

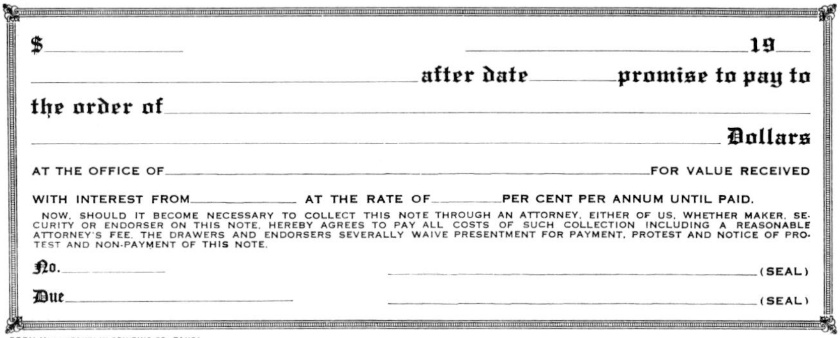

A promissory note is both a legal and a negotiable instrument. That is, in addition to a promise to pay, a note may be sold to a third party. In this sense a promissory note is similar to a personal check; it may be endorsed to a third party for cash, in payment for goods or services, or in retirement of a debt. Banks are the principal purchasers of promissory notes and do so at a discount. For instance, a businessperson may own a number of promissory notes that must be sold in order to meet unusual expenses. By discounting the notes at a bank, the businessperson obtains the needed cash and the bank earns a profit equal to the discount percentage.

When the payee of an interest-bearing note sells the note to a bank, he/she receives the proceeds of the newly discounted note. This is illustrated in the following examples.

Example 1

On March 1, Hal Miller loaned a friend $1,500 at a simple interest rate of 6½% with a due date of June 29. On April 10, Hal sold the note to a bank that discounted it at 8%. How much did Hal receive from the bank?

Solution:

By Appendix A there are 120 days from March 1 to June 29, and 80 days from April 10 to June 29. Before the proceeds of the discounted note can be found, it is necessary to calculate the maturity value of the simple interest loan using formula (9–10). $A = ?, P = \$1,500, r = 6\frac{1}{2}\%, t = \frac{120}{360} = \frac{1}{3}$, thus:

$$A = P\,(1 + rt)$$

$$= \$1{,}500\left(1 + \frac{13}{200}\cdot\frac{1}{3}\right)$$

$$= \$1{,}532.50$$

The proceeds are now calculated using formula (10–6). $P = ?$, $A = \$1{,}532.50$, $d = 8\%$, $t = \frac{80}{360}$

$$P = A\,(1 - dt)$$

$$= \$1{,}532.50\left(1 - \frac{8}{100}\cdot\frac{80}{360}\right)$$

$$= \$1{,}505.26$$

Hal receives $\$1{,}505.26$ from the bank and realizes $\$5.26$ on the loan despite having to sell the note prior to the maturity date. The bank realizes $\$1{,}532.50 - \$1{,}505.26 = \$27.24$ on the transaction.

Example 2

Thirty days before the due date of a $\$1{,}200$, 90-day loan discounted at 7%, the Granite City Bank rediscounted (sold) the note to the Franklin Federal Bank at a rate of 5%. (a) How much did the Granite City Bank receive from Franklin Federal? (b) How much did the Granite City Bank make on the transaction?

Solution:

a. $P = ?$, $A = \$1{,}200$, $d = 5\%$, $t = \dfrac{30}{360} = \dfrac{1}{12}$

$$P = A\,(1 - dt)$$

$$= \$1{,}200\left(1 - \frac{5}{100}\cdot\frac{1}{12}\right)$$

$$= \$1{,}195$$

b. First the proceeds of the original loan are calculated. $P = ?$, $A = \$1{,}200$, $d = 7\%$, $t = \dfrac{90}{360} = \dfrac{1}{4}$

$$P = A\,(1 - dt)$$

$$= \$1{,}200\left(1 - \frac{7}{100}\cdot\frac{1}{4}\right)$$

$$= \$1{,}179$$

The Granite City Bank earned $\$1{,}195 - \$1{,}179 = \$16$ on the transaction.

As illustrated in the last example, it is a common practice for financial institutions to charge each other a discount rate lower than that charged to individual borrowers and businesses.

A variation of discounting an interest-bearing note occurs when a merchant obtains a note from a bank in order to take advantage of a cash discount in the payment of a bill. Although a bill is not a promissory note, in a sense it is an interest-bearing document in that a higher price is paid if the purchaser fails to take advantage of the cash discount. In borrowing money to pay the bill, the merchant must pay interest, hence this action is prudent only if the bank discount is less than the cash discount. The maximum possible savings occur on the last day of the cash discount. Here are examples of this procedure.

9.8%   Corporate Bonds

8.0%   U.S. Government Guaranteed

8.2%   TAX FREE

Edward D. Jones & Co.
— Established 1871 —
Member New York Stock Exchange, Inc.

For Complete Details
Write or Call:

I would like further information
on Gov. Guaranteed Bonds ☐
Tax Free Bonds ☐
Corporate Bonds ☐

Name _____
Address _____
City _____
Phone _____

Example 3

The terms of a bill for $1,200 are 2/30, n/60. If the discount rate at a bank is 8%, (a) how much must be borrowed (proceeds) and (b) how much will be saved by taking advantage of the cash discount?

Solution:

a.   The cash discount is $1,200 × 0.02 = $24.00, hence:

$1,200 n/60
−   24 cash discount
—————
$1,176 amount to be borrowed (proceeds)

b. The net amount is due thirty days after the last day of the cash discount, thus it is necessary to calculate the maturity value necessary to generate proceeds of $1,176 in thirty days. $A = ?, P = \$1,176, d = 8\%, t = \frac{30}{360} = \frac{1}{12}$. Solving formula (10–6) for A,

$$A = \frac{P}{1 - dt}$$

$$= \frac{\$1,176}{1 - \left(\frac{8}{100} \cdot \frac{1}{12}\right)}$$

$$= \$1,183.89$$

The discount is $\$1,183.89 - \$1,176 = \$7.89$, thus the amount saved by borrowing is $\$24.00 - \$7.89 = \$16.11$.

Example 4

A merchant receives a consignment of goods for $840 with terms 1/10, n/30. At what discount rate could he afford to borrow money in order to take advantage of the cash discount?

Solution:

The cash discount is $\$840 \times 0.01 = \$8.40$, hence:

$$
\begin{array}{rl}
\$840.00 & \text{n/60} \\
- \quad 8.40 & \text{Cash discount} \\
\hline
\$831.60 & \text{Amount to be borrowed}
\end{array}
$$

The net amount is due twenty days after the last day of the cash discount. In borrowing from the bank, the discount percentage must not exceed $8.40 (the cash discount) or the merchant will lose money. Thus, using formula (10–4) with $D = \$8.40, A = \$840, d = ?$, and $t = \frac{20}{360} = \frac{1}{18}$

$$d = \frac{D}{At}$$

$$= \frac{\$8.40}{\$840 \times \frac{1}{18}}$$

$$= 0.18$$

$$= 18\%$$

The merchant could afford to borrow money at a discount rate up to 18% and still break even on the transaction.

1. Paul Prentice loaned Bill Butler $1,000 for ninety days at a simple interest rate of 7%. Then, sixty days later Paul sold the note to a bank that discounted it at 8%. How much did Paul receive from the bank? How much did Paul make on the loan?

2. A $1,400 note bearing 5% simple interest with a term of six months is sold to a bank two months before the due date. If the bank discounts the note at 7%, how much did the payee receive for the note? How much did the payee make on the loan?

3. Two months before the due date, the Gateway Bank purchased a one year, $2,000 note bearing 5½% simple interest. If the bank discounted the note at 7½%, how much did the bank make on the transaction? How much did the original owner of the note make?

4. On April 10, Mary Phillips loaned her sister $2,400 at a simple interest rate of 6¼%. The due date of the note was July 19, but on June 29 Mary sold the note to the bank, which discounted it at 8¾%. How much did Mary receive for the note? How much did she make on the loan? How much did the bank make on the transaction?

5. Jim Butler loaned his brother-in-law $1,800 on March 2 at a simple interest rate of 7¾%. The due date of the note was September 18, but because of an illness in his family Jim was forced to sell the note to the bank on April 1, and the bank discounted it at 9¼%. How much did Jim receive for the note? How much did he lose on the loan? How much did the bank make?

6. Forty-five days before the due date of an $800, 180-day loan discounted at 8%, the Pacific Bank sold the note to the Western Bank at a discount rate of 6%. How much did the Pacific Bank receive from Western? How much did the Pacific Bank make on the transaction?

7. On June 7, the Union Bank loaned $1,700 discounted at 7¼%. The due date of the note was November 4, but on September 5 Union sold the note to the Central Bank at a discount of 5¾%. How much did the Union Bank receive for the note? How much did the Union Bank make on the transaction?

8. The terms of a bill for $900 are 3/30, n/90. If the discount rate at a bank is 6%, how much must be borrowed (proceeds) to take advantage of the cash discount? How much is saved by taking advantage of the discount?

9. Packard Products receives a consignment of goods for $1,600 with terms of 2/10, n/30. The discount rate at the bank is 8¼%. How much should Packard borrow (proceeds) to take advantage of the cash discount? How much will Packard save by borrowing the money?

10. If the terms of a $1,400 bill are 1/20, n/50, find the maximum discount rate at which money could be borrowed to take advantage of the cash discount.

11. Howell Services, Inc., receives a bill for $2,100 with terms of 2/30, n/120. If the current discount rate for borrowing money is 9%, should the company borrow money to take advantage of the cash discount? Why?

12. Should a company borrow money at a discount rate of 10% to take advantage of the cash discount of an $1,800 bill with terms of 1/10, n/40? Why?

Simple Interest vs. Simple Discount

In Section 10.2 it was shown that for a given discount rate, it takes a higher simple interest rate to generate the same amount of interest. In this section the precise relationship between simple interest and simple discount is given by deriving formulas to convert from one rate to the other. If the formulas

$$A = P (1 + rt) \text{ and } P = A (1 - dt)$$

are solved for the common variable P, then:

$$P = \frac{A}{1 + rt} \qquad P = A (1 - dt)$$

Since P is equal to each of these quantities,

(10–7) $$\frac{A}{1 + rt} = A (1 - dt)$$

or

(10–8) $$\frac{1}{1 + rt} = 1 - dt \qquad \text{[dividing both sides of (10–7) by } A\text{]}$$

Solving (10–8) for r,

(10–9) $$r = \frac{d}{1 - dt}$$

Solving (10–8) for d,

(10–10) $$d = \frac{r}{1 + rt}$$

Formulas (10–9) and (10–10) give the relationship between simple interest and simple discount. Given one rate, we can solve for the other by using the appropriate formula. Note that only time affects the relation between the two rates; the maturity value has no effect.

Example 1

What simple interest rate corresponds (a) to a 6% discount rate on a loan for one year and (b) to an 8½% discount rate on a loan for ninety days?

Solution:

a. $d = 6\%, t = 1$

$$r = \frac{d}{1 - dt}$$

$$= \frac{\dfrac{6}{100}}{1 - \left(\dfrac{6}{100} \cdot 1\right)}$$

$$= 0.0638$$

$$= 6.38\%$$

(Compare with the calculations for the John Webster loan in Section 10.1.)

b. $d = 8½\%, t = \dfrac{90}{360} = \dfrac{1}{4}$

$$r = \frac{d}{1 - dt}$$

$$= \frac{\dfrac{17}{200}}{1 - \left(\dfrac{17}{200} \cdot \dfrac{1}{4}\right)}$$

$$= 0.086845$$

$$= 8.68\% \quad \text{(rounded)}$$

Example 2

Find the discount rate corresponding to a simple interest rate of (a) 6% and (b) 12¼% if the term of the loan is six months.

Solution:

a. $r = 6\%, t = \dfrac{6}{12}$

$$d = \frac{r}{1 + rt}$$

$$= \frac{\dfrac{6}{100}}{1 + \left(\dfrac{6}{100} \cdot \dfrac{1}{2}\right)}$$

$$= 0.05825$$

$$= 5.83\% \quad \text{(rounded)}$$

b. $d = 12\frac{1}{4}\%,\, t = \dfrac{1}{2}$

$$d = \frac{r}{1 + rt}$$

$$= \frac{\dfrac{49}{400}}{1 + \left(\dfrac{49}{400} \cdot \dfrac{1}{2}\right)}$$

$$= 0.11543$$

$$= 11.54\% \quad (\text{rounded})$$

Exercises for Section 10.5

In problems 1 through 8, find the simple interest rate that corresponds to the given discount rate for the given time.

1. 7%, 2 years

2. 8%, 6 months

3. 7¼%, 18 months

4. 11½%, 1 year

5. 9¾%, 90 days

6. 8¾%, 40 days

7. 10¼%, 100 days

8. 11¼%, 72 days

In problems 9 through 17, find the discount rate corresponding to the given simple interest rate for the given time.

9. 6%, 2 years

10. 8%, 18 months

11. 9¼%, 1 year

12. 8¾%, 4 years

13. 7¼%, 3 months

14. 6¾%, 40 days

15. 9½%, 180 days

16. 10¾%, 20 days

17. 8¼%, 60 days

18. Mary Miller needs to borrow some money for ninety days to cover expenses for opening a new clothing shop. She can obtain the money by borrowing it from a friend at 7% simple interest or she can borrow it from the bank at 6¾% discount. Where should she borrow the money?

19. John Parsons is opening a restaurant and wants to borrow some money to buy equipment. He plans to borrow the money for two years, and he can get it from the bank at 9¼% discount or he can borrow from a friend at 11¼% simple interest. Where should he get the money?

20. Jack Bentley can borrow money for two years from the bank at 8¾% discount or he can borrow money elsewhere at 10% simple interest. Should he borrow from the bank or obtain the money elsewhere?

21. C. J. Peterson wants to borrow money for four years so that she can remodel her gift shop. Should she obtain the money from the bank at 6½% discount or borrow from other sources at 9% simple interest?

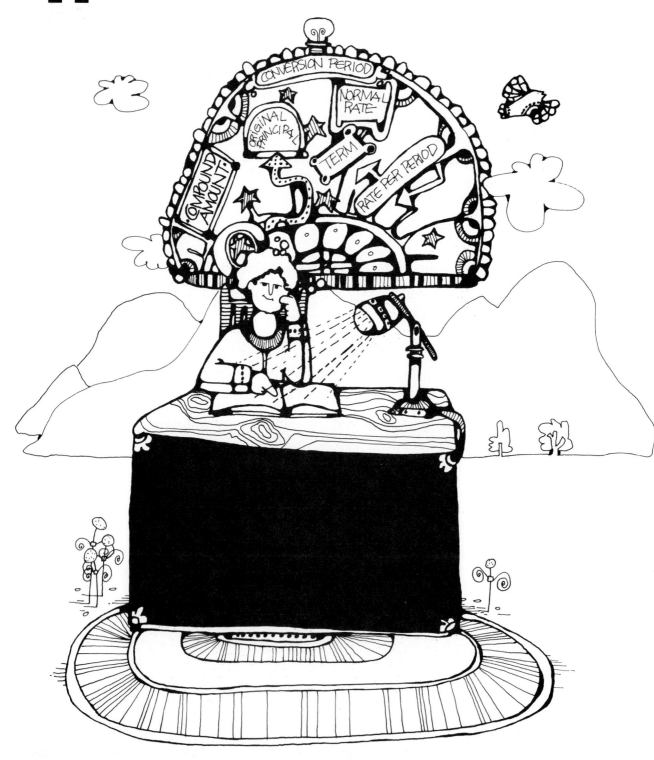

Compound Interest

Chapter Objectives for Chapter 11

I. Learn the meaning of the following terms:

A. *Compound Amount,* 287
B. *Original principal,* 287
C. *Nominal rate,* 287
D. *Term,* 287
E. *Conversion period,* 287
F. *Rate per period,* 288

II. Understand:

A. Compound interest, 286
B. Computing compound interest, 287
C. Present value for compound interest, 295
D. Daily compounding, 298
E. Effective interest rate, 301

III. Use:

A. The compound interest formula to compute compound interest, 291
B. Compound interest tables to solve compound interest problems, 291
C. Present value tables to compute present value at compound interest, 295
D. Daily interest table to compute interest compounded daily, 298

Compound interest differs from simple interest in that simple interest is computed on a principal that never changes, while compound interest is computed on the principal plus past interest. For this reason, compound interest is frequently described as "interest on interest."

To illustrate the difference between simple interest and compound interest, consider $100 invested for three years at 6% simple interest and 6% interest compounded annually. The calculations are as follows:

	*Simple Interest**	*Compound Interest*
1st Year	$100 Principal × 0.06 Rate × Time (0.06 × 1) ――― $6.00 Interest	$100 Principal × 0.06 Rate × Time (0.06 × 1) ――― $6.00 Interest
2nd Year	$100 Principal × 0.06 Rate × Time (0.06 × 1) ――― $6.00 Interest	$106 Principal ($100 + $6) × 0.06 Rate × Time (0.06 × 1) ――― $6.36 Interest
3rd Year	$100 Principal × 0.06 Rate × Time (0.06 × 1) ――― $6.00 Interest	$112.36 Principal ($106 + $6.36) × 0.06 Rate × Time (0.06 × 1) ――― $ 6.74 Interest

Note that the simple interest is $18.00 for the three years ($6 + $6 + $6) while the compound interest is $19.10 for the same period ($6 + $6.36 + $6.74) because interest is computed on interest for the last two years. Thus,

$$A = P + I \qquad\qquad A = P + I$$
$$= \$100 + \$18 \qquad\qquad = \$100 + \$19.10$$
$$= \$118 \qquad\qquad\quad = \$119.10$$

In the above illustration, compound interest generated more interest than the corresponding rate of simple interest, and in general, this is the case. Despite this, compound interest is the form of interest paid to investors by banks, savings and loan institutions, and the U.S. Government in its bond program. One reason for this is that compound interest encourages the investor to maintain the interest on deposit; the savings institution thus has funds to invest that they would otherwise be paying out in interest.

As demonstrated above, there is a close relation between simple interest and compound interest. As a result, some of interest terminology must be

---

* The simple interest calculation using $I = Prt$ is $100 × 0.06 × 3 = $18.00. However, for this illustration, the interest is calculated annually (the result is the same).

modified to distinguish between the two. For compound interest, the terms of the formula $A = P + I$ are called **compound amount, original principal,** and **compound interest,** respectively. The quoted interest rate is the **nominal rate** (rate per annum) and the length of an investment is the **term.** The intervals when interest is added to the principal are called **conversion periods,** or just **periods.** In the previous illustration, the compound amount is $119.10, the original principal is $100, the compound interest is $19.10, the nominal rate is 6%, the term is three years, and the conversion period is one year.

The most frequent conversion periods are monthly, quarterly, semi-annually, and annually. The greater the number of conversion periods, the greater the compound interest for a given investment.

11.2 **Computing Compound Interest**

One method of computing compound interest is the step-by-step calculation of the previous illustration. At the beginning of each period the earned interest is added to the principal of the previous period and interest is calculated using the formula $I = Prt$.

Example 1

Find the compound interest earned on $100 invested for two years at 6% compounded semiannually.

Solution:

$P = \$100, r = 0.06, t = \frac{1}{2}$

First Six Months	$100.00	Original principal
	$\times$ 0.03	Rate $\times$ Time ($0.06 \times \frac{1}{2}$)
	$ 3.00	Interest
Second Six Months	$103.00	Principal ($100 + $3)
	$\times$ 0.03	Rate $\times$ Time ($0.06 \times \frac{1}{2}$)
	$ 3.09	Interest
Third Six Months	$106.09	Principal ($103 + $3.09)
	$\times$ 0.03	Rate $\times$ Time ($0.06 \times \frac{1}{2}$)
	$ 3.18	Interest
Fourth Six Months	$109.27	Principal ($106.09 + $3.18)
	$\times$ 0.03	Rate $\times$ Time ($0.06 \times \frac{1}{2}$)
	$ 3.28	Interest

The compound interest is the sum of the interests for each period, or $3.00 + $3.09 + $3.18 + $3.28 = $12.55. Note that in applying the simple interest formula, it was convenient to multiply P by the combination *rt*. That is, $I = Prt$ is the same as $I = P \times (rt)$. In compound interest, this combination is called the **rate per period** and is equal to the product of the nominal rate and the reciprocal of the number of periods.* If $i =$ rate per period, then

(11–1)
$$i = \frac{\text{Nominal rate}}{\text{Number of periods per year}}$$

In Example 1, 6% per annum compounded semiannually is equal to $\frac{6\%}{2} = 3\%$ per period.

Example 2

Find the rate per period for (a) 4% per annum compounded semiannually, (b) 10% per annum compounded quarterly, and (c) 6% per annum compounded monthly.

Solution:

a. 4% compounded semiannually $= \frac{4\%}{2} = 2\%$ per six months

b. 10% compounded quarterly $= \frac{10\%}{4} = 2\frac{1}{2}\%$ per quarter

c. 6% compounded monthly $= \frac{6\%}{12} = \frac{1}{2}\%$ per month.

Example 3

Find the compound amount for \$600 invested for one year at 8% per annum compounded quarterly.

Solution:

The rate per period is $\frac{8\%}{4} = 2\%$ per quarter.

First Quarter		
	\$600.00	Original principal
$\times$	0.02	Rate per period
	\$ 12.00	Interest

Second Quarter		
	\$612.00	Principal (\$600 + \$12)
$\times$	0.02	Rate per period
	\$ 12.24	Interest

* Since $t = \frac{1}{p}$ where $t =$ time and $p =$ number of periods per year, then

$$r \times t = r \times \frac{1}{p} = \frac{r}{p}.$$

Third Quarter	$624.24	Principal ($612 + $12.24)
	× 0.02	Rate per period
	$12.4848	Interest

Fourth Quarter	$636.72	Principal ($624.24 + $12.48)
	× 0.02	Rate per period
	$12.7345	Interest

The compound interest is $12.00 + $12.24 + $12.4848 + $12.7345 = $49.4593.

$$A = P + I$$
$$= \$600 + \$49.4593 = \$649.46$$

Exercises for Section 11.2

In problems 1–10, find the rate per period i for the given nominal rate and conversion period.

1. 6% compounded semiannually
2. 8% compounded quarterly
3. 12% compounded monthly
4. 4% compounded monthly
5. 5% compounded semiannually

6. 6% compounded quarterly
7. 9% compounded monthly
8. 11% compounded semiannually
9. 6½% compounded semiannually
10. 8½% compounded quarterly

In problems 11–20, find the compound interest earned on the given original principal at the given compound interest rate for the indicated term.

11. $2,000 for two years at 8% compounded annually
12. $4,000 for one year at 12% compounded semiannually
13. $1,000 for one year at 4% compounded semiannually
14. $3,000 for two years at 8% compounded semiannually
15. $800 for two years at 10% compounded semiannually
16. $1,200 for one year at 9% compounded quarterly
17. $1,800 for one year at 6% compounded quarterly
18. $500 for one year at 6% compounded monthly
19. $600 for one year at 4% compounded monthly
20. $200 for six months at 5% compounded quarterly

In problems 21–25, find the compound amount for the given original amount invested at the given compound interest rate for the indicated term.

21. $500 for one year at 4% compounded quarterly
22. $900 for two years at 8% compounded semiannually

23. $1,600 for three years at 9% compounded annually

24. $4,000 for five years at 7% compounded annually

25. $2,400 for four years at 6% compounded semiannually

26. Lynn Bishop placed $2,000 in a new savings account that pays 6½% interest compounded quarterly. How much will be in the account after one year?

27. John Foster has $4,000 to invest for five years. He can either invest it at 6½% simple interest or at 6% interest compounded annually. Which interest rate should he choose?

Section **11.3** **The Compound Interest Formula**

In Example 3 of Section 11.2, if we multiply the principal $600 by $(1.02)^4$ where $(1.02)^4 = 1.02 \times 1.02 \times 1.02 \times 1.02,$* the result is:

$$\$600 \times (1.02)^4 = \$600 \times 1.082432$$
$$= \$649.4593$$
$$= \$649.46$$

This is the solution to Example 3 of Section 11.2.

The choice of multiplying $600 by $(1.02)^4$ to obtain $649.46 was not accidental. It is taken from a formula that can be derived to calculate compound amount.† The formula (11–2) is shown on page 291.

n factors

* In the algebra of exponents a^n is defined as: $a^n = \overbrace{a \cdot a \cdot a \cdots a}$. Thus $(1.02)^4 =$ $1.02 \times 1.02 \times 1.02 \times 1.02$.

† Let
I = Compound interest
P = Original principal
i = Rate per period
A_1 = Compound amount at the end of the first period

Then
$I = Pi$
$A_1 = P + I$
$\quad = P + Pi$ Substitution
$\quad = P(1 + i)$ Distributive Property

The compound amount A_2 at the end of the second period is
$A_2 = A_1 + A_1 i$
$\quad = A_1(1 + i)$ Distributive Property
$\quad = P(1 + i)(1 + i)$ Substitution for A_1
$\quad = P(1 + i)^2$ Where $(1+i)(1+i) = (1+i)^2$

At the end of the third period A_3,
$A_3 = A_2 + A_2 i$
$\quad = A_2(1 + i)$ Distributive Property
$\quad = P(1 + i)^2(1 + i)$ Substitution for A_2
$\quad = P(1 + i)^3$ Where $(1+i)^2(1+i) = (1+i)^3$

Continuing in this fashion, for an investment with a term of n periods, the compound amount A is:

$$A = P(1 + i)^n$$

(11–2) $$A = P(1 + i)^n$$

where

$$A = \text{compound amount}$$

$$P = \text{principal}$$

$$i = \text{rate per period}$$

$$n = \text{number of periods}$$

The entire subject of compound interest is contained in Formula (11–2).

Example 1

Find the compound amount and the compound interest in an investment of $2,000 for three years that pays 6% compounded semiannually.

Solution:

$$P = \$2,000,\ i = \frac{6\%}{2} = 3\%,\ n = 3 \times 2 = 6.$$

$$A = P(1 + i)^n$$

$$= \$2,000(1 + 0.03)^6$$

$$= \$2,000(1.03)^6$$

$$= \$2,000(1.1940523) \qquad (1.03 \times 1.03 \times 1.03 \times 1.03 \times$$
$$\qquad\qquad\qquad\qquad\qquad 1.03 \times 1.03 = 1.1940523)$$

$$= \$2,388.1046$$

$$= \$2,388.10$$

$$I = A - P$$

$$= \$2,388.10 - \$2,000.00$$

$$= \$388.10$$

Section 11.4 Compound Interest Tables

Applying formula (11–2) in the calculation of compound interest becomes unwieldy when n is a large number, as seen in the last example; finding $(1.03)^6$ is no small task. To simplify these calculations, tables have been prepared for combinations of $(1 + i)^n$. Such a table is Appendix B in the appendices, which provides the value of $(1 + i)^n$ for various combinations of i and n. In Example 1 in Section 11.3, $i = 3\%$ and $n = 6$. To find $(1.03)^6$, locate the appendix page labeled 3% and column B labeled "Compound Amount." Row 6 of this column is 1.1940523, which is the value of $(1.03)^6$.

Example 1

Find the compound interest on $4,000 at 7% compounded quarterly for five years.

Solution:

$$P = \$4,000, \; i = \frac{7\%}{4} = 1\frac{3}{4}\%, \; n = 20$$

$$A = P\,(1 + i)^n$$

$$= \$4,000\,(1.0175)^{20}$$

$$= \$4,000\,(1.4147782) \quad (\text{Appendix B})$$

$$= \$5,659.1128$$

$$= \$5,659.11$$

$$I = A - P$$

$$= \$5,659.11 - \$4,000.00$$

$$= \$1,659.11$$

Appendix B can also be used to find values of i or n.

Example 2

How long would it take for $2,000 to accumulate to $2,253.65 if money is worth 4% compounded quarterly?

Solution:

$$A = \$2,253.65, \; i = \frac{4\%}{4} = 1\%, \; P = \$2,000, \; n = ?$$

$$A = P(1 + i)^n$$

$$\frac{A}{P} = (1 + i)^n \quad (\text{Dividing both sides by } P)$$

$$\frac{\$2,253.65}{\$2,000.00} = (1.01)^n$$

$$1.12682503 = (1.01)^n$$

In Appendix B on the 1% page, 1.12682503 is the entry for $n = 12$, thus the term is twelve quarters or three years.

Example 3

What interest rate compounded semiannually would be required for $4,400 to accumulate to $14,111.40 in ten years?

Solution:

$A = \$14,111.40, P = \$4,400, i = ?, n = 10 \times 2 = 20$

$$A = P(1 + i)^n$$

$$\frac{A}{P} = (1 + i)^n \qquad \text{(Dividing both sides by } P)$$

$$\frac{\$14,111.40}{\$4,400.00} = (1 + i)^{20}$$

$$3.2071363 = (1 + i)^{20}$$

Scanning horizontally in the $n = 20$ line of Appendix B, the entry very close to 3.2071363 is on the page labeled $i = 6\%$. Since interest is compounded semiannually, the nominal rate is 12%.

Example 4

John Talbot invests $800 in a savings account paying 5% compounded semiannually. After two and one-half years he withdraws $1,000 from the account and invests in a certificate of deposit paying 6% compounded quarterly, leaving the remainder in the savings account. How much is his total compound amount two years after purchasing the certificate of deposit?

Solution:

First two and one-half years: $P = \$800, i = \dfrac{5\%}{2} = 2\tfrac{1}{2}\%, n = 2\tfrac{1}{2} \times 2 = 5$

$$A = P\,(1 + i)^n$$
$$= \$800\,(1.025)^5$$
$$= \$800\,(1.3140821) \qquad \text{(Appendix B)}$$
$$= \$1,051.27$$

Next two years: $P = \$1,000, i = \dfrac{6\%}{4} = 1\tfrac{1}{2}\%, n = 8$

$$A = P\,(1 + i)^n$$
$$= \$1,000\,(1 + 0.015)^8$$
$$= \$1,000\,(1.12649259) \qquad \text{(Appendix B)}$$
$$= \$1,126.49$$

$P = \$51.27, i = \dfrac{5\%}{2} = 2\tfrac{1}{2}\%, n = 4$

$$A = P(1 + i)^n$$
$$= \$51.27\,(1.025)^4$$
$$= \$51.27\,(1.10381289) \qquad \text{(Appendix B)}$$
$$= \$56.59$$

Total compound amount $= \$1,126.49 + \$56.59 = \$1,183.08.$

In problems 1–10, use the formula $A = P(1 + i)^n$ to find the compound amount and the compound interest for the given original principal at the given compound interest rate for the indicated term.

1. $1,000 for two years at 4% compounded annually

2. $500 for three years at 8% compounded annually

3. $400 for two years at 6% compounded semiannually

4. $700 for two years at 10% compounded semiannually

5. $1,200 for one year at 4% compounded quarterly

6. $500 for one year at 8% compounded quarterly

7. $800 for three months at 6% compounded monthly

8. $200 for five months at 12% compounded monthly

9. $1,400 for two years at 7% compounded semiannually

10. $2,200 for two years at 5% compounded semiannually

In problems 11–15, use Appendix B in the appendices to find the compound interest on the given original principal at the given compound interest rate for the indicated term.

11. $1,000 for five years at 8% compounded quarterly

12. $600 for two years at 12% compounded monthly

13. $1,200 for three years at 4% compounded quarterly

14. $800 for eight years at 12% compounded semiannually

15. $2,000 for ten years at 6% compounded quarterly

In problems 16–20, use Appendix B to find how long it would take for the given original principal to accumulate to the given amount at the given compound interest rate.

16. $1,000 to $1,084.43 at 2% compounded annually

17. $4,000 to $8,048.79 at 6% compounded semiannually

18. $500 to $742.97 at 8% compounded quarterly

19. $800 to $1,078.28 at 12% compounded monthly

20. $1,400 to $1,673.87 at 18% compounded monthly

In problems 21–25, find the compound interest rate that would make the given original principal accumulate to the given amount in the given length of time (Use Appendix B).

21. $400 to $477.62 in three years, interest compounded semiannually

22. $1,500 to $1,758.87 in four years, interest compounded quarterly

23. $3,000 to $3,787.43 in two years, interest compounded semiannually

24. $1,800 to $1,968.20 in six months, interest compounded monthly

25. $200 to $297.19 in five years, interest compounded quarterly

26. Mary Watkins places $450 in a savings account paying 4% compounded quarterly. After four years she withdraws $500 from the account and buys a certificate of deposit that pays 6% compounded semiannually, leaving the remainder in the savings account. How much is her total compound amount one year after purchasing the certificate of deposit?

27. Art Landon opens a savings account with $1,200. The account pays 6% interest compounded semiannually. After three and one-half years he withdraws $1,000 from the account and buys a certificate of deposit that pays 8% interest compounded quarterly, leaving the remainder in the savings account. How much is his total compound amount one and one-half years after purchasing his certificate of deposit?

Section **11.5** Present Value

In the chapter on simple interest, present value was defined as the current value of a future sum of money. This definition also applies to present value at compound interest. Also analogous is the procedure for finding present value; the formula for A is solved for P.

$$A = P(1 + i)^n$$

$$\frac{A}{(1 + i)^n} = \frac{P(1 + i)^n}{(1 + i)^n} \qquad \text{Dividing both sides by } (1 + i)^n$$

$$\frac{A}{(1 + i)^n} = P$$

or

(11–3) $P = A\,(1 + i)^{-n}$ where* $\dfrac{1}{(1 + i)^n} = (1 + i)^{-n}$

Calculating present value at compound interest is best done by using a table that lists the values of $(1 + i)^{-n}$. Such a table is Appendix C in the appendices. Similar to the compound interest table, an entry in Appendix C is found by locating the appendix page for the rate of interest i, then the nth row of column C "Present Value"; this entry is the value of $(1 + i)^{-n}$.

---

* In the algebra of exponents $\dfrac{1}{x^n}$ is defined as x^{-n} for any positive n and nonzero x.

Example 1

Find the principal that must be deposited at 6% compounded annually to have an amount of $10,000 in eight years.

Solution:

$P = ?$, $A = \$10,000$, $i = 6\%$, $n = 8$.

$$P = A (1 + i)^{-n}$$

$$= \$10,000 (1.06)^{-8}$$

$$= \$10,000 (0.62741237) \qquad \text{(Appendix C)}$$

$$= \$6,274.12$$

Example 2

Find the principal that must be deposited at 8% compounded annually to have an amount of $10,000 in five years.

Solution:

$P = ?$, $A = \$10,000$, $i = 8\%$, $n = 5$.

$$P = A (1 + i)^{-n}$$

$$= \$10,000 (0.6805832) \qquad \text{(Appendix C)}$$

$$= \$6,805.83$$

To check the calculation in the previous example, if a principal of $6,805.83 were invested at 8% compounded annually for five years, then by formula (11–2):

$$A = P (1 + i)^n$$

$$= \$6,805.83 (1.08)^5$$

$$= \$6,805.83 (1.46932808) \qquad \text{(Appendix B)}$$

$$= \$9,999.997$$

$$= \$10,000.00$$

Example 3

The parents of newly born Terry Morton wanted to establish a savings account that would provide $12,000 for college expenses for Terry at age eighteen. Their banker calculated the amount to be placed in an account that pays 5% compounded semiannually. How much was put in the savings account?

Solution:

$$P = ?, A = \$12,000, i = \frac{5\%}{2} = 2\frac{1}{2}\%, n = 18 \times 2 = 36$$

$$P = A (1 + i)^{-n}$$
$$= \$12,000 (1.025)^{-18}$$
$$= \$12,000 (0.64116591) \qquad (\text{Appendix C})$$
$$= \$7,693.99$$

Exercises for Section 11.5

In problems 1–10, find the principal that must be invested at the given interest rate in order to have the given amount after the given period of time.

1. $1,000 in two years at 6% compounded semiannually

2. $5,000 in five years at 3% compounded semiannually

3. $3,000 in three years at 4% compounded annually

4. $600 in one year at 8% compounded quarterly

5. $1,500 in ten years at 12% compounded quarterly

6. $2,000 in one year at 12% compounded monthly

7. $500 in four years at 18% compounded monthly

8. $4,000 in ten years at 4% compounded semiannually

9. $1,400 in six years at 6% compounded quarterly

10. $5,000 in ten years at 16% compounded quarterly

11. Ten years ago Jack Philips opened a savings account that paid 6% interest compounded quarterly. He made no deposits or withdrawals after his initial deposit. Today there is $3,083.83 in the account. How much did he place in the account initially?

12. John Foster, who is forty years old, wishes to place enough money in a savings account that pays 8% interest compounded annually so that when he is age sixty-five, he will have $20,000 in the account to use for retirement. How much should he put in the account?

13. Pam Shuster just inherited $15,000. She wishes to put enough of her inheritance into a savings account so that five years from now she will still have $15,000. If the account pays 6% compounded semiannually, how much should she put in the account?

14. Joyce Ruth is planning to tour Europe two years from now, and she estimates that she will need $3,000 for the trip. How much should she place in a savings account now in order to have enough money for her trip, if the account pays 8% compounded quarterly?

Daily Compounding

Traditionally, savings institutions offered interest at periods that were annual, semiannual, or quarterly. A recent innovation is the daily compounding of interest. Spreading east from California, this new trend offers the investor the advantages of higher interest for two reasons. It has already been demonstrated that the shorter the period, the greater the generated interest. Secondly, interest is earned for the time it is invested; there is no penalty for withdrawal during an interest period as there often is on accounts with periods of a quarter or longer.

Daily interest is calculated using formula (11–2), $A = P(1 + i)^n$, the same as for any other interest calculation. Since the conversion period is one day, $i = \dfrac{r}{365}$, where $r =$ the nominal rate. For ease of calculation, a table has been prepared for values of $\left(1 + \dfrac{r}{365}\right)^n$. This is Appendix H in the appendices. The headings at the top of the table are values of r; the values of n are given in the left-hand column. An appropriate entry in the table is multiplied by the principal P to obtain the compound amount A. The following examples illustrate the calculation of daily interest.

Example 1

Find the compound amount of $1,500 invested on July 14 and withdrawn on September 9 if interest is compounded daily at a rate of 5%.

Solution:

From Appendix A there are 57 days from July 14 to September 9. Thus:
$A = ?$, $P = \$1,500$, $r = 5\%$, $n = 57$.

$$A = P\left(1 + \frac{r}{365}\right)^n$$

$$= \$1,500\ (1.0078382) \qquad (\text{Appendix H})$$

$$= \$1,511.7573$$

$$= \$1,511.76$$

Example 2

Leslie Tormes invested $2,000 on July 24 in a credit union that pays interest at a rate of 4½% compounded daily. If the credit union credits the interest to her account quarterly, what was her balance at the end of the quarter?

Solution:

There are 68 days from July 24 to September 30.

$$A = P \left(1 + \frac{r}{365}\right)^n$$

$$= \$2,000 \ (1.0084183) \qquad \text{(Appendix H)}$$

$$= \$2,016.8366$$

$$= \$2,016.84$$

The balance as of September 30 is $2,016.84. The interest earned to this date is $2,016.84 − $2,000.00 = $16.84.

Example 3

Continental Federal pays investers interest at a rate of 5¼% compounded daily, and deposits made by the tenth of a month earn interest from the first of the month. Jim Click opened an account with a $500 deposit on April 8 and made an additional deposit of $700 on May 15. (a) What was the compound amount at the end of the quarter? (b) If Jim receives an interest check quarterly, how much did he receive at the end of the quarter?

Solution:

a. The first deposit earns interest from April 1, since it was made during the first 10 days of the month. There are ninety days from April 1 to June 30, and forty-six days from May 15 to June 30.

April Deposit	*May Deposit*

$$A_1 = P \left(1 + \frac{r}{365}\right)^n \qquad\qquad A_2 = P \left(1 + \frac{r}{365}\right)^n$$

$$\quad = \$500 \ (1.0130284) \qquad\qquad\quad = \$700 \ (1.0066379)$$

$$\quad = \$506.5142 \qquad\qquad\qquad\quad = \$704.64653$$

$$\quad = \$506.51 \qquad\qquad\qquad\qquad = \$704.65$$

The compound amount A is the sum $A_1 + A_2$; thus:

$$A = A_1 + A_2$$

$$= \$506.51 + \$704.65$$

$$= \$1,211.16$$

b. Interest is calculated using:

$$I = A - P$$

$$= \$1,211.16 - \$1,200 \qquad (\$1,200 = \$500 + \$700)$$

$$= \$11.16$$

In problems 1–10, find the compound amount of the given principal invested at the given compound interest rate when interest is compounded daily.

1. $500 from August 15 to December 7 at 4%

2. $1,000 from March 7 to September 14 at 5%

3. $750 from April 14 to June 27 at 4½%

4. $1,200 from October 11 to November 2 at 5½%

5. $1,500 from May 30 to August 23 at 4¾%

6. $900 from June 29 to September 5 at 5¾%

7. $1,450 from January 3 to September 13 at 5½% (Assume non-leap year.)

8. $1,575 from July 4 to October 29 at 4¼%

9. $815 from September 8 to January 27 at 5¼%

10. $682 from November 15 to January 18 at 4¾%

In problems 11–16, assume interest is compounded daily and credited quarterly. Find the amount at the end of the quarter when the given principal is placed in an account that pays the given rate of compound interest.

11. $500 deposited July 15 at 5%

12. $1,500 deposited October 9 at 4%

13. $1,800 deposited November 16 at 5½%

14. $2,200 deposited June 3 at 4½%

15. $600 deposited January 19 at 4¾% (non-leap year)

16. $1,470 deposited January 5 at 5¾% (non-leap year)

17. Pete Thomas opened an account at a savings and loan association that pays 5¼% interest compounded daily with deposits made by the 10th earning interest from the 1st. If Pete opened his account on August 7 with $600 and made an additional deposit on September 12 of $400, what was the balance in his account at the end of the quarter?

18. Carolyn James opened a savings account at Fiduciary Federal with $500 on October 9. On November 5, she made an additional deposit of $300. If Fiduciary Federal pays 4¾% interest compounded daily, with deposits made by the 10th earning interest from the 1st, what was the balance in her account at the end of the quarter?

Nominal Rate vs. Effective Rate

The rate quoted in a compound interest transaction is an annual rate, or **nominal rate.** When the conversion period is less than one year, the action of interest generating interest results in a rate greater than the nominal rate. For example, if $100 is invested for one year at 6% compounded quarterly, then:

$$A = P (1 + i)^n$$
$$= \$100 (1.015)^4$$
$$= \$100 (1.06136355) \qquad \text{(Appendix B)}$$
$$= \$106.14$$

The interest earned in one year is $6.14, which is 6.14% of $100. This is equivalent to $100 invested at 6.14% simple interest, since:

$$I = Prt$$
$$= \$100 \times 0.0614 \times 1$$
$$= \$6.14$$

Compared to the nominal rate of 6%, 6.14% is called the **effective rate** of interest or **true interest** rate, since it indicates the real earning power of the funds invested.

Example 1

If $1,200 is invested for one year at 8% compounded semiannually, find the effective rate.

Solution:

The nominal rate is 8%. $P = \$1,200$, $i = 4\%$, $n = 2$.

$$A = P (1 + i)^n$$
$$= \$1,200 (1.04)^2$$
$$= \$1,200 (1.0816)$$
$$= \$1,297.92$$
$$I = A - P$$
$$= \$1,297.92 - \$1,200.00$$
$$= \$97.92$$
$$r = \frac{I}{Pt}$$
$$= \frac{\$97.92}{\$1,200 \times 1}$$
$$= 0.0816$$
$$= 8.16\%$$

Example 2

A credit union announces the issuance of savings certificates paying an effective interest rate of 6.17%. If the minimum investment is $1,000 and interest is compounded monthly, what is the nominal rate?

Solution:

An effective rate of interest of 6.17% means that $1,000 \times 0.0617 \times 1 = $61.70 interest would be earned in one year, or an amount of $1,061.70.

$$(1 + i)^n = \frac{A}{P}$$

$$= \frac{\$1,061.70}{\$1,000.00}$$

$$= 1.0617$$

In Appendix B the entry for 1.0617 is $(1.005)^{12}$.

Thus:
$$\frac{r}{12} = 0.005$$

$$r = 12 \times 0.005 \qquad \text{(Multiplying both sides by 12)}$$

$$r = 0.06$$

$$r = 6\%$$

Exercises for Section 11.7

In problems 1–10, find the effective interest rates for the given rates of compound interest. (Use a principal of $1,000 invested for one year to perform the calculations.)

1. 6% compounded semiannually

2. 8% compounded quarterly

3. 12% compounded quarterly

4. 4% compounded quarterly

5. 12% compounded monthly

6. 12% compounded semiannually

7. 4% compounded semiannually

8. 3% compounded semiannually

9. 10% compounded quarterly

10. 18% compounded monthly

In problems 11–15, find the nominal interest rates for the given effective rates of interest.

11. 5.58%, interest compounded semiannually

12. 6.61%, interest compounded semiannually

13. 4.58%, interest compounded quarterly

14. 7.19%, interest compounded quarterly

15. 9.31%, interest compounded quarterly

16. A savings and loan association issues $1,000 savings certificates with an effective interest rate of 8.3%. If interest is compounded monthly, what is the nominal rate?

Consumer Credit

Chapter Objectives for Chapter 12

Credit has become an American institution. "Buy now—pay later" is an accepted way of life for the consumer, and Americans buy houses, automobiles, appliances, home furnishings, and clothing on credit. In fact, nearly anything may be obtained on credit. The extent to which Americans buy on credit is demonstrated in Figure 12–1.

Figure 12–1

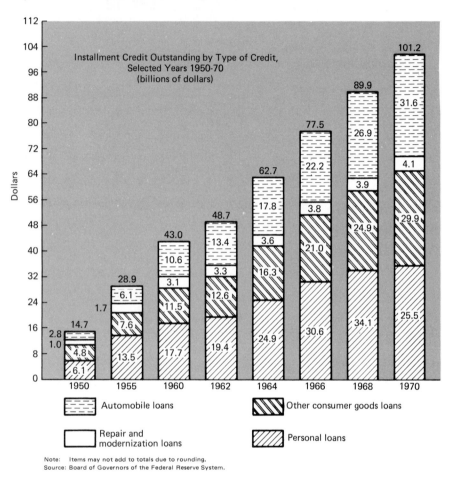

Installment Credit Outstanding by Type of Credit, Selected Years 1950-70 (billions of dollars)

Note: Items may not add to totals due to rounding.
Source: Board of Governors of the Federal Reserve System.

Partly as a result of credit, Americans enjoy the highest standard of living in the world, for it permits the purchase of items they might not otherwise be able to afford. By apportioning the cost of an item into a series of partial payments over a period of time, consumers are able to purchase items that would be impractical if cash were required.

Convenience is a second reason for the widespread acceptance of consumer credit. The ease of purchasing without the need to carry money has been a significant factor in the increase in credit sales. Americans often pay dearly for this convenience; nevertheless, credit purchases by consumers, business, and government are expected to continue to increase. Indeed, predictions of a "credit economy" and a "cashless-checkless" society are becoming widespread.

This chapter will focus on that segment of consumer credit dealing with charge accounts, credit cards, and installment contracts.

12.2 The United States Rule

There is a key difference in loans at simple interest and those retired by a series of partial payments. In the former, the borrower retains the principal for the entire term of the loan; in the latter a partial payment often includes a portion of the principal. As a result, the method of calculating interest can vary. To illustrate this, consider a loan for $1,000 for one year at 6% simple interest. If this loan is repaid in two installments, how is the interest calculated if $500 is paid at the end of six months? One method would be to calculate interest only after the entire principal is repaid; in this event, the interest is $60 ($1,000 × 0.06 × 1) and the second installment is $560. A second method would be to calculate interest after the first installment. Then:

Principal	Interest	Amount	Payment	New Principal
$1,000	$\left(\$30 \ (\$1,000 \times 0.06 \times \frac{1}{2}\right)$	$1,030	$500	$530
$ 530	$\left(\$15.90 \ (\$530 \times 0.06 \times \frac{1}{2}\right)$	$545.90	$545.90	——

Note by this method the total interest charge is only $30.00 + $15.90 = $45.90.

The variety of methods for crediting payments to principal and interest has led to numerous lawsuits, leading eventually to a decision by the United

States Supreme Court. In this decision, certain principles were established regarding partial payments that have become known as the **United States Rule.** The essence of the principles is:

1. Distribution of Partial Payments

    A. If the partial payment exceeds accumulated interest, the difference is deducted from the principal; this new principal is the basis for interest calculations of the next partial payment.

    B. If the partial payment does not exceed the accumulated interest, the interest continues to accrue until the sum of subsequent partial payments equals or exceeds the interest due.

2. Calculation of Interest

    A. Interest is calculated on the principal from the first day of the loan to the day of the first partial payment.

    B. For subsequent partial payments, interest is calculated on the remaining principal from the date of the previous payment to the date of the current payment.*

    C. On the maturity date, interest is calculated from the date of the last payment to the maturity date.*

While no time rule is specified by the court, Banker's Rule (exact time, 360-day year) is used most often. The second part of the previous illustration and the following example are applications of the United States Rule.

Example 1

On a $3,000 loan at 8%, payments of $300, $50, and $200 were made at 90-day intervals. What is the amount due if the loan is paid off in one year?

Solution:

Principal		$3,000.00
Payment 1	$300.00	
Less interest $\left(\$3,000 \times 0.08 \times \frac{1}{4}\right)$	60.00	
Applied to principal		240.00
New Principal		$2,760.00
Payment 2	$ 50.00	
Less interest $\left(\$2,760 \times 0.08 \times \frac{1}{4}\right)$	55.20	
Applied to principal		——

* An exception to this is 1B above.

New Principal		$2,760.00
Payment 3 ($200 + $50)*	$250.00	
Less interest $\left(\$2,760 \times 0.08 \times \frac{1}{2}\right)$	110.40	
Applied to principal		139.60
New Principal		$2,620.40
Interest $\left(\$2,620.40 \times 0.08 \times \frac{1}{4}\right)$		52.41
Amount Due		$2,672.81

The interest for a term of one year would have been $3,000 × 0.08 × 1 = $240; compared to the charges of $60 + $110.40 + $52.41 = $222.81, a savings of $17.19 was realized by making partial payments.

* Because the previous payment did not exceed the accrued interest, it is added to this payment and interest is calculated for 180 days.

Exercises for Section 12.2

In problems 1–10, find the amount due at the end of one year on the given loan when the indicated partial payments are made at 90-day intervals.

1. $1,000 loan at 6% interest; payments of $200, $200, and $400

2. $2,000 loan at 10% interest; payments of $400, $350, and $700

3. $5,000 loan at 9% interest; payments of $1,000, $2,000, and $400

4. $6,000 loan at 7% interest; payments of $2,000, $1,500, and $1,200

5. $8,000 loan at 12% interest; payments of $4,000, $100, and $2,000

6. $1,500 loan at 9% interest; payments of $400, $20, and $500

7. $800 loan at 7% interest; payments of $10, $80, and $100

8. $2,500 loan at 7½% interest; payments of $25, $400, and $600

9. $3,200 loan at 9¾% interest; payments of $50, $50, and $500

10. $2,700 loan at 6¼% interest; payments of $40, $30, and $100

11. Joan Reynolds borrowed $6,000 at 7% interest and made payments at 60-day intervals of $1,000, $500, $40, $1,200, and $30. How much was due on the loan at the end of the first year?

12. Bob Johnson borrowed $4,000 for two years at 8% interest so that he could remodel his clothing shop. If he made partial payments at 90-day intervals of $500, $50, $60, $300, $1,000, $40, and $1,000, how much did he owe at the end of two years?

The Truth-in-Lending Act

As the potential uses of credit are many, so are the potential abuses. Following World War II, credit sales rose phenomenally. A number of these purchases were made by men and women who were not aware of the true cost of credit. Lured by clever advertisements and catch phrases such as "no money down, small monthly payments," these individuals often purchased items solely on their ability to make the monthly payments, not realizing that the total purchase price sometimes included exorbitant fees and high interest rates. Unfortunately, those least able to afford such charges often were the most susceptible to this kind of sales approach, and in some instances persons and families incurred enormous debts due to repeated and unwise credit purchases.

In 1969, Congress acted to protect the public by passing legislation known as the Truth-in-Lending Act. Regulation Z of the Federal Reserve System carries out the provisions of this act.

Truth-in-Lending does not regulate interest charges; it is a disclosure act. The purpose of the law is to make consumers aware of the cost of consumer credit and to permit them to make comparisons of credit terms. As defined by the act, consumer credit is credit offered or extended for which a finance charge is or may be imposed or that is repayable in more than four installments. Thus Regulation Z applies to banks, savings and loans, credit card issuers, automobile dealers, residential mortgage brokers, and all other individuals or groups that offer or arrange for consumer credit.

Two important concepts embodied in Regulation Z are the finance charge and the annual percentage rate. These are discussed in relation to the two types of credit covered by the regulation.

The Finance Charge

In credit purchases covered by Regulation Z, the total price paid by the customer often includes fees other than interest charges. Examples of such fees are credit investigation fees, credit life insurance, or carrying charges. The latter (called carrying charges, time payment differential, or similar names) helps defray the additional bookkeeping expenses incurred by the seller in a credit transaction. Regulation Z lumps all such fees along with interest charges under the term **finance charge.** Thus, the finance charge is the total of all costs the buyer must pay for obtaining credit, whether direct or indirect. Regulation Z states that all such costs must be itemized and disclosed to the customer, clearly and conspicuously.

Not all charges are included in the finance charge. Costs that would be paid even if credit was not granted, such as taxes, licenses, and registration fees, may be excluded. However, these too must be itemized and disclosed to the buyer.

Open-End Credit

Open-end credit transactions are characterized by a finance charge on the unpaid balance each month. Typical of open-end credit are credit card accounts and the revolving charge accounts of most department stores and retail businesses. The finance charge is usually 1% or 1½% of the unpaid balance. The United States Rule is used in payments made on open-end credit accounts.

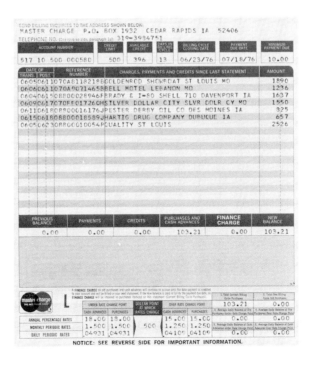

Example 1

The balance on a credit card account with a finance charge of 1% per month on the unpaid balance is $76.40. If monthly payments of $22.00, $12.00, $10.00, and $15.00 are made, find (a) the remaining balance due (b) the total paid in finance charges during this period.

Solution:

Month	Previous Balance	Current Purchases	Pay-ments	Finance Charge		Credited to Balance	New Balance
1	$76.40		$22.00	$0.76	($76.40 × 0.01)	$21.24	$55.16
2	55.16		12.00	0.55	($55.16 × 0.01)	11.45	43.71
3	43.71		10.00	0.44	($43.71 × 0.01)	9.56	34.15
4	34.15		15.00	0.34	($34.15 × 0.01)	14.66	19.49
				$2.09			

The remaining balance is $19.49 and a total finance charge of $2.09 was paid during the period.

Example 2

The outstanding balance, purchases, and payments made on a revolving charge account that carries a finance charge of 1% per month on the unpaid balance were as follows: Previous balance $36.20

Month	Purchases	Payments
1	$ 7.48	$15.00
2	22.60	10.00
3	—	20.00

What is the remaining balance following the third payment?

Solution:

Month	Previous Balance	Current Purchases	Pay-ments	Finance Charge	Credited to Balance	New Balance
1	$36.20	$ 7.48	$15.00	$0.36	$14.64	$29.04
2	29.04	22.60	10.00	0.29	9.71	41.93
3	41.93		20.00	0.42	19.58	22.35

A recent innovation in open-end credit is to calculate the finance charge as a percentage of the "average daily balance" rather than the unpaid balance. The average daily balance is defined as the sum of the daily balances during the billing period divided by the number of days in the billing period. Each daily balance is the previous balance plus cash advances* less any payments or credits, and excluding any unpaid finance charges and purchases made during the billing period.

* Bank sponsored credit cards often provide limited cash loans as a part of their credit services.

The next example illustrates calculation of the finance charge using this method.

Example 3

Rosemary Morley's latest monthly statement from Bank-a-Card contained the following information:

7–18	Closing Date	
	Previous Balance	$355.00
8–5	Payment	$155.00CR
8–8	Marshall's Dept. Store	42.18
8–10	Fancy French Restaurant	18.60
8–12	Cash Advance—Sunshine National Bank	100.00

If the finance charge is $1\frac{1}{2}\%$ per month of the average daily balance, find (a) the average daily balance and (b) the finance charge.

Solution:

a. There are 18 days from the closing date to the payment date, 7 days from the date of payment to the date of the cash advance, and 6 days from the date of the cash advance to the next closing date. Hence,

$$\$355 \times 18 = \$6,390$$
$$\$200 \times 7 = \$1,400\ (\$355 - \$155 = \$200)$$
$$\$300 \times \underline{6} = \$1,800\ (\$200 + \$100 = \$300)$$
$$\overline{31}\quad \$9,590$$

$$\$9,590 \div 31 = \$309.35 \text{ Average Daily Balance}$$

b. $\$309.35 \times 0.015 = \$4.64$ Finance Charge

The finance charge as a percentage of the average daily balance places a heavy penalty on the consumer who makes only a partial payment late in the billing period. To see this, suppose in the previous example Rosemary had no transactions other than a partial payment of $350 on August 15. Then the finance charge for the next statement, calculated on both the unpaid balance and the average daily balance, is as follows:

Unpaid Balance	*Average Daily Balance*
Unpaid Balance = $5	$355 \times 28 = \$9,940$
	$\$\ \ 5 \times \underline{\ \ 3} = \$\ \ \ \underline{15}$
	$\quad\quad\ \ 31\quad \$9,955$
	$\$9,955 \div 31 = \$321.13$ Average Daily Balance
$\$5 \times 0.015 = \$0.075$	$\$321.13 \times 0.015 = \$4.817$
$\quad\quad\quad = \$0.08$ Finance Charge	$\quad\quad\quad = \$4.82$ Finance Charge

Under the average daily balance, the finance charge is *60 times* that of the unpaid balance. While this example is admittedly an extreme case, it illustrates that the average daily balance permits a substantial increase in the finance charge without an increase in the interest rate.

Businesses offering open-end credit accounts are required by Regulation Z to provide new customers with a complete description of the financing, including conditions under which a finance charge can be made, how it is calculated, the periodic rate used, and the minimum periodic payment required. In addition, the seller must send a statement that contains the previous balance, amount and date of each purchase, payments, credits, the finance charge and periodic rate, and the annual percentage rate. Samples of such billing statements are shown in Figures 12–2 and 12–3.

Figure 12–2   Example of a retailer's statement, prepared by a manual billing operation, for an account on which the finance charge is determined by a single periodic rate or a minimum charge of 50 cents applicable to balances under a specific amount. It also assumes that the finance charge is computed on the previous balance before deducting payments and/or credits. Separate slips shall accompany each statement, identifying all charges and credits and showing the dates and amounts thereof.

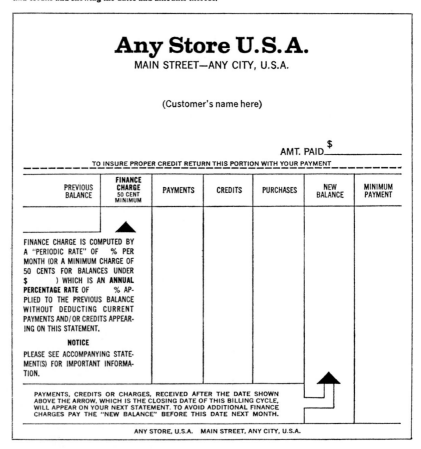

This form, when properly completed, will show how a creditor may comply with the disclosure requirements of the provisions of paragraphs (b) and (c) of §226.7 of Regulation Z for the type of credit extended in this example. This form is intended solely for purposes of demonstration and it is not the only format which will permit a creditor to comply with disclosure requirements of Regulation Z.

Figure 12–3 Example of a retailer's descriptive statement, prepared by an automated billing operation, for an account on which the finance charge is determined by a single periodic rate or a minimum charge of 50 cents applicable to balances under a specified amount. It also assumes that the finance charge is computed on the previous balance before deducting payments and/or credits.

(FACE OF FORM)

Any Store U.S.A.

MAIN STREET—ANY CITY, U.S.A.

(Customer's name here)

YOUR ACCOUNT NUMBER IS__________

TO INSURE PROPER CREDIT RETURN THIS PORTION WITH PAYMENT

BILLING DATES		To Your	We Added Your	We Deducted Your		We Added Your
NEXT MO.	THIS MO.	PREVIOUS BALANCE	**FINANCE CHARGE** 50¢ MINIMUM	PAYMENTS	CREDITS	PURCHASES

TRANSACTION NO.	DATE	STORE	DEPT. NO.	DEPARTMENT NAME	CHARGES	PAYMENTS & CREDITS

To Avoid Additional Finance Charges, Pay The "New Balance" Before Your Billing Date Next Month.	This Is Your NEW BALANCE	This Is Your MINIMUM PAYMENT	**ANNUAL PERCENTAGE RATE**
			%

NOTICE: SEE REVERSE SIDE FOR IMPORTANT INFORMATION

(REVERSE SIDE OF FORM)

PAYMENTS, CREDITS OR CHARGES RECEIVED AFTER YOUR BILLING DATE "THIS MONTH" WILL APPEAR ON YOUR NEXT STATEMENT. YOUR **FINANCE CHARGE** IS COMPUTED BY A SINGLE PERIODIC RATE OF % (OR A MINIMUM CHARGE OF 50 CENTS FOR BALANCES UNDER $) WHICH IS AN **ANNUAL PERCENTAGE RATE** OF % APPLIED TO YOUR "PREVIOUS BALANCE" WITHOUT DEDUCTING CURRENT PAYMENTS AND/OR CREDITS APPEARING ON THE FACE OF THIS STATEMENT.

DEPT. NO.	DEPT. NAME	DEPT. NO.	DEPT. NAME	DEPT. NO.	DEPT. NAME
1	MEN'S ACCESSORIES (Shirts, Ties, Socks, etc.)	(In this form of billing, this side of the statement contains a listing of all departments and a brief description of the merchandise sold in each.)			
2	MEN'S CLOTHING (Suits, Sportcoats, Outerwear, etc.)				

ANY STORE, U.S.A., MAIN ST., ANY CITY, U.S.A.

This form, when properly completed, will show how a creditor may comply with the disclosure requirements of the provisions of paragraphs (b) and (c) of §226.7 of Regulation Z for the type of credit extended in this example. This form is intended solely for purposes of demonstration and it is not the only format which will permit a creditor to comply with disclosure requirements of Regulation Z

Exercises for Section 12.5

A description of a credit card account, including the amount of the unpaid balance and the rate of the monthly finance charge is given in each of problems 1–10. Find the remaining balance due and the total paid in finance charges based on unpaid balance when the indicated monthly payments are made on the account.

1. Unpaid balance of $212.40; 1% per month finance charge; monthly payments of $30, $40, and $50
2. Unpaid balance of $147.32; 1% per month finance charge; monthly payments of $10, $14, and $25

3. Unpaid balance of $171.52; 1½% per month finance charge; monthly payments of $25, $40, and $70

4. Unpaid balance of $314.27; 1½% per month finance charge; monthly payments of $50, $60, and $40

5. Unpaid balance of $273.18; 1% per month finance charge; monthly payments of $30, $70, $40, and $50

6. Unpaid balance of $362.41; 1% per month finance charge; monthly payments of $90, $75, $80, and $100

7. Unpaid balance of $416.14; 1¼% per month finance charge; monthly payments of $85, $90, $60, and $120

8. Unpaid balance of $423.81; 1¼% per month finance charge; monthly payments of $110, $65, $85, and $100

9. Unpaid balance of $517.63; 1½% per month finance charge; monthly payments of $105, $115, $70, $80, and $115

10. Unpaid balance of $605.42; 1½% per month finance charge; monthly payments of $115, $100, $125, $80, and $110

In each of problems 11–16, the outstanding balance, rate of finance charge, purchases, and payments are given for a revolving charge account. Find the remaining balance of each account after the indicated payments and purchases are made.

11. Previous balance of $202.02; 1% per month finance charge

Month	Purchases	Payments
1	$11.56	$20.00
2	$23.41	$40.00
3	$17.85	$50.00

12. Previous balance of $151.42; 1% per month finance charge

Month	Purchases	Payments
1	$19.47	$25.00
2	$43.15	$50.00
3	$11.72	$50.00

13. Previous balance of $94.27; 1½% per month finance charge

Month	Purchases	Payments
1	$17.21	$15.00
2	$ 7.62	$40.00
3	$21.14	$30.00

14. Previous balance of $114.21; 1½% per month finance charge

Month	Purchases	Payments
1	$32.14	$25.00
2	$14.21	$20.00
3	$27.86	$25.00

15. Previous balance of $202.11; 1½% per month finance charge

Month	Purchases	Payments
1	$17.28	$25.00
2	$42.81	$50.00
3	$37.96	$25.00
4	$ 5.11	$75.00

16. Previous balance of $311.49; 1½% per month finance charge

Month	Purchases	Payments
1	$58.41	$100.00
2	$62.83	$ 75.00
3	$19.27	$ 50.00
4	$41.52	$ 75.00

In problems 17–20, the closing date, previous balance, rate of finance charge, and dates of purchases and payments are given for a charge account. Find the average daily balance for the month and compute the finance charge based on the average daily balance.

17. Closing date 4–15, previous balance $240.14, 1% per month finance charge

    4–20, charge—$50.72
    4–28, charge—$24.72
    5–10, payment—$140.00

18. Closing date 2–20, previous balance $360.24, 1½% per month finance charge

    2–26, charge—$24.16
    3–2, payment—$175.00
    3–15, payment—$20.00

19. Closing date 8–10, previous balance $416.18, 1% per month finance charge

    8–20, payment—$200.00
    8–25, cash advance—$50.00
    9–4, charge—$16.72
    9–8, charge—$72.42

20. Closing date 6–1, previous balance $182.78, 1½% per month finance charge

    6–12, cash advance—$100.00
    6–20, payment—$40.00
    6–28, charge—$17.42
    6–30, payment—$50.00

21. The closing date of a charge account is 4–10, with a balance of $316.40. The finance charge is 1½% per month. Find (a) the

finance charge based on the average daily balance and (b) the new balance as of 5–10 if the following transactions are recorded:

    4–20, payment—$150.00
    4–22, charge—$27.16
    4–28, cash advance—$50.00
    4–30, charge—$84.15
    5–4, payment—$100.00

22. The closing balance of a charge account is $512.16 as of 7–20, the closing date. If the finance charge is $1\frac{1}{2}\%$ per month based on the average daily balance, find (a) the finance charge and (b) the new balance as of 8–20 if the following transactions are recorded:

    7–22, charge—$17.29
    7–28, charge—$110.12
    7–29, payment—$300.00
    8–7, charge—$17.29
    8–12, cash advance—$75.00
    8–16, charge—$41.16

What would the new balance be as of 8–20 if the finance charge is computed on the unpaid balance rather than the average daily balance?

12.6   The Installment Plans

A second type of consumer credit is credit in return for a series of equal payments at equal intervals over a fixed period of time. This credit, called the **installment plan,** is used in the purchase of "big ticket" items such as automobiles, furniture, and major appliances. The major features of the installment plan are the down payment, the amount financed, and the amount and schedule of payments.

An accepted principle of the installment plan is that the buyer pay a part of the cash price in the form of a **down payment** or **trade-in.** This creates a sense of ownership for the buyer and provides a safety margin for the vendor. The amount of down payment will vary according to the item purchased; for furniture and appliances, 10% of the cash price is a common figure.*

The cash price minus the down payment or trade-in is the **amount financed.**† The sum of the cash price, the finance charge, and any other charges are called the **deferred payment price.**

The **schedule of payments** is determined by dividing the deferred payment price minus the total down payment into a series of equal partial payments. There are two factors to consider: the amount of the payment

---

* The credit rating of the customer may also influence the amount of the down payment.
† The amount financed is also called the unpaid balance of the cash price. Actually, the amount financed may include other items, but these will not be discussed in this text.

should be relative to the buyer's income and credit status and should correlate with the buyer's pay period; secondly, the unpaid balance should be no greater than the resale value of the merchandise.

Example 1

To purchase a used car, Terry Bacon agreed to pay $200 down and a finance charge of 9% of the cash price of $1,895.00. If Terry paid off the debt in 24 monthly payments, what was (a) the amount of the finance charge, (b) the deferred payment price, and (c) the monthly payment?

Solution:

a. $1,895 × 0.09 = $170.55 Amount of finance charge

b.
$$
\begin{array}{r}
\$1,895.00 \text{ Cash price} \\
+\quad 170.55 \text{ Finance charge} \\
\hline
\$2,065.55 \text{ Deferred payment price}
\end{array}
$$

c.
$$
\begin{array}{r}
\$2,065.55 \text{ Deferred payment price} \\
-\quad 200.00 \text{ Down payment} \\
\hline
\$1,865.55
\end{array}
$$

$1,865.55 ÷ 24 = $77.73125

Since the division does not result in an even number of cents, the monthly payment would likely be $77.73 for 23 months and $77.76 for the final month.

$$
\begin{array}{r}
\$1,787.79 = \$77.73 \times 23 \\
+\quad 77.76 \\
\hline
\$1,865.55
\end{array}
$$

Example 2

Sarah Compton purchased a refrigerator with a cash price of $468.95 from a department store. Sarah paid $46.90 down and $26.26 per month for 18 months. Find (a) the amount financed, (b) the deferred payment price, and (c) the finance charge.

Solution:

a.
$$
\begin{array}{r}
\$468.95 \text{ Cash price} \\
-\quad 46.90 \text{ Down payment} \\
\hline
\$422.05 \text{ Amount financed}
\end{array}
$$

b.
$$
\begin{array}{r}
\$472.68 \text{ (\$26.26} \times 18) \\
+\quad 46.90 \text{ Down payment} \\
\hline
\$519.58 \text{ Deferred payment price}
\end{array}
$$

c.
$$
\begin{array}{r}
\$519.58 \text{ Deferred payment price} \\
-\quad 468.95 \text{ Cash price} \\
\hline
\$\ 50.63 \text{ Finance charge}
\end{array}
$$

Businesses offering installment plans must provide their customers with a description of the financing, similar to the open-end credit plans. It must be in printed form (usually a sales contract) and clearly state the terms of the plan, including the items covered in the previous examples along with the annual rate and the charge for default, delinquency, or penalty for prepayment of principal. A sample of the disclosure information required by Regulation Z is shown in Figure 12–4.

Figure 12–4

Seller's Name: _____   Contract #_____

RETAIL INSTALLMENT CONTRACT AND SECURITY AGREEMENT

The undersigned (herein called Purchaser, whether one or more) purchases from _____(seller) and grants to _____ a security interest in, subject to the terms and conditions hereof, the following described property.

QUANTITY	DESCRIPTION	AMOUNT

Description of Trade-in:

	Sales Tax	
	Total	

PURCHASER'S NAME_____
PURCHASER'S ADDRESS_____
CITY_____STATE_____ZIP_____

1. CASH PRICE $_____
2. LESS: CASH DOWN PAYMENT $_____
3.   TRADE-IN   _____
4.   TOTAL DOWN PAYMENT _____$_____
5. UNPAID BALANCE OF CASH PRICE $_____
6. OTHER CHARGES:

   _____ $_____
   _____

7. AMOUNT FINANCED $_____
8. FINANCE CHARGE $_____
9. TOTAL OF PAYMENTS $_____
10. DEFERRED PAYMENT PRICE (1+6+8) $_____
11. ANNUAL PERCENTAGE RATE   _____%

Insurance Agreement

The purchase of insurance coverage is voluntary and not required for credit.   (Type of Ins.) insurance coverage is available at a cost of $_____ for the term of credit.

I desire insurance coverage

Signed_____ Date_____

I do not desire insurance coverage

Signed_____ Date_____

Purchaser hereby agrees to pay to_____
_____ at their .offices shown above the "TOTAL OF PAYMENTS" shown above in _____ monthly installments of $_____(final payment to be $_____) the first installment being payable _____ 19_____, and all subsequent installments on the same day of each consecutive month until paid in full. The finance charge applies from ___(Date)

Signed_____

Notice to Buyer: You are entitled to a copy of the contract you sign. You have the right to pay in advance the unpaid balance of this contract and obtain a partial refund of the finance charge based on the "Actuarial Method." [Any other method of computation may be so identified, for example, "Rule of 78's," "Sum of the Digits," etc.]

This form, when properly completed, will show how a creditor may comply with the disclosure requirements of the provisions of paragraphs (b) and (c) of §226.8 of Regulation Z for the type of credit extended in this example. This form is intended solely for purposes of demonstration and it is not the only format which will permit a creditor to comply with disclosure requirements of Regulation Z.

In problems 1–10, the cash price of an item is given, along with the percent of the cash price that is the finance charge. For the given down payment and a number of monthly payments, find (a) the amount of the finance charge, (b) the deferred payment price, and (c) the monthly payment.

1. Cash price $772.14, finance charge 7% of cash price, down payment $100, 18 monthly payments

2. Cash price $611.23, finance charge 8% of cash price, down payment $50, 12 monthly payments

3. Cash price $927.18, finance charge 11% of cash price, down payment $125.00, 12 monthly payments

4. Cash price $1,421.87, finance charge 9% of cash price, down payment $201.47, 18 monthly payments

5. Cash price $1,387.26, finance charge 7% of cash price, down payment $225, 12 monthly payments

6. Cash price $2,147.62, finance charge 9½% of cash price, down payment $401.72, 24 monthly payments

7. Cash price $2,896.14, finance charge 8½% of cash price, down payment $375.46, 24 monthly payments

8. Cash price $4,276.18, finance charge 7¼% of cash price, down payment $647.18, 36 monthly payments

9. Cash price $3,721.18, finance charge 8¾% of cash price, down payment $518.27, 36 monthly payments

10. Cash price $3,911.42, finance charge 9¾% of cash price, down payment $421.18, 36 monthly payments

In problems 11–20, the cash price of an item is given, along with the down payment, the amount paid per month, and the number of months payments are to be made. Find (a) the amount financed, (b) the deferred payment price and, (c) the finance charge.

11. Cash price $511.25, down payment $75, monthly payments of $20.78 for 24 months

12. Cash price $824.11, down payment $122.14, monthly payments of $43.04 for 18 months

13. Cash price $421.18, down payment $45.26, monthly payments of $34.54 for 12 months

14. Cash price $729.18, down payment $63.63, monthly payments of $40.92 for 18 months

15. Cash price $1,214.18, down payment $172.18, monthly payments of $49.34 for 24 months

16. Cash price $1,021.11, down payment $221.14, monthly payments of $75.17 for 12 months

17. Cash price $992.95, down payment $110.72, monthly payments of $57.71 for 18 months

18. Cash price $1,795.92, down payment $333.21, monthly payments of $55.77 for 30 months

19. Cash price $2,892.11, down payment $463.81, monthly payments of $77.71 for 36 months

20. Cash price $2,214.87, down payment $385.75, monthly payments of $71.86 for 30 months

21. Judy Anderson purchased a living room suite for $321.18 down and a finance charge of 10% of the cash price of $1,842.15. If Judy paid off the furniture in 20 monthly payments, find (a) the amount of finance charge, (b) the deferred payment price, and (c) the monthly payment.

22. Tom Phillips purchased a washing machine for $40.00 down and $25.00 per month for 12 months. If the cash price of the machine was $312.42, find (a) the amount financed, (b) the deferred payment price, and (c) the finance charge.

12.7 The Annual Percentage Rate

A key feature of the truth-in-lending legislation is the requirement that the seller disclose not only the amount of the finance charge but also the annual percent. Because interest is normally expressed as a rate per annum, the requirement that finance charges also be expressed as an annual rate provides the consumer a truer picture of the cost of consumer credit.

As defined by Regulation Z, the annual percentage rate is found by multiplying the unit-period rate by the number of unit-periods in a given year. The regulation further states that the computation must be accurate to the nearest quarter of 1 percent and that payments are applied first to the finance charge and any remainder to the unpaid balance of the amount financed.

In open-end credit, the unit period is normally one month, and the unit-period rate is the percent per month charge on the unpaid balance. Thus, a charge of 1% per month is an annual percentage rate of 1% × 12 = 12%, 1½% per month is an annual percentage rate (APR) of 1½% × 12 = 18% and 3½% per month is an APR of 42%.

For installment plans, the computation is more involved and APR tables have been prepared by the government to simplify the computation. A portion of this table is Table 12–1. To calculate the APR by this table:

Step 1: Divide the finance charge by the total amount financed and multiply by $100. (This gives the finance charge per $100 of amount to be financed.)

Step 2: Find the number of payments in the first column. Follow horizontally across this line to the amount nearest the value obtained in Step 1. Reading the top of this column gives the annual percentage rate.

Table 12–1

SAMPLE PAGE FROM TABLE FOR COMPUTING ANNUAL PERCENTAGE RATE FOR LEVEL MONTHLY PAYMENT PLANS

NUMBER OF PAYMENTS	ANNUAL PERCENTAGE RATE															
	14.00%	14.25%	14.50%	14.75%	15.00%	15.25%	15.50%	15.75%	16.00%	16.25%	16.50%	16.75%	17.00%	17.25%	17.50%	17.75%
	(FINANCE CHARGE PER $100 OF AMOUNT FINANCED)															
1	1.17	1.19	1.21	1.23	1.25	1.27	1.29	1.31	1.33	1.35	1.37	1.40	1.42	1.44	1.46	1.48
2	1.75	1.78	1.82	1.85	1.88	1.91	1.94	1.97	2.00	2.04	2.07	2.10	2.13	2.16	2.19	2.22
3	2.34	2.38	2.43	2.47	2.51	2.55	2.59	2.64	2.68	2.72	2.76	2.80	2.85	2.89	2.93	2.97
4	2.93	2.99	3.04	3.09	3.14	3.20	3.25	3.30	3.36	3.41	3.46	3.51	3.57	3.62	3.67	3.73
5	3.53	3.59	3.65	3.72	3.78	3.84	3.91	3.97	4.04	4.10	4.16	4.23	4.29	4.35	4.42	4.48
6	4.12	4.20	4.27	4.35	4.42	4.49	4.57	4.64	4.72	4.79	4.87	4.94	5.02	5.09	5.17	5.24
7	4.72	4.81	4.89	4.98	5.06	5.15	5.23	5.32	5.40	5.49	5.58	5.66	5.75	5.83	5.92	6.00
8	5.32	5.42	5.51	5.61	5.71	5.80	5.90	6.00	6.09	6.19	6.29	6.38	6.48	6.58	6.67	6.77
9	5.92	6.03	6.14	6.25	6.35	6.46	6.57	6.68	6.78	6.89	7.00	7.11	7.22	7.32	7.43	7.54
10	6.53	6.65	6.77	6.88	7.00	7.12	7.24	7.36	7.48	7.60	7.72	7.84	7.96	8.08	8.19	8.31
11	7.14	7.27	7.40	7.53	7.66	7.79	7.92	8.05	8.18	8.31	8.44	8.57	8.70	8.83	8.96	9.09
12	7.74	7.89	8.03	8.17	8.31	8.45	8.59	8.74	8.88	9.02	9.16	9.30	9.45	9.59	9.73	9.87
13	8.36	8.51	8.66	8.81	8.97	9.12	9.27	9.43	9.58	9.73	9.89	10.04	10.20	10.35	10.50	10.66
14	8.97	9.13	9.30	9.46	9.63	9.79	9.96	10.12	10.29	10.45	10.62	10.78	10.95	11.11	11.28	11.45
15	9.59	9.76	9.94	10.11	10.29	10.47	10.64	10.82	11.00	11.17	11.35	11.53	11.71	11.88	12.06	12.24
16	10.20	10.39	10.58	10.77	10.95	11.14	11.33	11.52	11.71	11.90	12.09	12.28	12.46	12.65	12.84	13.03
17	10.82	11.02	11.22	11.42	11.62	11.82	12.02	12.22	12.42	12.62	12.83	13.03	13.23	13.43	13.63	13.83
18	11.45	11.66	11.87	12.08	12.29	12.50	12.72	12.93	13.14	13.35	13.57	13.78	13.99	14.21	14.42	14.64
19	12.07	12.30	12.52	12.74	12.97	13.19	13.41	13.64	13.86	14.09	14.31	14.54	14.76	14.99	15.22	15.44
20	12.70	12.93	13.17	13.41	13.64	13.88	14.11	14.35	14.59	14.82	15.06	15.30	15.54	15.77	16.01	16.25
21	13.33	13.58	13.82	14.07	14.32	14.57	14.82	15.06	15.31	15.56	15.81	16.06	16.31	16.56	16.81	17.07
22	13.96	14.22	14.48	14.74	15.00	15.26	15.52	15.78	16.04	16.30	16.57	16.83	17.09	17.36	17.62	17.88
23	14.59	14.87	15.14	15.41	15.68	15.96	16.23	16.50	16.78	17.05	17.32	17.60	17.88	18.15	18.43	18.70
24	15.23	15.51	15.80	16.08	16.37	16.65	16.94	17.22	17.51	17.80	18.09	18.37	18.66	18.95	19.24	19.53
25	15.87	16.17	16.46	16.76	17.06	17.35	17.65	17.95	18.25	18.55	18.85	19.15	19.45	19.75	20.05	20.36
26	16.51	16.82	17.13	17.44	17.75	18.06	18.37	18.68	18.99	19.30	19.62	19.93	20.24	20.56	20.87	21.19
27	17.15	17.47	17.80	18.12	18.44	18.76	19.09	19.41	19.74	20.06	20.39	20.71	21.04	21.37	21.69	22.02
28	17.80	18.13	18.47	18.80	19.14	19.47	19.81	20.15	20.48	20.82	21.16	21.50	21.84	22.18	22.52	22.86
29	18.45	18.79	19.14	19.49	19.83	20.18	20.53	20.88	21.23	21.58	21.94	22.29	22.64	22.99	23.35	23.70
30	19.10	19.45	19.81	20.17	20.54	20.90	21.26	21.62	21.99	22.35	22.72	23.08	23.45	23.81	24.18	24.55
31	19.75	20.12	20.49	20.87	21.24	21.61	21.99	22.37	22.74	23.12	23.50	23.88	24.26	24.64	25.02	25.40
32	20.40	20.79	21.17	21.56	21.95	22.33	22.72	23.11	23.50	23.89	24.28	24.68	25.07	25.46	25.86	26.25
33	21.06	21.46	21.85	22.25	22.65	23.06	23.46	23.86	24.26	24.67	25.07	25.48	25.88	26.29	26.70	27.11
34	21.72	22.13	22.54	22.95	23.37	23.78	24.19	24.61	25.03	25.44	25.86	26.28	26.70	27.12	27.54	27.97
35	22.38	22.80	23.23	23.65	24.08	24.51	24.94	25.36	25.79	26.23	26.66	27.09	27.52	27.96	28.39	28.83
36	23.04	23.48	23.92	24.35	24.80	25.24	25.68	26.12	26.57	27.01	27.46	27.90	28.35	28.80	29.25	29.70
37	23.70	24.16	24.61	25.06	25.51	25.97	26.42	26.88	27.34	27.80	28.26	28.72	29.18	29.64	30.10	30.57
38	24.37	24.84	25.30	25.77	26.24	26.70	27.17	27.64	28.11	28.59	29.06	29.53	30.01	30.49	30.96	31.44
39	25.04	25.52	26.00	26.48	26.96	27.44	27.92	28.41	28.89	29.38	29.87	30.36	30.85	31.34	31.83	32.32
40	25.71	26.20	26.70	27.19	27.69	28.18	28.68	29.18	29.68	30.18	30.68	31.18	31.68	32.19	32.69	33.20
41	26.39	26.89	27.40	27.91	28.41	28.92	29.44	29.95	30.46	30.97	31.49	32.01	32.52	33.04	33.56	34.08
42	27.06	27.58	28.10	28.62	29.15	29.67	30.19	30.72	31.25	31.78	32.31	32.84	33.37	33.90	34.44	34.97
43	27.74	28.27	28.81	29.34	29.88	30.42	30.96	31.50	32.04	32.58	33.13	33.67	34.22	34.76	35.31	35.86
44	28.42	28.97	29.52	30.07	30.62	31.17	31.72	32.28	32.83	33.39	33.95	34.51	35.07	35.63	36.19	36.76
45	29.11	29.67	30.23	30.79	31.36	31.92	32.49	33.06	33.63	34.20	34.77	35.35	35.92	36.50	37.08	37.66
46	29.79	30.36	30.94	31.52	32.10	32.68	33.26	33.84	34.43	35.01	35.60	36.19	36.78	37.37	37.96	38.56
47	30.48	31.06	31.66	32.25	32.84	33.44	34.03	34.63	35.23	35.83	36.43	37.04	37.64	38.25	38.86	39.46
48	31.17	31.77	32.37	32.98	33.59	34.20	34.81	35.42	36.03	36.65	37.27	37.88	38.50	39.13	39.75	40.37
49	31.86	32.48	33.09	33.71	34.34	34.96	35.59	36.22	36.84	37.47	38.10	38.74	39.37	40.01	40.65	41.29
50	32.55	33.18	33.82	34.45	35.09	35.73	36.37	37.01	37.65	38.30	38.94	39.59	40.24	40.89	41.55	42.20
51	33.25	33.89	34.54	35.19	35.84	36.49	37.15	37.81	38.46	39.12	39.79	40.45	41.11	41.78	42.45	43.12
52	33.95	34.61	35.27	35.93	36.60	37.27	37.94	38.61	39.28	39.96	40.63	41.31	41.99	42.67	43.36	44.04
53	34.65	35.32	36.00	36.68	37.36	38.04	38.72	39.41	40.10	40.79	41.48	42.17	42.87	43.57	44.27	44.97
54	35.35	36.04	36.73	37.42	38.12	38.82	39.52	40.22	40.92	41.63	42.33	43.04	43.75	44.47	45.18	45.90
55	36.05	36.76	37.46	38.17	38.88	39.60	40.31	41.03	41.74	42.47	43.19	43.91	44.64	45.37	46.10	46.83
56	36.76	37.48	38.20	38.92	39.65	40.38	41.11	41.84	42.57	43.31	44.05	44.79	45.53	46.27	47.02	47.77
57	37.47	38.20	38.94	39.68	40.42	41.16	41.91	42.65	43.40	44.15	44.91	45.66	46.42	47.18	47.94	48.71
58	38.18	38.93	39.68	40.43	41.19	41.95	42.71	43.47	44.23	45.00	45.77	46.54	47.32	48.09	48.87	49.65
59	38.89	39.66	40.42	41.19	41.96	42.74	43.51	44.29	45.07	45.85	46.64	47.42	48.21	49.01	49.80	50.60
60	39.61	40.39	41.17	41.95	42.74	43.53	44.32	45.11	45.91	46.71	47.51	48.31	49.12	49.92	50.73	51.55

Some questions and answers about open end credit

Q: Are periodic statements necessary on open end accounts?
A: Yes, but only where there is an unpaid balance over $1 or where a finance charge is made. (Reg. Z/226.7 (b))

Q: What sort of information must accompany a monthly statement?
A: Where applicable, you must give customers this information: (Reg. Z/226.7 (b))
1. The unpaid balance at the start of the billing period.
2. The amount and date of each extension of credit and identification of each item bought.
3. Payments made by a customer and other credits: this includes returns, rebates and adjustments.
4. The finance charge shown in dollars and cents.
5. The rates used in calculating the finance charge plus the range of balances to which they apply.
6. The annual percentage rate.
7. The unpaid balance on which the finance charge was calculated.
8. The closing date of the billing cycle and the unpaid balance at that time.

Q: Where must this information appear?
A: Some items must appear on the actual face of the statement. Others may be shown on the reverse side; or, on a separate form enclosed in the same envelope. (Reg. Z/226.7 (c))

Q: How is the annual percentage rate determined on open end credit?
A: The finance charge is divided by the unpaid balance to which it applies. This gives the rate per month or whatever time period is used.
The result is multiplied by 12 or the other number of time periods used by you during the year. (Reg. Z/226.5 (a))

Here's an example:

A typical charge of 1½ % is made on an unpaid balance where bills are sent out monthly. The annual percentage rate would be twelve times 1½% or 18%.
Other methods for calculating the annual percentage rate on open end credit are detailed in Reg. Z/226.5 (a) and Reg. Z/226.7 (b) (6).

Example 1

An installment contract for a color TV set contains the following information: cash price $695.00, total down payment $150.00, deferred payment price $799.25. What is the annual percentage rate if the plan calls for 24 monthly payments?

Solution:

$799.25 Deferred payment price
− 695.00 Cash price
———————
$104.25 Finance charge

$695.00   Cash price
$\underline{-\ 150.00}$ Down payment
$545.00   Amount financed

Step 1: $\dfrac{\$104.25}{\$545.00} \times \$100 = \$19.13$

Step 2:   In line 24 of Table 12–1, the nearest value to $19.13 is $19.24. At the top of this column, the annual percentage rate is 17.50%.

Example 2

Gene Roberts purchased a set of four automobile tires by making 16 monthly payments of $13.44. He received $12.00 credit for his old tires as a trade-in. The cash price was $51.00 per tire including all state and federal taxes. What annual percentage rate did Gene pay as a result of buying on credit?

Solution:

$215.08   ($13.44 × 16)
$\underline{+\ \ \ 12.00}$ Trade-in
$227.08   Deferred payment price

$227.08   Deferred payment price
$\underline{-\ 204.00}$ Cash price ($51.00 × 4)
$ 23.08   Finance charge

$204.00   Cash price
$\underline{-\ \ \ 12.00}$ Trade-in
$192.00   Amount financed

$\dfrac{\$\ 23.08}{\$192.00} \times 100 = \$12.02$

In line 16 the nearest value to $12.02 is $12.09; hence, the APR is 16.5%.

12.8   The Constant Ratio Method

Prior to the Truth-in-Lending law, the most common method for calculating an annual interest rate was by a formula called the **constant ratio** method. This formula computes an interest rate higher than the tables used to compute the APR, but can be used as a rough approximation. The constant ratio method owes its name to the fact that the ratio of the interest to the total partial payment remains constant for each payment. The constant ratio formula is

$$i = \frac{2md}{B(n+1)}$$

where

$$i = \text{annual interest rate}$$

$$m = \text{number of possible payments in one year}$$

$$n = \text{total number of payments}$$

$$d = \text{finance charge}$$

$$B = \text{amount financed}$$

Example 1

Thelma Fricks purchased a vacuum cleaner by paying $15.00 down and $8.26 per month for 6 months. If the cash price was $59.95, find an annual interest rate using the constant ratio formula.

Solution:

$59.95 Cash price
− 15.00 Down payment

$44.95 Amount financed

$49.56 ($8.26 × 6)
− 44.95 Amount financed

$ 4.61 Finance charge

$m = 12, n = 6, d = 4.61, B = \$44.95$

$$i = \frac{2md}{B(n+1)}$$

$$= \frac{2 \times 12 \times 4.61}{44.95 \times 7}$$

$$= 0.352$$

$$= 35.2\%$$

Exercises for Sections 12.7 and 12.8   In problems 1–6, find the annual percentage rate for revolving charge accounts with the given monthly interest rate.

1. 1¼%   4. 2¾%

2. 2¼%   5. ¾%

3. 2½%   6. 1¾%

In problems 7–15, use Table 12–1 to find the annual percentage rate for the given installment contract.

7. Cash price $472.00, down payment $75.00, deferred payment price $525.00, 18 monthly payments

8. Cash price $782.40, down payment $110, deferred payment price $896.62, 24 monthly payments

9. Cash price $1,287.40, down payment $325, deferred payment price $1,575.80, 40 monthly payments

10. Cash price $1,896.52, down payment $425.50, deferred payment price $2,145.80, 24 monthly payments

11. Cash price $2,692.49, down payment $510.25, deferred payment price $3,082.75, 26 monthly payments

12. Cash price $979.42, down payment $220.15, deferred payment price $1,142.60, 30 monthly payments

13. Cash price $1,475.83, down payment $283.49, deferred payment price $1,695.43, 28 monthly payments

14. Cash price $1,064.89, down payment $187.72, deferred payment price $1,210.87, 25 monthly payments

15. Cash price $4,287.50, down payment $723.89, deferred payment price $4,893.80, 22 monthly payments

In problems 16–20, use Table 12–1 to find the annual percentage rate when an item with the given cash price is paid for by making the given payments.

16. Cash price $485.42, 24 monthly payments of $23.45 each

17. Cash price $859.63, 12 monthly payments of $77.82 each

18. Cash price $1,152.16, 15 monthly payments of $85.86 each

19. Cash price $987.24, 30 monthly payments of $39.33 each

20. Cash price $647.83, 18 monthly payments of $40.96 each

In problems 21–25, use the constant ratio formula to compute the annual interest rate.

21. Cash price $743.85, down payment $50.00, 18 monthly payments of $44.65 each

22. Cash price $1,142.86, down payment $225, 12 monthly payments of $83.15 each

23. Cash price $1,857.64, down payment $410, 24 monthly payments of $71.20 each

24. Cash price $858.19, down payment $95.00, 20 monthly payments of $43.66 each

25. Cash price $1,042.80, down payment $140, 18 monthly payments of $58.11 each

26. Bob Johnson purchased a new outboard motor by paying $75.00 down and $56.03 a month for 18 months. If the cash price was $957.75, find the annual interest rate Bob is paying by (a) using Table 12–1 and (b) using the constant ratio formula.

27. Sylvia Stephens purchased a new sewing machine by paying $50.00 down and $27.66 a month for 24 months. If the cash price was $621.80, find the annual interest rate Sylvia is paying by (a) using Table 12–1 and (b) using the constant ratio formula.

Section **12.9** Rule of 78

Installment contracts are designed to pay off the principal and interest charge by a series of partial payments; thus, each payment is part principal and part interest. Should the full amount of the obligation be paid prior to the maturity date, the borrower may be entitled to a rebate on the unearned interest.

The Truth-in-Lending Act requires the lender to disclose the method of calculating such a rebate when the loan is initiated. In the language of the act, the lender must give ". . . a statement of the amount or method of computation of any charge that may be deducted from the amount of any rebate of such unearned finance charge that will be credited to an obligation or refunded to the customer."*

A method commonly used to calculate this rebate is called the Rule of 78, or the sum-of-the-balances method. This method assumes that on a 12-month loan, 12 units of principal are outstanding on the first month, 11 units are outstanding the second month, 10 units are outstanding the third month, and so on, to the last or twelfth month when 1 unit of principal would be outstanding. Since the sum of the numbers from 1 to 12 is 78, the total interest charge is divided into 78 units (hence the name Rule of 78).

Division of the interest charge into 78 units has the following effect on the amount of the rebate. Clearly, there is no rebate if the loan is not paid off until the end of the twelfth month or the maturity date, but if the loan is paid off at the end of the eleventh month, the borrower is entitled to a rebate of $\frac{1}{78}$ of the interest charge. If the loan is paid off at the end of the tenth month, the borrower is entitled to a rebate of $\frac{1}{78} + \frac{2}{78} = \frac{1+2}{78} = \frac{3}{78}$

---

* If the credit contract does not provide for any rebate of unearned finance charges upon prepayment in full, this must be disclosed.

of the finance charge, and if the loan is paid off at the end of the ninth month, the borrower is entitled to a rebate of $\dfrac{1+2+3}{78}$ of the interest charge. In general, if a 12-month loan is paid in full at the end of the nth month, then the amount of the rebate R is given by the formula

$$(12\text{--}1) \qquad R = \frac{1 + 2 + \ldots + (12\text{-}n)}{78} \times \text{Interest Charge}$$

Example 1

Beverly McMillan purchased a set of golf clubs on an installment contract that included a finance charge of $40.00. If she decided to pay off the entire contract at the end of the seventh month, how much would her rebate be under the Rule of 78?

Solution:

$n = 7$ and $12 - n = 12 - 7 = 5$, hence by formula (12–1),

$$R = \frac{1 + 2 + 3 + 4 + 5}{78} \times \$40.00$$

$$= \frac{15}{78} \times \$40.00$$

$$= \$7.692$$

$$= \$7.69$$

Rebate calculations for contracts other than twelve months duration are the same, except that the number of units is different. For a six-month loan there are $1 + 2 + 3 + 4 + 5 + 6 = 21$ units, for an 18-month loan there are 171 units, for a two-year loan there are 300 units, etc.

A general formula for the amount of rebate under the sum-of-the-balances method is as follows:

If $R =$ amount of rebate

$m =$ total number of months

$n = m$ minus number of months before prepay

then

$$(12\text{--}2) \qquad R = \frac{n(n+1)}{m(m+1)} \times \text{Interest Charge}$$

In Example 1 of this section, $m = 12$, $n = 12 - 7 = 5$, and the finance charge was $40.00, thus

$$R = \frac{5(6)}{12(13)} \times \$40.00$$

$$= \frac{5}{26} \times \$40.00$$

$$= \$7.69$$

Example 2

To get a new roof put on his house Danny Swisshelm signed a contract calling for a finance charge of $234.00 and 24 monthly payments of $84.75. At the end of the fifteenth month, Danny decided to pay off the entire debt. Under the sum-of-the-balances method, what rebate did Danny receive?

Solution:

$m = 24, n = 24 - 15 = 9$

$$R = \frac{9(10)}{24(25)} \times \$234.00$$

$$= \frac{3}{20} \quad \times \$234.00$$

$$= \$35.10$$

Example 3

K. May McCluskey purchased a vacuum cleaner for a finance charge of $18.00 and 6 payments of $23.00 per month. At the end of the fourth month, Mrs. McCluskey decided to pay off the entire amount of the obligation. Find (a) the amount of the rebate and (b) the amount of the final payment.

Solution:

a. $m = 6, n = 6 - 4 = 2$

$$R = \frac{2(3)}{6(7)} \times \$18.00$$

$$= \frac{1}{7} \times \$18.00$$

$$= \$2.57$$

b. If the debt is to be paid off at the end of the fourth month, three payments have been made with three remaining. The remaining payments total $3 \times \$23.00 = \$69.00$; with the rebate, the final payment is $\$69.00 - \$2.57 = \$66.43$.

Exercises for Section 12.9

In problems 1–5, use the Rule of 78 to compute the rebate when a twelve-month installment contract with the given finance charge is paid off at the end of the given month.

1. Finance charge $60, paid off at the end of the fifth month

2. Finance charge $18, paid off at the end of the third month

3. Finance charge $24, paid off at the end of the tenth month

4. Finance charge $38, paid off at the end of the fourth month

5. Finance charge $42, paid off at the end of the eighth month

In problems 6–10, use the sum-of-the-balances method to compute the rebate when an installment contract of the given duration with the given finance charge is paid off at the end of the given month.

6. Two-year contract, $180 finance charge, paid off at the end of the twelfth month

7. Eighteen-month contract, $110 finance charge, paid off at the end of the eighth month

8. Six-month contract, $24 finance charge, paid off at the end of the third month

9. Fourteen-month contract, $90 finance charge, paid off at the end of the fifth month

10. Twenty-month contract, $140 finance charge, paid off at the end of the fourteenth month

11. Bob Jacobs purchased a color television set on a one-year installment contract that included a finance charge of $86. If Bob paid off the contract at the end of the eighth month, what was his rebate?

12. Jennifer Childress signed a one-year installment contract to purchase some furniture. If the contract included a finance charge of $74, and if Jennifer paid off the contract at the end of the fifth month, what was her rebate?

13. Craig Ross bought some new equipment for his radiator shop on a 20-month installment contract that included a finance charge of $236. He was then able to pay off the contract at the end of the 12th month. How much was his rebate?

14. Diane Dennis signed an 18-month installment contract to buy some new display items for her clothing shop. If the contract included a finance charge of $210, and if Diane paid off the contract at the end of the 14th month, what was her rebate?

15. Ralph Thomas bought a fishing boat on an installment plan of $52 a month for one year. At the end of the seventh month, Ralph paid off the contract. If the finance charge was $46, find the amount of the final payment.

16. Marcia Brennan purchased a refrigerator for a finance charge of $36 and 8 monthly payments of $63 each. At the end of the sixth month, Marcia paid off the contract. What was the amount of the final payment?

13

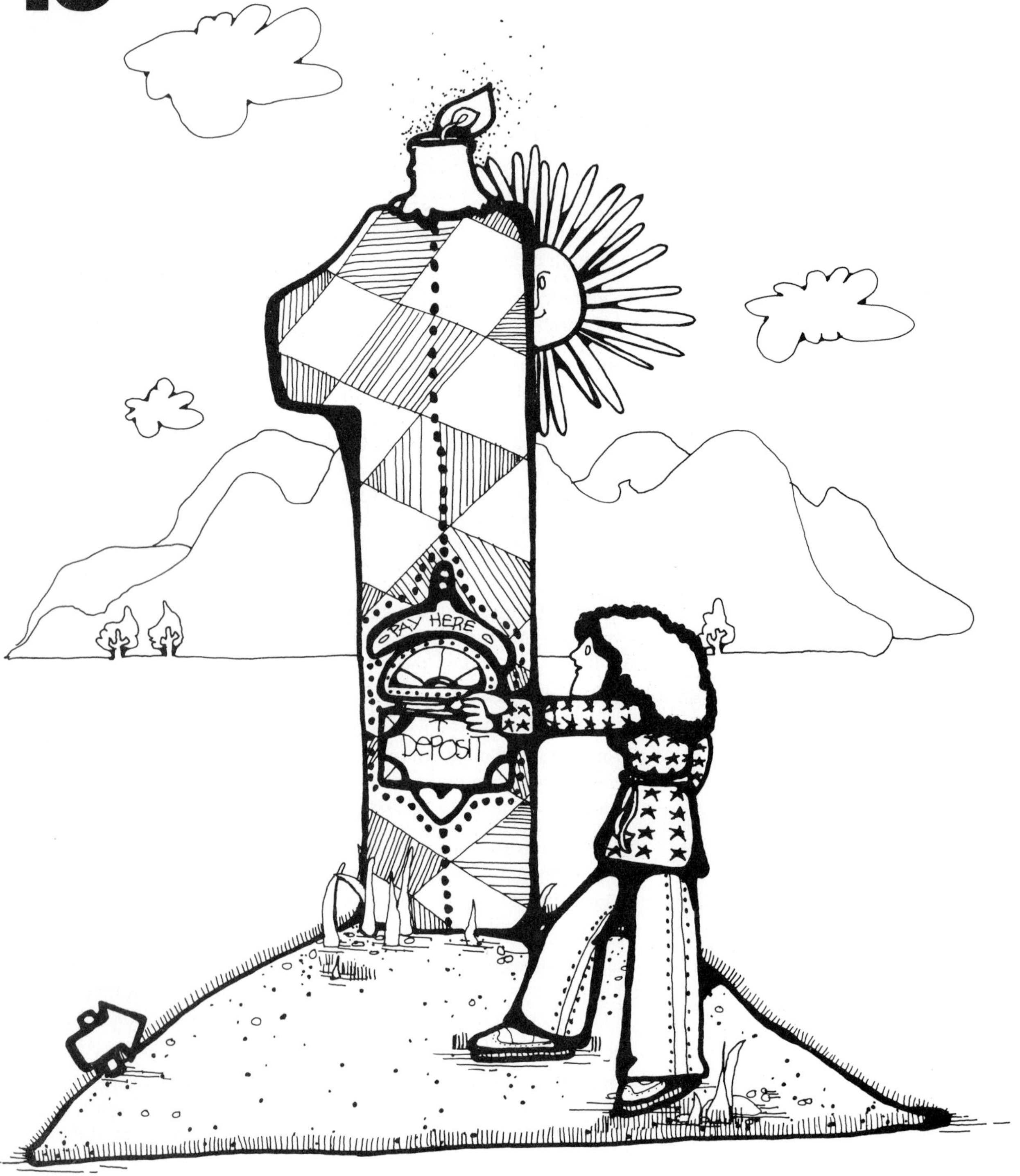

Annuities

Chapter Objectives for Chapter 13

I. Learn the meaning of the following terms:

A. *Annuity*, 334
B. *Period of an annuity*, 334
C. *Term of an annuity*, 334
D. *Annuity certain*, 334
E. *Ordinary annuity*, 334
F. *Annuity due*, 334
G. *Present value of an annuity*, 341

II. Understand:

A. The difference between an ordinary annuity and an annuity due, 334
B. The accumulated amount of an ordinary annuity, 335
C. The present value of an ordinary annuity, 341
D. The accumulated amount of an annuity due, 345
E. The present value of an annuity due, 348

III. Calculate:

A. The accumulated amount of an ordinary annuity, 335
B. The number of payments of an ordinary annuity, 339, 342
C. The present value of an ordinary annuity, 342
D. The accumulated amount of an annuity due, 345
E. The present value of an annuity due, 348

Introduction

An **annuity** is a series of payments at regular intervals. The payments are normally equal, but need not be so. The time interval between payments is called the **period,** and the **term** of an annuity is the time from the beginning of the first period to the end of the last period. Examples of annuities are social security payments, mortgage payments on a house, endowments, and installment plan payments.

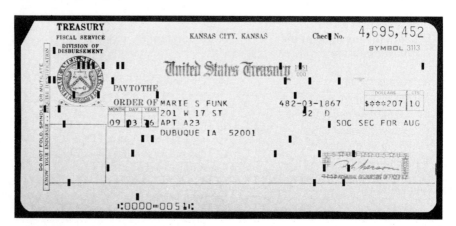

The type of annuity to be studied in this chapter is the **annuity certain,** in which the beginning and ending dates are specified.* There are two basic kinds of annuities certain. If the payment is made at the end of a period, the annuity is called an **ordinary annuity;** if the payment is made at the beginning of a period, the annuity is called an **annuity due.** (See Figure 13–1.)

Figure 13–1

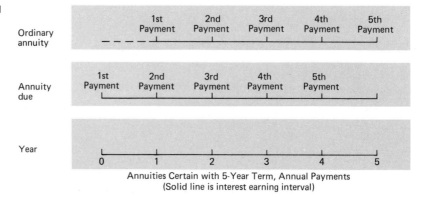

Annuities Certain with 5-Year Term, Annual Payments
(Solid line is interest earning interval)

---

* If either the beginning or ending date is not specified, then the annuity is called a **contingent** annuity. Proceeds of a life insurance policy that are paid in installments are an example of this kind of annuity, in that the beginning payment is contingent on the death of the insured.

Ordinary Annuities

To understand this annuity and its formulas, suppose on May 1 of each year for five years, $1 is deposited in a savings account paying 6% interest compounded annually. What is the accumulated amount at the *end* of the last deposit?

The fifth deposit, having just been made, earns no interest; the fourth deposit earns one year's interest, the third two years' interest, etc. By formula (11–1) for compound interest,

$$
\begin{array}{lll}
\text{Fifth deposit} & \$1 & = \$1.00000000 \\
\text{Fourth deposit} & \$1\,(1.06)^1 = & 1.06000000 \\
\text{Third deposit} & \$1\,(1.06)^2 = & 1.12360000 \\
\text{Second deposit} & \$1\,(1.06)^3 = & 1.19101600 \\
\text{First deposit} & \$1\,(1.06)^4 = & \underline{1.26247696} \\
\text{Accumulated deposit} & & = \$5.63709296
\end{array}
$$

The accumulated amount for deposits of $1 is $5.63709296; by the same reasoning it can be shown that had the deposits been $100 per year the accumulated amount would be $100 × 5.63709296 = $563.709296, and that deposits of $1,000 per year would result in an accumulated amount of $1,000 × 5.63709296 = $5,637.09296.

This special case leads to a generalization. Consider an ordinary annuity with n payments of $1 each ($n$ = a counting number) made at intervals of one a year, and let the annual compound interest rate be i. Then, if the accumulated amount is denoted by $s_{\overline{n}|\,i}$,

(13–1) $s_{\overline{n}|\,i} = 1 + (1+i) + (1+i)^2 + (1+i)^3 + \cdots + (1+i)^{n-1}$

The right-hand side of this equation can be simplified;* the result is

(13–2) $$s_{\overline{n}|\,i} = \frac{(1+i)^n - 1}{i}$$

To demonstrate formula (13–2), consider the previous illustration:

$$
\begin{aligned}
s_{\overline{5}|\,.06} &= \frac{(1.06)^5 - 1}{0.06} \\
&= \frac{1.33822558 - 1}{0.06} \qquad (\text{Appendix B}) \\
&= \frac{0.33822558}{0.06} \\
&= 5.63709296
\end{aligned}
$$

* The right-hand side of the equation is in the form of a geometric progression
$a + ar + ar^2 + \cdots + ar^{n-1}$, which is equal to $\dfrac{a(r^n - 1)}{r - 1}$.

One final step in the generalization remains. Formula (13–2) is the accumulated amount for payments of $1; if the payments are P dollars per year, and if the accumulated amount is denoted by S, then

(13–3) $$S = P \cdot s_{\overline{n}|\,i}$$

Annuity Tables

It is clear that annuity computations can be made using a compound interest table such as Appendix B. However, the computations are tedious; for that reason a table has been prepared for values of $s_{\overline{n}|\,i}$. Such a table is Appendix D in the appendix. The heading of each page is the value for i; the values of n are in the left-hand column.

Example 1

What is the accumulated amount for annual deposits of $1,000 in an account paying 8% compounded annually following the 12th deposit?

Solution:

$S = ?, P = \$1,000, n = 12, i = 0.08$

$$S = P \cdot s_{\overline{n}|\,i}$$
$$= \$1,000 \cdot s_{\overline{12}|\,.08}$$
$$= \$1,000 \times 18.97712646 \qquad \text{(Appendix D)}$$
$$= \$18,977.12646$$
$$= \$18,977.13$$

Exercises for Section 13.3

In problems 1 through 19, use Appendix D and the formula $S = P \cdot s_{\overline{n}|\,i}$ to find the accumulated amount S when P dollars are invested annually n times in an account paying the given interest rate i compounded annually.

1. $P = \$500, n = 4, i = 6\%$

2. $P = \$800, n = 6, i = 4\%$

3. $P = \$1,200, n = 5, i = 8\%$

4. $P = \$1,200, n = 8, i = 8\%$

5. $P = \$1,600, n = 10, i = 7\%$

6. $P = \$600, n = 15, i = 5\%$

7. $P = \$750, n = 15, i = 4\frac{1}{2}\%$

8. $P = \$400, n = 20, i = 6\%$

9. $P = \$900, n = 40, i = 3\frac{1}{2}\%$

10. $P = \$300, n = 10, i = 7\%$

11. $P = \$350, n = 14, i = 6\%$

12. $P = \$750, n = 12, i = 5\%$

13. $P = \$1,250, n = 15, i = 7\%$

14. $P = \$1,000, n = 20, i = 8\%$

15. $P = \$1,600, n = 18, i = 7\%$

16. $P = \$1,750, n = 14, i = 6\%$

17. $P = \$950, n = 12, i = 8\%$

18. $P = \$650, n = 25, i = 7\%$

19. $P = \$700, n = 30, i = 4\frac{1}{2}\%$

20. Carl Jennings decides to start a savings plan for his retirement by placing $1,000 a year in a savings account that pays 7% interest compounded annually. How much will Carl have in his savings account after he makes his twentieth deposit?

21. Myra Miller is working in a woman's clothing store. She wants to open her own shop, so she decides to put $1,200 a year into a savings account that pays 8% interest compounded annually. How much will she have in her account after she makes her fifth deposit? After she makes her eighth deposit?

22. John Atkins is placing $800 a year in an account that pays 8% interest compounded annually. He intends to use this savings plan to educate his children. How much will John have in the account after he makes his fifteenth deposit?

23. Sarah Stephens is putting $1,600 a year into an account that pays 6% interest compounded annually in order to save money for a new house. How much will she have in the account after she makes her sixth deposit? After she makes her twelfth deposit?

24. Mechanic Jack Ruse places $2,000 a year in an account paying 7% compounded annually in order to save money to purchase his own auto repair shop. How much will Jack have in the account after he makes his seventh deposit? After he makes his tenth deposit?

25. Janet Richards has decided to put $1,500 a year into an account that pays 8% interest compounded annually, so that one day she will be able to open her own business. How much will she have in the account after she makes her fourth deposit? After she makes her seventh deposit?

Nominal Rate

The word annuity implies annual payments and a nominal rate; in practice the payments and conversion period may be semiannual, quarterly, or monthly.* Analogous to compound interest, formula (13–3) may be used in any annuity calculation as long as the conversion period and the payment period are the same time interval.

Example 1

Payments of $1,000 are made twice a year, and are accumulated at 5% compounded semiannually. What is the accumulated amount following the tenth payment?

Solution:

$$S = ?, P = \$1,000, n = 10, i = \frac{5\%}{2} = 2\tfrac{1}{2}\%$$

$$
\begin{aligned}
S &= P \cdot s_{\overline{n}|\,i} \\
&= \$1,000 \cdot s_{\overline{10}|\,.025} \\
&= \$1,000 \cdot 11.20338177 \qquad (\text{Appendix D}) \\
&= \$11,203.38177 \\
&= \$11,203.38
\end{aligned}
$$

Example 2

To provide for the replacement of machinery, the Krane Company made quarterly deposits of $1,800 in an account that pays 6% interest compounded quarterly. How much was in the fund after the twelfth deposit, and how much interest was earned?

Solution:

$$S = ?, P = \$1,800, n = 12, i = \frac{6\%}{4} = 1\tfrac{1}{2}\%$$

$$
\begin{aligned}
S &= P \cdot s_{\overline{n}|\,i} \\
&= \$1,800 \cdot s_{\overline{12}|\,.015} \\
&= \$1,800 \times 13.04121143 \qquad (\text{Appendix D}) \\
&= \$23,474.18052 \\
&= \$23,474.18
\end{aligned}
$$

The total of the deposits is $12 \times \$1,800 = \$21,600$, thus the interest earned is $\$23,474.18 - \$21,600 = \$1,874.18$.

---

* **Nominal rate** and **conversion period** were discussed in Section 11.1.

Example 3

How many monthly payments of $150 would it take to accumulate $5,000 if the payments are deposited in an account paying 4% compounded monthly?

Solution:

$$S = \$5,000, \ P = \$150, \ n = \ ?, \ i = \frac{4\%}{12} = \frac{1}{3}\%$$

$$S = P \cdot s_{\overline{n}| \, i}$$

$$P \cdot s_{\overline{n}| \, i} = S$$

$$s_{\overline{n}| \, i} = \frac{S}{P} \qquad \text{(Dividing both sides by } P\text{)}$$

$$s_{\overline{n}| \, \frac{1}{3}\%} = \frac{\$5,000}{150}$$

$$= 33.33333333$$

Using Appendix D on the page headed ⅓%, the entry nearest to but larger than 33.33333333 is 33.70980154, for $n = 32$. Thus, a minimum of $n = 32$ payments are required. This will result in an accumulation of $150 × 33.70980154 = $5,056.47.

Exercises for Section 13.4

In problems 1 through 10, find the accumulated amount S at the end of the n equal payments of P dollars each into an account that pays the given nominal interest rate.

1. Semiannual payments of $P = \$200$ each, $n = 10$ payments, 8% interest compounded semiannually

2. Semiannual payments of $P = \$350$ each, $n = 15$ payments, 6% interest compounded semiannually

3. Quarterly payments of $P = \$100$ each, $n = 20$ payments, 8% interest compounded quarterly

4. Quarterly payments of $P = \$75$ each, $n = 24$ payments, 10% interest compounded quarterly

5. Monthly payments of $P = \$50$ each, $n = 50$ payments, 12% interest compounded monthly

6. Monthly payments of $P = \$80$ each, $n = 25$ payments, 6% interest compounded monthly

7. Semiannual payments of $P = \$350$ each, $n = 12$ payments, 9% interest compounded semiannually

8. Monthly payments of $P = \$200$ each, $n = 40$ payments, 9% interest compounded monthly

9. Quarterly payments of $P = \$175$ each, $n = 16$ payments, 10% interest compounded quarterly

10. Quarterly payments of $P = \$225$ each, $n = 30$ payments, 6% interest compounded quarterly

11. How many quarterly payments of $500 each would it take to accumulate $20,000 if the payments are deposited in an account paying 8% interest compounded quarterly?

12. Find the number of quarterly payments of $250 each that must be paid into an account earning 4% interest compounded quarterly in order for there to be $8,000 in the account.

13. John Peterson has decided to place $100 each month in a credit union savings account that pays 6% compounded monthly, so that he can purchase a new car that costs $4,500. How long will it take for the accumulated amount in the account to reach $4,500? How much interest will be earned by the time the account accumulates to $4,500?

14. To offset future expansion expenses, Martin Industries, Inc., made semiannual deposits of $1,500 each into an account that paid 8% interest compounded semiannually. How much was in the account after the 15th deposit? How much interest was earned?

15. Taylor's Transit Co. is making quarterly payments of $750 into an account that pays 6% interest compounded quarterly, in order to accumulate $20,000 for the purchase of new equipment. How long will it take for the account to accumulate to $20,000? How much interest will be earned by that time?

16. To provide for future remodeling expenses, the owner of a restaurant made semiannual payments of $500 into an account that pays 8% interest compounded semiannually. How much was in the account after the 10th deposit? How much interest was earned?

17. The Phillips Produce Company is making monthly payments of $600 into an account that pays 9% interest compounded monthly, in order to provide funds for business expansion. How much will be in the account after the 20th deposit? How much interest will be earned at that time?

18. In order to provide funds for new research equipment, Conco Labs, Inc., made semiannual payments of $2,000 each into an account that paid 12% interest compounded semiannually. How long did it take for the account to accumulate to $30,000? How much interest was earned at that time? How much was in the account after the twentieth deposit?

Present Value of an Ordinary Annuity

The **present value** of an annuity is that current amount that if invested at a given rate will result in a series of future payments. To understand the formulas for the present value of an ordinary annuity, consider the special case of how much must be deposited now in a bank paying 6% compounded annually to provide for five annual withdrawals of $1, the first withdrawal to be made in one year. See Figure 13–1.

The amount to be deposited is the sum of the present values of the separate withdrawals. That is:

First withdrawal	$1(1.06)^{-1} =$	$0.94339623
Second withdrawal	$1(1.06)^{-2} =$	0.88999644
Third withdrawal	$1(1.06)^{-3} =$	0.83961928
Fourth withdrawal	$1(1.06)^{-4} =$	0.79209366
Fifth withdrawal	$1(1.06)^{-5} =$	0.74725817
Amount deposited now	$=$	$4.21236378

Thus, a deposit of slightly more than $4.21 in an account paying 6% compounded annually would provide a fund that would permit $1 to be withdrawn annually for five years. To withdraw $100 a year for five years, the deposit would have to be $100 \times 4.2123638 = \$421.23638$, and to withdraw $1,000 a year for five years, a deposit of $1,000 \times 4.2123638 = \$4,212.3638$ would be required.

There is a similarity between the above discussion and that for the accumulated amount of an ordinary annuity. This similarity extends to the development of a formula for the present value of an annuity. The formula is:

(13–4) $\qquad A = P \cdot a_{\overline{n}|i}$

where $\qquad A =$ present value of an ordinary annuity

$\qquad P =$ payment or deposit

$\qquad a_{\overline{n}|i} =$ present value of a deposit of $1 at interest rate

$\qquad\qquad$ per period i for n conversion periods*

The values of $a_{\overline{n}|i}$ can be found in a table which is similar to Appendix D used for the values of $s_{\overline{n}|i}$. This table is Appendix E in the appendix. The values in this table are multiplied by P to obtain A.

---

* For n withdrawals of $1 each ($n$ a counting number) made annually at compound interest rate i, the present value $a_{\overline{n}|\,i}$ is:

$$a_{\overline{n}|\,i} = (1+i)^{-1} + (1+i)^{-2} + (1+i)^{-3} + \cdots + (1+i)^{-n}$$
$$= \frac{1-(1+i)^{-n}}{i}$$

For n withdrawals of P dollars each, the present value is $P \cdot a_{\overline{n}|\,i}$

Example 1

Carl Jefferson sold his business and retired on his 60th birthday. He used a part of the money from the sale to purchase an annuity that would pay him $1,500 a quarter until he begins to receive social security at age 65. If money is worth 6% compounded quarterly, how much did the annuity cost?

Solution:

$$A = ?, P = \$1,500, n = 20, i = \frac{6\%}{4} = 1\frac{1}{2}\%$$

$$
\begin{aligned}
A &= P \cdot a_{\overline{n}|i} \\
&= \$1,500 \cdot a_{\overline{20}|.015} \\
&= \$1,500 \times 17.16863879 \qquad \text{(Appendix E)} \\
&= \$25,752.958185 \\
&= \$25,752.96
\end{aligned}
$$

Note that Carl received $20 \times \$1,500 = \$30,000$ in payments, thus $\$30,000 - \$25,752.96 = \$4,247.04$ was earned in interest.

Example 2

For her corner lot, Con Oil offered Margaret Prescott $10,000 and semiannual payments of $5,000 for the next five years. If money is worth 8% compounded semiannually, what is the equivalent cash price of the lot?

Solution:

$$A = ?, P = \$5,000, n = 10, i = \frac{8\%}{2} = 4\%.$$

$$
\begin{aligned}
A &= P \cdot a_{\overline{n}|i} \\
&= \$5,000 \cdot a_{\overline{10}|.04} \\
&= \$5,000 \cdot 8.11089578 \qquad \text{(Appendix E)} \\
&= \$40,554.4789 \\
&= \$40,554.48
\end{aligned}
$$

Thus the cash price of the lot is $\$10,000 + \$40,554.48 = \$50,554.48$.

Example 3

If $22,600 is used to purchase an annuity that pays $500 a month, and if the interest rate is 3% compounded monthly, approximately how many payments are possible?

Solution:

$$A = \$22{,}600,\ P = \$500,\ n = ?,\ i = \frac{3\%}{12} = \frac{1}{4}\%$$

$$A = P \cdot a_{\overline{n}|i}$$

$$P \cdot a_{\overline{n}|i} = A$$

$$a_{\overline{n}|i} = \frac{A}{P} \qquad (\text{Dividing both sides by } P)$$

$$a_{\overline{n}|\frac{1}{4}\%} = \frac{\$22{,}600}{500}$$

$$= 45.2$$

Using Appendix E on the page headed ¼%, the value for $a_{\overline{48}|\frac{1}{4}\%}$ is

45.17869463; this is the largest entry in the table which is still less than 45.2. Thus $n = 48$ payments are possible.

Exercises for Section 13.5   In problems 1 through 10, find the present value of an annuity that will provide the given payments for the given length of time when money is worth the given nominal compound interest rate.

1. $2,000 per year for 10 years, 6% interest compounded annually

2. $3,500 per year for 8 years, 8% interest compounded annually

3. $800 per quarter for 4 years, 8% interest compounded quarterly

4. $1,200 per quarter for 2 years, 4% interest compounded quarterly

5. $400 semiannually for 6 years, 6% interest compounded semiannually

6. $750 semiannually for 12 years, 10% interest compounded semiannually

7. $150 per month for 4 years, 9% interest compounded monthly

8. $175 per month for $3\frac{1}{2}$ years, 12% interest compounded monthly

9. $300 per quarter for 6 years, 6% interest compounded quarterly

10. $475 per quarter for 5 years, 10% interest compounded quarterly

11. If $15,000 is used to purchase an annuity that pays $400 a month, and if the interest rate is 12% compounded monthly, how many full payments will be received from the annuity?

12. How many full payments will be received from an annuity that costs $10,000 if the payments are $750 semiannually and money is worth 8% compounded semiannually?

13. Bob Brewster sold some real estate for $5,000 down and quarterly payments of $500 for ten years. If money is worth 8% compounded quarterly, what is the equivalent cash price of the real estate?

14. Ron Johnson purchased an annuity that would pay his son $200 per month while he was getting his education. How much did the annuity cost, if the payments were to continue for four years and money was worth 6% compounded monthly?

15. Jesse Phillips won $20,000 in a sweepstakes and purchased an annuity with the money that would pay him $750 a month. If money was worth 10% compounded quarterly at the time he purchased the annuity, how many full payments will he receive?

16. Sarah Steadman sold her retail clothing store for $20,000 in cash and monthly payments of $500 for four years. If money is worth 12% compounded monthly, what was the equivalent cash selling price of the store?

17. Carol Jackson purchased an annuity that would pay her daughter $150 a month for forty months. How much did the annuity cost, if money was worth 9% compounded monthly?

18. Ron Jacobson sold one of the branch stores of his business for $65,000 and used the money to purchase an annuity that would pay him $5,000 semiannually. If money was worth 12% compounded semiannually at the time he purchased the annuity, how many full payments will he receive?

Section **13.6** **Annuities Due**

The second type of annuity certain is the annuity due. In an annuity due, payments are made at the beginning of the period. Mortgage payments, insurance premiums, and installment payments are common examples of annuities due.

PATRICIA L. A. HAGEMEIER
437 DOBSON HALL
PLATTEVILLE, WI 53818

196

0715-0205

January 3, 1977

PAY TO THE ORDER OF *Independent Auto Insurance Co.* $98.87

Ninety eight dollars and 87/100 cents DOLLARS

STATE NATIONAL BANK
· PLATTEVILLE, WISCONSIN 53818 ·

FOR *6 months ins. premium*   *Patricia L. A. Hagemeier*

⑆0715⑆0205⑆   360⑈356⑈

The accumulated amount and the present value of an annuity due have the same meanings as for an ordinary annuity, thus formulas for these values can be derived from the formulas and tables of the ordinary annuity.

To determine a formula for the accumulated amount of an annuity due, consider Figure 13–1 and our first illustration of a $1 annual payment for five years. Note that the annuity due has five interest earning periods, one more than for the ordinary annuity. This is true in general; i.e., if an ordinary annuity has n interest earning periods, then for the same term an annuity due will have $n + 1$ interest earning periods. Secondly, the formulas for $s_{\overline{n}|i}$ include the last payment of an ordinary annuity that earns no interest (this is the first term in equation 13–1). The annuity due has no such payment, thus it must be deducted from $s_{\overline{n}|i}$.

Combining this information, the accumulated amount of an annuity due is

(13–5) $$\overline{S} = P \cdot (s_{\overline{n+1}|i} - 1)$$

where $\overline{S}$ = accumulated amount of annuity due*

   P = payment

   n = number of payments

   i = rate per period

Example 1

For ten years an annual deposit of $4,000 was made on April 1 in an account paying 8% compounded annually. Find the accumulated amount on April 1 of the 11th year.

Solution:

$\overline{S} = ?, P = \$4,000, n = 10, i = 8\%$

$$\overline{S} = P(s_{\overline{n+1}|i} - 1)$$

$$= \$4,000 \, (s_{\overline{11}|.08} - 1)$$

$$= \$4,000 \, (16.64548746 - 1) \qquad \text{(Appendix D)}$$

$$= \$4,000 \, (15.64548746)$$

$$= \$62,581.948$$

$$= \$62,581.95$$

---

* It is customary to designate the accumulated amount and the present value of an annuity due by boldface letters **S** and **A**. For ease of writing, the notation $\overline{S}$ and $\overline{A}$ will be used in this text.

Example 2

How long would it take to accumulate $25,000 if $1,620 is deposited at the beginning of each month in an account that pays interest at 4% compounded monthly?

Solution:

$$\bar{S} = \$25,000, P = \$1,620, n = ?, i = \frac{4\%}{12} = \frac{1}{3}\%$$

$$\bar{S} = P(s_{\overline{n+1}|\,i} - 1)$$

$$P(s_{\overline{n+1}|\,i} - 1) = \bar{S}$$

$$s_{\overline{n+1}|\,i} - 1 = \frac{\bar{S}}{P} \qquad \text{(Dividing both sides by } P)$$

$$s_{\overline{n+1}|\,i} = \frac{\bar{S}}{P} + 1 \qquad \text{(Adding 1 to both sides)}$$

$$s_{\overline{n+1}|\,\frac{1}{3}\%} = \frac{\$25,000}{\$1,620} + 1$$

$$s_{\overline{n+1}|\,\frac{1}{3}\%} = 16.43209877$$

Using Appendix D on the page headed $\frac{1}{3}$%, the smallest entry greater than 16.4320987 is $s_{\overline{17}|\,\frac{1}{3}\%} = 17.46097781$. Since $n+1 = 17$, $n = 16$.

Thus, sixteen months would be required.

Example 3

For twenty semiannual deposits of $1,800 invested at 7% compounded semiannually, find the accumulated amount of (a) an ordinary annuity and (b) an annuity due.

Solution:

a. $S = ?, P = \$1,800, n = 20, i = \dfrac{7\%}{2} = 3\frac{1}{2}\%$

$$S = P \cdot s_{\overline{n}|\,i}$$

$$= \$1,800 \cdot s_{\overline{20}|\,.035}$$

$$= \$1,800 \times 28.27968181 \qquad \text{(Appendix D)}$$

$$= \$50,903.42724$$

$$= \$50,903.43$$

b. $\bar{S} = ?, P = \$1,800, n = 20, i = \dfrac{7\%}{2} = 3\frac{1}{2}\%$

$$\bar{S} = P \left(s_{\overline{n+1}|\,i} - 1\right)$$

$$= \$1,800 \left(s_{\overline{21}|\,.035} - 1\right)$$

$$= \$1,800 \left(30.26947068 - 1\right) \qquad (\text{Appendix D})$$

$$= \$1,800 \times 29.26947068$$

$$= \$52,685.04708$$

$$= \$52,685.05$$

Note that the accumulated amount for the annuity due is greater than that of the ordinary annuity. This is true in general.

Exercises for Section 13.6

In problems 1–10, find the accumulated amount of the given annuities due when n payments of P dollars each are deposited in an account that pays the given nominal interest rate.

1. $1,000 per year for 5 years, 6% interest compounded annually

2. $1,500 per year for 15 years, 8% interest compounded annually

3. $700 semiannually for 5 years, 8% interest compounded semiannually

4. $400 semiannually for 12 years, 10% interest compounded semiannually

5. $200 per month for 3 years, 6% interest compounded monthly

6. $150 per month for 1 year, 12% interest compounded monthly

7. $450 per quarter for 4 years, 8% interest compounded quarterly

8. $600 per quarter for 5 years, 6% interest compounded quarterly

9. $100 per month for 4 years, 9% interest compounded monthly

10. $175 per quarter for 5 years, 10% interest compounded quarterly

11. A deposit of $50 is made each month for 24 months into an account that pays 6% interest compounded monthly. Find the accumulated amount in the account at the beginning of the 25th month.

12. For five years a deposit of $550 is made at the beginning of each quarter into an account that pays 6% interest compounded quarterly. What is the accumulated amount in the account at the beginning of the first quarter of the sixth year?

13. How long would it take to accumulate $10,000 if $700 is deposited at the beginning of each year into an account that pays interest at 6% compounded annually?

14. $500 is paid quarterly into an account that pays 4% interest compounded quarterly. How many years will it take to accumulate $15,000 in the account?

15. For 10 quarterly deposits of $600 each invested at 8% compounded quarterly, find the accumulated amount of (a) an ordinary annuity and (b) an annuity due.

16. For 20 monthly deposits of $75 each invested at 6% compounded monthly, find the accumulated amount of (a) an ordinary annuity and (b) an annuity due.

17. To provide funds for an expected increase in operating expenses at her restaurant, Myra Cole decides to deposit $200 each month into an account that pays 6% interest compounded monthly. How much will she have in the account 24 months from now, if she immediately makes the first deposit?

18. Bob Schwartz decides to begin a savings plan by depositing $125 each quarter into an account that pays 6% interest compounded quarterly. If he makes his first deposit now, how much will be in the account 3 years from now?

13.7 Present Value of an Annuity Due

To determine a formula for the present value of an annuity due, again consider Figure 13–1 on page 334. In the annuity due, the present value of the first payment of $1 is $1, since there is no interest-earning period. As a result, there are only four periods for calculation of present value, one less than the ordinary annuity. This is true in the general case; if an ordinary annuity has n periods, the annuity due will have $n-1$ periods when calculating present value. The initial payment is then added to this calculation.

Combining this information

(13–6) $$\overline{A} = P(a_{\overline{n-1}|i} + 1)$$

where $\overline{A}$ = present value of an annuity due

P = payment

n = number of payments

i = rate per period

Example 1

Find the present value of an annuity due with semiannual payments of $3,000 invested at 7% compounded semiannually for a term of ten years.

Solution:

$$\bar{A} = ?, P = \$3,000, n = 20, i = \frac{7\%}{2} = 3\frac{1}{2}\%$$

$$\bar{A} = P(a_{\overline{n-1}|i} + 1)$$

$$= \$3,000 \ (a_{\overline{19}|.035} + 1)$$

$$= \$3,000 \ (13.70983742 + 1) \qquad \text{(Appendix E)}$$

$$= \$3,000 \ (14.70983742)$$

$$= \$44,129.511$$

$$= \$44,129.51$$

Example 2

A company retirement fund pays Bob Simmons $480 at the beginning of each month. If money is worth 3% compounded monthly, what is the present value of the pension for (a) one year and (b) four years?

Solution:

a. $\quad \bar{A} = ?, P = \$480, n = 12, i = \dfrac{3\%}{12} = \dfrac{1}{4}\%$

$$\bar{A} = P \ (a_{\overline{n-1}|i} + 1)$$

$$= \$480 \ (a_{\overline{11}|\frac{1}{4}\%} + 1)$$

$$= \$480 \ (10.83677198 + 1) \qquad \text{(Appendix E)}$$

$$= \$480 \ (11.83677198)$$

$$= \$5,681.6506$$

$$= \$5,681.65$$

b. $\quad \bar{A} = ?, P = \$480, n = 48, i = \dfrac{3\%}{12} = \dfrac{1}{4}\%$

$$\bar{A} = P \ (a_{\overline{n-1}|i} + 1)$$

$$= \$480 \ (a_{\overline{47}|\frac{1}{4}\%} + 1)$$

$$= \$480 \ (44.29164137 + 1) \qquad \text{(Appendix E)}$$

$$= \$480 \ (45.29164137)$$

$$= \$21,739.9878576$$

$$= \$21,739.99$$

Example 3

What is the present value of (a) an ordinary annuity and (b) an annuity due if $P = \$750$ per month, the term is 30 months, and interest is compounded at 6% monthly?

Solution:

a. $A = ?, P = \$750, n = 30, i = \dfrac{6\%}{12} = \dfrac{1}{2}\%$

$$A = P \cdot a_{\overline{n}|i}$$

$$= \$750 \cdot a_{\overline{30}|\frac{1}{2}\%}$$

$$= \$750 \times 27.79405397 \qquad \text{(Appendix E)}$$

$$= \$20,845.539$$

$$= \$20,845.54$$

b. $\overline{A} = ?, P = \$750, n = 30, i = \dfrac{6\%}{12} = \dfrac{1}{2}\%$

$$\overline{A} = P\,(a_{\overline{n-1}|i} + 1)$$

$$= \$750\,(a_{\overline{29}|\frac{1}{2}\%} + 1)$$

$$= \$750\,(26.93302423 + 1) \qquad \text{(Appendix E)}$$

$$= \$750\,(27.93302423)$$

$$= \$20,949.77$$

Note that the present value of the annuity due is greater than that of the ordinary annuity. It can be shown that this is true in general.

Exercises for Section 13.7   In problems 1 through 10, find the present value for each annuity due using the information provided.

1. $800 per year for 5 years, 8% interest compounded annually

2. $1,400 per year for 10 years, 6% interest compounded annually

3. $700 per quarter for 4 years, 8% interest compounded quarterly

4. $400 per quarter for 5 years, 4% interest compounded quarterly

5. $1,200 semiannually for 5 years, 6% interest compounded semiannually

6. $2,000 semiannually for 8 years, 8% interest compounded semiannually

7. $200 per month for 15 months, 6% interest compounded monthly

8. $350 per month for 20 months, 12% interest compounded monthly

9. $1,250 per quarter for 3 years, 10% interest compounded quarterly

10. $3,400 semiannually for 8 years, 9% interest compounded semiannually

11. Find the present value of (a) an ordinary annuity and (b) an annuity due if $P = \$4,200$ semiannually, the term is 10 years, and interest is compounded at 7% semiannually.

12. What is the present value of (a) an ordinary annuity and (b) an annuity due if $P = \$250$ monthly, the term is 3 years, and interest is compounded at 9% monthly.

13. As payment to satisfy an old debt, John Baker agrees to pay his neighbor $400 semiannually for 5 years, with the first payment to be made immediately. If money is worth 10% compounded semiannually, what is the equivalent cash value of his debt to his neighbor?

14. Some teenagers vandalized Lisa Carter's clothing store, and their parents agree to pay Lisa $50 per month for two years to cover damages with the first payment to be made immediately. What is the equivalent cash amount of damage done to the store, if money is worth 6% compounded monthly?

15. When Ella Richards graduated from college, her father gave her $50 and promised to pay her $50 each month for the next 12 months. If money is worth 9% compounded monthly, what is the equivalent cash value of Ella's gift?

16. To satisfy a debt to one of its creditors, a company agrees to pay $3,000 semiannually for six years with the first payment to be made immediately. If money is worth 5% compounded semiannually, what is the amount of the debt?

17. Atlas Plumbing Supply agreed to pay Richard Simmons $250 quarterly for 5 years as compensation for injuries Richard received on the job. If the first payment was made immediately and if money was worth 12% compounded quarterly, what was the equivalent cash value of the settlement?

18. Bob Jacobs, a truck driver, lost control of his truck and knocked down a wall of a restaurant while making a delivery. In order to pay for the damages, Bob paid the owner of the restaurant $100 a month for two years with the first payment made immediately. If money was worth 18% compounded monthly, what was the equivalent cash value of the damage?

14

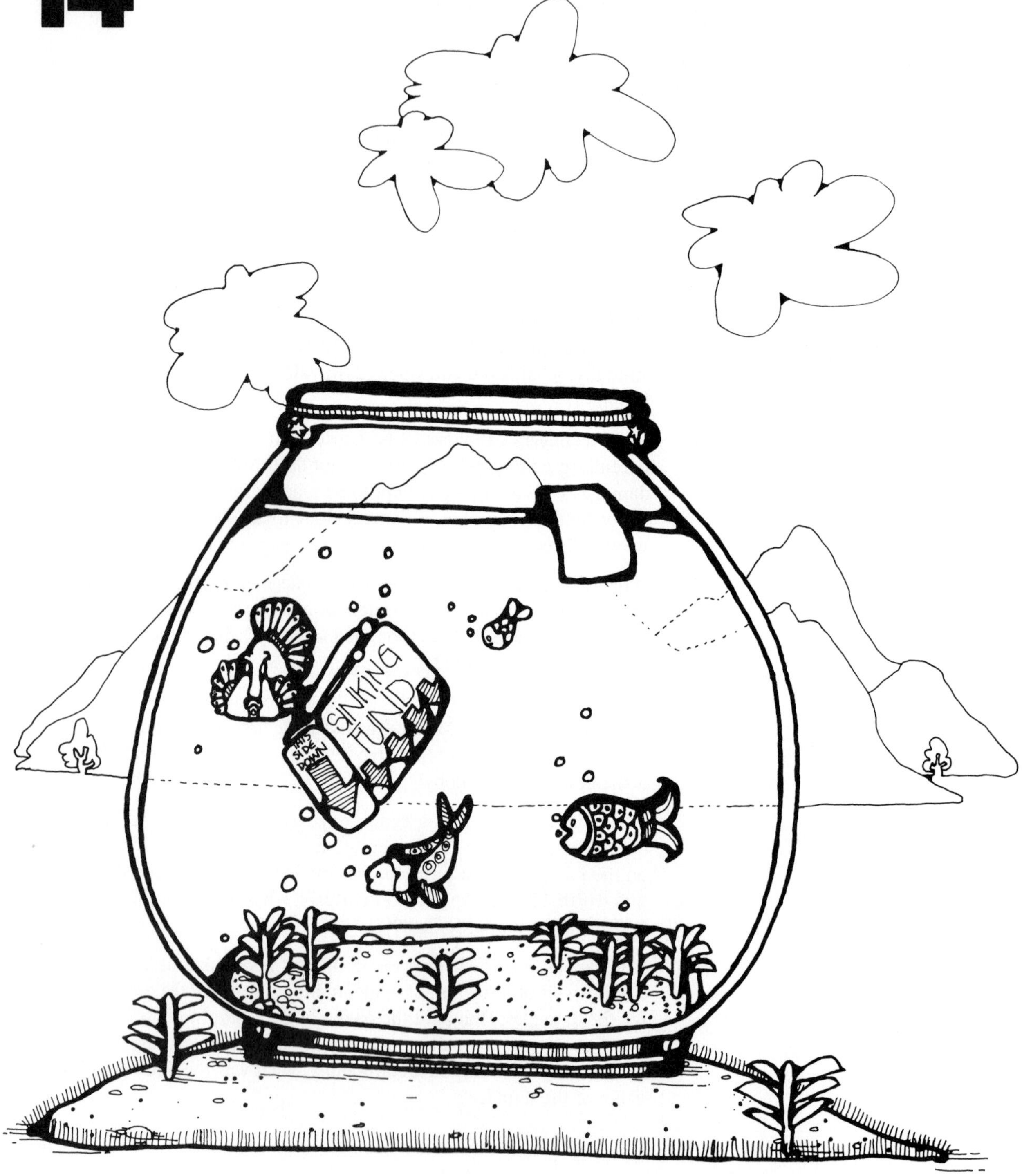

Sinking Funds and Amortization

Chapter Objectives for Chapter 14

I. Learn the meaning of the following terms:

A. *Sinking Fund,* 354
B. *Amortization,* 358

II. Understand:

A. The difference between amortization and sinking funds, 354
B. The preparation of a Schedule of Payments for a sinking fund, 356
C. The preparation of an Amortization Schedule, 360

III. Calculate:

A. The periodic payment of a sinking fund, 354
B. The periodic payment to amortize a debt, 360

Introduction

An annuity established to meet a future obligation is called a **sinking fund.** Businesses establish sinking funds to redeem bonds, to replace worn-out equipment, to expand facilities, or to meet a future debt or anticipated expense.

In general, sinking funds retire only the principal of a debt; if both the principal and accrued interest are gradually retired by partial payments, the process is called **amortization.** This chapter will examine the fundamentals of these two payment plans. While the methods developed are applicable to both kinds of annuities certain, the discussion is limited to the ordinary annuity.

Section **14.2** **Sinking Funds**

In a sinking fund, the amount of the obligation, the term, and the current interest rate are known, hence the problem is to determine the amount of the periodic payment P.* This means solving the annuity formula for P. The result is: †

(14–1)
$$P = S \times \frac{1}{s_{\overline{n}|i}}$$

To facilitate calculations, a table of values for $\frac{1}{s_{\overline{n}|i}}$ has been prepared; this is Appendix F in the appendix. The following examples illustrate the use of formula (14–1).

Example 1

The Scorpio Corporation estimates that its plant machinery will be obsolete in another three years. The replacement cost is $240,000 and the current interest rate is 8% compounded quarterly. How much should the company invest at the end of each quarter to be prepared to purchase new equipment in three years?

Solution:

$$S = \$240,000, P = ?, n = 12, i = \frac{8\%}{4} = 2\%$$

$$P = S \times \frac{1}{s_{\overline{n}|i}}$$

---

* The periodic payment to a sinking fund is often called the **rent.**

†
$$S = P \times s_{\overline{n}|i}$$
$$P \times s_{\overline{n}|i} = S$$
$$P = \frac{S}{s_{\overline{n}|i}} \qquad \text{(dividing both sides by } s_{\overline{n}|i}\text{)}$$
$$P = S \times \frac{1}{s_{\overline{n}|i}}$$

$$= \$240{,}000 \times \frac{1}{s_{\overline{12}|\,0.02}}$$

$$= \$240{,}000 \times .07455960 \qquad (\text{Appendix F})$$

$$= \$17{,}894.304$$

$$= \$17{,}894.30^*$$

Example 2

Grey Enterprises, Inc., plans to replace its fleet of trucks in three years at an estimated cost of $140,000. The company establishes a sinking fund in an account that earns interest at 9% compounded semiannually. What is the amount of the payment at the end of each six months?

Solution:

$$S = \$140{,}000, \ P = ?, \ n = 6, \ i = \frac{9\%}{2} = 4\frac{1}{2}\%$$

$$P = S \times \frac{1}{s_{\overline{n}|\,i}}$$

$$= \$140{,}000 \times \frac{1}{s_{\overline{6}|\,0.045}}$$

$$= \$140{,}000 \times 0.14887839 \qquad (\text{Appendix F})$$

$$= \$20{,}842.9746$$

$$= \$20{,}842.97$$

Example 3

The Davidson Corporation borrowed $200,000 by issuing bonds redeemable in ten years. To redeem the bonds at maturity, the company established a sinking fund into which payments were made at the end of each quarter. If the interest rate is 6% compounded quarterly, (a) what was the amount of each payment and (b) how much total interest was earned?

Solution:

$$S = \$200{,}000, \ P = ?, \ n = 40, \ i = 1\frac{1}{2}\%$$

a. $$P = S \times \frac{1}{s_{\overline{n}|\,i}}$$

$$= \$200{,}000 \times \frac{1}{s_{\overline{40}|\,.015}}$$

$$= \$200{,}000 \times 0.0184271 \qquad (\text{Appendix F})$$

$$= \$3{,}685.42$$

b. $200,000.00 Accumulated Amount

− 147,416.80 Total Payments ($3,685.42 × 40)

$ 52,583.20 Earned Interest

---

* Actually, the fund will accumulate to only $17,894.30 × 13.41208973 = $239,999.94 because of rounding. If the firm chose to invest $17,894.31, the fund would be $240,000.02.

Frequently, it is convenient to have a schedule showing the operation of the sinking fund.

Example 4

In order to remodel their display rooms eighteen months from now, the Regency Company established a sinking fund by making regular payments into an account paying 6% compounded quarterly. Prepare a schedule for a remodeling cost of $28,000.

Solution:

$S = \$28,000, P = ?, n = 6, i = 1\frac{1}{2}\%$

$$P = S \times \frac{1}{s_{\overline{n}|i}}$$

$$= \$28,000 \times \frac{1}{s_{\overline{6}|0.015}}$$

$$= \$28,000 \times 0.16052521 \qquad \text{(Appendix F)}$$

$$= \$4,494.7028$$

$$= \$4,494.70$$

Figure 14–1

	Beginning of Period	End of Period		
Period	Accumulated Amount (1)	Earned Interest (2)	Periodic Payment (3)	Accumulated Amount (1)+(2)+(3)
1	0	0	$4,494.70	$ 4,494.70
2	$ 4,494.70	$ 67.42	4,494.70	9,056.82
3	9,056.82	135.85	4,494.70	13,687.37
4	13,687.37	205.31	4,494.70	18,387.38
5	18,387.38	275.81	4,494.70	23,157.89
6	25,157.89	347.37	4,494.70	28,000.00

Since each line in Figure 14–1 is a separate interest problem, the interest can be computed using the simple interest formula.* The remaining entries are self-explanatory.

---

* Recall that compound interest is simply an accumulation of simple interest calculations (See Section 11.2).

In problems 1–6, find the amount of the periodic payment P for the given sinking fund.

1. $S = \$70,000$, quarterly payments for 5 years, 8% interest compounded quarterly

2. $S = \$40,000$, semiannual payments for 10 years, 5% interest compounded semiannually

3. $S = \$90,000$, quarterly payments for 6 years, 6% interest compounded quarterly

4. $S = \$27,000$, semiannual payments for 8 years, 7% interest compounded semiannually

5. $S = \$16,000$, monthly payments for 3 years, 9% interest compounded monthly

6. $S = \$35,000$, monthly payments for 2 years, 6% interest compounded monthly

In problems 7–12, find the amount of the periodic payment P for the given sinking fund, set up a schedule showing the operation of the fund, and compute the total interest earned by the fund.

7. $S = \$22,000$, quarterly payments for two years, 8% interest compounded quarterly

8. $S = \$31,000$, semiannual payments for 3 years, 6% interest compounded semiannually

9. $S = \$8,000$, monthly payments for 6 months, 12% interest compounded monthly

10. $S = \$40,000$, semiannual payments for 4 years, 8% interest compounded semiannually

11. $S = \$36,000$, quarterly payments for 20 months, 10% interest compounded quarterly

12. $S = \$42,000$, annual payments for 5 years, 6% interest compounded annually

Fill in the missing entries in the following sinking fund schedules.

13.

Period	Beginning of Period Accumulated Amount (1)	End of Period Earned Interest (2)	Periodic Payment (3)	Accumulated Amount (1)+(2)+(3)
1	0	0	$2,073.72	$2,073.72
2	$2,073.72	$207.37		
3				
4				
5				
6				

14.

| Period | Beginning of Period | | End of Period | |
	Accumulated Amount (1)	Earned Interest (2)	Periodic Payment (3)	Accumulated Amount (1)+(2)+(3)
1	0	0		
2	$1,332.62	$59.97		
3				
4				
5				
6				
7				
8				

15. The Hudson Manufacturing Company plans to replace some of its machinery in two years at an estimated cost of $220,000. The company establishes a sinking fund in an account that earns interest at 10% compounded quarterly. Find the amount of each quarterly payment.

16. Scott Processors, Inc., issued bonds totalling $125,000 to raise capital for plant modifications. The bonds were redeemable in six years, and the company established a sinking fund, into which payments were made semiannually, to redeem the bonds. If the interest rate was 8% compounded semiannually, (a) find the amount of each payment and (b) find the total interest earned.

17. The owner of an appliance store established a sinking fund so that she could remodel her display room in two years. If the account earned interest at 9% compounded monthly, and if the remodeling cost was $4,000, find the amount of the monthly payments into the account.

18. The Harris Company plans to open a branch office in three years at an estimated cost of $230,000. To provide the funds, the company establishes a sinking fund in an account that pays 9% interest compounded semiannually. Find the amount of the semiannual payments into the fund. Prepare a schedule showing the operation of the fund.

Section 14.3 Amortization

In Example 3 of Section 14.2 a sinking fund was established to redeem bonds that had been issued. But investors buy bonds because they are interest bearing; that is, the bondholder not only receives the original cost of the bond at maturity (principal), but also periodic interest while the bond is in force. Example 3 created a sinking fund to pay off the principal;

the interest on the bonds would have to be paid from another source. If both the principal and accrued interest had been retired by partial payments, the debt would have been **amortized.*** Perhaps the most common example of amortization is mortgage payments on a real estate loan. A portion of each payment is applied to accrued interest, with the remainder to the outstanding principal, in accordance with the United States Rule. Other examples of amortization occurred in the section on installment plans (Chapter 12); although the interest calculation is different, the partial payments pay off the entire debt, both principal and carrying charges.

43 758

ACCOUNT NO.

DATE	ESCROW CHARGES	ESCROW PAYMENTS	ESCROW BALANCE	INT. & MISC. CHARGES	LOAN PAYMENTS	LOAN BALANCE	TELLER
05 20 76NB	141.00		21.82-		.01	21,224.37	D3B
05 26 76NB		19.00	2.82-	159.18	211.00	21,172.55	D3B
06 25 76NB		200.00	197.18			21,172.55	D2A
06 25 76NB			197.18	200.00		21,372.55	D2A
JUL 1,76LC		49.00	246.18	160.29	182.00	21,350.84	D2A
JUL 30,76LC		49.00	295.18	160.13	182.00	21,328.97	D5B
AUG30,76LC		49.00	344.18	159.97	182.00	21,306.94	D5A

Consider a debt A drawing interest at rate i per period. To pay off the entire debt in n periodic payments of amount P, the present value of these future payments must equal A. That is,

(14–2)
$$P \cdot a_{\overline{n}|i} = A$$

Solving 14–2 for P is†

(14–3)
$$P = A \times \frac{1}{a_{\overline{n}|i}}$$

Each payment using equation 14–3 is distributed between principal and interest according to the United States Rule. A table of values for $\frac{1}{a_{\overline{n}|i}}$ is Appendix G in the appendix.

---

* In accounting, amortization may have a broader meaning. However, in this text, amortization means the elimination of both the principal and interest of a debt by a series of equal payments at regular intervals.

† $P \times a_{\overline{n}|i} = A$,

$$P = \frac{A}{a_{\overline{n}|i}} \quad \text{(dividing both sides by } a_{\overline{n}|i}\text{)}$$

$$P = A \times \frac{1}{a_{\overline{n}|i}}.$$

Example 1

The Growth Corporation acquired a piece of property for $750,000 by paying $150,000 down and signing a mortgage for 48 quarterly payments (payments to be made at the end of each quarter). What is the amount of each payment if the nominal rate is 6%?

Solution:

$A = \$750,000 - \$150,000 = \$600,000, P = ?, n = 48, i = 1\frac{1}{2}\%$

$$P = A \times \frac{1}{a_{\overline{n}|i}}$$

$$= \$600,000 \times \frac{1}{a_{\overline{48}|.015}}$$

$$= \$600,000 \times 0.029375 \qquad (\text{Appendix G})$$

$$= \$17,625$$

Example 2

A debt of $4,850 bears interest at 7% compounded annually. What annual payment is required to amortize the debt in 5 years if the payments are made at the end of each year?

Solution:

$A = \$4,850, P = ?, n = 5, i = 7\%$.

$$P = A \times \frac{1}{a_{\overline{n}|i}}$$

$$= \$4,850 \times \frac{1}{a_{\overline{5}|.07}}$$

$$= \$4,850 \times 0.24389069 \qquad (\text{Appendix G})$$

$$= \$1,182.8694$$

$$= \$1,182.87$$

Example 3

Construct a schedule showing the distribution of payments in Example 2 of this section.

Solution:

To determine the interest in column (3) of Figure 14-2, again recall that compound interest is a series of simple interest calculations, with the simple interest formula applied to the principal plus interest of the preceding period (column (1)).

Figure 14–2

	Beginning of Period	End of Period			
Period	Amount of Debt (1)	Payment (2)	Interest (3)	Applied to Principal (4)=(2)−(3)	Remaining Debt (5)=(1)−(4)
1	$4,850.00	$1,182.87	$339.50	$ 843.37	$4,006.63
2	4,006.63	1,182.87	280.46	902.41	3,104.22
3	3,104.22	1,182.87	217.30	965.57	2,138.65
4	2,138.65	1,182.87	149.71	1,033.16	1,105.49
5	1,105.49	1,182.87	77.38	1,105.49	0.00

The above schedule showing the distribution of the payments is called an **amortization schedule.** Amortization schedules are frequently presented to debtors, particularly in the case of real estate loans.

Exercises for Section 14.3

In problems 1–6, find the periodic payment required to amortize the given debt in the given time.

1. $4,000 debt bearing interest at 5% compounded annually, annual payments for 10 years

2. $10,000 debt bearing interest at 8% compounded quarterly, quarterly payments for 12 years

3. $16,000 debt bearing interest at 10% compounded semiannually, semiannual payments for 20 years

4. $12,500 debt bearing interest at 6% compounded monthly, monthly payments for $3\frac{1}{2}$ years

5. $7,500 debt bearing interest at 9% compounded monthly, monthly payments for 3 years

6. $25,000 debt bearing interest at 7% compounded semiannually, semiannual payments for 10 years

In problems 7–12, find the periodic payment required to amortize the given debt in the given time, and construct a schedule showing the distribution of payments.

7. $5,250 debt bearing interest at 8% compounded annually, annual payments for 4 years

8. $7,420 debt bearing interest at 6% compounded semiannually, semiannual payments for 3 years

9. $3,200 debt bearing interest at 6% compounded quarterly, quarterly payments for 2 years

10. $9,450 debt bearing interest at 12% compounded monthly, monthly payments for 10 months

11. $8,700 debt bearing interest at 9% compounded monthly, monthly payments for 1 year

12. $2,400 debt bearing interest at 5% compounded semiannually, semiannual payments for 6 years

13. Fill in the missing entries in the following amortization schedule.

Period	Beginning of Period Amount of Debt (1)	End of Period			
		Payment (2)	Interest (3)	Applied to Principal (4)=(2)−(3)	Remaining Debt (5)=(1)−(4)
1	$1,500.00		$75.00		
2					
3					
4					

14. Fill in the missing entries in the following amortization schedule.

Period	Beginning of Period Amount of Debt (1)	End of Period			
		Payment (2)	Interest (3)	Applied to Principal (4)=(2)−(3)	Remaining Debt (5)=(1)−(4)
1	$5,000.00		$200.00		
2					
3					
4					
5					

15. Johnson Properties, Inc, acquired some acreage for $340,000 by paying $100,000 down and signing a mortgage for 24 quarterly payments. If the interest rate is 8% compounded quarterly, what is the amount of each quarterly payment?

16. The Centaur Corporation borrowed $200,000 to open a new branch office. If the interest rate is 6% compounded semiannually, and if the debt is to be amortized by semiannual payments for 10 years, find the amount of each payment.

17. The Everwear Carpet Outlet borrowed $175,000 to construct a new warehouse. The company is to amortize the loan in 4 years by making quarterly payments. If the interest rate is 10% compounded quarterly, find the amount of each payment.

15

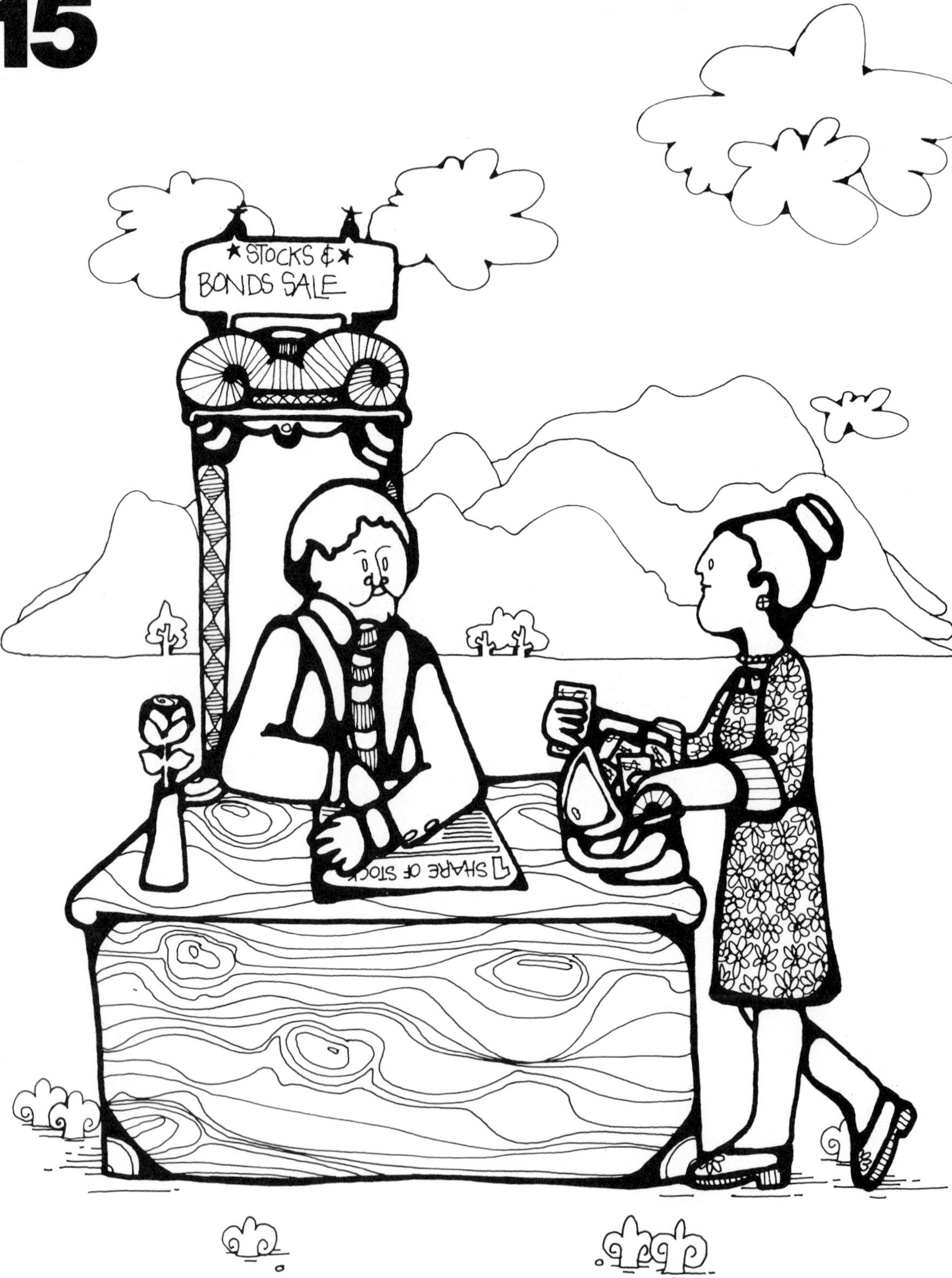

Securities

Chapter Objectives for Chapter 15

Introduction

There are times when a corporation may need funds in excess of those in the company treasury. Plant expansion, acquisition of another company, modernization of facilities, even the birth of the corporation itself may require capital beyond the ability of the company to supply. It may be possible to borrow the money from a lending institution, but there are more advantageous methods of raising capital. Corporations often raise money by selling securities to the public; two of these, corporate stocks and corporate bonds, are the subject of this chapter.

Common Stock

When a company issues common stock, it offers for sale to the public part ownership in the company. The word "common" in common stock means that the stockholders own the company in common. If, for example, an individual owns 1,000 shares* of a total of 100,000 shares of stock, then that person owns 1% of the corporation. If 100 persons each bought 1,000 shares, then the company is owned by the 100 persons. As part owners of the corporation, stockholders have a voice in management. Although the direction of the company is determined by a board of directors, this board is elected by the stockholders, and stockholders have the opportunity to vote on company matters and to suggest changes in corporate policy at the annual meeting of the company.

* A share is the unit of issue of stock. Evidence of stock ownership is the stock certificate, an engraved or lithographed document on which are entered the owner's name, the number of shares, and the date of issue.

However, most individuals do not invest in common stock because of part ownership. Instead, the following reasons are cited for buying stock: (1) Dividends, (2) Capital Gain, (3) Liquidity and Minimum Management, and (4) Inflation Protection.

1. *Dividends.* A percentage of the after tax profits of a corporation is usually distributed by the board of directors to the stockholders on a per share basis. Dividends are normally in cash, but may be in additional shares of stock, or even in property. As an example, a dividend of $0.25 per share to a stockholder who owns 1,000 shares means a payment of $0.25 × 1,000 = $250.00. The amount of a dividend often exceeds returns from other forms of investment (e.g., bonds or savings accounts), but it should be understood that dividends come from the company's net earnings; a firm that has made no money or that is in financial stress may reduce the amount of the dividend or declare no dividend at all. The per share dividend is calculated by dividing the total profits to be distributed by the number of outstanding shares.

Example 1

The board of directors of the Craft Corporation voted to distribute 60% of the company's net profits of $600,000 to its stockholders. If there are 450,000 outstanding shares, what was the amount of the declared dividend?

Solution:

The amount to be distributed is $600,000 × 0.60 = $360,000.

$$\frac{\$360,000}{450,000} = \$0.80 \text{ Dividend per share}$$

2. *Appreciation.* It is possible for the value of stock to increase, thus allowing an individual to sell the stock for more than its purchase price. This is called **capital gain.**

Example 2

John Jacobs purchased 500 shares of stock at $38.00 a share and later sold them for $42.50 a share. What was his capital gain?

Solution:

$$
\begin{array}{ll}
\$21,250 & \text{Selling price (\$42.50 × 500)} \\
- 19,000 & \text{Cost price (\$38.00 × 500)} \\
\hline
\$2,250 & \text{Capital gain}
\end{array}
$$

3. *Liquidity and Minimum Management.* Stocks require little attention and may be sold readily for cash. This is not true for all investments —real estate, for example.

4. *Inflation Protection.* In general, the prices for stocks increase as prices rise for other commodities, thus protecting the buyer from devaluation of the dollar. Some investments, savings accounts for example, do not afford this protection.

15.3 Preferred Stock

Another class of stock that may be issued by a company is called **preferred stock.** Preferred stock differs from common stock in three important ways:

1. Preferred stock dividends are fixed and are paid before any dividends are paid to common stockholders.

2. Preferred stock dividends are usually cumulative; i.e., should the company earnings be insufficient to pay the full dividend per share, the difference is carried over to subsequent dividend distribution payments.

3. In the event of liquidation, preferred stockholders have a claim to the company assets prior to that of common stockholders.

Example 1

The board of directors of the Orion Corporation voted $362,000 in dividends for the fourth quarter. The company has issued 70,000 shares of preferred stock which pays a quarterly dividend of $0.60 per share, and there are 640,000 shares of common stock outstanding. Determine the dividend distribution.

Solution:

The preferred stock dividends are distributed first. This is already fixed at $0.60 per share.

$$
\begin{array}{rl}
\$362,000 & \text{Amount to be distributed} \\
-\quad 42,000 & \text{Preferred stock dividends } (\$0.60 \times 70,000) \\
\hline
\$320,000 & \text{For distribution to common stockholders}
\end{array}
$$

$$\frac{\$320,000}{640,000} = \$0.50 \text{ per share dividend—common stock}$$

Preferred stock is often described as a hybrid stock, because it has characteristics of both common stock and bonds. The chief advantage of preferred stock is its dividend, but there are several disadvantages. Participation in management is restricted, the right to buy additional shares is limited, and the dividend is fixed regardless of the prosperity of the company. Preferred stocks were issued in large numbers in the latter part of the nineteenth century when many bankrupt railroads were being reorganized. This type of stock was issued in lieu of common stock in order to attract investors who wanted a smaller risk than provided by common stock, but a greater return than from bonds. Preferred stock thus occupies an intermediate position between common stock and bonds and must be considered a moderately conservative investment.

Exercises for Sections 15.2 and 15.3

1. The Huron Company is distributing 70% of its net profits of $450,000 to its stockholders. There are 200,000 outstanding shares of stock in the company. What is the dividend per share?

2. John Porter owns 200 shares of stock in the Martin Mining Company. The company has decided to distribute 50% of its first quarter profits of $700,000 to its stockholders. If there are 500,000 outstanding shares, how much will John receive in dividends?

3. Lucille Porter purchased 100 shares of stock in the Owens Corporation. The company's board of directors voted to distribute 55% of the company's profits of $225,000 to its stockholders, and there are 300,000 outstanding shares of stock. How much did Lucille receive?

4. There are 220,000 outstanding shares of stock in the Otis Manufacturing Company. The company's quarterly profits in 1976 were

Quarter I:	$210,000
Quarter II:	$160,000
Quarter III:	$140,000
Quarter IV:	$170,000

If the company distributed 60% of its profits to its 180,000 stockholders, what was the annual dividend per share in 1976?

5. Myron Industries recorded the following profits in 1976, with the given percentages distributed among the company's stockholders:

Quarter I:	$110,000; 60%
Quarter II:	$180,000; 65%
Quarter III:	$ 90,000; 40%
Quarter IV:	$105,000; 45%

If there are 210,000 outstanding shares of stock, what was the annual dividend per share in 1976?

6. Joan Richards purchased 150 shares of stock in Continental Industries at $22.25 per share and a year later sold the stock for $23.75 per share. What was her capital gain?

7. At the beginning of the second quarter Tim O'Connor bought 300 shares of Data Systems stock at $14.75 per share. The board of

directors of the company voted to distribute 65% of the company's second quarter profits of $350,000 among its stockholders, and there are 400,000 outstanding shares of stock. Tim sold his stock at the end of the quarter for $17.25 per share. What was his capital gain? How much did he receive in dividends? What was his total profit on the transaction?

8. The board of directors of the Babson Company voted $150,000 in dividends for the third quarter. The company has issued 30,000 shares of preferred stock that pays a quarterly dividend of $0.20 per share, and there are 400,000 shares of common stock outstanding. Determine the dividend distribution.

9. There are 800,000 outstanding shares of common stock in the Lyonkraft Company and 70,000 shares of preferred stock that pay a quarterly dividend of $0.50 per share. For the second quarter, the company will distribute $420,000 in dividends. Determine the dividend distribution.

10. Rhonda Myer has 100 shares of preferred and 400 shares of common stock in the Scott Manufacturing Company. For the first quarter, the company will distribute $320,000 in dividends. If the preferred stock pays a quarterly dividend of $0.60 a share and if there are 650,000 shares of common and 50,000 shares of preferred stock outstanding, how much will Rhonda receive in dividends?

15.4 Transactions in Stocks

After a share of stock becomes publicly held, the issuing company can no longer control its ownership or its price. As a result, stock is bought and sold like any other commodity. For major corporations, the principal market for stocks is a stock exchange. In the United States, the largest stock exchanges are the New York Stock Exchange and the American Stock

Exchange. At a stock exchange, the price of a stock is determined by the most fundamental of economic concepts, the law of supply and demand. Shares are sold by a two-way auction; buyers compete with other buyers for the lowest price, and sellers compete with other sellers for the highest price.

The actual trading (buying and selling) of a stock is executed by members of a stock exchange called brokers. To buy or sell a share of stock, an order must be placed with a broker, usually via a local brokerage office. Once placed, it is the responsibility of the broker to bargain for the best possible price, whether it is a purchase or a sale.

Because the trading of stocks is subject to supply and demand, the price of a share fluctuates almost daily. To keep abreast of these variations, the financial sections of many daily newspapers carry an account of the previous day's activity on an exchange. A portion of such an account is shown in Figure 15–1. For an interpretation of this information, consider the underlined entry. The meaning of this line is as follows:

Figure 15–1

Monsan—Abbreviation for the Monsanto Chemical Company

2.60 —The amount of the annual dividend.

9 —The price-earnings ratio. This will be discussed in a later section.

568 —The number of reported shares sold for the day, in hundreds.

$75\frac{3}{8}$ —The highest selling price of the day. Stocks are sold in whole dollars and units of eighths of a dollar ($12\frac{1}{2}$¢ or $0.125). Thus, the high for the day was $75.375 per share.

$74\frac{1}{8}$ —The lowest selling price of the day, $74.125.

$74\frac{1}{2}$ —The last or closing price of the day, $74.50.

$+\frac{1}{4}$ —The difference between today's closing price and the closing price of the last session in which the stock was traded. Today's closing price was $74\frac{1}{2}$; the last closing price was $74\frac{1}{4}$.

Note the line immediately below the one just discussed. This is a second issue of Monsanto, a preferred stock issue. The same information is provided as for common stock.

Section 15.5 Buying and Selling Costs—Stocks

In addition to the trading price, the cost of buying or selling a share of stock includes a commission for the broker. For the seller, there are additional fees imposed by the Federal government and often by state or local governments. These costs are illustrated in the examples to follow.

A. Broker Commission

All investors who buy or sell stocks on an exchange pay a commission to the broker who executes the order. The commission schedule* shown in Figure 15–2 is based on round-lot orders. A round-lot is usually 100 shares or a multiple thereof, but for low volume stocks it may be 10 shares.

Figure 15–2

On orders of less than $100, the commission is as mutually agreed. On that portion of an order exceeding $300,000, the commission may be negotiated between broker and customer. An order for less than the customary unit of trading, usually 100 shares, incurs an additional cost per share, known as the odd-lot differential, of ⅛-point (12½ cents).

(a) On orders of 100 shares the rates are:

Money Involved	Percent of Money Involved	Plus Stated Amount
Under $ 100	As mutually agreed	—
$ 100–but under $ 800	2.0%	$ 6.40
$ 800–but under $ 2,500	1.3%	$ 12.00
$ 2,500–and above	0.9%	$ 22.00

Notwithstanding the foregoing, the commission on any order for 100 shares shall not exceed $65.

On multiple round-lot orders the rates are:

Money Involved	Percent of Money Involved	Plus Stated Amount
Under $ 100	As mutually agreed	—
$ 100–but under $ 2,500	1.3%	$ 12.00
$ 2,500–but under $20,000	0.9%	$ 22.00
$20,000–but under $30,000	0.6%	$ 82.00
$30,000 to and including $300,000	0.4%	$142.00

Plus a charge for each round-lot of 100 shares within the order of:

First to tenth round lot	$6.00 per round lot
Eleventh round lot and above	$4.00 per round lot

On odd-lot orders, the rates are the same as for orders of 100 shares except that the added, stated amount is $2 less. Further, the commission on any odd-lot order cannot exceed $65.

* Present-day commission schedules are flexible and vary from broker to broker. Figure 15–2 illustrates the basic principles of a commission schedule and will be used in the examples and problems of this section.

Orders for other than round lots are called **odd-lots.** For odd-lot orders, add $\frac{1}{8}$ point ($12\frac{1}{2}$¢) per share to the schedule in Figure 15–2. This is called the **odd-lot differential.**

Example 1

Find the commission for an order of 100 shares at $4.00.

Solution:

The trading price is $4.00 \times 100 = \$400.00$.

$ 8.00	Percentage of money involved ($400 × 0.02)
+ 6.40	Stated amount
$14.40	Commission

Example 2

Find the commission on a sale of 600 shares at $35\frac{1}{8}$.

Solution:

The trading price is $35.125 \times 600 = \$21,075$.

$126.45	Percentage of money involved ($21,075 × 0.006)
+ 82.00	Stated amount
+ 36.00	Round-lot charge ($6 × 6)
$244.45	Commission

Example 3

What is the commission on a purchase of 40 shares at $20\frac{1}{4}$?

Solution:

The trading price is $20.25 \times 40 = \$810.00$.

$10.53	Percentage of money involved ($810 × 0.013)
+ 5.00	Odd-lot differential ($0.125 × 40)
+ 10.00	Stated amount ($12.00 − $2.00)
$25.53	Commission

B. Taxes and Fees   In addition to a broker's commission, the seller of a stock must pay certain fees and taxes. The Securities and Exchange Commission levies a fee on the trading price of 1¢ per $500 in value or fraction thereof.* In addition, state or local governments may impose transfer taxes. These are usually on a graduated scale, according to the trading price of the stock.

* The Securities and Exchange Commission is a Federal regulatory agency created by Congress in 1934 to help protect investors.

Example 4

Janis McGuire sold 200 shares of stock at $37\frac{5}{8}$. If the state transfer taxes were $11.00, what did Janis net from the sale?

Solution:

The trading price is $37.625 \times 200 = \$7,525$.

Commission:
$\quad$ $ 67.73 Percentage of money involved ($7,525 × 0.009)
$\quad$ + $\quad$ 22.00 Stated amount
$\quad$ + $\quad$ 12.00 Round-lot charge ($6 × 2)
$\quad$ $\overline{}$
$\quad$ $101.73 Commission

SEC fee: $\quad$ $ 0.16 ($7,525 ÷ 500 = $15.05; $15.05 × 0.01 = $0.1505)

Thus
$\quad$ $7,525.00 Trading price
$\quad$ − $\quad$ 101.73 Commission
$\quad$ − $\quad$ 0.16 SEC fee
$\quad$ − $\quad$ 11.00 Transfer taxes
$\quad$ $\overline{}$
$\quad$ $7,412.11 Net to Janis

Exercises for Sections 15.4 and 15.5

In problems 1–10, use the information given in Figure 15–2 to find the commission for an order of the indicated number of shares of stock when purchased at the given price per share.

1. 100 shares at $7.00 per share

2. 100 shares at $22.50 per share

3. 100 shares at $42\frac{1}{8}$ per share

4. 400 shares at $3.25 per share

5. 900 shares at $57\frac{3}{8}$ per share

6. 1,300 shares at $40\frac{5}{8}$ per share

7. 60 shares at $18.50 per share

8. 55 shares at $32\frac{7}{8}$ per share

9. 120 shares at $15\frac{3}{8}$ per share (100 round lot, 20 odd lot)

10. 225 shares at $60\frac{5}{8}$ per share (200 round lot, 25 odd lot)

11. Ron Jacobs sold 400 shares of stock at $22.25 per share. The state transfer taxes were $13.00. What amount did John net from the sale?

12. Find the net sale price of 100 shares of stock at $18\frac{3}{8}$ per share if local transfer taxes amount to $2.30.

13. Cliff Harris purchased 200 shares of stock at $17\frac{1}{4}$ per share and later sold the stock at $26\frac{1}{8}$ per share. The state transfer taxes when he sold the stock amounted to $4.25. How much net profit (capital gain less all commissions and fees) did Cliff realize from the purchase and sale of the stock?

14. Eugenia Rasmussen bought 40 shares of stock at $42\frac{7}{8}$ and later sold the stock at $41\frac{1}{4}$. If the transfer taxes on the sale of the stock were $5.40, how much did Eugenia lose (capital loss plus all commissions and fees) from the purchase and sale of the stock?

Section 15.6

Valuation Indices

Because of the fluctuation in stock prices, it is possible to make a great amount of money in the stock market; it is also possible to lose a great amount of money.* Consequently, investors have long sought methods to predict market behavior. While some formulas have been successful over a long period of time, no one has yet found a way to "beat the market." The old axiom is still true: "The market can do anything."

Nevertheless, there are several indicators used by investors to evaluate a stock. Among these are (A) earnings per share, (B) price-earnings ratio, and (C) the yield.

A. Earnings per Share

The **earnings per share** for common stock is found by dividing earnings available for common stock by the number of outstanding shares. That is,

$$(15\text{--}1) \qquad E/S = \frac{\text{Net profit} - \text{Preferred dividends}}{\text{Outstanding shares}}$$

Example 1

In the previous fiscal year, Gartco Corporation had a net profit of $4,600,000 from which preferred stock dividends were $520,000. If there are 1.8 million outstanding shares, what is the earnings per share?

Solution:

$$E/S = \frac{\$4,600,000 - \$520,000}{1,800,000}$$

$$= \frac{\$4,080,000}{1,800,000}$$

$$= \$2.266$$

$$= \$2.27$$

---

* Two examples of this are Bernard Baruch and Daniel Drew. Baruch once made $700,000 on one stock, Amalgamated Copper. On the other hand, "Uncle Daniel," one of the most ruthless men in Wall Street history and who amassed a fortune of some $13,000,000, lost it all in the market and died with assets of less than $1,000.

Earnings per share represents the theoretical portion of total earnings owned by a holder of one share of stock. It is not to be confused with dividends, which are actually distributed to stockholders. In examining earnings per share, investors look for an upward trend.

B. Price-Earnings Ratio

The **price-earnings ratio** is a number found by dividing the current market price of a share by the earnings per share. That is,

$$(15\text{--}2) \qquad P/E = \frac{\text{Current Market Price}}{\text{Earnings per Share}}$$

Example 2

Find the price-earnings ratio of a stock selling for $64 with earnings per share of $4.

Solution:

$$P/E = \frac{\$64}{\$4} = \frac{16}{1} = 16$$

The price-earnings ratio is 16 to 1.

The price-earnings ratio is the most frequently used indicator of the relation between stock prices and earnings. The P/E ratio represents the amount investors are currently paying for $1 of that company's earnings. In general, a high P/E stock is bought for growth, a low P/E stock for income. Over a period of time, the P/E ratio of a given stock tends to fluctuate over a wide range. It is the task of the investor to estimate the "normal" P/E ratio.

C. Yield

Another simple tool for measuring stock valuation is the yield. The **yield** is that percent found by dividing the annual dividend by the current market price. That is,

$$(15\text{--}3) \qquad \text{Yield} = \frac{\text{Annual Dividend}}{\text{Current Market Price}}$$

Example 3

Find the yield of a stock if it is currently selling at $36\frac{1}{4}$ and paying an annual dividend of $1.60.

Solution:

$$\text{Yield} = \frac{\$1.60}{\$36.25}$$

$$= 0.044$$

$$= 4.4\%$$

Yield is considered a definite indicator of the reasonableness of a stock price. Slow growth stocks may be expected to yield as much as 5% while future growth stocks may average only 2% to 3%.

Exercises for Section 15.6

In problems 1–4, find the earnings per share.

1. Net profit $2,300,000; preferred dividends $410,000; outstanding shares 900,000

2. Net profit $4,800,000; preferred dividends $1,100,000; outstanding shares 1,500,000

3. Net profit $3,750,000; preferred dividends $820,000; outstanding shares 1,400,000

4. Net profit $6,255,000; preferred dividends $2,150,000; outstanding shares 2,300,000

In problems 5–8, find the price-earnings ratio of the given stock.

5. Selling price of stock, $23.50; earnings per share $1.85

6. Selling price of stock, $43\frac{1}{8}$; earnings per share $2.15

7. Net profit of company, $5,620,000; preferred dividends $750,000; outstanding shares, 1,100,000; selling price of stock, $62\frac{3}{8}$

8. Net profit of company, $4,750,000; preferred dividends $1,150,000; outstanding shares 875,000; selling price of stock, $52\frac{7}{8}$

In problems 9–13, find the yield of the given stock.

9. Annual dividend per share, $0.60; selling price $22.25.

10. Annual dividend per share, $1.20; selling price $31.25.

11. Annual dividend per share, $1.45; selling price $18\frac{1}{8}$.

12. Total annual dividends paid, $2,300,000; outstanding shares, 1,875,000; selling price $19\frac{7}{8}$.

13. Total annual dividends paid, $3,111,000; outstanding shares, 920,000; selling price $64\frac{3}{8}$.

14. Jane Travis is deciding which of three stocks to purchase. Stock A pays dividends of $1.80 and sells for $28\frac{1}{8}$; stock B pays dividends of $0.20 and sells for $3\frac{1}{4}$; stock C pays dividends of $0.90 and sells for $14\frac{1}{8}$. If Jane is interested in income, which stock should she purchase?

Section 15.7 Bonds

Bonds are a second way corporations may acquire capital. When a company issues bonds, it is borrowing money from investors; thus a bond is like a long-term promissory note. Each bond is an agreement to repay the principal (face value) at a specified time and to pay a set annual rate of interest from the day of issue to the day of redemption.*

As an investment, corporate bonds differ from corporate stocks in the following ways:

1. A stockholder is a part owner of the company and has a voice in management; a person who buys bonds simply lends his or her money to the company.

2. The stockholder expects to share in the company's profits; the bondholder expects to receive only a fixed interest payment. However, dividends may fluctuate or may not be paid at all, but a bondholder will receive interest payments when due; failure to do so constitutes insolvency of the company.

3. In the event of insolvency, bondholders have a prior claim to the company's assets. The claims of bondholders come first, then preferred stockholders, and last, common stockholders.

It is clear from the above that bonds are a more conservative investment than common stock. But, as the risk is smaller, so is the return; the interest paid on bonds is almost always less than the dividends paid on common stock. The element of financial risk plays a definite role in both the price and profits of corporate securities. The additional investment security of bonds makes them popular with insurance companies, banks, pension funds, and other investors seeking guaranteed incomes. Common stocks are for investors willing to accept financial risk for potential growth and increased profits.

There are several types of corporate bonds, but the most popular is the **mortgage bond,** which pledges the physical property of the corporation as security. This is an example of a secured bond. Unsecured bonds, called **debentures,** are backed only by the general credit of the corporation. Since the quality of a bond is a measure of its security, it is a practice to rate bonds according to their security features. A triple A bond as rated by an investor service company offers the ultimate safety in principal and income to the investor. Bonds in the B range are medium to fair security risks, while C rated bonds are considered highly speculative.

Section **15.8** **Transactions in Bonds**

Bonds are sold in denominations ranging from $50 to $10,000, but the most popular denomination is $1,000. Bonds are marketed at a securities exchange or on the over-the-counter market.† Bond transactions at an

---

* Although the set interest rate is nominal (annual), it is customary to pay the interest semiannually.

† An over-the-counter market is made up of securities dealers who may or may not be members of an exchange. In addition to bonds, stock of companies with insufficient financial qualifications to be listed on an exchange are also traded on over-the-counter markets.

exchange are reported daily in the financial section of many newspapers. Figure 15–3 is a sample portion of such a report. The meaning of the underlined entry is as follows:

Figure 15–3

A FrP 4.80s87	BB	8.0	8	59⅞+	⅞	Gen E18½s04	AAA	8.7	29	98 — ⅝	Pepsico8¼85	A 8.6
AmInv8¾s89	BBB	11.7	110	75 +	4	Gen E17½s96	AAA	8.2	30	91⅞+ 2⅜	Pet Inc8s91	A 8.8
A M F 10s85	BBB	10.0	5	100 +	¼	Gen E16¼s79	AAA	6.7	55	93¼— ½	Pfizer 9¼s20	AA 9.2
AmMedi 5s97	B	11.2	1	44¾	...	Gen E13½s76	AAA	3.6	22	98½+ ½	Pfizer 8⅞s85	AA 8.7
A Motor 6s88	B	9.4	17	64 +	½	GECrd8⅞s92	A	8.8	5	101 + ¼	Pfizer In 4s97	A 5.5
A Sug 5.30s93	BB	7.5	15	71 +	¾	GECr8.60s85	A	8.8	5	97½ ...	PhilE 12¾s81	..... 12.0
AT&T 8¾s20	AAA	8.8	347	99½+	½	GECrd8½s76	A	8.5	5 100	9-16+17-32	PhilE 11⅝s20	A 11.2
AT&T 8.70s02	AAA	8.9	95	97½+	½	GECr8.40s81	A	8.4	10	99⅞— ⅛	PhilElc 11s20	A 11.0
AT&T 8.80s05	AAA	8.9	278	99¾+	⅝	GECrd7⅞s78	A	7.4	20	96 — ½	PhilElc 11s80	A 10.6
AT&T 8⅝s07	AAA	8.9	765	96⅞—	⅛	GenElCr7s79	A	7.4	10	94 + 2	PhilEl8½s04	A 10.6
AT&T 7¾s82	AAA	7.9	115	98½+	¾	GenFd8⅞s90	AAA	8.9	31	99½— 1	PhilEl8¼s96	A 10.0
AT&T 7¾s77	AAA	7.7	35	100⅜+	⅜	GnHost 11s88	CCC	11.5	13	95⅞— ⅛	PhilE16½s93	A 9.8
AT&T 7⅛s03	AAA	8.6	78	82½	...	GenHost7s94	CCC	13.0	20	53¾+ ¾	PhilMo 8½ 85	A 8.6
AT&T 7s2001	AAA	8.5	77	82	...	GenInstr 5s92	BB	9.2	5	54½+ ⅝	PhilPt 7⅝s01	AA 9.0
AT&T 6½s79	AAA	6.9	64	94 —	1	GMAC 8.70s83	A	8.7	1	100¼ ...	Pittston 4s97	BBB 7.8
AT&T 4⅝s85	AAA	6.0	10	73½+	⅜	GMAC 8⅞s99	AA	9.1	5	97½+ 1¼	PizzaH 6¼ 95	....
AT&T 3⅞s90	AAA	6.4	12	61 +	1⅛	GMAC 7¾s94	AA	8.9	17	87½+ ½	PortGE 10s82	BBB 9.8
AT&T 3¼s84	AAA	4.8	2	67¾—	1¼	GMAC 7⅛s92	AA	8.6	15	82⅝+ 1⅛	PortG 10½ 80	BBB 10.1
AT&T 2¾s80	AAA	3.4	35	80¾—	¼	GMAC 6¼s88	AA	7.9	15	79⅛— ⅜	Pot E19½s05	A 10.1
AT&T 2¾s82	AAA	3.7	20	74	...	G M A C 5s77	AA	5.3	4	95 + ¼	PubSvE 12 04	AA 10.9

AT & T—Abbreviation for American Telephone and Telegraph

$7\frac{3}{4}$s —The annual interest rate of the bond, $7\frac{3}{4}\%$

82   —The maturity date of the bond, 1982

AAA —The bond rating or quality

7.9 —The bond yield (This will be discussed in a later section.)

115 —The volume of sales in hundreds

$98\frac{1}{2}$ —The closing price in % of $1,000 face value; i.e., the price is $1,000 \times .985 = \$985$

$+\frac{3}{4}$ —The change in closing price from the last trading session

Section 15.9 Bond Costs

Although most bonds are issued with a face value or par value of $1,000, the actual trading price may be more or less than this amount. There are two reasons for this, financial risk and interest rates. The best protection against financial risk is to purchase only high grade bonds; the interest rate risk is more difficult to estimate.

Since the interest rate of a bond is fixed, bonds can be marketed competitively against current interest rates only by adjusting the selling price. To illustrate, in order to sell a $1,000 bond paying 4% interest when the current rate is 6%, the owner would have to accept less than the face value, so that the bond interest plus the difference between the face value and selling price would equal or exceed the return on money invested at 6%. Thus, the trading price of a bond fluctuates with the changes in current interest rates.

A second factor in the cost of a bond is accrued interest. Because interest is paid only to the owner of a bond, the purchaser pays the seller for all accrued interest since the last interest payment. The interest is computed by the simple interest formula $I = Prt$, using the financial calendar of a 30-day month and a 360-day year. Most bond interest is paid semiannually.

Both buyer and seller pay a broker's commission which also adds to the cost of a bond. A typical commission is $5.00 per $1,000 bond.* Finally, the seller of a bond is subject to an SEC fee of 1¢ per $500 quotation or fraction thereof.

The costs of buying and selling bonds can be summarized as follows:

Purchase = Trading price + accrued interest + commission.

Sale = Trading price + accrued interest − commission − SEC fee.

In the examples to follow, the face value of the bonds is $1,000.

Example 1

Find the cost of buying 5 Con Oil 6s quoted at $89\frac{1}{2}$ if the date of the sale is March 1 and interest is paid on January 1 and July 1.

Solution:

The accrued interest is calculated first. January 1 to March 1 is 60 days, thus $t = \dfrac{60}{360} = \dfrac{1}{6}$.

$$I = Prt$$
$$= \$1,000 \times 0.06 \times \frac{1}{6}$$
$$= \$10$$

$$
\begin{array}{rl}
\$4,475.00 & \text{Trading price (\$895} \times 5) \\
+\quad 50.00 & \text{Accrued interest (\$10} \times 5) \\
+\quad 25.00 & \text{Commission (\$5.00} \times 5) \\
\hline
\$4,550.00 & \text{Cost}
\end{array}
$$

Example 2

Alice Blake bought 10 BLT 11½s quoted at 104¼. If the date of the sale is October 1 and interest is paid on January 1 and July 1, what did Alice pay for the bonds?

Solution:

July 1 to October 1 is 90 days, thus $t = \dfrac{90}{360} = ¼$.

$$I = Prt$$
$$= \$1,000 \times 0.115 \times ¼$$
$$= \$28.75$$

---

* Bond commissions vary, often according to the number of bonds purchased. However, a fixed rate of $5.00 per $1,000 bond will be used in the examples and problems of this section.

$$\begin{array}{rl}
\$10,425.00 & \text{Trading price } (\$1,042.50 \times 10) \\
+\quad 287.50 & \text{Accrued interest } (\$28.75 \times 10) \\
+\qquad 50.00 & \text{Commission } (\$5.00 \times 10) \\
\hline
\$10,762.50 & \text{Cost}
\end{array}$$

Example 3

Richard Whitlock sold four TLT $8\frac{1}{4}$s bonds on November 25. The bonds were quoted at $91\frac{1}{8}$ and paid interest semiannually on March 1 and September 1. How much did Richard net from the sale?

Solution:

The time from the last interest payment is 2 months and 24 days or 84 days.*

$$I = Prt$$

$$= \$1,000 \times 0.0825 \times \frac{84}{360}$$

$$= \$19.25$$

$$\begin{array}{rl}
\$3,645.00 & \text{Trading price } (\$911.25 \times 4) \\
+\quad 77.00 & \text{Accrued interest } (\$19.25 \times 4) \\
-\quad 20.00 & \text{Commission } (\$5.00 \times 4) \\
-\qquad 0.08 & \text{SEC fee } (\$3,645 \div 500 = 7.29; 8 \times 1\cent = 8\cent) \\
\hline
\$3,701.92 & \text{Net to Richard}
\end{array}$$

* The **settlement date** is the date that the buyer makes payment and acquires title to the bond. Thus the interest period is

$$\begin{array}{ll}
\text{September 1 to November 1} & = 2 \text{ months} = 60 \text{ days} \\
\text{November 1 to November 25} & \qquad\qquad\;\; = 24 \text{ days} \\
\hline
\text{Interest period} & \qquad\qquad\;\; = 84 \text{ days}
\end{array}$$

Exercises for Sections 15.7 through 15.9

In problems 1–8, find the cost of buying the given bonds (the face value is $1,000).

1. 10 LBT 7s quoted at $72\frac{1}{2}$; date of sale April 1; interest paid on January 1 and July 1

2. 6 AML 9s quoted at $87\frac{1}{4}$; date of sale October 1; interest paid on January 1 and July 1

3. 8 KBJ $8\frac{1}{8}$s quoted at $82\frac{1}{8}$; date of sale July 1; interest paid on April 1 and October 1

4. 15 MLE $7\frac{1}{8}$s quoted at $91\frac{1}{4}$; date of sale July 14; interest paid on January 1 and July 1

5. 9 SBR $6\frac{7}{8}$s quoted at $57\frac{1}{2}$; date of sale April 22; interest paid on February 1 and August 1

6. 4 PTT $7\frac{5}{8}$s quoted at $64\frac{1}{2}$; date of sale August 28; interest paid on April 1 and October 1

7. 8 MTE 10½s quoted at 103; date of sale April 1; interest paid on January 1 and July 1

8. 12 PPR 11¼s quoted at 105¼; date of sale May 18; interest paid on February 1 and August 1

In problems 9–16, find the net proceeds from the sale of the given bonds (the face value is $1,000).

9. 3 RLL $7\frac{1}{4}$s quoted at 78; date of sale May 1; interest paid on January 1 and July 1

10. 5 COL $5\frac{1}{4}$s quoted at $41\frac{1}{8}$; date of sale December 1; interest paid on January 1 and July 1

11. 6 AOW $6\frac{7}{8}$s quoted at $52\frac{3}{8}$; date of sale February 16; interest paid on February 1 and August 1

12. 9 WKP $9\frac{1}{8}$s quoted at $95\frac{1}{2}$; date of sale May 27; interest paid on May 1 and November 1

13. 15 OCC $8\frac{7}{8}$s quoted at $88\frac{1}{4}$; date of sale June 18; interest paid on March 1 and September 1

14. 12 TPL $7\frac{5}{8}$s quoted at $74\frac{1}{4}$; date of sale May 19; interest paid on February 1 and August 1

15. 15 DLC 12¼s quoted at 108⅛; date of sale June 12; interest paid on March 1 and September 1

16. 10 PLL 11¾s quoted at 110½; date of sale February 12; interest paid on February 1 and August 1

17. David Truitt sold 4 LNN $7\frac{1}{8}$s bonds on April 14. The bonds were quoted at $82\frac{1}{4}$ and paid semiannual interest on February 1 and August 1. That same day, he used part of the proceeds to purchase 3 PCC $8\frac{7}{8}$s bonds quoted at $92\frac{1}{8}$. If the PCC bonds paid interest on January 1 and July 1, how much did he have left of the proceeds from the sale of the LNN bonds?

18. Janis Boyd sold 5 NTT $8\frac{1}{4}$s bonds on March 23. The bonds were quoted at $87\frac{1}{8}$ and paid semiannual interest on January 1 and July 1. That same day, she decided to use the proceeds to purchase some LCC $9\frac{1}{8}$s quoted at $98\frac{1}{2}$. If the LCC bonds paid interest on March 1 and September 1, how many LCC bonds was she able to buy? How much did she have left of the proceeds from the sale of the NTT bonds?

Valuation Indices—Bonds

Aside from the yield stated on the bond itself, which is the **nominal yield,** there are two other valuation indices commonly used by bond investors. The **current yield** is that percent found by dividing the annual interest by the current trading price. That is,

(15–4) $$\text{Current Yield} = \frac{\text{Annual interest}}{\text{Current trading price}}$$

The current yield is the yield quoted in the financial section of a newspaper.

Example 1

Verify the yield for GnMtr $8\frac{5}{8}$s 05 in Figure 15–3.

Solution:

Since $8\frac{5}{8}$s $= 8.625\%$, the annual interest is $\$1,000 \times 0.08625 = \$86.25$. The trading price is $\$1,000 \times 0.99 = \$990$, thus

$$\begin{aligned} \text{Current yield} &= \frac{\$86.25}{\$990} \\ &= 0.0871212 \\ &= 8.7\% \end{aligned}$$

The most common measure of bond yield is the yield to maturity. The **yield to maturity** is that percent found by dividing the combined annual gain by the average investment. Yields to maturity are normally published in especially prepared bond tables, but may be approximated by the following formula:

(15–5)   Yield to Maturity $= \dfrac{\text{Annual interest} + \text{average capital gain}}{500 + \frac{1}{2} \text{ trading price}}$

where the average capital gain (or loss) is the difference between the face value and the trading price divided by the remaining term of the bond.*

Example 2

Find the yield to maturity on a $1,000 bond purchased at 80 if the interest rate is 7% and the term of the bond is 20 years.

Solution:

Annual interest $= \$1,000 \times 0.07 = \$70$

Average Capital gain $= \dfrac{\$1,000 - \$800}{20} = \$10$

$500 + \frac{1}{2}$ purchase price $= \$500 + \$400 = \$900$

Yield to maturity $= \dfrac{\$70 + \$10}{\$900}$

$= 0.08888$

$= 8.9\%$

Exercises for Section 15.10

In problems 1–8, compute the current yield for the given bonds (with face value $1,000).

1. TCC $8\frac{1}{2}$s quoted at 93

2. BTL $7\frac{1}{8}$s quoted at 82

3. KTT $6\frac{3}{8}$s quoted at $71\frac{1}{8}$

4. SMP $7\frac{5}{8}$s quoted at $84\frac{3}{8}$

5. RCK $8\frac{7}{8}$s quoted at $97\frac{1}{2}$

6. GWM $6\frac{1}{8}$s quoted at $67\frac{3}{8}$

---

* If there is an average capital loss rather than an average capital gain, then the formula is

Yield to Maturity $= \dfrac{\text{Annual Interest} - \text{average capital loss}}{500 + \frac{1}{2} \text{ trading price}}$

7. PAA $7\frac{3}{8}$s quoted at $85\frac{1}{4}$

8. ALM $8\frac{3}{8}$s quoted at $89\frac{1}{8}$

In problems 9–15, find the yield to maturity for the given bond.

9. HNN $7\frac{1}{4}$s quoted at 83; remaining term 10 years

10. TPL $8\frac{1}{2}$s quoted at 91; remaining term 20 years

11. PCC $9\frac{1}{8}$s quoted at 94; remaining term 15 years

12. CPL $6\frac{7}{8}$s quoted at $71\frac{1}{4}$; remaining term 8 years

13. LTP $7\frac{5}{8}$s quoted at $83\frac{1}{8}$; remaining term 14 years

14. TAP $8\frac{3}{8}$s quoted at $92\frac{5}{8}$; remaining term 12 years

15. BPL $6\frac{3}{8}$s quoted at $68\frac{7}{8}$; remaining term 6 years

16. John Boswell is considering purchasing DTT $7\frac{7}{8}$s bonds at $87\frac{5}{8}$. The remaining term of the bonds is 22 years. Compute the current yield and the yield to maturity.

17. Kathy Forbes is trying to decide whether to buy GPL $6\frac{1}{8}$s bonds at $71\frac{1}{8}$ or NLL $8\frac{1}{4}$s bonds at $87\frac{1}{8}$. If the remaining term of the GPL bonds is 12 years and the remaining term of the NLL bonds is 8 years, which of the bonds has the greatest yield to maturity?

4 Selected Topics

16

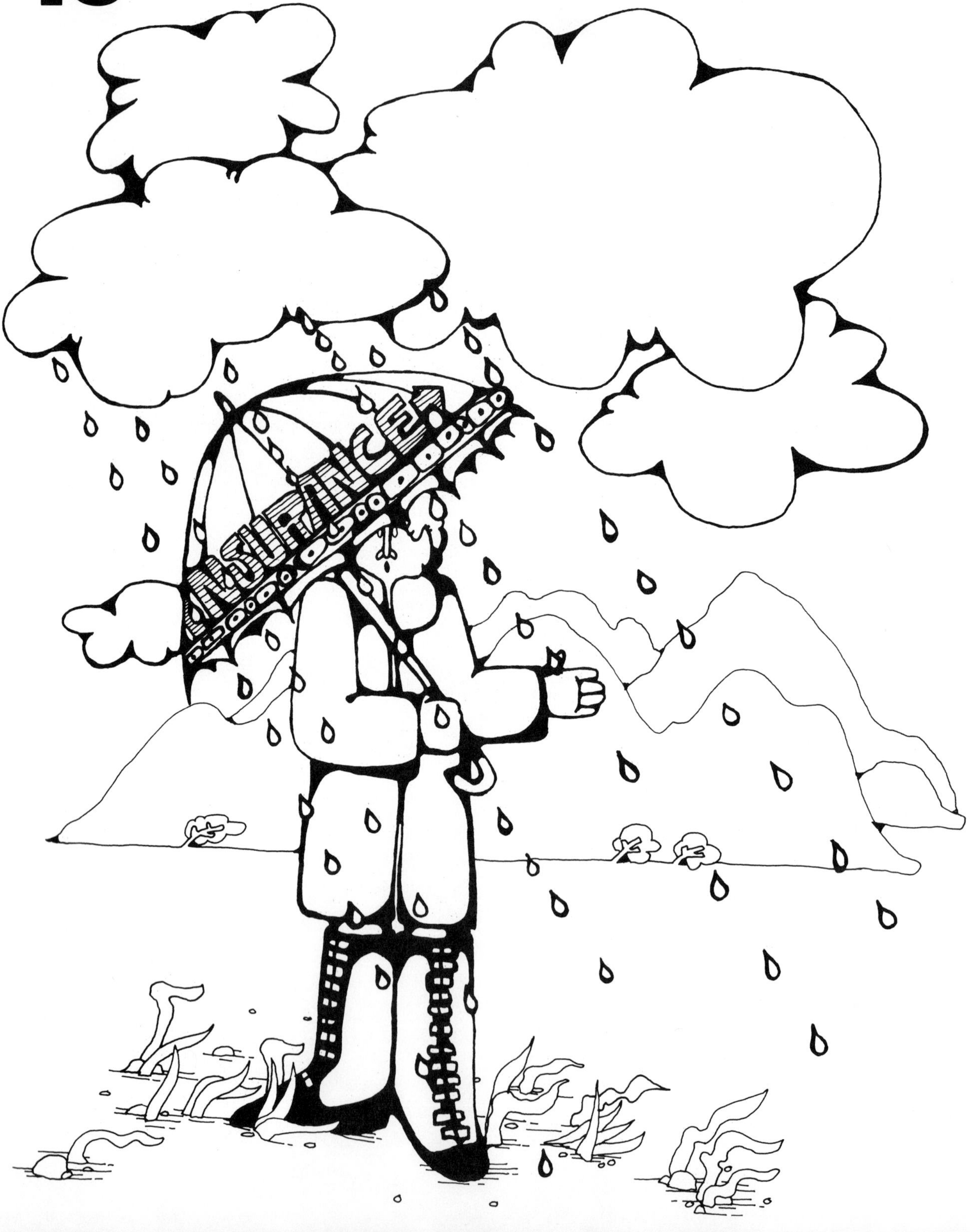

Insurance

Chapter Objectives for Chapter 16

The financial loss resulting from illness, death, fire, theft, flood, or countless other hazards can be catastrophic. For protection from such losses, individuals and businesses turn to insurance. Insurance is a means of avoiding possible economic loss.

The fundamental principle of insurance is group sharing of losses. People subject to a particular risk combine their resources and share losses on an equitable basis. This permits each member of the group to be protected against a substantial loss for a relatively small cost. This basic insurance principle is quite old and is found in the earliest written records. Today, insurance can be purchased for almost any peril, and the insurance industry is one of the largest and most influential businesses in the world.

Because of its unique product, a specialized vocabulary has developed. The following terminology is common to all types of insurance and must be understood to properly interpret an insurance contract:

peril—an event that causes a loss (fire, accident, illness, etc.).

hazard—a condition that may create a peril or increase its probability of occurrence.

insurance—a contract whereby a party undertakes to guarantee another against loss by an accidental event.

insurance policy—the contract wherein the terms and conditions of the insurance are stated.

insured (or **policyholder**)—the person or organization that has purchased an insurance policy.

insurer (or **underwriter**)—the organization that sells an insurance policy.

premium—the cost of the insurance policy.

A typical insurance policy will consist of four parts:

1. The **declaration** contains descriptive material indicating who is covered, what is covered, the amount of coverage, and the premium.
2. The **insuring agreement** sets forth exactly what perils are covered.
3. The **exclusions** state what the policy does not cover in the insuring agreement.
4. The **conditions** the insured must fulfill to receive the insurance.

Most policies follow the foregoing format with the parts clearly identified. Some deviations from the standard format may be found, but a knowledge of their contents will make them recognizable in any policy.

Every policy should be carefully read to be sure that the coverage desired is so stated, that nothing is excluded from the desired coverage, and that the person or property is described correctly and completely.

The kinds and varieties of insurance could easily be the subject of an entire textbook. In this chapter, the discussion is limited to three forms of insurance common to business operations: life insurance, group insurance, and fire insurance.

The primary purpose of life insurance is to offset financial need resulting from the death of a person. An individual who buys life insurance joins a risk-sharing group by purchasing a life insurance contract. Upon the death of the individual, the insurance company promises to pay a specified amount of money (the face value of the policy) to a person or persons (the beneficiary) named by the insured.

There are two categories of life insurance, term insurance and cash-value insurance. Term insurance is pure protection, while cash-value insurance combines protection with a savings account. Cash-value insurance comes in three basic forms: ordinary life, limited pay life, and endowments.

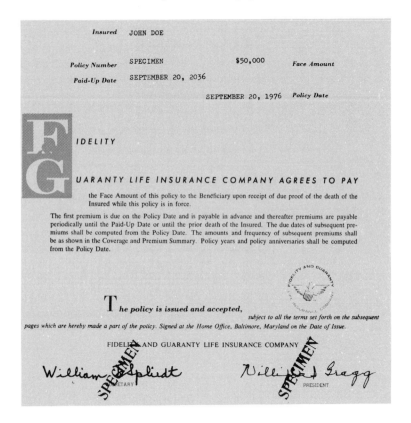

A. Term Insurance

Term insurance is protection for a limited period. The period may be as short as one year or may extend to age sixty-five or seventy, but most policies are written for five, ten, fifteen, or twenty years. Term insurance is analogous to rent; it provides protection, but develops no equity. The advantage of term insurance is that it provides the maximum life insurance protection for the premium dollars.

Term insurance may be renewable and/or convertible. Renewable term insurance means the insured has the option of renewing the contract for a limited number of additional periods. Convertibility means the insured may exchange the term policy for a form of cash-value insurance. This conversion is guaranteed regardless of the physical condition of the insured at the time of conversion.

B. Cash-Value Insurance

One thing all individual life insurance policies have in common is that they are constructed on a framework of increasing cost with increasing age. That is, the premium per $1,000 increases each year (See Section 16–3). Because of the unpopularity of an annual price increase, insurance companies have developed the level premium plan. A level premium is the same for each installment, higher than the actual cost of the protection in the lower ages, but considerably less than the cost of the protection at the upper ages. The excess premium at the lower ages is invested at compound interest and the accumulated amount is used to offset the higher protection cost at the upper ages. The fund thus accumulated is held in trust for the insured and represents a savings element called the **cash value.** Cash-value insurance thus combines insurance protection with an investment feature. The three forms of cash-value insurance are discussed here in order of increasing premium cost.

1. Ordinary Life Insurance

Also known as whole or straight life insurance, ordinary life insurance is characterized by the payment of premiums as long as the insured lives. It is the basic policy of most life insurance companies and usually the most widely sold. In the sense that the policy never has to be renewed or converted, it is often referred to as "permanent" protection.

The extended payment period makes the ordinary life policy the least expensive of the cash-value plans, but most individuals do not plan to pay premiums beyond a certain age. At that point they hope to exercise one of the nonforfeiture options contained in the policy (See Section 16.5). Insurance protection ceases with the last payment, but the accumulated cash value may be used to purchase an annuity, to buy other forms of insurance, or in a variety of other ways. This flexibility is one of the advantages of cash-value insurance.

2. Limited Payment Life Insurance

Limited payment life insurance plans have the same features as ordinary life insurance, except that premium payments are limited to a specified period of years. The idea is to pay for a lifetime of coverage during the peak income earning years. Thus limited pay policies are sold with payment periods of ten, fifteen, twenty, twenty-five, or thirty years, or to a specified age such as sixty-five or seventy. Unless the policyholder exercises one of the settlement options, upon completion of the payments the insurance remains in force, thus providing permanent or lifetime insurance protection. The higher premiums necessitated by a shorter payment period are offset by greater cash values than for an ordinary policy of the same face value, thus providing a larger fund for use if needed.

3. *Endowment Insurance*

In contrast to term insurance and the other forms of cash-value insurance that pay the face amount of the policy only in the event of death, endowment insurance pays the face amount if the insured is alive as of a specified date called the maturity date. That is, if the policyholder dies during the endowment period, the beneficiary receives the face amount; if the policyholder survives the endowment period, he or she receives the face value. Typical endowment periods are ten, fifteen, or twenty years, or may be specified as a particular age, for example sixty or sixty-five. Endowment insurance emphasizes the investment feature of cash-value insurance. A traditional use of endowment policies is to provide educational funds for children. However, the "can't miss" feature of this form of insurance makes it the most expensive of the cash-value forms (See Section 16.4). Note also that endowment insurance is not permanent insurance; insurance protection ceases upon payment of the face value to the policyholder at the maturity date. Essentially, endowment insurance is a savings plan with insurance to protect the savings program against premature death.

Life Insurance Premiums

The instrument used by a life insurance company to price its product is called a mortality table. A **mortality table** indicates the probability of death at each age. Insurance companies have kept careful records of groups of people, recording the number living and dying at each age. These statistics form the basis of a mortality table and are sufficiently accurate to estimate future deaths.

A mortality table widely used by insurance companies is that shown in Table 16–1. The table indicates the number of deaths and survivors of a hypothetical group of 10,000,000 males from age 0 to age 100 and also gives the probability of dying at each age.

The use of a mortality table can be illustrated in the calculation of the premium of a one-year term policy.

Suppose 100,000 males, all age thirty, purchased $1,000 of term life insurance for one year. What premium should the insurance company charge for the insurance? According to Table 16–1, 213 of this group would die before reaching age thirty-one, thus the insurance company would have to pay out a total of

$$\$1,000 \times 213 = \$213,000$$

in claims.* Thus, the per insured share of the cost is:

$$\$213,000 \div 100,000 = \$2.13.$$

In other words, if each of the 100,000 members of the group pays $2.13 to be insured, the total of $213,000 collected will be exactly the amount needed to pay the beneficiaries of those who died during the year. Actually, the

---

* In calculating premiums using Table 16–1, insurance actuaries make the following assumptions: (1) premiums are paid in advance, (2) claims are paid at the end of the year, and (3) the death rate is uniform throughout the year.

Table 16–1

Age	Number living	Number dying	Deaths per 1000	Expec- tation	Age	Number living	Number dying	Deaths per 1000	Expec- tation
0	10,000,000	70,800	7.08	68.30	50	8,762,306	72,902	8.32	23.63
1	9,929,200	17,475	1.76	67.78	51	8,689,404	79,160	9.11	22.82
2	9,911,725	15,066	1.52	66.90	52	8,610,244	85,758	9.96	22.03
3	9,896,659	14,449	1.46	66.00	53	8,524,486	92,832	10.89	21.25
4	9,882,210	13,835	1.40	65.10	54	8,431,654	100,337	11.90	20.47
5	9,868,375	13,322	1.35	64.19	55	8,331,317	108,307	13.00	19.71
6	9,855,053	12,812	1.30	63.27	56	8,223,010	116,849	14.21	18.97
7	9,842,241	12,401	1.26	62.35	57	8,106,161	125,970	15.54	18.23
8	9,829,840	12,091	1.23	61.43	58	7,980,191	135,663	17.00	17.51
9	9,817,749	11,879	1.21	60.51	59	7,844,528	145,830	18.59	16.81
10	9,805,870	11,865	1.21	59.58	60	7,698,698	156,592	20.34	16.12
11	9,794,005	12,047	1.23	58.65	61	7,542,106	167,736	22.24	15.44
12	9,781,958	12,325	1.26	57.72	62	7,374,370	179,271	24.31	14.78
13	9,769,633	12,896	1.32	56.80	63	7,195,099	191,174	26.57	14.14
14	9,756,737	13,562	1.39	55.87	64	7,003,925	203,394	29.04	13.51
15	9,743,175	14,225	1.46	54.95	65	6,800,531	215,917	31.75	12.90
16	9,728,950	14,983	1.54	54.03	66	6,584,614	228,749	34.74	12.31
17	9,713,967	15,737	1.62	53.11	67	6,355,865	241,777	38.04	11.73
18	9,698,230	16,390	1.69	52.19	68	6,114,088	254,835	41.68	11.17
19	9,681,840	16,846	1.74	51.28	69	5,859,253	267,241	45.61	10.64
20	9,664,994	17,300	1.79	50.37	70	5,592,012	278,426	49.79	10.12
21	9,647,694	17,655	1.83	49.46	71	5,313,586	287,731	54.15	9.63
22	9,630,039	17,912	1.86	48.55	72	5,025,855	294,766	58.65	9.15
23	9,612,127	18,167	1.89	47.64	73	4,731,089	299,289	63.26	8.69
24	9,593,960	18,324	1.91	46.73	74	4,431,800	301,894	68.12	8.24
25	9,575,636	18,481	1.93	45.82	75	4,129,906	303,011	73.37	7.81
26	9,557,155	18,732	1.96	44.90	76	3,826,895	303,014	79.18	7.39
27	9,538,423	18,981	1.99	43.99	77	3,523,881	301,997	85.70	6.98
28	9,519,442	19,324	2.03	43.08	78	3,221,884	299,829	93.06	6.59
29	9,500,118	19,760	2.08	42.16	79	2,922,055	295,683	101.19	6.21
30	9,480,358	20,193	2.13	41.25	80	2,626,372	288,848	109.98	5.85
31	9,460,165	20,718	2.19	40.34	81	2,337,524	278,983	119.35	5.51
32	9,439,447	21,239	2.25	39.43	82	2,058,541	265,902	129.17	5.19
33	9,418,208	21,850	2.32	38.51	83	1,792,639	249,858	139.38	4.89
34	9,396,358	22,551	2.40	37.60	84	1,542,781	231,433	150.01	4.60
35	9,373,807	23,528	2.51	36.69	85	1,311,348	211,311	161.14	4.32
36	9,350,279	24,685	2.64	35.78	86	1,100,037	190,108	172.82	4.06
37	9,325,594	26,112	2.80	34.88	87	909,929	168,455	185.13	3.80
38	9,299,482	27,991	3.01	33.97	88	741,474	146,997	198.25	3.55
39	9,271,491	30,132	3.25	33.07	89	594,477	126,303	212.46	3.31
40	9,241,359	32,622	3.53	32.18	90	468,174	106,809	228.14	3.06
41	9,208,737	35,362	3.84	31.29	91	361,365	88,813	245.77	2.82
42	9,173,375	38,253	4.17	30.41	92	272,552	72,480	265.93	2.58
43	9,135,122	41,382	4.53	29.54	93	200,072	57,881	289.30	2.33
44	9,093,740	44,741	4.92	28.67	94	142,191	45,026	316.66	2.07
45	9,048,999	48,412	5.35	27.81	95	97,165	34,128	351.24	1.80
46	9,000,587	52,473	5.83	26.95	96	63,037	25,250	400.56	1.51
47	8,948,114	56,910	6.36	26.11	97	37,787	18,456	488.42	1.18
48	8,891,204	61,794	6.95	25.27	98	19,331	12,916	668.15	.83
49	8,829,410	67,104	7.60	24.45	99	6,415	6,415	1000.00	.50

SOURCE: 1958 Commissioners Standard Ordinary Mortality Table.

premium charged would be less than $2.13; since insurance premiums are paid in advance, the company could invest the money for one year. The present value of $213,000 at a conservative rate of 3% compounded annually is:

$$\$213,000 \times 0.97087379 = \$206,796.16 \qquad \text{(Appendix C)}$$

which amounts to:

$$\$206,796.16 \div 100,000 = \$2.0679616 = \$2.07$$

per insured member.

The above calculation is called the **net premium** because it does not take into consideration the expenses of the company. The premium actually paid is called the **gross premium** and includes the cost of the insurance, the company's overhead expenses and contingency reserves.

With a net premium of $2.07 per member, the insurance company records the following:

$$
\begin{array}{rll}
\$207,000 & \text{Premium Collected } (\$2.07 \times 100,000) \\
+\quad 6,210 & \text{Interest on Invested Premium } (\$207,000 \times 0.03) \\
\hline
\$213,210 & \\
-\quad 213,000 & \text{Claims Paid } (\$1,000 \times 213) \\
\hline
\$\quad 210 & \text{Surplus (due to rounding of premium)}
\end{array}
$$

It is not necessary to insure 100,000 people to determine the premium per individual. This may be found in another way using Table 16–1. At age 30 there are 2.13 deaths per 1,000. This is equivalent to $\dfrac{2.13}{1,000}$ or 0.00213.

Multiplying this by the face value of the policy determines the premium; i.e.,

$$\$1,000 \times 0.00213 = \$2.13.$$

At an assumed rate of 3% per annum, the present value of $2.13 for one year is:

$$\$2.13 \times 0.97087379 = \$2.06796117$$
$$= \$2.07 \text{ (net premium)}$$

Example 1

Find the premium for a one-year term policy of $5,000 sold to a male age 40 if the assumed interest rate is 3% per annum.

Solution:

From Table 16–1, the death rate is 3.53 per 1,000, or 0.00353. Thus,

$$\$5,000 \times 0.00353 \times 0.97087379 = \$17.14.$$

Face	Death	Present Value
Value	Rate	for 1 year at 3%

Table 16–1 is based on the experiences of 10 million men. Since women have a longer life expectancy than men, an adjustment must be made if this table is to be used in calculating premiums for female policyholders. One approach is to base the premium on an age less than the applicant's actual age. For example, a female age twenty-five may have her premiums calculated as though she were age twenty-two.

Example 2

Joan Jacobs (age 25) purchased a one-year term policy for $15,000 from the Presidential Insurance Company. Presidential uses a three-year age reduction on the 1958 C.S.O. table and assumes an interest rate of 3% per annum. Find the net premium.

Solution:

From Table 16–1, the death rate at age $25 - 3 = 22$ is 1.86 per 1,000 or 0.00186. Thus, the net premium is:

$$\$15,000 \times 0.00186 \times 0.97087379 = \$27.09$$

Exercises for Sections 16.1 through 16.3

In problems 1–10, find the net premium for a one-year term policy with the given face amount and the given interest rate issued to a male of the given age.

1. $12,000; 3%; age 40

2. $8,000; 4%; age 24

3. $15,000; 5%; age 42

4. $7,000; $3\frac{1}{2}$%; age 36

5. $14,000; $4\frac{1}{2}$%; age 52

6. $13,000; 5%; age 49

7. $8,500; $2\frac{1}{2}$%; age 27

8. $17,500; $3\frac{1}{2}$%; age 56

9. $16,500; $4\frac{1}{2}$%; age 28

10. $19,500; $3\frac{1}{2}$%; age 37

In problems 11–16, one-year term policies of the given face amount are issued to females. Find the net premium for the given interest rate and the given age reduction.

11. $9,500; 4%; age 24; 3 year age reduction

12. $13,000; 3%; age 42; 4 year age reduction

13. $20,000; 5%; age 34; 3 year age reduction

14. $18,000; $4\frac{1}{2}$%; age 46; 5 year age reduction

15. $25,000; $3\frac{1}{2}$%; age 52; 4 year age reduction

16. $15,000; $2\frac{1}{2}$%; age 39; 3 year age reduction

17. Eloise Clark, age twenty-two, purchased a one-year term policy for $2,500 from a company that uses a two-year age reduction for females. If the interest rate is 4% per annum, what was the net premium for the policy?

18. Find the premium for a one-year term policy of $8,000 sold to a female age thirty-seven if the assumed rate of interest is 5% per annum and the company uses a three-year age reduction for females.

19. Bob Forester has been assigned to do extensive travelling for his company during the coming year. He decides to purchase a $25,000 one-year term policy. If the interest rate is 3% per annum and if Bob is thirty-four years old, what is the net premium for the policy?

20. Mary Johnson, age forty-six, purchased a $30,000 one-year term policy from a company that uses a three-year age reduction for females. At an interest rate of $3\frac{1}{2}$% per annum, find the net premium for the policy.

Section 16.4 Level Premiums

Premium calculations in the previous section were for a one-year term policy. The premiums change each year and escalate rapidly in the later years.* Figure 16–1 graphs the net premium per $1,000 of a renewable one-year term policy issued at age thirty and assuming an interest rate of 3% per annum.

An annual price increase would make insurance a difficult commodity to sell; furthermore, at the later years the cost may well be prohibitive. To overcome this difficulty, insurance companies have developed the level premium plan.

A **level premium** is a premium that is the same for each payment. Figure 16–2 illustrates the level premium of a term policy to age sixty compared to the yearly renewable term policy. Both are issued at age thirty and the rates are based on an interest rate of 3% per annum. Note that the level premium is greater than the renewable premium at the early ages, but less at the later ages. The insurance company invests the excess premium from the early ages at compound interest and uses the interest to offset the difference in premium at the higher ages. The excess premium is also used to generate the cash value in cash-value policies.

---

* This is true for all life insurance plans.

Figure 16–1

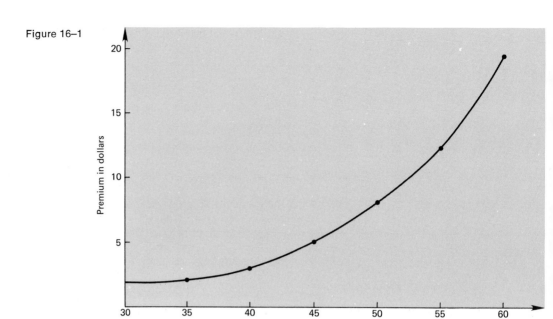

Figure 16–2

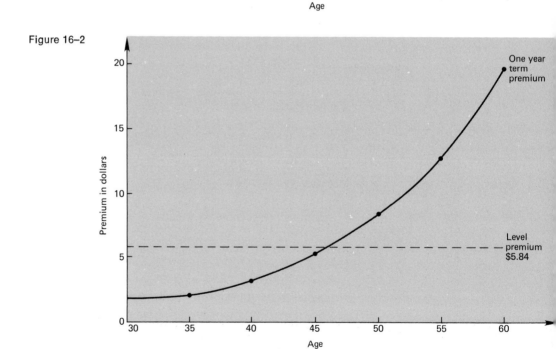

The methods used to calculate the level premium are beyond the scope of this text, but Table 16–2 illustrates the annual gross level premium per $1,000 for four policies at selected ages. The total gross premium is found by multiplying the face value of the policy (in thousands) by the appropriate entry in the table.

Table 16–2

Annual Level Premium Rates per $1,000
Face Value

Age	Renewable Term	Ordinary Life	20-Pay Life	20-Year Endowment
25	$ 9.97	$12.95	$21.50	$43.13
30	11.79	15.31	24.34	43.55
35	14.17	18.40	27.78	44.24
40	17.22	22.36	31.75	45.32
45	21.13	27.44	36.77	46.89
50	25.87	33.60	42.34	49.12
55	31.90	41.44	48.90	52.94
60	40.74	52.31	58.06	59.26

Example 1

Using Table 16–2, what is the annual premium for an ordinary life policy of $15,000 issued to a fifty-year-old man?

Solution:

$33.60 × 15 = $504.00.

Example 2

Vicky Williams (age thirty) purchased a 20-pay life policy from Megapolis Life Insurance Company, which uses a five-year setback in calculating rates for females. If the face value of the policy is $20,000 and Megapolis uses the rates of Table 16–2, what is Vicky's annual premium?

Solution:

A five-year setback means Megapolis would use the rate for age twenty-five. Hence

$$ \$21.50 \times 20 = \$430.00. $$

The level premiums discussed thus far are annual premiums. However, payment periods may also be semiannual, quarterly, or monthly. These rates are a percentage of the annual rate and may be approximated according to the following table.*

* It is possible to circumvent the increased semiannual and quarterly premiums by the use of multiple policies. For example, in lieu of a single policy of $10,000 with semiannual payments, two $5,000 policies each with an annual premium could be purchased at six-month intervals. Not only does this avoid increased premium costs, but it provides greater flexibility for the insured or the beneficiary.

Table 16–3

Payment Period	% of Annual Premium
Semiannual	52
Quarterly	26
Monthly	9

Example 3

At age forty, John Higgins purchased a 20-year endowment policy for $25,000. If the rates are based on Tables 16–2 and 16–3, what is the amount of John's monthly premium?

Solution:

$$\$45.32 \times 25 \times 0.09 = \$101.97$$

Although insurance companies are conservative in their estimates of death rates and interest earnings, premiums are based on probabilities, and actual claims could exceed income. One method of guarding against this eventuality is to charge a premium greater than the company expects to need under normal circumstances. The company will later refund a portion of this surplus in the form of dividends. Policies with dividend provisions are called **participating** and are usually marketed by mutual insurance companies.* Generally, dividends begin from one to three years after purchase and increase in size each year. Over a period of time, dividends can substantially reduce the actual insurance cost.

A life insurance policy without the dividend feature is said to be **nonparticipating.** Here the risk of adverse claims is borne by the owners of the company, normally the stockholders. As a rule, nonparticipating premiums are considerably less than for corresponding participating policies, but there are no provisions for dividends.

Exercises for Section 16.4

In problems 1–10, use Table 16–2 to find the annual premium for the given policy if the purchaser is a male of the given age.

1. $20,000   Renewable Term;   age 40

2. $30,000   20-Year Endowment;   age 30

3. $10,000   20-Pay Life;   age 35

4. $12,000   Ordinary Life;   age 55

5. $25,000   20-Pay Life;   age 25

6. $40,000   Renewable Term;   age 60

* A mutual life insurance company is owned by the policyholders who share in the company's surplus earnings in the form of dividends. Nonparticipating policies are usually sold by a stock life insurance company, which is a corporation owned by the stockholders. Surplus earnings of a stock company are distributed to the stockholders as dividends.

7. $35,000   Ordinary Life;   age 45
8. $10,000   20-Year Endowment;   age 60
9. $15,000   Ordinary Life;   age 35
10. $50,000   Renewable Term;   age 40

In problems 11–16, find the annual premium for the given policy if the purchaser is a female and the company uses a five-year age reduction.

11. $40,000   20-Pay Life;   age 40
12. $50,000   Ordinary Life;   age 30
13. $25,000   Renewable Term;   age 55
14. $60,000   20-Year Endowment;   age 45
15. $15,000   20-Pay Life;   age 35
16. $20,000   Renewable Term;   age 50

In problems 17–22, use Tables 16–2 and 16–3 to find the net premium for the given periodic payment on the given policy if the purchaser is a male.

17. $40,000   Ordinary Life;   age 35;   Monthly Payment
18. $20,000   Renewable Term;   age 50;   Quarterly Payment
19. $50,000   20-Year Endowment;   age 40;   Semiannual Payment
20. $60,000   20-Pay Life;   age 25;   Monthly Payment
21. $15,000   Renewable Term;   age 60;   Semiannual Payment
22. $20,000   Ordinary Life;   age 45;   Quarterly Payment

In problems 23–28, use Tables 16–2 and 16–3 to find the net premium for the given periodic payment on the given policy if the purchaser is a female. (Use a five-year age reduction.)

23. $30,000   20-Year Endowment;   age 40;   Monthly Payment
24. $25,000   20-Pay Life;   age 35;   Quarterly Payment
25. $28,000   Renewable Term;   age 45;   Semiannual Payment
26. $45,000   20-Pay Life;   age 35;   Monthly Payment
27. $40,000   Ordinary Life;   age 30;   Quarterly Payment
28. $25,000   20-Year Endowment;   age 35;   Semiannual Payment

29. Mary Johnson, age thirty-five, purchased a 20-Pay Life policy for $30,000. The company uses a five-year age reduction for females. How much is the semiannual premium?

30. Preston French bought a $50,000 Ordinary Life Policy upon the birth of his first child. If he was twenty-five years old at the time, what was his quarterly premium?

31. Victoria Peters decides to buy a 20-Year Endowment for $35,000. She is forty-five years old and the company uses a five-year age reduction for females. How much is her monthly premium?

32. When Elvin Harrison was married, he purchased a $100,000 Renewable Term Policy. If he was thirty years old at the time, how much was his quarterly premium?

Section 16.5 Nonforfeiture Values

A cash-value insurance policy contains three nonforfeiture or surrender options in the event of nonpayment of premiums.

1. Cash Value. The policyholder may receive the cash value of the policy in cash. This terminates the contract and the company has no other obligation under the policy. Normally, cash values begin to accrue after one or two years.

2. Reduced Paid-up Insurance. Under this option, the cash value is used to purchase protection without further premiums. The face amount of the new policy depends on the amount of cash value and the attained age of the insured, but will be less than the original policy. If the original policy was a life policy, the protection is for life; if an endowment, the protection continues to the maturity date at which time the policyholder receives the reduced face value as a cash settlement.

3. Extended Term Insurance. This option is used to continue the insurance protection at the face amount by using the cash value to purchase a paid-up term policy. The length of the term depends on the attained age of the insured and the amount of the cash value. This option automatically goes into effect if the policyholder does not elect an option within a specified number of days after the failure to make a premium payment.

Table 16–4 illustrates minimum paid-up nonforfeiture values per $1,000 face value for a policy issued at age thirty-five.

Table 16–4

Issued at Age 35 on Basis of the 1958 C.S.O. Table and $2\frac{1}{2}$ Percent

| End of Year | Ordinary Life | | | | 20-Payment Life | | | | 20-Year Endowment | | | | |
| | Cash Values | Extended Term* | | Reduced Paid-Up | Cash Values | Extended Term* | | Reduced Paid-Up | Cash Values | Extended Term* | | Pure Endow-ment* | Reduced Paid-Up |
		Years	Days			Years	Days			Years	Days		
3	$ 17.00	4	38	$ 37.97	$ 45.93	9	190	$102.57	$ 84.12	14	313	—	$125.76
5	51.31	9	47	109.84	103.95	15	125	222.53	172.42	15	—	$119.14	246.02
10	140.96	14	91	272.40	259.55	21	291	501.56	412.23	10	—	462.39	523.45
15	235.14	15	183	412.25	431.88	24	352	757.17	684.38	5	—	755.79	772.52
20	331.58	15	72	530.91	624.55	Fully	Paid	Up	1,000.00	At		Maturity	
25	427.84	14	60	630.46	—	—	—	—	—	—	—	—	—
30	520.74	12	310	712.57	—	—	—	—	—	—	—	—	—

* Based on 1958 C.E.T. Table.

Example 1

Twenty-five years after purchase, Herb Goldberg elected to surrender his $40,000 ordinary life policy for the cash value. How much did Herb receive? (Refer to Table 16–4.)

Solution:

The per $1,000 cash value at the end of twenty-five years is $427.84. Hence:

$$\$427.84 \times 40 = \$17{,}113.60$$

16.6   Settlement Options

It is the prerogative of the insured (or in some cases the beneficiary) to designate the manner in which the proceeds are distributed, and insurance companies offer a variety of options called settlement options.* Typically, the options fall into four categories.

A.   *Cash.* The beneficiary may receive the proceeds in cash, generally referred to as a lump-sum payment. Technically, this is not an option, for the policy usually provides for this payment unless another option is selected.

B.   *Interest Option.* Under this option, the proceeds remain with the company and only interest earned on the proceeds is paid to the beneficiary, with provisions for later lump-sum payment or gradual withdrawal.

C.   *Installment Option.* This option liquidates the principal and interest of the proceeds according to one of two plans:

    1.   Fixed Period. The payments are spread over a given period of time, with the longer the period, the smaller the installment.
    2.   Fixed Amount. Each payment is for a specified amount, with the larger the amount, the shorter the time until the fund is exhausted.

D.   *Life Income Annuity.* The proceeds are converted to a life annuity form of income. Several plans are available, and may include a *period certain* that provides for a guaranteed number of payments to the beneficiary or to a second beneficiary in the event the primary beneficiary dies before the guaranteed time elapses.

Tables of settlement values often appear in the policy; Table 16–5 illustrates such tables for selected ages.

---

* Because of dividends or policy loans, the actual amount paid by the insurance company may be more or less than the face value of the policy, hence the term proceeds is used to designate the payment to the beneficiary.

Table 16–5 **Monthly Payment Per $1,000 of Proceeds**

Option C		Option D					
Fixed Period Payments					Life Income with Payments Certain		
					Number of Installments		
Years	Payment	Male	Female	Life Income	100	120	240
1	$84.32	20	25	$2.95	$2.93	$2.92	$2.86
2	42.71	25	30	3.09	3.07	3.06	2.99
3	28.84	30	35	3.26	3.23	3.22	3.15
4	21.91	35	40	3.49	3.46	3.45	3.35
5	17.75	40	45	3.77	3.73	3.72	3.59
6	14.98	45	50	4.12	4.04	4.02	3.85
7	13.00	50	55	4.58	4.50	4.47	4.19
8	11.52	55	60	5.16	5.02	4.97	4.52
9	10.37	60	65	5.90	5.68	5.50	4.86
10	9.45	65	70	6.88	6.40	6.23	5.13

Example 1

Nell Butterfield (age 50) is the beneficiary of a $20,000 ordinary life policy. She selects the life income option with 100 payments certain. Find the monthly payment using Table 16–5.

Solution:

For a female age 50, the payment per $1,000 is $4.04. Hence:

$$\$4.04 \times 20 = \$80.80.$$

Section **16.7** **Business Uses of Life Insurance**

While the primary use of life insurance is to protect the dependents of the insured against financial loss, businesses also need protection against the loss of a valuable worker. For example, consider a drug company with a chemist who is developing a drug anticipated to be highly successful and profitable to the company. The unexpected loss of this individual may curtail production, affect credit, reduce dividends, or damage the company in other ways. To offset the estimated financial loss, the company may purchase a life insurance policy for this key employee. The company is the beneficiary of the policy and pays the premiums. This form of insurance is called "key man insurance" and is designed to provide cash for the company during the readjustment period following the death of a key employee.

A second use of life insurance in business is for business continuation. For example, in a partnership form of business organization, the general rule of law calls for the dissolution and liquidation upon death of a general partner, with the surviving partners responsible for paying the estate of the deceased his/her share of the business. Because forced liquidation is costly, many partnerships enter into an agreement that binds the surviving partners to purchase at a predetermined price the interest of the first partner to die. One method of purchase is with a life insurance policy. Each partner is insured for his/her share, the policy being owned by the other partners. In the event of death, the proceeds of the policy are used to purchase the deceased partner's share of the business. All parties benefit by this arrangement and it eliminates the need for liquidation.

Exercises for Sections 16.5 through 16.7

In problems 1–11, use Table 16–4 to find the cash value received when the given policy is surrendered after the given number of years.

1. $20,000   Ordinary Life;   15 years

2. $10,000   20-Year Endowment;   10 years

3. $30,000   20-Payment Life;   5 years

4. $ 5,000   20-Year Endowment;   5 years

5. $50,000   Ordinary Life;   30 years

6. $15,000   20-Payment Life;   15 years

7. A $35,000 Ordinary Life Policy is surrendered after fifteen years for reduced paid-up insurance. What is the face amount of the new policy?

8. If a $10,000 20-Year Endowment Policy is surrendered after five years for extended term insurance, what is the length of the term of the new policy? What is the face amount of the new term insurance policy?

9. Russ Overmeyer surrendered his $40,000 20-Payment Life Policy after ten years for reduced paid-up insurance. Find the face amount of the new policy.

10. Find the length of the term when a $25,000 Ordinary Life Policy is surrendered for extended term insurance after twenty-five years. What is the face amount of the new term insurance policy?

11. A 20-Year Endowment Policy is surrendered after three years for reduced paid-up insurance. If the face amount of the endowment policy was $15,000, what is the face amount of the new policy?

In problems 12–23, use Table 16–5 to find the amount of the monthly payment to the beneficiary of a policy with the given proceeds when the given settlement option is selected.

12. Proceeds: $20,000; Payee: Male age 40; Settlement option: Life income.

13. Proceeds: $35,000; Payee: Female age 60; Settlement option: Fixed period payments for five years.

14. Proceeds: $10,000; Payee: Male age 20; Settlement option: Life income, payments certain, 120 installments.

15. Proceeds: $30,000; Payee: Female age 45; Settlement option: Life income.

16. Proceeds: $40,000; Payee: Female age 35; Settlement option: Life income, payments certain, 240 installments.

17. Proceeds: $50,000; Payee: Male age 55; Settlement option: Life income, payments certain, 100 installments.

18. Proceeds: $25,000; Payee: Male age 40; Settlement option: Life income.

19. Proceeds: $40,000; Payee: Male age 25; Settlement option: Fixed period payments for ten years.

20. Proceeds: $15,000; Payee: Female age 50; Settlement option: Fixed period payments for six years.

21. Pasco Phillips, age 35, is the beneficiary of a $25,000 Ordinary Life Policy, payable as life income. Find the monthly payments that Pasco will receive.

22. Jean Tatum is to receive the proceeds of $40,000 from her father's life insurance in fixed period payments for eight years. If Jean is 45 when her father dies, what are her monthly payments?

23. Find the monthly payments to the beneficiary (male, age 50) of a life insurance policy with proceeds of $30,000 if the proceeds are payable as life income with payments certain in 120 installments.

Group Insurance

Group insurance provides insurance protection to the employees of an organization. Under a group plan, a master contract issued to a company may provide both life insurance and nonoccupational disability insurance to participating employees. Many plans also provide coverage for dependents of employees.

Compared to individual insurance, a group insurance plan contains a number of unique features. Among these are:

1. Medical examinations usually are not required for employees actively at work.

2. Benefits are automatically determined by wage bracket, position, or some other employee classification.

3. The cost is shared by the employer. Most plans call for the employer to pay a portion of the total premium. This lowers the cost to the employee and encourages participation in the plan. A

minimum employee participation is required to originate the contract and keep it in force, usually 75 percent.

4. The actual cost of the insurance is based on the experience of the organization rather than the experience of the insurance company.

FIDELITY AND GUARANTY *Life Insurance Company*

BALTIMORE, MARYLAND

(Herein called the Company)

APPLICATION is hereby made to the Company for Group Policy No._____

by _____

whose Main Office Address is _____

Said Group Policy is hereby approved and the terms thereof are hereby accepted.

This Application is executed in duplicate, one counterpart being attached to said Group Policy and the other being returned to the Company.

It is agreed that this Application supersedes _____ application for the said Group Policy.

"SPECIMEN COPY"

_____

(Full or Corporate Name of Applicant)

Signed at _____By_____

(Signature and Title)

On _____Witness_____

(To be signed by Resident Agent where required by law)

This Copy is to Remain Attached to the Policy

FGL 388G (11-68)

Group contracts may include a variety of coverages. Among these are:

1. Term Life Insurance. The basic plan is yearly renewable term insurance with the same features as individual policies.

2. In-Hospital Expense. This coverage pays a specified amount for hospital daily room and board and for miscellaneous hospital charges.

3. Surgical Expense. This benefit pays a surgeon for fees resulting from a surgical procedure. The amount paid is usually specified by a surgical schedule. The maximum benefit on such a schedule may range from $200 to $900.

4. Major Medical Expense. This coverage pays a percent (usually 80 percent) of all covered expenses in excess of a deductible.* Designed to cover the catastrophic illness, maximum benefits under this coverage may be written for $10,000, $15,000, or higher. In a typical plan, benefits under this coverage become payable only after exhaustion of other health benefits and satisfaction of the deductible.

* A deductible is a portion of covered expenses paid by the insured.

Other coverages available under a group plan include:

5. Accidental Death and Dismemberment

6. Weekly Indemnity

7. Long-Term Disability

8. In-Hospital Medical Care

9. Diagnostic Expense

10. Dental Care

Section 16.9   Group Insurance Premiums

Net premiums for group term life insurance are found by multiplying the rate per $1,000 at each age by the number of thousands of insurance at that age, adding the results and dividing by the total amount of insurance to obtain an average rate per $1,000. This rate is charged every employee, regardless of age.* The premium is the product of the rate and the number of thousands of insurance. Premiums are paid monthly.

Example 1

Rainbow Industries has the following group life insurance coverage for its employees:

Officers	$10,000
Foremen	$ 5,000
All Other Employees	$ 2,000

What is the monthly premium for each classification if the total premium is $164.00 and total insurance is $200,000.

Solution:

The rate per $1,000 is $\dfrac{\$164}{200} = \$0.82$. Thus:

Officers	$0.82 \times 10 = \$8.20$
Foremen	$0.82 \times 5 = \$4.10$
All Other Employees	$0.82 \times 2 = \$1.64$

The premium for other group benefits is the sum of the rates for each benefit. The rates will vary according to the amount of coverage and the characteristics of the group. The actual premium paid by the employee will depend upon (1) the contribution of the employer and (2) whether or

---

* In a company with a normal flow of new, young employees replacing retiring or
deceased employees, the average age will remain relatively constant, resulting in an
almost level premium for the group each year.

not dependents are also covered. For the next example, the premiums listed in Table 16–6 will be used.

Table 16–6

| Coverage | Monthly Premiums | |
	Employee	Dependents
A. Life Insurance	$0.52/$1,000	—
B. Accidental Death & Dismemberment	0.12/$1,000	—
C. Weekly Indemnity	4.84	—
D. Hospitalization	12.68	24.56
E. Surgical Expense	4.04	10.36
F. In-Hospital Medical Care	0.80	1.44
G. Major Medical	3.72	5.80

Example 2

Harry Wurts works for a company which carries coverages A ($5,000), B ($5,000), D, E, and G. (See Table 16–6.) Harry insures his family and the company contributes 75 percent of the employee (only) premium. How much is Harry's monthly premium?

Solution:

The total employer and dependent monthly premiums are:

Coverage	Employer	Dependents
A	$ 2.60	—
B	0.60	—
D	12.68	$24.56
E	4.04	10.36
G	3.72	5.80
Total	$23.64	$40.72

Harry pays 25% of the employee premium, or $23.64 \times 0.25 = $5.91, plus the dependent premium for a total of $5.91 + $40.72 = $46.63.

Exercises for Sections 16.8 and 16.9

1. A company provides $10,000 worth of group term life insurance for each of its employees. Find the monthly premium for each employee if the total monthly premium is $285.00 and the total insurance is $300,000.

2. If $15,000 worth of group term life insurance is provided to each employee of a company, and if the total monthly premium is $292.00 and the total insurance is $400,000, what is the monthly premium for each employee?

3. Find the monthly group life insurance premium for each employee of a company that provides all employees with $10,000 worth of group term life insurance, if the total monthly premium is $335.00 and the total insurance is $500,000.

4. The executives of Rockford Enterprises, Inc., are eligible for $25,000 worth of group term life insurance. All other employees are eligible for $10,000 worth of insurance. Find the monthly premium for the executives and for the other employees if the total premium is $195.00 and the total insurance is $250,000.

5. The Minton Company has the following group life insurance coverage for its employees:

Executives	$20,000
Supervisors	$15,000
Other employees	$10,000

What is the monthly premium for each classification if the total premium is $504.00 and the total insurance is $800,000?

6. Find the monthly premium for each classification of employee at the Buford Corporation, if the total premium is $996.00, the total insurance is $1,200,000, and the company provides the following coverages:

Officers	$40,000
Foremen	$20,000
Other employees	$15,000

In problems 7–12, use Table 16–6 to compute the monthly premium for an employee with the given insurance coverage.

7. Coverage: A ($10,000), B ($10,000), D & E; No dependents; Company contributes 60 percent of the premium.

8. Coverage: A ($10,000), B ($10,000), C,D,E; Dependents insured; Company contributes 70 percent of the employee (only) premium.

9. Coverage: A ($5,000), B ($5,000), D,E,F,G; No dependents; Company contributes 80 percent of the premium.

10. Coverage: A ($7,500), B ($7,500), C,D,E,F; Dependents insured; Company contributes 70 percent of the employee (only) premium.

11. Coverage: A ($4,000), B ($4,000), D,E,F; Dependents insured; Company contributes 100 percent of the employee (only) premium.

12. Coverage: A ($5,000), B ($5,000), C,D,E,F,G; Dependents insured; Company contributes 100 percent of the employee (only) premium.

16.10   Fire Insurance

In addition to people, businesses need to protect their property from loss. Insurance of this type is called property and liability insurance. This section will review one of the basic coverages of property and liability insurance, fire insurance.

Fire insurance indemnifies the insured for direct losses arising from uncontrolled fire, lightning, and damage to property suffered while the insured is moving it to safety. Most fire insurance policies conform to a standard fire contract. This contract came into existence because of confusion resulting when every company wrote its own policy; every word and phrase of the standard policy has been interpreted by the courts. The standard policy indicates who is insured, where, when, what property is covered and what is not covered, the amount of coverage, the premium, and the conditions under which coverage is suspended.

Two factors affect the actual amount paid by the insurance company in the event of a loss, (1) the actual damage to the property, and (2) coinsurance. While fire insurance policies have a fixed face value that establishes the maximum liability of the company, most fires seldom cause total destruction, and the insurance company is responsible only for the value of the actual loss, or the cost to repair or replace.

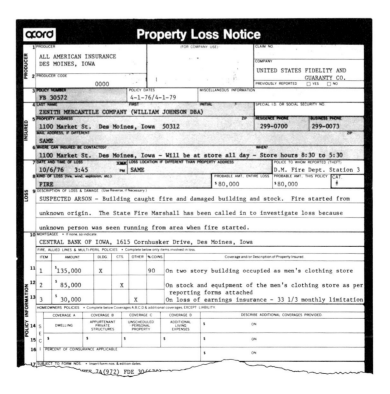

The probability of a fire causing only a partial loss has led many businesses to insure their property for only a fraction of its total value. However, an insurance company cannot afford to pay a loss in full if the premiums are based on the partial value of the property. This situation has led to the practice of coinsurance.

As used in this context, **coinsurance** means that the company and the insured share the risk. The most common ratio is 80 percent − 20 percent; that is, the insured agrees to carry insurance equal to at least 80 percent of the value of the property. Thus, for a property worth $100,000, the insured would carry a policy of $80,000; in the event of a total loss, the company would pay $80,000, while the insured would absorb $20,000 of the loss.

The coinsurance clause places a penalty on the insured who carries a face value less than the coinsurance percent. The amount paid by the company in the event of a loss is according to the following formula:*

$$(16\text{--}1) \quad \text{Insurer's Liability} = \frac{\text{Amount of Insurance Carried}}{\text{Property Value} \times \text{Coinsurance \%}} \times \text{Loss (up to face value)}$$

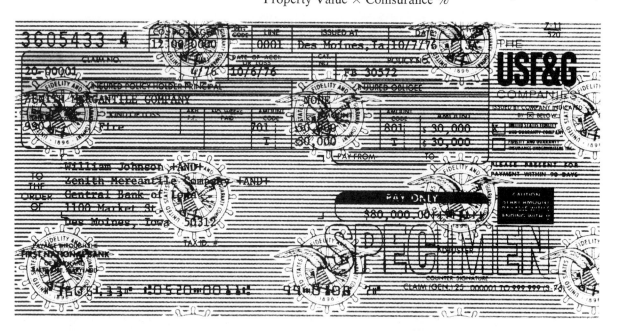

Example 1

Property worth $100,000 is insured for $60,000. If the policy contains an 80 percent coinsurance clause and a fire causes $30,000 damage, what is the liability of the insurance company?

* It should be noted that the insurer will pay the least of (1) the face value, (2) the actual loss, (3) the formula computations.

Solution:

Using Formula (16–1),

$$\text{Insurer's Liability} = \frac{\$60,000}{\$100,000 \times 0.80} \times \$30,000$$

$$= \frac{\$60,000}{\$80,000} \times \$30,000$$

$$= \frac{3}{4} \times \$30,000$$

$$= \$22,500$$

Had the insured carried the full amount of insurance required by the coinsurance clause ($80,000), the company would have paid the full amount of the loss, $30,000. To encourage the insureds to carry insurance equal to the coinsurance percent, companies offer a rate reduction for this amount of insurance.

Section 16.11 **Fire Insurance Premiums**

A number of factors affect the premium charged for fire insurance. Among these are:

1. Construction (brick, frame, etc.)
2. Occupancy (flammability of contents)
3. Protection Facilities (fire-fighting equipment, water supply, etc.)
4. Exposure (congestion of area, hazardous property nearby, etc.)
5. Geographical Location (losses vary by state)

Fire insurance premiums are quoted as a rate per $100 of insurance coverage, and the calculation is an application of the basic percentage formula with P = premium, B = face value of the policy in hundreds, and R = rate per $100. Premium calculations are rounded to the nearest dollar in the last step.

Example 1

What is the premium for a fire insurance policy with a face value of $140,000 if the rate per $100 is $0.86?

Solution:

$P = ?, B = 1400, R = \$0.86.$

$$P = BR$$

$$= 1400 \times \$0.86$$

$$= \$1,204.00$$

While premiums are quoted for one year, policies may be in force for less than one year.* In this event, the premium charged is a percentage of the annual premium, according to a Short-Term Rate Table. An abbreviated version of such a table is illustrated in Table 16–7.

Table 16–7

Time in Force	% of Annual Rate
5 Days	7
10 Days	10
15 Days	13
20 Days	16
25 Days	18
1 Month	20
2 Months	30
3 Months	40
4 Months	50
5 Months	60
6 Months	70
7 Months	75
8 Months	80
9 Months	85
10 Months	90
11 Months	95
12 Months	100

Example 2

The need for additional space caused Alan Labeda to sell his property and move to a new location for his electronics store. He cancelled a $78,000 fire insurance policy five months after paying a premium at a rate of $0.63 per $100. What refund will Alan receive?

Solution:

First, the annual premium is calculated. $P = ?$, $B = \$780$, $R = \$0.63$

$$P = BR$$

$$= 780 \times \$0.63$$

$$= \$491.40$$

$$= \$491.00 \text{ (Rounded)}$$

Using Table 16–7, the premium is 60% of the annual premium; Alan receives the difference. That is,

$$
\begin{array}{ll}
\$491.00 & \text{Annual Premium} \\
-\ 294.60 & \text{Short-Term Premium } (\$491 \times 0.60) \\
\hline
\$196.40 & \text{Refund to Alan}
\end{array}
$$

* Policies in force for less than one year may be due to (1) temporary protection need, (2) cancellation by the insured, (3) cancellation by the insurance company.

In problems 1–8, use Formula (16–1) to compute the insurer's liability for a fire that causes the given amount of damage.

1. Property value: $120,000; amount of insurance: $78,000; coinsurance clause: 80%; fire causes $20,000 damage.

2. Property value: $320,000; amount of insurance: $224,000; coinsurance clause: 80%; fire causes $190,000 damage.

3. Property value: $150,000; amount of insurance: $110,000; coinsurance clause: 80%; fire causes $60,000 damage.

4. Property value: $400,000; amount of insurance: $200,000; coinsurance clause: 80%; fire causes $300,000 damage.

5. Property value: $180,000; amount of insurance: $120,000; coinsurance clause: 80%; fire causes $180,000 damage.

6. Property value: $260,000; amount of insurance: $200,000; coinsurance clause: 80%; fire causes $220,000 damage.

7. Property value: $300,000; amount of insurance: $220,000; coinsurance clause: 80%; fire causes $260,000 damage.

8. Property value: $340,000; amount of insurance: $250,000; coinsurance clause: 80%; fire causes $300,000 damage.

9. Find the premium for a fire insurance policy with a face value of $230,000 if the rate per $100 is $0.82.

10. Sam Donaldson opened a sporting goods store and purchased a $280,000 fire insurance policy. If the rate per $100 was $0.78, how much was the premium for the policy?

11. When Jennifer Smith opened her clothing store, she insured it for $175,000. What was her insurance premium if the rate per $100 was $0.72?

In problems 12–21, use Table 16–8 to find the premium for a fire insurance policy of the given face amount when the policy is in force for the given period of time.

12. Face amount: $50,000; time in force: 4 months; annual rate per $100: $0.62.

13. Face amount: $115,000; time in force: 10 months; annual rate per $100: $0.81.

14. Face amount: $320,000; time in force: 2 months; annual rate per $100: $0.77.

15. Face amount: $210,000; time in force: 20 days; annual rate per $100: $0.87.

16. Face amount: $72,000; time in force: 7 months; annual rate per $100: $0.66.

17. Face amount: $145,000; time in force: 5 days; annual rate per $100: $0.68.

18. Face amount: $82,000; time in force: 8 months; annual rate per $100: $0.72.

19. John Dirkson insured his business for $250,000, but after six months he went out of business and cancelled his policy. If the annual rate per $100 was $0.84, how much did John pay for his insurance coverage for the six months that he was in business?

20. Find the premium for a $170,000 fire insurance policy in force for eight months if the annual rate per $100 is $0.75.

21. Laura Nesbitt insured her beauty parlor for $46,000 with a fire insurance policy that cost $0.89 per $100. Eleven months later the company cancelled her policy because she failed to correct fire hazards in her business. How much did Laura have to pay for the eleven months of coverage?

Statistics

Chapter Objectives for Chapter 17

I. Learn the meaning of the following terms:

A. *Array*, 420
B. *Frequency distribution,* 420
C. *Relative frequency distribution,* 421
D. *Cumulative frequency distribution,* 421
E. *Ogive,* 422
F. *The Greek letter* Σ, 425
G. *Measures of location,* 426
H. *Arithmetic mean,* 427, 431
I. *Median,* 428, 432
J. *Mode,* 429, 436
K. *Bimodal,* 429
L. *Modal Class,* 434

II. Understand:

A. How to summarize data into
   1. An array, 420
   2. A frequency distribution, 420
   3. A relative frequency distribution, 421
   4. A cumulative frequency distribution, 421
B. The advantages and disadvantages of the mean, median, and mode, 427, 429

III. Calculate:

A. The mean, median, and mode of
   1. Ungrouped data, 427–429
   2. A frequency distribution, 431–434
B. The standard deviation, 437

17.1 Introduction

The word *statistics* has more than one meaning. In its most common usage, statistics refers to a collection of numerical data. Statistics may also refer to the analysis and interpretation of such data. In the singular, the word statistic may denote a particular data item or a measure calculated from data.

Each of these connotations has an application in business. A characterization of the contemporary business enterprise is the accumulation of numerous reports, graphs, and other forms of numerical data, from both internal and external sources. The proper utilization of this data is crucial to successful business practices. In this chapter, several of the basic methods used to summarize and categorize numerical data are introduced.

17.2 Data Organization

Before statistical analysis can take place, the data to be analyzed must be arranged in a usable form. One such arrangement is called an **array,** where the data is ordered from high to low or from low to high. For example, the number of sales at register 9 of the R. D. Davis Company for a two-week period is recorded as follows:

Figure 17–1

Week	M	T	W	T	F	S
1	10	12	15	9	22	32
2	7	15	16	17	20	29

An array of the data in Figure 17–1 is shown in Table 17–1.

Table 17–1

7, 9, 10, 12, 15, 15, 16, 17, 20, 22, 29, 32

An array serves to detail the overall pattern, but its usefulness is limited to sets with a small number of values; the ordering of data with a large number of values is tedious unless data processing equipment is available.

A second method of summarizing or describing a set of data is to arrange the values in a frequency distribution. In a **frequency distribution,** the values are grouped into classes, then a tally is made of the number or frequency of the values in each class.

Table 17–2 shows a frequency distribution of the data in Figure 17–1.

Frequency distributions are described as **numerical** when the data are grouped according to numerical size (such as Table 17–2), and **categorical** when sorted according to a qualitative description.* The

* One example of a categorical distribution would be to arrange the data according to categories of sales such as records, tapes, phonographs, televisions, etc.

Table 17–2

Class	Tally	Frequency
5–9	/ /	2
10–14	/ /	2
15–19	/ / / /	4
20–24	/ /	2
25–29	/	1
30–34	/	1

number of classes in a frequency distribution is arbitrary, but should range from six to fifteen. It is also desirable to make class intervals of equal length whenever possible.

Of the numerous other methods of presenting data, two others will be mentioned. One is the **relative frequency distribution** in which relative class frequencies are found by dividing class frequencies by the total number in the sample. Table 17–3 is a relative frequency distribution of the data in Figure 17–1.

Table 17–3

Class	Frequency	Relative Frequency	Percent
5–9	2	0.1667	16.67
10–14	2	0.1667	16.67
15–19	4	0.3333	33.33
20–24	2	0.1667	16.67
25–29	1	0.0833	8.33
30–34	1	0.0833	8.33
	12	1.0000	

A **cumulative frequency distribution** is one in which the frequency of each line in the table is the class frequency plus the sum of the frequencies of all preceding lines. A cumulative frequency distribution of the data of Figure 17–1 is shown in Table 17–4.

Table 17–4

Class	Number
Less than 10	2
Less than 15	4
Less than 20	8
Less than 25	10
Less than 30	11
Less than 35	12

Visual presentations of frequency distributions are possible using bar graphs, line graphs, and pictograms. The data of Table 17–2 and Table 17–4 are graphed in Figures 17–2 through 17–4. The first is a bar

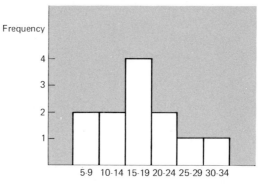

Figure 17–2

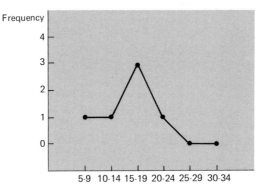

Figure 17–3

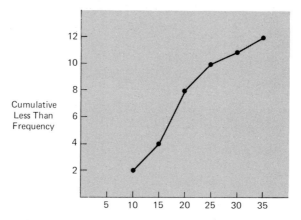

Figure 17–4

graph of Table 17–2, the second is a line graph of Table 17–2 using class midpoints as abcissas, and the third is a graph of Table 17–4. A graph such as Figure 17–4 is called an **ogive.**

Exercises for Section 17.2

Use the following data to solve problems 1 through 12.

A	5	21	14	33	19	27	9	15
B	7	13	24	15	32	37	41	11
C	43	12	8	26	31	23	39	18
D	9	18	27	25	29	19	8	23

1. Arrange the data in line A in an array.

2. Arrange the data in line D in an array.

3. Arrange the data in lines A,C in an array.

4. Arrange the data in lines B,D in an array.

5. Arrange the data in lines B,C in an array.

6. Complete the following table using the data in lines A,C.

Class	Frequency
0–9	
10–19	
20–29	
30–39	
40–49	

7. Complete the following table using the data in lines B,D.

Class	Frequency
0–9	
10–19	
20–29	
30–39	
40–49	

8. Complete the following table using the data in lines B,C.

Class	Frequency
0–9	
10–19	
20–29	
30–39	
40–49	

9. Complete the following table using the data in lines A,D.

Class	Frequency	Relative Frequency	Percent
0–9			
10–19			
20–29			
30–39			
40–49			

10. Complete the following table using the data in lines A,B.

Class	Frequency	Relative Frequency	Percent
0–9			
10–19			
20–29			
30–39			
40–49			

11. Complete the following table for the data in lines A,D.

Class	Frequency	Cumulative Frequency
0–9		
10–19		
20–29		
30–39		
40–49		

12. Complete the following table for the data in lines, B,D.

Class	Frequency	Cumulative Frequency
0–9		
10–19		
20–29		
30–39		
40–49		

13. The number of sales reported by each of ten salepeople at a used car outlet last week are given in the following table:

Sales-person	Number of Sales	Sales-person	Number of Sales
J.H.	15	R.S.	16
A.B.	7	B.A.	12
D.T.	11	C.D.	9
P.Z.	4	E.T.	8
D.D.	13	E.S.	5

Construct a frequency distribution of this data using class intervals of 5.

14. The following numbers represent the number of years that the ten employees at the Simpson Company have yet to work before being eligible for retirement: 5, 11, 14, 2, 21, 8, 14, 9, 18, 12. Construct a frequency distribution of this data using class intervals of 4.

15. Construct a relative frequency distribution of the data in problem 13.

16. Construct a relative frequency distribution of the data in problem 14.

17. The biweekly net earnings of twelve employees at the Concord Company are: $390, $420, $405, $470, $510, $475, $460, $492, $505, $435, $425, $395. Construct a cumulative frequency distribution of this data using class intervals of $20 starting with $380.

18. The following numbers represent the scores made by the students in a class on a final exam:

62	59	91	80	87	56
72	68	78	87	76	75
42	98	72	75	70	55
52	83	72	71	99	89
69	73	74	59	63	91

Construct a cumulative frequency distribution of this data using class intervals of 10 starting with 40.

17.3 The Sigma Notation

Statisticians use a number of techniques to describe quantitative data. Numerical and graphical displays were covered in the previous section. The sections to follow cover arithmetic methods. Before describing these arithmetic techniques, it is necessary to introduce the mathematical notation used in these measures.

The Greek letter Σ is a notation used for "sum" or "add." For example, if the values in a distribution are x_1, x_2, x_3, x_4, and x_5, the sum of these values can be denoted by $\sum_{i=1}^{5} x_i$. That is,

(17–1)
$$\sum_{i=1}^{5} x_i = x_1 + x_2 + x_3 + x_4 + x_5$$

The notation Σx_i means sum (add) all of the x_i's. The notation below and above the sigma symbol indicates the range of the x_i's, in this case from 1 to 5.

The notation $\sum_{i=1}^{7} y_i$ means the sum of y_1 through y_7; that is,

(17–2)
$$\sum_{i=1}^{7} y_i = y_1 + y_2 + y_3 + y_4 + y_5 + y_6 + y_7$$

Example 1

Find: $\sum_{i=1}^{4} x_i$ if $x_1 = 2, x_2 = 4, x_3 = 9, x_4 = 16$

Solution:

$$\sum_{i=1}^{4} x_i = x_1 + x_2 + x_3 + x_4$$

$$= 2 + 4 + 9 + 16$$

$$= 31$$

Example 2

Find: $\displaystyle\sum_{i=1}^{3} (x_i + y_i)$ if $x_1 = 4$, $x_2 = 9$, $x_3 = 14$, $y_1 = 8$, $y_2 = 22$, $y_3 = 7$

Solution:

$$\sum_{i=1}^{3} (x_i + y_i) = (x_1+y_1) + (x_2+y_2) + (x_3+y_3) + (x_4+y_4)$$
$$= (4 + 8) + (9 + 22) + (14 + 7)$$
$$= 12 + 31 + 21$$
$$= 64$$

Exercises for Section 17.3

1. Compute $\displaystyle\sum_{i=1}^{3} x_i$ if $x_1 = 2$, $x_2 = 3$, and $x_3 = 7$.

2. If $y_1 = 10$, $y_2 = 13$, $y_3 = 4$, and $y_4 = 6$, find $\displaystyle\sum_{i=1}^{4} y_i$.

3. Find $\displaystyle\sum_{i=1}^{3} (y_i-2)$ when $y_1 = 6$, $y_2 = 8$, and $y_3 = 10$.

4. Find $\displaystyle\sum_{i=1}^{4} (2x_i)$ when $x_1 = 3$, $x_2 = 2$, $x_3 = 5$, and $x_4 = 8$.

5. If $x_1 = 6$, $x_2 = 12$, $x_3 = 8$, and $x_4 = 4$, what is the value of
   $\displaystyle\sum_{i=1}^{4} (3x_i-1)$?

6. If $x_1 = 10$, $x_2 = 12$, $x_3 = 20$, $y_1 = 4$, $y_2 = 6$, and $y_3 = 11$, find
   $\displaystyle\sum_{i=1}^{3} (x_i+y_i)$.

7. In problem 6, find $\displaystyle\sum_{i=1}^{3} (x_i \cdot y_i)$.

8. In problem 6, find $\displaystyle\sum_{i=1}^{3} (4x_i-y_i)$.

9. Find $\displaystyle\sum_{i=1}^{4} (2x_i+4) + \sum_{i=1}^{3} (4y_i-1)$ when $x_1 = 2$, $x_2 = 7$, $x_3 = 11$,
   $x_4 = 6$, $y_1 = 2$, $y_2 = 5$, and $y_3 = 8$.

10. Find $\displaystyle\sum_{i=1}^{3} (6x_i-1) - \sum_{i=1}^{4} (3y_i+2)$ when $x_1 = 2$, $x_2 = 3$, $x_3 = 1$,
    $y_1 = 1$, $y_2 = 1$, $y_3 = 3$, and $y_4 = 2$.

Section 17.4 Measures of Location

Measures of location are numbers indicative of the "center" or "average" of a set of data. The statistics used for this purpose are also called **measures of central tendency.** The measures of location to be studied in this section are : (1) the arithmetic mean, (2) the median, and (3) the mode. There are advantages and disadvantages for each measure, hence more than one may be utilized for a given set of data.

The Arithmetic Mean The arithmetic mean is the most popular measure of location and is that value usually associated with the word "average." Average weight, batting average, and average sales are examples of the arithmetic mean. The **arithmetic mean** or **mean** is the sum of the values of a set of data divided by the total number of values. That is, for a set containing n values, the arithmetic mean is given by the formula

(17–3)
$$\bar{x} = \frac{\sum\limits_{i=1}^{n} x_i}{n}$$

Example 1

Find the mean of the data in Table 17–1.

Solution:

$x_1 = 7, x_2 = 9, x_3 = 12, \ldots, x_{12} = 32$, hence

$$\bar{x} = \frac{\sum\limits_{i=1}^{12} x_i}{12}$$
$$= \frac{204}{12}$$
$$= 17$$

Example 2

Sixteen pieceworkers of the Hudgins Company produced the following number of pieces in one day's work: 22,24,20,22,26,26,23,30,28,22,20, 24,28,27,26,24. What was the mean number of pieces produced by the sixteen workers?

Solution:

$$\bar{x} = \frac{\sum\limits_{i=1}^{16} x_i}{16}$$
$$= \frac{392}{16}$$
$$= 24.5$$

As a measure of central tendency, the mean has several advantages. The mean always exists; it is unique,* and it takes into account each item

* It is unique in the sense that a set of data has only one mean.

of the data. A disadvantage of the mean is that it is affected by extreme values; that is, an unusually high or low value shifts the mean towards this value. The mean of the set $\{2,3,4,5,6\}$ is $\frac{20}{5} = 4$, but the mean of the set $\{2,3,4,5,16\}$ is $\frac{30}{5} = 6$; the mean of the second set was shifted towards the extreme value.

The Median Consider an array of n values. The **median** is (a) the middle value of the array if n is odd and (b) the mean of the two middle values if n is even.

Example 3

Find the median of (a) $\{2,4,6,8,10\}$ and (b) $\{2,4,6,8,10,12\}$

Solution:

a. $n = 5$, thus, the median is the middle value 6

b. $n = 6$, thus, the median is the mean of the two middle values; i.e.,

$$\frac{6 + 8}{2} = 7.$$

Example 4

Find the median of the data in Table 17–1.

Solution:

$n = 12$, hence the median is the mean of the 6th and 7th values.

$$\frac{15 + 16}{2} = \frac{31}{2}, \text{ thus the median is } 15.5.$$

Example 5

During an eleven-day period, the closing stock prices of the Hanson Corporation were:

$$21\tfrac{1}{4}, 21\tfrac{3}{8}, 21\tfrac{1}{4}, 21\tfrac{1}{2}, 21\tfrac{5}{8}, 21\tfrac{1}{2}, 21\tfrac{3}{4}, 22, 22\tfrac{1}{4}, 21\tfrac{7}{8}, 21\tfrac{5}{8}.$$

What was the median price of the stock during this period?

Solution:

Arranging the prices in an array,

$$21\tfrac{1}{4}, 21\tfrac{1}{4}, 21\tfrac{3}{8}, 21\tfrac{1}{2}, 21\tfrac{1}{2}, 21\tfrac{5}{8}, 21\tfrac{5}{8}, 21\tfrac{3}{4}, 21\tfrac{7}{8}, 22, 22\tfrac{1}{4},$$

the sixth or middle value is $21\tfrac{5}{8}$; this is the median closing price of the stock.

Like the mean, the median is unique and always exists. The median requires a minimum of calculation; unlike the mean, it is not affected by extreme values. On the other hand, to find the median the values must be arranged in an array, a tedious task for large values of n. A more significant disadvantage is that in statistical problems of estimation and tests of hypotheses, the median is less reliable than the mean.

The Mode　A third measure of location is the mode. The **mode** is that value, class, or category that has the highest frequency.

Example 6

Find the mode of the data in Table 17–1.

Solution:

The value with the highest frequency is 15, which occurs twice.

The chief advantage of the mode is that it requires no calculation. On the other hand, the mode may not exist,* or if it does exist it may not be unique. The array 2,4,4,6,6,8 has two modes 4 and 6, and is said to be **bimodal.** The principal value of the mode lies with categorical data. Suppose a poll indicated the following preferences for package size:

$$\text{Size A} = 157$$
$$\text{Size B} = 84$$
$$\text{Size C} = 120$$
$$\text{Size D} = 95$$

The frequency of 157 clearly indicates that size A is the mode.

Exercises for Section 17.4　The following data is to be used for problems 1 through 12.

A:　7,11,5,19,6,12,12,21,14,12,14
B:　18,4,7,2,16,23,15,15,9,14
C:　6,11,15,14,13,7,13,24,18,17,16
D:　15,9,12,18,7,10,14,15,11,13

1. Find the mean of the data in line A.

2. Find the mean of the data in line B.

3. Find the mean of the data in line C.

4. What is the median of line A?

5. What is the median of line B?

6. What is the median of line C?

* The set {4,5,6,7} has no mode.

7. Find the mode of A.

8. Find the mode of B.

9. Find the mode of C.

10. Find the mean, median, and mode of line D.

11. Find the mean, median, and mode of lines A,B.

12. Find the mean, median, and mode of lines C,D.

13. A sales representative for the Burns Corporation reported the following daily sales for the past week: Monday, $7,200; Tuesday, $6,200; Wednesday, $10,400; Thursday, $12,100; and Friday, $8,400. Find the mean daily sales for the week.

14. Twelve pieceworkers at Parker Industries produced the following number of pieces in one day's work: 42, 51, 46, 44, 38, 40, 49, 53, 46, 47, 44, 48. What was the mean number of pieces produced by the workers?

15. The prices of nine stocks on the New York Stock Exchange are: $14,$52,$60,$22,$12,$38,$67,$54, and $58. Find the median price of the stock.

16. The six employees of the Central Variety Store earn weekly salaries of $160, $165, $180, $140, $144, and $210. Find the median salary.

17. Earl Bowers decided to purchase a new television set and priced the set in seven different stores. The prices he found were $465,$420, $455,$435,$455,$440, and $470. Find (a) the mean price and (b) the mode of the prices.

18. The annual salaries of the employees at the Dunfield Company are given in the following table. Find (a) the mean annual salary, (b) the median of the salaries, and (c) the mode of the annual salaries.

Annual Salary	Frequency
$14,200	2
15,500	4
15,800	8
15,900	3
16,400	1
17,200	3

17.5 **Frequency Distributions and Measures of Location**

When a set of data contains a large number of values, measures of location are more efficiently calculated using a frequency distribution.

The Mean   The mean of a distribution with k classes is found using the formula

(17–4)
$$\bar{x} = \frac{\sum\limits_{i=1}^{k} f_i x_i}{\sum\limits_{i=1}^{k} f_i}$$

where $f_i =$ class frequency

$x_i =$ midpoint of class interval

Example 1

Find the mean of the data in Table 17–2.

Solution:

There are six classes, hence $k = 6$.

Class	Frequency (f_i)	Class Midpoint (x_i)	$f_i x_i$
5–9	2	7	14
10–14	2	12	24
15–19	4	17	68
20–24	2	22	44
25–29	1	27	27
30–34	1	32	32
	12		209

$$\bar{x} = \frac{\sum\limits_{i=1}^{6} f_i x_i}{\sum\limits_{i=1}^{6} f_i}$$

$$= \frac{209}{12}$$

$$= 17.416$$

$$= 17.42$$

The difference between 17.42 and the actual mean of 17 results from using the midpoint of the class intervals in place of the actual values. If the sample contains a large number of values, this error will be quite small.

Example 2

Gasoline sales at a station of the Sure Oil Company were recorded as follows:

Amount	Number of Sales
Less than $4.00	26
$ 4.00– 7.99	52
8.00–11.99	37
12.00–15.99	18
16.00–20.00	4

Find the mean sale at the station.

Solution:

Class	f_i	x_i	$f_i x_i$
$ 0.00–$ 3.99	26	$ 2.00	$ 52.00
4.00– 7.99	52	6.00	312.00
8.00– 11.99	37	10.00	370.00
12.00– 15.99	18	14.00	252.00
16.00– 19.99	4	18.00	72.00
	137		$1,058.00

$$\bar{x} = \frac{\sum\limits_{i=1}^{5} f_i x_i}{\sum\limits_{i=1}^{5} f_i}$$

$$= \frac{\$1,058}{137}$$

$$= \$7.72$$

The Median If a set of data contains n values, the median is a number that is neither greater than $\frac{n}{2}$ of the values nor less than $\frac{n}{2}$ of the values. To find the median of the frequency distribution shown in Table 17–2, $\frac{n}{2} = \frac{12}{2} = 6$, which means that the median must occur in the class 15–19. Assuming that the values are equally distributed in that interval, the following formula can be used to find the median:

(17–5) $$m = b + \frac{cd}{f_m}$$

where m = median

b = lower boundary of the class containing the median

c = class interval

f_m = frequency of the class containing the median

d = the difference between $\frac{n}{2}$ and the cumulative frequency up to b.

Example 3

Using Formula (17–5), find the median of the data in Table 17–2.

Solution:

$\frac{n}{2} = 6, b = 15, c = 5, f_m = 4, d = 6-4 = 2.$

$$m = b + \frac{cd}{f_m}$$

$$= 15 + \frac{10}{4}$$

$$= 15 + 2.5$$

$$= 17.5$$

The discrepancy between 17.5 and the median of 15.5 in Example 4 of Section 7.4 results from assuming the values in the class are uniformly distributed over the interval.* For data with a large number of values this is more likely to occur, and the calculated value will approximate the median with little error.

Example 4

The following table records the reliability of an electronic component:

Hours	Number
700– 799	86
800– 899	82
900– 999	64
1,000–1,099	32
1,100–1,199	10

* In class 15–19, the values were distributed as follows:

/ /	/	/		
15	16	17	18	19

What is the median number of hours the component may be expected to perform?

Solution:

$\frac{n}{2} = \frac{274}{2} = 137$, hence the median class is 800–899. $b = 800$, $c = 10$, $f_m = 82$, $d = 137 - 86 = 51$

$$m = b + \frac{cd}{f_m}$$
$$= 800 + \frac{10 \cdot 51}{82}$$
$$= 800 + 6.22$$
$$= 806.22 \text{ hours}$$

The Mode   The mode of a frequency distribution cannot be identified, hence it is customary to report only the modal class. The **modal class** of a frequency distribution is the class with the highest frequency.

Example 5

Find the modal class of the data in Table 17–2.

Solution:

The class with the greatest frequency is the class 15–19, hence it is the modal class.

If a single value of the mode is necessary the midpoint of the modal class may be used. In this event, the mode of the data in Table 17–2 is

$$\frac{15 + 19}{2} = 17$$

Example 6

A survey indicated the following number of flavors of ice cream carried by area supermarkets and drugstores:

Number of Flavors	Frequency
1–5	2
6–10	11
11–15	9
16–20	1

Find (a) the modal class and (b) a single modal value.

Solution:

a.   The modal class is 6–10.

b.   The modal value is $\dfrac{6+10}{2} = 8$.

**Exercises
for Section 17.5**

In problems 1 through 5, fill in the missing entries in the given frequency distribution and use the formula $\bar{x} = \left(\sum\limits_{i=1}^{k} f_i x_i \right) / \left(\sum\limits_{i=1}^{k} f_i \right)$ to find the mean of the data in the distribution.

1.

Class	Frequency (f_i)	Class Midpoint (x_i)	f_i x_i
5–9	1	_____	_____
10–14	3	_____	_____
15–19	4	_____	_____
20–24	4	_____	_____
25–29	2	_____	_____

2.

Class	Frequency (f_i)	Class Midpoint (x_i)	f_i x_i
0–4	2	_____	_____
5–9	6	_____	_____
10–14	8	_____	_____
15–19	8	_____	_____
20–24	10	_____	_____
25–29	7	_____	_____
30–34	6	_____	_____
35–39	3	_____	_____

3.

Class	Frequency (f_i)	Class Midpoint (x_i)	f_i x_i
0–9	2	_____	_____
10–19	3	_____	_____
20–29	2	_____	_____
30–39	4	_____	_____
40–49	1	_____	_____

4.

Class	Frequency (f_i)	Class Midpoint (x_i)	f_i x_i
0–8	1	_____	_____
9–17	2	_____	_____
18–26	3	_____	_____
27–35	2	_____	_____
36–44	4	_____	_____
45–53	1	_____	_____
54–62	1	_____	_____

5.

Class	Frequency (f_i)	Class Midpoint (x_i)	$f_i x_i$
0–10	2	_____	_____
11–21	4	_____	_____
22–32	6	_____	_____
33–43	5	_____	_____
44–54	7	_____	_____
55–65	3	_____	_____
66–76	1	_____	_____

6. Use the formula $m = b + \dfrac{cd}{f_m}$ to find the median of the data given in problem 1.

7. Repeat problem 6 for the data given in problem 2.

8. Repeat problem 6 for the data given in problem 3.

9. Repeat problem 6 for the data given in problem 4.

10. Find the modal class of the frequency distribution in problem 1. What is the modal value?

11. Find the modal class and the modal value for the frequency distribution in problem 2.

12. Find the modal class and the modal value for the frequency distribution in problem 5.

13. A survey of the number of brands of cereal carried by area supermarkets yielded the following data:

Number of Brands	Frequency
1–5	4
6–10	11
11–15	14
16–20	3

Find (a) the mean, (b) the median, and (c) the modal class.

14. The Eltec Company manufactures light bulbs. The number of hours of useful life of one of the company's products is indicated by the following data:

Hours	Frequency
160–179	12
180–199	102
200–219	120
220–239	110
240–259	60
260–279	4

Find (a) the mean, (b) the median, and (c) the modal class.

15. Sales at a local convenience store were recorded as follows:

Amount	Number of Sales
Less than $2.00	42
$ 2.00– 3.99	126
4.00– 5.99	130
6.00– 7.99	72
8.00– 9.99	84
10.00–11.99	20

Find (a) the mean, (b) the median, and (c) the modal class.

16. A survey of the employees at a manufacturing plant yielded the following frequency distribution of the weekly amount spent for food:

Amount Spent	Frequency
$30–39	38
40–49	62
50–59	74
60–69	46
70–79	23
80–89	18
90–99	5

Find (a) the mean, (b) the median, and (c) the modal class.

17.6 Measures of Variation

Equally important to measures of location that describe the "center" of a set of data are measures of variation that describe the amount of scatter or variation among the values. The most important of the measures of variation is the standard deviation. The **standard deviation** is defined by the formula*

(17–6)
$$s = \sqrt{\frac{\sum\limits_{i=1}^{n} (x_i - \overline{x})^2}{(n-1)}}$$

but is more easily calculated by the formula

(17–7)
$$s = \sqrt{\frac{n \cdot \sum\limits_{i=1}^{n} x_i^2 - (\sum\limits_{i=1}^{n} x_i)^2}{n(n-1)}}$$

* $\sqrt{}$ denotes the square root. The square root of a nonnegative number a is that nonnegative number b such that $b \times b = a$. For example, $\sqrt{36} = 6$ because $6 \times 6 = 36$.

where s = standard deviation
n = total number of values
x_i = data values

The use of Formula (17–7) is demonstrated in the next example.

Example 1

Find the standard deviation of the data in Table 17–1, using Table 17–5 to find the necessary square root.

Solution:

x_i	x_i^2
7	49
9	81
10	100
12	144
15	225
15	225
16	256
17	289
20	400
22	484
29	841
32	1,024
$\sum\limits_{i=1}^{12} x_i = 204$	$\sum\limits_{i=1}^{12} x_i^2 = 4,118$

$$s = \sqrt{\frac{12(4,118) - (204)^2}{12(11)}}$$

$$= \sqrt{\frac{49,416 - 41,616}{132}}$$

$$= \sqrt{\frac{7,800}{132}}$$

$$= \sqrt{59.09} \approx \sqrt{59} = 7.68 \qquad \text{(Table 17–5)}$$

The standard deviation describes the amount of scatter in a set of data in that the larger the number the greater the amount of scatter. In addition, the following occurs for many sets of data:

Approximately 68% of the values will differ from the mean by less than one standard deviation.
About 95% of the values will differ from the mean by less than two standard deviations.
About 99% of the values will differ from the mean by less than three standard deviations.

Table 17–5

n	$\sqrt{n}$	n	$\sqrt{n}$	n	$\sqrt{n}$	n	$\sqrt{n}$
1	1	51	7.14	101	10.05	151	12.29
2	1.41	52	7.21	102	10.10	152	12.33
3	1.73	53	7.28	103	10.15	153	12.37
4	2.00	54	7.35	104	10.20	154	12.41
5	2.24	55	7.41	105	10.25	155	12.45
6	2.45	56	7.48	106	10.30	156	12.49
7	2.65	57	7.55	107	10.34	157	12.53
8	2.83	58	7.62	108	10.39	158	12.57
9	3.00	59	7.68	109	10.44	159	12.61
10	3.16	60	7.75	110	10.49	160	12.65
11	3.32	61	7.81	111	10.54	161	12.69
12	3.46	62	7.87	112	10.58	162	12.73
13	3.61	63	7.94	113	10.63	163	12.77
14	3.74	64	8.00	114	10.68	164	12.81
15	3.87	65	8.06	115	10.72	165	12.85
16	4.00	66	8.12	116	10.77	166	12.88
17	4.12	67	8.19	117	10.82	167	12.92
18	4.24	68	8.25	118	10.86	168	12.96
19	4.36	69	8.31	119	10.91	169	13.00
20	4.47	70	8.37	120	10.95	170	13.04
21	4.58	71	8.43	121	11.00	171	13.08
22	4.69	72	8.49	122	11.05	172	13.11
23	4.80	73	8.54	123	11.09	173	13.15
24	4.90	74	8.60	124	11.14	174	13.19
25	5.00	75	8.66	125	11.18	175	13.23
26	5.10	76	8.72	126	11.22	176	13.27
27	5.20	77	8.77	127	11.27	177	13.30
28	5.29	78	8.83	128	11.31	178	13.34
29	5.39	79	8.89	129	11.36	179	13.38
30	5.48	80	8.94	130	11.40	180	13.42
31	5.57	81	9.00	131	11.46	181	13.45
32	5.66	82	9.06	132	11.49	182	13.49
33	5.74	83	9.11	133	11.53	183	13.53
34	5.83	84	9.17	134	11.58	184	13.56
35	5.92	85	9.22	135	11.62	185	13.60
36	6.00	86	9.27	136	11.66	186	13.64
37	6.08	87	9.33	137	11.70	187	13.67
38	6.16	88	9.38	138	11.75	188	13.71
39	6.25	89	9.43	139	11.79	189	13.75
40	6.32	90	9.49	140	11.83	190	13.78
41	6.40	91	9.54	141	11.87	191	13.82
42	6.48	92	9.59	142	11.92	192	13.86
43	6.55	93	9.64	143	11.96	193	13.89
44	6.63	94	9.70	144	12.00	194	13.93
45	6.71	95	9.75	145	12.04	195	13.96
46	6.78	96	9.80	146	12.08	196	14.00
47	6.86	97	9.85	147	12.12	197	14.04
48	6.92	98	9.90	148	12.17	198	14.07
49	7.00	99	9.95	149	12.21	199	14.11
50	7.07	100	10.00	150	12.25	200	14.14

For a frequency distribution with k classes, a formula for the standard deviation s is

(17–8)
$$s = \sqrt{\frac{\sum\limits_{i=1}^{k} (x_i - \overline{x})^2 \cdot f_i}{n - 1}}$$

where the variables have the same meaning as in Formula (17–4).

Exercises for Section 17.6

In problems 1 through 5, use Formula (17–7) to compute the standard deviation of the given data.

1. 11,4,23,16,4,15

2. 6,2,12,8,4,8

3. 5,11,15,14,13,6,12,11

4. 10,15,11,20,25,14,16,21

5. 4,6,2,8,5,12,9,7,8,6,10,8

6. The weekly salaries of the employees at the Curtis Company are given in the following table.

Weekly Salary	Frequency
$120	3
$130	9
$150	6
$160	2

Compute the standard deviation for this data.

7. The number of sales reported by each of eight salespeople at a furniture store last week were 12,8,10,11,15,6,10, and 8. Compute the standard deviation for this data.

8. The number of years of service of the ten employees of the Quality Clothing Store are 23,5,10,16,4,8,14,8,17, and 8. Compute the standard deviation for this data. What percent of the employees have served a number of years that is within one standard deviation of the mean?

9. A class of 40 students was given an examination. If the mean score on the exam was 75 and the standard deviation was 10, approximately how many students scored between 65 and 85 on the exam? How many scored between 55 and 95?

10. An analysis of the weekly salaries paid to the assembly-line workers at a manufacturing plant revealed a mean weekly salary of $173 with a standard deviation of $12. If the plant employs 72 assembly-line workers, approximately how many earn between $161 and $185 per week? How many earn between $149 and $197 per week?

The Binary System

Chapter Objectives for Chapter 18

I. Learn the meaning of the following terms:

A. *Binary number,* 444, 445
B. *Binary mode,* 450

II. Understand:

A. How positional notation is used in the binary system, 445
B. Conversion of binary numbers to decimal numbers, 445
C. Conversion of decimal numbers to binary numbers, 446
D. How the binary system is used in computers, 450

III. Perform:

A. Calculations with binary numbers, 447–449

Introduction

The decimal system is an integral part of modern commerce. As demonstrated in this text, it is the core of business mathematics. The decimal system is also the base for our currency system, and it is the foundation of the measuring system used by most of the world, the metric system.

However, the decimal system is not the only numbering system. Our use of this system is a product of biology, not necessity. We count by tens probably because we have ten fingers and ten toes, and had our ancestors been born with some other combination, our numbering system might be quite different today. In this chapter, we explore another number system called the binary system. The binary system is used in computer logic, thus an understanding of this system will enhance understanding the operation of an electronic computer.

Section **18.2** **Positional Notation**

The decimal system has two central parts, the digits 0,1,2,3,4,5,6,7,8,9 and the Hindu-Arabic positional notation. The latter permits us to establish a system of counting whereby all numbers are written with these same ten digits. Because all numbers are written with ten digits, the decimal system is said to be of base 10.

The binary system has the same central parts as the decimal system, except that all numbers are written with only two digits 0 and 1. The word **binary** means "something made up of two parts," thus the binary system is a number system of base 2.

The construction of a number in the binary system uses the Hindu-Arabic positional notation, except the base is 2 instead of 10. A comparison of the positional columns is shown in Figure 18–1.

Figure 18–1

Decimal

Ten thousands	Thousands	Hundreds	Tens	Ones
10x10x10x10	10x10x10	10x10	10	1
		1	0	1

Binary

Sixteens	Eights	Fours	Twos	Ones
2x2x2x2	2x2x2	2x2	2	1
		1	0	1

The decimal number 101 means 1 hundred + 0 tens + 1 one, which is the number named one-hundred one. In the binary system, the number 101 means 1 four + 0 twos + 1 one; it is equivalent to the decimal number 5. The positional procedure of both systems is the same; only the base is changed.

In the decimal system, positional notation becomes necessary upon reaching the number ten. The digits 0 through 9 having been used, a two-digit number is constructed to designate the number after the number 9. Similarly, a three-digit number is constructed after the number 99 because all two-digit combinations have been used. The same procedure is followed in the binary system. As a result, the beginning numbers in each system appear as follows:

Decimal	Binary	Binary Positional Interpretation
0	0	0 ones
1	1	1 one
2	10	1 two + 0 ones
3	11	1 two + 1 one
4	100	1 four + 0 twos + 0 ones
5	101	1 four + 0 twos + 1 one
6	110	1 four + 1 two + 0 ones
7	111	1 four + 1 two + 1 one
8	1000	1 eight + 0 fours + 0 twos + 0 ones
9	1001	1 eight + 0 fours + 0 twos + 1 one
10	1010	1 eight + 0 fours + 1 two + 0 ones
11	1011	1 eight + 0 fours + 1 two + 1 one
12	1100	1 eight + 1 four + 0 twos + 0 ones
13	1101	1 eight + 1 four + 0 twos + 1 one
14	1110	1 eight + 1 four + 1 two + 0 ones
15	1111	1 eight + 1 four + 1 two + 1 one

Because numbers in each system may have the same appearance, a subscript is used for identification. Thus 10_2 is the binary number corresponding to the decimal number 2_{10}, and 10_{10} is the decimal number equivalent to the binary number 1010_2.

18.3   Conversion from Binary to Decimal Numbers

Positional notation permits easy conversion of a binary number to a decimal number. For example,

$$101101_2$$

means 1 thirty-two + 0 sixteens + 1 eight + 1 four + 0 twos + 1 one, or $32 + 8 + 4 + 1 = 45$. Thus:

$$101101_2 = 45_{10}$$

Example 1

Convert   a. 111_2 b. 1011_2 to their equivalent decimal numbers.

Solution:

a. 111_2 means 1 four + 1 two + 1 one, or $4 + 2 + 1 = 7$.
$111_2 = 7_{10}$

b. 1011_2 means 1 eight + 0 fours + 1 two + 1 one, or
$8 + 0 + 2 + 1 = 11$.
$1011_2 = 11_{10}$.

Section **18.4**   **Conversion of Decimal Numbers to Binary Numbers**

The conversion of a decimal number to a binary number is best explained by illustration. Consider the decimal number 19_{10}.

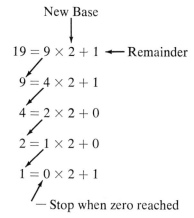

Writing the remainders from bottom to top we have 10011. Thus, $19_{10} = 10011_2$. This may be checked as follows: $10011_2 = 1$ sixteen + 0 eights + 0 fours + 1 two + 1 one, or $16 + 2 + 1 = 19$.

Example 1

Find the binary numbers equivalent to   a. 20_{10} b. 37_{10}.

Solution:

a. $20 = 10 \times 2 + 0$ b. $37 = 18 \times 2 + 1$
$\quad 10 = 5 \times 2 + 0$ $\quad 18 = 9 \times 2 + 0$
$\quad 5 = 2 \times 2 + 1$ $\quad 9 = 4 \times 2 + 1$
$\quad 2 = 1 \times 2 + 0$ $\quad 4 = 2 \times 2 + 0$
$\quad 1 = 0 \times 2 + 1$ $\quad 2 = 1 \times 2 + 0$
$\quad 9 = 4 \times 2 + 1$
$20_{10} = 10100_2$ $37_{10} = 100101_2$

In problems 1–10, convert the binary number to its equivalent decimal number.

1.	101_2	6.	10000_2
2.	1110_2	7.	101100_2
3.	1010_2	8.	11100011_2
4.	11011_2	9.	11000001_2
5.	10001_2	10.	111110110_2

In problems 11–20, convert the decimal number to its equivalent binary number.

11.	9_{10}	16.	133_{10}
12.	14_{10}	17.	150_{10}
13.	22_{10}	18.	200_{10}
14.	56_{10}	19.	225_{10}
15.	111_{10}	20.	$4,000_{10}$

Section 18.5 Binary Arithmetic

With only two digits in the system, binary arithmetic becomes quite streamlined. For instance, the addition and multiplication tables appear as follows:

+	0	1
0	0	1
1	1	10

×	0	1
0	0	0
1	0	1

Arithmetic problems in the binary system are solved by the same algorithms used in decimal arithmetic. As in the decimal system, care must be exercised to use the "carrying process" in addition, and the "borrowing process" in subtraction.

Example 1

Find: a. $111_2 + 10_2$ b. $1011 + 1101_2$

Solution:

```
        1                    111
a.     111          b.      1011
     +  10                + 1101
      ----                 -----
      1001                 11000
```

Example 2

Find and check your results: a. $1011_2 - 110_2$

b. $1110_2 - 101_2$

Solution:

a.   1011   b.   1110
        − 110   − 101
          101   1001

The check is performed by adding the subtrahend and the difference.

a.   110   b.   1001
       + 101   + 101
        1011   1110

Example 3

Find: a. $1010_2 \times 111_2$ b. $1011_2 \times 101_2$

Solution:

a.   1010   b.   1011
     ×   111   ×   101
       1010   1011
      1010   0000
     1010   1011
   1000110   110111

Example 4

Find and check your results: a. $1111_2 \div 101_2$

b. $101011_2 \div 1101_2$

Solution:

a.
```
          11
   101) 1111
        101
        101
        101
          0
```

b.
```
              11
   1101) 101011
         1101
        10001
         1101
          100
```

$1111_2 \div 101_2 = 11_2$ $101011_2 \div 1101_2 = 11_2$ with remainder 100_2

The check is performed by multiplying the divisor by the quotient and adding the remainder.

a.
$$\begin{array}{r} 101 \\ \times\ 11 \\ \hline 101 \\ 101 \\ \hline 1111 \end{array}$$

b.
$$\begin{array}{r} 1101 \\ \times\ 11 \\ \hline 1101 \\ 1101 \\ \hline 100111 \\ 100 \\ \hline 101011 \end{array}$$

Exercises for Section 18.5 Solve:

1. $111_2 + 110_2$

2. $101_2 + 100_2$

3. $1001_2 + 110_2$

4. $1101_2 + 111_2$

5. $1111_2 + 1001_2$

6. $1010_2 + 1101_2$

7. $10111_2 + 111_2$

8. $11011_2 + 1001_2$

9. $10101_2 + 11100_2$

10. $1111011_2 + 110001_2$

11. $111_2 - 10_2$

12. $1110_2 - 111_2$

13. $1111_2 - 1001_2$

14. $101100_2 - 101001_2$

15. $111011_2 - 1011_2$

16. $111010_2 - 101110_2$

17. $1101111_2 - 100011_2$

18. $101010101_2 - 1100110_2$

19. $110110110_2 - 100100100_2$

20. $111011101_2 - 10101101_2$

21. $101_2 \times 10_2$

22. $110_2 \times 100_2$

23. $1101_2 \times 1101_2$

24. $1110_2 \times 1010_2$

25. $11101_2 \times 10001_2$

26. $10010_2 \times 11101_2$

27. $11001100_2 \times 1100_2$

28. $1101011_2 \times 11110_2$

29. $111111_2 \times 11011_2$

30. $1100011000_2 \times 111000_2$

31. $1110_2 \div 10_2$

32. $10100_2 \div 101_2$

33. $110010_2 \div 11001_2$

34. $100110_2 \div 10011_2$

35. $1011000_2 \div 1011_2$

36. $111_2 \div 10_2$

37. $1001_2 \div 110_2$

38. $11110_2 \div 1001_2$

39. $101101_2 \div 11011_2$

40. $11100111_2 \div 10101_2$

18.6 Computers and the Binary System

Consider an ordinary light bulb connected in a circuit with an off-on switch. As such, there are only two states for the light and only one state can exist at any time; it is either on or off. This is an illustration of what computer technicians call a binary mode. A **binary mode** is a set of two conditions, only one of which may exist at any point in time. The components of an electronic computer (the transistors, the magnetic tape, the punched cards, etc.) indicate only one of two possible states at any point in time; they are either activated ("on") or not activated ("off").

The binary mode can be used to construct a number with light bulbs. Suppose it is agreed that when a bulb is lit it represents the digit 1, and when it is not lit it represents the digit 0. Thus by using four bulbs side-by-side, any decimal number from 0 to 9 can be represented by its binary equivalent. This is shown in Figure 18–2.

Figure 18–2

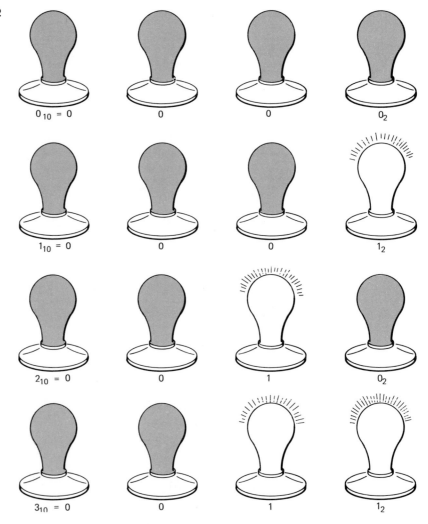

Figure 18–2 (*continued*)

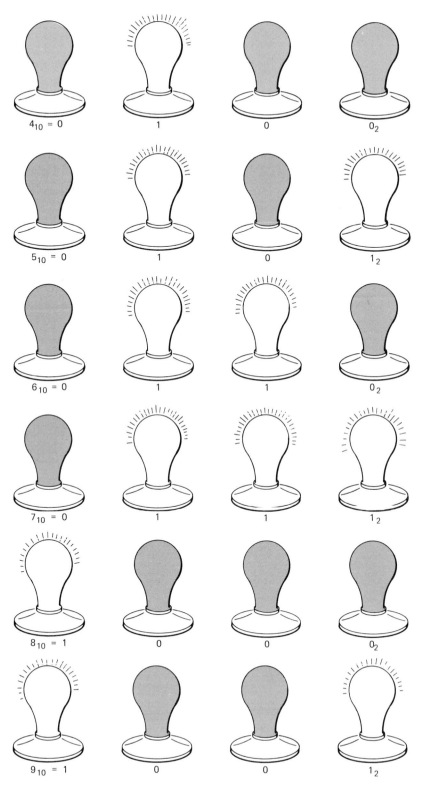

$$4_{10} = 0 \quad 1 \quad 0 \quad 0_2$$

$$5_{10} = 0 \quad 1 \quad 0 \quad 1_2$$

$$6_{10} = 0 \quad 1 \quad 1 \quad 0_2$$

$$7_{10} = 0 \quad 1 \quad 1 \quad 1_2$$

$$8_{10} = 1 \quad 0 \quad 0 \quad 0_2$$

$$9_{10} = 1 \quad 0 \quad 0 \quad 1_2$$

The position of the lights side by side is the same as the columnar arrangement in the Hindu-Arabic positional notation.

If the lights in the above illustration are replaced by computer components—the transistors, magnetic cores, magnetic tapes, punched cards, etc., we have the binary mode in computer operation. In a computer system, components that are activated correspond to the digit 1 in the binary system. When a component is not activated, it corresponds to the digit 0 in the binary system. Most computer codes are based on this binary coded method of data representation.

The Metric System

Chapter Objectives for Chapter 19

I. Learn the meaning of the following terms:

II. Understand:

III. Perform:

Introduction

The system of weights and measures used in the United States has its heritage in the English system of weights and measures, which in turn can be traced to ancient Roman and Egyptian customs. These ancient standards were imprecise and largely based on anatomical dimensions. For example, in Egypt, a basic unit of length was the cubit, the distance from the elbow to the tip of the middle finger. The Egyptians divided the cubit into seven palms and each palm into four digits, a word also meaning finger. Thus, every person carried his own measuring system, but because these lengths vary among individuals, everyone had a different "ruler."

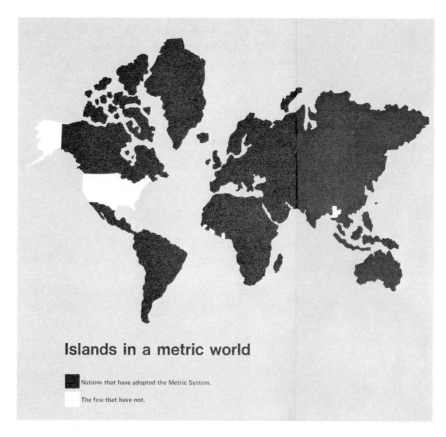

Islands in a metric world

■ Nations that have adopted the Metric System.

□ The few that have not.

In the latter part of the eighteenth century, a commission of French scientists developed a system that has become the international standard of weights and measures. Called the metric system, it has been adopted by almost every civilized country except the United States.* The metric system has two distinct advantages over other forms of measurement; it has a fixed, invariable base, and its numerical system is decimal based.

* American scientists already express scientific measurements in metric units, but the general public continues to use the system of feet, miles, pounds, gallons, etc. Serious discussions are now taking place on plans to convert to the metric system for the entire country.

Figure 19–1

Australian Stamps Promoting
Metric Conversion

The basic unit of measurement is the **meter,** which was defined to be $\frac{1}{10,000,000}$ of the distance from the equator to either the North or South Pole.* In the U.S. system, this is 39.37 inches or approximately 1.093 yards. This unit of length is also used to establish units of area, capacity, and weight, as will be seen in the sections to follow.

In establishing a decimal based system of weights and measure, decimal multiples and fractions of the basic unit were designated by Greek and Latin prefixes. The value and meaning of these designations are shown in Table 19–1.

* A more recent definition of the meter is 1,650,763.73 wave lengths of the orange-red light of krypton 86.

Table 19–1	Prefix (Abbreviation)	Meaning	Numerical Value
	Giga (G)	one billion	1,000,000,000
	Mega (M)	one million	1,000,000
	kilo (k)	one thousand	1,000
	hecto (h)	one hundred	100
	Deca (da)	ten	10
	Deci (d)	one tenth	$\frac{1}{10} = 0.1$
	Centi (c)	one hundredth	$\frac{1}{100} = 0.01$
	Milli (m)	one thousandth	$\frac{1}{1,000} = 0.001$
	Micro (u)	one millionth	$\frac{1}{1,000,000} = 0.000001$
	Nano (n)	one billionth	$\frac{1}{1,000,000,000} = 0.000000001$

Thus, a decameter is 10 meters, a kilometer is 1,000 meters, a centimeter is $\frac{1}{100}$ of a meter, and a millimeter is $\frac{1}{1,000}$ of a meter. The decimal base makes calculations with the metric system much simpler than with the U.S. system. For example, any denominations can be changed to the next higher by moving the decimal point to the left, and changed to the next lower by moving the decimal point to the right. Thus,

$$1.725 \text{ decameters} = 17.25 \text{ meters} = 172.5 \text{ decimeters}$$

Section 19.2 Metric Units of Length

The meter is the basic unit of length in the metric system. The kilometer is used to measure long distances, while for small lengths, the centimeter and the millimeter are the most common forms. It is standard practice to abbreviate metric terms. Abbreviations for the above terms are:

meter m

kilometer km (k = kilo and m = meter)

centimeter cm (c = centi and m = meter)

millimeter mm (m = milli and m = meter)

The relation between these units and their U.S. counterparts is shown in Table 19–2.

Table 19–2

Length

Meter (m)	= 1.093 yards	Yard = 0.9144 meter
	= 3.281 feet	Foot = 0.3048 meter
	= 39.370 inches	Inch = 0.0254 meter
Kilometer (km)	= 0.621 mile	Mile = 1.609 kilometers

Surface

Square meter (m²)	= 1.196 square yards	Square yard = 0.836 square meter
	= 10.764 square feet	Square foot = 0.092 square meter
Square centimeter (cm²)	= 0.155 square inch	Square inch = 6.45 square centimeters
Square kilometer (km²)	= 0.386 square mile	Square mile = 2.590 square kilometers
Hectare (ha)	= 2.471 acres	Acre = 0.405 hectare

Capacity

Liter (l)	= 1.056 U.S. liquid quarts	U.S. liquid quart = 0.946 liter
	= 0.908 dry quart	Dry quart = 1.111 liters
	= 0.264 U.S. gallon	U.S. gallon = 3.785 liters
Hectoliter (hl)	= 2.837 U.S. bushels	U.S. bushel = 0.352 hectoliter

Weight

Gram (g)	= 15.432 grains	Grain = 0.0648 gram
	= 0.0352 avoirdupois ounce	Avoirdupois ounce = 28.35 grams
Kilogram (kg)	= 2.2046 pounds avoirdupois	Pound = 0.4536 kilogram
Metric ton (t)	= 2204.62 pounds avoirdupois	Short ton = 0.907 metric ton

Example 1

Karl's Auto Parts specializes in foreign car parts. A voltage regulator 10.1 cm in length is to be mailed to a customer. How long a box (in inches) is required if one-half inch packing is used on both ends?

Solution:

1 cm	$= 0.3937$ inches	(Table 19–2)
10.1 cm	$= 10.1 \times 0.3937$	
	$= 3.98$ inches	
packing	$= 1.00$ inches	
Total length	$= 4.98$ inches	

Karl will no doubt use a five-inch box to mail the part.

19.3 **Metric Unit of Area**

The unit of area in the metric system is the **square meter,** which is the area of a square whose sides are one meter in length. See Figure 19–2. For most land measurements, the **are** (100 square meters), the **hectare** (100 ares), and the square kilometer are used. For small areas, the square meter and the square centimeter are common. Abbreviations for the above units are:

square meter	m²
are	a
hectare	ha
square centimeter	cm²

The relation between these units and their U.S. counterparts is shown in Table 19–2.

Figure 19–2

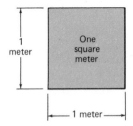

Example 1

The Sikes Company purchased 150 ha of land in Spain for construction of a branch factory. If the total price was $70,000, what was the cost per acre?

Solution:

$$1 \text{ ha} = 2.4711 \text{ acres}$$

$$150 \text{ ha} = 150 \times 2.4711$$

$$= 370.665 \text{ acres}$$

$$\frac{\$70,000}{370.665} = \$188.85 \text{ per acre.}$$

19.4 **Metric Units of Capacity**

The unit of capacity in the metric system is the liter. A **liter** is the capacity of a cubic container measuring ten centimeters on each side. See Figure 19–3. The liter is slightly larger than a quart. For large measurement, the **hectoliter** (100 liters) is used. Abbreviations for the above units are:

liter	l
hectoliter	hl

The relation between these units and their U.S. counterparts is shown in Table 19–2.

Figure 19–3

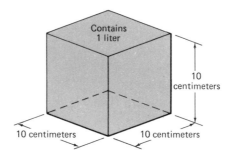

Example 1

The Moroni Import Company received a shipment of 50hl of olive oil. What was the shipment in gallons?

Solution:

$$1 \text{ hl} = 100 \text{ liters}$$

$$50 \text{ hl} = 50 \times 100$$

$$= 5,000 \text{ liters}$$

$$1 \text{ gallon} = 3.7853 \text{ liters}$$

$$\frac{5,000}{3.7853} = 1,320.9 \text{ gallons}$$

19.5 Metric Units of Weight

The unit of weight in the metric system is the gram. A **gram** is the weight of one cubic centimeter of distilled water at its greatest density, which is at 39.2°F (4°C) at sea level. Because a gram weighs only 0.353 ounces, the **kilogram** (1,000 grams) is the standard for most small weights. For heavy items, the **metric ton** (1,000 kilograms) is used. Abbreviations for the above units are:

gram	g
kilogram	kg
metric ton	t

The relation between these units and their U.S. counterparts is shown in Table 19–2.

Metric recipe

Queen cakes

100 g butter or margarine
100 g castor sugar
150 g self-raising flour
pinch of salt
2 eggs
25 mℓ milk
100 g currants

Cream the fat and sugar together until light and fluffy.

Sieve or mix the flour and salt.

Add the eggs, one at a time, to the creamed mixture with a spoonful of flour, stir then beat.

Beat in the milk with a little more flour.

Stir in the currants with the remaining flour.

Divide the mixture evenly between about 20 baking cases, smooth level.

Bake for 15–20 minutes at 190 °C (375 °F) gas mark 5.

Recipe supplied by the United Kingdom Home Economics Federation.

Metric recipe leaflets are on sale from UKFEHE, 36 Ravenscroft Avenue, London NW11 8AU.

Example 1

A poor grain harvest forced the Russian government to purchase 3 million metric tons of wheat on the open market. What is the U.S. equivalent in tons?

Solution:

$$1 \text{ t} = 1.1023 \text{ tons} \qquad \text{(Table 19–2)}$$

$$3 \text{ million t} = 3,000,000 \times 1.1023$$

$$= 3,306,900 \text{ tons}$$

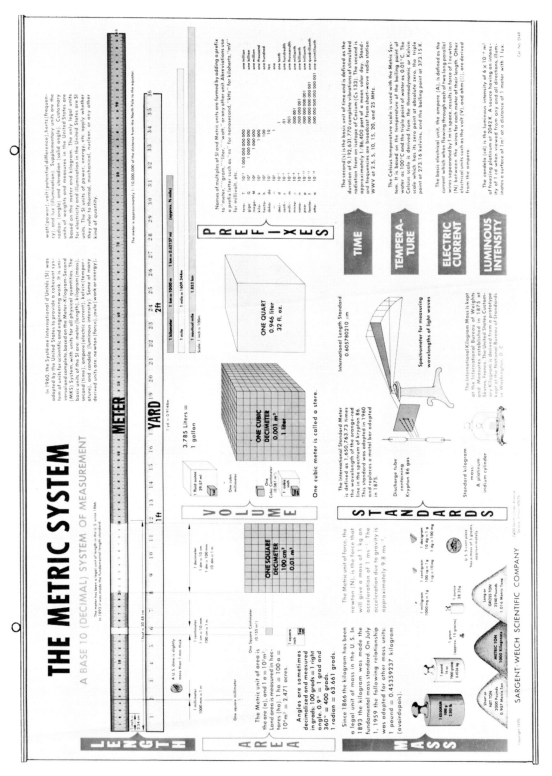

Figure 19-4

In exercises 1–20, convert the given measure or weight to the equivalent metric unit specified.

1. 2 meters to centimeters

2. 12 hectometers to kilometers

3. 412.5 millimeters to micrometers

4. 170 hectoliters to centiliters

5. 120.4 centimeters to decimeters

6. 261.3 grams to kilograms

7. 130.8 decameters to decimeters

8. 1,248 milligrams to micrograms

9. 463.7 gigameters to kilometers

10. 383.4 liters to centiliters

11. 5 km = ____m = ____mm

12. 9 kg = ____g = ____t

13. 40m² = ____a = ____ha

14. 14 km² = ____m² = ____cm²

15. 42hl = ____l = ____ml

16. 122.5 cm² = ____m² = ____a

17. 27.25 cl = ____l = ____hl

18. 147.8 mg = ____kg = ____g

19. 183.2 m = ____mm = ____cm

20. 481.7 a = ____ha = ____km²

In exercises 21–48, fill in the blanks. Round your answers to the second decimal place.

21. 10 meters = _____ feet.

22. 1,500 meters = _____ miles.

23. 45 millimeters = _____ inches.

24. 60 kilometers = _____ miles.

25. 4,500 meters = _____ yards.

26. 48 inches = _____ centimeters.

27. 100 yards = _____ meters.

28. 12 miles = _____ kilometers.

29. 6 feet = _____ meters.

30. 350 feet = _____ decameters.

31. 12 square meters = _____ square yards.

32. 66 square centimeters = _____ square inches.

33. 4 square kilometers = _____ square miles.

34. 7 square meters = _____ square feet.

35. 44 hectares = _____ acres.

36. 12 square yards = _____ square meters.

37. 144 square inches = _____ square centimeters.

38. $4\frac{1}{2}$ square miles = _____ square kilometers.

39. 30 square feet = _____ square meters.

40. 75 acres = _____ hectares.

41. 6 liters = _____ quarts.

42. $2\frac{1}{2}$ liters = _____ pints.

43. 16 liters = _____ gallons.

44. 110 hectoliters = _____ bushels.

45. 36 gallons = _____ liters.

46. 14 quarts = _____ liters.

47. 62 bushels = _____ hectoliters.

48. 24 quarts = _____ liters.

49. The Ferris Company sold 200 gallons of molasses to a European firm for $4.40 per gallon. What is the price per liter?

50. Visitors to a country in the Middle East are advised that the speed limit is 90 kilometers per hour. What is the speed limit in miles per hour?

51. A British plant consumes 12 metric tons of coal every 8 hours. How many pounds of coal per hour is this?

52. The Wheeling Tool and Die Company received an order for some brass fittings from a foreign firm. One of the specifications called for a hole of 32 millimeters in diameter. What is the size of the hole in inches?

53. A buyer for the Romulus Corporation can buy an item at $0.26 per pound or $0.12 per kilogram. Which is the best price?

54. The Monroe Packing Company sold a total of 120 metric tons of citrus products to a Japanese import company in one year. Find the number of pounds of citrus products sold.

55. The engine of a foreign car is rated at 1,500 cubic centimeters. How many cubic inches is this? (Note: 1 cubic inch = 16.387 cubic centimeters.)

Appendix

Appendix A The Number of Each Day of the Year

Day of Month	Jan.	Feb.	Mar.	April	May	June	July	Aug.	Sept.	Oct.	Nov.	Dec.	Day of Month
1	1	32	60	91	121	152	182	213	244	274	305	335	1
2	2	33	61	92	122	153	183	214	245	275	306	336	2
3	3	34	62	93	123	154	184	215	246	276	307	337	3
4	4	35	63	94	124	155	185	216	247	277	308	338	4
5	5	36	64	95	125	156	186	217	248	278	309	339	5
6	6	37	65	96	126	157	187	218	249	279	310	340	6
7	7	38	66	97	127	158	188	219	250	280	311	341	7
8	8	39	67	98	128	159	189	220	251	281	312	342	8
9	9	40	68	99	129	160	190	221	252	282	313	343	9
10	10	41	69	100	130	161	191	222	253	283	314	344	10
11	11	42	70	101	131	162	192	223	254	284	315	345	11
12	12	43	71	102	132	163	193	224	255	285	316	346	12
13	13	44	72	103	133	164	194	225	256	286	317	347	13
14	14	45	73	104	134	165	195	226	257	287	318	348	14
15	15	46	74	105	135	166	196	227	258	288	319	349	15
16	16	47	75	106	136	167	197	228	259	289	320	350	16
17	17	48	76	107	137	168	198	229	260	290	321	351	17
18	18	49	77	108	138	169	199	230	261	291	322	352	18
19	19	50	78	109	139	170	200	231	262	292	323	353	19
20	20	51	79	110	140	171	201	232	263	293	324	354	20
21	21	52	80	111	141	172	202	233	264	294	325	355	21
22	22	53	81	112	142	173	203	234	265	295	326	356	22
23	23	54	82	113	143	174	204	235	266	296	327	357	23
24	24	55	83	114	144	175	205	236	267	297	328	358	24
25	25	56	84	115	145	176	206	237	268	298	329	359	25
26	26	57	85	116	146	177	207	238	269	299	330	360	26
27	27	58	86	117	147	178	208	239	270	300	331	361	27
28	28	59	87	118	148	179	209	240	271	301	332	362	28
29	29		88	119	149	180	210	241	272	302	333	363	29
30	30		89	120	150	181	211	242	273	303	334	364	30
31	31		90		151		212	243		304		365	31

Note. In leap years, after February 28, add 1 to the tabulated number.

Rate ¼%	B Compound Amount	C Present Value	D Amount of Annuity	E Present Value of Annuity	F Sinking Fund	G Amortization	
n	$(1 + i)^n$	$(1 + i)^{-n}$	$S_{\overline{n}|i}$	$A_{\overline{n}|i}$	$1/S_{\overline{n}|i}$	$1/A_{\overline{n}|i}$	n
1	1.0025 0000	0.9975 0623	1.0000 0000	0.9975 0623	1.0000 0000	1.0025 0000	1
2	1.0050 0625	0.9950 1869	2.0025 0000	1.9925 2492	0.4993 7578	0.5018 7578	2
3	1.0075 1877	0.9925 3734	3.0075 0625	2.9850 6227	0.3325 0139	0.3350 0139	3
4	1.0100 3756	0.9900 6219	4.0150 2502	3.9751 2446	0.2490 6445	0.2515 6445	4
5	1.0125 6266	0.9875 9321	5.0250 6258	4.9627 1766	0.1990 0250	0.2015 0250	5
6	1.0150 9406	0.9851 3038	6.0376 2523	5.9478 4804	0.1656 2803	0.1681 2803	6
7	1.0176 3180	0.9826 7370	7.0527 1930	6.9305 2174	0.1427 8928	0.1442 8928	7
8	1.0201 7588	0.9802 2314	8.0703 5110	7.9107 4487	0.1239 1035	0.1264 1035	8
9	1.0227 2632	0.9777 7869	9.0905 2697	8.8885 2357	0.1100 0462	0.1125 0462	9
10	1.0252 8313	0.9753 4034	10.1132 5329	9.8638 6391	0.0988 8015	0.1013 8015	10
11	1.0278 4634	0.9729 0807	11.1385 3642	10.8367 7198	0.0897 7840	0.0922 7840	11
12	1.0304 1596	0.9704 8187	12.1663 8277	11.8072 5384	0.0821 9370	0.0846 9370	12
13	1.0329 9200	0.9680 6171	13.1967 9872	12.7753 1555	0.0767 7595	0.0782 7595	13
14	1.0355 7448	0.9656 4759	14.2297 9072	13.7409 6314	0.0702 7510	0.0727 7510	14
15	1.0381 6341	0.9632 3949	15.2653 6520	14.7042 0264	0.0655 0777	0.0680 0777	15
16	1.0407 5882	0.9608 3740	16.3035 2861	15.6650 4004	0.0613 3642	0.0638 3642	16
17	1.0433 6072	0.9584 4130	17.3442 8743	16.6234 8133	0.0576 5587	0.0601 5587	17
18	1.0459 6912	0.9560 5117	18.3876 4815	17.5795 3250	0.0543 8433	0.0568 8433	18
19	1.0485 8404	0.9536 6700	19.4336 1727	18.5331 9950	0.0514 5722	0.0539 5722	19
20	1.0512 0550	0.9512 8878	20.4822 0131	19.4844 8828	0.0488 2288	0.0513 2288	20
21	1.0538 3352	0.9489 1649	21.5334 0682	20.4334 0477	0.0464 3947	0.0489 3947	21
22	1.0564 6810	0.9465 5011	22.5872 4033	21.3799 5488	0.0442 7278	0.0467 7278	22
23	1.0591 0927	0.9441 8964	23.6437 0843	22.3241 4452	0.0422 9455	0.0447 9455	23
24	1.0617 5704	0.9418 3505	24.7028 1770	23.2659 7957	0.0404 8121	0.0429 8121	24
25	1.0644 1144	0.9394 8634	25.7645 7475	24.2054 6591	0.0388 1298	0.0413 1298	25
26	1.0670 7247	0.9371 4348	26.8289 8619	25.1426 0939	0.0372 7312	0.0397 7312	26
27	1.0697 4015	0.9348 0646	27.8960 5865	26.0774 1585	0.0358 4736	0.0383 4736	27
28	1.0724 1450	0.9324 7527	28.9657 9880	27.0098 9112	0.0345 2347	0.0370 2347	28
29	1.0750 9553	0.9301 4990	30.0382 1330	27.9400 4102	0.0332 9093	0.0357 9093	29
30	1.0777 8327	0.9278 3032	31.1133 0883	28.8678 7134	0.0321 4059	0.0346 4059	30
31	1.0804 7773	0.9255 1653	32.1910 9210	29.7933 8787	0.0310 6449	0.0335 6449	31
32	1.0831 7892	0.9232 0851	33.2715 6983	30.7165 9638	0.0300 5569	0.0325 5569	32
33	1.0858 8687	0.9209 0624	34.3547 4876	31.6375 0262	0.0291 0806	0.0316 0806	33
34	1.0886 0159	0.9186 0972	35.4406 3563	32.5561 1234	0.0282 1620	0.0307 1620	34
35	1.0913 2309	0.9163 1892	36.5292 3722	33.4724 3126	0.0273 7533	0.0298 7533	35
36	1.0940 5140	0.9140 3384	37.6205 6031	34.3864 6510	0.0265 8121	0.0290 8121	36
37	1.0967 8653	0.9117 5445	38.7146 1171	35.2982 1955	0.0258 3004	0.0283 3004	37
38	1.0995 2850	0.9094 8075	39.8113 9824	36.2077 0030	0.0251 1843	0.0276 1843	38
39	1.1022 7732	0.9072 1272	40.9109 2673	37.1149 1302	0.0244 4335	0.0269 4335	39
40	1.1050 3301	0.9049 5034	42.0132 0405	38.0198 6336	0.0238 0204	0.0263 0204	40
41	1.1077 9559	0.9026 9361	43.1182 3706	38.9225 5697	0.0231 9204	0.0256 9204	41
42	1.1105 6508	0.9004 4250	44.2260 3265	39.8229 9947	0.0226 1112	0.0251 1112	42
43	1.1133 4149	0.8981 9701	45.3365 9774	40.7211 9648	0.0220 5724	0.0245 5724	43
44	1.1161 2485	0.8959 5712	46.4499 3923	41.6171 5359	0.0215 2855	0.0240 2855	44
45	1.1189 1516	0.8937 2281	47.5660 6408	42.5108 7640	0.0210 2339	0.0235 2339	45
46	1.1217 1245	0.8914 9407	48.6849 7924	43.4023 7047	0.0205 4022	0.0230 4022	46
47	1.1245 1673	0.8892 7090	49.8066 9169	44.2916 4137	0.0200 7762	0.0225 7762	47
48	1.1273 2802	0.8870 5326	50.9312 0842	45.1786 9463	0.0196 3433	0.0221 3433	48
49	1.1301 4634	0.8848 4116	52.0585 3644	46.0635 3580	0.0192 0915	0.0217 0915	49
50	1.1329 7171	0.8826 3457	53.1886 8278	46.9461 7037	0.0188 0099	0.0213 0099	50

Rate 1/3%	B Compound Amount	C Present Value	D Amount of Annuity	E Present Value of Annuity	F Sinking Fund	G Amortization	
n	$(1 + i)^n$	$(1 + i)^{-n}$	$S_{\overline{n}|i}$	$A_{\overline{n}|i}$	$1/S_{\overline{n}|i}$	$1/A_{\overline{n}|i}$	n
1	1.0033 3333	0.9966 7774	1.0000 0000	0.9966 7744	1.0000 0000	1.0033 3333	1
2	1.0066 7778	0.9933 6652	2.0033 3333	1.9900 4426	0.4991 6805	0.5025 0139	2
3	1.0100 3337	0.9900 6630	3.0100 1111	2.9801 1056	0.3322 2469	0.3355 5802	3
4	1.0134 0015	0.9867 7704	4.0200 4448	3.9668 8760	0.2487 5347	0.2520 8680	4
5	1.0167 7815	0.9834 9871	5.0334 4463	4.9503 8631	0.1986 7110	0.2020 0444	5
6	1.0201 6741	0.9802 3127	6.0502 2278	5.9306 1759	0.1652 8317	0.1686 1650	6
7	1.0235 6797	0.9769 7469	7.0703 9019	6.9075 9228	0.1414 3491	0.1447 6824	7
8	1.0269 7986	0.9737 2893	8.0939 5816	7.8813 2121	0.1235 4895	0.1268 8228	8
9	1.0304 0313	0.9704 9395	9.1209 3802	8.8518 1516	0.1096 3785	0.1129 7118	9
10	1.0338 3780	0.9672 6972	10.1513 4114	9.8190 8487	0.0985 0915	0.1018 4248	10
11	1.0372 8393	0.9640 5620	11.1851 7895	10.7831 4107	0.0894 0402	0.0927 3736	11
12	1.0407 4154	0.9608 5335	12.2224 6288	11.7439 9442	0.0818 1657	0.0851 4990	12
13	1.0442 1068	0.9576 6115	13.2632 0442	12.7016 5557	0.0753 9656	0.0787 2989	13
14	1.0476 9138	0.9544 7955	14.3074 1510	13.6561 3512	0.0698 9383	0.0732 2716	14
15	1.0511 8369	0.9513 0852	15.3551 0648	14.6074 4364	0.0651 2491	0.0684 5825	15
16	1.0546 8763	0.9481 4803	16.4062 9017	15.5555 9167	0.0609 5223	0.0642 8557	16
17	1.0582 0326	0.9449 9803	17.4609 7781	16.5005 8970	0.0572 7056	0.0606 0389	17
18	1.0617 3060	0.9418 5851	18.5191 8107	17.4424 4821	0.0539 9807	0.0573 3140	18
19	1.0652 6971	0.9387 2941	19.5809 1167	18.3811 7762	0.0510 7015	0.0544 0348	19
20	1.0688 2060	0.9356 1071	20.6461 8137	19.3167 8832	0.0484 3511	0.0517 6844	20
21	1.0723 8334	0.9325 0236	21.7150 0198	20.2492 9069	0.0460 5111	0.0493 8445	21
22	1.0759 5795	0.9294 0435	22.7873 8532	21.1786 9504	0.0438 8393	0.0472 1726	22
23	1.0795 4448	0.9263 1663	23.8633 4327	22.1050 1167	0.0419 0528	0.0452 3861	23
24	1.0831 4296	0.9232 3916	24.9428 8775	23.0282 5083	0.0400 9159	0.0434 2492	24
25	1.0867 5344	0.9201 7192	26.0260 3071	23.9484 2275	0.0384 2307	0.0417 5640	25
26	1.0903 7595	0.9171 1487	27.1127 8414	24.8655 3763	0.0368 8297	0.0402 1630	26
27	1.0940 1053	0.9140 6798	28.2031 6009	25.7796 0561	0.0354 5702	0.0387 9035	27
28	1.0976 5724	0.9110 3121	29.2971 7062	26.6906 3682	0.0341 3299	0.0374 6632	28
29	1.1013 1609	0.9080 0453	30.3948 2786	27.5986 4135	0.0329 0033	0.0362 3367	29
30	1.1049 8715	0.9049 8790	31.4961 4395	28.5036 2925	0.0317 4992	0.0350 8325	30
31	1.1086 7044	0.9019 8130	32.6011 3110	29.4056 1055	0.0306 7378	0.0340 0712	31
32	1.1123 6601	0.8989 8468	33.7098 0154	30.3045 9523	0.0296 6496	0.0329 9830	32
33	1.1160 7389	0.8959 9802	34.8221 6754	31.2005 9325	0.0287 1734	0.0320 5067	33
34	1.1197 9414	0.8930 2128	35.9382 4143	32.0936 1454	0.0278 2551	0.0311 5885	34
35	1.1235 2679	0.8900 5444	37.0580 3557	32.9836 6898	0.0269 8470	0.0303 1803	35
36	1.1272 7187	0.8870 9745	38.1815 6236	33.8707 6642	0.0261 9065	0.0295 2399	36
37	1.1310 2945	0.8841 5028	39.3088 3423	34.7549 1670	0.0254 3957	0.0287 7291	37
38	1.1347 9955	0.8812 1290	40.4398 6368	35.6361 2960	0.0247 2808	0.0280 6141	38
39	1.1385 8221	0.8782 8528	41.5746 6322	36.5144 1488	0.0240 5311	0.0273 8644	39
40	1.1423 7748	0.8753 6739	42.7132 4543	37.3897 8228	0.0234 1194	0.0267 4527	40
41	1.1461 8541	0.8724 5920	43.8556 2292	38.2622 4147	0.0228 0209	0.0261 3543	41
42	1.1500 0603	0.8695 6066	45.0018 0833	39.1318 0213	0.0222 2133	0.0255 5466	42
43	1.1538 3938	0.8666 7175	46.1518 1436	39.9984 7389	0.0216 6762	0.0250 0095	43
44	1.1576 8551	0.8637 9245	47.3056 5374	40.8622 6633	0.0211 3912	0.0244 7246	44
45	1.1615 4446	0.8609 2270	48.4633 3925	41.7231 8903	0.0206 3415	0.0239 6749	45
46	1.1654 1628	0.8580 6249	49.6248 8371	42.5812 5153	0.0201 5118	0.0234 8451	46
47	1.1693 0100	0.8552 1179	50.7902 9999	43.4364 6332	0.0196 8880	0.0230 2213	47
48	1.1731 9867	0.8523 7055	51.9596 0099	44.2888 3387	0.0192 4572	0.0225 7905	48
49	1.1771 0933	0.8495 3876	53.1327 9966	45.1383 7263	0.0188 2077	0.0221 5410	49
50	1.1810 3303	0.8467 1637	54.3099 0899	45.9850 8900	0.0184 1285	0.0217 4618	50

Rate ½%	B Compound Amount	C Present Value	D Amount of Annuity	E Present Value of Annuity	F Sinking Fund	G Amortization	
n	$(1 + i)^n$	$(1 + i)^{-n}$	$S_{\overline{n}|i}$	$A_{\overline{n}|i}$	$1/S_{\overline{n}|i}$	$1/A_{\overline{n}|i}$	n
1	1.0050 0000	0.9950 2488	1.0000 0000	0.9950 2488	1.0000 0000	1.0050 0000	1
2	1.0100 2500	0.9900 7450	2.0050 0000	1.9850 9938	0.4987 5312	0.5037 5312	2
3	1.0150 7513	0.9851 4876	3.0150 2500	2.9702 4814	0.3316 7221	0.3366 7221	3
4	1.0201 5050	0.9802 4752	4.0301 0013	3.9504 9566	0.2481 3279	0.2531 3279	4
5	1.0252 5125	0.9753 7067	5.0502 5063	4.9258 6633	0.1980 0998	0.2030 0997	5
6	1.0303 7751	0.9705 1808	6.0755 0188	5.8963 8441	0.1645 9546	0.1695 9546	6
7	1.0355 2940	0.9656 8963	7.1058 7939	6.8620 7404	0.1407 2854	0.1457 2854	7
8	1.0407 0704	0.9608 8520	8.1414 0879	7.8229 5924	0.1228 2886	0.1278 2886	8
9	1.0459 1058	0.9561 0468	9.1821 1583	8.7790 6392	0.1089 0736	0.1139 0736	9
10	1.0511 4013	0.9513 4794	10.2280 2641	9.7304 1186	0.0977 7057	0.1027 7057	10
11	1.0563 9583	0.9466 1487	11.2791 6654	10.6770 2673	0.0886 5903	0.0936 5903	11
12	1.0616 7781	0.9419 0534	12.3355 6237	11.6189 3207	0.0810 6643	0.0860 6643	12
13	1.0669 8620	0.9372 1924	13.3972 4018	12.5561 5131	0.0746 4224	0.0796 4224	13
14	1.0723 2113	0.9325 5646	14.4642 2639	13.4887 0777	0.0691 3609	0.0741 3609	14
15	1.0776 8274	0.9279 1688	15.5365 4752	14.4166 2465	0.0643 6436	0.0693 6436	15
16	1.0830 7115	0.9233 0037	16.6142 3026	15.3399 2502	0.0601 8937	0.0651 8937	16
17	1.0884 8651	0.9187 0684	17.6973 0141	16.2586 3186	0.0565 0579	0.0615 0579	17
18	1.0939 2894	0.9141 3616	18.7857 8791	17.1727 6802	0.0532 3173	0.0582 3173	18
19	1.0993 9858	0.9095 8822	19.8797 1685	18.0823 5624	0.0503 0253	0.0553 0253	19
20	1.1048 9558	0.9050 6290	20.9791 1544	18.9874 1915	0.0476 6645	0.0526 6645	20
21	1.1104 2006	0.9005 6010	22.0840 1101	19.8879 7925	0.0452 8163	0.0502 8163	21
22	1.1159 7216	0.8960 7971	23.1944 3107	20.7840 5896	0.0431 1380	0.0481 1380	22
23	1.1215 5202	0.8916 2160	24.3104 0322	21.6756 8055	0.0411 3465	0.0461 3465	23
24	1.1271 5978	0.8871 8567	25.4319 5524	22.5628 6622	0.0393 2061	0.0443 2061	24
25	1.1327 9558	0.8827 7181	26.5591 1502	23.4456 3803	0.0376 5186	0.0426 5186	25
26	1.1384 5955	0.8783 7991	27.6919 1059	24.3240 1794	0.0361 1163	0.0411 1163	26
27	1.1441 5185	0.8740 0986	28.8303 7015	25.1980 2780	0.0346 8565	0.0396 8565	27
28	1.1498 7261	0.8696 6155	29.9745 2200	26.0676 8936	0.0333 6167	0.0383 6167	28
29	1.1556 2197	0.8653 3488	31.1243 9461	26.9330 2423	0.0321 2914	0.0371 2914	29
30	1.1614 0008	0.8610 2973	32.2800 1658	27.7940 5397	0.0309 7892	0.0359 7892	30
31	1.1672 0708	0.8567 4600	33.4414 1666	28.6507 9997	0.0299 0304	0.0349 0304	31
32	1.1730 4312	0.8524 8358	34.6086 2375	29.5032 8355	0.0288 9453	0.0338 9453	32
33	1.1789 0833	0.8482 4237	35.7816 6686	30.3515 2592	0.0279 4727	0.0329 4727	33
34	1.1848 0288	0.8440 2226	36.9605 7520	31.1955 4818	0.0270 5586	0.0320 5586	34
35	1.1907 2689	0.8398 2314	38.1453 7807	32.0353 7132	0.0262 1550	0.0312 1550	35
36	1.1966 8052	0.8356 4492	39.3361 0496	32.8710 1624	0.0254 2194	0.0304 2194	36
37	1.2026 6393	0.8314 8748	40.5327 8549	33.7025 0372	0.0246 7139	0.0296 7139	37
38	1.2086 7725	0.8273 5073	41.7354 4942	34.5298 5445	0.0239 6045	0.0289 6045	38
39	1.2147 2063	0.8232 3455	42.9441 2666	35.3530 8900	0.0232 8607	0.0282 8607	39
40	1.2207 9424	0.8191 3886	44.1588 4730	36.1722 2786	0.0226 4552	0.0276 4552	40
41	1.2268 9821	0.8150 6354	45.3796 4153	36.9872 9141	0.0220 3631	0.0270 3631	41
42	1.2330 3270	0.8110 0850	46.6065 3974	37.7982 9991	0.0214 5622	0.0264 5622	42
43	1.2391 9786	0.8069 7363	47.8395 7244	38.6052 7354	0.0209 0320	0.0259 0320	43
44	1.2453 9385	0.8029 5884	49.0787 7030	39.4082 3238	0.0203 7541	0.0253 7541	44
45	1.2516 2082	0.7989 6402	50.3241 6415	40.2071 9640	0.0198 7117	0.0248 7117	45
46	1.2578 7892	0.7949 8907	51.5757 8497	41.0021 8547	0.0193 8894	0.0243 8894	46
47	1.2641 6832	0.7910 3390	52.8336 6390	41.7932 1937	0.0189 2733	0.0239 2733	47
48	1.2704 8916	0.7870 9841	54.0978 3222	42.5803 1778	0.0184 8503	0.0234 8503	48
49	1.2768 4161	0.7831 8250	55.3683 2138	43.3635 0028	0.0180 6087	0.0230 6087	49
50	1.2832 2581	0.7792 8607	56.6451 6299	44.1427 8635	0.0176 5376	0.0226 5376	50

Rate ¾%	B Compound Amount	C Present Value	D Amount of Annuity	E Present Value of Annuity	F Sinking Fund	G Amortization	
n	$(1+i)^n$	$(1+i)^{-n}$	$S_{\overline{n}|i}$	$A_{\overline{n}|i}$	$1/S_{\overline{n}|i}$	$1/A_{\overline{n}|i}$	n
1	1.0075 0000	0.9925 5583	1.0000 0000	0.9925 5583	1.0000 0000	1.0075 0000	1
2	1.0150 5625	0.9851 6708	2.0075 0000	1.9777 2291	0.4981 3201	0.5056 3201	2
3	1.0226 6917	0.9778 3333	3.0225 5625	2.9555 5624	0.3308 4579	0.3383 4579	3
4	1.0303 3919	0.9705 5417	4.0452 2542	3.9261 1041	0.2472 0501	0.2547 0501	4
5	1.0380 6673	0.9633 2920	5.0755 6461	4.8894 3961	0.1970 2242	0.2045 2242	5
6	1.0458 5224	0.9561 5802	6.1136 3135	5.8455 9763	0.1635 6891	0.1710 6891	6
7	1.0536 9613	0.9490 4022	7.1594 8358	6.7946 3785	0.1396 7488	0.1471 7488	7
8	1.0615 9885	0.9419 7540	8.2131 7971	7.7366 1325	0.1217 5552	0.1292 5552	8
9	1.0695 6084	0.9349 6318	9.2747 7856	8.6715 7642	0.1078 1929	0.1153 1929	9
10	1.0775 8255	0.9280 0315	10.3443 3940	9.5995 7958	0.0966 7123	0.1041 7123	10
11	1.0856 6441	0.9210 9494	11.4219 2194	10.5206 7452	0.0875 5094	0.0950 5094	11
12	1.0938 0690	0.9142 3815	12.5075 8636	11.4349 1267	0.0799 5148	0.0874 5148	12
13	1.1020 1045	0.9074 3241	13.6013 9325	12.3423 4508	0.0735 2188	0.0810 2188	13
14	1.1102 7553	0.9006 7733	14.7034 0370	13.2430 2242	0.0680 1146	0.0755 1146	14
15	1.1186 0259	0.8939 7254	15.8136 7923	14.1369 9495	0.0632 3639	0.0707 3639	15
16	1.1269 9211	0.8873 1766	16.9322 8183	15.0243 1261	0.0590 5879	0.0665 5879	16
17	1.1354 4455	0.8807 1231	18.0592 7394	15.9050 2492	0.0553 7321	0.0628 7321	17
18	1.1439 6039	0.8741 5614	19.1947 1849	16.7791 8107	0.0520 9766	0.0595 9766	18
19	1.1525 4009	0.8676 4878	20.3386 7888	17.6468 2984	0.0491 6740	0.0566 6740	19
20	1.1611 8414	0.8611 8985	21.4912 1897	18.5080 1969	0.0465 3063	0.0540 3063	20
21	1.1698 9302	0.8547 7901	22.6524 0312	19.3627 9870	0.0441 4543	0.0516 4543	21
22	1.1786 6722	0.8484 1589	23.8222 9614	20.2112 1459	0.0419 7748	0.0494 7748	22
23	1.1875 0723	0.8421 0014	25.0009 6336	21.0533 1473	0.0399 9846	0.0474 9846	23
24	1.1964 1353	0.8358 3140	26.1884 7059	21.8891 4614	0.0381 8474	0.0456 8474	24
25	1.2053 8663	0.8296 0933	27.3848 8412	22.7187 5547	0.0365 1650	0.0440 1650	25
26	1.2144 2703	0.8234 3358	28.5902 7075	23.5421 8905	0.0349 7693	0.0424 7693	26
27	1.2235 3523	0.8173 0380	29.8046 9778	24.3594 9286	0.0335 5176	0.0410 5176	27
28	1.2327 1175	0.8112 1966	31.0282 3301	25.1707 1251	0.0322 2871	0.0397 2871	28
29	1.2419 5709	0.8051 8080	32.2609 4476	25.9758 9331	0.0309 9723	0.0384 9723	29
30	1.2512 7176	0.7991 8690	33.5029 0184	26.7750 8021	0.0298 4816	0.0373 4816	30
31	1.2606 5630	0.7932 3762	34.7541 7361	27.5683 1783	0.0287 7352	0.0362 7352	31
32	1.2701 1122	0.7873 3262	36.0148 2991	28.3556 5045	0.0277 6634	0.0352 6634	32
33	1.2796 3706	0.7814 7158	37.2849 4113	29.1371 2203	0.0268 2048	0.0343 2048	33
34	1.2892 3434	0.7756 5418	38.5645 7819	29.9127 7621	0.0259 3053	0.0334 3053	34
35	1.2989 0359	0.7698 8008	39.8538 1253	30.6826 5629	0.0250 9170	0.0325 9170	35
36	1.3086 4537	0.7641 4896	41.1527 1612	31.4468 0525	0.0242 9973	0.0317 9973	36
37	1.3184 6021	0.7584 6051	42.4613 6149	32.2052 6576	0.0235 5082	0.0310 5082	37
38	1.3283 4866	0.7528 1440	43.7798 2170	32.9580 8016	0.0228 4157	0.0303 4157	38
39	1.3383 1128	0.7472 1032	45.1081 7037	33.7052 9048	0.0221 6893	0.0296 6893	39
40	1.3483 4861	0.7416 4796	46.4464 8164	34.4469 3844	0.0215 3016	0.0290 3016	40
41	1.3584 6123	0.7361 2701	47.7948 3026	35.1830 6545	0.0209 2277	0.0284 2276	41
42	1.3686 4969	0.7306 4716	49.1532 9148	35.9137 1260	0.0203 4452	0.0278 4452	42
43	1.3789 1456	0.7252 0809	50.5219 4117	36.6389 2070	0.0197 9338	0.0272 9338	43
44	1.3892 5642	0.7198 0952	51.9008 5573	37.3587 3022	0.0192 6751	0.0267 6751	44
45	1.3996 7584	0.7144 5114	53.2901 1215	38.0731 8136	0.0187 6521	0.0262 6521	45
46	1.4101 7341	0.7091 3264	54.6897 8799	38.7823 1401	0.0182 8495	0.0257 8495	46
47	1.4207 4971	0.7038 5374	56.0999 6140	39.4861 6775	0.0178 2532	0.0253 2532	47
48	1.4314 0533	0.6986 1414	57.5207 1111	40.1847 8189	0.0173 8504	0.0248 8504	48
49	1.4421 4087	0.6934 1353	58.9521 1644	40.8781 9542	0.0169 6292	0.0244 6292	49
50	1.4529 5693	0.6882 5165	60.3942 5732	41.5664 4707	0.0165 5787	0.0240 5787	50

Rate 1%	B Compound Amount	C Present Value	D Amount of Annuity	E Present Value of Annuity	F Sinking Fund	G Amortization	
n	$(1 + i)^n$	$(1 + i)^{-n}$	$S_{\overline{n}|i}$	$A_{\overline{n}|i}$	$1/S_{\overline{n}|i}$	$1/A_{\overline{n}|i}$	n
1	1.0100 0000	0.9900 9901	1.0000 0000	0.9900 9901	1.0000 0000	1.0100 0000	1
2	1.0201 0000	0.9802 9605	2.0100 0000	1.9703 9506	0.4975 1244	0.5075 1244	2
3	1.0303 0100	0.9705 9015	3.0301 0000	2.9409 8521	0.3300 2211	0.3400 2211	3
4	1.0406 0401	0.9609 8034	4.0604 0100	3.9019 6555	0.2462 8109	0.2562 8109	4
5	1.0510 1005	0.9514 6569	5.1010 0501	4.8534 3124	0.1960 3980	0.2060 3980	5
6	1.0615 2015	0.9420 4524	6.1520 1506	5.7954 7647	0.1625 4837	0.1725 4837	6
7	1.0721 3535	0.9327 1805	7.2135 3521	6.7281 9453	0.1386 2828	0.1486 2828	7
8	1.0828 5671	0.9234 8322	8.2856 7056	7.6516 7775	0.1206 9029	0.1306 9029	8
9	1.0936 8527	0.9143 3982	9.3685 2727	8.5660 1758	0.1067 4036	0.1167 4036	9
10	1.1046 2213	0.9052 8695	10.4622 1254	9.4713 0453	0.0955 8208	0.1055 8208	10
11	1.1156 6835	0.8963 2372	11.5668 3467	10.3676 2825	0.0864 5408	0.0964 5408	11
12	1.1268 2503	0.8874 4923	12.6825 0301	11.2550 7747	0.0788 4879	0.0888 4879	12
13	1.1380 9328	0.8786 6260	13.8093 2804	12.1337 4007	0.0724 1482	0.0824 1482	13
14	1.1494 7421	0.8699 6297	14.9474 2132	13.0037 0304	0.0669 0117	0.0769 0117	14
15	1.1609 6896	0.8613 4947	16.0968 9554	13.8650 5252	0.0621 2378	0.0721 2378	15
16	1.1725 7864	0.8528 2126	17.2578 6449	14.7178 7378	C 0579 4460	0.0679 4460	16
17	1.1843 0443	0.8443 7749	18.4304 4314	15.5622 5127	0.0542 5806	0.0642 5806	17
18	1.1961 4748	0.8360 1731	19.6147 4757	16.3982 6858	0.0509 8205	0.0609 8205	18
19	1.2081 0895	0.8277 3992	20.8108 9504	17.2260 0850	0.0480 5175	0.0580 5175	19
20	1.2201 9004	0.8195 4447	22.0190 0399	18.0455 5297	0.0454 1531	0.0554 1531	20
21	1.2323 9194	0.8114 3017	23.2391 9403	18.8569 8313	0.0430 3075	0.0530 3075	21
22	1.2447 1586	0.8033 9621	24.4715 8598	19.6603 7934	0.0408 6372	0.0508 6372	22
23	1.2571 6302	0.7954 4179	25.7163 0183	20.4558 2113	0.0388 8584	0.0488 8584	23
24	1.2697 3465	0.7875 6613	26.9734 6485	21.2433 8726	0.0370 7347	0.0470 7347	24
25	1.2824 3200	0.7797 6844	28.2431 9950	22.0231 5570	0.0354 0675	0.0454 0675	25
26	1.2952 5631	0.7720 4796	29.5256 3150	22.7952 0366	0.0338 6888	0.0438 6888	26
27	1.3082 0888	0.7644 0392	30.8208 8781	23.5596 0759	0.0324 4553	0.0424 4553	27
28	1.3212 9097	0.7568 3557	32.1290 9669	24.3164 4316	0.0311 2444	0.0411 2444	28
29	1.3345 0388	0.7493 4215	33.4503 8766	25.0657 8530	0.0298 9502	0.0398 9502	29
30	1.3478 4892	0.7419 2292	34.7848 9153	25.8077 0822	0.0287 4811	0.0387 4811	30
31	1.3613 2740	0.7345 7715	36.1327 4045	26.5422 8537	0.0276 7573	0.0376 7573	31
32	1.3749 4068	0.7273 0411	37.4940 6785	27.2695 8947	0.0266 7089	0.0366 7089	32
33	1.3886 9009	0.7201 0307	38.8690 0853	27.9896 9255	0.0257 2744	0.0357 2744	33
34	1.4025 7699	0.7129 7334	40.2576 9862	28.7026 6589	0.0248 3997	0.0348 3997	34
35	1.4166 0276	0.7059 1420	41.6602 7560	29.4085 8009	0.0240 0368	0.0340 0368	35
36	1.4307 6878	0.6989 2495	43.0768 7836	30.1075 0504	0.0232 1431	0.0332 1431	36
37	1.4450 7647	0.6920 0490	44.5076 4714	30.7995 0994	0.0224 6805	0.0324 6805	37
38	1.4595 2724	0.6851 5337	45.9527 2361	31.4846 6330	0.0217 6150	0.0317 6150	38
39	1.4741 2251	0.6783 6967	47.4122 5085	32.1630 3298	0.0210 9160	0.0310 9160	39
40	1.4888 6373	0.6716 5314	48.8863 7336	32.8346 8611	0.0204 5560	0.0304 5560	40
41	1.5037 5237	0.6650 0311	50.3752 3709	33.4996 8922	0.0198 5102	0.0298 5102	41
42	1.5187 8989	0.6584 1892	51.8789 8946	34.1581 0814	0.0192 7563	0.0292 7563	42
43	1.5339 7779	0.6518 9992	53.3977 7936	34.8100 0806	0.0187 2737	0.0287 2737	43
44	1.5493 1757	0.6454 4546	54.9317 5715	35.4554 5352	0.0182 0441	0.0282 0441	44
45	1.5648 1075	0.6390 5492	56.4810 7472	36.0945 0844	0.0177 0505	0.0277 0505	45
46	1.5804 5885	0.6327 2764	58.0458 8547	36.7272 3608	0.0172 2775	0.0272 2775	46
47	1.5962 6344	0.6264 6301	59.6263 4432	37.3536 9909	0.0167 7111	0.0267 7111	47
48	1.6122 2608	0.6202 6041	61.2226 0777	37.9739 5949	0.0163 3384	0.0263 3384	48
49	1.6283 4834	0.6141 1921	62.8348 3385	38.5880 7871	0.0159 1474	0.0259 1474	49
50	1.6446 3182	0.6080 3882	64.4631 8218	39.1961 1753	0.0155 1273	0.0255 1273	50

Rate 1¼%	B Compound Amount	C Present Value	D Amount of Annuity	E Present Value of Annuity	F Sinking Fund	G Amortization	
n	$(1+i)^n$	$(1+i)^{-n}$	$S_{\overline{n}|i}$	$A_{\overline{n}|i}$	$1/A_{\overline{n}|i}$	$1/S_{\overline{n}|i}$	n
1	1.0125 0000	0.9876 5432	1.0000 0000	0.9876 5432	1.0000 0000	1.0125 0000	1
2	1.0251 5625	0.9754 6106	2.0125 0000	1.9631 1538	0.4968 9441	0.5093 9441	2
3	1.0379 7070	0.9634 1833	3.0376 5625	2.9265 3371	0.3292 0117	0.3417 0117	3
4	1.0509 4534	0.9515 2428	4.0756 2695	3.8780 5798	0.2453 6102	0.2578 6102	4
5	1.0640 8215	0.9397 7706	5.1265 7229	4.8178 3504	0.1950 6211	0.2075 6211	5
6	1.0773 8318	0.9281 7488	6.1906 5444	5.7460 0992	0.1615 3381	0.1740 3381	6
7	1.0908 5047	0.9167 1593	7.2680 3762	6.6627 2585	0.1375 8872	0.1500 8872	7
8	1.1044 8610	0.9053 9845	8.3588 8809	7.5681 2429	0.1196 3314	0.1321 3314	8
9	1.1182 9218	0.8942 2069	9.4633 7420	8.4623 4498	0.1056 7055	0.1181 7055	9
10	1.1322 7083	0.8831 8093	10.5816 6637	9.3455 2591	0.0945 0307	0.1070 0307	10
11	1.1464 2422	0.8722 7746	11.7139 3720	10.2178 0337	0.0853 6839	0.9078 6839	11
12	1.1607 5452	0.8615 0860	12.8603 6142	11.0793 1197	0.0777 5831	0.0902 5831	12
13	1.1752 6395	0.8508 7269	14.0211 1594	11.9301 8466	0.0713 2100	0.0838 2100	13
14	1.1899 5475	0.8403 6809	15.1963 7988	12.7705 5275	0.0658 0515	0.0783 0515	14
15	1.2048 2918	0.8299 9318	16.3863 3463	13.6005 4592	0.0610 2646	0.0735 2646	15
16	1.2198 8955	0.8197 4635	17.5911 6382	14.4202 9227	0.0568 4672	0.0693 4672	16
17	1.2351 3817	0.8096 2602	18.8110 5336	15.2299 1829	0.0531 6023	0.0656 6023	17
18	1.2505 7739	0.7996 3064	20.0461 9153	16.0295 4893	0.0498 8479	0.0623 8479	18
19	1.2662 0961	0.7897 5866	21.2967 6893	16.8193 0759	0.0469 5548	0.0594 5548	19
20	1.2820 3723	0.7800 0855	22.5629 7854	17.5993 1613	0.0443 2039	0.0568 2039	20
21	1.2980 6270	0.7703 7881	23.8450 1577	18.3696 9495	0.0419 3749	0.0544 3749	21
22	1.3142 8848	0.7608 6796	25.1430 7847	19.1305 6291	0.0397 7238	0.0522 7238	22
23	1.3307 1709	0.7514 7453	26.4573 6695	19.8820 3744	0.0377 9666	0.0502 9666	23
24	1.3473 5105	0.7421 9707	27.7880 8403	20.6242 3451	0.0359 8665	0.0484 8665	24
25	1.3641 9294	0.7330 3414	29.1354 3508	21.3572 6865	0.0343 2247	0.0468 2247	25
26	1.3812 4535	0.7239 8434	30.4996 2802	22.0812 5299	0.0327 8729	0.0452 8729	26
27	1.3985 1092	0.7150 4626	31.8808 7337	22.7962 9925	0.0313 6677	0.0438 6677	27
28	1.4159 9230	0.7062 1853	33.2793 8429	23.5025 1778	0.0300 4863	0.0425 4863	28
29	1.4336 9221	0.6974 9978	34.6953 7659	24.2000 1756	0.0288 2228	0.0413 2228	29
30	1.4516 1336	0.6888 8867	36.1290 6880	24.8889 0623	0.0276 7854	0.0401 7854	30
31	1.4697 5853	0.6803 8387	37.5806 8216	25.5692 9010	0.0266 0942	0.0391 0942	31
32	1.4881 3051	0.6719 8407	39.0504 4069	26.2412 7418	0.0256 0791	0.0381 0791	32
33	1.5067 3214	0.6636 8797	40.5385 7120	26.9049 6215	0.0246 6787	0.0371 6786	33
34	1.5255 6629	0.6554 9429	42.0453 0334	27.5604 5644	0.0237 8387	0.0362 8387	34
35	1.5446 3587	0.6474 0177	43.5708 6963	28.2078 5822	0.0229 5111	0.0354 5111	35
36	1.5639 4382	0.6394 0916	45.1155 0550	28.8472 6737	0.0221 6533	0.0346 6533	36
37	1.5834 9312	0.6315 1522	46.6794 4932	29.4787 8259	0.0214 2270	0.0339 2270	37
38	1.6032 8678	0.6237 1873	48.2629 4243	30.1025 0133	0.0207 1983	0.0332 1983	38
39	1.6233 2787	0.6160 1850	49.8662 2921	30.7185 1983	0.0200 5365	0.0325 5365	39
40	1.6436 1946	0.6084 1334	51.4895 5708	31.3269 3316	0.0194 2141	0.0319 2141	40
41	1.6641 6471	0.6009 0206	53.1331 7654	31.9278 3522	0.0188 2063	0.0313 2063	41
42	1.6849 6677	0.5934 8352	54.7973 4125	32.5213 1874	0.0182 4906	0.0307 4906	42
43	1.7060 2885	0.5861 5656	56.4823 0801	33.1074 7530	0.0177 0466	0.0302 0466	43
44	1.7273 5421	0.5789 2006	58.1883 3687	33.6863 9536	0.0171 8557	0.0296 8557	44
45	1.7489 4614	0.5717 7290	59.9156 9108	34.2581 6825	0.0166 9012	0.0291 9012	45
46	1.7708 0797	0.5647 1397	61.6646 3721	34.8228 8222	0.0162 1675	0.0287 1675	46
47	1.7929 4306	0.5577 4219	63.4354 4518	35.3806 2442	0.0157 6406	0.0282 6406	47
48	1.8153 5485	0.5508 5649	65.2283 8824	35.9314 8091	0.0153 3075	0.0278 3075	48
49	1.8380 4679	0.5440 5579	67.0437 4310	36.4755 3670	0.0149 1564	0.0274 1563	49
50	1.8610 2237	0.5373 3905	68.8817 8989	37.0128 7575	0.0145 1763	0.0270 1763	50

Rate 1½%	B Compound Amount	C Present Value	D Amount of Annuity	E Present Value of Annuity	F Sinking Fund	G Amortization	
n	$(1 + i)^n$	$(1 + i)^{-n}$	$S_{\overline{n}|i}$	$A_{\overline{n}|i}$	$1/S_{\overline{n}|i}$	$1/A_{\overline{n}|i}$	n
1	1.0150 0000	0.9852 2167	1.0000 0000	0.9852 2167	1.0000 0000	1.0150 0000	1
2	1.0302 2500	0.9706 6175	2.0150 0000	1.9558 8342	0.4962 7792	0.5112 7792	2
3	1.0456 7838	0.9563 1699	3.0452 2500	2.9122 0042	0.3283 8296	0.3433 8296	3
4	1.0613 6355	0.9421 8423	4.0909 0338	3.8543 8465	0.2444 4479	0.2594 4479	4
5	1.0772 8400	0.9282 6033	5.1522 6693	4.7826 4497	0.1940 8932	0.2090 8932	5
6	1.0934 4326	0.9145 4219	6.2295 5093	5.6971 8717	0.1605 2521	0.1755 2521	6
7	1.1098 4491	0.9010 2679	7.3229 9419	6.5982 1396	0.1365 5616	0.1515 5616	7
8	1.1264 9259	0.8877 1112	8.4328 3911	7.4859 2508	0.1185 8402	0.1335 8402	8
9	1.1433 8998	0.8745 9224	9.5593 3169	8.3605 1732	0.1046 0982	0.1196 0982	9
10	1.1605 4083	0.8616 6723	10.7027 2167	9.2221 8455	0.0934 3418	0.1084 3418	10
11	1.1779 4894	0.8489 3323	11.8632 6249	10.0711 1779	0.0842 9384	0.0992 9384	11
12	1.1956 1817	0.8363 8742	13.0412 1143	10.9075 0521	0.0766 7999	0.0916 7999	12
13	1.2135 5244	0.8240 2702	14.2368 2960	11.7315 3222	0.0702 4036	0.0852 4036	13
14	1.2317 5573	0.8118 4928	15.4503 8205	12.5433 8150	0.0647 2332	0.0797 2332	14
15	1.2502 3207	0.7998 5150	16.6821 3778	13.3432 3301	0.0599 4436	0.0749 4436	15
16	1.2689 8555	0.7880 3104	17.9323 6984	14.1312 6405	0.0557 6508	0.0707 6508	16
17	1.2880 2033	0.7763 8526	19.2013 5539	14.9076 4931	0.0520 7966	0.0670 7966	17
18	1.3073 4064	0.7649 1159	20.4893 7572	15.6725 6089	0.0488 0578	0.0638 0578	18
19	1.3269 5075	0.7536 0747	21.7967 1636	16.4261 6837	0.0458 7847	0.0608 7847	19
20	1.3468 5501	0.7424 7042	23.1236 6710	17.1686 3879	0.0432 4574	0.0582 4574	20
21	1.3670 5783	0.7314 9795	24.4705 2211	17.9001 3673	0.0408 6550	0.0558 6550	21
22	1.3875 6370	0.7206 8763	25.8375 7994	18.6208 2437	0.0387 0332	0.0537 0332	22
23	1.4083 7715	0.7100 3708	27.2251 4364	19.3308 6145	0.0367 3075	0.0517 3075	23
24	1.4295 0281	0.6995 4392	28.6335 2080	20.0304 0537	0.0349 2410	0.0499 2410	24
25	1.4509 4535	0.6892 0583	30.0630 2361	20.7196 1120	0.0332 6345	0.0482 6345	25
26	1.4727 0953	0.6790 2052	31.5139 6896	21.3986 3172	0.0317 3196	0.0467 3196	26
27	1.4948 0018	0.6689 8574	32.9866 7850	22.0676 1746	0.0303 1527	0.0453 1527	27
28	1.5172 2218	0.6590 9925	34.4814 7867	22.7267 1671	0.0290 0108	0.0440 0108	28
29	1.5399 8051	0.6493 5887	35.9987 0085	23.3760 7558	0.0277 7878	0.0427 7878	29
30	1.5630 8022	0.6397 6243	37.5386 8137	24.0158 3801	0.0266 3919	0.0416 3919	30
31	1.5865 2642	0.6303 0781	39.1017 6159	24.6461 4582	0.0255 7430	0.0405 7430	31
32	1.6103 2432	0.6209 9292	40.6882 8801	25.2671 3874	0.0245 7710	0.0395 7710	32
33	1.6344 7918	0.6118 1568	42.2986 1233	25.8789 5442	0.0236 4144	0.0386 4144	33
34	1.6589 9637	0.6027 7407	43.9330 9152	26.4817 2849	0.0227 6189	0.0377 6189	34
35	1.6838 8132	0.5938 6608	45.5920 8789	27.0755 9458	0.0219 3363	0.0369 3363	35
36	1.7091 3954	0.5850 8974	47.2759 6921	27.6606 8431	0.0211 5240	0.0361 5240	36
37	1.7347 7663	0.5764 4309	48.9851 0874	28.2371 2740	0.0204 1437	0.0354 1437	37
38	1.7607 9828	0.5679 2423	50.7198 8538	28.8050 5163	0.0197 1613	0.0347 1613	38
39	1.7872 1025	0.5595 3126	52.4806 8366	29.3645 8288	0.0190 5463	0.0340 5463	39
40	1.8140 1841	0.5512 6232	54.2678 9391	29.9158 4520	0.0184 2710	0.0334 2710	40
41	1.8412 2868	0.5431 1559	56.0819 1232	30.4589 6079	0.0178 3106	0.0328 3106	41
42	1.8688 4712	0.5350 8925	57.9231 4100	30.9940 5004	0.0172 6426	0.0322 6426	42
43	1.8968 7982	0.5271 8153	59.7919 8812	31.5212 3157	0.0167 2465	0.0317 2465	43
44	1.9253 3302	0.5193 9067	61.6888 6794	32.0406 2223	0.0162 1038	0.0312 1038	44
45	1.9542 1301	0.5117 1494	63.6142 0096	32.5523 3718	0.0157 1976	0.0307 1976	45
46	1.9835 2621	0.5041 5265	65.5684 1398	33.0564 8983	0.0152 5125	0.0302 5125	46
47	2.0132 7910	0.4967 0212	67.5519 4018	33.5531 9195	0.0148 0342	0.0298 0342	47
48	2.0434 7829	0.4893 6170	69.5652 1929	34.0425 5365	0.0143 7500	0.0293 7500	48
49	2.0741 3046	0.4821 2975	71.6086 9758	34.5246 8339	0.0139 6478	0.0289 6478	49
50	2.1052 4242	0.4750 0468	73.6828 2804	34.9996 8807	0.0135 7168	0.0285 7168	50

Rate 1¾%	B Compound Amount	C Present Value	D Amount of Annuity	E Present Value of Annuity	F Sinking Fund	G Amortization	
n	$(1+i)^n$	$(1+i)^{-n}$	$S_{\overline{n}|i}$	$A_{\overline{n}|i}$	$1/S_{\overline{n}|i}$	$1/A_{\overline{n}|i}$	n
1	1.0175 0000	0.9828 0098	1.0000 0000	0.9828 0098	1.0000 0000	1.0175 0000	1
2	1.0353 0625	0.9658 9777	2.0175 0000	1.9486 9875	0.4956 6295	0.5131 6295	2
3	1.0534 2411	0.9492 8528	3.0528 0625	2.8979 8403	0.3275 6746	0.3450 6746	3
4	1.0718 5903	0.9329 5851	4.1062 3036	3.8309 4254	0.2435 3237	0.2610 3237	4
5	1.0906 1656	0.9169 1254	5.1780 8939	4.7478 5508	0.1931 2142	0.2106 2142	5
6	1.1097 0235	0.9011 4254	6.2687 0596	5.6489 9762	0.1595 2256	0.1770 2256	6
7	1.1291 2215	0.8856 4378	7.3784 0831	6.5346 4139	0.1355 3059	0.1530 3059	7
8	1.1488 8178	0.8704 1157	8.5075 3045	7.4050 5297	0.1175 4292	0.1350 4292	8
9	1.1689 8721	0.8554 4135	9.6564 1224	8.2604 9432	0.1035 5813	0.1210 5813	9
10	1.1894 4449	0.8407 2860	10.8253 9945	9.1012 2291	0.0923 7534	0.1098 7534	10
11	1.2102 5977	0.8262 6889	12.0148 4394	9.9274 9181	0.0832 3038	0.1007 3038	11
12	1.2314 3931	0.8120 5788	13.2251 0371	10.7395 4969	0.0756 1378	0.0931 1377	12
13	1.2529 8950	0.7980 9128	14.4565 4303	11.5376 4097	0.0691 7283	0.0866 7283	13
14	1.2749 1682	0.7843 6490	15.7095 3253	12.3220 0587	0.0636 5562	0.0811 5562	14
15	1.2972 2786	0.7708 7459	16.9844 4935	13.0928 8046	0.0588 7739	0.0763 7739	15
16	1.3199 2935	0.7576 1631	18.2816 7721	13.8504 9677	0.0546 9958	0.0721 9958	16
17	1.3430 2811	0.7445 8605	19.6016 0656	14.5950 8282	0.0510 1623	0.0685 1623	17
18	1.3665 3111	0.7317 7990	20.9446 3468	15.3268 6272	0.0477 4492	0.0652 4492	18
19	1.3904 4540	0.7191 9401	22.3111 6578	16.0460 5673	0.0448 2061	0.0623 2061	19
20	1.4147 7820	0.7068 2458	23.7016 1119	16.7528 8130	0.0421 9122	0.0596 9122	20
21	1.4395 3681	0.6946 6789	25.1163 8938	17.4475 4919	0.0398 1464	0.0573 1464	21
22	1.4647 2871	0.6827 2028	26.5559 2620	18.1302 6948	0.0376 5638	0.0551 5638	22
23	1.4903 6146	0.6709 7817	28.0206 5490	18.8012 4764	0.0356 8796	0.0531 8796	23
24	1.5164 4279	0.6594 3800	29.5110 1637	19.4606 8565	0.0338 8565	0.0513 8565	24
25	1.5429 8054	0.6480 9632	31.0274 5915	20.1087 8196	0.0322 2952	0.0497 2952	25
26	1.5699 8269	0.6369 4970	32.5704 3969	20.7457 3166	0.0307 0269	0.0482 0269	26
27	1.5974 5739	0.6259 9479	34.1404 2238	21.3717 2644	0.0292 9079	0.0467 9079	27
28	1.6254 1290	0.6152 2829	35.7378 7977	21.9869 5474	0.0279 8151	0.0454 8151	28
29	1.6538 5762	0.6046 4697	37.3632 9267	22.5916 0171	0.0267 6424	0.0442 6424	29
30	1.6828 0013	0.5942 4764	39.0171 5029	23.1858 4934	0.0256 2975	0.0431 2975	30
31	1.7122 4913	0.5840 2716	40.6999 5042	23.7698 7650	0.0245 7005	0.0420 7005	31
32	1.7422 1349	0.5739 8247	42.4121 9955	24.3438 5897	0.0235 7812	0.0410 7812	32
33	1.7727 0223	0.5641 1053	44.1544 1305	24.9079 6951	0.0226 4779	0.0401 4779	33
34	1.8037 2452	0.5544 0839	45.9271 1527	25.4623 7789	0.0217 7363	0.0392 7363	34
35	1.8352 8970	0.5448 7311	47.7308 3979	26.0072 5100	0.0209 5082	0.0384 5082	35
36	1.8674 0727	0.5355 0183	49.5661 2949	26.5427 5283	0.0201 7507	0.0376 7507	36
37	1.9000 8689	0.5262 9172	51.4335 3675	27.0690 4455	0.0194 4257	0.0369 4257	37
38	1.9333 3841	0.5172 4002	53.3336 2365	27.5862 8457	0.0187 4990	0.0362 4990	38
39	1.9671 7184	0.5083 4400	55.2669 6206	28.0946 2857	0.0180 9399	0.0355 9399	39
40	2.0015 9734	0.4996 0098	57.2341 3390	28.5942 2955	0.0174 7209	0.0349 7209	40
41	2.0366 2530	0.4910 0834	59.2357 3124	29.0852 3789	0.0168 8170	0.0343 8170	41
42	2.0722 6624	0.4825 6348	61.2723 5654	29.5678 0135	0.0163 2057	0.0338 2057	42
43	2.1085 3090	0.4742 6386	63.3446 2278	30.0420 6522	0.0157 8666	0.0332 8666	43
44	2.1454 3019	0.4661 0699	65.4531 5367	30.5081 7221	0.0152 7810	0.0327 7810	44
45	2.1829 7522	0.4580 9040	67.5985 8386	30.9662 6261	0.0147 9321	0.0322 9321	45
46	2.2211 7728	0.4502 1170	69.7815 5908	31.4164 7431	0.0143 3043	0.0318 3043	46
47	2.2600 4789	0.4424 6850	72.0027 3637	31.8589 4281	0.0138 8836	0.0313 8836	47
48	2.2995 9872	0.4348 5848	74.2627 8425	32.2938 0129	0.0134 6570	0.0309 6569	48
49	2.3398 4170	0.4273 7934	76.5623 8298	32.7211 8063	0.0130 6124	0.0305 6124	49
50	2.3807 8893	0.4200 2883	78.9022 2468	33.1412 0946	0.0126 7391	0.0301 7391	50

Rate 2%	B Compound Amount	C Present Value	D Amount of Annuity	E Present Value of Annuity	F Sinking Fund	G Amortization	
n	$(1 + i)^n$	$(1 + i)^{-n}$	$S_{\overline{n}|i}$	$A_{\overline{n}|i}$	$1/S_{\overline{n}|i}$	$1/A_{\overline{n}|i}$	n
1	1.0200 0000	0.9803 9216	1.0000 0000	0.9803 9216	1.0000 0000	1.0200 0000	1
2	1.0404 0000	0.9611 6878	2.0200 0000	1.9415 6094	0.4950 4951	0.5150 4950	2
3	1.0612 0800	0.9423 2233	3.0604 0000	2.8838 8327	0.3267 5467	0.3467 5467	3
4	1.0824 3216	0.9238 4543	4.1216 0800	3.8077 2870	0.2426 2375	0.2626 2375	4
5	1.1040 8080	0.9057 3081	5.2040 4016	4.7134 5951	0.1921 5839	0.2121 5839	5
6	1.1261 6242	0.8879 7138	6.3081 2096	5.6014 3089	0.1585 2581	0.1785 2581	6
7	1.1486 8567	0.8705 6018	7.4342 8338	6.4719 9107	0.1345 1196	0.1545 1196	7
8	1.1716 5938	0.8534 9037	8.5829 6905	7.3254 8144	0.1165 0980	0.1365 0980	8
9	1.1950 9257	0.8367 5527	9.7546 2843	8.1622 3671	0.1025 1544	0.1225 1544	9
10	1.2189 9442	0.8203 4830	10.9497 2100	8.9825 8501	0.0913 2653	0.1113 2653	10
11	1.2433 7431	0.8042 6304	12.1687 1542	9.7868 4805	0.0821 7794	0.1021 7794	11
12	1.2682 4179	0.7884 9318	13.4120 8973	10.5753 4122	0.0745 5960	0.0945 5960	12
13	1.2936 0663	0.7730 3253	14.6803 3152	11.3483 7375	0.0681 1835	0.0881 1835	13
14	1.3194 7876	0.7578 7502	15.9739 3815	12.1062 4877	0.0626 0197	0.0826 0197	14
15	1.3458 6834	0.7430 1473	17.2934 1692	12.8492 6350	0.0578 2547	0.0778 2547	15
16	1.3727 8571	0.7284 4581	18.6392 8525	13.5777 0931	0.0536 5013	0.0736 5013	16
17	1.4002 4142	0.7141 6256	20.0120 7096	14.2918 7188	0.0499 6984	0.0699 6984	17
18	1.4282 4625	0.7001 5937	21.4123 1238	14.9920 3125	0.0467 0210	0.0667 0210	18
19	1.4568 1117	0.6864 3076	22.8405 5863	15.6784 6201	0.0437 8177	0.0637 8177	19
20	1.4859 4740	0.6729 7133	24.2973 6980	16.3514 3334	0.0411 5672	0.0611 5672	20
21	1.5156 6634	0.6597 7582	25.7833 1719	17.0112 0916	0.0387 8477	0.0587 8477	21
22	1.5459 7967	0.6468 3904	27.2989 8354	17.6580 4820	0.0366 3140	0.0566 3140	22
23	1.5768 9926	0.6341 5592	28.8449 6321	18.2922 0412	0.0346 6810	0.0546 6810	23
24	1.6084 3725	0.6217 2149	30.4218 6247	18.9139 2560	0.0328 7110	0.0528 7110	24
25	1.6406 0599	0.6095 3087	32.0302 9972	19.5234 5647	0.0312 2044	0.0512 2044	25
26	1.6734 1811	0.5975 7928	33.6709 0572	20.1210 3576	0.0296 9923	0.0496 9923	26
27	1.7068 8648	0.5858 6204	35.3443 2383	20.7068 9780	0.0282 9309	0.0482 9309	27
28	1.7410 2421	0.5743 7455	37.0512 1031	21.2812 7236	0.0269 8967	0.0469 8967	28
29	1.7758 4469	0.5631 1231	38.7922 3451	21.8443 8466	0.0257 7836	0.0457 7836	29
30	1.8113 6158	0.5520 7089	40.5680 7921	22.3964 5555	0.0246 4992	0.0446 4992	30
31	1.8475 8882	0.5412 4597	42.3794 4079	22.9377 0152	0.0235 9635	0.0435 9635	31
32	1.8845 4059	0.5306 3330	44.2270 2961	23.4683 3482	0.0226 1061	0.0426 1061	32
33	1.9222 3140	0.5202 2873	46.1115 7020	23.9885 6355	0.0216 8653	0.0416 8653	33
34	1.9606 7603	0.5100 2817	48.0338 0160	24.4985 9172	0.0208 1867	0.0408 1867	34
35	1.9998 8955	0.5000 2761	49.9944 7763	24.9986 1933	0.0200 0221	0.0400 0221	35
36	2.0398 8734	0.4902 2315	51.9943 6719	25.4888 4248	0.0192 3285	0.0392 3285	36
37	2.0806 8509	0.4806 1093	54.0342 5453	25.9694 5341	0.0185 0678	0.0385 0678	37
38	2.1222 9879	0.4711 8719	56.1149 3962	26.4406 4060	0.0178 2057	0.0378 2057	38
39	2.1647 4477	0.4619 4822	58.2372 3841	26.9025 8883	0.0171 7114	0.0371 7114	39
40	2.2080 3966	0.4528 9042	60.4019 8318	27.3554 7924	0.0165 5575	0.0365 5575	40
41	2.2522 0046	0.4440 1021	62.6100 2284	27.7994 8945	0.0159 7188	0.0359 7188	41
42	2.2972 4447	0.4353 0413	64.8622 2330	28.2347 9358	0.0154 1729	0.0354 1729	42
43	2.3431 8936	0.4267 6875	67.1594 6777	28.6615 6233	0.0148 8993	0.0348 8993	43
44	2.3900 5314	0.4184 0074	69.5026 5712	29.0799 6307	0.0143 8794	0.0343 8794	44
45	2.4378 5421	0.4101 9680	71.8927 1027	29.4901 5987	0.0139 0962	0.0339 0962	45
46	2.4866 1129	0.4021 5373	74.3305 6447	29.8923 1360	0.0134 5342	0.0334 5342	46
47	2.5363 4352	0.3942 6836	76.8171 7576	30.2865 8196	0.0130 1792	0.0330 1792	47
48	2.5870 7039	0.3865 3761	79.3535 1927	30.6731 1957	0.0126 0184	0.0326 0184	48
49	2.6388 1179	0.3789 5844	81.9405 8966	31.0520 7801	0.0122 0396	0.0322 0396	49
50	2.6915 8803	0.3715 2788	84.5794 0145	31.4236 0589	0.0118 2321	0.0318 2321	50

Rate 2¼%	B Compound Amount	C Present Value	D Amount of Annuity	E Present Value of Annuity	F Sinking Fund	G Amortization	
n	$(1 + i)^n$	$(1 + i)^{-n}$	$S_{\overline{n}|i}$	$A_{\overline{n}|i}$	$1/S_{\overline{n}|i}$	$1/A_{\overline{n}|i}$	n
1	1.0225 0000	0.9779 9511	1.0000 0000	0.9779 9511	1.0000 0000	1.0225 0000	1
2	1.0455 0625	0.9564 7444	2.0225 0000	1.9344 6955	0.4944 3758	0.5169 3758	2
3	1.0690 3014	0.9354 2732	3.0680 0625	2.8698 9687	0.3259 4458	0.3484 4458	3
4	1.0930 8332	0.9148 4335	4.1370 3639	3.7847 4021	0.2417 1893	0.2642 1893	4
5	1.1176 7769	0.8947 1232	5.2301 1971	4.6794 5253	0.1912 0021	0.2137 0021	5
6	1.1428 2544	0.8750 2427	6.3477 9740	5.5544 7680	0.1575 3496	0.1800 3496	6
7	1.1685 3901	0.8557 6946	7.4906 2284	6.4102 4626	0.1335 0025	0.1560 0025	7
8	1.1948 3114	0.8369 3835	8.6591 6186	7.2471 8461	0.1154 8462	0.1379 8462	8
9	1.2217 1484	0.8185 2161	9.8539 9300	8.0657 0622	0.1014 8170	0.1239 8170	9
10	1.2492 0343	0.8005 1013	11.0757 0784	8.8662 1635	0.0902 8768	0.1127 8768	10
11	1.2773 1050	0.7828 9499	12.3249 1127	9.6491 1134	0.0811 3649	0.1036 3649	11
12	1.3060 4999	0.7656 6748	13.6022 2177	10.4147 7882	0.0735 1740	0.0960 1740	12
13	1.3354 3611	0.7488 1905	14.9082 7176	11.1635 9787	0.0670 7686	0.0895 7686	13
14	1.3654 8343	0.7323 4137	16.2437 0788	11.8959 3924	0.0615 6230	0.0840 6230	14
15	1.3962 0680	0.7162 2628	17.6091 9130	12.6121 6551	0.0567 8853	0.0792 8852	15
16	1.4276 2146	0.7004 6580	19.0053 9811	13.3126 3131	0.0526 1663	0.0751 1663	16
17	1.4597 4294	0.6850 5212	20.4330 1957	13.9976 8343	0.0489 4039	0.0714 4039	17
18	1.4925 8716	0.6699 7763	21.8927 6251	14.6676 6106	0.0456 7720	0.0681 7720	18
19	1.5261 7037	0.6552 3484	23.3853 4966	15.3228 9590	0.0427 6182	0.0652 6182	19
20	1.5605 0920	0.6408 1647	24.9115 2003	15.9637 1237	0.0401 4207	0.0626 4207	20
21	1.5956 2066	0.6267 1538	26.4720 2923	16.5904 2775	0.0377 7572	0.0602 7572	21
22	1.6315 2212	0.6129 2457	28.0676 4989	17.2033 5232	0.0356 2821	0.0581 2821	22
23	1.6682 3137	0.5994 3724	29.6991 7201	17.8027 8955	0.0336 7097	0.0561 7097	23
24	1.7057 6658	0.5862 4668	31.3674 0338	18.3890 3624	0.0318 8023	0.0543 8023	24
25	1.7441 4632	0.5733 4639	33.0731 6996	18.9623 8263	0.0302 3599	0.0527 3599	25
26	1.7833 8962	0.5607 2997	34.8173 1628	19.5231 1260	0.0287 2134	0.0512 2134	26
27	1.8235 1588	0.5483 9117	36.6007 0590	20.0715 0376	0.0273 2188	0.0498 2188	27
28	1.8645 4499	0.5363 2388	38.4242 2178	20.6078 2764	0.0260 2525	0.0485 2525	28
29	1.9064 9725	0.5245 2213	40.2887 6677	21.1323 4877	0.0248 2081	0.0473 2081	29
30	1.9493 9344	0.5129 8008	42.1952 6402	21.6453 2985	0.0236 9934	0.0461 9934	30
31	1.9932 5479	0.5016 9201	44.1446 5746	22.1470 2186	0.0226 5280	0.0451 5280	31
32	2.0381 0303	0.4906 5233	46.1379 1226	22.6376 7419	0.0216 7415	0.0441 7415	32
33	2.0839 6034	0.4798 5558	48.1760 1528	23.1175 2977	0.0207 5722	0.0432 5722	33
34	2.1308 4945	0.4692 9641	50.2599 7563	23.5868 2618	0.0198 9655	0.0423 9655	34
35	2.1787 9356	0.4589 6960	52.3908 2508	24.0457 9577	0.0190 8731	0.0415 8731	35
36	2.2278 1642	0.4488 7002	54.5696 1864	24.4946 6579	0.0183 2522	0.0408 2522	36
37	2.2779 4229	0.4389 9268	56.7974 3506	24.9336 5848	0.0176 0643	0.0401 0643	37
38	2.3291 9599	0.4293 3270	59.0753 7735	25.3629 9118	0.0169 2753	0.0394 2753	38
39	2.3816 0290	0.4198 8528	61.4045 7334	25.7828 7646	0.0162 8543	0.0387 8543	39
40	2.4351 8897	0.4106 4575	63.7861 7624	26.1935 2221	0.0156 7738	0.0381 7738	40
41	2.4899 8072	0.4016 0954	66.2213 6521	26.5951 3174	0.0151 0087	0.0376 0087	41
42	2.5460 0528	0.3927 7216	68.7113 4592	26.9879 0390	0.0145 5364	0.0370 5364	42
43	2.6032 9040	0.3841 2925	71.2573 5121	27.3720 3316	0.0140 3364	0.0365 3364	43
44	2.6618 6444	0.3756 7653	73.8606 4161	27.7477 0969	0.0135 3901	0.0360 3901	44
45	2.7217 5639	0.3674 0981	76.5225 0605	28.1151 1950	0.0130 6805	0.0355 6805	45
46	2.7829 9590	0.3593 2500	79.2442 6243	28.4744 4450	0.0126 1921	0.0351 1921	46
47	2.8456 1331	0.3514 1809	82.0272 5834	28.8258 6259	0.0121 9107	0.0346 9107	47
48	2.9096 3961	0.3436 8518	84.8728 7165	29.1695 4777	0.0117 8233	0.0342 8233	48
49	2.9751 0650	0.3361 2242	87.7825 1126	29.5056 7019	0.0113 9179	0.0338 9179	49
50	3.0420 4640	0.3287 2608	90.7576 1776	29.8343 9627	0.0110 1836	0.0335 1836	50

Rate 2½%	B Compound Amount	C Present Value	D Amount of Annuity	E Present Value of Annuity	F Sinking Fund	G Amortization	
n	$(1 + i)^n$	$(1 + i)^{-n}$	$S_{\overline{n}\mid i}$	$A_{\overline{n}\mid i}$	$1/S_{\overline{n}\mid i}$	$1/A_{\overline{n}\mid i}$	n
1	1.0250 0000	0.9756 0976	1.0000 0000	0.9756 0976	1.0000 0000	1.0250 0000	1
2	1.0506 2500	0.9518 1440	2.0250 0000	1.9274 2415	0.4938 2716	0.5188 2716	2
3	1.0768 9063	0.9285 9941	3.0756 2500	2.8560 2356	0.3251 3717	0.3501 3717	3
4	1.1038 1289	0.9059 5064	4.1525 1563	3.7619 7421	0.2408 1788	0.2658 1788	4
5	1.1314 0821	0.8838 5429	5.2563 2852	4.6458 2850	0.1902 4686	0.2152 4686	5
6	1.1596 9342	0.8622 9687	6.3877 3673	5.5081 2536	0.1565 4997	0.1815 4997	6
7	1.1886 8575	0.8412 6524	7.5474 3015	6.3493 9060	0.1324 9543	0.1574 9543	7
8	1.2184 0290	0.8207 4657	8.7361 1590	7.1701 3717	0.1144 6735	0.1394 6735	8
9	1.2488 6297	0.8007 2836	9.9545 1880	7.9708 6553	0.1004 5689	0.1254 5689	9
10	1.2800 8454	0.7811 9840	11.2033 8177	8.7520 6393	0.0892 5876	0.1142 5876	10
11	1.3120 8666	0.7621 4478	12.4834 6631	9.5142 0871	0.0801 0596	0.1051 0596	11
12	1.3448 8882	0.7435 5589	13.7955 5297	10.2577 6460	0.0724 8713	0.0974 8713	12
13	1.3785 1104	0.7254 2038	15.1404 4179	10.9831 8497	0.0660 4827	0.0910 4827	13
14	1.4129 7382	0.7077 2720	16.5189 5284	11.6909 1217	0.0605 3652	0.0855 3652	14
15	1.4482 9817	0.6904 6556	17.9319 2666	12.3813 7773	0.0557 6646	0.0807 6646	15
16	1.4845 0562	0.6736 2493	19.3802 2483	13.0550 0266	0.0515 9899	0.0765 9899	16
17	1.5216 1826	0.6571 9506	20.8647 3045	13.7121 9772	0.0479 2777	0.0729 2777	17
18	1.5596 5872	0.6411 6591	22.3863 4871	14.3533 6363	0.0446 7008	0.0696 7008	18
19	1.5986 5019	0.6255 2772	23.9460 0743	14.9788 9134	0.0417 6062	0.0667 6062	19
20	1.6386 1644	0.6102 7094	25.5446 5761	15.5891 6229	0.0391 4713	0.0641 4713	20
21	1.6795 8185	0.5953 8629	27.1832 7405	16.1845 4857	0.0367 8733	0.0617 8733	21
22	1.7215 7140	0.5808 6467	28.8628 5590	16.7654 1324	0.0346 4661	0.0596 4661	22
23	1.7646 1068	0.5666 9724	30.5844 2730	17.3321 1048	0.0326 9638	0.0576 9638	23
24	1.8087 2595	0.5528 7535	32.3490 3798	17.8849 8583	0.0309 1282	0.0559 1282	24
25	1.8539 4410	0.5393 9059	34.1577 6393	18.4243 7642	0.0292 7592	0.0542 7592	25
26	1.9002 9270	0.5262 3472	36.0117 0803	18.9506 1114	0.0277 6875	0.0527 6875	26
27	1.9478 0002	0.5133 9973	37.9120 0073	19.4640 1087	0.0263 7687	0.0513 7687	27
28	1.9964 9502	0.5008 7778	39.8598 0075	19.9648 8866	0.0250 8793	0.0500 8793	28
29	2.0464 0739	0.4886 6125	41.8562 9577	20.4535 4991	0.0238 9127	0.0488 9127	29
30	2.0975 6758	0.4767 4269	43.9027 0316	20.9302 9259	0.0227 7764	0.0477 7764	30
31	2.1500 0677	0.4651 1481	46.0002 7074	21.3954 0741	0.0217 3900	0.0467 3900	31
32	2.2037 5694	0.4537 7055	48.1502 7751	21.8491 7796	0.0207 6831	0.0457 6831	32
33	2.2588 5086	0.4427 0298	50.3540 3445	22.2918 8094	0.0198 5938	0.0448 5938	33
34	2.3153 2213	0.4319 0534	52.6128 8531	22.7237 8628	0.0190 0675	0.0440 0675	34
35	2.3732 0519	0.4213 7107	54.9282 0744	23.1451 5734	0.0182 0558	0.0432 0558	35
36	2.4325 3532	0.4110 9372	57.3014 1263	23.5562 5107	0.0174 5158	0.0424 5158	36
37	2.4933 4870	0.4010 6705	59.7339 4794	23.9573 1812	0.0167 4090	0.0417 4090	37
38	2.5556 8242	0.3912 8492	62.2272 9664	24.3486 0304	0.0160 7012	0.0410 7012	38
39	2.6195 7448	0.3817 4139	64.7829 7906	24.7303 4443	0.0154 3615	0.0404 3615	39
40	2.6850 6384	0.3724 3062	67.4025 5354	25.1027 7505	0.0148 3623	0.0398 3623	40
41	2.7521 9043	0.3633 4695	70.0876 1737	25.4661 2200	0.0142 6786	0.0392 6786	41
42	2.8209 9520	0.3544 8483	72.8398 0781	25.8206 0683	0.0137 2876	0.0387 2876	42
43	2.8915 2008	0.3458 3886	75.6608 0300	26.1664 4569	0.0132 1688	0.0382 1688	43
44	2.9638 0808	0.3374 0376	78.5523 2308	26.5038 4945	0.0127 3037	0.0377 3037	44
45	3.0379 0328	0.3291 7440	81.5161 3116	26.8330 2386	0.0122 6751	0.0372 6751	45
46	3.1138 5086	0.3211 4576	84.5540 3443	27.1541 6962	0.0118 2676	0.0368 2676	46
47	3.1916 9713	0.3133 1294	87.6678 8530	27.4674 8255	0.0114 0669	0.0364 0669	47
48	3.2714 8956	0.3056 7116	90.8595 8243	27.7731 5371	0.0110 0599	0.0360 0599	48
49	3.3532 7680	0.2982 1576	94.1310 7199	28.0713 6947	0.0106 2348	0.0356 2348	49
50	3.4371 0872	0.2909 4221	97.4843 4879	28.3623 1168	0.0102 5806	0.0352 5806	50

Rate 2¾%	B Compound Amount	C Present Value	D Amount of Annuity	E Present Value of Annuity	F Sinking Fund	G Amortization	
n	$(1 + i)^n$	$(1 + i)^{-n}$	$S_{\overline{n}\rvert i}$	$A_{\overline{n}\rvert i}$	$1/S_{\overline{n}\rvert i}$	$1/A_{\overline{n}\rvert i}$	n
1	1.0275 0000	0.9732 3601	1.0000 0000	0.9732 3601	1.0000 0000	1.0275 0000	1
2	1.0557 5625	0.9471 8833	2.0275 0000	1.9204 2434	0.4932 1825	0.5207 1825	2
3	1.0847 8955	0.9218 3779	3.0832 5625	2.8422 6213	0.3243 3243	0.3518 3243	3
4	1.1146 2126	0.8971 6573	4.1680 4580	3.7394 2787	0.2399 2059	0.2674 2059	4
5	1.1452 7334	0.8731 5400	5.2826 6706	4.6125 8186	0.1892 9832	0.2167 9832	5
6	1.1767 6836	0.8497 8491	6.4279 4040	5.4623 6678	0.1555 7083	0.1830 7083	6
7	1.2091 2949	0.8270 4128	7.6047 0876	6.2894 0806	0.1314 9748	0.1589 9747	7
8	1.2423 8055	0.8049 0635	8.8138 3825	7.0943 1441	0.1134 5795	0.1409 5795	8
9	1.2765 4602	0.7833 6385	10.0562 1880	7.8776 7826	0.0994 4095	0.1269 4095	9
10	1.3116 5103	0.7623 9791	11.3327 6482	8.6400 7616	0.0882 3972	0.1157 3972	10
11	1.3477 2144	0.7419 9310	12.6444 1585	9.3820 6926	0.0790 8629	0.1065 8629	11
12	1.3847 8378	0.7221 3440	13.9921 3729	10.1042 0366	0.0714 6871	0.0989 6871	12
13	1.4228 6533	0.7028 0720	15.3769 2107	10.8070 1086	0.0650 3252	0.0925 3252	13
14	1.4619 9413	0.6839 9728	16.7997 8639	11.4910 0814	0.0595 2457	0.0870 2457	14
15	1.5021 9896	0.6656 9078	18.2617 8052	12.1566 9892	0.0547 5917	0.0822 5917	15
16	1.5435 0944	0.6478 7424	19.7639 7948	12.8045 7315	0.0505 9710	0.0780 9710	16
17	1.5859 5595	0.6305 3454	21.3074 8892	13.4351 0769	0.0469 3186	0.0744 3186	17
18	1.6295 6973	0.6136 5892	22.8934 4487	14.0487 6661	0.0436 8063	0.0711 8063	18
19	1.6743 8290	0.5972 3496	24.5230 1460	14.6460 0157	0.0407 7802	0.0682 7802	19
20	1.7204 2843	0.5812 5057	26.1973 9750	15.2272 5213	0.0381 7173	0.0656 7173	20
21	1.7677 4021	0.5656 9398	27.9178 2593	15.7929 4612	0.0358 1941	0.0633 1941	21
22	1.8163 5307	0.5505 5375	29.6855 6615	16.3434 9987	0.0336 8640	0.0611 8640	22
23	1.8663 0278	0.5358 1874	31.5019 1921	16.8793 1861	0.0317 4410	0.0592 4410	23
24	1.9176 2610	0.5214 7809	33.3682 2199	17.4007 9670	0.0299 6863	0.0574 6863	24
25	1.9703 6082	0.5075 2126	35.2858 4810	17.9083 1795	0.0283 3997	0.0558 3997	25
26	2.0245 4575	0.4939 3796	37.2562 0892	18.4022 5592	0.0268 4116	0.0543 4116	26
27	2.0802 2075	0.4807 1821	39.2807 5467	18.8829 7413	0.0254 5776	0.0529 5776	27
28	2.1374 2682	0.4678 5227	41.3609 7542	19.3508 2640	0.0241 7738	0.0516 7738	28
29	2.1962 0606	0.4553 3068	43.4984 0224	19.8061 5708	0.0229 8935	0.0504 8935	29
30	2.2566 0173	0.4431 4421	45.6946 0830	20.2493 0130	0.0218 8442	0.0493 8442	30
31	2.3186 5828	0.4312 8391	47.9512 1003	20.6805 8520	0.0208 5453	0.0483 5453	31
32	2.3824 2138	0.4197 4103	50.2698 6831	21.1003 2623	0.0198 9263	0.0473 9263	32
33	2.4479 3797	0.4085 0708	52.6522 8969	21.5088 3332	0.0189 9253	0.0464 9253	33
34	2.5152 5626	0.3975 7380	55.1002 2765	21.9064 0712	0.0181 4875	0.0456 4875	34
35	2.5844 2581	0.3869 3314	57.6154 8391	22.2933 4026	0.0173 5645	0.0448 5645	35
36	2.6554 9752	0.3765 7727	60.1999 0972	22.6699 1753	0.0166 1132	0.0441 1132	36
37	2.7285 2370	0.3664 9856	62.8554 0724	23.0364 1609	0.0159 0953	0.0434 0953	37
38	2.8035 5810	0.3566 8959	65.5839 3094	23.3931 0568	0.0152 4764	0.0427 4764	38
39	2.8806 5595	0.3471 4316	68.3874 8904	23.7402 4884	0.0146 2256	0.0421 2256	39
40	2.9598 7399	0.3378 5222	71.2681 4499	24.0781 0106	0.0140 3151	0.0415 3151	40
41	3.0412 7052	0.3288 0995	74.2280 1898	24.4069 1101	0.0134 7200	0.0409 7200	41
42	3.1249 0546	0.3200 0968	77.2692 8950	24.7269 2069	0.0129 4175	0.0404 4175	42
43	3.2108 4036	0.3114 4495	80.3941 9496	25.0383 6563	0.0124 3871	0.0399 3871	43
44	3.2991 3847	0.3031 0944	83.6050 3532	25.3414 7507	0.0119 6100	0.0394 6100	44
45	3.3898 6478	0.2949 9702	86.9041 7379	25.6364 7209	0.0115 0693	0.0390 0693	45
46	3.4830 8606	0.2871 0172	90.2940 3857	25.9235 7381	0.0110 7493	0.0385 7493	46
47	3.5788 7093	0.2794 1773	93.7771 2463	26.2029 9154	0.0106 6358	0.0381 6358	47
48	3.6772 8988	0.2719 3940	97.3559 9556	26.4749 3094	0.0102 7158	0.0377 7158	48
49	3.7784 1535	0.2646 6122	101.0332 8544	26.7395 9215	0.0098 9773	0.0373 9773	49
50	3.8823 2177	0.2575 7783	104.8117 0079	26.9971 6998	0.0095 4092	0.0370 4092	50

Rate 3%	B Compound Amount	C Present Value	D Amount of Annuity	E Present Value of Annuity	F Sinking Fund	G Amortization	
n	$(1 + i)^n$	$(1 + i)^{-n}$	$S_{\overline{n}|i}$	$A_{\overline{n}|i}$	$1/S_{\overline{n}|i}$	$1/A_{\overline{n}|i}$	n
1	1.0300 0000	0.9708 7379	1.0000 0000	0.9708 7379	1.0000 0000	1.0300 0000	1
2	1.0609 0000	0.9425 9591	2.0300 0000	1.9134 6970	0.4926 1084	0.5226 1084	2
3	1.0927 2700	0.9151 4166	3.0909 0000	2.8286 1135	0.3235 3036	0.3535 3036	3
4	1.1255 0881	0.8884 8705	4.1836 2700	3.7170 9840	0.2390 2705	0.2690 2705	4
5	1.1592 7407	0.8626 0878	5.3091 3581	4.5797 0719	0.1883 5457	0.2183 5457	5
6	1.1940 5230	0.8374 8426	6.4684 0988	5.4171 9144	0.1545 9750	0.1845 9750	6
7	1.2298 7387	0.8130 9151	7.6624 6218	6.2302 8296	0.1305 0635	0.1605 0635	7
8	1.2667 7008	0.7894 0923	8.8923 3605	7.0196 9219	0.1124 5639	0.1424 5639	8
9	1.3047 7318	0.7664 1673	10.1591 0613	7.7861 0892	0.0984 3386	0.1284 3386	9
10	1.3439 1638	0.7440 9391	11.4638 7931	8.5302 0284	0.0872 3051	0.1172 3051	10
11	1.3842 3387	0.7224 2128	12.8077 9569	9.2526 2411	0.0780 7745	0.1080 7745	11
12	1.4257 6089	0.7013 7988	14.1920 2956	9.9540 0399	0.0704 6209	0.1004 6209	12
13	1.4685 3371	0.6809 5134	15.6177 9045	10.6349 5533	0.0640 2954	0.0940 2954	13
14	1.5125 8972	0.6611 1781	17.0863 2416	11.2960 7314	0.0585 2634	0.0885 2634	14
15	1.5579 6742	0.6418 6195	18.5989 1389	11.9379 3509	0.0537 6658	0.0837 6658	15
16	1.6047 0644	0.6231 6694	20.1568 8130	12.5611 0203	0.0496 1085	0.0796 1085	16
17	1.6528 4763	0.6050 1645	21.7615 8774	13.1661 1847	0.0459 5253	0.0759 5253	17
18	1.7024 3306	0.5873 9461	23.4144 3537	13.7535 1308	0.0427 0870	0.0727 0870	18
19	1.7535 0605	0.5702 8603	25.1168 6844	14.3237 9911	0.0398 1388	0.0698 1388	19
20	1.8061 1123	0.5536 7575	26.8703 7449	14.8774 7486	0.0372 1571	0.0672 1571	20
21	1.8602 9457	0.5375 4928	28.6764 8572	15.4150 2414	0.0348 7178	0.0648 7178	21
22	1.9161 0341	0.5218 9250	30.5367 8030	15.9369 1664	0.0327 4739	0.0627 4739	22
23	1.9735 8651	0.5066 9175	32.4528 8370	16.4436 0839	0.0308 1390	0.0608 1390	23
24	2.0327 9411	0.4919 3374	34.4264 7022	16.9355 4212	0.0290 4742	0.0590 4742	24
25	2.0937 7793	0.4776 0557	36.4592 6432	17.4131 4769	0.0274 2787	0.0574 2787	25
26	2.1565 9127	0.4636 9473	38.5530 4225	17.8768 4242	0.0259 3829	0.0559 3829	26
27	2.2212 8901	0.4501 8906	40.7096 3352	18.3270 3147	0.0245 6421	0.0545 6421	27
28	2.2879 2768	0.4370 7675	42.9309 2252	18.7641 0823	0.0232 9323	0.0532 9323	28
29	2.3565 6551	0.4243 4636	45.2188 5020	19.1884 5459	0.0221 1467	0.0521 1467	29
30	2.4272 6247	0.4119 8676	47.5754 1571	19.6004 4135	0.0210 1926	0.0510 1926	30
31	2.5000 8035	0.3999 8715	50.0026 7818	20.0004 2849	0.0199 9893	0.0499 9893	31
32	2.5750 8276	0.3883 3703	52.5027 5852	20.3887 6553	0.0190 4662	0.0490 4662	32
33	2.6523 3524	0.3770 2625	55.0778 4128	20.7657 9178	0.0181 5612	0.0481 5612	33
34	2.7319 0530	0.3660 4490	57.7301 7652	21.1318 3668	0.0173 2196	0.0473 2196	34
35	2.8138 6245	0.3553 8340	60.4620 8181	21.4872 2007	0.0165 3929	0.0465 3929	35
36	2.8982 7833	0.3450 3243	63.2759 4427	21.8322 5250	0.0158 0379	0.0458 0379	36
37	2.9852 2668	0.3349 8294	66.1742 2259	22.1672 3544	0.0151 1162	0.0451 1162	37
38	3.0747 8348	0.3252 2615	69.1594 4927	22.4924 6159	0.0144 5934	0.0444 5934	38
39	3.1670 2698	0.3157 5355	72.2342 3275	22.8082 1513	0.0138 4385	0.0438 4385	39
40	3.2620 3779	0.3065 5684	75.4012 5973	23.1147 7197	0.0132 6238	0.0432 6238	40
41	3.3598 9893	0.2976 2800	78.6632 9753	23.4123 9997	0.0127 1241	0.0427 1241	41
42	3.4606 9589	0.2889 5922	82.0231 9645	23.7013 5920	0.0121 9167	0.0421 9167	42
43	3.5645 1677	0.2805 4294	85.4838 9234	23.9819 0213	0.0116 9811	0.0416 9811	43
44	3.6714 5227	0.2723 7178	89.0484 0911	24.2542 7392	0.0112 2985	0.0412 2985	44
45	3.7815 9584	0.2644 3862	92.7198 6139	24.5187 1254	0.0107 8518	0.0407 8518	45
46	3.8950 4372	0.2567 3653	96.5014 5723	24.7754 4907	0.0103 6254	0.0403 6254	46
47	4.0118 9503	0.2492 5876	100.3965 0095	25.0247 0783	0.0099 6051	0.0399 6051	47
48	4.1322 5188	0.2419 9880	104.4083 9598	25.2667 0664	0.0095 7777	0.0395 7777	48
49	4.2562 1944	0.2349 5029	108.5406 4785	25.5016 5693	0.0092 1314	0.0392 1314	49
50	4.3839 0602	0.2281 0708	112.7968 6729	25.7297 6401	0.0088 6549	0.0388 6549	50

Rate 3½%	B Compound Amount	C Present Value	D Amount of Annuity	E Present Value of Annuity	F Sinking Fund	G Amortization	
n	$(1+i)^n$	$(1+i)^{-n}$	$S_{\overline{n}|i}$	$A_{\overline{n}|i}$	$1/S_{\overline{n}|i}$	$1/A_{\overline{n}|i}$	n
1	1.0350 0000	0.9661 8357	1.0000 0000	0.9661 8357	1.0000 0000	1.0350 0000	1
2	1.0712 2500	0.9335 1070	2.0350 0000	1.8996 9428	0.4914 0049	0.5264 0049	2
3	1.1087 1788	0.9019 4271	3.1062 2500	2.8016 3698	0.3219 3418	0.3569 3418	3
4	1.1475 2300	0.8714 4223	4.2149 4288	3.6730 7921	0.2372 5114	0.2722 5114	4
5	1.1876 8631	0.8419 7317	5.3624 6588	4.5150 5238	0.1864 8137	0.2214 8137	5
6	1.2292 5533	0.8135 0064	6.5501 5218	5.3285 5302	0.1526 6821	0.1876 6821	6
7	1.2722 7926	0.7859 9096	7.7794 0751	6.1145 4398	0.1285 4449	0.1635 4449	7
8	1.3168 0904	0.7594 1156	9.0516 8677	6.8739 5554	0.1104 7665	0.1454 7665	8
9	1.3628 9735	0.7337 3097	10.3684 9581	7.6076 8651	0.0964 4601	0.1314 4601	9
10	1.4105 9876	0.7089 1881	11.7313 9316	8.3166 0532	0.0852 4137	0.1202 4137	10
11	1.4599 6972	0.6849 4571	13.1419 9192	9.0015 5104	0.0760 9197	0.1110 9197	11
12	1.5110 6866	0.6617 8330	14.6019 6164	9.6633 3433	0.0684 8395	0.1034 8395	12
13	1.5639 5606	0.6394 0415	16.1130 3030	10.3027 3849	0.0620 6157	0.0970 6157	13
14	1.6186 9452	0.6177 8179	17.6769 8636	10.9205 2028	0.0565 7073	0.0915 7073	14
15	1.6753 4883	0.5968 9062	19.2956 8088	11.5174 1090	0.0518 2507	0.0868 2507	15
16	1.7339 8604	0.5767 0591	20.9710 2971	12.0941 1681	0.0476 8483	0.0826 8483	16
17	1.7946 7555	0.5572 0378	22.7050 1575	12.6513 2059	0.0440 4313	0.0790 4313	17
18	1.8574 8920	0.5383 6114	24.4996 9130	13.1896 8173	0.0408 1684	0.0758 1684	18
19	1.9225 0132	0.5201 5569	26.3571 8050	13.7098 3742	0.0379 4033	0.0729 4033	19
20	1.9897 8886	0.5025 6588	28.2796 8181	14.2124 0330	0.0353 6108	0.0703 6108	20
21	2.0594 3147	0.4855 7090	30.2694 7068	14.6979 7420	0.0330 3659	0.0680 3659	21
22	2.1315 1158	0.4691 5063	32.3289 0215	15.1671 2484	0.0309 3207	0.0659 3207	22
23	2.2061 1448	0.4532 8563	34.4604 1373	15.6204 1047	0.0290 1865	0.0640 1880	23
24	2.2833 2849	0.4379 5713	36.6665 2821	16.0583 6760	0.0272 7283	0.0622 7283	24
25	2.3632 4498	0.4231 4699	38.9498 5669	16.4815 1459	0.0256 7404	0.0606 7404	25
26	2.4459 5856	0.4088 3767	41.3131 0168	16.8903 5226	0.0242 0540	0.0592 0540	26
27	2.5315 6711	0.3950 1224	43.7590 6024	17.2853 6451	0.0228 5241	0.0578 5241	27
28	2.6201 7196	0.3816 5434	46.2906 2734	17.6670 1885	0.0216 0265	0.0566 0265	28
29	2.7118 7798	0.3687 4815	48.9107 9930	18.0357 6700	0.0204 4538	0.0554 4538	29
30	2.8067 9370	0.3562 7841	51.6226 7728	18.3920 4541	0.0193 7133	0.0543 7133	30
31	2.9050 3148	0.3442 3035	54.4294 7098	18.7362 7576	0.0183 7240	0.0533 7240	31
32	3.0067 0759	0.3325 8971	57.3345 0247	19.0688 6547	0.0174 4150	0.0524 4150	32
33	3.1119 4235	0.3213 4271	60.3412 1005	19.3902 0818	0.0165 7242	0.0515 7242	33
34	3.2208 6033	0.3104 7605	63.4531 5240	19.7006 8423	0.0157 5966	0.0507 5966	34
35	3.3335 9045	0.2999 7686	66.6740 1274	20.0006 6110	0.0149 9835	0.0499 9835	35
36	3.4502 6611	0.2898 3272	70.0076 0318	20.2904 9381	0.0142 8416	0.0492 8416	36
37	3.5710 2543	0.2800 3161	73.4578 6930	20.5705 2542	0.0136 1325	0.0486 1325	37
38	3.6960 1132	0.2705 6194	77.0288 9472	20.8410 8736	0.0129 8214	0.0479 8214	38
39	3.8253 7171	0.2614 1250	80.7249 0604	21.1024 9987	0.0123 8775	0.0473 8775	39
40	3.9592 5972	0.2525 7247	84.5502 7775	21.3550 7234	0.0118 2728	0.0468 2728	40
41	4.0978 3381	0.2440 3137	88.5095 3747	21.5991 0371	0.0112 9822	0.0462 9822	41
42	4.2412 5799	0.2357 7910	92.6073 7128	21.8348 8281	0.0107 9828	0.0457 9828	42
43	4.3897 0202	0.2278 0590	96.8486 2928	22.0626 8870	0.0103 2539	0.0453 2539	43
44	4.5433 4160	0.2201 0231	101.2383 3130	22.2827 9102	0.0098 7768	0.0448 7768	44
45	4.7023 5855	0.2126 5924	105.7816 7290	22.4954 5026	0.0094 5343	0.0444 5343	45
46	4.8669 4110	0.2054 6787	110.4840 3145	22.7009 1813	0.0090 5108	0.0440 5108	46
47	5.0372 8404	0.1985 1968	115.3509 7255	22.8994 3780	0.0086 6919	0.0436 6919	47
48	5.2135 8898	0.1918 0645	120.3882 5659	23.0912 4425	0.0083 0646	0.0433 0646	48
49	5.3960 6459	0.1853 2024	125.6018 4557	23.2765 6450	0.0079 6167	0.0429 6167	49
50	5.5849 2686	0.1790 5337	130.9979 1016	23.4556 1787	0.0076 3371	0.0426 3371	50

Rate 4%	B Compound Amount	C Present Value	D Amount of Annuity	E Present Value of Annuity	F Sinking Fund	G Amortization	
n	$(1 + i)^n$	$(1 + i)^{-n}$	$S_{\overline{n}|i}$	$A_{\overline{n}|i}$	$1/S_{\overline{n}|i}$	$1/A_{\overline{n}|i}$	n
1	1.0400 0000	0.9615 3846	1.0000 0000	0.9615 3846	1.0000 0000	1.0400 0000	1
2	1.0816 0000	0.9245 5621	2.0400 0000	1.8860 9467	0.4901 9608	0.5301 9608	2
3	1.1248 6400	0.8889 9636	3.1216 0000	2.7750 9103	0.3203 4854	0.3603 4854	3
4	1.1698 5856	0.8548 0419	4.2464 6400	3.6298 9522	0.2354 9005	0.2754 9005	4
5	1.2166 5290	0.8219 2711	5.4163 2256	4.4518 2233	0.1846 2711	0.2246 2711	5
6	1.2653 1902	0.7903 1453	6.6329 7546	5.2421 3686	0.1507 6190	0.1907 6190	6
7	1.3159 3178	0.7599 1781	7.8982 9448	6.0020 5467	0.1266 0961	0.1666 0961	7
8	1.3685 6905	0.7306 9021	9.2142 2626	6.7327 4487	0.1085 2783	0.1485 2783	8
9	1.4233 1181	0.7025 8674	10.5827 9531	7.4353 3161	0.0944 9299	0.1344 9299	9
10	1.4802 4428	0.6755 6417	12.0061 0712	8.1108 9578	0.0832 9094	0.1232 9094	10
11	1.5394 5406	0.6495 8093	13.4863 5141	8.7604 7671	0.0741 4904	0.1141 4904	11
12	1.6010 3222	0.6245 9705	15.0258 0546	9.3850 7376	0.0665 5217	0.1065 5217	12
13	1.6650 7351	0.6005 7409	16.6268 3768	9.9856 4785	0.0601 4373	0.1001 4373	13
14	1.7316 7645	0.5774 7508	18.2919 1119	10.5631 2293	0.0546 6897	0.0946 6897	14
15	1.8009 4351	0.5552 6450	20.0235 8764	11.1183 8743	0.0499 4110	0.0899 4110	15
16	1.8729 8125	0.5339 0818	21.8245 3114	11.6522 9561	0.0458 2000	0.0858 2000	16
17	1.9479 0050	0.5133 7325	23.6975 1239	12.1656 6885	0.0421 9852	0.0821 9852	17
18	2.0258 1652	0.4936 2812	25.6454 1288	12.6592 9697	0.0389 9333	0.0789 9333	18
19	2.1068 4918	0.4746 4242	27.6712 2940	13.1339 3940	0.0361 3862	0.0761 3862	19
20	2.1911 2314	0.4563 8695	29.7780 7858	13.5903 2634	0.0335 8175	0.0735 8175	20
21	2.2787 6807	0.4388 3360	31.9692 0172	14.0291 5995	0.0312 8011	0.0712 8011	21
22	2.3699 1879	0.4219 5539	34.2479 6979	14.4511 1533	0.0291 9881	0.0691 9881	22
23	2.4647 1554	0.4057 2633	36.6178 8858	14.8568 4167	0.0273 0906	0.0673 0906	23
24	2.5633 0416	0.3901 2147	39.0826 0412	15.2469 6314	0.0255 8683	0.0655 8683	24
25	2.6658 3633	0.3751 1680	41.6459 0829	15.6220 7994	0.0240 1196	0.0640 1196	25
26	2.7724 6978	0.3606 8923	44.3117 4462	15.9827 6918	0.0225 6738	0.0625 6738	26
27	2.8833 6858	0.3468 1657	47.0842 1440	16.3295 8575	0.0212 3854	0.0612 3854	27
28	2.9987 0332	0.3334 7747	49.9675 8298	16.6630 6322	0.0200 1298	0.0600 1298	28
29	3.1186 5145	0.3206 5141	52.9662 8630	16.9837 1463	0.0188 7993	0.0588 7993	29
30	3.2433 9751	0.3083 1867	56.0849 3775	17.2920 3330	0.0178 3010	0.0578 3010	30
31	3.3731 3341	0.2964 6026	59.3283 3526	17.5884 9356	0.0168 5535	0.0568 5535	31
32	3.5080 5875	0.2850 5794	62.7014 6867	17.8735 5150	0.0159 4859	0.0559 4859	32
33	3.6483 8110	0.2740 9417	66.2095 2742	18.1476 4567	0.0151 0357	0.0551 0357	33
34	3.7943 1634	0.2635 5209	69.8579 0851	18.4111 9776	0.0143 1477	0.0543 1477	34
35	3.9460 8899	0.2534 1547	73.6522 2486	18.6646 1323	0.0135 7732	0.0535 7732	35
36	4.1039 3255	0.2436 6872	77.5983 1385	18.9082 8195	0.0128 8688	0.0528 8688	36
37	4.2680 8986	0.2342 9685	81.7022 4640	19.1425 7880	0.0122 3957	0.0522 3957	37
38	4.4388 1345	0.2252 8543	85.9703 3626	19.3678 6423	0.0116 3192	0.0516 3192	38
39	4.6163 6599	0.2166 2061	90.4091 4971	19.5844 8484	0.0110 6083	0.0510 6083	39
40	4.8010 2063	0.2082 8904	95.0255 1570	19.7927 7388	0.0105 2349	0.0505 2349	40
41	4.9930 6145	0.2002 7793	99.8265 3633	19.9930 5181	0.0100 1738	0.0500 1738	41
42	5.1927 8391	0.1925 7493	104.8195 9778	20.1856 2674	0.0095 4020	0.0495 4020	42
43	5.4004 9527	0.1851 6820	110.0123 8169	20.3707 9494	0.0090 8989	0.0490 8990	43
44	5.6165 1508	0.1780 4635	115.4128 7696	20.5488 4129	0.0086 6454	0.0486 6454	44
45	5.8411 7568	0.1711 9841	121.0293 9204	20.7200 3970	0.0082 6246	0.0482 6246	45
46	6.0748 2271	0.1646 1386	126.8705 6772	20.8846 5356	0.0078 8205	0.0478 8205	46
47	6.3178 1562	0.1582 8256	132.9453 9043	21.0429 3612	0.0075 2189	0.0475 2189	47
48	6.5705 2824	0.1521 9476	139.2632 0604	21.1951 3088	0.0071 8065	0.0471 8065	48
49	6.8333 4937	0.1463 4112	145.8337 3429	21.3414 7200	0.0068 5712	0.0468 5712	49
50	7.1066 8335	0.1407 1262	152.6670 8366	21.4821 8462	0.0065 5020	0.0465 5020	50

Rate 4½%	B Compound Amount	C Present Value	D Amount of Annuity	E Present Value of Annuity	F Sinking Fund	G Amortization	
n	$(1 + i)^n$	$(1 + i)^{-n}$	$S_{\overline{n}\rceil i}$	$A_{\overline{n}\rceil i}$	$1/S_{\overline{n}\rceil i}$	$1/A_{\overline{n}\rceil i}$	n
1	1.0450 0000	0.9569 3780	1.0000 0000	0.9569 3780	1.0000 0000	1.0450 0000	1
2	1.0920 2500	0.9157 2995	2.0450 0000	1.8726 6775	0.4889 9756	0.5339 9756	2
3	1.1411 6613	0.8762 9660	3.1370 2500	2.7489 6435	0.3187 7336	0.3637 7336	3
4	1.1925 1860	0.8385 6134	4.2781 9113	3.5875 2570	0.2337 4365	0.2787 4365	4
5	1.2461 8194	0.8024 5105	5.4707 0973	4.3899 7674	0.1827 9164	0.2277 9164	5
6	1.3022 6012	0.7678 9574	6.7168 9166	5.1578 7248	0.1488 7839	0.1938 7839	6
7	1.3608 6183	0.7348 2846	8.0191 5179	5.8927 0094	0.1247 0147	0.1697 0147	7
8	1.4221 0061	0.7031 8513	9.3800 1362	6.5958 8607	0.1066 0965	0.1516 0965	8
9	1.4860 9514	0.6729 0443	10.8021 1423	7.2687 9050	0.0925 7447	0.1375 7447	9
10	1.5529 6942	0.6439 2768	12.2882 0937	7.9127 1818	0.0813 7882	0.1263 7882	10
11	1.6228 5305	0.6161 9874	13.8411 7879	8.5289 1692	0.0722 4818	0.1172 4818	11
12	1.6958 8143	0.5896 6386	15.4640 3184	9.1185 8078	0.0646 6619	0.1096 6619	12
13	1.7721 9610	0.5642 7164	17.1599 1327	9.6828 5242	0.0582 7535	0.1032 7535	13
14	1.8519 4492	0.5399 7286	18.9321 0937	10.2228 2528	0.0537 2032	0.0978 2032	14
15	1.9352 8244	0.5167 2044	20.7840 5429	10.7395 4573	0.0481 1381	0.0931 1381	15
16	2.0223 7015	0.4944 6932	22.7193 3673	11.2340 1505	0.0440 1537	0.0890 1537	16
17	2.1133 7681	0.4731 7639	24.7417 0689	11.7071 9143	0.0404 1758	0.0854 1758	17
18	2.2084 7877	0.4528 0037	26.8550 8370	12.1599 9180	0.0372 3690	0.0822 3690	18
19	2.3078 6031	0.4333 0179	29.0635 6246	12.5932 9359	0.0344 0734	0.0794 0734	19
20	2.4117 1402	0.4146 4286	31.3714 2277	13.0079 3645	0.0318 7614	0.0768 7614	20
21	2.5202 4116	0.3967 8743	33.7831 3680	13.4047 2388	0.0296 0057	0.0746 0057	21
22	2.6336 5201	0.3797 0089	36.3033 7795	13.7844 2476	0.0275 4565	0.0725 4565	22
23	2.7521 6635	0.3633 5013	38.9370 2996	14.1477 7489	0.0256 8249	0.0706 8249	23
24	2.8760 1383	0.3477 0347	41.6891 9631	14.4954 7837	0.0239 8703	0.0689 8703	24
25	3.0054 3446	0.3327 3060	44.5652 1015	14.8282 0896	0.0224 3903	0.0674 3903	25
26	3.1406 7901	0.3184 0248	47.5706 4460	15.1466 1145	0.0210 2137	0.0660 2137	26
27	3.2820 0956	0.3046 9137	50.7113 2361	15.4513 0282	0.0197 1946	0.0647 1946	27
28	3.4296 9999	0.2915 7069	53.9933 3317	15.7428 7351	0.0185 2081	0.0635 2081	28
29	3.5840 3649	0.2790 1502	57.4230 3316	16.0218 8853	0.0174 1461	0.0624 1461	29
30	3.7453 1813	0.2670 0002	61.0070 6966	16.2888 8854	0.0163 9154	0.0613 9154	30
31	3.9138 5745	0.2555 0241	64.7523 8779	16.5443 9095	0.0154 4345	0.0604 4345	31
32	4.0899 8104	0.2444 9991	68.6662 4524	16.7888 9086	0.0145 6320	0.0595 6320	32
33	4.2740 3018	0.2339 7121	72.7562 2628	17.0228 6207	0.0137 4453	0.0587 4453	33
34	4.4663 6154	0.2238 9589	77.0302 5646	17.2467 5796	0.0129 8191	0.0579 8191	34
35	4.6673 4781	0.2142 5444	81.4966 1800	17.4610 1240	0.0122 7045	0.0572 7045	35
36	4.8773 7846	0.2050 2817	86.1639 6581	17.6660 4058	0.0116 0578	0.0566 0578	36
37	5.0968 6049	0.1961 9921	91.0413 4427	17.8622 3979	0.0109 8402	0.0559 8402	37
38	5.3262 1921	0.1877 5044	96.1382 0476	18.0499 9023	0.0104 0169	0.0554 0169	38
39	5.5658 9908	0.1796 6549	101.4644 2398	18.2296 5572	0.0098 5567	0.0548 5567	39
40	5.8163 6454	0.1719 2870	107.0303 2306	18.4015 8442	0.0093 4315	0.0543 4315	40
41	6.0781 0094	0.1645 2507	112.8466 8760	18.5661 0949	0.0088 6158	0.0538 6158	41
42	6.3516 1548	0.1574 4026	118.9247 8854	18.7235 4975	0.0084 0868	0.0534 0868	42
43	6.6374 3818	0.1506 6054	125.2764 0402	18.8742 1029	0.0079 8235	0.0529 8235	43
44	6.9361 2290	0.1441 7276	131.9138 4220	19.0183 8305	0.0075 8071	0.0525 8071	44
45	7.2482 4843	0.1379 6437	138.8499 6510	19.1563 4742	0.0072 0202	0.0522 0202	45
46	7.5744 1961	0.1320 2332	146.0982 1353	19.2883 7074	0.0068 4471	0.0518 4471	46
47	7.9152 6849	0.1263 3810	153.6726 3314	19.4147 0884	0.0065 0734	0.0515 0734	47
48	8.2714 5557	0.1208 9771	161.5879 0163	19.5356 0654	0.0061 8858	0.0511 8858	48
49	8.6436 7107	0.1156 9158	169.8593 5720	19.6512 9813	0.0058 8722	0.0508 8722	49
50	9.0326 3627	0.1107 0965	178.5030 2828	19.7620 0778	0.0056 0215	0.0506 0215	50

Rate 5%	B Compound Amount	C Present Value	D Amount of Annuity	E Present Value of Annuity	F Sinking Fund	G Amortization	
n	$(1 + i)^n$	$(1 + i)^{-n}$	$S_{\overline{n}|i}$	$A_{\overline{n}|i}$	$1/S_{\overline{n}|i}$	$1/A_{\overline{n}|i}$	n
1	1.0500 0000	0.9523 8095	1.0000 0000	0.9523 8095	1.0000 0000	1.0500 0000	1
2	1.1025 0000	0.9070 2948	2.0500 0000	1.8594 1043	0.4878 0488	0.5378 0488	2
3	1.1576 2500	0.8638 3760	3.1525 0000	2.7232 4803	0.3172 0856	0.3672 0856	3
4	1.2155 0625	0.8227 0247	4.3101 2500	3.5459 5050	0.2320 1183	0.2820 1183	4
5	1.2762 8156	0.7835 2617	5.5256 3125	4.3294 7667	0.1809 7480	0.2309 7480	5
6	1.3400 9564	0.7462 1540	6.8019 1281	5.0756 9207	0.1470 1747	0.1970 1747	6
7	1.4071 0042	0.7106 8133	8.1420 0845	5.7863 7340	0.1228 1982	0.1728 1982	7
8	1.4774 5544	0.6768 3936	9.5491 0888	6.4632 1276	0.1047 2181	0.1547 2181	8
9	1.5513 2822	0.6446 0892	11.0265 6432	7.1078 2168	0.0906 9008	0.1406 9008	9
10	1.6288 9463	0.6139 1325	12.5778 9254	7.7217 3493	0.0795 0458	0.1295 0458	10
11	1.7103 3936	0.5846 7929	14.2067 8716	8.3064 1422	0.0703 8889	0.1203 8889	11
12	1.7958 5633	0.5568 3742	15.9171 2652	8.8632 5164	0.0628 2541	0.1128 2541	12
13	1.8856 4914	0.5303 2135	17.7129 8285	9.3935 7299	0.0564 5577	0.1064 5577	13
14	1.9799 3160	0.5050 6795	19.5986 3199	9.8986 4094	0.0510 2397	0.1010 2397	14
15	2.0789 2818	0.4810 1710	21.5785 6359	10.3796 5804	0.0463 4229	0.0963 4229	15
16	2.1828 7459	0.4581 1152	23.6574 9177	10.8377 6956	0.0422 6991	0.0922 6991	16
17	2.2920 1832	0.4362 9669	25.8403 6636	11.2740 6625	0.0386 9914	0.0886 9914	17
18	2.4066 1923	0.4155 2065	28.1323 8467	11.6895 8690	0.0355 4622	0.0855 4622	18
19	2.5269 5020	0.3957 3396	30.5390 0391	12.0853 2086	0.0327 4501	0.0827 4501	19
20	2.6532 9771	0.3768 8948	33.0659 5410	12.4622 1034	0.0302 4259	0.0802 4259	20
21	2.7859 6259	0.3589 4236	35.7192 5181	12.8211 5271	0.0279 9611	0.0779 9611	21
22	2.9252 6072	0.3418 4987	38.5052 1440	13.1630 0258	0.0259 7051	0.0759 7051	22
23	3.0715 2376	0.3255 7131	41.4304 7512	13.4885 7388	0.0241 3682	0.0741 3682	23
24	3.2250 9994	0.3100 6791	44.5019 9887	13.7986 4179	0.0224 7090	0.0724 7090	24
25	3.3863 5494	0.2953 0277	47.7270 9882	14.0939 4457	0.0209 5246	0.0709 5246	25
26	3.5556 7269	0.2812 4073	51.1134 5376	14.3751 8530	0.0195 6432	0.0695 6432	26
27	3.7334 5632	0.2678 4832	54.6691 2645	14.6430 3362	0.0182 9186	0.0682 9186	27
28	3.9201 2914	0.2550 9364	58.4025 8277	14.8981 2726	0.0171 2253	0.0671 2253	28
29	4.1161 3560	0.2429 4632	62.3227 1191	15.1410 7358	0.0160 4551	0.0660 4551	29
30	4.3219 4238	0.2313 7745	66.4388 4750	15.3724 5103	0.0150 5144	0.0650 5144	30
31	4.5380 3949	0.2203 5947	70.7607 8988	15.5928 1050	0.0141 3212	0.0641 3212	31
32	4.7649 4147	0.2098 6617	75.2988 2937	15.8026 7667	0.0132 8042	0.0632 8042	32
33	5.0031 8854	0.1998 7254	80.0637 7084	16.0025 4921	0.0124 9004	0.0624 9004	33
34	5.2533 4797	0.1903 5480	85.0669 5938	16.1929 0401	0.0117 5545	0.0617 5545	34
35	5.5160 1537	0.1812 9029	90.3203 0735	16.3741 9429	0.0110 7171	0.0610 7171	35
36	5.7918 1614	0.1726 5741	95.8363 2272	16.5468 5171	0.0104 3446	0.0604 3446	36
37	6.0814 0694	0.1644 3563	101.6281 3886	16.7112 8734	0.0098 3979	0.0598 3979	37
38	6.3854 7729	0.1566 0536	107.7095 4580	16.8678 9271	0.0092 8423	0.0592 8423	38
39	6.7047 5115	0.1491 4797	114.0950 2309	17.0170 4067	0.0087 6462	0.0587 6462	39
40	7.0399 8871	0.1420 4568	120.7997 7424	17.1590 8635	0.0082 7816	0.0582 7816	40
41	7.3919 8815	0.1352 8160	127.8397 6295	17.2943 6796	0.0078 2229	0.0578 2229	41
42	7.7615 8756	0.1288 3962	135.2317 5110	17.4232 0758	0.0073 9471	0.0573 9471	42
43	8.1496 6693	0.1227 0440	142.9933 3866	17.5459 1198	0.0069 9333	0.0569 9333	43
44	8.5571 5028	0.1168 6133	151.1430 0559	17.6627 7331	0.0066 1625	0.0566 1625	44
45	8.9850 0779	0.1112 9651	159.7001 5587	17.7740 6982	0.0062 6173	0.0562 6173	45
46	9.4342 5818	0.1059 9668	168.6851 6366	17.8800 6650	0.0059 2820	0.0559 2820	46
47	9.9059 7109	0.1009 4921	178.1194 2185	17.9810 1571	0.0056 1421	0.0556 1421	47
48	10.4012 6965	0.0961 4211	188.0253 9294	18.0771 5782	0.0053 1843	0.0553 1843	48
49	10.9213 3313	0.0915 6391	198.4266 6259	18.1687 2173	0.0050 3965	0.0550 3965	49
50	11.4673 9979	0.0872 0373	209.3479 9572	18.2559 2546	0.0047 7674	0.0547 7674	50

Rate 6%	B Compound Amount	C Present Value	D Amount of Annuity	E Present Value of Annuity	F Sinking Fund	G Amortization	
n	$(1 + i)^n$	$(1 + i)^{-n}$	$S_{\overline{n}|i}$	$A_{\overline{n}|i}$	$1/A_{\overline{n}|i}$	$1/S_{\overline{n}|i}$	n
1	1.0600 0000	0.9433 9623	1.0000 0000	0.9433 9623	1.0000 0000	1.0600 0000	1
2	1.1236 0000	0.8899 9644	2.0600 0000	1.8333 9267	0.4854 3689	0.5454 3689	2
3	1.1910 1600	0.8396 1928	3.1836 0000	2.6730 1195	0.3141 0981	0.3741 0981	3
4	1.2624 7696	0.7920 9366	4.3746 1600	3.4651 0561	0.2285 9149	0.2885 9149	4
5	1.3382 2558	0.7472 5817	5.6370 9296	4.2123 6379	0.1773 9640	0.2373 9640	5
6	1.4185 1911	0.7049 6054	6.9753 1854	4.9173 2433	0.1433 6263	0.2033 6263	6
7	1.5036 3026	0.6650 5711	8.3938 3765	5.5823 8144	0.1191 3502	0.1791 3502	7
8	1.5938 4807	0.6274 1237	9.8974 6791	6.2097 9381	0.1010 3594	0.1610 3594	8
9	1.6894 7896	0.5918 9846	11.4913 1598	6.8016 9227	0.0870 2224	0.1470 2224	9
10	1.7908 4770	0.5583 9478	13.1807 9494	7.3600 8705	0.0758 6796	0.1358 6796	10
11	1.8982 9856	0.5267 8753	14.9716 4264	7.8868 7458	0.0667 9294	0.1267 9294	11
12	2.0121 9647	0.4969 6936	16.8699 4120	8.3838 4394	0.0592 7703	0.1192 7703	12
13	2.1329 2826	0.4688 3902	18.8821 3767	8.8526 8296	0.0529 6011	0.1129 6011	13
14	2.2609 0396	0.4423 0096	21.0150 6593	9.2949 8393	0.0475 8491	0.1075 8491	14
15	2.3965 5819	0.4172 6506	23.2759 6988	9.7122 4899	0.0429 6276	0.1029 6276	15
16	2.5403 5168	0.3936 4628	25.6725 2808	10.1058 9527	0.0389 5214	0.0989 5214	16
17	2.6927 7279	0.3713 6442	28.2128 7976	10.4772 5969	0.0354 4480	0.0954 4480	17
18	2.8543 3915	0.3503 4379	30.9056 5255	10.8276 0348	0.0323 5654	0.0923 5654	18
19	3.0255 9950	0.3305 1301	33.7599 9170	11.1581 1649	0.0296 2086	0.0896 2086	19
20	3.2071 3547	0.3118 0473	36.7855 9120	11.4699 2122	0.0271 8456	0.0871 8456	20
21	3.3995 6360	0.2941 5540	39.9927 2668	11.7640 7662	0.0250 0455	0.0850 0455	21
22	3.6035 3742	0.2775 0510	43.3922 9028	12.0415 8172	0.0230 4557	0.0830 4557	22
23	3.8197 4966	0.2617 9726	46.9958 2769	12.3033 7898	0.0212 7848	0.0812 7848	23
24	4.0489 3464	0.2469 7855	50.8155 7735	12.5503 5753	0.0196 7901	0.0796 7900	24
25	4.2918 7072	0.2329 9863	54.8645 1200	12.7833 5616	0.0182 2672	0.0782 2672	25
26	4.5493 8296	0.2198 1003	59.1563 8272	13.0031 6619	0.0169 0435	0.0769 0435	26
27	4.8223 4594	0.2073 6795	63.7057 6568	13.2105 3414	0.0156 9717	0.0756 9717	27
28	5.1116 8670	0.1956 3014	68.5281 1162	13.4061 6428	0.0145 9255	0.0745 9255	28
29	5.4183 8790	0.1845 5674	73.6397 9832	13.5907 2102	0.0135 7961	0.0735 7961	29
30	5.7434 9117	0.1741 1013	79.0581 8622	13.7648 3115	0.0126 4891	0.0726 4891	30
31	6.0881 0064	0.1642 5484	84.8016 7739	13.9290 8599	0.0117 9222	0.0717 9222	31
32	6.4533 8668	0.1549 5740	90.8897 7803	14.0840 4339	0.0110 0234	0.0710 0234	32
33	6.8405 8988	0.1461 8622	97.3431 6471	14.2302 2961	0.0102 7294	0.0702 7293	33
34	7.2510 2528	0.1379 1153	104.1837 5460	14.3681 4114	0.0095 9843	0.0695 9843	34
35	7.6860 8679	0.1301 0522	111.4347 7987	14.4982 4636	0.0089 7386	0.0689 7386	35
36	8.1472 5200	0.1227 4077	119.1208 6666	14.6209 8713	0.0083 9483	0.0683 9483	36
37	8.6360 8712	0.1157 9318	127.2681 1866	14.7367 8031	0.0078 5743	0.0678 5743	37
38	9.1542 5235	0.1092 3885	135.9042 0578	14.8460 1916	0.0073 5812	0.0673 5812	38
39	9.7035 0749	0.1030 5552	145.0584 5813	14.9490 7468	0.0068 9377	0.0668 9377	39
40	10.2857 1794	0.0972 2219	154.7619 6562	15.0462 9687	0.0064 6154	0.0664 6154	40
41	10.9028 6101	0.0917 1905	165.0476 8356	15.1380 1592	0.0060 5886	0.0660 5886	41
42	11.5570 3267	0.0865 2740	175.9505 4457	15.2245 4332	0.0056 8342	0.0656 8342	42
43	12.2504 5463	0.0816 2962	187.5075 7724	15.3061 7294	0.0053 3312	0.0653 3312	43
44	12.9854 8191	0.0770 0908	199.7580 3188	15.3831 8202	0.0050 0606	0.0650 0606	44
45	13.7646 1083	0.0726 5007	212.7435 1379	15.4558 3209	0.0047 0050	0.0647 0050	45
46	14.5904 8748	0.0685 3781	226.5081 2462	15.5243 6990	0.0044 1485	0.0644 1485	46
47	15.4659 1673	0.0646 5831	241.0986 1210	15.5890 2821	0.0041 4768	0.0641 4768	47
48	16.3938 7173	0.0609 9840	256.5645 2882	15.6500 2661	0.0038 9765	0.0638 9765	48
49	17.3775 0403	0.0575 4566	272.9584 0055	15.7075 7227	0.0036 6356	0.0636 6356	49
50	18.4201 5427	0.0542 8836	290.3359 0458	15.7618 6064	0.0034 4429	0.0634 4429	50

Rate 7%	B Compound Amount	C Present Value	D Amount of Annuity	E Present Value of Annuity	F Sinking Fund	G Amortization	
n	$(1+i)^n$	$(1+i)^{-n}$	$S_{\overline{n}|i}$	$A_{\overline{n}|i}$	$1/S_{\overline{n}|i}$	$1/A_{\overline{n}|i}$	n
1	1.0700 0000	0.9345 7944	1.0000 0000	0.9345 7944	1.0000 0000	1.0700 0000	1
2	1.1449 0000	0.8734 3873	2.0700 0000	1.8080 1817	0.4830 9179	0.5530 9179	2
3	1.2250 4300	0.8162 9788	3.2149 0000	2.6243 1604	0.3110 5167	0.3810 5167	3
4	1.3107 9601	0.7628 9521	4.4399 4300	3.3872 1126	0.2252 2812	0.2952 2812	4
5	1.4025 5173	0.7129 8618	5.7507 3901	4.1001 9744	0.1738 9069	0.2438 9069	5
6	1.5007 3035	0.6663 4222	7.1532 9074	4.7665 3966	0.1397 9580	0.2097 9580	6
7	1.6057 8148	0.6227 4974	8.6540 2109	5.3892 8940	0.1155 5322	0.1855 5322	7
8	1.7181 8618	0.5820 0910	10.2598 0257	5.9712 9851	0.0974 6776	0.1674 6776	8
9	1.8384 5921	0.5439 3374	11.9779 8875	6.5152 3225	0.0834 8647	0.1534 8647	9
10	1.9671 5136	0.5083 4929	13.8164 4796	7.0235 8154	0.0723 7750	0.1423 7750	10
11	2.1048 5195	0.4750 9280	15.7835 9932	7.4986 7434	0.0633 5690	0.1333 5690	11
12	2.2521 9159	0.4440 1196	17.8884 5127	7.9426 8630	0.0559 0199	0.1259 0199	12
13	2.4098 4500	0.4149 6445	20.1406 4286	8.3576 5074	0.0496 5085	0.1196 5085	13
14	2.5785 3415	0.3878 1724	22.5504 8786	8.7454 6799	0.0443 4494	0.1143 4494	14
15	2.7590 3154	0.3624 4602	25.1290 2201	9.1079 1401	0.0397 9462	0.1097 9462	15
16	2.9521 6375	0.3387 3460	27.8880 5355	9.4466 4860	0.0358 5765	0.1058 5765	16
17	3.1588 1521	0.3165 7439	30.8402 1730	9.7632 2299	0.0324 2519	0.1024 2519	17
18	3.3799 3228	0.2958 6392	33.9990 3251	10.0590 8691	0.0294 1260	0.0994 1260	18
19	3.6165 2754	0.2765 0833	37.3789 6479	10.3355 9524	0.0267 5301	0.0967 5301	19
20	3.8696 8446	0.2584 1900	40.9954 9232	10.5940 1425	0.0243 9293	0.0943 9293	20
21	4.1405 6237	0.2415 1309	44.8651 7678	10.8355 2733	0.0222 8900	0.0922 8900	21
22	4.4304 0174	0.2257 1317	49.0057 3916	11.0612 4050	0.0204 0577	0.0904 0577	22
23	4.7405 2986	0.2109 4688	53.4361 4090	11.2721 8738	0.0187 1393	0.0887 1393	23
24	5.0723 6695	0.1971 4662	58.1766 7076	11.4693 3400	0.0171 8902	0.0871 8902	24
25	5.4274 3264	0.1842 4918	63.2490 3772	11.6535 8318	0.0158 1052	0.0858 1052	25
26	5.8073 5292	0.1721 9549	68.6764 7036	11.8257 7867	0.0145 6103	0.0845 6103	26
27	6.2138 6763	0.1609 3037	74.4838 2328	11.9867 0904	0.0134 2573	0.0834 2573	27
28	6.6488 3836	0.1504 0221	80.6976 9091	12.1371 1125	0.0123 9193	0.0823 9193	28
29	7.1142 5705	0.1405 6282	87.3465 2927	12.2776 7407	0.0114 4865	0.0814 4865	29
30	7.6122 5504	0.1313 6712	94.4607 8632	12.4090 4118	0.0105 8640	0.0805 8640	30
31	8.1451 1290	0.1227 7301	102.0730 4137	12.5318 1419	0.0097 9691	0.0797 9691	31
32	8.7152 7080	0.1147 4113	110.2181 5426	12.6465 5532	0.0090 7292	0.0790 7292	32
33	9.3253 3975	0.1072 3470	118.9334 2506	12.7537 9002	0.0084 0807	0.0784 0807	33
34	9.9781 1354	0.1002 1934	128.2587 6481	12.8540 0936	0.0077 9674	0.0777 9674	34
35	10.6765 8148	0.0936 6294	138.2368 7835	12.9476 7230	0.0072 3396	0.0772 3396	35
36	11.4239 4219	0.0875 3546	148.9134 5984	13.0352 0776	0.0067 1531	0.0767 1531	36
37	12.2236 1814	0.0818 0884	160.3374 0202	13.1170 1660	0.0062 3685	0.0762 3685	37
38	13.0792 7141	0.0764 5686	172.5610 2017	13.1934 7345	0.0057 9505	0.0757 9505	38
39	13.9948 2041	0.0714 5501	185.6402 9158	13.2649 2846	0.0053 8676	0.0753 8676	39
40	14.9744 5784	0.0667 8038	199.6351 1199	13.3317 0884	0.0050 0914	0.0750 0914	40
41	16.0226 6989	0.0624 1157	214.6095 6983	13.3941 2041	0.0046 5962	0.0746 5962	41
42	17.1442 5678	0.0583 2857	230.6322 3972	13.4524 4898	0.0043 3591	0.0743 3591	42
43	18.3443 5475	0.0545 1268	247.7764 9650	13.5069 6167	0.0040 3590	0.0740 3590	43
44	19.6284 5959	0.0509 4643	266.1208 5125	13.5579 0810	0.0037 5769	0.0737 5769	44
45	21.0024 5176	0.0476 1349	285.7493 1084	13.6055 2159	0.0034 9957	0.0734 9957	45
46	22.4726 2338	0.0444 9859	306.7517 6260	13.6500 2018	0.0032 5997	0.0732 5996	46
47	24.0457 0702	0.0415 8747	329.2243 8598	13.6916 0764	0.0030 3744	0.0730 3744	47
48	25.7289 0651	0.0388 6679	353.2700 9300	13.7304 7443	0.0028 3070	0.0728 3070	48
49	27.5299 2997	0.0363 2410	378.9989 9951	13.7667 9853	0.0026 3853	0.0726 3853	49
50	29.4570 2506	0.0339 4776	406.5289 2947	13.8007 4629	0.0024 5985	0.0724 5985	50

Rate 8%	B Compound Amount	C Present Value	D Amount of Annuity	E Present Value of Annuity	F Sinking Fund	G Amortization	
n	$(1 + i)^n$	$(1 + i)^{-n}$	$S_{\overline{n}|i}$	$A_{\overline{n}|i}$	$1/S_{\overline{n}|i}$	$1/A_{\overline{n}|i}$	n
1	1.0800 0000	0.9259 2593	1.0000 0000	0.9259 2593	1.0000 0000	1.0800 0000	1
2	1.1664 0000	0.8573 3882	2.0800 0000	1.7832 6475	0.4807 6923	0.5607 6923	2
3	1.2597 1200	0.7938 3224	3.2464 0000	2.5770 9699	0.3080 3351	0.3880 3351	3
4	1.3604 8896	0.7350 2985	4.5061 1200	3.3121 2684	0.2219 2080	0.3019 2080	4
5	1.4693 2808	0.6805 8320	5.8666 0096	3.9927 1004	0.1704 5645	0.2504 5645	5
6	1.5868 7432	0.6301 6963	7.3359 2904	4.6228 7966	0.1363 1539	0.2163 1539	6
7	1.7138 2427	0.5834 9040	8.9228 0336	5.2063 7006	0.1120 7240	0.1920 7240	7
8	1.8509 3021	0.5402 6888	10.6366 2763	5.7466 3894	0.0940 1476	0.1740 1476	8
9	1.9990 0463	0.5002 4897	12.4875 5784	6.2468 8791	0.0800 7971	0.1600 7971	9
10	2.1589 2500	0.4631 9349	14.4865 6247	6.7100 8140	0.0690 2949	0.1490 2949	10
11	2.3316 3900	0.4288 8286	16.6454 8746	7.1389 6426	0.0600 7634	0.1400 7634	11
12	2.5181 7012	0.3971 1376	18.9771 2646	7.5360 7802	0.0526 9502	0.1326 9502	12
13	2.7196 2373	0.3676 9792	21.4952 9658	7.9037 7594	0.0465 2181	0.1265 2181	13
14	2.9371 9362	0.3404 6104	24.2149 2030	8.2442 3698	0.0412 9685	0.1212 9685	14
15	3.1721 6911	0.3152 4170	27.1521 1393	8.5594 7869	0.0368 2954	0.1168 2954	15
16	3.4259 4264	0.2918 9047	30.3242 8304	8.8513 6916	0.0329 7687	0.1129 7687	16
17	3.7000 1805	0.2702 6895	33.7502 2569	9.1216 3811	0.0296 2943	0.1096 2943	17
18	3.9960 1950	0.2502 4903	37.4502 4374	9.3718 8714	0.0267 0210	0.1067 0210	18
19	4.3157 0106	0.2317 1206	41.4462 6324	9.6035 9920	0.0241 2763	0.1041 2763	19
20	4.6609 5714	0.2145 4821	45.7619 6430	9.8181 4741	0.0218 5221	0.1018 5221	20
21	5.0338 3372	0.1986 5575	50.4229 2144	10.0168 0316	0.0198 3225	0.0998 3225	21
22	5.4365 4041	0.1839 4051	55.4567 5516	10.2007 4366	0.0180 3207	0.0980 3207	22
23	5.8714 6365	0.1703 1528	60.8932 9557	10.3710 5895	0.0164 2217	0.0964 2217	23
24	6.3411 8074	0.1576 9934	66.7647 5922	10.5287 5828	0.0149 7796	0.0949 7796	24
25	6.8484 7520	0.1460 1790	73.1059 3995	10.6747 7619	0.0136 7878	0.0936 7878	25
26	7.3963 5321	0.1352 0176	79.9544 1515	10.8099 7795	0.0125 0713	0.0925 0713	26
27	7.9880 6147	0.1251 8682	87.3507 6836	10.9351 6477	0.0114 4810	0.0914 4810	27
28	8.6271 0639	0.1159 1372	95.3388 2983	11.0510 7849	0.0104 8891	0.0904 8891	28
29	9.3172 7490	0.1073 2752	103.9659 3622	11.1584 0601	0.0096 1854	0.0896 1854	29
30	10.0626 5689	0.0993 7733	113.2832 1111	11.2577 8334	0.0088 2743	0.0888 2743	30
31	10.8676 6944	0.0920 1605	123.3458 6800	11.3497 9939	0.0081 0728	0.0881 0728	31
32	11.7370 8300	0.0852 0005	134.2135 3744	11.4349 9944	0.0074 5081	0.0874 5081	32
33	12.6760 4964	0.0788 8893	145.9506 2044	11.5138 8837	0.0068 5163	0.0868 5163	33
34	13.6901 3361	0.0730 4531	158.6266 7007	11.5869 3367	0.0063 0411	0.0863 0411	34
35	14.7853 4429	0.0676 3454	172.3168 0368	11.6545 6822	0.0058 0326	0.0858 0326	35
36	15.9681 7184	0.0626 2458	187.1021 4797	11.7171 9279	0.0053 4467	0.0853 4467	36
37	17.2456 2558	0.0579 8572	203.0703 1981	11.7751 7851	0.0049 2440	0.0849 2440	37
38	18.6252 7563	0.0536 9048	220.3159 4540	11.8288 6899	0.0045 3894	0.0845 3894	38
39	20.1152 9768	0.0497 1341	238.9412 2103	11.8785 8240	0.0041 8513	0.0841 8513	39
40	21.7245 2150	0.0460 3093	259.0565 1871	11.9246 1333	0.0038 6016	0.0838 6016	40
41	23.4624 8322	0.0426 2123	280.7810 4021	11.9672 3457	0.0035 6149	0.0835 6149	41
42	25.3394 8187	0.0394 6411	304.2435 2342	12.0066 9867	0.0032 8684	0.0832 8684	42
43	27.3666 4042	0.0365 4084	329.5830 0530	12.0432 3951	0.0030 3414	0.0830 3414	43
44	29.5559 7166	0.0338 3411	356.9496 4572	12.0770 7362	0.0028 0152	0.0828 0152	44
45	31.9204 4939	0.0313 2788	386.5056 1738	12.1084 0150	0.0025 8728	0.0825 8728	45
46	34.4740 8534	0.0290 0730	418.4260 6677	12.1374 0880	0.0023 8991	0.0823 8991	46
47	37.2320 1217	0.0268 5861	452.9001 5211	12.1642 6741	0.0022 0799	0.0822 0799	47
48	40.2105 7314	0.0248 6908	490.1321 6428	12.1891 3649	0.0020 4027	0.0820 4027	48
49	43.4274 1899	0.0230 2693	530.3427 3742	12.2121 6341	0.0018 8557	0.0818 8557	49
50	46.9016 1251	0.0213 2123	573.7701 5642	12.2334 8464	0.0017 4286	0.0817 4286	50

Appendix H Compound Daily Interest Factors for 365–Day Year

Day	4.00%	4.25%	4.50%	4.75%	5.00%	5.25%	5.50%	5.75%
1	1.0001 0958	1.0001 1643	1.0001 2328	1.0001 3013	1.0001 3698	1.0001 4383	1.0001 5068	1.0001 5753
2	1.0002 1919	1.0002 3289	1.0002 4659	1.0002 6029	1.0002 7399	1.0002 8769	1.0003 0139	1.0003 1509
3	1.0003 2880	1.0003 4935	1.0003 6990	1.0003 9046	1.0004 1101	1.0004 3156	1.0004 5212	1.0004 7267
4	1.0004 3842	1.0004 6583	1.0004 9324	1.0005 2064	1.0005 4805	1.0005 7546	1.0006 0287	1.0006 3028
5	1.0005 4806	1.0005 8232	1.0006 1659	1.0006 5085	1.0006 8511	1.0007 1938	1.0007 5365	1.0007 8791
6	1.0006 5771	1.0006 9883	1.0007 3995	1.0007 8107	1.0008 2219	1.0008 6332	1.0009 0445	1.0009 4557
7	1.0007 6737	1.0008 1535	1.0008 6333	1.0009 1131	1.0009 5929	1.0010 0728	1.0010 5527	1.0011 0326
8	1.0008 7704	1.0009 3188	1.0009 8672	1.0010 4157	1.0010 9641	1.0011 5126	1.0012 0611	1.0012 6096
9	1.0009 8673	1.0010 4843	1.0011 1013	1.0011 7184	1.0012 3355	1.0012 9526	1.0013 5698	1.0014 1870
10	1.0010 9643	1.0011 6499	1.0012 3356	1.0013 0213	1.0013 7070	1.0014 3928	1.0015 0787	1.0015 7645
11	1.0012 0614	1.0012 8156	1.0013 5700	1.0014 3243	1.0015 0788	1.0015 8333	1.0016 5878	1.0017 3424
12	1.0013 1586	1.0013 9815	1.0014 8045	1.0015 6276	1.0016 4507	1.0017 2739	1.0018 0971	1.0018 9204
13	1.0014 2559	1.0015 1475	1.0016 0392	1.0016 9310	1.0017 8228	1.0018 7147	1.0019 6067	1.0020 4988
14	1.0015 3533	1.0016 3137	1.0017 2741	1.0018 2345	1.0019 1951	1.0020 1558	1.0021 1165	1.0022 0773
15	1.0016 4509	1.0017 4799	1.0018 5091	1.0019 5383	1.0020 5676	1.0021 5970	1.0022 6265	1.0023 6562
16	1.0017 5486	1.0018 6464	1.0019 7442	1.0020 8422	1.0021 9403	1.0023 0385	1.0024 1368	1.0025 2352
17	1.0018 6464	1.0019 8129	1.0020 9795	1.0022 1463	1.0023 3132	1.0024 4802	1.0025 6473	1.0026 8145
18	1.0019 7444	1.0020 9796	1.0022 2150	1.0023 4505	1.0024 6862	1.0025 9220	1.0027 1580	1.0028 3941
19	1.0020 8424	1.0022 1464	1.0023 4506	1.0024 7560	1.0026 0595	1.0027 3641	1.0028 6689	1.0029 9739
20	1.0021 9406	1.0023 3134	1.0024 6864	1.0026 0595	1.0027 4329	1.0028 8064	1.0030 1801	1.0031 5540
21	1.0023 0389	1.0024 4805	1.0025 9223	1.0027 3643	1.0028 8065	1.0030 2489	1.0031 6915	1.0033 1343
22	1.0024 1373	1.0025 6477	1.0027 1584	1.0028 6692	1.0030 1803	1.0031 6916	1.0033 2031	1.0034 7149
23	1.0025 2358	1.0026 8151	1.0028 3946	1.0029 9743	1.0031 5543	1.0033 1345	1.0034 7150	1.0036 2957
24	1.0026 3345	1.0027 9826	1.0029 6310	1.0031 2796	1.0032 9285	1.0034 5777	1.0036 2271	1.0037 8767
25	1.0027 4333	1.0029 1502	1.0030 8675	1.0032 5851	1.0034 3029	1.0036 0210	1.0037 7394	1.0039 4581
26	1.0028 5322	1.0030 3180	1.0032 1042	1.0033 8907	1.0035 6774	1.0037 4645	1.0039 2519	1.0041 0396
27	1.0029 6312	1.0031 4859	1.0033 3410	1.0035 1964	1.0037 0522	1.0038 9083	1.0040 7647	1.0042 6214
28	1.0030 7303	1.0032 6540	1.0034 5780	1.0036 5024	1.0038 4271	1.0040 3522	1.0042 2777	1.0044 2035
29	1.0031 8269	1.0033 8222	1.0035 8152	1.0037 8085	1.0039 8023	1.0041 7964	1.0043 7909	1.0045 7858
30	1.0032 9290	1.0034 9905	1.0037 0524	1.0039 1148	1.0041 1776	1.0043 2407	1.0045 3043	1.0047 3683
31	1.0034 0285	1.0036 1590	1.0038 2899	1.0040 4213	1.0042 5531	1.0044 6853	1.0046 8180	1.0048 9511
32	1.0035 1281	1.0037 3275	1.0039 5275	1.0041 7279	1.0043 9288	1.0046 1301	1.0048 3319	1.0050 5342
33	1.0036 2278	1.0038 4963	1.0040 7652	1.0043 0347	1.0045 3046	1.0047 5751	1.0049 8460	1.0052 1175
34	1.0037 3277	1.0039 6651	1.0042 0031	1.0044 3417	1.0046 6807	1.0049 0203	1.0051 3604	1.0053 7010
35	1.0038 4277	1.0040 8341	1.0043 2412	1.0045 6488	1.0048 0570	1.0050 4657	1.0052 8750	1.0055 2848
36	1.0039 5278	1.0042 0033	1.0044 4794	1.0046 9561	1.0049 4334	1.0051 9113	1.0054 3898	1.0055 8689
37	1.0040 6280	1.0043 1726	1.0045 7178	1.0048 2636	1.0050 8101	1.0053 3571	1.0055 0049	1.0058 4532
38	1.0041 7883	1.0044 3420	1.0046 9563	1.0049 5712	1.0052 1869	1.0054 8032	1.0057 4201	1.0060 0378
39	1.0042 8288	1.0045 5115	1.0048 1949	1.0050 8791	1.0053 5639	1.0056 2494	1.0058 9356	1.0061 6226
40	1.0043 9294	1.0046 6812	1.0049 4338	1.0052 1871	1.0054 9411	1.0057 6959	1.0060 4514	1.0063 2076
41	1.0045 0301	1.0047 8510	1.0050 6727	1.0053 4952	1.0056 3185	1.0059 1425	1.0061 9673	1.0064 7829
42	1.0046 1309	1.0049 0210	1.0051 9119	1.0054 8035	1.0057 6961	1.0060 5894	1.0063 4835	1.0066 3785
43	1.0047 2318	1.0050 1911	1.0053 1511	1.0056 1121	1.0059 0738	1.0062 0364	1.0064 0999	1.0067 9643
44	1.0048 3329	1.0051 1361	1.0054 3906	1.0057 4207	1.0060 4518	1.0063 4837	1.0066 5166	1.0069 5503
45	1.0049 4341	1.0052 5317	1.0055 6301	1.0058 7296	1.0061 8299	1.0064 9312	1.0068 0334	1.0071 1366
46	1.0050 5354	1.0053 7022	1.0056 8699	1.0060 0386	1.0063 2083	1.0066 3789	1.0069 5505	1.0072 7231
47	1.0051 6368	1.0054 8728	1.0058 1098	1.0061 3478	1.0064 5868	1.0067 8768	1.0071 0679	1.0074 3099
48	1.0052 7384	1.0056 0436	1.0059 3498	1.0062 6571	1.0065 9655	1.0069 2749	1.0072 5854	1.0075 8970
49	1.0053 8401	1.0057 2145	1.0060 5900	1.0063 9666	1.0067 3444	1.0070 7232	1.0074 1032	1.0077 4843
50	1.0054 9418	1.0058 3855	1.0061 8303	1.0065 2763	1.0068 7235	1.0072 1718	1.0075 6212	1.0079 0718

Day	4.00%	4.25%	4.50%	4.75%	5.00%	5.25%	5.50%	5.75%
51	1.0056 0438	1.0059 5567	1.0063 0708	1.0066 5862	1.0070 1028	1.0073 6205	1.0077 1395	1.0080 6596
52	1.0057 1458	1.0060 7280	1.0064 3115	1.0067 8962	1.0071 4822	1.0075 0695	1.0078 6579	1.0082 2477
53	1.0058 2479	1.0061 8995	1.0065 5523	1.0069 2064	1.0072 8619	1.0076 5186	1.0080 1757	1.0083 8360
54	1.0059 3502	1.0063 0711	1.0066 7933	1.0070 5168	1.0074 2417	1.0077 9680	1.0081 6956	1.0085 4245
55	1.0060 4526	1.0064 2428	1.0068 0344	1.0071 8274	1.0075 6218	1.0079 4175	1.0083 2147	1.0087 0133
56	1.0061 5551	1.0065 4147	1.0069 2756	1.0073 1381	1.0077 0020	1.0080 8673	1.0084 7341	1.0088 6024
57	1.0062 6578	1.0066 5867	1.0070 5171	1.0074 4490	1.0078 3824	1.0082 3173	1.0086 2537	1.0090 1917
58	1.0063 7605	1.0067 7588	1.0071 7586	1.0075 7600	1.0079 7630	1.0083 7675	1.0087 7736	1.0091 7812
59	1.0064 8634	1.0068 9311	1.0073 0004	1.0077 0713	1.0081 1438	1.0085 2179	1.0089 2937	1.0093 3710
60	1.0065 9664	1.0070 1035	1.0074 2422	1.0078 3827	1.0082 5248	1.0086 6685	1.0090 8140	1.0094 9611
61	1.0067 0695	1.0071 2760	1.0075 4843	1.0079 6942	1.0083 9059	1.0088 1193	1.0092 3345	1.0096 5514
62	1.0068 1728	1.0072 4487	1.0076 7264	1.0081 0060	1.0085 2873	1.0089 5704	1.0093 8553	1.0098 1419
63	1.0069 2761	1.0073 6215	1.0077 9688	1.0082 3179	1.0086 6688	1.0091 0216	1.0095 3763	1.0099 7328
64	1.0070 3796	1.0074 7945	1.0079 2113	1.0083 6300	1.0088 0506	1.0092 4731	1.0096 8975	1.0101 3238
65	1.0071 4832	1.0075 9676	1.0080 4539	1.0084 9422	1.0089 4325	1.0093 9247	1.0098 4189	1.0102 9151
66	1.0072 5869	1.0077 1408	1.0081 6967	1.0086 2546	1.0090 8146	1.0095 3766	1.0099 9406	1.0104 5067
67	1.0073 6908	1.0078 3142	1.0082 9397	1.0087 5672	1.0092 1969	1.0096 8287	1.0101 4625	1.0106 0985
68	1.0074 7947	1.0079 4877	1.0084 1828	1.0088 8800	1.0093 5794	1.0098 2809	1.0102 9847	1.0107 6905
69	1.0075 8988	1.0080 6613	1.0085 4260	1.0090 1929	1.0094 9621	1.0099 7334	1.0104 5070	1.0109 2828
70	1.0077 0030	1.0081 8351	1.0086 6694	1.0091 5060	1.0096 3449	1.0101 1861	1.0106 0296	1.0110 8754
71	1.0078 1074	1.0083 0090	1.0087 9130	1.0092 8193	1.0097 7280	1.0102 6390	1.0107 5525	1.0112 4682
72	1.0079 2118	1.0084 1830	1.0089 1567	1.0094 1328	1.0099 1113	1.0104 0922	1.0109 0755	1.0114 0613
73	1.0080 3164	1.0085 3572	1.0090 4006	1.0095 4464	1.0100 4947	1.0105 5455	1.0110 5988	1.0115 6546
74	1.0081 4211	1.0086 5315	1.0091 6446	1.0096 7602	1.0101 8783	1.0106 9990	1.0112 1223	1.0117 2481
75	1.0082 5259	1.0087 7060	1.0092 8888	1.0098 0741	1.0103 2621	1.0108 4528	1.0113 6461	1.0118 8419
76	1.0083 6308	1.0088 8806	1.0094 1331	1.0099 3883	1.0104 6462	1.0109 9067	1.0115 1700	1.0120 4360
77	1.0084 7359	1.0090 0553	1.0095 3776	1.0100 7026	1.0106 0304	1.0111 3609	1.0116 6942	1.0122 0303
78	1.0085 8411	1.0091 2302	1.0096 6222	1.0102 0170	1.0107 4147	1.0112 8153	1.0118 2187	1.0123 6249
79	1.0086 9464	1.0092 4052	1.0097 8670	1.0103 3317	1.0108 7993	1.0114 2699	1.0119 7433	1.0125 2197
80	1.0088 0518	1.0093 5804	1.0099 1119	1.0104 6465	1.0110 1841	1.0115 7246	1.0121 2682	1.0126 8148
81	1.0089 1573	1.0094 7556	1.0100 3570	1.0105 9615	1.0111 5690	1.0117 1797	1.0122 7933	1.0128 4101
82	1.0090 2630	1.0095 9311	1.0101 6023	1.0107 2767	1.0112 9542	1.0118 6349	1.0124 3187	1.0130 0057
83	1.0091 3688	1.0097 1066	1.0102 8477	1.0108 5920	1.0114 3395	1.0120 0903	1.0125 8443	1.0131 6015
84	1.0092 4747	1.0098 2823	1.0104 0932	1.0109 9075	1.0115 7251	1.0121 5459	1.0127 3701	1.0133 1976
85	1.0093 5807	1.0099 4581	1.0105 3390	1.0111 2232	1.0117 1108	1.0123 0017	1.0128 8961	1.0134 7939
86	1.0094 6868	1.0100 6341	1.0106 5848	1.0112 5390	1.011 84967	1.0124 4578	1.0130 4224	1.0136 3905
87	1.0095 7931	1.0101 8102	1.0107 8308	1.0113 8550	1.0119 8828	1.0125 9141	1.0131 9489	1.0137 9873
88	1.0096 8995	1.0102 9864	1.0109 0770	1.0115 1712	1.0121 2691	1.01273 705	1.0133 4756	1.0139 5844
89	1.0098 0060	1.0104 1628	1.0110 3233	1.0116 4876	1.0122 6555	1.0128 8272	1.0135 0026	1.0141 1817
90	1.0099 1126	1.0105 3393	1.0111 5698	1.0117 8041	1.0124 0422	1.0130 2841	1.0136 5298	1.0142 7793
91	1.0100 2194	1.0106 5160	1.0112 8164	1.0119 1208	1.0125 4290	1.0131 7412	1.0138 0572	1.0144 3771
92	1.0101 3262	1.0107 6927	1.0114 0632	1.0120 4377	1.0126 8161	1.0133 1985	1.0139 5849	1.0145 9752
93	1.0102 4332	1.0108 8697	1.0115 3102	1.0121 7547	1.0128 2033	1.0134 5560	1.0141 1127	1.0147 5736
94	1.0103 5404	1.0110 0467	1.0116 5573	1.0123 0719	1.0129 5908	1.0136 1137	1.0142 6409	1.0149 1721
95	1.0104 4676	1.0111 2239	1.0117 8045	1.0124 3893	1.0130 9784	1.0137 5717	1.0144 1692	1.0150 7710
96	1.0105 7550	1.0112 4013	1.0119 0519	1.0125 7069	1.0132 3662	1.0139 0298	1.0145 6978	1.0152 3701
97	1.0106 8624	1.0113 5787	1.0120 2995	1.0127 0246	1.0133 7542	1.0140 4882	1.0147 2266	1.0153 9694
98	1.0107 9700	1.0114 7563	1.0121 5472	1.0128 3425	1.0135 1424	1.0141 9467	1.0148 7556	1.0155 5690
99	1.0109 0778	1.0115 9341	1.0122 7950	1.0129 6606	1.0136 5307	1.0143 4055	1.0150 2849	1.0157 1689
100	1.0110 1856	1.0117 1120	1.0124 0430	1.0130 9788	1.0137 9193	1.0144 8645	1.0151 8144	1.0158 7690

Day	4.00%	4.25%	4.50%	4.75%	5.00%	5.25%	5.50%	5.75%
101	1.0111 2936	1.0118 2900	1.0125 2912	1.0132 2972	1.0139 3081	1.0146 3237	1.0153 3441	1.0160 3693
102	1.0112 4017	1.0119 4681	1.0126 5395	1.0133 6158	1.0140 6970	1.0147 7831	1.0154 8741	1.0161 9699
103	1.0113 5099	1.0120 6464	1.0127 7880	1.0134 9346	1.0142 0861	1.0149 2427	1.0156 4042	1.0163 5708
104	1.0114 6182	1.0121 8249	1.0129 0366	1.0136 2535	1.0143 4755	1.0150 7025	1.0157 9347	1.0165 1719
105	1.0115 7266	1.0123 0034	1.0130 2854	1.0137 5726	1.0144 8650	1.0152 1625	1.0159 4653	1.0166 7733
106	1.0116 8352	1.0124 1821	1.0131 5344	1.0138 8919	1.0146 2547	1.0153 6228	1.0160 9962	1.0168 3749
107	1.0117 9439	1.0125 3610	1.0132 7835	1.0140 2113	1.0147 6446	1.0155 0832	1.0162 5273	1.0169 9767
108	1.0119 0527	1.0126 5400	1.0134 0327	1.0141 5309	1.0149 0347	1.0156 5439	1.0164 0586	1.0171 5789
109	1.0120 1617	1.0127 7191	1.0135 2821	1.0142 8507	1.0150 4250	1.0158 0048	1.0165 5902	1.0173 1812
110	1.0121 2707	1.0128 8983	1.0136 5317	1.0144 1707	1.0151 8154	1.0159 4658	1.0167 1220	1.0174 7839
111	1.0122 3799	1.0130 0777	1.0137 7814	1.0145 4908	1.0153 2061	1.0160 9271	1.0168 6540	1.0176 3867
112	1.0123 4892	1.0131 2573	1.0139 0312	1.0146 8111	1.0154 5969	1.0162 3886	1.0170 1863	1.0177 9899
113	1.0124 5986	1.0132 4369	1.0140 2813	1.0148 1316	1.0155 9880	1.0163 8504	1.0171 7188	1.0179 5933
114	1.0125 7082	1.0133 6167	1.0141 5314	1.0149 4522	1.0157 3792	1.0165 3123	1.0173 2515	1.0181 1969
115	1.0126 8178	1.0134 7967	1.0142 7818	1.0150 7731	1.0158 7706	1.0166 7744	1.0174 7845	1.0182 8008
116	1.0127 9276	1.0135 9768	1.0144 0322	1.0152 0941	1.0160 1622	1.0168 2368	1.0176 3177	1.0184 4049
117	1.0129 0375	1.0137 1570	1.0145 2829	1.0153 4152	1.0161 5540	1.0169 6993	1.0177 8511	1.0186 0093
118	1.0130 1476	1.0138 3373	1.0146 5337	1.0154 7366	1.0162 9460	1.0171 1621	1.0179 3847	1.0187 6139
119	1.0131 2577	1.0139 5178	1.0147 7846	1.0156 0581	1.0164 3382	1.0172 6251	1.0180 9186	1.0189 2188
120	1.0132 3680	1.0140 6984	1.0149 0357	1.0157 3797	1.0165 7306	1.0174 0882	1.0182 4527	1.0190 8240
121	1.0133 4784	1.0141 8792	1.0150 2869	1.0158 7016	1.0167 1232	1.0175 5516	1.0183 9871	1.0192 4294
122	1.0134 5889	1.0143 0601	1.0151 5384	1.0160 0236	1.0168 5159	1.0177 0152	1.0185 5216	1.0194 0351
123	1.0135 6996	1.0144 2412	1.0152 7899	1.0161 3458	1.0169 9089	1.0178 4791	1.0187 0564	1.0195 6410
124	1.0136 8103	1.0145 4223	1.0154 0416	1.0162 6682	1.0171 3020	1.0179 9431	1.0188 5915	1.0197 2471
125	1.0137 9212	1.0146 6037	1.0155 2935	1.0163 9907	1.0172 6953	1.0181 4073	1.0190 1267	1.0198 8535
126	1.0139 0322	1.0147 7851	1.0156 5455	1.0165 3134	1.0174 0888	1.0182 8718	1.0191 6622	1.0200 4602
127	1.0140 1433	1.0148 9667	1.0157 7977	1.0166 6363	1.0175 4826	1.0184 3364	1.0193 1980	1.0202 0671
128	1.0141 2546	1.0150 1484	1.0159 0500	1.0167 9594	1.0176 8765	1.0185 8013	1.0194 7339	1.0203 6743
129	1.0142 3659	1.0151 3303	1.0160 3025	1.0169 2826	1.0178 2706	1.0187 2664	1.0196 2701	1.0205 2817
130	1.0143 4774	1.0152 5123	1.0161 5552	1.0170 6060	1.0179 6648	1.0188 7317	1.0197 8065	1.0206 8894
131	1.0144 5891	1.0153 6944	1.0162 8079	1.0171 9296	1.0181 0593	1.0190 1972	1.0199 3432	1.0208 4974
132	1.0145 7008	1.0154 8767	1.0164 0609	1.0173 2533	1.0182 4540	1.0191 6629	1.0200 8801	1.0210 1055
133	1.0146 8126	1.0156 0591	1.0165 3140	1.0174 5772	1.0138 8488	1.0193 1288	1.0202 4172	1.0211 7140
134	1.0147 9246	1.0157 2417	1.0166 5678	1.0175 9013	1.0185 2439	1.0194 5950	1.0203 9546	1.0213 3227
135	1.0149 0367	1.0158 4244	1.0167 8207	1.0177 2256	1.0186 6391	1.0196 0613	1.0205 4921	1.0214 9316
136	1.0150 1489	1.0159 6072	1.0169 0742	1.0178 5500	1.0188 0345	1.0197 5279	1.0270 0300	1.0216 5408
137	1.0151 2613	1.0160 7902	1.0170 3280	1.0179 8746	1.0189 4302	1.0198 9946	1.0208 5680	1.0218 1503
138	1.0152 3736	1.0161 9733	1.0171 5818	1.0181 1994	1.0190 8260	1.0200 4616	1.0210 1063	1.0219 7600
139	1.0153 4864	1.0163 1565	1.0172 8359	1.0182 5243	1.0192 2220	1.0201 9288	1.0211 6448	1.0221 3700
140	1.0154 5991	1.0164 3399	1.0174 0900	1.0183 8495	1.0193 6182	1.0203 3962	1.0213 1835	1.0222 9802
141	1.0155 7119	1.0165 5234	1.0175 3444	1.0185 1748	1.0195 0146	1.0204 8638	1.0214 7225	1.0224 5906
142	1.0156 8248	1.0166 7071	1.0176 5989	1.0186 5002	1.0196 4111	1.0206 3316	1.0216 2617	1.0226 2014
143	1.0157 9379	1.0167 8909	1.0177 8535	1.0187 8259	1.0197 8079	1.0207 7997	1.0217 8011	1.0227 8123
144	1.0159 0511	1.0169 0748	1.0179 1083	1.0189 1517	1.0199 2049	1.0209 2679	1.0219 3408	1.0229 4236
145	1.0160 1644	1.0170 2589	1.0180 3633	1.0190 4777	1.0200 6020	1.0210 7364	1.0220 8807	1.0231 0351
146	1.0161 2779	1.0171 4431	1.0181 6184	1.0191 8038	1.0201 9994	1.0212 2050	1.0222 4208	1.0232 6458
147	1.0162 3915	1.0172 6274	1.0182 8737	1.0193 1302	1.0203 3969	1.0213 6739	1.0223 9612	1.0234 2588
148	1.0163 5051	1.0173 8119	1.0184 1291	1.0194 4567	1.0204 7946	1.0215 1430	1.0225 5018	1.0235 8710
149	1.0164 6189	1.0174 9965	1.0185 3847	1.0195 7833	1.0206 1925	1.0216 6123	1.0227 0426	1.0237 4835
150	1.0165 7329	1.0176 1813	1.0186 6404	1.0197 1102	1.0207 5907	1.0218 0818	1.0228 5837	1.0239 0963

Day	4.00%	4.25%	4.50%	4.75%	5.00%	5.25%	5.50%	5.75%
151	1.0166 8469	1.0177 3662	1.0187 8963	1.0198 4372	1.0208 9890	1.0219 5515	1.0230 1250	1.0240 7093
152	1.0167 9611	1.0178 5512	1.0189 1523	1.0199 7644	1.0210 3874	1.0221 0215	1.0231 6665	1.0242 3226
153	1.0169 0754	1.0179 7364	1.0190 4085	1.0201 0918	1.0211 7861	1.0222 4916	1.0233 2083	1.0243 9361
154	1.0170 1898	1.0180 9217	1.0191 6649	1.0202 4193	1.0231 1850	1.0223 9620	1.0234 7503	1.0245 5498
155	1.0171 3044	1.0182 1072	1.0192 9214	1.0203 7470	1.0214 5841	1.0225 4325	1.0236 2925	1.0247 1639
156	1.0172 4190	1.0183 2928	1.0194 1781	1.0205 0749	1.0215 9833	1.0226 9033	1.0237 8349	1.0248 7781
157	1.0173 5338	1.0184 4785	1.0195 4349	1.0206 4030	1.0217 3828	1.0228 3743	1.0239 3776	1.0250 3927
158	1.0174 6487	1.0185 6643	1.0196 6918	1.0207 7312	1.0218 7824	1.0229 8455	1.0240 9205	1.0252 0075
159	1.0175 7637	1.0186 8503	1.0197 9490	1.0209 0596	1.0220 1823	1.0231 3169	1.0242 4637	1.0253 6225
160	1.0176 8789	1.0188 0365	1.0199 2062	1.0210 3882	1.0221 5823	1.0232 7886	1.0244 0071	1.0255 2378
161	1.0177 9942	1.0189 2228	1.0200 4637	1.0211 7169	1.0222 9825	1.0234 2604	1.0245 5507	1.0256 8534
162	1.0179 1096	1.0190 4092	1.0201 7213	1.0213 0458	1.0224 3829	1.0235 7325	1.0247 0946	1.0258 4692
163	1.0180 2251	1.0191 5957	1.0202 9790	1.0214 3749	1.0225 7835	1.0237 2047	1.0248 6386	1.0260 0852
164	1.0181 3407	1.0192 7824	1.0204 2369	1.0215 7042	1.0227 1843	1.0238 6772	1.0250 1829	1.0261 7015
165	1.0182 4565	1.0193 9693	1.0205 4950	1.0217 0336	1.0228 5853	1.0240 1499	1.0251 7275	1.0263 3181
166	1.0183 5724	1.0195 1562	1.0206 7532	1.0218 3633	1.0229 9865	1.0241 6228	1.0253 2723	1.0264 9349
167	1.0184 6884	1.0196 3433	1.0208 0116	1.0219 6930	1.0231 3878	1.0243 0959	1.0254 8173	1.0266 5520
168	1.0185 8045	1.0197 5306	1.0209 2701	1.0221 0230	1.0232 7894	1.0244 5692	1.0256 3625	1.0268 1695
169	1.0186 9208	1.0198 7180	1.0210 5288	1.0222 3531	1.0234 1911	1.0246 0427	1.0257 9080	1.0269 7869
170	1.0188 0371	1.0199 9055	1.0211 7876	1.0223 6834	1.0235 5931	1.0247 5165	1.0259 4537	1.0271 4048
171	1.0189 1536	1.0201 0931	1.0213 0466	1.0225 0139	1.0236 9952	1.0248 9904	1.0260 9997	1.0273 0229
172	1.0190 2703	1.0202 2809	1.0214 3057	1.0226 3446	1.0238 3975	1.0250 4646	1.0262 5459	1.0274 6412
173	1.0191 3870	1.0203 4689	1.0215 5650	1.0227 6754	1.0239 8001	1.0251 9390	1.0264 0923	1.0276 2598
174	1.0192 5039	1.0204 6570	1.0216 8245	1.0229 0064	1.0241 2028	1.0253 4136	1.0265 6389	1.0277 8787
175	1.0193 6209	1.0205 8452	1.0218 0841	1.0230 3376	1.0242 6057	1.0254 8884	1.0267 1858	1.0279 4978
176	1.0194 7380	1.0207 0335	1.0219 3430	1.0231 6680	1.0244 0088	1.0256 3634	1.0268 7329	1.0281 1172
177	1.0195 8552	1.0208 2220	1.0220 6038	1.0233 0004	1.0245 4121	1.0257 8386	1.0270 2802	1.0282 7368
178	1.0196 9726	1.0209 4106	1.0221 8638	1.0234 3321	1.0246 8155	1.0259 3141	1.0271 8278	1.0284 3567
179	1.0198 0900	1.0210 5994	1.0223 1241	1.0235 6640	1.0248 2191	1.0260 7897	1.0273 3756	1.0285 0768
180	1.0199 2076	1.0211 7883	1.0224 3845	1.0236 9960	1.0249 6231	1.0262 2656	1.0274 9237	1.0287 5972
181	1.0200 3253	1.0212 9774	1.0225 6450	1.0238 3282	1.0251 0271	1.0263 7417	1.0276 4719	1.0289 2179
182	1.0201 4432	1.0214 1665	1.0226 9057	1.0239 6606	1.0252 4314	1.0265 2180	1.0278 0205	1.0290 8388
183	1.0202 5612	1.0215 3559	1.0228 1665	1.0240 9932	1.0253 8358	1.0266 6945	1.0279 5692	1.0292 4599
184	1.0203 6792	1.0216 5453	1.0229 4275	1.0242 3250	1.0255 2405	1.0268 1712	1.0281 1182	1.0294 0814
185	1.0204 7975	1.0217 7349	1.0230 6887	1.0243 6588	1.0256 6453	1.0269 6481	1.0282 6674	1.0295 7030
186	1.0205 9158	1.0218 9247	1.0231 9500	1.0244 9919	1.0258 0503	1.0271 1253	1.0284 2168	1.0297 3250
187	1.0207 0342	1.0220 1145	1.0233 2115	1.0246 3251	1.0259 4555	1.0272 6026	1.0285 7665	1.0298 9471
188	1.0208 1528	1.0221 3045	1.0234 4731	1.0247 6586	1.0260 8609	1.0274 0807	1.0287 3164	1.0300 5696
189	1.0209 2715	1.0222 4947	1.0235 7349	1.0248 9922	1.0262 2665	1.0275 5580	1.0288 8666	1.0302 1923
190	1.0210 3904	1.0223 6850	1.0236 9969	1.0250 3259	1.0263 6723	1.0277 0360	1.0290 4159	1.0303 8152
191	1.0211 5093	1.0224 8754	1.0238 2589	1.0251 6599	1.0265 0783	1.0278 5142	1.0291 9675	1.0305 4384
192	1.0212 6284	1.0226 0660	1.0239 5212	1.0252 9940	1.0266 4845	1.0279 9926	1.0293 5184	1.0307 0619
193	1.0213 7476	1.0227 2567	1.0240 7836	1.0254 3283	1.0267 8908	1.0281 4712	1.0295 0695	1.0308 6856
194	1.0214 8669	1.0228 4475	1.0242 0462	1.0255 6628	1.0269 2974	1.0282 9501	1.0296 6208	1.0310 3096
195	1.0215 9863	1.0229 6385	1.0243 3089	1.0256 9974	1.0270 7042	1.0284 4291	1.0298 1723	1.0311 9338
196	1.0217 1059	1.0230 8296	1.0244 5718	1.0258 3322	1.0272 1111	1.0285 9084	1.0299 7241	1.0313 5583
197	1.0218 2256	1.0232 0209	1.0245 8348	1.0259 6672	1.0273 5182	1.0287 3879	1.0301 2761	1.0315 1830
198	1.0219 3454	1.0233 2123	1.0247 0980	1.0261 0024	1.0274 9256	1.0288 8675	1.0302 8284	1.0316 8080
199	1.0220 4653	1.0234 4038	1.0248 3613	1.0262 3377	1.0276 3331	1.0290 3475	1.0304 3808	1.0318 4333
200	1.0221 5853	1.0235 5955	1.0249 6248	1.0263 6732	1.0277 7408	1.0291 8276	1.0305 9336	1.0320 0588

Appendix H Compound Daily Interest Factors for 365–Day Year—*Cont.*

Day	4.00%	4.25%	4.50%	4.75%	5.00%	5.25%	5.50%	5.75%
201	1.0222 7055	1.0236 7873	1.0250 8885	1.0265 0089	1.0279 1487	1.0293 3079	1.0307 4865	1.0321 6845
202	1.0223 8258	1.0237 9739	1.0252 1523	1.0266 3448	1.0280 5568	1.0294 7884	1.0309 0397	1.0323 3105
203	1.0224 9462	1.0239 1714	1.0253 4162	1.0267 6808	1.0281 9651	1.0296 2692	1.0310 5931	1.0324 9368
204	1.0226 0668	1.0240 3636	1.0254 6804	1.0269 0170	1.0283 3736	1.0297 7502	1.0312 1468	1.0326 5633
205	1.0227 1874	1.0241 5560	1.0255 9446	1.0270 3534	1.0284 7823	1.0299 2314	1.0313 7006	1.0328 1901
206	1.0228 3082	1.0242 7485	1.0257 2091	1.0271 6899	1.0286 1912	1.0300 7128	1.0315 2548	1.0329 8172
207	1.0229 4291	1.0243 9411	1.0258 4737	1.0273 0267	1.0287 6002	1.0302 1944	1.0316 8091	1.0331 4445
208	1.0230 5502	1.0245 1339	1.0259 7384	1.0274 3636	1.0289 0095	1.0303 6762	1.0318 3637	1.0333 0720
209	1.0231 6713	1.0246 3269	1.0261 0033	1.0275 7006	1.0290 4189	1.0305 1582	1.0319 9185	1.0334 6998
210	1.0232 7926	1.0247 5199	1.0262 2683	1.0277 0379	1.0291 8286	1.0306 6405	1.0321 4736	1.0336 3279
211	1.0233 9140	1.0248 7131	1.0263 5336	1.0278 3753	1.0293 2384	1.0308 1229	1.0323 0289	1.0337 9562
212	1.0235 0355	1.0249 9065	1.0264 7989	1.0279 7129	1.0294 6485	1.0309 6056	1.0324 5844	1.0339 5848
213	1.0236 1572	1.0251 0999	1.0266 0645	1.0281 0507	1.0296 0587	1.0311 0885	1.0326 1402	1.0341 2137
214	1.0237 2789	1.0252 2936	1.0267 3301	1.0282 3886	1.0297 4691	1.0312 5716	1.0327 6961	1.0342 8428
215	1.0238 4008	1.0253 4873	1.0268 5960	1.0283 7267	1.0298 8797	1.0314 0549	1.0329 2524	1.0344 4721
216	1.0239 5229	1.0254 6812	1.0269 8620	1.0285 0650	1.0300 2905	1.0315 5384	1.0330 8088	1.0346 1017
217	1.0240 6450	1.0255 8753	1.0271 1281	1.0286 4035	1.0301 7015	1.0317 0222	1.0332 3655	1.0347 7316
218	1.0241 7673	1.0257 0694	1.0272 3944	1.0287 7421	1.0303 1127	1.0318 5061	1.0333 9225	1.0349 3617
219	1.0242 8896	1.0258 2638	1.0273 6609	1.0289 0810	1.0304 5241	1.0319 9903	1.0335 4796	1.0350 9921
220	1.0244 0122	1.0259 4582	1.0274 9275	1.0290 4199	1.0305 9357	1.0321 4747	1.0337 0370	1.0352 6227
221	1.0245 1348	1.0260 6528	1.0276 1943	1.0291 7591	1.0307 3475	1.0322 9593	1.0338 5947	1.0354 2536
222	1.0246 2575	1.0261 8475	1.0277 4612	1.0293 0984	1.0308 7594	1.0324 4441	1.0340 1525	1.0355 8848
223	1.0247 3804	1.0263 0424	1.0278 7283	1.0294 4380	1.0310 1716	1.0325 9291	1.0341 7106	1.0357 5162
224	1.0248 5034	1.0264 2374	1.0279 9955	1.0295 7776	1.0311 5839	1.0327 4144	1.0343 2690	1.0359 1478
225	1.0249 6265	1.0265 4326	1.0281 2629	1.0297 1175	1.0312 9965	1.0328 8998	1.0344 8276	1.0360 7797
226	1.0250 7498	1.0266 6279	1.0282 5305	1.0298 4575	1.0314 4092	1.0330 3855	1.0346 3864	1.0362 4119
227	1.0251 8732	1.0267 8233	1.0283 7982	1.0299 7978	1.0315 8221	1.0331 8713	1.0347 9454	1.0364 0444
228	1.0252 9987	1.0269 0189	1.0285 0660	1.0301 1381	1.0317 2353	1.0333 3574	1.0349 5047	1.0365 6771
229	1.0254 1203	1.0270 2146	1.0286 3341	1.0302 4787	1.0318 6486	1.0334 8437	1.0351 0642	1.0367 3100
230	1.0255 2440	1.0271 4104	1.0287 6022	1.0303 8194	1.0320 0621	1.0336 3303	1.0352 6240	1.0368 9432
231	1.0256 3679	1.0272 6064	1.0288 8706	1.0305 1603	1.0321 4758	1.0337 8170	1.0354 1839	1.0370 5767
232	1.0257 4919	1.0273 8025	1.0290 1391	1.0306 5014	1.0322 8897	1.0339 3039	1.0355 7442	1.0372 2104
233	1.0258 6160	1.0274 9988	1.0291 4077	1.0307 8427	1.0324 3038	1.0340 7911	1.0357 3046	1.0373 8444
234	1.0259 7402	1.0276 1952	1.0292 6765	1.0309 1841	1.0325 7181	1.0342 2785	1.0358 8653	1.0375 4786
235	1.0260 8645	1.0277 3917	1.0293 9455	1.0310 5257	1.0327 1326	1.0343 7661	1.0360 4262	1.0377 1131
236	1.0261 9890	1.0278 5884	1.0295 2146	1.0311 8675	1.0328 5473	1.0345 2539	1.0361 9874	1.0378 7479
237	1.0263 1136	1.0279 7852	1.0296 4839	1.0313 2095	1.0329 9621	1.0346 7419	1.0363 5488	1.0380 3829
238	1.0264 2384	1.0280 9822	1.0297 7533	1.0314 5516	1.0331 3772	1.0348 2301	1.0365 1104	1.0382 0181
239	1.0265 3632	1.0282 1793	1.0299 0229	1.0315 8939	1.0332 7924	1.0349 7185	1.0366 6723	1.0383 6536
240	1.0266 4882	1.0283 3765	1.0300 2926	1.0317 2364	1.0334 2079	1.0351 2072	1.0368 2344	1.0385 2894
241	1.0267 6133	1.0284 5739	1.0301 5625	1.0318 5790	1.0335 6235	1.0352 6961	1.0369 7967	1.0386 9255
242	1.0268 7385	1.0285 7714	1.0302 8326	1.0319 9218	1.0337 0394	1.0354 1852	1.0371 3593	1.0388 5618
243	1.0269 8638	1.0286 9691	1.0304 1028	1.0321 2649	1.0338 4554	1.0355 6745	1.0372 9221	1.0390 1983
244	1.0270 9893	1.0288 1669	1.0305 3731	1.0322 6080	1.0339 8716	1.0357 1640	1.0374 4851	1.0391 8351
245	1.0272 1149	1.0289 3648	1.0306 6437	1.0323 9514	1.0341 2881	1.0358 6537	1.0376 0484	1.0393 4722
246	1.0273 2406	1.0290 5629	1.0307 9144	1.0325 2949	1.0342 7047	1.0360 1437	1.0377 6119	1.0395 1095
247	1.0274 3664	1.0291 7611	1.0309 1852	1.0326 6386	1.0344 1215	1.0361 6338	1.0379 1757	1.0396 7471
248	1.0275 4924	1.0292 9595	1.0310 4562	1.0327 9825	1.0345 5385	1.0363 1242	1.0380 7397	1.0398 3850
249	1.0276 6185	1.0294 1580	1.0311 7273	1.0329 3265	1.0346 9557	1.0364 6148	1.0382 3039	1.0400 0231
250	1.0277 7447	1.0295 3566	1.0312 9987	1.0330 6708	1.0348 3731	1.0366 1056	1.0383 8683	1.0401 6614

Day	4.00%	4.25%	4.50%	4.75%	5.00%	5.25%	5.50%	5.75%
251	1.0278 8710	1.0296 5554	1.0314 2701	1.0332 0152	1.0349 7907	1.0367 5966	1.0385 4330	1.0403 3000
252	1.0279 9974	1.0297 7543	1.0315 5417	1.0333 3597	1.0351 2084	1.0369 0878	1.0386 9980	1.0404 9389
253	1.0281 1240	1.0298 9534	1.0316 8135	1.0334 7045	1.0352 6264	1.0370 5793	1.0388 5631	1.0406 5780
254	1.0282 2507	1.0300 1526	1.0318 0855	1.0336 0494	1.0354 0446	1.0372 0709	1.0390 1285	1.0408 2174
255	1.0283 3775	1.0301 3519	1.0319 3575	1.0337 3945	1.0355 4629	1.0373 5628	1.0391 6942	1.0409 8571
256	1.0284 5045	1.0302 5514	1.0320 6298	1.0338 7398	1.0356 8815	1.0375 0549	1.0393 2600	1.0411 4970
257	1.0285 6316	1.0303 7510	1.0321 9022	1.0340 0853	1.0358 3002	1.0376 5472	1.0394 8261	1.0413 1372
258	1.0286 7588	1.0304 9507	1.0323 1748	1.0341 4309	1.0359 7192	1.0378 0397	1.0396 3925	1.0414 7776
259	1.0298 8861	1.0306 1506	1.0324 4475	1.0342 7767	1.0361 1383	1.0379 5324	1.0397 9591	1.0416 4183
260	1.0289 0135	1.0307 3506	1.0325 7204	1.0344 1227	1.0362 5577	1.0381 0254	1.0399 5259	1.0418 0592
261	1.0290 1411	1.0308 5508	1.0326 9934	1.0345 4688	1.0363 9772	1.0382 5185	1.0401 0929	1.0419 7004
262	1.0291 2688	1.0309 7511	1.0328 2666	1.0346 8151	1.0365 3969	1.0384 0119	1.0402 6602	1.0421 3419
263	1.0292 3966	1.0310 9516	1.0329 5399	1.0348 1617	1.0366 8168	1.0385 5055	1.0404 2277	1.0422 9836
264	1.0293 5245	1.0312 1522	1.0330 8134	1.0349 5083	1.0368 2369	1.0386 9993	1.0405 7955	1.0424 6256
265	1.0294 6526	1.0313 3529	1.0332 0871	1.0350 8552	1.0369 6573	1.0388 4933	1.0407 3635	1.0426 2678
266	1.0295 7807	1.0314 5538	1.0333 3609	1.0352 2022	1.0371 0778	1.0389 9876	1.0408 9817	1.0427 9103
267	1.0296 9090	1.0315 7548	1.0334 6349	1.0353 5494	1.0372 4985	1.0391 4820	1.0410 5002	1.0429 5531
268	1.0298 0375	1.0316 9559	1.0335 9090	1.0354 8968	1.0373 9193	1.0392 9767	1.0412 0689	1.0431 1961
269	1.0299 1660	1.0318 1572	1.0337 1833	1.0356 2444	1.0375 3404	1.0394 4716	1.0413 6379	1.0432 8393
270	1.0300 2947	1.0319 3586	1.0338 4578	1.0357 5921	1.0376 7617	1.0395 9667	1.0415 2070	1.0434 4879
271	1.0301 4235	1.0320 5602	1.0339 7324	1.0358 9400	1.0378 1832	1.0397 4620	1.0416 7764	1.0436 1267
272	1.0302 5524	1.0321 7619	1.0341 0071	1.0360 2881	1.0379 6048	1.0398 9575	1.0418 3461	1.0437 7707
273	1.0303 6815	1.0322 9638	1.0342 2821	1.0361 6363	1.0381 0267	1.0400 4532	1.0419 9160	1.0439 6150
274	1.0304 8106	1.0324 1658	1.0343 5571	1.0362 9848	1.0382 4488	1.0401 9492	1.0421 4861	1.0441 0596
275	1.0305 9399	1.0325 3679	1.0344 8234	1.0364 3334	1.0383 8710	1.0403 4454	1.0423 0565	1.0442 7044
276	1.0307 0694	1.0326 5702	1.0346 1078	1.0365 6821	1.0385 2935	1.0404 9417	1.0424 6271	1.0444 3495
277	1.0308 1989	1.0327 7726	1.0347 3833	1.0367 0311	1.0386 7161	1.0406 4383	1.0426 1979	1.0445 9948
278	1.0309 3286	1.0328 9751	1.0348 6590	1.0368 3807	1.0388 1390	1.0407 9352	1.0427 7690	1.0447 6404
279	1.0310 4583	1.0330 1778	1.0349 9349	1.0369 7295	1.0389 5620	1.0409 4322	1.0429 3403	1.0449 2863
280	1.0311 5883	1.0331 3806	1.0351 2109	1.0371 0790	1.0390 9852	1.0410 9294	1.0430 9118	1.0450 9324
281	1.0312 7183	1.0332 5886	1.0352 4871	1.0372 4287	1.0392 4086	1.0412 4269	1.0432 4836	1.0452 5788
282	1.0313 8485	1.0333 7867	1.0353 7634	1.0373 7785	1.0393 8323	1.0413 9246	1.0434 0556	1.0454 2254
283	1.0314 9787	1.0334 9900	1.0355 0399	1.0375 1285	1.0395 2561	1.0415 4225	1.0435 6279	1.0455 8723
284	1.0316 1092	1.0336 1933	1.0356 3165	1.0376 4787	1.0396 6801	1.0416 9206	1.0437 2004	1.0457 5195
285	1.0317 2397	1.0337 3969	1.0357 5933	1.0377 8291	1.0398 1043	1.0418 4189	1.0438 7731	1.0459 1669
286	1.0318 3703	1.0338 6005	1.0358 8703	1.0379 1796	1.0399 5287	1.0419 9174	1.0440 3461	1.0460 8146
287	1.0319 5011	1.0339 8044	1.0360 1474	1.0380 5304	1.0400 9533	1.0421 4162	1.0441 9193	1.0462 4625
288	1.0320 6320	1.0341 0083	1.0361 4247	1.0381 8812	1.0402 3781	1.0422 9152	1.0443 4927	1.0464 1107
289	1.0321 7631	1.0342 2124	1.0362 7021	1.0383 2323	1.0403 8030	1.0424 4144	1.0445 0664	1.0465 7592
290	1.0322 8942	1.0343 4166	1.0363 9797	1.0384 5836	1.0405 2282	1.0425 9138	1.0446 6403	1.0467 4079
291	1.0324 0255	1.0344 6210	1.0365 2575	1.0385 9350	1.0406 6536	1.0427 4134	1.0448 2145	1.0469 0569
292	1.0325 1569	1.0345 8255	1.0366 5354	1.0387 2866	1.0408 0792	1.0428 9132	1.0449 7888	1.0470 7061
293	1.0326 2884	1.0347 0302	1.0367 8135	1.0388 6383	1.0409 5049	1.0430 4133	1.0451 3635	1.0472 3556
294	1.0327 4201	1.0348 2349	1.0369 0917	1.0389 9903	1.0410 9309	1.0431 9135	1.0452 9383	1.0474 0053
295	1.0328 5518	1.0349 4399	1.0370 3701	1.0391 3424	1.0412 3570	1.0433 4140	1.0454 5134	1.0475 6554
296	1.0329 6837	1.0350 6450	1.0371 6486	1.0392 6947	1.0413 7834	1.0434 9147	1.0456 0888	1.0477 3056
297	1.0330 8157	1.0351 8502	1.0372 9273	1.0394 0472	1.0415 2099	1.0436 4156	1.0457 6643	1.0478 9562
298	1.0331 9479	1.0353 0555	1.0374 2062	1.0395 3998	1.0416 6367	1.0437 9167	1.0459 2402	1.0480 6070
299	1.0333 0802	1.0354 2610	1.0375 4852	1.0396 7526	1.0418 0636	1.0439 4181	1.0460 8162	1.0482 2580
300	1.0334 2125	1.0355 4666	1.0376 7643	1.0398 1057	1.0419 4907	1.0440 9196	1.0462 3925	1.0483 9093

Day	4.00%	4.25%	4.50%	4.75%	5.00%	5.25%	5.50%	5.75%
301	1.0335 3451	1.0356 6724	1.0378 0437	1.0399 4588	1.0429 9181	1.0442 4214	1.0463 9690	1.0485 5609
302	1.0336 4777	1.0357 8783	1.0379 3231	1.0400 8122	1.0422 3456	1.0443 9234	1.0465 5458	1.0487 2127
303	1.0337 6105	1.0359 0844	1.0380 6028	1.0402 1657	1.0423 7733	1.0445 4256	1.0467 1228	1.0488 8648
304	1.0338 7434	1.0360 2906	1.0381 8826	1.0403 5194	1.0425 2012	1.0446 9280	1.0468 7000	1.0490 5172
305	1.0339 8764	1.0361 4969	1.0383 1625	1.0404 8733	1.0426 6293	1.0448 4307	1.0470 2775	1.0492 1698
306	1.0341 0095	1.0362 7034	1.0384 4427	1.0406 2274	1.0428 0576	1.0449 9335	1.0471 8552	1.0493 8227
307	1.0342 1428	1.0363 9100	1.0385 7229	1.0407 5816	1.0429 4861	1.0451 4366	1.0473 4332	1.0495 4758
308	1.0343 2762	1.0365 1168	1.0387 0034	1.0408 9360	1.0430 9148	1.0452 9399	1.0475 0113	1.0497 1292
309	1.0344 4097	1.0366 3237	1.0388 2840	1.0410 2906	1.0432 3437	1.0454 4434	1.0476 5898	1.0498 7829
310	1.0345 5433	1.0367 5307	1.0389 5647	1.0411 6454	1.0433 7728	1.0455 9471	1.0478 1684	1.0500 4368
311	1.0346 6771	1.0368 7379	1.0390 8456	1.0413 0003	1.0435 2021	1.0457 4511	1.0479 7473	1.0502 0910
312	1.0347 8109	1.0369 9452	1.0392 1267	1.0414 3554	1.0436 6316	1.0458 9552	1.0481 3255	1.0503 7454
313	1.0348 9449	1.0371 1527	1.0393 4079	1.0415 7107	1.0438 0613	1.0460 4596	1.0482 9059	1.0505 4001
314	1.0350 0791	1.0372 3603	1.0394 6893	1.0417 0662	1.0439 4911	1.0461 9642	1.0484 4855	1.0507 0551
315	1.0351 2133	1.0373 5680	1.0395 9708	1.0418 4218	1.0440 9212	1.0463 4690	1.0486 0653	1.0508 7103
316	1.0352 3477	1.0374 7759	1.0397 2525	1.0419 7776	1.0442 3515	1.0464 9740	1.0487 6454	1.0510 3658
317	1.0353 4822	1.0375 9839	1.0398 5344	1.0421 1336	1.0443 7819	1.0466 4792	1.0489 2257	1.0512 3215
318	1.0354 6168	1.0377 1921	1.0399 8164	1.0422 4898	1.0445 2126	1.0467 9847	1.0490 8053	1.0513 6775
319	1.0355 7516	1.0378 4004	1.0401 0985	1.0423 8462	1.0446 6434	1.0469 4904	1.0492 3871	1.0515 3338
320	1.0356 8865	1.0379 6088	1.0402 3809	1.0425 2027	1.0448 0745	1.0470 9962	1.0493 9682	1.0516 7903
321	1.0358 0215	1.0380 8174	1.0403 6634	1.0426 5594	1.0449 5057	1.0472 5023	1.0495 5494	1.0518 6471
322	1.0359 1566	1.0382 0261	1.0404 9460	1.0427 9163	1.0450 9372	1.0474 0087	1.0497 1310	1.0520 3041
323	1.0360 2918	1.0383 2350	1.0406 2288	1.0429 2733	1.0452 3688	1.0475 5152	1.0498 7127	1.0521 7614
324	1.0361 4272	1.0384 4440	1.0407 5118	1.0430 6306	1.0453 8006	1.0477 0219	1.0500 2947	1.0523 6190
325	1.0362 5627	1.0385 6531	1.0408 7949	1.0431 9880	1.0455 2326	1.0478 5289	1.0501 8770	1.0525 2768
326	1.0363 6983	1.0386 8624	1.0410 0781	1.0433 3456	1.0456 6649	1.0480 0361	1.0503 4594	1.0526 9349
327	1.0364 8341	1.0388 0719	1.0411 3616	1.0434 7033	1.0458 0973	1.0481 5435	1.0505 0422	1.0528 5933
328	1.0365 9700	1.0389 2814	1.0412 6452	1.0436 0613	1.0459 5299	1.0483 0511	1.0506 6251	1.0529 2519
329	1.0367 1060	1.0390 4911	1.0413 9289	1.0437 4194	1.0460 9627	1.0484 5590	1.0508 2083	1.0531 3188
330	1.0368 2421	1.0391 7010	1.0415 2128	1.0438 7777	1.0462 3957	1.0486 0670	1.0509 7917	1.0533 5699
331	1.0369 3783	1.0392 9110	1.0416 4969	1.0440 1362	1.0463 8289	1.0487 5753	1.0511 3754	1.0535 7293
332	1.0370 5147	1.0394 1211	1.0417 7811	1.0441 4948	1.0465 2623	1.0489 0838	1.0512 9593	1.0536 5870
333	1.0371 6512	1.0395 3314	1.0419 0655	1.0442 8536	1.0466 6959	1.0490 5925	1.0514 5434	1.0538 5489
334	1.0372 7878	1.0396 5418	1.0420 3501	1.0444 2126	1.0468 1297	1.0492 1014	1.0516 1278	1.0540 2091
335	1.0373 9246	1.0397 7524	1.0421 6348	1.0445 5718	1.0469 5637	1.0493 6105	1.0517 7124	1.0541 8695
336	1.0375 0614	1.0398 9631	1.0422 9195	1.0446 9312	1.0470 9979	1.0495 1199	1.0519 2973	1.0543 5302
337	1.0376 1984	1.0400 1739	1.0424 2046	1.0448 2907	1.0472 4323	1.0496 6295	1.0520 8824	1.0545 1912
338	1.0377 3355	1.0401 3849	1.0425 4898	1.0449 6504	1.0473 8669	1.0498 1392	1.0522 4677	1.0546 3524
339	1.0378 4728	1.0402 5960	1.0426 7751	1.0451 0103	1.0475 3016	1.0499 6493	1.0524 0533	1.0548 5139
340	1.0379 6101	1.0403 8072	1.0428 0606	1.0452 3704	1.0476 7366	1.0501 1595	1.0525 6391	1.0550 1757
341	1.0380 7476	1.0405 0187	1.0429 3463	1.0453 7306	1.0478 1718	1.0502 6699	1.0527 2252	1.0551 8377
342	1.0381 8853	1.0406 2302	1.0430 6321	1.0455 0910	1.0479 6072	1.0504 1806	1.0528 8115	1.0553 4989
343	1.0383 0230	1.0407 4419	1.0431 9181	1.0456 4516	1.0481 0427	1.0505 6914	1.0530 3980	1.0555 1625
344	1.0384 1609	1.0408 6537	1.0433 2042	1.0457 8124	1.0482 4785	1.0507 2025	1.0531 9848	1.0556 8253
345	1.0385 2988	1.0409 8657	1.0434 4905	1.0459 1733	1.0483 9144	1.0508 7139	1.0533 5718	1.0558 4883
346	1.0386 4370	1.0411 0778	1.0435 7769	1.0460 5344	1.0485 3506	1.0510 2254	1.0535 1591	1.0560 1517
347	1.0387 5752	1.0412 2900	1.0437 0635	1.0461 8958	1.0486 7869	1.0511 7371	1.0536 7465	1.0561 8153
348	1.0388 7136	1.0413 5024	1.0438 3503	1.0463 2572	1.0488 2235	1.0513 2491	1.0538 3343	1.0563 4791
349	1.0389 8521	1.0414 7149	1.0439 6372	1.0464 6189	1.0489 6602	1.0514 7613	1.0539 9222	1.0565 1432
350	1.0390 9907	1.0415 9276	1.0440 9243	1.0465 9807	1.0491 0972	1.0516 2737	1.0541 5104	1.0566 8076

Day	4.00%	4.25%	4.50%	4.75%	5.00%	5.25%	5.50%	5.75%
351	1.0392 1294	1.0417 1404	1.0442 2115	1.0467 3427	1.0492 5343	1.0517 7863	1.0543 0989	1.0568 4722
352	1.0393 2683	1.0418 3534	1.0443 4989	1.0468 7049	1.0493 9716	1.0519 2991	1.0544 6876	1.0570 1371
353	1.0394 4073	1.0419 5665	1.0444 7865	1.0470 0673	1.0495 4092	1.0520 8122	1.0546 2765	1.0571 8023
354	1.0395 5464	1.0420 7797	1.0446 0742	1.0471 4298	1.0496 8469	1.0522 3254	1.0547 8657	1.0573 4677
355	1.0396 6856	1.0421 9931	1.0447 3621	1.0472 7926	1.0498 2848	1.0523 8389	1.0549 4551	1.0575 1334
356	1.0397 8250	1.0423 2066	1.0448 6501	1.0474 1554	1.0499 7229	1.0525 3526	1.0551 0447	1.0576 7993
357	1.0398 9645	1.0424 4203	1.0449 9383	1.0475 5185	1.0501 1612	1.0526 8665	1.0552 6346	1.0578 4655
358	1.0400 1041	1.0425 6341	1.0451 2266	1.0476 8818	1.0502 5998	1.0528 3807	1.0554 2247	1.0580 1320
359	1.0401 2438	1.0426 8480	1.0452 5151	1.0478 2452	1.0504 0385	1.0529 8950	1.0555 8151	1.0581 7987
360	1.0402 3837	1.0428 0621	1.0453 8038	1.0479 6088	1.0505 4774	1.0531 4096	1.0557 4057	1.0583 4657
361	1.0403 5237	1.0429 2763	1.0455 0926	1.0480 9726	1.0506 9165	1.0532 9244	1.0558 9965	1.0585 1330
362	1.0404 6638	1.0430 4907	1.0456 3816	1.0482 3366	1.0508 3558	1.0534 4394	1.0560 5876	1.0586 8005
363	1.0405 8040	1.0431 7052	1.0457 6707	1.0483 7007	1.0509 7953	1.0535 9546	1.0562 1789	1.0588 4683
364	1.0406 9444	1.0432 9199	1.0458 9601	1.0485 0650	1.0511 2350	1.0537 4701	1.0563 7705	1.0590 1363
365	1.0408 0849	1.0434 1347	1.0460 2495	1.0486 4295	1.0512 6749	1.0538 9857	1.0565 3623	1.0591 8046

Appendix I Answers to Odd–Numbered Exercises

Chapter 1

Section 1.2

1. 754
3. 8,853
5. 1,473,385
7. 1,269
9. 840
11. 921
13. 1,320
15. 8,383,520
17. 2,147
19. 84,756,989
21. 2,637
23. 10,523
25. 21,869
27. 625
29. 2,640
31. 19,831
33. $464
35. $19,656
37. 13,441
39. $10,682
41. 39,368
43. $164,730,781
45. Horizontal:
      Office — $11,987
      Showroom — $4,817
      Sales — $19,711
      Storage — $3,269
    Vertical:
      Jan. — $ 6,505
      Feb. — $ 6,301
      Mar. — $ 6,457
      Apr. — $ 7,010
      May — $ 6,645
      June — $ 6,866
      Total — $39,784

Section 1.3

1. 12
3. 132

5. 5,223
7. 714
9. 5,559
11. 3,079
13. 12,573
15. 27,288
17. $35,400
19. $13,747
21. $389
23. $2,899
25. $55,179

Section 1.4

1. 36
3. 1,504
5. 38,793
7. 288,695
9. 871,641
11. 19,503,603
13. 17,522,898
15. 5,461
17. $255
19. $39,606
21. $736,268

Sections 1.5 and 1.6

1. 12
3. 47
5. 83
7. 14
9. 14
11. 67
13. 56
15. 754
17. 859
19. 652
21. 27
23. 54
25. 40

27.	65	41.	$35
29.	95	43.	$1,127
31.	8	45.	$14
33.	9	47.	$18
35.	23	49.	$25
37.	0	51.	$213
39.	4	53.	$253,071

Chapter 2

Section 2.2

1.	1/6
3.	6/15
5.	54/49
7.	108/187
9.	(2/6)/(9/8)
11.	6/28 laid off; 22/28 worked
13.	5/36 junk; 31/36 sold
15.	36/42
17.	21/32
19.	5/24

Section 2.3

1.	6/8, 9/12, 12/16
3.	6/4, 9/6, 12/8
5.	30/32, 45/48, 60/64
7.	10/34, 15/51, 20/68
9.	18/8, 27/12, 36/16
11.	36/62, 54/93, 72/124
13.	19/41, 76/164, 114/246
15.	21/24, 7/8, 210/240
17.	25/60
19.	28/60
21.	45/60
23.	84/90
25.	360/90
27.	39/90
29.	equal
31.	unequal
33.	equal
35.	equal
37.	1/2
39.	3/4
41.	4/3

43.	59/62
45.	3/2
47.	1/2
49.	9/2
51.	168
53.	1/2
55.	4/9
57.	2/3
59.	3/8
61.	1/9
63.	7/55
65.	252/575
67.	2/3

Section 2.4

1.	7/2
3.	4/9
5.	9/4
7.	5/7
9.	7/8
11.	40/21
13.	26/27
15.	224/247
17.	2/1
19.	45
21.	305/143
23.	1/2
25.	21/32
27.	40/7
29.	1/15
31.	19/7
33.	6
35.	57/63
37.	6
39.	12

41. 1050
43. 20
45. 8

Sections 2.5 and 2.6

1. 8, 5/8
3. 12, $1\frac{1}{12}$
5. 35, $1\frac{23}{35}$
7. 34, 1/2
9. 69, $1\frac{2}{69}$
11. 18/5
13. 29/8
15. 40/13
17. 80/11
19. 307/22
21. $4\frac{2}{3}$
23. $2\frac{1}{2}$
25. $1\frac{3}{4}$
27. $1\frac{11}{13}$
29. $3\frac{2}{5}$
31. 31/70
33. 21/40
35. $1\frac{47}{70}$
37. $3\frac{25}{57}$
39. 15/38
41. $8\frac{1}{8}$
43. $\frac{1}{2}$
45. $13\frac{17}{24}$
47. $11\frac{2}{3}$
49. $6\frac{5}{6}$
51. $12\frac{31}{40}$
53. $30\frac{5}{6}$
55. 136/153
57. $24\frac{16}{21}$
59. $1\frac{21}{26}$
61. 11/30
63. 45/56, 5/168
65. 29/35, 6/35
67. 53/63, 4/63
69. 31/35, 4/35
71. $164.15
73. 7
75. $53.20

Section 2.7

1. 59.7
3. 248.3

5. 55.94
7. 819.081
9. 150.598
11. 946.35
13. 420.246
15. 445.63
17. 66.7288
19. 8.59210
21. 129.3705
23. 3206.4014
25. 17.8311456
27. 31.193
29. 19.565
31. 84.534
33. $527.03
35. $54,899.88
37. $1,940.37
39. $14,847.80
41. $482,850.72
43. $4,696.12
45. Total Profit $12,817.35
    $6,975.15 more profit
47. $4,576.04

Section 2.8

1. (a) 23
   (b) 23.4
   (c) 23.41
3. (a) 217.0
   (b) 217.5
   (c) 217.48
5. (a) 4,220
   (b) 4,219.8
   (c) 4,219.79
7. (a) 217,500
   (b) 217,500.0
   (c) 217,499.98
9. (a) 23,453
   (b) 23,452.9
   (c) 23,452.90
11. (a) 5,000
    (b) 4,900
    (c) 4,872.58
13. (a) 7,000
    (b) 7,000
    (c) 6,975.007
15. (a) 20,000

(b) 19,900
(c) 19,942.19

17. (a) 927,000
    (b) 927,400
    (c) 927,399.95

19. (a) 150,000

(b) 149,900
(c) 149,891.69

21. $37.33
23. $533.46
25. $37.30
27. $407.70

Chapter 3

Sections 3.2 and 3.3

1. $4 \cdot 2 + 2 = 10$
3. $5 \cdot 0 + 2 = 3 \cdot 0 + (2 \cdot 0 + 2)$
5. $3 \cdot 2 + 3 = 3 + 2 \cdot 3$
7. $2(3+5) = 2 \cdot 3 + 2 \cdot 5$
9. one, conditional
11. two, identity
13. two, conditional
15. three, identity
17. four, identity
19. three, conditional
21. $x - 5 = 0$

5. Smith—$911
   Porter—$839
7. March—$412
   Feb.—$221
9. T.V.—$7,040
   Other—$2,200
11. Sand—$32.12
    Gravel—$9.88
13. A—330,000
    B—110,000
15. $16,000
17. 65
19. 38

Section 3.4

1. 7
3. 3
5. 7/6
7. 10
9. 10
11. 10/21
13. 2
15. 20/7
17. 23
19. 2
21. 3
23. 2/3
25. 45/28
27. 9/16
29. 56/19
31. No

Section 3.5

1. 25
3. $99.60

Section 3.6

1. 23
3. 20
5. 200
7. 1
9. $z = (y-x)/2$, 2
11. $c = 4KR/ab$, 8
13. $x = (z+2y)/yz$, 7/6
15. $x = (y - yz + z)/z$, $\frac{1}{6}$
17. $x = zy + 5y$, 24
19. $x = 1/[yz(y+2z)]$, 1/48
21. $n = G/P$, 400
23. $R = I/Pt$, 0.05
25. (a) $1.25
    (b) $1.30
    (c) $1.40
27. (a) $6,000
    (b) $7,200
    (c) $11,000
29. (a) $37
    (b) $61
    (c) $73

31. (a) 2,200
    (b) 2,000
    (c) 1,800

33. (a) 14,000
    (b) 11,500
    (c) 7,750

Chapter 4

Section 4.2

1. 0.04
3. 0.52
5. 0.926
7. 0.0731
9. 0.9242
11. 0.115
13. 0.0025
15. 3.21
17. 1.725
19. 1%
21. 53%
23. 70%
25. 5.3%
27. 59.34%
29. 0.52%
31. 432%
33. 624.1%
35. 702.63%
37. 7/50
39. 7/20
41. 1/500
43. 1/400
45. 11/2,500
47. 7/800
49. 3/500
51. 7/400
53. 51/50
55. 61/50
57. 123/125
59. 833/500
61. 25%
63. 75%
65. 35%
67. 87.5%
69. 93.75%
71. $81\frac{9}{11}\%$
73. $6\frac{2}{3}\%$
75. 225%

Section 4.3

1. 8
3. 4.8
5. 6.72
7. 240
9. 68.1
11. 31.21
13. 5%
15. 3%
17. 7%
19. $41.25
21. 20%
23. $800
25. 112 reconditioned
        8 junked
27. $160
29. $1,800
31. 8%
33. 80%
35. 43%
37. 21%
39. $61.95

Section 4.4

1. 50% increase
3. 25% decrease
5. 7% increase
7. 30% increase
9. 13% decrease
11. 63
13. 287.02
15. 137.76
17. 101.52
19. 5,267.18
21. 10% decrease
23. 30% increase
25. 13% increase
27. 9% increase

29. 9% decrease
31. 9% savings
33. 26% increase
35. 10% increase

37. 6% decrease
39. $1,228.81
41. $858.33
43. $136.36

Chapter 5

Section 5.2

1. (a) $.75
   (b) $1.25

3.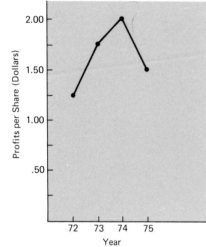

5.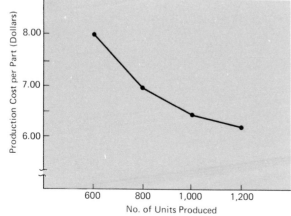

7.

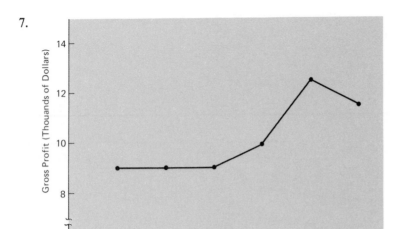

9.

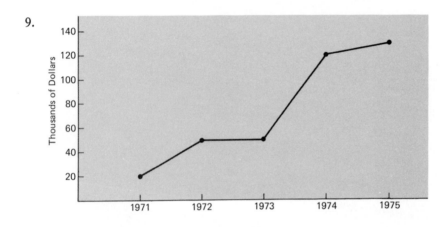

11.

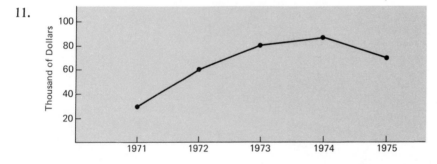

13.

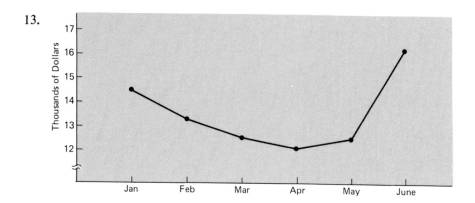

Section 5.3

1. (a) $75,000 (Approx.)
    (b) $17,500 (Approx.)
    (c) March

3.

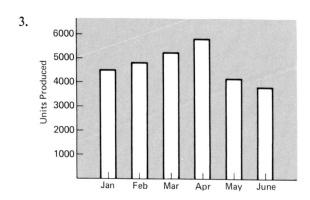

5.

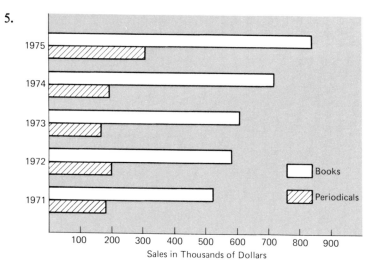

7.

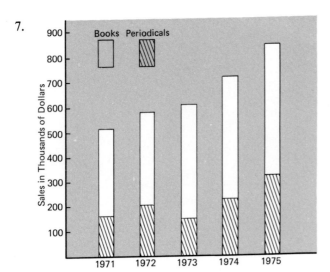

9.

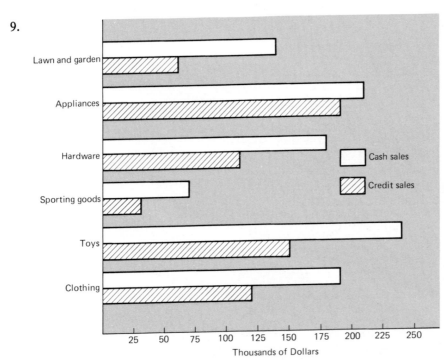

11.

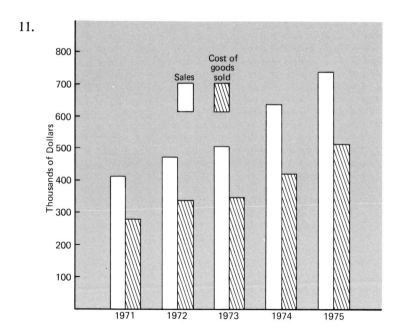

13.

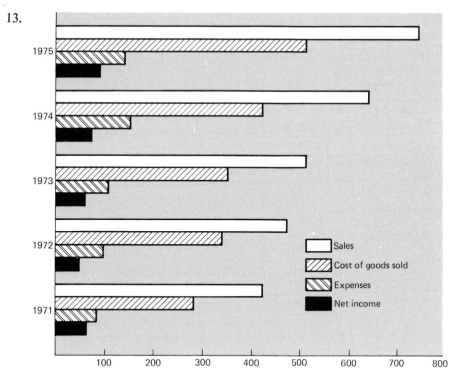

15.

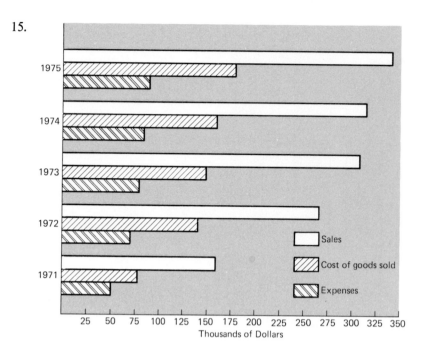

Thousands of Dollars

Section 5.4

1.

= 10,000 Tractors

3.

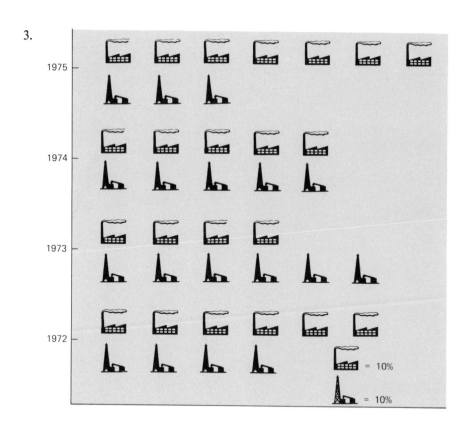

1975

1974

1973

1972

= 10%

= 10%

5.

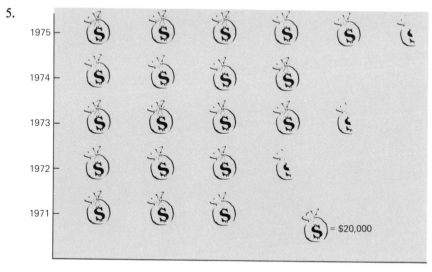

1975

1974

1973

1972

1971

= $20,000

Section 5.5

1. (a) 36 (b) 54
3. (a) 18 (b) 306
5. (a) 133 (rounded)
   (b) 43 (rounded)

7.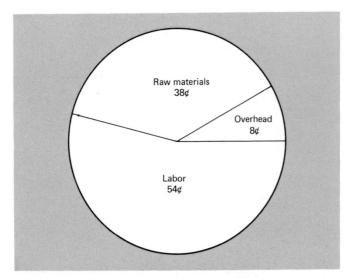

9.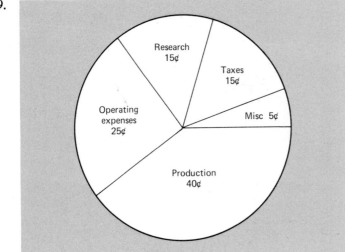

11.

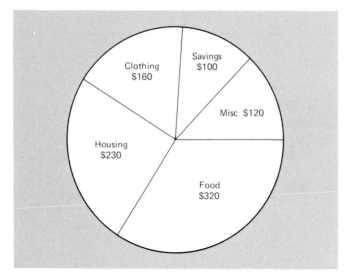

13.

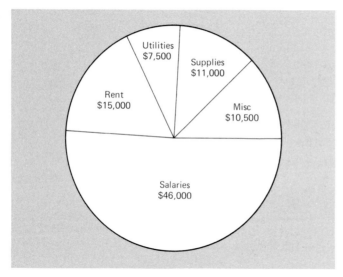

Section 5.6

1. Graph C; Graph A—
   Horizontal scale is too
   spread out, Graph B—
   Vertical scale is too spread
   out

3. Graph B

5. Graph C; Graph A—
   Horizontal scale is too
   compressed, Graph B—
   Horizontal scale is too
   spread out and it does not
   begin at zero

Chapter 6

Section 6.2

1. $184, $391
3. $173.60, $446.40
5. (a) $497
   (b) $559.70
7. 26%, 74%
9. $73, $146
11. $950
13. $372

Section 6.3

1. $312.80
3. $228.48
5. $126.68
7. $467.78
9. (a) 64%
   (b) 85.6%
   (c) 56.8%
   (d) 43.5%
11. $478.80
13. $224.00
15. $779.76
17. $354.44

Section 6.4

1. $910
3. $564.12
5. $1,105.19
7. $1,560.17

Sections 6.5 and 6.6

1. (a) $361.42
   (b) $372.60
3. $917.28
5. (a) $1,382.25
   (b) $1,411.35
   (c) $1,455.00
7. $1,792.92 and $1,810.25
9. $502.10

Section 6.7

1. (a) $453.66
   (b) $472.56
   (c) May 31
3. (a) $453.60
   (b) $472.50
5. 874.50
7. (a) $324.75
   (b) $315.01
   (c) $318.26
   (d) $311.76

Sections 6.8 and 6.9

1. (a) $56.40
   (b) $59.22
3. (a) $110.60
   (b) $114.55
5. Cost Price—$248.18
   Selling Price—$384.67
7. $63.33
9. $177.50
11. 20%
13. (a) 43%
   (b) 54%
15. (a) 61%
   (b) $229.43

Sections 6.10 and 6.11

1. 25%
3. (a) $250
   (b) $175
5. $10.25 Profit
7. $2.01 Profit
9. $71.75
11. 15% Markdown Percent
    $27 Cost Price
    Sale at $30.60 will not result
       in operating loss; will
       result in profit of $1.40.

Chapter 7

Section 7.2A

1. $307.69
3. $438.46
5. $2,153.85
7. $1,576.92
9. $339.23
11. $1,126.67
13. $801.67

Section 7.2B

1. $1,358.50
3. $1,065.54
5. $1,259.19
7. $78.60
9. $\frac{3}{4}\%$

11.

	1	2	3	4	5	6
Jan.	$5,200	$468	0	$468	$575	$107
Feb.	6,850	616.50	107	509.50	575	65.50
March	8,450	760.50	65.50	695.00	695	0

13.

	1	2	3	4	5	6
April	$8,842	$530.52	$70.00	$460.52	$550	$89.48
May	11,540	692.40	89.48	602.92	602.92	0
June	12,760	765.60	0	765.60	765.60	0

15. $537.30
17. $526.80
19. $1,255.41
21. $120.00
23. $610.20
25. $213.94
27. $209.33, $239.96, $216.54, $276.40, $241.04

Section 7.2C

1. $228.60
3. $479.05
5. $22.68
7. $132.00
9. $105.00
11. $3.33

13. $116.71
15. $107.20
17. $105.12
19. (a) $30.40
    (b) $35.87

Section 7.3

1. $120.08
3. $508.22
5. $543.63
7. $157.78
9. $146.80
11. $247
13. $180.00
15. $318.45
17. $162.89
19. $124.95
21. $121.87

Section 7.4

1. $40.90
3. $94.60
5. $38.60
7. $49.20
9. $25.80
11. $17.60
13. (a) $61.88
    (b) 14
15. $22.38
17. $231.15
19. $176.58
21. March: $415.89
    October: $458.08

Chapter 8

Sections 8.2—8.4

1.

The Topkin Company
Income Statement for the Year Ended
December 31, 1976

Revenue		
Sales		$870,000
Rental Income		73,500
Interest		17,400
	Total	$960,900
Expenses		
Cost of Merchandise Sold		$642,500
Operating Expenses		122,000
Interest Expenses		7,200
Federal and State Taxes		97,000
	Total	$868,700
Net Income		$ 92,200

3.

The Elkhorn Company
Balance Sheet
December 31, 1976

Assets

Current Assets

Cash	$ 47,500
Marketable Securities	82,000
Accounts Receivable	218,400
Inventories	249,000
Total Current Assets	$ 596,900

Fixed Assets

Land	$ 98,000
Plant and Equipment	430,000
Total Fixed Assets	528,000
Total Assets	$1,124,900

Equities

Current Liabilities

Payables	$ 748,200
Accrued Taxes	37,400

Long-term Liabilities

Long-term Debts	257,000

Owner's Equity

P. H. Elkhorn, Owner	$ 82,300
Total Equities	$1,124,900

5.

Houser Wholesalers
Income Statement
December 31, 1976

	Amount	Percent
Revenue		
Sales	$730,000	91.6
Rentals	60,000	7.5
Interest	7,000	0.9
Total Income	$797,000	100.0
Expenses		
Cost of Merchandise	$540,000	67.8
Operating Expenses	92,000	11.5
Interest Expenses	6,000	0.8
Taxes	46,000	5.8
Total Expenses	$684,000	85.8
Net Income	$113,000	14.2

7.

Oswald Enterprises
Income Statement for Years
Ending December 31, 1975 and 1976

	1976	1975	Increase or Decrease Amount	Increase or Decrease Percent
Net Sales	$450,000	$370,000	$80,000	21.6
Less:				
Cost of Sales	310,000	240,000	70,000	29.2
Depreciation	8,000	6,200	1,800	29.0
Maintenance	5,200	4,800	400	8.3
Total Cost and Operating Expenses	323,200	251,000	72,200	28.8
Operating Income	126,800	119,000	7,800	6.6
Interest Expense	14,000	12,000	2,000	16.7
Federal Taxes	22,000	18,000	4,000	22.2
Net Income	90,800	89,000	1,800	2.0

9.

			Increase or Decrease		Percent of Total Assets	
	1976	1975	Amount	Percent	1976	1975
Brooker Enterprises Balance Sheet for Years Ending December 31, 1975 and 1976						
Assets						
Cash	$ 3,220,000	$ 4,110,000	$ 890,000	(21.7)	7.9	11.5
Marketable Securities	11,700,000	9,100,000	2,600,000	28.6	28.9	25.4
Accounts Receivable	8,756,000	8,386,000	370,000	4.4	21.6	23.4
Inventory	16,750,000	14,200,000	2,550,000	18.0	41.3	39.6
Total Current Assets	$40,426,000	$35,796,000	$4,630,000	12.9	99.7	99.8
Fixed Assets	110,000	70,000	40,000	57.1	0.3	0.2
Total Assets	$40,536,000	$35,866,000	$4,670,000	13.0	100.0	100.0
Equities						
Payables	$15,700,000	$14,100,000	$1,600,000	11.3	38.7	39.3
Accrued Taxes	2,700,000	2,200,000	500,000	22.7	6.7	6.1
Dividends Payable	4,100,000	3,476,000	624,000	18.0	10.1	9.7
Deposits	1,842,000	1,040,000	802,000	77.1	4.5	2.9
Total Current Liabilities	24,342,000	20,816,000	3,526,000	16.9	60.1	58.0
Long-term Debt	6,214,000	5,470,000	744,000	13.6	15.3	15.3
Total Liabilities	30,556,000	26,286,000	4,270,000	16.2	75.4	73.3
Common Stock	$ 9,740,000	$ 8,840,000	$ 900,000	10.2	24.0	24.6
Retained Earnings	240,000	740,000	500,000	(67.6)	0.6	2.1
Total Stock-holders' Equity	9,980,000	9,580,000	400,000	4.2	24.6	26.7
Total Liabilities and Stock-holders' Equity	$40,536,000	$35,866,000	$4,670,000	13.0	100.0	100.0

Section 8.5

1. 2.8:1
3. Current Ratio 2.5:1
   Acid-Test Ratio 1.4:1
5. Gross Profit Margin—41%
   Operating Ratio—96%
7. 70%
9. Stockholder's Equity Ratio—65%: Debt-Equity Ratio—35%

11. Total Current Assets— $80,250
    Total Current Liabilities— $25,150
    Land—$21,700
    Retained Earnings—$2,900
    Net Income—$36,000
    Interest Charges—$2,400
13. Gross Profit Margin—43%
    Operating Ratio—85%
15. 31%

Section 8.6

1. $900.00

3. $2,437.50

5.

Year	Depreciation	Accumulated Depreciation	Book Value
0	—	—	$18,000.00
1	$3,600.00	$3,600.00	$14,400.00
2	2,880.00	6,480.00	11,520.00
3	2,304.00	8,784.00	9,216.00
4	1,843.20	10,627.20	7,372.80
5	1,474.56	12,101.76	5,898.24
6	1,179.65	13,281.41	4,718.59

7.

Year	Depreciation	Accumulated Depreciation	Book Value
0	—	—	$36,000.00
1	$5,400.00	$5,400.00	30,600.00
2	4,590.00	9,990.00	26,010.00
3	3,901.50	13,891.50	22,108.50
4	3,316.28	17,207.78	18,792.22
5	2,818.83	20,026.61	15,973.39
6	2,396.01	22,422.62	13,577.38
7	2,036.61	24,459.23	11,540.77
8	1,731.12	26,190.35	9,809.65

9.

Year	Depreciation	Accumulated Depreciation	Book Value
0	—	—	$16,000.00
1	$3,111.11	$3,111.11	12,889.89
2	2,722.22	5,833.33	10,166.67
3	2,333.33	8,166.66	7,833.34
4	1,944.44	10,111.10	5,888.90
5	1,555.56	11,666.66	4,333.34
6	1,166.67	12,833.33	3,166.67
7	777.78	13,611.11	2,388.89
8	388.89	14,000.00	2,000.00

11. (a)

Year	Depreciation	Accumulated Depreciation	Book Value
0	—	—	$10,000.00
1	$1,200.00	$1,200.00	8,800.00
2	1,200.00	2,400.00	7,600.00
3	1,200.00	3,600.00	6,400.00
4	1,200.00	4,800.00	5,200.00
5	1,200.00	6,000.00	4,000.00

11. (b)

Year	Depreciation	Accumulated Depreciation	Book Value
0	—	—	$10,000.00
1	$2,500.00	$2,500.00	7,500.00
2	1,875.00	4,375.00	5,625.00
3	1,406.25	5,781.25	4,218.75
4	1,054.69	6,835.94	3,164.06
5	791.02	7,626.96	2,373.04

11. (c)

Year	Depreciation	Accumulated Depreciation	Book Value
0	—	—	$10,000.00
1	$2,000.00	$2,000.00	8,000.00
2	1,600.00	3,600.00	6,400.00
3	1,200.00	4,800.00	5,200.00
4	800.00	5,600.00	4,400.00
5	400.00	6,000.00	4,000.00

13. $15,000 x 0.20 = $3,000 $15,000 — $3,000 = $12,000

$$d = \frac{c - f}{n}$$

$$d = \frac{\$12,000 - \$5,000}{8} = \frac{\$7,000}{8} = \$875$$

Year	Depreciation	Accumulated Depreciation	Book Value
0	—	—	$15,000
1	$3,875 ($3,000 + $875)	$ 875	11,125
2	875	4,750	10,250
3	875	5,625	9,375
4	875	6,500	8,500
5	875	7,375	7,625
6	875	8,250	6,750
7	875	9,125	5,875
8	875	10,000	5,000

15.

Year	Depreciation	Accumulated Depreciation	Book Value
0	—	—	$15,000.00
1	$4,555.56	$4,555.56	10,444.44
2	1,361.11	5,916.67	9,083.33
3	1,166.67	7,083.34	7,916.66
4	972.22	8,055.56	6,944.44
5	777.78	8,833.34	6,166.66
6	583.33	9,416.67	5,583.33
7	388.89	9,805.56	5,194.44
8	194.44	10,000.00	5,000.00

Section 8.7

1. Offices—$800.00
   Accounting—$2,400.00
   Production—$12,800.00
   Warehouse—$16,000.00
3. Clothing—$1,041.25
   Hardware—$531.25
   Appliances—$680.00
   Toys—$276.25
   Home Furnishings—$871.25
5. Office Supplies—$910.00
   Furnishings—$625.63
   Floor Coverings—$422.50
   Office Machines—$1,291.88
7. Office Equipment—$1,513.08
   Business Forms—$302.62
   Art Supplies—$406.37
   Chemicals—$1,392.03

Chapter 9

Section 9.2

1. $15,000.00
3. 8%
5. $7,500
7. 6 3/4%
9. $4,166.67
11. 3
13. $288
15. $65.63
17. $65.63
19. $5,000
21. 4
23. 6 1/2%
25. $2,278.13
27. No—Interest would be $1,080
29. 7 1/2%

Section 9.3

1. (a) 220
   (b) 216
3. (a) 113
   (b) 111
5. (a) 159
   (b) 159
7. (a) 281
   (b) 276
9. (a) 300
   (b) 295

11. (a) August 24
    (b) August 24
13. (a) October 20
    (b) October 21
15. (a) May 11
    (b) May 10
17. (a) August 16
    (b) August 18
19. (a) May 16
    (b) May 18

Section 9.4

1. (a) $110.96
   (b) $112.50
3. (a) $43.40
   (b) $44.00
5. (a) $60.41
   (b) $61.25
7. (a) $36.99
   (b) $37.50
9. (a) $168.29
   (b) $170.63
11. (a) $187.52
    (b) $190.13
13. (a) $222.99
    (b) $226.09
15. (a) $241.77
    (b) $245.13
17. 8%
19. 6%

21. 9 1/2%
23. 7 1/4%
25. 9 1/4%
27. 60 days
29. 240 days
31. 150 days
33. $4,000
35. $2,500
37. $4,200
39. $5,600

Section 9.5

1. $87.50
3. $36.00
5. $21.20
7. $142.80
9. $1,008.00
11. $17.20
13. $19.20
15. $56.80
17. $280.00
19. $102.67
21. $30.00

23. $608.00
25. $181.50
27. $195.30
29. $214.50

Section 9.6

1. $2,300
3. $2,340
5. $1,921.69
7. $2,919.58
9. $2,000
11. $3,000
13. $2,800
15. $1,966.81
17. $1,815
19. $5,850
21. $1,702.13
23. $2,476.78
25. $1,432.84
27. $2,009.25
29. 10%
31. 4 years
33. 9 1/4%

Chapter 10

Section 10.2

1. $210, $790
3. $54, $666
5. $75.94, $2,174.06
7. $63.80, $811.20
9. $143.44, $1,131.56
11. $5.25, $894.75
13. $3.77, $346.23
15. $58.97, $1,291.03
17. 8.79%
19. 8.92%
21. $225, $1,275
23. $112.29, $1,887.71, 8.74%

Section 10.3

1. 2
3. $8\frac{1}{2}\%$

5. 8%
7. $1,700
9. $20
11. $1,400
13. $661.50
15. $1,067.02
17. $2,127.66
19. $8\frac{1}{2}\%$
21. 6.2%

Section 10.4

1. $10.72, $1,010.72
3. $26.37, $83.63
5. $1,795.49, $4.51, $82.01
7. $1,683.71, $35.06
9. $1,575.22, $24.78
11. No

Section 10.5

1. 8.14%
3. 8.13%
5. 9.99%
7. 10.55%
9. 5.36%

11. 8.47%
13. 7.12%
15. 9.07%
17. 8.14%
19. Friend
21. Bank

Chapter 11

Section 11.2

1. 3%
3. 1%
5. $2\frac{1}{2}$%
7. $\frac{3}{4}$%
9. $3\frac{1}{4}$%
11. $332.80
13. $40.40
15. $172.41
17. $110.46
19. $24.44
21. $520.30
23. $2,072.05
25. $3,040.25
27. 6% compounded annually

Sections 11.3 and 11.4

1. $1,081.60, $81.60
3. $450.20, $50.20
5. $1,248.72, $48.72
7. $812.06, $12.06
9. $1,606.53, $206.53
11. $485.95
13. $352.19
15. $1,628.04
17. 12 years
19. 30 months
21. 12%
23. 12%
25. 8%
27. $1,646.13

Section 11.5

1. $888.49
3. $2,666.99
5. $459.84
7. $204.65
9. $979.36
11. $1,700.00
13. $11,161.41

Section 11.6

1. $506.29
3. $756.87
5. $1,516.68
7. $1,506.34
9. $831.70
11. $505.30
13. $1,812.25
15. $605.57
17. $1,006.24

Section 11.7

1. 6.09%
3. 12.55%
5. 12.68%
7. 4.04%
9. 10.38%
11. $5\frac{1}{2}$%
13. 4.50%
15. 9%

Chapter 12

Section 12.2

1. $240.19
3. $1,896.37
5. $2,466.23
7. $662.31
9. $2,903.08
11. $3,537.83

Section 12.5

1. $97.82, $5.43
3. $43.00, $6.48
5. $91.55, $8.37
7. $76.10, $14.95
9. $57.62, $25.00
11. $150.63
13. $59.13
15. $142.30
17. $216.81, $2.17
19. $306.50, $3.07
21. (a) $3.25
    (b) $230.96

Section 12.6

1. (a) $54.05
   (b) $826.19
   (c) $40.34
3. (a) $101.99
   (b) $1,029.17
   (c) $75.35
5. (a) $97.11
   (b) $1,484.37
   (c) $104.95
7. (a) $246.17
   (b) $3,142.31
   (c) $115.29
9. (a) $325.60
   (b) $4,046.78
   (c) $98.01
11. (a) $436.25
    (b) $573.72
    (c) $62.47

13. (a) $375.92
    (b) $459.74
    (c) $38.56
15. (a) $1,042.00
    (b) $1,356.34
    (c) $142.16
17. (a) $882.23
    (b) $1,149.50
    (c) $156.55
19. (a) $2,428.30
    (b) $3,261.37
    (c) $369.26
21. (a) $184.22
    (b) $2,026.37
    (c) $85.26

Sections 12.7 and 12.8

1. 15%
3. 30%
5. 9%
7. 16.25%
9. 16.25%
11. 15.00%
13. 14.50%
15. 17.00%
17. 15.50%
19. 14.25%
21. 20%
23. 17.32%
25. 20.03%
27. (a) 14.75%
    (b) 15.45%

Section 12.9

1. $21.54
3. $0.92
5. $5.38
7. $35.38
9. $38.57
11. $11.03
13. $40.46
15. $8.85

Chapter 13

Section 13.3

1. $2,187.31
3. $7,039.92
5. $22,106.32
7. $15,588.04
9. $76,095.25
11. $7,355.27
13. $31,411.28
15. $57,083.82
17. $18,571.79
19. $42,704.95
21. $7,110.45, $12,996.77
23. $12,037.34, $32,225.15
25. $6,784.18, $13,487.06

Section 13.4

1. $2,401.22
3. $2,429.74
5. $4,083.48
7. $5,412.41
9. $3,391.54
11. 30
13. 41 months, $437.96
15. 23, $3,168.86
17. $12,894.73, $894.73

Section 13.5

1. $14,720.17
3. $10,862.17

5. $3,981.60
7. $6,027.72
9. $6,009.12
11. 47
13. $18,677.74
15. 44
17. $5,167.04

Section 13.6

1. $5,975.32
3. $10,951.84
5. $7,906.56
7. $8,555.43
9. $5,795.21
11. $1,277.96
13. 11
15. $6,569.83
17. $5,111.82

Section 13.7

1. $3,449.70
3. $9,694.48
5. $10,543.33
7. $2,897.74
9. $13,142.76
11. $59,692.09
13. $3,243.13
15. $621.75
17. $3,830.95

Chapter 14

Section 14.2

1. $2,880.97
3. $3,143.17
5. $388.80

7.

Period	Accum. Amt.	Interest	Payment	Accum. Amt.
1	—	—	$2,563.22	$ 2,563.22
2	$ 2,563.22	$ 51.26	2,563.22	5,177.70
3	5,177.70	103.55	2,563.22	7,844.47
4	7,844.47	156.89	2,563.22	10,564.58
5	10,564.58	211.29	2,563.22	13,339.09
6	13,339.09	266.78	2,563.22	16,169.09
7	16,169.09	323.38	2,563.22	19,055.69
8	19,055.69	381.11	2,563.22	22,000.02
Total		$1,494.26		

9.

Period	Accum. Amt.	Interest	Payment	Accum. Amt.
1	—	—	$1,300.39	$1,300.39
2	$1,300.39	$ 13.00	1,300.39	2,613.78
3	2,613.78	26.14	1,300.39	3,940.31
4	3,940.31	39.40	1,300.39	5,280.10
5	5,280.10	52.80	1,300.39	6,633.29
6	6,633.29	66.33	1,300.39	8,000.01
Total		$197.67		

11.

Period	Accum. Amt.	Interest	Payment	Accum. Amt.
1	—	—	$6,848.89	$ 6,848.89
2	$ 6,848.89	$ 171.22	6,848.89	13,689.00
3	13,869.00	346.73	6,848.89	21,064.62
4	21,064.62	526.62	6,848.89	28,440.13
5	28,440.13	711.00	6,848.89	36,000.02
Total		$1,755.57		

13.

Period	Accum. Amt.	Interest	Payment	Accum. Amt.
1	—	—	$2,073.72	$ 2,073.72
2	$ 2,073.72	$ 207.37	2,073.72	4,354.81
3	4,354.81	435.48	2,073.72	6,864.01
4	6,864.01	686.40	2,073.72	9,624.13
5	9,624.13	962.41	2,073.72	12,660.26
6	12,660.26	1,266.03	2,073.72	16,000.01

15. $25,182.82

17. $152.74

Section 14.3

1. $518.02
3. $932.45
5. $ 95.01

7.

Period	Amt. of Debt	Payment	Interest	App. to Prin.	Remaining Debt
1	$5,250.00	$1,585.08	$420.00	$1,165.08	$4,084.92
2	4,084.92	1,585.08	326.79	1,258.29	2,826.63
3	2,826.63	1,585.08	226.13	1,358.95	1,467.68
4	1,467.68	1,585.08	117.41	1,467.67	0.01

9.

Period	Amt. of Debt	Payment	Interest	App. to Prin.	Remaining Debt
1	$3,200.00	$427.47	$48.00	$379.47	$2,820.53
2	2,820.53	427.47	42.31	385.16	2,435.37
3	2,435.37	427.47	36.53	390.94	2,044.43
4	2,044.43	427.47	30.67	396.80	1,647.63
5	1,647.63	427.47	24.71	402.76	1,244.87
6	1,244.87	427.47	18.67	408.80	836.07
7	836.07	427.47	12.54	414.93	421.14
8	421.14	427.47	6.32	421.15	—0.01

11.

Period	Amt. of Debt	Payment	Interest	App. to Prin.	Remaining Debt
1	$8,700.00	$760.83	$65.25	$695.58	$8,004.42
2	8,004.42	760.83	60.03	700.80	7,303.62
3	7,303.62	760.83	54.78	706.05	6,597.57
4	6,597.57	760.83	49.48	711.35	5,886.22
5	5,886.22	760.83	44.15	716.68	5,169.54
6	5,169.54	760.83	38.77	722.06	4,447.48
7	4,447.48	760.83	33.36	727.47	3,720.01
8	3,720.01	760.83	27.90	732.93	2,987.08
9	2,987.08	760.83	22.40	738.43	2,248.65
10	2,248.65	760.83	16.86	743.97	1,504.68
11	1,504.68	760.83	11.29	749.54	755.14
12	755.14	760.83	5.66	755.17	—0.03

13.

Period	Amt. of Debt	Payment	Interest	App. to Prin.	Remaining Debt
1	$1,500.00	$423.02	$75.00	$348.02	$1,151.98
2	1,151.98	423.02	57.60	365.42	786.56
3	786.56	423.02	39.33	383.69	402.87
4	402.87	423.02	20.14	402.88	—0.01

15. $12,689.06
17. $13,404.82

Chapter 15

Sections 15.2 and 15.3

1. $1.58
3. $41.25
5. $1.27
7. $750.00, $170.63, $920.63
9. $0.48

Sections 15.4 and 15.5

1. $20.40
3. $59.91
5. $402.55
7. $31.93
9. $45.04
11. $8,760.72
13. $1,624.56

Section 15.6

1. $2.10
3. $2.09
5. 13:1
7. 14:1
9. 2.7%
11. 8%
13. 5.3%

Sections 15.7–15.9

1. $7,475.00
3. $6,775.04
5. $5,359.23
7. $8,490.00
9. $2,397.46
11. $3,129.59
13. $13,557.93
15. $16,658.97
17. $472.81

Section 15.10

1. 9.1%
3. 9.0%
5. 9.1%
7. 8.7%
9. 9.8%
11. 9.8%
13. 9.6%
15. 13.7%
17. NLL

Chapter 16

Sections 16.1–16.3

1. $41.13
3. $59.57
5. $133.44
7. $16.50
9. $32.05
11. $16.72
13. $41.71
15. $167.87
17. $4.30
19. $58.25

Section 16.4

1. $344.40
3. $277.80
5. $537.50
7. $960.40
9. $276.00
11. $1,111.20
13. $646.75
15. $365.10
17. $66.24
19. $1,178.32

21.	$317.77	5.	Executives $12.60
23.	$119.45		Supervisors $9.45
25.	$250.72		Other Employees $6.30
27.	$134.68	7.	$9.25
29.	$379.70	9.	$4.89
31.	$142.76	11.	$36.36

Sections 16.5–16.7

1.	$4,702.80
3.	$3,118.50
5.	$26,037.00
7.	$14,428.75
9.	$20,062.40
11.	$1,886.40
13.	$621.25
15.	$113.10
17.	$251.00
19.	$378.00
21.	$87.25
23.	$134.10

Sections 16.10 and 16.11

1.	$16,250
3.	$55,000
5.	$150,000
7.	$238,333.33
9.	$1,886.00
11.	$1,260.00
13.	$838.35
15.	$239.32
17.	$69.02
19.	$1,470
21.	$388.93

Sections 16.8 and 16.9

| 1. | $9.50 |
| 3. | $6.70 |

Chapter 17

Section 17.2

1. 5, 9, 14, 15, 19, 21, 27, 33
3. 5, 8, 9, 12, 14, 15, 18, 19, 21, 23, 26, 27, 31, 33, 39, 43
5. 7, 8, 11, 12, 13, 15, 18, 23, 24, 26, 31, 32, 37, 39, 41, 43

7. Frequency
   3
   5
   5
   2
   1

9.

Frequency	Relative Frequency	Percent
4	0.25	25
5	0.3125	31.25
6	0.375	37.5
1	0.0625	6.25
0	0.0	0
16	1.0	

11.

Frequency	Cumulative Frequency
4	4
5	9
6	15
1	16
0	0

13.

Class	Frequency
0-4	1
5-9	4
10-14	3
15-19	2

15.

Frequency	Relative Frequency	Percent
1	0.1	10
4	0.4	40
3	0.3	30
2	0.2	20
10	1.0	

17.

Class	Frequency	Cumulative Frequency
380-399	2	2
400-419	1	3
420-439	2	5
440-459	1	6
460-479	3	9
480-499	1	10
500-519	2	12

Section 17.3

1. 12
3. 18
5. 86
7. 332
9. 125

5. 14.5
7. 12
9. 13
11. Median = 12.19
    Mean = 12
    Mode: None
13. $8,860
15. $52
17. Mean = $448.57
    Mode = $455

Section 17.4

1. 12.09
3. 14

Section 17.5

1.
Class Midpoint (x_i)	$f_i x_i$
7	7
12	36
17	68
22	88
27	54
	253

   Mean = 253/14 = 18.07

3.
Class Midpoint (x_i)	$f_i x_i$
4.5	9
14.5	43.5
24.5	49
34.5	138
44.5	44.5
	284

   Mean = 284/12 = 23.67

5.
Class Midpoint (x_i)	$f_i x_i$
5	10
16	64
27	162
38	190
49	343
60	180
71	71
	1020

   Mean = 1020/28 = 36.49

7. 20.5
9. 31.5
11. Modal Class: None
    Modal Value: None
13. Mean = 10.5
    Median = 11.36
    Modal class: 11-15
15. Mean = $5.37
    Median = $5.06
    Modal Class: $4.00–$5.99

Section 17.6

1. 7.41
3. 3.61
5. 2.65
7. 2.83
9. (a) 27 students
   (b) 38 students

Chapter 18

Sections 18.3 and 18.4

1. 5_{10}
3. 10_{10}
5. 17_{10}
7. 44_{10}
9. 193_{10}
11. 1001_2
13. 10110_2
15. 1101111_2
17. 10010110_2
19. 11100001_2

Section 18.5

1. 1101_2
3. 1111_2
5. 11000_2
7. 11110_2
9. 110001_2
11. 101_2
13. 110_2
15. 110000_2
17. 1001100_2
19. 10010010_2

21. 1010_2
23. 10101001_2
25. 111101101_2
27. 100110010000_2
29. 11010100101_2

31. 111_2
33. 10_2
35. 1000_2
37. 1_2R11_2
39. $1_2R10010_2$

Chapter 19

Sections 19.1–19.5

1. 200 cm
3. 0.4125 um
5. 12.04 dm
7. 13,080 dm
9. 463,700,000 km
11. 5,000 m, 5,000,000 mm
13. 0.4 a, 0.004 ha
15. 4,200 l, 4,200,000 ml
17. 0.2725 l, 0.002725 hl
19. 183,200 mm, 18,320 cm
21. 32.81 ft.
23. 1.77 in.
25. 4,918.50 yds.
27. 91.44 m

29. 1.83 m
31. 14.35 sq. yds.
33. 1.54 sq. miles
35. 108.72 acres
37. 928.80 cm^2
39. 2.76 m^2
41. 6.34 qts.
43. 4.22 gal.
45. 136.26 1
47. 21.82 hl
49. $1.16 per liter
51. 3,306.93 lbs./hr.
53. $0.12 per kg. is better
55. 91.536 cu. in.

Index